Microsoft® Project
2007 Bible

Microsoft® Project 2007 Bible

Elaine Marmel

Wiley Publishing, Inc.

Microsoft® Project 2007 Bible

Published by
Wiley Publishing, Inc.
111 River Street
Hoboken, NJ 07030
www.wiley.com

Copyright © 2007 by Wiley Publishing, Inc., Indianapolis, Indiana

Published simultaneously in Canada

Library of Congress Control Number: 2006936837

ISBN-13: 978-0-470-00992-5
ISBN-10: 0-470-00992-6

Manufactured in the United States of America

10 9 8 7 6 5 4 3 2 1

1O/SX/RS/QW/IN

To my brother and sister-in-law, Jim and Mariann Marmel, who always believe in me, and to the memories of my mother, Susan Marmel (1914-2003) and my father Harry Marmel (1914-1985), who always made me feel loved and cherished.

About the Author

Elaine Marmel is President of Marmel Enterprises, LLC, an organization that specializes in technical writing and software training. Elaine has an MBA from Cornell University and worked on projects to build financial management systems for New York City and Washington, D.C. This prior experience provided the foundation for Marmel Enterprises, LLC to help small businesses implement computerized accounting systems.

Elaine left her native Chicago for the warmer climes of Arizona (by way of Cincinnati, OH; Jerusalem, Israel; Ithaca, NY; Washington, D.C., and Tampa, FL) where she basks in the sun with her PC and her dog Josh and her cats, Cato, Watson, and Buddy, and sings barbershop harmony with the 2006 International Championship Scottsdale Chorus.

Elaine spends most of her time writing; she has authored and co-authored more than 30 books about Microsoft Project, QuickBooks, Peachtree, Quicken for Windows, Quicken for DOS, Microsoft Excel, Microsoft Word for Windows, Microsoft Word for the Mac, Windows 98, 1-2-3 for Windows, and Lotus Notes. From 1994 to 2006, she also was the contributing editor to monthly publications *Peachtree Extra* and *QuickBooks Extra*.

Credits

Acquisitions Editor
Kyle Looper

Project Editor
Susan Christophersen

Technical Editors
Jim Peters, Brian Kennemer, Thuy Le, T.R. Sloan

Copy Editor
Susan Christophersen

Editorial Manager
Jodi Jensen

Vice President & Executive Group Publisher
Richard Swadley

Vice President and Publisher
Andy Cummings

Editorial Director
Mary C. Corder

Project Coordinator
Kristie Rees

Graphics and Production Specialists
Carrie A. Foster
Joyce Haughey
Jennifer Mayberry
Barbara Moore
Heather Pope
Rashell Smith
Alicia South

Quality Control Technician
Brian Walls

Media Development Project Supervisor
Laura Moss

Media Development Specialist
Kate Jenkins

Proofreading and Indexing
Techbooks

Contents at a Glance

Contents

Contents

Contents

Part III: Refining Your Project   159

Chapter 6: Understanding the Basics of Views 161

Rollup views 195
    Using the summary task bar 196
    Using the Rollup_Formatting macro 198
    Switching rollup views 201
Task Details Form 203
Task Entry 204
Task Form 205
Task Name Form 206
Task Sheet 207
Task Usage 208
Printing Your Project 209
Summary 213

Chapter 7: Using Views to Gain Perspective **215**
Customizing Views 215
  Changing tables 215
    Changing row height and column width 215
    Hiding and inserting columns 217
    Adding fields to a usage view 218
    Switching tables 220
    Creating new tables or editing existing tables 221
  Working with views 224
    Adding views 225
    Creating a combination view 227
Ordering Tasks in a View 229
  Sorting tasks 229
  Creating WBS codes 232
  Renumbering WBS codes 235
  Defining outline numbers 238
Filtering Views to Gain Perspective 242
  Applying a filter to a view 246
  Creating custom filters 247
  Using AutoFilters 248
  Using grouping 249
Summary 253

Chapter 8: Modifying the Appearance of Your Project **255**
Changing Project's Looks 255
Using the Gantt Chart Wizard 257
Formatting Elements One by One 261
  Working with text 261
    Formatting selected text 261
    Applying formatting to categories of text 263

Contents

Part IV: Tracking Your Progress   347

Chapter 11: Understanding Tracking 349

Chapter 12: Recording Actuals 367

Contents

Contents

Contents

Contents

Preface

Managing projects can be as exciting as scheduling the next space shuttle or as mundane as planning routine production-line maintenance. A project can be as rewarding as striking oil or as disastrous as the maiden voyage of the Titanic. Projects can have budgets of $5 or $5,000,000. One thing that all projects have in common, however, is their potential for success or failure — the promise that if you do it right, you'll accomplish your goal.

Why You Need This Book

Microsoft Project is a tool for implementing project management principles and practices that can help you succeed. That's why this book provides not only the information about which buttons to press and where to type project dates but also the conceptual framework to make computerized project management work for you.

How it's designed

This book strives to offer real-world examples of projects from many industries and disciplines. You'll see yourself and your own projects somewhere in this book. A wealth of tips and advice show you how to address, control, and overcome real-world constraints. The book is designed to work for you in two ways:

- **As a tutorial.** You can use *Microsoft Project 2007 Bible* as a linear tool to learn Project — from the ground up.
- **As a reference.** You can put it on the shelf and use it as your Project reference book, to be pulled down as needed — for advice, information, and step-by-step procedures.

Either way, this book will enrich your Microsoft Project experience and make you a better project manager.

Whom it's for

Unlike word processing or spreadsheet software, many of you may have come to project management software never having used anything quite like it before. You may also have used earlier versions of Project or other project management software.

■ **If you're new to project management:** This book is for you. The early chapters explain the basic concepts of computerized project management and what it can do for you so that you have a context in which to learn Project.

■ **If you're experienced with project management:** This book is also for you. It explains what's new in the latest version of Project and shows you techniques for using the software that you may not have considered before.

You will benefit most from this book if you have at least a basic understanding of the Windows environment, have mastered standard Windows software conventions, and are comfortable using a mouse. But beyond that, you need only the desire to succeed as a project manager, which this book will help you do.

The Special Features of This Book

To help you maximize your use of this book, I've included many special features in its design and conception. The following sections show you how they work.

Formatting conventions

To streamline your learning experience, I've used the following formatting conventions:

■ Text you're asked to type: When you're asked to enter text into a Project schedule, for example, it appears in **boldface**.

■ When using the mouse: A click indicates a left mouse-button click and right-click indicates a right mouse-button click. Double-click designates two quick, successive clicks of the left mouse button.

■ Keystroke combinations: These look like this: Alt+Tab. Hold down the first key and, without letting it go, press the second key.

■ Menu commands: These are shown with the command arrow — for example, Choose File ➪ Open.

■ New terms: When a new term or concept is introduced, it appears in *italics*.

Margin icons

Throughout the book, I've included special icons in the margins to call your attention to added information, shortcuts and advice, warnings about potentially disastrous courses of action, the new features of Project 2007, references to additional wisdom, and how to access the wonderful software on the CD-ROM that accompanies this book. Here's how they look:

 The Note icon signals additional information about a point under discussion or background information that may be of interest to you.

TIP A tip is a bit of advice or a hint to save you time and indicate the best way to get things done.

NEW FEATURE This icon highlights a new feature in Project 2007.

CROSS-REF This helpful icon clues you in to sources of additional information on a topic under discussion. It points to another chapter or a specific heading elsewhere in the book.

ON the CD-ROM The CD-ROM icon flags useful software and templates that you'll find on the accompanying CD-ROM.

Sagacious Sidebars

Sidebars, such as this one, are departures into background details or interesting information. They're designed so that you may read around them if you're in a hurry to accomplish a specific task.

When you have the time for a more comprehensive approach to the subject, however, the concepts that you find in sidebars may prove invaluable — providing the context and depth necessary to achieve a fuller understanding of Project's functions.

How This Book Is Organized

This book is organized in the way that you will use Microsoft Project. It begins with some basic concepts and progresses through the features that you need to build a typical schedule and then track its progress. The later chapters provide more advanced information for customizing Project, using it in workgroup settings, and taking Project online.

Part I: Project Management Basics

Part I of the book explains the basic project management concepts and terminology that you'll need to learn Project. In Chapter 1, you take a look at the nature of projects themselves, how Microsoft Project can help you control them, and the life cycle of a typical project. In Chapter 2, you get your first glimpse of the Project software environment.

Part II: Getting Your Project Going

Here's where you learn about the type of information that Project needs in order to do its job. In Chapter 3, you begin to build your first schedule and add tasks in an outline structure. In Chapter 4, you assign timing and construct timing relationships among those tasks. In Chapter 5, you begin assigning people and other resources to your project. This chapter is also where you learn to determine how these resources add costs to a project and how to handle issues such as overtime and shift work.

Part III: Refining Your Project

Before your project is ready for prime time, you need to tweak some things, just as you check spelling in a word-processed document. Chapter 6 explains how to view that information to gain perspective on your project, and Chapter 7 helps you to manipulate and customize views to make them work for you. Chapter 8 shows you how to make your project schedule look more professional by formatting the text and modifying the appearance of chart elements. The next two chapters delve into the tools that Project provides to resolve conflicts in your schedule. Chapter 9 explores resolving conflicts in the timing of your schedule so that you can meet your deadlines. Chapter 10 considers the issue of resolving resource conflicts, such as overworked people and underutilized equipment.

Part IV: Tracking Your Progress

Here's where you get the payoff for all your data entry and patient resolution of problems in your schedule. After you set your basic schedule and the project begins, you can track its progress and check data on your status from various perspectives. Chapter 11 gives you an overview of the tracking process. Chapter 12 shows you how to track progress on your individual tasks and view that progress in various ways. In Chapter 13, you explore the power of generating reports on your projects for everyone from management to individual project team members. Chapter 14 gives advice and methods for analyzing your progress and making adjustments as needed to stay on schedule and within your budget.

Part V: Working in Groups

Most projects worth the effort of tracking in Project aren't done by a single person; workgroups, teams, and committees often form a day-to-day working project team. Chapter 15 shows you how to set up multiple projects to run concurrently or to consolidate smaller projects into larger schedules, and in Chapters 16 through 21, you learn how to plan, implement, and manage projects using Project, Project Web Access, and Project Server, Microsoft's Web-based project-managed solution.

Part VI: Advanced Microsoft Project

Part VI provides advice and information to make your use of Microsoft Project easier. Learn about customizing the Project environment in Chapter 22. Chapter 23 provides information on macros, which are simple programs that enable you to record and automatically play back series of steps that you use frequently, thus saving you time and effort. Chapter 24 shows you how to use VBA and VBScript to customize Project so that it works the way you work. Chapter 25 deals with importing and exporting information into and out of Project. Importing information from other software can save you the time and expense of reentering existing data. And in Chapter 26, you'll find some case studies that show you ways in which Project has been used by a variety of companies.

Appendixes

Appendixes B–D provide resources and other additional materials to make your work easier. Appendix A covers the contents of and installation for the companion CD-ROM, which contains trial software, time-saving templates, and a Web page with links to sites of interest in the project management world — including sites for partners of Microsoft Project.

Project Management Glossary

The glossary at the end of the book contains many specifically project management–related terms and concepts that have evolved over time. These terms are defined when they are first used in the book, but you may want to look them up at a later date. Use this handy alphabetical listing to do so.

Acknowledgments

No man (or woman) is an island, and this book is the product of the efforts of several people. Thank you, Kyle Looper, for your support and for making things smooth and easy and for having faith in me. Thank you, Robin Drake, for starting this project with me and keeping me on track while you could. I'm sorry we couldn't finish together, but I hope there will be projects in our future. Thank you, Susan Christophersen, for the wonderful job you did of picking up where Robin left off and keeping me sane, and for keeping the manuscript readable. My thanks also go to the CD team at Wiley for producing the Web page on the CD and handling the details of compiling the CD.

Thank you, Jim Peters, for keeping me technically accurate and for the wonderful insights you added. As always, it was a delight to work with you and I look forward to our next venture together. Jim is a PMP and president of SoftwareMatters.com, Inc., a Microsoft Project Partner focused on integrating project management and software development methods with Microsoft's Enterprise Project Management solutions and tools. Jim has extensive experience designing and implementing enterprise project management software solutions, delivering project management training, and developing project management reporting systems. He can be reached by phone at (877) 257-1982 or by e-mail at jmpeters@softwarematters.com. For more information about SoftwareMatters.com, Inc., see its Web site, www.softwarematters.com. Many thanks also to the additional technical reviewers who helped out in a time crunch and contributed their expertise to this project: Brian Kennemer, Thuy Le, and T.R. Sloan.

Thanks to Ira Brown and Roger Butler of Project Assistants, who co-authored Chapter 24. Ira is the Executive Vice President, CTO, and co-founder of Project Assistants, Inc., a Premier Microsoft Project Partner and Solution Provider specializing in implementation services, integration, training, and custom software development for Microsoft Project. He has extensive project management and application development experience and is recognized as a leading authority in developing custom solutions for Microsoft Project and Microsoft Project Server. Roger is a Senior Solution Architect with Project Assistants who specializes in custom software development for Microsoft Project and Microsoft Project Web Access and is an integration expert to a variety of third-party project management–related applications. Ira can be contacted by phone at (800) 642-9259 or e-mail at ibrown@projectassistants.com. Roger can be contacted by phone at (610) 305-4572 or e-mail at roger@projectassistants.com. For more information about Project Assistants, visit their Web site at www.projectassistants.com.

You all helped me make the Project 2007 Bible a better book than I could have produced by myself.

Part I

Project Management Basics

Chapter 1

The Nature of Projects

Everybody does projects. Building a tree house is a project; so is putting a man on the moon. From the simplest home improvement to the most complex business or scientific venture, projects are a part of most of our lives. But exactly what is a project, and what can you do to manage all its facets?

IN THIS CHAPTER

Understanding projects

The life cycle of a project

Some projects are defined by their randomness. Missed deadlines, unpleasant surprises, and unexpected problems seem to be as unavoidable as the weekly staff meeting. Other projects have few problems. Nevertheless, the project that goes smoothly from beginning to end is rare. Good planning and communication can go a long way toward avoiding disaster. And although no amount of planning can prevent all possible problems, good project management enables you to deal with those inevitable twists and turns in the most efficient manner possible.

In this chapter, you begin exploring tools and acquiring skills that can help you become a more efficient and productive project manager. The goal of this chapter is to provide a survey of what a project is, what project management is, and how Microsoft Project 2007 fits into the picture.

Understanding Projects

When you look up the word *project* in the dictionary, you see definitions such as "plan" and "concerted effort." A project in the truest sense isn't a simple one-person endeavor to perform a task. By this definition, getting yourself dressed — difficult though that task may seem on a Monday morning — isn't a project.

A project is a series of steps that are typically performed by more than one person. In addition, a project has the following characteristics:

- **A project has a specific and measurable goal.** You know you have finished the project when you have successfully met your project goal.

- **Projects have a specific time frame.** The success of a project is often measured by how successfully the project has been completed within the amount of time allotted to it.

- **Projects use resources.** Resources aren't just people; resources can include money, machinery, materials, and more. How well these resources are allocated and orchestrated is another key measure of a project's success or failure.

- **All projects consist of interdependent, yet individual, steps called *tasks*.** No piece of a project exists in a vacuum. If one task runs late or over budget, it typically affects other tasks, the overall schedule, and the total cost of the project.

Projects can last for months or even years. By their nature, projects are dynamic; they tend to grow, change, and behave in ways that you can't always predict. Consequently, you, as a project manager, have to remain alert to the progress and vagaries of your projects or you will never reach your goals. Documentation and communication are your two key tools for staying on top of a project throughout its life.

Exploring project management

Project management is a discipline that examines the nature of projects and offers ways to control their progress. Project management attempts to organize and systematize the tasks in a project to minimize the number of surprises that you may encounter.

Project management and project managers concern themselves with the following key areas:

- Scheduling
- Budgeting
- Managing resources
- Tracking and reporting progress

To manage these aspects of projects, certain tools have evolved over the years. Some of these are conceptual, such as the critical path; others involve specific formats for charting progress, such as a Gantt Chart. The following sections introduce some key project management concepts and tools.

Critical path and slack

The critical path marks the series of tasks in a project that must be completed on time for the overall project to stay on schedule. For example, suppose that you are planning a going-away party at your office. You have three days to plan the party. The following table lists some of the tasks that are involved and indicates their time frames.

Task	Duration
Signing the good-bye card	Three days
Ordering food	One day
Reserving a room	One hour
Buying a good-bye gift	One day

The shortest task, reserving a room, takes only one hour. Assuming that plenty of rooms are available for holding the party, you can delay reserving the room until the last hour of the third day. Delaying this task doesn't cause any delay in holding the party — as long as you accomplish this task by the end of the longest task, which is getting everyone to sign the good-bye card. Therefore, the task of reserving a room isn't on the critical path. However, you can't delay the task of signing the good-bye card, which is projected to take three days to accomplish, without delaying the party. Therefore, the card-signing task is on the critical path. (Of course, this example is very simple; typically, a whole series of tasks that can't afford delay form an entire critical path.)

The following points further define and clarify these concepts:

- The critical path changes as the project progresses. Remember that a *critical path* is a means of identifying tasks that have no leeway in their timing to ensure that they don't run late and affect your overall schedule. Knowing where your critical path tasks are at any point during the project is crucial to staying on track. Figures 1.1 and 1.2 show the same schedule — first with all tasks displayed and then filtered to show only the tasks that are on the critical path.

CROSS-REF See Chapter 7 to find out how to filter for only critical tasks and to see more information about changing the view of your project.

- *Slack,* also called *float,* is the amount of time that you can delay a task before that task moves onto the critical path. In the preceding example, the one-hour-long task — reserving a room — has slack. This task can slip a few hours, even a couple of days, and the party will still happen on time. However, if you wait until the last half-hour of the third day to reserve a room, that task will have used up its slack and it then moves onto the critical path.

FIGURE 1.1

Tasks with slack displayed alongside those on the critical path.

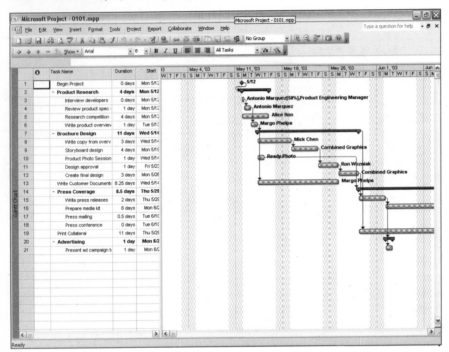

FIGURE 1.2

When you apply the appropriate filter, only the tasks that can't afford delay appear in your schedule.

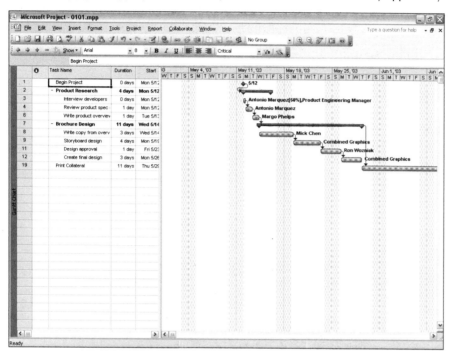

Durations and milestones

Most tasks in a project take a specific amount of time to accomplish. Tasks can take anywhere from five minutes to five months. The length of time needed to complete a task is called the task's *duration.* You should always try to break the long tasks in a project into smaller tasks of shorter duration so that you can track their progress more accurately. For example, break a five-month-long task into five one-month tasks. Checking off the completion of the smaller tasks each month reduces the odds of a serious surprise five months down the road — and makes you feel as though you're getting something done.

Some tasks, called *milestones,* have no (0) duration. Milestones are merely points in time that mark the start or completion of some phase of a project. For example, if your project involves designing a new brochure, the approval of the initial design may be considered a milestone. You can assign a duration to the process of routing the design to various people for review, but assigning a length of time to the moment when you have everyone's final approval is probably impossible. Therefore, this task has a duration of 0 — that is, approval of the design is a milestone that simply marks a key moment in the project.

Resource-driven schedules and fixed-duration tasks

Some tasks take the same amount of time — no matter how many people or other resources you devote to them. Flying from San Francisco to New York is likely to take about five hours, regardless of how many pilots or flight attendants you add. You can't speed up a test on a mixture of two solvents that must sit for six hours to react by adding more solvent or by hiring more scientists to work in the laboratory. These tasks have a *fixed duration,* meaning that their timing is set by the nature of the task.

On the other hand, the number of available resources can affect the duration of some tasks. For example, if one person needs two hours to dig a ditch, adding a second person will likely cut the time in half. The project still requires two hours of effort, but two resources can perform the task simultaneously. Tasks whose durations are affected by the addition or subtraction of resources are called *resource-driven tasks.*

NOTE In real-world projects, this calculation is seldom so exact. Because people have different skill levels and perform work at different speeds, two people don't always cut the time of a task exactly in half. In addition, the more people you add to a task, the more communication, cooperation, and training may be involved. Microsoft Project handles additional assignments of resources strictly as a mathematical calculation, but you can still use your judgment of the resources that are involved to modify this calculation (see Chapter 10).

Diagrams that aid project management

Gantt Charts, network diagrams, and work breakdown structures (WBSs) are tools of project management that have evolved over many years. These tools are simply charts that you can use to track different aspects of your project. Figure 1.3 shows a Microsoft Project Gantt Chart, and Figure 1.4 shows a Microsoft Project network diagram. Figure 1.5 shows a typical WBS, although Microsoft Project does not include a WBS chart as one of its standard views.

The Gantt Chart bars represent timing of the tasks in a project.

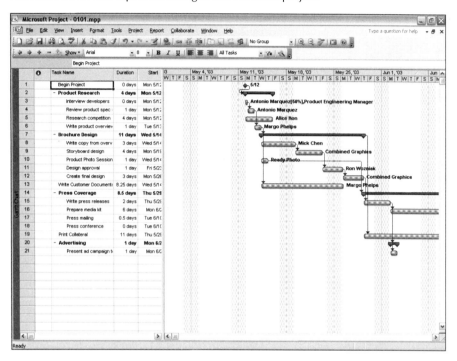

You can purchase an add-on product (WBS Chart Pro) to create a WBS chart from a Microsoft Project file. The CD-ROM that is included with this book features a sample of the program.

Before people used computers to manage their projects, managers drew these charts by hand. Any self-respecting project war room had a 10-foot network diagram, WBS, or Gantt Chart tacked to the wall. By the end of the project, this chart was as marked up and out of date as last year's appointment calendar. Thankfully, project management software makes these charts easier to generate, update, and customize.

A Gantt Chart represents the tasks in a project with bars that reflect the duration of individual tasks. Milestones are shown as diamond-shaped objects.

FIGURE 1.4

The network diagram resembles a flow chart for work in a project.

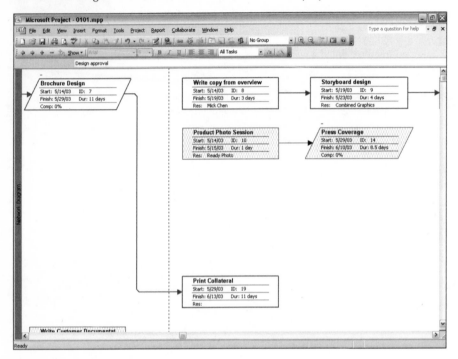

FIGURE 1.5

The work breakdown structure chart reminds you of a typical company's organization chart.

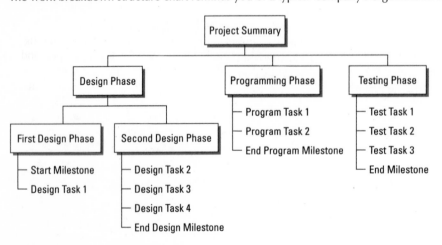

CROSS-REF You can find out more about the various elements of the Gantt Chart in Chapter 2. For this chapter's purposes, you simply need to know that a Gantt Chart enables you to visualize and track the timing of a project.

Network diagrams, on the other hand, don't accurately detail the timing of a project. Instead, a network diagram shows the flow of tasks in a project and the relationships of tasks to each other. Each task is contained in a box called a *node*, and lines that flow among the nodes indicate the flow of tasks.

NOTE In Project 98 and prior versions of Project, network diagrams were called PERT charts. PERT stands for *Program Evaluation and Review Technique.* The Special Projects Office of the U.S. Navy devised this method for tracking the flow of tasks in a project when it was designing the Polaris submarine in the late 1950s.

The U.S. defense establishment uses the WBS as its primary tool for managing projects and describes the WBS in Military Standard (MIL-STD) 881B (25 Mar 93) as follows: "A work breakdown structure is a product-oriented family tree composed of hardware, software, services, data and facilities . . . [It] displays and defines the product(s) to be developed and/or produced and relates the elements of work to be accomplished to each other and to the end product(s)."

NOTE MIL-STD 881B was superseded by MIL-HDBK 881A, 30 July 2005. The foreword of the newer documents states that there were "no substantive changes in work breakdown structure definition." The full text is available on many DOD sites (for example, `http://dcarc .pae.osd.mil/881handbook/881a.pdf`).

ON the CD-ROM Project doesn't contain a PERT chart view. However, on the enclosed CD-ROM, you can find a sample version of PERT Chart EXPERT, a program that converts the information in any Project file to a PERT view.

Dependencies

The final project management concept that you should understand is dependencies. The overall timing of a project isn't simply the sum of the durations of all tasks, because all tasks in a project don't usually happen simultaneously. For example, in a construction project, you must pour the foundation of a building before you can build the structure. You also have to enclose the building with walls and windows before you lay carpeting. In other words, project managers anticipate and establish relationships among the tasks in a project. These relationships are called *dependencies*. Only after you have created tasks, assigned durations to them, and established dependencies can you see the overall timing of your project.

CROSS-REF Chapter 4 covers several kinds of dependencies.

Managing projects with project management software

Many people manage projects with stacks of outdated to-do lists and colorful hand-drawn wall charts. They scribble notes on calendars in pencil, knowing — more often than not — that dates and tasks will change over time. They hold numerous meetings to keep everyone in the project informed. People have developed these simple organizational tools because projects typically have so many bits and pieces that no one can possibly remember them all.

To manage a project, you need a set of procedures. Project management software automates many of these procedures. With project management software, you can do the following:

- **Plan upfront:** By preplanning the various elements of your project, you can more accurately estimate the time and resources that are required to complete the project.

- **View your progress:** By examining your progress on an ongoing basis from various perspectives, you can see whether you are likely to meet your goal.

- **Recognize conflicts:** By identifying time and resource conflicts early, you can try out various what-if scenarios to resolve them before the project gets out of hand.

- **Make adjustments:** You can make adjustments to task timing and costs, and automatically update all other tasks in the project to reflect the impact of your changes.

- **Generate professional-looking reports:** You can create reports on the status of your project to help team members prioritize and to help management make informed decisions.

CROSS-REF To effectively manage projects with many participants, often based in many locations, consider using Project 2007 in conjunction with its companion server product, Project Server. Using Project Server and Project 2007, you can manage projects in a Web-based environment, simplifying collaboration. For more details, see Chapters 16 through 21.

What's required of you

Many people contemplate using project management software with about as much relish as they contemplate having surgery. They anticipate hours of data-entry time before they can get anything out of the software. To some extent, that vision is true. You have to provide a certain amount of information about your project for any software to estimate schedules and generate reports, just as you have to enter numbers for a spreadsheet to calculate a budget or a loan payback schedule.

On the other hand, after you enter your basic project information into Microsoft Project, the ongoing maintenance of that data is far easier than generating handwritten to-do lists that become obsolete almost immediately. In addition, the accuracy and professionalism of reports that you generate with Project can make the difference between a poorly managed project and a successful one. As with a quarterly budget that you create with spreadsheet software, after you enter the data, Project performs its calculations automatically. And, using Project makes it easy for you to quickly spot potential problems and to test alternative solutions.

So, exactly what do you have to do to manage your project with Microsoft Project? To create a schedule in Microsoft Project, you must enter the following information about your tasks:

- Individual task names
- Task durations
- Task dependencies

To track the costs of these tasks, you add certain information about resources, including the following:

- The list of human and material resources and their costs for both standard and overtime hours
- The assignment of resources to specific tasks

To track a project over its lifetime, you need to enter the following information:

- Progress on tasks
- Changes in task timing or dependencies
- Changes in resources — that is, resources that are added to or removed from the project
- Changes in resource time commitments and costs

What Microsoft Project can do to help

Even though you still must enter a great deal of information into your project schedule, Microsoft Project has ways to make the job easier:

- **Project templates:** If you often do similar types of projects, you can create project templates with typical project tasks already in place; you can then modify the templates for individual projects. Project comes with templates to help you get started.

ON the CD-ROM You can take advantage of sample project templates, which can be found on this book's companion CD-ROM. These templates represent a cross section of typical industries and project types.

- **Automate repeated tasks:** If you have tasks that repeat throughout the life of a project, such as weekly meetings or regular reviews, you can create a single repeating task, and Project duplicates it for you.
- **Import existing task lists:** You can create projects from tasks that you've set up in Outlook, or you can use Excel to start your project and then easily import the spreadsheet into Project.
- **Exchange task information with Outlook:** You can download project tasks into Outlook from Project Web Access, work on them, record the work in Outlook, and then upload the updated information to Project Web Access.

CROSS-REF See Chapter 25 for more information about starting projects in Outlook and Excel and then moving them into Project 2007.

- **Advanced reporting and analytical capabilities:** In addition to the reports Project provides, you can easily use Project data to prepare reports in Visio and Excel, providing you with additional analytical capabilities.
- **Consolidate projects:** You can break projects into smaller pieces that team members can use to enter and track progress. By tracking with this method, no individual person has

to enter an overwhelming amount of data. Also, team members feel more accountable and involved in the project.

CROSS-REF See Part V of this book, "Working in Groups," for detailed information about working in groups in Project 2007 alone or in conjunction with Project Server.

■ **Macros:** You can take advantage of Microsoft Visual Basic to build macros that automate repetitive tasks, such as generating weekly reports.

CROSS-REF See Chapter 23 for more information about using macros to speed your work.

The Life Cycle of a Project

Projects typically consist of several phases. Understanding the nature of each phase can help you relate the features of Microsoft Project to your own projects.

Identifying your goal and the project's scope

Before you can begin to plan a project, you have to identify the goal, which isn't always as obvious as it sounds. Various participants may define a project's goal differently. In fact, many projects fail because the team members are unwittingly working toward different goals. For example, is the team's goal to perform a productivity study or to actually improve productivity? Is the outcome for your project to agree on the final building design, or is it to complete the actual construction of the building? As you analyze your goal and factor in the perspectives of other team members, make sure that your project isn't just one step in a series of projects to reach a larger, longer-term goal.

To identify your goal, you can communicate in various ways, such as meetings, e-mail, and conference calls. Most important, you should conduct a dialogue at various levels (from management through front-line personnel) that gets ideas on the table and answers questions. Take the time to write a goal statement and circulate it among the team members to make sure that everyone understands the common focus of the project.

NOTE Be careful not to set a long-range goal that is likely to change before the project ends. Smaller projects or projects that have been broken into various phases are more manageable and more flexible.

CROSS-REF See Chapter 16 for tips on avoiding pitfalls during project planning.

After you understand your goal, you should also gather the information that you need to define the project's scope. This endeavor may take some research on your part. The *scope* of a project is a statement of more specific parameters or constraints for its completion. The constraints of a project usually fall within the areas of time, quality, and cost, and they often relate directly to project deliverables.

The following are some sample goal and scope statements:

Project A:

- **Goal:** To locate a facility for our warehouse.
- **Scope:** By October 15, to find a modern warehouse facility of approximately 5,200 square feet, with a lease cost of no more than $3,000 per month, in a location that is convenient to our main office.

Project B:

- **Goal:** To launch a new cleaning product.
- **Scope:** Includes test-marketing the product, designing packaging, and creating and launching an advertising campaign. The launch must be completed before the end of the third quarter of 2007 and can cost no more than $750,000.

Notice that the second scope statement designates major phases of the project (conducting test marketing, designing packaging, and creating an ad campaign). This statement provides a starting point for planning the tasks in the project. In fact, you may eventually decide to break this project into smaller projects of conducting test marketing, designing packaging, and launching an advertising campaign. Writing the scope of the project may encourage you to redefine both the goal and the scope to make the project more manageable.

TIP Keep your goal and scope statements brief. If you can't explain your goal or scope in a sentence or two, your project may be overly ambitious and complex. Consider breaking the project into smaller projects.

Writing a simple goal and scope statement ensures that you've gathered key data — such as deliverables, timing, and budget — and that you and your team agree on the focus of everyone's efforts. These activities are likely to occur before you ever open a Microsoft Project file.

Planning

When you understand the goal and scope of a project, you can begin to work backward to determine the steps that you need to take to reach the goal. Look for major phases first, and then break each phase into a logical sequence of steps.

Planning for resources is one aspect of planning the entire project. Resources can include equipment of limited availability, materials, individual workers, and groups of workers. Don't forget to take into account various schedules issues, such as overtime, vacations, and resources that are shared among projects. Time, money, and resources are closely related: You may be able to save time with more resources, but resources typically cost money. You need to understand the order of priority among time, quality, and money.

NOTE There's truth to the old joke: Time, budget, or quality — pick two. Devoting resources (which usually become costs) to a project schedule can decrease the time but can also cause loss of quality control. Extending the time can improve quality but usually causes resource conflicts and added costs. Microsoft Project helps you see the trade-offs among these three important criteria throughout the life of your project.

Planning is the point at which you begin to enter data in Microsoft Project and see your project take shape. Figure 1.6 shows an initial Microsoft Project schedule.

Revising

Most of the time, you send an initial project schedule to various managers or coworkers for approval or input so that you can refine the schedule based on different factors. You can use the reporting features of Microsoft Project to generate several drafts of your plan.

CROSS-REF Chapter 13 explains more about the reports that are available in Project.

FIGURE 1.6

The outline format of a Project schedule clearly shows the various phases of your project. Dependencies among tasks have not yet been established; every task starts at the same time, which isn't always possible.

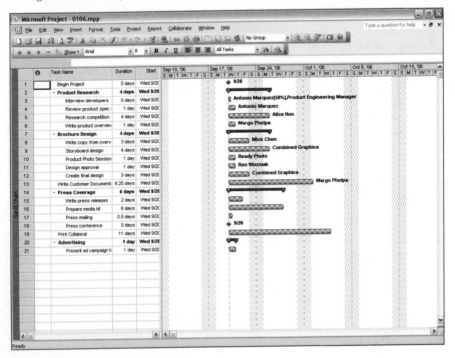

Be prepared to revise your plan after everyone has a chance to review it. You may want to create and save multiple Project files to generate what-if scenarios based on the input that you receive. Seeing your plans from various perspectives is a great way to take advantage of Project's power.

CROSS-REF Find out more about what-if analysis in Chapter 6.

Finding resolutions to conflicts in timing and resource allocation is another aspect of planning and revising. Project helps you pinpoint these conflicts, which may include the following:

- A team member or resource that is booked on several projects at one time
- A task that begins before another task that must precede it
- An unusually high use of expensive equipment in one phase that is upsetting your budget

CROSS-REF This book contains many tips and techniques for resolving conflicts. In particular, Chapters 9 and 10 focus on using Microsoft Project features to resolve scheduling and resource problems.

When your project plan seems solid, you can take a picture of it, called a *baseline*, against which you can track actual progress.

CROSS-REF Chapter 11 explains how to set (and, if necessary, clear) baselines.

Tracking

You should try to solidify your tracking methods before your project begins. Ask yourself the following questions:

- Do you want to track your progress once a week or once a month?
- Do project participants track their own work or merely report their progress to you?
- Do you want to roll those smaller reports into a single, less-detailed report for management?

TIP The answers to these questions can also help you determine whether you need to use Project Standard, Project Professional, or Project Server. See Chapter 2 for more information on choosing the Project product that best suits your needs.

Knowing how you are going to track your project's progress, and who needs to know what and when, helps your team establish efficient tracking mechanisms from the outset; this reduces frustration.

The Microsoft Project schedule shown in Figure 1.7 uses the Tracking Gantt view to show the original baseline (the bottom bar of each task) tracked against actual progress (the top bar of each task).

FIGURE 1.7

The darker portion of each upper taskbar and the percentage figure to the right of each upper taskbar indicate the percentage of each task that is complete.

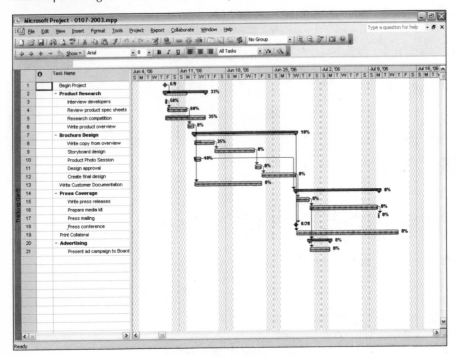

TIP You can save interim baselines of a schedule at various points during your project. This approach helps you see where major shifts occurred and shows how you accommodated those shifts. See Chapter 11 for more information on baselines.

Learning from your mistakes

Learning project management software isn't like learning to use a word processor because project management as a discipline entails conceptual layers that transcend the tools and features of the software. Having the experience and wisdom to use these features effectively comes from repeated use. You probably won't be a proficient Microsoft Project user right away. You have to work through one or more projects before you really know the most effective way to enter information about your project. You can expect to develop efficient tracking methods over time. Don't worry — it took you time to learn all you know about managing projects. If you pay attention to what goes on during your projects when you first implement Microsoft Project schedules, you can learn from your mistakes.

Microsoft Project enables you to review your projects and to clearly see where you estimated incorrectly, made adjustments too slowly, or didn't break phases into manageable chunks. Project keeps your original schedule's baseline in a single file, along with interim baselines and your final tracked schedule. When planning future projects, you can use these older baselines to help gauge the duration of tasks and the cost of certain items and to know how many resources are enough resources.

In the end, you'll be a more successful and efficient project manager. You can easily show your boss the specific actions that you've taken to avoid problems and provide solutions. In addition, you'll have the tools that you need to help you and your manager understand the issues that you face and to get the support that you need.

Summary

This chapter presented a survey of the discipline known as *project management* and explained the role that project management software can play to help you manage projects. The following topics were covered:

- Projects involve a stated goal, a specific time frame, and multiple resources (which can include people, equipment, and materials).

- Project management seeks to control issues of time, quality, and money.

- Critical path, slack, task durations, milestones, fixed tasks, resource-driven tasks, and dependencies are project management elements that help you build and monitor a project.

- Project management software can assist you in planning, tracking, and communicating with team members and in reporting on projects with tools such as Gantt Charts and network diagrams.

- Although using Project takes some effort on your part, this effort pays off in increased productivity and efficiency.

- Projects typically have five activities: Setting the goal and defining the scope, planning, revising, tracking, and reviewing to learn from your mistakes.

Chapter 2 takes a closer look at the Project environment and provides information about some of the tools that you can use to manage a project.

Chapter 2

Exploring the Microsoft Project Environment

IN THIS CHAPTER

Taking a first look at Project

The basics of entering information in Project

This chapter introduces Project's environment as well as the powerful tools that Project places at your disposal. You practice moving among different views, and you work with some of the tools and on-screen elements that you can use to create schedules.

Although Microsoft considers Project to be part of the Microsoft Office family, you will notice that Project does not sport the new interface found in Word, Excel, PowerPoint, and other Office products. Many of the changes to Project 2007 are "under the hood" changes.

Taking a First Look at Project

Two versions of Microsoft Project 2007 are available. You can purchase Project 2007 Standard or Project 2007 Professional. These products differ only in the way that they support Project Server, which is Project's tool to manage projects on the Web.

The functionality of Project Server has again been expanded. As with Project 2003, you can't use Project Server with Project Standard. Instead, to use Project Server 2007, you must also use Project Professional 2007. In this book, I assume that you're using Project Professional.

CROSS-REF See Part V for more information on using Project Server.

NOTE If you are not connected to Project Server, you'll see no difference in functionality between Project 2007 Standard and Project 2007 Professional. You see commands in Project 2007 Professional that you don't see in Project 2007 Standard, but the commands aren't available for use. So, if you're using Project Standard, most of this book also applies to you.

What Is Project Server?

Project Server enables you to manage projects on your company's intranet or on the Internet — and only the manager installs and uses Microsoft Project Professional. Everyone else on the project uses Project Web Access, the Web-based product that connects to the Project Server database that contains your project data. You open Project Web Access by typing the URL to the Project Server database into Internet Explorer version 6 (or later). Using Project Web Access instead of Microsoft Project, resources can, among other things, do the following:

- View a project's Gantt Chart
- Receive, refuse, and delegate work assignments
- Update assignments with progress and completion information
- Attach supporting documentation, such as budget estimates or feasibility studies, to a project
- Receive notices about task status
- Send status reports to the project manager

Project managers can do even more than resources. For example, by using Project Server, project managers have access to a company-wide resource pool (called the Enterprise Resource Pool) that tracks resource allocations across projects. If a project manager finds that a specific resource is unavailable, he or she can define the requirements for the job and let Project Server tools search the Enterprise Resource Pool to find another resource with the same skills.

CROSS-REF See Part V for more information about Project Server and Project Web Access.

Project uses the menu and toolbar structure found in Office 2003 and earlier products.

TIP Project contains a View bar that functions similarly to the one in Outlook, Microsoft's organizer, e-mail, and calendar program. The View bar enables you to switch among views and functions in the software. You can choose to hide or display the View bar. Open the View menu; if a check appears next to View Bar, Project displays the View bar. Click View Bar to remove the check and hide the View bar.

NOTE The figures throughout this book don't show the View bar.

Starting Project

When you open Microsoft Project from the `Programs` folder of the Windows Start menu, Project initially displays the main screen for Project 2007, as shown in Figure 2.1. On the left, you see the Project Guide pane. The Project Guide pane helps users set up and work with a project.

FIGURE 2.1

The first screen that you see when you start Project shows the Project Guide pane, which can help you set up a project.

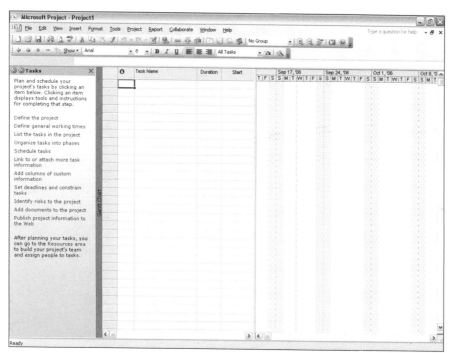

 **TIP**   You also can open Project by double-clicking any Project file. Project files are saved with the extension .mpp.

Working with the Project Guide

The Project Guide is a goal-based user interface that helps you build projects. In addition to the Project Guide pane on the left side of the screen, you also can display the Project Guide toolbar, which appears just above the Project Guide pane. To display the Project Guide toolbar, right-click anywhere in the toolbar area at the top of the screen and choose Project Guide (see Figure 2.2). Using the buttons on the Project Guide toolbar, you can limit the choices that appear in the Project Guide pane.

At this point, you can use the Project Guide toolbar and the Project Guide pane to begin building your project. Click a button on the Project Guide toolbar to start working in the associated area. The choices listed in the Project Guide pane change, based on the Project Guide toolbar button that you click.

FIGURE 2.2

The buttons on the Project Guide toolbar control the information that appears in the Project Guide pane.

Project Guide toolbar

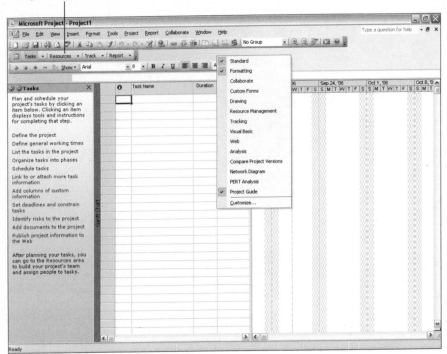

When you click a link in the Project Guide, a wizard starts and walks you through the process that's suggested by the link. For example, if you click the Tasks button on the Project Guide toolbar and then click the Define the project link, a three-step wizard walks you through starting a project. The first step helps you to establish the starting date for your project. After setting the date, click the right arrow at the top of the pane or click Save and go to Step 2 at the bottom of the Project Guide pane to continue (see Figure 2.3). In Step 2 of the Define the Project Wizard, you identify whether you intend to use Project Server. In Step 3, you return to the Project Guide.

FIGURE 2.3

The Define the Project Wizard walks you through a three-step process to begin a project.

If you click the Resources button on the Project Guide taskbar and then click Specify people and equipment for the project, the Project Guide helps you set up resources for your project (see Figure 2.4).

The Project Guide can help you set up resources for your project.

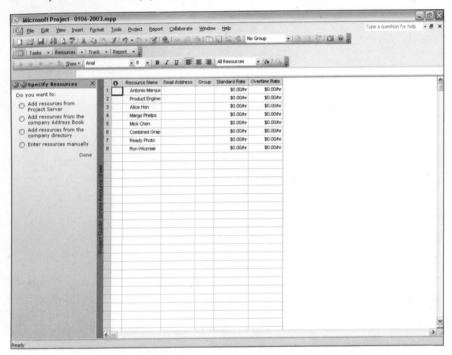

When you click the Track button on the Project Guide toolbar, you can perform a variety of tasks that are associated with tracking your project, including setting a baseline (see Figure 2.5).

FIGURE 2.5

You can use the Project Guide to help you track project information.

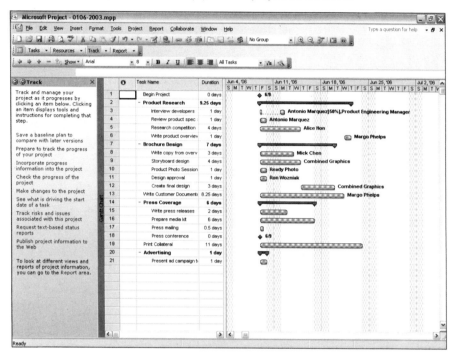

CROSS-REF Read about using Project to track your project in Part IV.

If you click the Report button on the Project Guide toolbar, you find links that help you report on your project, including a link that enables you to print what you see — the <u>Print current view as a report</u> link (see Figure 2.6). The four-step process helps you do the following:

- Determine the number of pages for the report
- Change the size of the report by modifying elements such as the timescale or the columns
- Set up the header, footer, and legend
- Set other options to change the margins, print notes, configure manual page breaks, and more

FIGURE 2.6

The Print current view as a report link walks you through a four-step process to print what you see on-screen.

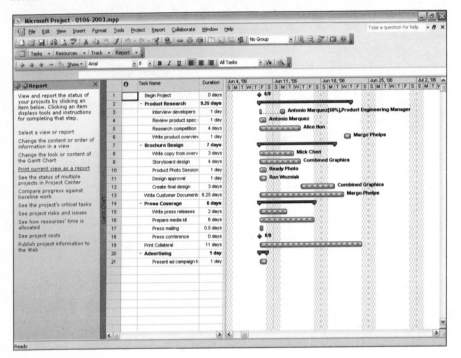

You also can preview the report on-screen before you print.

CROSS-REF You can customize the Project Guide so that it offers you options to work the way that your organization works. See Chapter 24 for some examples on customizing the Project Guide.

If you decide that you don't want to use the Project Guide (perhaps it eats up too much screen real estate for your taste), you can hide the pane and the toolbar. To temporarily hide the pane, click the X in the upper-right corner of the pane. You can redisplay the Project Guide by clicking the leftmost button on the Project Guide toolbar. To temporarily hide the toolbar, right-click any toolbar and click Project Guide to remove the check mark that appears next to it.

To turn off the Project Guide feature entirely, open the Options dialog box (choose Tools ➪ Options) and click the Interface tab. Then, remove the check mark from the Display Project Guide box.

Examining the Gantt Chart view

CROSS-REF See Chapter 22 for more information on setting options in Project.

After you've hidden the pane, you see the blank Project screen in the Gantt Chart view, as shown in Figure 2.7.

By default, Project opens a new project in the Gantt Chart view. You see other views throughout this book, but you're likely to spend a great deal of your time in the Gantt Chart view. This view offers a wealth of information about your project in a single snapshot. In most table views, you find a fill handle, which you can use to populate columns, just as you use a fill handle in Excel.

CROSS-REF For details about the other views that are available in Project, see Chapter 6.

FIGURE 2.7

A blank project contains no project information. When you enter information in the Gantt Chart view, the split pane displays the data both textually and graphically.

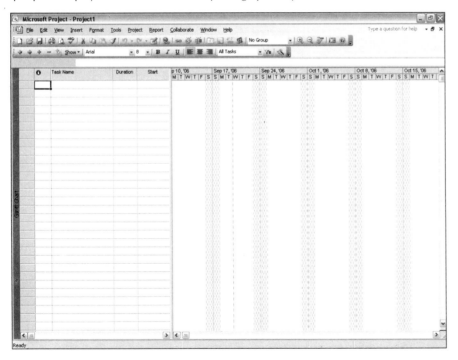

The Gantt Chart view has two main sections: the Gantt table and the Gantt Chart. After you enter task information, the Gantt table (in the left pane) holds columns of information about your project, such as the task name, duration, start date, and more. The Gantt Chart (in the right pane) is a graphic representation that helps you see the timing and relationships among tasks, as shown in Figure 2.8.

The timescale along the top of the Gantt Chart acts like a horizontal calendar. Think of it as a ruler against which you draw the tasks in your project. Instead of marking off inches, however, this ruler marks off the hours, days, weeks, and months of your project. Project enables you to display up to three timescales along the top of the Gantt Chart — a top, middle, and bottom timescale. In Figure 2.8, you see two timescales. The top timescale shows months; the bottom timescale shows weeks. Multiple timescales help you to see the multiple levels of timing simultaneously, such as the day and hour or the month, week, and day.

FIGURE 2.8

A sample project with task details in the Gantt table and bars representing tasks in the Gantt Chart.

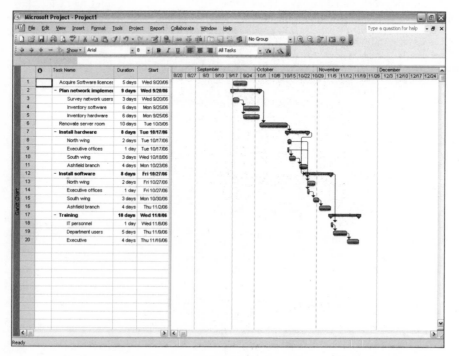

NOTE You can customize your timescale to increase or reduce the amount of information that appears on the right side of the Gantt Chart or to show unusual time increments, such as thirds of months. In Figure 2.8, I customized the timescale to show week increments. Double-click the timescale itself to display the Timescale dialog box. You can adjust settings for all three timescales in the Timescale dialog box. Also, note that Project uses default settings for the number of hours in a workday, days in a week, and so on. To adjust these settings to display or hide nonworking days, you can use the settings on the Non-working Time tab in the Timescale dialog box.

CROSS-REF In Chapter 3, I explain how to modify the calendars that control a project, and in Chapter 4, I explain how to set the timescale.

You can modify what you see on-screen in the Gantt Chart view, and Project carries those modifications to other views. After you practice moving among these views, you can see information about timing, budget, or resource assignments in detail, or you can just look at the big picture. You also can customize what each view shows you. For example, you can use the divider that runs between the Gantt table and Gantt Chart to adjust the amount of space that each pane occupies. Dragging this divider to the right reveals more columns of project data in the Gantt table. Dragging the divider to the left displays more of the project's taskbars in the Gantt Chart.

In addition to modifying how much of each pane you display on-screen, you can zoom in or out to view larger or smaller time increments for different perspectives of your project's schedule. You can show smaller time increments in the Gantt Chart by clicking the Zoom In button, or you can show larger increments of time by clicking the Zoom Out button. A daily perspective on a three-year project enables you to manage day-to-day tasks, whereas a quarterly representation of your project may be more useful when you're discussing larger issues with your management team.

Notice that the two panes of the Gantt Chart view have their own sets of scroll bars at the bottom of the window. To make changes, you must use the appropriate scroll bar and select objects in the appropriate pane.

Using Project menus

The menus in Project 2007 appear at the top of the screen and work like the menus in Office XP and Office 2003; by default, commands are available "on demand." That is, when you open a menu, you see a small subset of commands that Microsoft believes you'll use most often. In addition, at the bottom of the menu, you see a pair of downward-pointing arrows, as shown in Figure 2.9. If you highlight the pair of arrows (or pause the mouse over them for a few moments), Project displays the other commands that usually appear on the menu, as shown in Figure 2.10. After you select a command, that command appears on the menu as soon as you open the menu.

FIGURE 2.9

Initially, only a subset of commands appears on a menu.

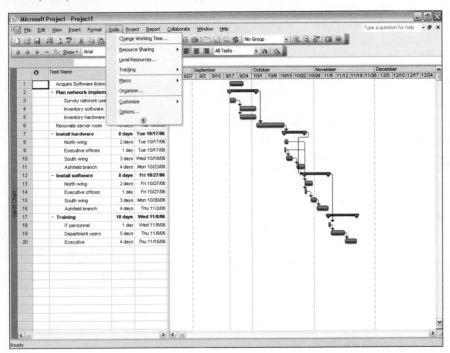

FIGURE 2.10

When you pause the mouse over or click the downward-pointing arrows at the bottom of the menu, the rest of the menu commands appear.

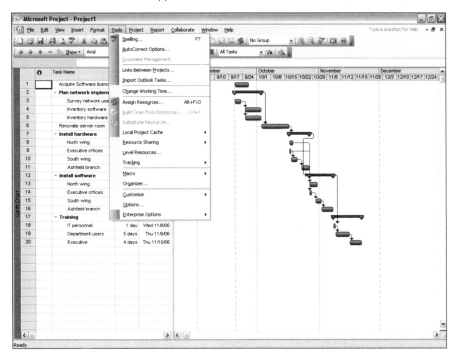

You can change this menu behavior so that all commands appear on a menu when you open it. To do this, use the Customize dialog box.

CROSS-REF The Customize dialog box is described in detail in Chapter 22.

Several of the menus in Project offer commands that are probably quite familiar to you, such as Save, Print, and Copy. Other menus on the menu bar are specific to the tasks that you perform with Project.

Table 2.1 shows the various types of functions that you can perform from each menu.

TABLE 2.1

Microsoft Project Menus

Menu	Types of Functions Available
File	Open and close new and existing files; save and print files; adjust page setup and document properties; and route files to e-mail recipients.
Edit	Cut, copy, and paste text or objects; manipulate data with Fill, Clear, and Delete commands; link and unlink task relationships; and locate information with Find, Replace, and Go To commands.
View	Select various default views of your project; access standard report formats; choose to display or hide various toolbars; use the Zoom feature; and enter header and footer information.
Insert	Insert new tasks, another Project file, or columns in various views and insert various objects into your schedule, including drawings, Excel charts, Word documents, media clips, and even hyperlinks to Web sites.
Format	Adjust the appearance of text, taskbars, and the Timescale display and change the overall appearance of a view's layout.
Tools	Run or modify Spelling and AutoCorrect functions to proofread your schedule; access workgroup features; establish links between projects; and modify your working calendar or resources. You can also customize standard views and functions with the Organizer, Options, or Customize commands; record macros; and initiate tracking functions. If you're using Project 2007 Professional, you can set Enterprise options.
Project	Display task or project information or notes, and use commands to sort or filter tasks to see specific details. You can also control outlining features of your project tasks.
Report	Contains commands to copy a picture of your project to another Office application. Also contains commands to prepare standard text reports and visual reports if you also use Excel 2007 or Visio Professional 2007.
Collaborate	Publish project information to Project Server, request or update progress information, view the Project Center and Resource Center, analyze or model a portfolio, discuss risks and issues, view documents posted by other users, and set Collaboration options. If you're using Project Standard, you don't see this menu.

The remaining two menus, Window and Help, contain commands to arrange windows on-screen and to access Help features, respectively.

CROSS-REF See Chapter 3 for more information on the Help system in Project.

Microsoft has placed corresponding tool symbols and keyboard shortcuts (such as Delete or Ctrl+F) next to the menu commands, as shown in Figure 2.11. This display helps you to get things done more quickly in Project. Notice also that the main menus sometimes open submenus (also called *side menus* or *cascading menus*). A black arrow to the right of a command indicates the presence of a submenu. Finally, if you choose a menu command followed by an ellipsis (. . .), such as Find . . . or Replace . . ., Project displays a dialog box.

FIGURE 2.11

Tool symbols appear to the left and keyboard shortcuts appear to the right of commands on Project menus. Submenus offer more choices, and dialog boxes appear if you click a menu command that is followed by an ellipsis.

Examining the toolbars

You're probably already familiar with tools in Windows programs and the way in which they appear by category on toolbars. When you open Project, two default toolbars are visible: the Standard toolbar and the Formatting toolbar. These appear in Figure 2.12.

FIGURE 2.12

The Standard toolbar and the Formatting toolbar are the default toolbars in Project.

You may see both toolbars appear on one row when you open Project. In this case, you also don't see all the tools that appear in Figure 2.12. You can change the appearance so that the toolbars appear on two rows, as I've done throughout this book. If you choose to keep both toolbars on one row, you can access the buttons that don't appear by clicking the Toolbar Options down arrow, which appears at the end of each toolbar, and then clicking the button that you want to use.

TIP If you move your mouse over the Toolbar Options down arrow and pause, a ScreenTip appears to help you identify it.

CROSS-REF To change the appearance of the toolbars in Project, use the Customize dialog box, which is discussed in Chapter 22.

In some software programs, the available tools are context sensitive, that is, they change according to the function that you're performing. In Project, the default toolbars are fairly consistent. Some tools become unavailable when you perform certain functions or change views. In these cases, the tools appear grayed out, and nothing happens when you click them.

NOTE If you insert an object into your project from another Microsoft application, such as Excel or PowerPoint, the other program's environment replaces the toolbars and menus in Project when you select that object. Therefore, you can use the other program's tools to modify the object without leaving Project. The toolbars and menus in Project reappear when you click outside the inserted object.

In addition to the Standard and Formatting toolbars, Project contains several other toolbars, some of which appear automatically when you're performing certain types of activities. However, you can also display any of these toolbars at any time by choosing View ⇨ Toolbars and selecting from the toolbar submenu that appears.

TIP These toolbars appear anchored at the top of the Project window with the Standard and Formatting toolbars, but you can float any toolbar — including the Standard and Formatting toolbars — anywhere on your screen by positioning the mouse pointer over the leftmost edge of the toolbar; when the pointer changes to a four-headed arrow, drag the toolbar and it will float on-screen. When floating, each toolbar displays a title bar, and you can move floating toolbars by dragging their title bars. To anchor a floating toolbar in the area where the Standard and Formatting toolbars appear, simply drag the floating toolbar (using its title bar) to the top of the screen.

Entering information

Several views or portions of views in Project, such as the Gantt table, use a familiar spreadsheet-style interface. Information appears in columns and rows. The intersection of a column and a row is a *cell*, just as in Excel. Project assigns each task in your project an ID number, which corresponds to the task's row number running along the left of the spreadsheet. You can enter project information either in dialog boxes or directly into cells. When you select a cell, the Entry bar, which appears immediately above the column names of the table, displays the information in the cell.

NOTE When you press Delete, Project deletes just the selected cell. Prior to Project 2002, Project deleted an entire row instead of a single cell.

If you've ever used Microsoft Excel or one of the other popular spreadsheet programs, you already know how to enter and edit information in Project. When you begin typing in a cell, the insertion point appears in the cell to the right of any text that you enter. To edit text in a cell, click once to select the cell and then press F2 or click a second time at the location in the cell where you want to begin editing. If you press F2, the insertion point appears at the right edge of the text in the cell. If you click a second time, the insertion point appears in the cell at the location where you clicked the second time.

As you enter information into a cell, the information also appears in the Entry bar, which runs along the top of the screen directly under the Formatting toolbar. The Entry bar in Project serves the same purpose as the Entry bar in Excel. You can type new text or edit existing text by clicking anywhere within the text in the Entry bar. Two buttons on the left of the bar (an X and a check mark) enable you to cancel or accept an entry, as shown in Figure 2.13.

CROSS-REF Chapter 4 covers entering and editing text in greater detail.

NEW FEATURE Project 2007 introduces the Change Highlighting feature; when you make a change to timing information in a project, Project highlights all tasks in your project that are affected by the change you made. If you don't like the effects, you can click the Undo button on the Standard toolbar. In fact, beginning with Project 2007, you can click the Undo button an unlimited number of times to "go back" to the state of your project before you made any changes. See Chapters 3 and 4 for more details on both of these features.

FIGURE 2.13

You can enter or edit text in individual cells or in the Entry bar.

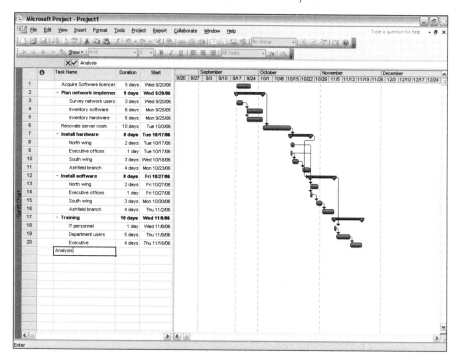

Changing views

Project offers multiple views in which you can display project information. A single view can't possibly show all the information that you need to see regarding timing, relationships among tasks, resource allocations, and project progress. In fact, to interpret each type of information accurately, you need special kinds of graphical and textual displays. Think of a project as a small business. As in any business, different people attend to various aspects of the work. The accounting department thinks mainly of the costs of doing business. The plant supervisor focuses on operations and having enough machinery and manpower to get the job done. Your human resources department thinks of people — their salaries, hours, benefits, and so on. As the owner of your project, you are likely to wear all these hats (and more) during the project. With Project, switching to another view to see your work from a different perspective is the equivalent of changing hats as you move from one responsibility to another. Each view helps you to focus on a different aspect of your project. The View bar or the View menu enables you to jump from view to view, as shown in Figure 2.14.

FIGURE 2.14

The View bar and View menu offer several predefined views of your project.

The View bar contains icons for eight views; you can display any of the views by clicking them in the View bar. Similarly, the View menu contains commands for the same eight views; you can display any of the views that are listed on the View menu by clicking the command.

At the bottom of the View bar and on the View menu, you can see an item called More Views. Click More Views to open the More Views window, shown in Figure 2.15.

FIGURE 2.15

The More Views dialog box lists 24 built-in views; you can add your own as well.

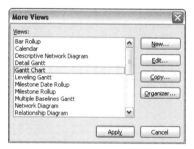

CROSS-REF In Chapter 6, you find out more about all of Project's views and how you can use them to gain perspective on your project. In Chapter 7, you discover how to create custom views by clicking New in the More Views dialog box.

What's New in Project 2007

Most of the new features in Project 2007 revolve around Project Server, with improvements both to the interface and under the hood. For example, in Project Server, you can now update the OLAP cube process incrementally instead of needing to build an entirely new cube to update the cube's information.

But there also are a few fairly powerful new features in Project Standard Professional that users have anxiously awaited.

For example, Project 2007 introduces a multilevel Undo capability — a long-awaited feature. And, the Gantt Chart view and the Calendar views have been enhanced.

The new Change Highlighting feature helps you see the effects that changes to one task's timing has on other tasks.

The Task Driver feature helps you identify, quickly and easily, the scheduling factors that drive individual tasks.

Rather than describe all the new features in Project 2007 at this point in the book, I've provided Table 2.2, which shows you where you can find more information in this book on new features.

NEW FEATURE You can easily find the new features in the chapters in which I discuss them in detail. Simply look for the New Feature icon that appears next to the discussion of a new feature in Project.

NOTE The features for which you find descriptions in Chapters 16–21 are not available in Project Standard.

TABLE 2.2

New Features in Project 2003

Feature	Chapter
Create named calendar exceptions	3
Define recurring calendar exceptions	3
Task Driver	4
Multilevel Undo	3 and 4
Change Highlighting	3 and 4
Cost resources	5
Budgeting using cost resources	5
Gantt Chart view enhancements	6
Calendar view enhancements	6
Visual reporting	13
Active cache to improve the offline experience for Project 2007 users connected to Project Server.	16
Import tasks from a Windows SharePoint Services Version 3 Project Tracking List	19
Improvements to resource substitution	19
Commitments	19

Summary

This chapter introduced the Project 2007 environment and the many ways in which you can display project information. This chapter also described the following techniques:

- Understanding the Project screen
- Using Project menus and toolbars
- Entering information in your project

Chapter 3 covers how to get help in Project and how to save Project files.

Part II

Getting Your
Project Going

Chapter 3

Creating a New Project

N ow that you have some project management concepts under your belt and you've taken a stroll around Project's environment, you are ready to create your first schedule. Before you type any information into a Project schedule, however, you should first assemble the relevant information about your project. Then you can open a new Project file and begin to build your project tasks by using a simple outline structure.

In this chapter, you begin to build your first Project schedule and find out how to save your project. At the end of the chapter, you read about how to take advantage of Project's various Help features.

Gathering Information

As you read in Chapter 1, several elements must be in place before you can begin to build a project schedule. First, you must understand the overall goal and scope of the project so that you can clearly see the steps that lie between you and that goal. You'll find delineating the major steps of the project a good place to start. Don't worry about the order of the tasks at this point — just brainstorm all the major areas of activity. Suppose that you've been given the project of organizing an annual meeting for your company. You may take the following steps:

- Book the meeting space
- Schedule speakers
- Arrange for audiovisual equipment
- Order food
- Send out invitations
- Mail out annual reports

IN THIS CHAPTER

Gathering information

Opening a Project file

Looking at Project calendars

Entering tasks

Adding subtasks

Saving Project files

Getting help

The last item on that list raises the question of scope: Is it within the scope of your project to create the annual report, or are you simply supposed to obtain copies of a report from the marketing department, for example, and mail them to stockholders before the meeting? In some corporations, the person who is responsible for organizing the annual meeting is also responsible for overseeing the production of the annual report. Be sure to answer questions of scope and responsibility at this stage of your planning.

For this example, you can assume that another department is creating the annual report. You simply need to make sure that someone mails copies of the report to all stockholders before the annual meeting.

Determining detail tasks

After you have prepared a list of major tasks, break them into more detailed tasks. Take one of the items on the list — Order food, for example — and consider how you can break down this task. How detailed should you get? The following is one possible breakdown of the Order food task:

- Create a budget.
- Determine a menu.
- Select a caterer.
    - Send out requests for bids.
    - Receive all estimates.
    - Review estimates and award contract.
- Give final head count to caterer.
- Confirm menu one week before the meeting.

Could you do without the detailed tasks under Select a caterer? Do you need more details under Create a budget? Those decisions are up to you, based on your knowledge of your project and procedures. However, keep the following points in mind:

- Create tasks that remind you of major action items, but don't overburden yourself with items of such detail that keeping track of your schedule becomes a full-time job. That's the purpose of daily to-do lists.

- Include milestones to mark off points in your project. For example, the Review estimates and reward contract task under the summary task Select a caterer is a milestone — it marks a point in time by which you want to have made a major decision. If that time comes and goes and you haven't selected the caterer, will missing this deadline affect other subsequent tasks? If so, including that milestone could be vital to your success.

- Include tasks that management should know about, because you'll use the Project schedule to report progress. If your boss wants to see that you've sent out a purchase order to the caterer per your new Accounting department procedures, you may want to include the task (even if you don't think that this level of detail is important).

Establishing time limits

After you have an idea of the tasks that are involved in your project, you need to have some idea of the timing of these tasks. Should you allow two weeks for caterers to reply with bids? Not if you have only three weeks to organize the meeting. You may want to approach determining task timing by building an initial schedule in Project, assigning time to tasks, and seeing how close you can come to your deadline. If you're way off, you can go back and tweak the timing for individual tasks until your schedule works.

CAUTION You may be tempted to trim time off your tasks to make them fit a deadline, but this approach tends to produce an unrealistic schedule. What should you do? Use the initial schedule to convince your boss that you need more time, money, or resources to complete this project on time. If he or she wants to trim time from a specific task to meet the deadline, you may have grounds to ask for more help.

At this early planning stage, get any information that you need to assign timing to tasks. For example, contact vendors or subcontractors to get their timing estimates, which you need to reflect in your schedule. If your project has a drop-dead completion date, you should be aware of it. However, leave it to Project to show you whether your estimates work in an overall schedule.

Lining up your resources

Before you can build a Project schedule, you need to know what resources are available to you, as well as their costs. You don't necessarily need to know these resources by name, but you should know, for example, that your construction project needs three engineers at a cost of $75 per hour and one piece of earthmoving equipment at a daily rental cost of $450.

You need to identify these resources and assign them to individual tasks early in the project-planning process. Find out anything you can about the availability of these resources: Are some resources available only half-time for your project? Will all the engineers be unavailable during the third week of August because of a professional conference? Research the cost and availability of resources as much as possible as you begin to build a project.

CROSS-REF For more information about identifying resources and assigning them to individual tasks, see Chapters 5 and 19.

Looking at dependencies

Finally, before you enter project information into a schedule, be aware of relationships among tasks. Does the CEO have to approve the menu before you book the caterers? Are you required to wait three weeks after applying for a permit before starting construction on a building? If your project faces issues involving the order and relationships of tasks, you will save yourself some headaches down the line and build a more realistic schedule if you can identify these obstacles now.

Opening a Project File

You can start a project file in a couple of different ways. In this section, you first see the "usual" way to start a file. Then, I cover how to use templates with project files.

Opening a project file — the usual way

Okay, you've done your homework. You've made some notes about your upcoming project's tasks, timing, resources, and dependencies. You're ready to start building your first schedule in Project. Choose Start ➪ All Programs ➪ Microsoft Office ➪ Microsoft Office Project 2007. You see the main Project window, where you can begin building a task outline.

NOTE When you first open Microsoft Office Project — depending on how you have your Enterprise options set — you may be prompted to connect to Project Server or to work offline. To work offline, simply click My Computer and then click the Work Offline button.

CROSS-REF To learn how to set Project Server options, see Chapter 19.

Other ways to open or start projects

You can base your project on one of the templates available in Project 2007. Templates contain "standard" information to help you get started quickly. Instead of entering tasks, you may need only to edit tasks. Choose File ➪ New. In the New Project task pane that appears (see Figure 3.1), click one of the three links that are available to search for templates. You can search at the Office Online Web site, on your computer, or on your Web sites. To use one of the templates that comes with Project, click On computer. Project displays the Templates dialog box; click the Project Templates tab to see the templates available to you.

FIGURE 3.1

Project comes with several predefined template projects that you can use as the basis of a project.

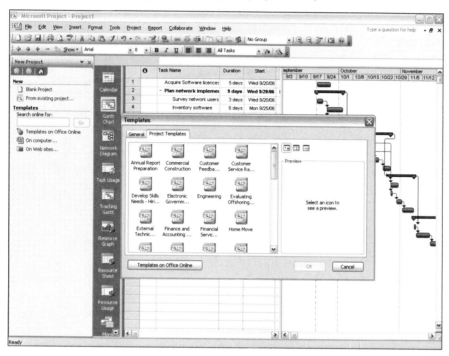

Select a template and click OK. Project displays a new project that contains tasks relevant to the title of the template you selected (see Figure 3.2). You can use this project as a starting point for your project and modify it as needed.

FIGURE 3.2

When you use a template, Project creates a new project that already contains tasks.

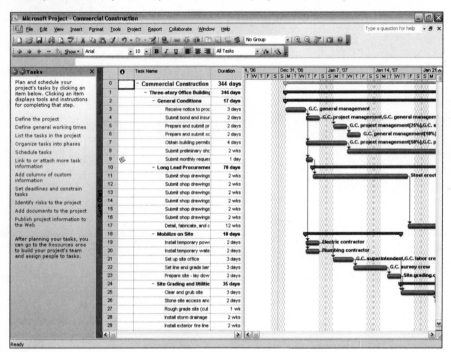

NOTE   You may need your Project 2007 CD to install a template.

The last four files you opened previously appear at the bottom of the File menu; click the File menu, and if the file you want to open appears at the bottom of the list, click it to open it.

TIP   You can change the number of files that Project displays at the bottom of the File menu. Choose Tools ⇨ Options and click the General tab. Then, modify the Recently used file list option.

You also can open a project that you previously saved if you click the Open button on the Standard toolbar to display the Open dialog box, shown in Figure 3.3, and navigate to the folder where you store projects to open the project.

FIGURE 3.3

Use the Open dialog box to navigate to the folder where you store projects and select a project to open.

Open

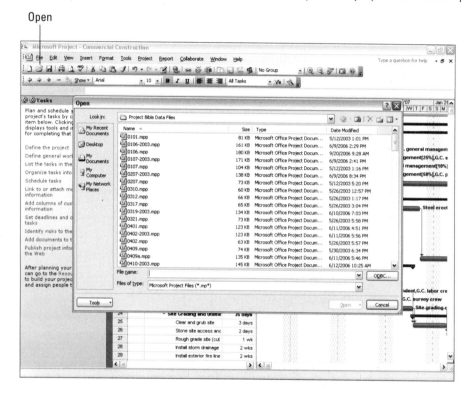

Establishing Basic Project Information

Use the Project Information dialog box, shown in Figure 3.4, to supply basic information about the new project that you want to set up. If this box doesn't automatically appear, choose Project ➪ Project Information to display it.

TIP You can make the Project Information dialog box appear automatically whenever you start a new project by checking the Prompt for project info for new projects box on the General tab of the Options dialog box. Choose Tools ➪ Options to open the dialog box.

FIGURE 3.4

The Project Information dialog box tracks basic information about each project.

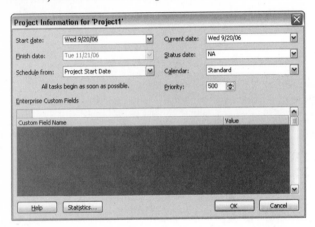

You can enter the following eight pieces of information in the Project Information dialog box:

- **Start Date:** If you set a start date for the project, all tasks begin on that date until you assign timing or dependencies to them.

- **Finish Date:** If you know your project's deadline, you can enter it here and then work backward to schedule your project. You must change the setting in the Schedule from field to make this option available.

- **Schedule From:** You can build schedules from completion to start by setting this field to Project Finish Date. Alternatively, you can build your schedule from the start date forward by accepting the default setting, Project Start Date.

- **Current Date:** Project uses your computer's current date setting for the default entry in this field. To use a different date, change the date in this field. You can adjust this setting to generate reports that provide information on your project as of a certain date or to go back and track your project's progress from an earlier date.

- **Status Date:** This field sets the date used in the earned-value calculations and identifies the complete-through date in the Update Project dialog box. The status date also enables Project to place progress lines in your project. If you leave the status date set at NA, Project sets the status date using your computer's current date setting.

- **Calendar:** You can select the calendar on which to base your schedule. The Standard calendar is the default — it schedules work eight hours a day, five days a week.

- **Priority:** You can establish a priority for each project in addition to setting priorities for tasks. For priorities, Project uses a numerical value between 1 and 1,000. The project level priority plays a role when you use shared resources across multiple projects. Setting a project priority helps you to better control how resource leveling adjusts tasks when you share resources across projects.

Leveling is a technique you can use to smooth out the use of resources so that you use resources most efficiently. Leveling is particularly useful when your resources are over-allocated; Project can help you reallocate your resources' efforts and potentially eliminate conflicts.

For more information on resource leveling, see Chapter 10.

- **Enterprise Custom Fields:** If your organization uses Project Server, you may need to assign values to project-level custom fields or outline codes that are defined in the Project Server database. You see an asterisk (*) next to any required custom field or outline code. Enter either a start or finish date — only one is available to you, depending on the choice that you've made in the Schedule From field. If you schedule from the project start date, Project defaults the constraint type for all new tasks to As Soon As Possible (ASAP). And, as you would expect, if you schedule from the project finish date, Project defaults the constraint type for all new tasks to As Late As Possible (ALAP).

To enter one of these dates, click the down arrow next to the text box. (The arrow is not available if the Schedule From field isn't set for that choice.) Select a date from the pop-up calendar, as shown . in Figure 3.5.

FIGURE 3.5

Use the arrow keys at the top of this calendar to choose other months.

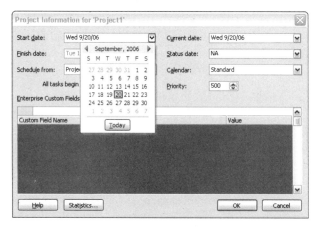

If you decide to schedule backward from the finish date, Project can't use tools such as resource leveling to resolve conflicts in your schedule.

You can change the project's start date during the planning phase, trying out alternative what-if scenarios by modifying this field. As you build your tasks going forward, Project identifies the project finish date as dictated by the length of your tasks and their timing relationships. When you're satisfied with the overall time frame, you can set the start date that works best when you're ready to begin.

TIP   If you have already begun the project, you can set the start date to a date in the past to accurately reflect the real start date.

If you know the date by which something must be completed (as with the annual meeting project, for example, or a Christmas party that must happen on December 25), you can schedule tasks by moving backward from the finish date. When you do this, Project builds the tasks going back in time. You may be surprised when Project generates a schedule telling you that you should have started three weeks earlier to finish on time. In that case, you can either add resources to get the work done faster or reduce the scope of the project.

CROSS-REF   In Chapters 9 and 10, you can read about techniques that you can use to help you resolve scheduling and resource problems.

When beginning a new schedule, you typically accept the default settings for Current date and Status date. After your project is under way, changing these default settings affects project tracking and the material that is generated in project reports.

For now, you can keep all the default settings (that is, scheduling from the start of the project, having the current date be today, and starting the project today, as well as basing your schedule on the standard calendar). Click OK to close the Project Information dialog box.

Looking at Project Calendars

The Project Information dialog box enables you to set the basic parameters of the project's timing. Those parameters and the information that you're about to enter for specific tasks are based on the Standard calendar, also called the base calendar because it serves as the basis for the calendar scheduling calculations Project makes.

You can create a Standard calendar for each group of resources in your project. For example, if the plant employees work a nine-hour day from 6:00 a.m. to 3:00 p.m., and the office employees work an eight-hour day from 8:00 a.m. to 5:00 p.m., you can create two calendars. When you assign one day of an office employee's time, Project understands it to be an eight-hour day. In the Project Information dialog box, you designate whether you want your project to use a standard, 24-hour, or night-shift calendar for most of your work assignments.

NOTE   If you're using Project Standard, the preceding information is absolutely true. If you're using Project Professional, it's *almost* all true. When using Project Professional, you can create your own calendars (for both projects and tasks) if you're working offline and storing the project locally (not in the Project Server database). If you store the project in the Project Server database, you can create calendars only if the administrator has given you the rights to do so.

Project also supports resource calendars and task calendars that you can use when a resource's calendar or a task's calendar don't follow the Standard calendar for the project. Resource and task calendars work well for resources or tasks in your project with work hours that are different from the rest of the resources or tasks.

CROSS-REF You find out more about task calendars in Chapter 4 and more about resource calendars in Chapter 5.

Setting calendar options

Project makes default assumptions about certain items that form the basis of the default project calendar. For example, Project assumes that the default week contains five working days and 40 working hours. Project uses this calendar for resources unless you assign a different calendar to them. You can see the assumptions that Project uses on the Calendar tab of the Options dialog box.

NOTE The Calendar tab of the Options dialog box does not affect scheduling. The options that you see in this dialog box show you the defaults that Project uses to convert durations into corresponding time amounts. For example, if you enter 1mo for a task's duration, Project assumes that you are allotting one month (which is equal to 20 days) for that task.

To view the default calendar options, choose Tools ➪ Options. Click the Calendar tab in the Options dialog box, as shown in Figure 3.6.

FIGURE 3.6

By reviewing the settings on the Calendar tab in the Options dialog box, you ensure that you and Project are speaking the same language when you enter task-duration information.

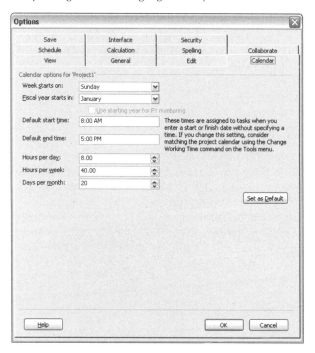

 Any changes that you make to these options apply to the current schedule only. To save your changes across all schedules, click the Set as Default button on the Calendar tab.

You can select any day of the week as your start day. For example, if you run a restaurant that closes on Sundays and Mondays, you may want to designate a work week of Tuesday through Saturday. In that case, you would set the Week Starts On field to Tuesday.

If your company uses a fiscal year other than the calendar year (January through December), you may want to set the Fiscal Year Starts In option. This setting is especially useful when you generate reports that show costs per quarter or year.

The final five settings on the Calendar tab of the Options dialog box enable you to designate specific start and end times for each day, the number of hours in a day and in a week, and the number of days in a month. For example, you can set the work day to start at 9:00 a.m. and end at 6:00 p.m., assign 9 hours to your work day (no lunch for you!), and end up with a 45-hour week.

Setting schedule options

You also can modify the way in which Project enters task information. In the Options dialog box (if it isn't open, choose Tools ➪ Options), click the Schedule tab to change the default settings for entering tasks, as shown in Figure 3.7. On this tab, you determine the default unit of time for entering task durations (the default is days), work time (hours), and whether new tasks start on the project start date or the current date. For example, if you are working on a five-year project in which most tasks run for months — not days — you may want to change the default setting for the Duration Is Entered In field. If you prefer to have any new tasks begin no earlier than the current date, you can adjust the setting for New tasks. As you gain experience in entering information, you will find ways to customize Project to match your work style.

When you are satisfied with the settings on the Schedule tab, click OK to close the Options dialog box.

Creating a new calendar

The Standard calendar may not work for your project under all circumstances. For example, suppose that you run a print shop and each project that you complete requires you to use the printing press, but the press requires cleaning and maintenance each week for two hours on Thursday afternoon. To make sure that each printing project takes the maintenance requirement of the printing press in consideration, you can create a Press calendar that covers the need to shut the press down for cleaning and maintenance. Then you can assign the Press calendar to the Press Time task that you create for each project.

FIGURE 3.7

The Schedule tab is where you modify the default settings for entering tasks.

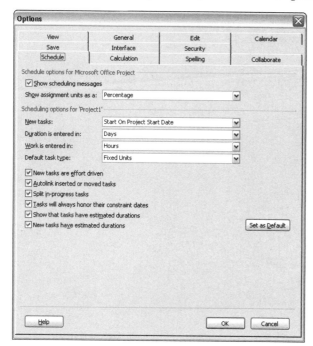

NOTE   As previously mentioned, if you're using Project Standard, everything you're about to read works automatically. However, if you're using Project Professional, you can create your own calendars (for both projects and tasks) if you're working offline and storing the project locally and not in the Project Server database. If you store the project in the Project Server database, you can create calendars only if the administrator has given you the rights to do so. Also, the privilege to create calendars doesn't permit you to change the Standard calendar.

To create a new, project-wide calendar, choose Tools ➪ Change Working Time to display the Change Working Time dialog box, as shown in Figure 3.8. The Legend panel on the left side of the dialog box identifies Working, Nonworking, Edited working hours, and exception days and non-default work weeks.

FIGURE 3.8

By default, Project displays the settings for Standard (Project Calendar) in the Change Working Time dialog box.

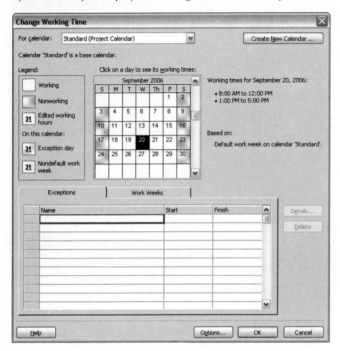

If other calendars exist, you see them listed in the For calendar list box. You can create a custom calendar by clicking the Create New Calendar button. Project then displays the Create New Base Calendar dialog box, shown in Figure 3.9.

To model your calendar on an existing calendar, select the existing calendar from the Make a copy of drop-down box. Provide a name for the new calendar in the Name box.

TIP By default, Project suggests that you copy the calendar that you were viewing when you chose the Create New Calendar button. In particular, I suggest that you make a copy of the Standard calendar rather than modify it. That way, you can always use the original Standard calendar if you need it.

Click OK to create the new calendar.

FIGURE 3.9

From the Create New Base Calendar dialog box, you can create a copy of an existing calendar or you can create a new Standard calendar.

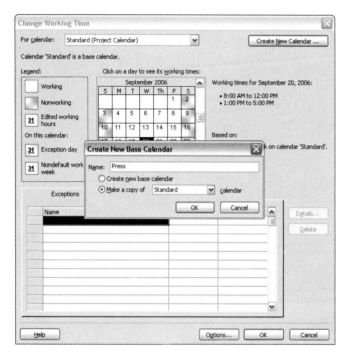

Adjusting the calendar

You can create exceptions to the Standard calendar or any other calendar using the tabs at the bottom of the Change Working Time dialog box. To accommodate the maintenance time needed for the printing press, you would modify the work week for the printing press by following these steps:

1. Click the Work Weeks tab.
2. Click the [Default] work week already defined for the calendar by Project (see Figure 3.10).
3. Click Details. Project displays the Details dialog box (see Figure 3.11).
4. Select the day you want to change on the left side of the dialog box.
5. Select the Set day(s) to these specific working times option.
6. In the Working times section, define the working time for the selected day.
7. Click OK. Project redisplays the Change Working Time dialog box.

FIGURE 3.10

To modify the default work week, select [Default] on the Work Weeks tab.

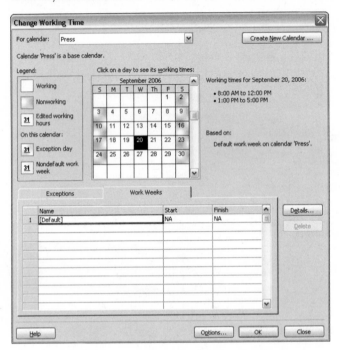

FIGURE 3.11

Use this dialog box to redefine a work week.

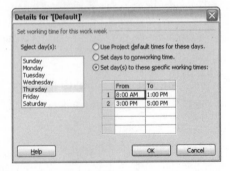

When you change the work week, the change you make is not considered an exception; instead, it is considered the normal work week. So, you won't notice any changes to the calendar in the Change Working Time dialog box. However, you can identify the working time for any day by clicking that day on the calendar; the working time appears to the right.

Suppose, however, that your child has swimming lessons every Wednesday afternoon during the month of July and you, as the owner of the business, have decided to close the shop and take your child to swimming lessons because business is slow in the summer anyway. To set up a working time exception like this one, follow these steps:

1. In the Name column on the Exceptions tab, type a name that helps you remember the purpose of the exception.

2. In the Start column, select the date on which the exception starts.

3. In the Finish column, select the date on which the exception ends. Project sets every day between the starting and ending dates as an exception on the calendar, and the Details button and the Delete button become available (see Figure 3.12).

FIGURE 3.12

To set up a working time exception, type a name for the exception and set dates.

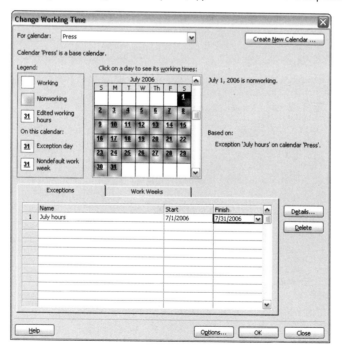

4. Click the Details button. Project displays the Details for dialog box shown in Figure 3.13.

FIGURE 3.13

Use this dialog box to define the working time exception.

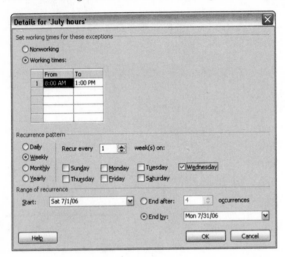

5. In the top section of the dialog box, click the Working Times option button and then set the working times; in this example, I set the working time from 8:00 a.m. to 1:00 p.m.

6. To repeat this working time pattern every Wednesday, click Weekly in the Recurrence pattern section and check the Wednesday check box.

7. In the Range of recurrence section, Project set the starting and ending dates for the working time exception using the dates you supplied in Steps 2 and 3. You can change these dates if you want.

8. Click OK. When Project redisplays the Change Working Time dialog box, every Wednesday between the beginning and ending dates you specified appears as an exception on the calendar (see Figure 3.14).

FIGURE 3.14

Project marks exceptions to the typical schedule with an underscore.

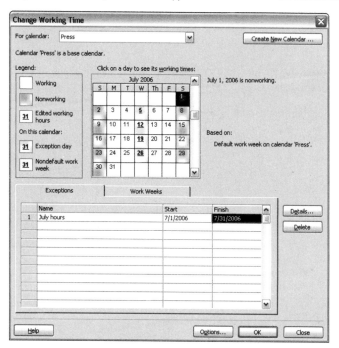

Entering Tasks

To begin building a project, enter the major steps to reach your goal in roughly the same order that you expect them to occur. (Don't worry if you're not quite accurate about the sequence of events; Project makes it easy to reorganize tasks in your schedule at any time.)

NOTE You can use the Project Guide to help you enter tasks. Display the Project Guide tool-bar (simply right-click any toolbar and click Project Guide) and click the Tasks button. In the Project Guide pane, click the List the tasks in the project link. You see helpful information on entering tasks.

For the sample project (organizing a corporate annual meeting), follow these steps to create your first task — booking the meeting space:

1. Click the Task Name column in the first row of the Gantt table.

2. Type **Book Meeting Space**. The text appears in the cell and in the entry bar that is above the Gantt table.

3. Press Enter to accept the text.

> **TIP** You also can accept an entry in a cell by clicking the check mark button that's located to the left of the entry bar, by pressing a directional arrow key on your keyboard to move to another cell, by clicking another cell with your mouse pointer, or by pressing Tab.

Information begins to appear in your schedule. Project lists the task name in the Task Name column and makes a corresponding entry in the Duration column. The question mark in the Duration column represents an estimated duration. According to the Start column, the task begins today, and a taskbar reflects the one-day duration of the task graphically. And, as you work, Project highlights any change you make that affects the schedule (see Figure 3.15).

> **NOTE** Remember the default setting in the Schedule tab of the Options dialog box? The default length of new tasks is estimated at one day. The question mark that you see in the Duration column represents the estimation that Project makes. Chapter 4 contains more information about estimated durations.

FIGURE 3.15

Project highlights the duration and dates of any changes you make that affect the project schedule.

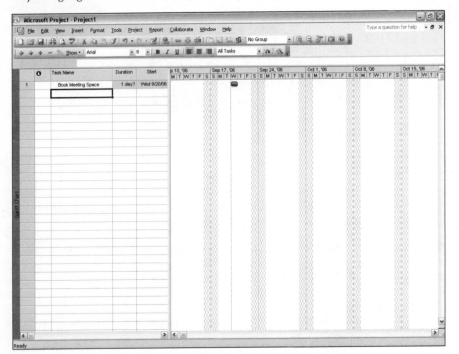

 The Change Highlighting feature, new to Project 2007, highlights the duration and date information for any task affected by a change you make in a project schedule. As you make different changes, Project highlights the duration and date information of different tasks so that you can easily identify the tasks affected by each change you make. You can turn this feature on and off using the Change Highlighting button on the Standard toolbar or by opening the View menu and clicking Show Change Highlighting or Hide Change Highlighting.

If you use the scroll bar that is located at the bottom of the Gantt table to move to the right, you see the Finish Date entry. Because this is a one-day task, it will be completed by the end of the day.

TIP You also can drag the bar that divides the Gantt table from the Gantt Chart to expand the visible area of the Gantt table.

Using either your mouse pointer or the down-arrow key, move to the second row in the Task Name column and enter **Schedule Speakers** as the next task. Then enter the following tasks in the next four rows: **Arrange for Audio/Visual Equipment**, **Order Food**, **Send Invitations**, and **Mail Annual Reports**. Your schedule should now look like that shown in Figure 3.16.

FIGURE 3.16

Note that each task is the same length by default, and each begins on the project start date.

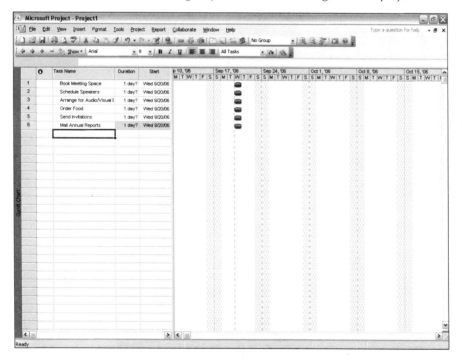

NEW FEATURE If you make a mistake, you can click the Undo button. Each time you click the Undo button, Project 2007 displays an earlier version of your project. You can click the Undo button a multiple number of times.

Adding Subtasks

After you enter the major tasks in your project, you can begin to flesh out the details by adding subordinate tasks, also referred to as *subtasks*. When you add subtasks, the upper-level task becomes a summary task. Summary tasks and subtasks provide an easy-to-apply outline structure for your schedule.

Project's outline approach also enables you to display and print your project information with various levels of detail. For example, with only summary tasks showing, you see a higher-level overview of the project that you may want to present to management. On the other hand, you can reveal the details of only one or two phases of a project so that you can discuss those tasks with the people who will be performing them. The outline structure gives you a lot of flexibility in working with your schedule.

NEW FEATURE You can use the Project Guide to help you organize your project outline. On the Project Guide toolbar (to display the toolbar, right-click any toolbar and then click Project Guide), click Tasks. Then click the Organize tasks into phases link.

When you insert a new task, it appears above the currently selected task. Begin by adding subtasks under the Book meeting space task. Follow these steps to insert a new task:

1. Click the Schedule Speakers task.
2. Choose Insert ➪ New Task. Row 2 becomes a blank row, all the other tasks move down one row, and Project selects the new task row.
3. Type **Request purchase order** and click the check mark button to accept the new task.
4. Click the Indent button on the Formatting toolbar to indent the subtask, as shown in Figure 3.17.

NOTE By default, summary tasks appear in boldface type and subtasks appear in normal type. However, some people like to differentiate these task types even more. In traditional outlining, the capitalization of items may vary, depending on their level. For example, you can capitalize the first letters of all the words in the summary tasks (headline style) and capitalize only the first letter of the first word in the subtasks (sentence style), as in this example. The choice is yours. However, if you decide to use some special effect as you enter text, be consistent so that others looking at your schedule can recognize your system. And, if others are to work on your schedule, make sure that they follow the formats that you have established.

FIGURE 3.17

The summary task now appears in boldface type.

Indent button

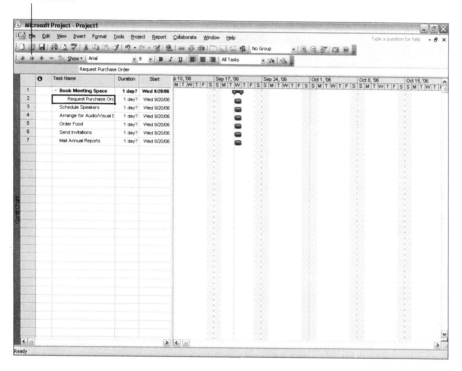

Notice that the summary task (Book meeting space) now displays a black bar on the Gantt Chart, with a down arrow shape marking its beginning and end. When a task becomes a summary task (that is, when it contains subtasks), the timing of the summary task reflects the total amount of time that is required to complete its subtasks. If a task has a duration assigned to it and you make it into a summary task, the timing of the subtasks overrides the assigned duration. If you change the timing of a subtask, the summary task duration changes to reflect the change.

You can add other subtasks by following these steps:

1. Click the Schedule Speakers task.

2. Press Insert (which is a shortcut to choosing Insert ➪ New Task). A new blank row appears.

3. Type **Select Room** and press Enter to accept the new task. The new task uses the same level of indentation as the task above it.

4. Press Insert. A new blank row appears.

5. Type **Confirm Space** and press Enter to accept the new task. The new task uses the same level of indentation as the task above it.

6. Press Insert.

7. Type **Order Flowers** and press Enter to accept the new task.

Each of these new tasks indents to the subordinate level. However, the third new task is not a sub-task of the Book Meeting Space summary task. To move the task higher in the outline hierarchy, simply select the new task and use the Outdent button on the toolbar. You can also use your mouse to move the task as follows:

1. Move your mouse over the first few letters of the Order Flowers task name until the mouse pointer becomes a two-way pointing arrow.

2. Drag the task to the left until a thick, gray line indicates that the task is lined up with the upper-level tasks in the outline, as shown in Figure 3.18.

FIGURE 3.18

You can use your mouse to drag tasks in or out in the outline hierarchy.

Outdent button

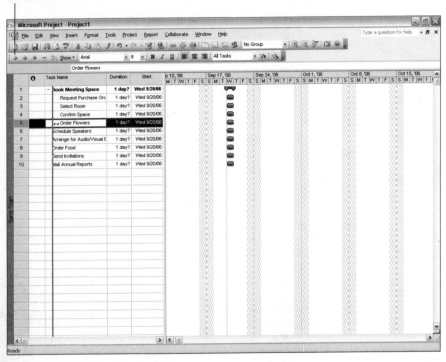

3. Release the mouse button to complete the move.

NOTE Project didn't use any Change Highlighting when you outdented the task because out-denting didn't affect any task dates or durations.

Your schedule now looks like the schedule shown in Figure 3.19. Adding details is as simple as inserting new tasks wherever you want them and then moving the tasks in or out in the outline structure.

FIGURE 3.19

The outline structure enables you to see summary tasks and subtasks as manageable chunks of work.

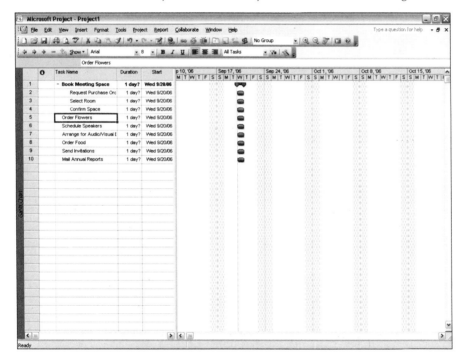

Saving Project Files

Of course, you should always save your work frequently. With the often-mission-critical informa-tion that is centralized in a Project file, frequent saving is even more important. When saving Project files, you have the option of setting up protection for them. You can also save your files as templates, that is, files on which you can base other schedules.

Saving files

To save a Project file for the first time, choose File ➪ Save or click the Save tool on the Standard toolbar. In the Save As dialog box, specify the name of the file, where to save the file, and what format you want to use, as shown in Figure 3.20.

Use the buttons and tools of the Save As dialog box to tell Project where to save a file and what format to use.

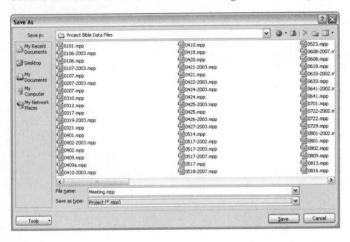

In the File name box, type a name for the file. Click the arrow at the right edge of the Save in list box to display a hierarchy of your computer's drive and directory organization. Click the Up One Level tool to move up one level in that hierarchy. Or, select one of the Save in choices (for example, My Recent Documents, Desktop, My Documents, My Computer, or My Network Places) to select a folder in which to save the file. To place this project file in a new folder, navigate to the drive or folder in which you want Project to store the new folder and then use the Create New Folder tool.

NOTE Project 2003, Project, 2002, and Project 2000 all use the same file format, but Project 2007 uses a different file format. If you need to share your files with users of earlier versions of Project, you can save your file using the file format for Project 2000 – 2003. Any features or formatting exclusive to Project 2007 will be lost. Also note that Project 2007 *cannot* save to the Project 98 file format.

By default, Project saves files in Project 2007 format with the extension .mpp. To save a file in a different format, such as a Microsoft Access database (.mdb) or a Project 2000 - 2003 file (also .mpp), you can select that format in the Save as type drop-down list. After you enter a name for your file and designate its location and type, click Save to save the file.

After you save a project for the first time, you can simply click the Save button to save the file; Project doesn't display this dialog box. If you want to change a setting or save the file with a new name, choose File ⇨ Save As to display this dialog box again.

Saving files as templates

One format in the Save as type drop-down list is template. Template files have an .mpt extension. The template feature is especially useful in project management because most companies perform projects that are similar to each other. A template file saves all the settings that you may have made for a particular project, such as formatting, commonly performed tasks, and calendar choices. Keeping template files on hand can save your coworkers (and you) from having to reinvent the wheel each time that you want to build a similar project.

You may ask, "Can't I just save my previous project's file with a new name and use that for my next project?" Yes, you can, but after you track progress on tasks, opening that final project file and stripping it back to its baseline settings is a cumbersome process — a project in and of itself. Saving the initial schedule as a template on which you can build new schedules is a much better approach. To create a new schedule, simply open the template and save the file as a standard Project file with a new name.

To save a project file as a template, use the Save As dialog box shown in the preceding section; in the Save as type list, select Template (*.mpt).

Protecting files

Some projects are as top secret as an FBI file. In a case such as this, some people within the organization — and certainly people from outside the organization — should not have access to the details. If your projects fit this mold, you need a way to keep your Project files secure from prying eyes. You can set a measure of security for Project 2007 files by clicking the Tools button in the Save As dialog box and choosing General Options to display the Save Options dialog box, as shown in Figure 3.21.

FIGURE 3.21

Don't use your phone extension, birthday, or spouse's name as a password — such passwords are much too easy to break!

Assigning a password in the Protection password box safeguards the file from being opened. Only someone with the assigned password can open a file that is protected in this way. If you assign a Write reservation password, on the other hand, anyone can open the file without a password, but as a *read-only* file (that is, no one else can make changes to the file). Finally, if you check the Read-Only recommended option, Project displays a message recommending that anyone opening the file not make changes to it. However, this choice doesn't prevent someone from making changes.

> **TIP** What kind of passwords should you use? Consider two factors: You must be able to remember the password, and you must make it something that the average person can't guess. (No password is perfect; if someone really wants to break into your files, he or she will.) Try using passwords such as an address or phone number that you had as a child—information that you remember but others are not likely to know.

> **CAUTION** Both the Protection password and Write reservation password are case sensitive. If you assign a password of JoeS, you can't open the file if you enter joes.

Closing Project

When you're finished working in Project, you can save your files as described previously and then use one of the following methods to close the program:

- Click the Close button in the upper-right corner of the Project window.
- Choose File ➪ Exit.

If you haven't saved any open files, Project prompts you to do so.

Working with a Project Outline

After you build a project outline, reorganizing the sequence of individual tasks is easy. You can also manipulate the outline to show more or less detail about your project. Outlining features work the same way in many software products. For example, Microsoft Office Word, PowerPoint, and Project all have the same outlining tools and features. In Project, you can (as you may expect) move, copy, hide, and display tasks.

Adjusting tasks in an outline

To move tasks in an outline, you can cut and paste (as you see in the following Steps 1 through 4) or you can drag and drop (as you see in the following Steps 5 through 7). You also can change the relative position of tasks in the hierarchy of the outline by promoting or demoting them (outdenting or indenting). In Step 8, you see an example of demoting a task.

To move tasks, you must first select them. Use any of the following techniques to select tasks:

You can select a task by clicking its Gantt bar.

- To select a single task, click its ID number.

- To select several contiguous tasks, select the first task. Then hold down Shift and click the last task that you want to select.

- To select several noncontiguous tasks, hold down Ctrl as you click the ID numbers of the tasks that you want to select.

Moving tasks and subtasks can be a little tricky. It's important to remember that although you can move tasks wherever you like, when you move a summary task, its subtasks move with it. Furthermore, if you move a task at the highest level of the outline to a new location just below a task with subtasks, Project demotes the task that you move. Similarly, if you move a subtask so that it appears below a task at the highest level of the outline, Project promotes the subtask that you move. To get a feel for this behavior, try the following steps:

To move a summary task only (without moving any of its subtasks), you must first promote all its subtasks to a higher level.

1. Click the ID number (in the leftmost column) for the Order Flowers task. Project highlights (selects) the entire row.

2. Click the Cut tool on the Standard toolbar.

3. Click the Gantt bar for the Send Invitations task. Project selects the row.

4. Click the Paste tool on the Standard toolbar. The Order Flowers task appears selected in its new location above the Send Invitations task.

5. Click the ID number of the Request Purchase Order task to select the task.

6. Move the mouse pointer over the ID number of the selected task; the pointer changes to a four-way arrow.

7. Press and hold down the left mouse button while you drag the Request Purchase Order task below the Order Food task. A horizontal gray line appears on-screen, indicating the new proposed position as you drag (see Figure 3.22). When you release the mouse button, Project moves the Request Purchase Order task below the Order Food task — and promotes the Request Purchase Order task in accordance with its new position in the outline.

You can promote or demote tasks by dragging. Dragging a task to the left promotes the task in the project outline. Similarly, dragging a task to the right demotes the task. You see the same gray vertical line when you promote or demote tasks that you see when you move tasks up or down in the outline.

FIGURE 3.22

Project indicates the proposed position of the task with a horizontal gray line.

Indent button

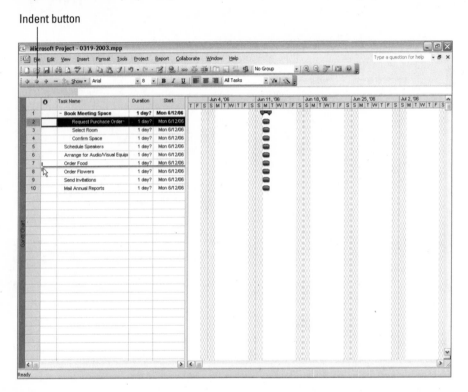

8. With the Request Purchase Order task selected (either the entire row or just the task name), click the Indent button on the Formatting toolbar to make the task subordinate.

NOTE You also can promote or demote by dragging. Move the mouse pointer over the first few letters of the subtask name until the pointer becomes a double arrow. Then drag the task to the left or right.

Your schedule now has two tasks with subtasks beneath them (see Figure 3.23).

FIGURE 3.23

FIGURE 3.23

Both Book Meeting Space and Order Food tasks have subtasks beneath them.

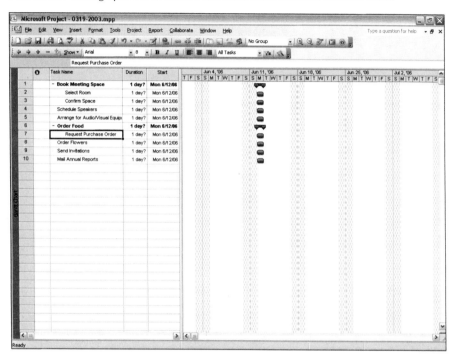

Copying tasks

Copying tasks also is simple to do and can come in handy while building a project outline. For example, suppose that you were entering tasks in a project to test various versions of a compound to see which works best as a fixative. You may repeat the same series of tasks (Obtain compound sample, Test in various environments, Write up test results, Analyze results, and so on) several times. Instead of typing those tasks 10 or 20 times, you can save time by copying them.

To copy tasks, you must first select them using any of the techniques that I described in the previous section. You can copy tasks in the following two ways:

■ Use the Edit ➪ Copy and Edit ➪ Paste commands (or their corresponding tools on the Standard toolbar) to copy the selected task(s) to another location.

> **TIP** Remember, to copy a summary task and its subtasks, you need only select the summary task and copy it. Project automatically copies the summary's subtasks for you.

■ Press and hold the left mouse button followed by the Ctrl key; then, drag the task(s) to another location. Release the mouse button to complete the copy.

If you have several repetitive phases of a project, such as the development and production of several models of a single product, you can use the fill handle to copy the tasks. In Figure 3.24, you see three tasks: Design, Development, and Production. To copy a group of tasks such as Development and Production, follow these steps:

1. Select their task names.

2. Place the mouse pointer over the fill handle in the lower-right corner of the selection.

   The mouse pointer changes to a plus sign (+).

3. Drag the fill handle down until you have selected the group of rows that you want to contain the repetitive tasks.

> **CAUTION** The fill handle copies tasks into a contiguous range. However, if the range already contains information, using the fill handle to copy overwrites the existing information. To avoid this problem, insert blank rows in the project before using the fill handle. Select the task that you want to appear beneath the new row, and choose Insert ➪ New Task. To insert more than one blank row, select the number of rows that you want to insert before choosing Insert ➪ New Task.

When you release the mouse pointer, Project copies the tasks into the selected range, as shown in Figure 3.25.

FIGURE 3.24

Take advantage of the fill handle for contiguous copy tasks.

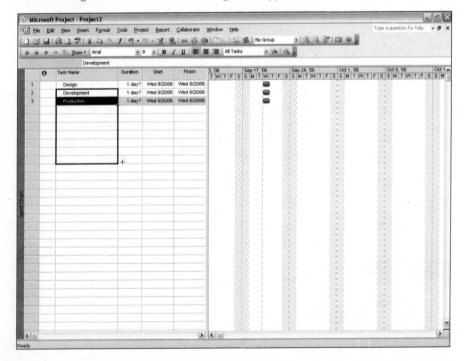

FIGURE 3.25

Project fills the range with the selected tasks.

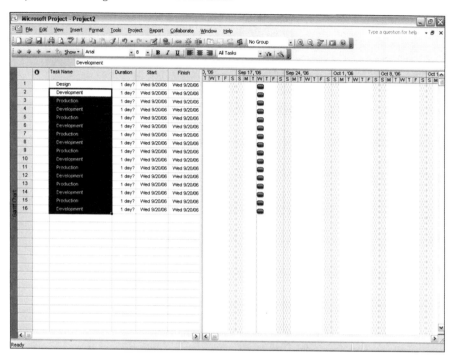

TIP Suppose that you're using WBS codes and you set up the WBS codes to automatically assign codes when you create new tasks. When you copy tasks by using any of the methods described here, Project automatically assigns incremental WBS codes to the new tasks. See Chapter 7 for details on creating WBS codes.

Displaying and hiding tasks

The outline structure enables you to view your project at different levels of detail by expanding or collapsing the summary tasks. You can use the Show button on the Formatting toolbar to quickly hide or display subtasks based on their outline level, as shown in Figure 3.26. By using the Show button, you also can quickly display all the detail tasks in your schedule.

FIGURE 3.26

Use the Show button on the Formatting toolbar to easily determine the level of detail that you want to view in a project.

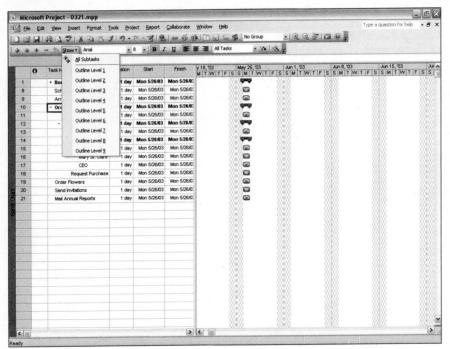

Figure 3.27 shows a minus sign (–) appearing to the left of each summary task. This symbol indicates that all subtasks are in view. If you click the minus sign, any subtasks disappear from view and a plus sign replaces the minus sign next to the summary task name. The plus sign indicates that the task is associated with some hidden detail tasks. Click the plus sign to reveal the "hidden" subtasks.

How many levels of detail can an outline have? Just about as many as you need. For example, the schedule that is shown in Figure 3.27 has several levels of detail regarding the annual meeting project. Any task that has subtasks also has the plus and minus sign mechanism for displaying or hiding the subtasks.

FIGURE 3.27

You can expand or collapse any task that has a subtask.

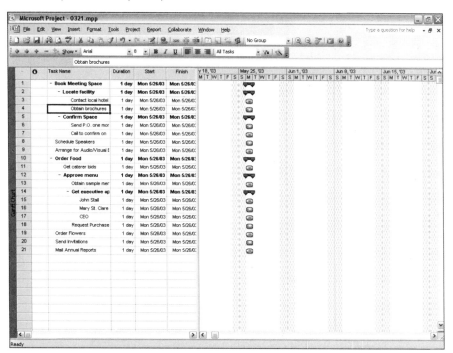

CAUTION   Using too many levels of outline indentation (usually more than three or four) makes it difficult to see your entire schedule on-screen. In fact, a very detailed project outline may indicate that you need to rethink the scope of the project and break it into smaller, more manageable projects.

You can use the hide and show features of the outline to focus on just the amount of detail that you want. You can take the same schedule that you saw in Figure 3.27, for example, and show just the highest level of detail for a report to management to summarize project activity, as shown in Figure 3.28.

FIGURE 3.28

The detailed tasks are now hidden. The plus signs and the summary-style taskbar, however, indicate that more is here than meets the eye.

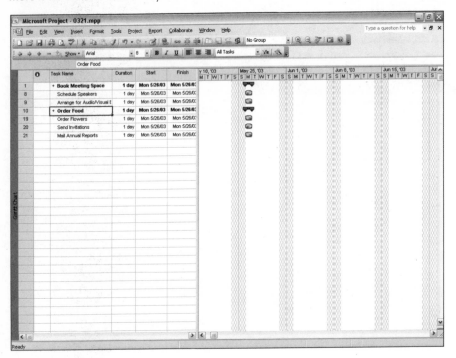

Getting Help

As you begin to build tasks in a schedule, you're likely to have questions about using Project 2007 that the Help system can answer. Project's Help is similar to the Help feature in Microsoft Office 2007 products.

Using the Help system

You click the Microsoft Office Project Help button located on the end of the Standard toolbar and choose Help ⇨ Microsoft Office Project Help to display the Help window (see Figure 3.29).

FIGURE 3.29

You can use the Project Help window to search both online and offline sources for help.

From the Help window, you can click a subject on which you want help, and Project displays a list of topics associated with the subject you selected (see Figure 3.30).

FIGURE 3.30

Project displays a list of topics after you select a subject.

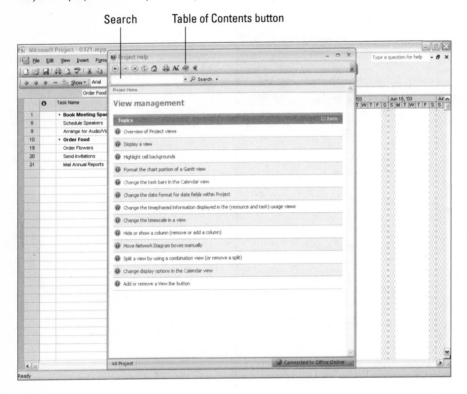

When you click a topic, Project displays the Help text associated with that topic (see Figure 3.31).

If you prefer, you can type a keyword in the Search box at the top of the Help window and click the arrow next to the box; Project searches for Help topics that include your keyword.

The Table of Contents is a good way to view the structure of the Project Help file and see the topics under each subject. Click the Show Table of Contents button on the Help window toolbar to display the Table of Contents (see Figure 3.32). Click any book in the Table of Contents to see the topics associated with that subject. To hide the Table of Contents, click the Hide Table of Contents button on the Help window toolbar.

TIP Use the buttons across the top of the Help window to go back and forward between help topics or click the Home icon to return to the opening Help window.

FIGURE 3.31

A typical Help topic.

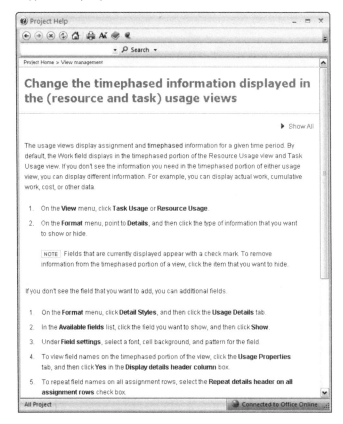

Finding online help

You can find a world of support, information, and even freeware, shareware, or products for a price that work along with Project on the Internet.

ON the CD-ROM This book's companion CD-ROM includes several products from third-party vendors that work with Project to enhance it.

You can open the Help menu and click Microsoft Office Online to follow a link to the Microsoft Office Online Web site. At this site, you can find things such as update information, files to download, and software companies that provide add-on products or specialize in the use of Microsoft Office Project. You also can find links on this page to the Microsoft Office Project discussion groups, experts, and solution providers.

FIGURE 3.32

Use the Table of Contents to view the structure of the Project Help file.

Hide Table of Contents button

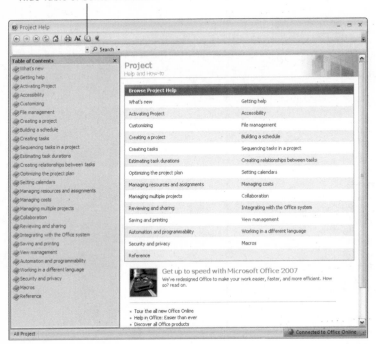

Summary

In this chapter, you started to build your first project by creating summary tasks and subtasks. You learned about the following aspects of Project:

- Gathering the data that you need to begin creating your schedule
- Entering Project information and setting up some calendar defaults
- Creating summary and subtasks
- Saving files and closing Project
- Working with the outlining hierarchy to move, copy, and display subtasks
- Using the Help system to search for information and obtain online help

In Chapter 4, you begin to add details about task types, add timing, and establish relationships among your tasks.

Chapter 4

Building Tasks

Hesiod, that classic Greek project manager, once said, "Observe due measure, for right timing is in all things the most important factor." You could do worse than to use this truism from around 700 B.C. as your personal project management mantra today. When it comes to projects, timing is, indeed, everything.

In Chapter 3 you created several tasks and used the outlining feature of Project to organize them. But every task in your schedule has the default length (one estimated day), and they all occur on the same day. In essence, you have listed the steps to get to your goal, but with no related timing information, your schedule is more like a to-do list than a project schedule.

You have to add durations to your tasks. In other words, you must establish how long (or how many hours of effort) each task will take. However, timing consists of more than determining how many hours, days, or weeks it takes to complete each task. Timing for your project becomes clear only when you've set a duration for each task and when you've established the relationships, called *dependencies,* among the tasks. Only then can you accurately predict the amount of time that you will need to complete the project.

Establishing Timing for Tasks

Your boss asks how long it will take to write that report, and you tell her it will take about a week. Your coworker calls and asks when you will be finished repairing the computer network, and you tell him it will take another day. You make estimates about task durations every day. You know your own business, and you're probably pretty good at setting the timing for everyday tasks based on many factors.

Exactly how do you figure out the timing for a task in a project? The method is virtually identical to the seemingly automatic process that you go through when someone asks you how long it will take to complete a task, such as placing an order for materials. Consider the following example:

1. You estimate that you will spend about 40 minutes doing the research and performing the calculations to determine how many square feet of lumber you'll need for the job.

2. You consider how long the actual task (placing a phone order for materials) will take. This duration could be a matter of only minutes, but if you factor in playing a few rounds of phone tag, you may want to allow half a day.

3. You also think about what's involved in getting a purchase order. With your system, cutting a purchase order can take up to four days. Some of that time requires your presence, but most of it consists of waiting.

So how long is your task? You could say that you need exactly four days, four hours, and 40 minutes, but just to be safe, you should probably allow about five days. In addition, Project uses some specific methods that you need to understand to estimate task durations accurately.

Fixed-unit tasks

By default, Project creates resource-driven tasks that are referred to as *fixed-unit tasks*. Here's a simple example. You have to plant a tree. One person needs two hours to plant a tree. If you add another person (another resource), together they need only one hour to complete the task. That is, two resources, each putting in an hour of effort, complete the two hours of work in only one hour. With resource-driven scheduling, when you add resources, the task duration becomes shorter; if you take away resources, the task takes longer to complete. And, on the flip side, the resource assignments to a task don't change when the work increases or decreases. By default, each task that you create in Project is a resource-driven, fixed-unit task type.

CAUTION The reduction of time required on a resource-driven task is strictly a mathematical calculation in Project. For example, ten people get work done in one-tenth the time of one person. However, whenever two or more people work on a task, the time savings are seldom so straightforward. You must also factor in the time for those people to communicate, miscommunicate, hold meetings, and so on.

Fixed-duration tasks

You also can use the *fixed-duration task* type in Project. The number of resources does not affect the timing of this type of task. To allow a week for a committee to review the company's new ad campaign — no matter how many people are on the committee — give the task a fixed duration. You can't shorten the task's duration by adding resources to it. In fact, adding people to the review process may lengthen the task, because their effort has no impact on getting the work done more quickly, and coordinating their efforts can add time.

To Pad or Not to Pad?

Although most people agree that delays are inevitable and that you should allow for them, people who schedule projects accommodate these delays in various ways.

Some schedulers build in extra time at the task level, adding a day or two to each task's duration — just in case. Unfortunately, padding each task may leave you with an impossibly long schedule, and it may suggest to your boss that you're not very efficient. Why should it take two days to run a three-hour test? It doesn't — but because you know that setting up the test parameters properly the first time is an error-prone process, you allow a couple of work days to complete the testing. Just make sure that your boss understands that you're building a worst-case scenario; when you bring the project in early, he or she will be glad to share the praise.

One school of thought on estimating task duration suggests that you take your estimate, double it, and then add 10%. If you are new to estimating, you might want to try this approach — as long as your project fits within the timeframe allotted for it — until you have an opportunity to track the progress of a few projects and learn just how accurately you estimate.

Some project managers add one long task, maybe two weeks or so in duration, at the end of the schedule, and they name it something like Critical Issues Resolution Period. This task acts as a place-holder that covers you if individual tasks run late. This approach can help you see how the overall time left for delays is being used as the project proceeds. For example, if the final two-week task is running a week late because of earlier delays, you know that you've eaten up half of the slack that the task represents.

Or, you can build a schedule with best-case timing. Then you can document any problems and delays that occur, and request additional time as needed. In the case of a project that you must complete quickly, you may need to work this way. However, best-case timing sets you up for potential missed deadlines.

Which approach should you use? Possibly a combination. For example, try building a best-case schedule. If the completion date is one week earlier than your deadline, by all means add a little time to the tasks that are most likely to encounter problems, such as those that are performed by outside vendors.

Fixed-work tasks

When you create a *fixed-work task*, you set the duration of the task, and Project assigns a percentage of effort that is sufficient to complete the task in the time that is allotted for each resource that you assign to the task. For example, if you assigned three people to work on a one-day task, Project would say that each person should spend 33 percent of his or her time on the task to complete it in one day. Similarly, a task may take 48 hours to complete (its fixed-work value). With one resource assigned working eight hours a day, the task will require six days to complete. With two resources assigned working eight hours a day, the task will require three days to complete. In either case, the amount of work that's required remains constant. The task's duration changes based on the number of resources that are assigned to the task.

Effort-driven tasks

For fixed-duration and fixed-unit tasks, you can tell Project to modify the percentage of total work that is allocated to each resource, based on the number of assigned resources, if the number of resources changes. In effect, you create an *effort-driven task*. The work that's required to complete the task remains the same, but Project redistributes the work equally among all assigned resources.

NOTE   Fixed-work tasks are always effort driven. You can choose to make fixed-duration and fixed-unit tasks effort driven, or you can make Project retain the original allocation of work.

In this chapter, I use Project's default settings: The durations that you assign to tasks are resource driven. Therefore, a five-day task requires five days of resource effort to complete.

CROSS-REF   In Chapter 5, you find out more about how resource assignments modify task timing.

Assigning Task Timing

You now understand the basics of estimating task timing, and you understand how task timing relates to effort that is expended on the task by resources. The actual process of assigning durations is simple. To assign a duration to a task, you can use one of the following three methods:

- Enter a duration in the Duration column of the Gantt table.
- Use the Task Information dialog box to enter and view information about all aspects of a task, including its timing, constraints, dependencies, resources, and priority in the overall project.
- Use your mouse to drag a task bar to the required length.

NOTE   You also can enter the work value after assigning the resources to the task. Project then calculates the duration and provides smart tag help, giving you the option to change the method of calculation.

Using the Gantt table

To enter a task's duration in the Entry table portion of the Gantt Chart view, simply click the Duration column and enter the duration. You may have noticed that Project uses estimated durations — a question mark (?) — by default when you type a task name but no duration. Even though Project initially assigns estimated durations to tasks, when you type a duration, Project assumes that you want a planned rather than an estimated duration — unless you enter a question mark (?).

TIP   You can change Project's default behavior (and use planned rather than estimated durations) on the Schedule tab of the Options dialog box. See the next section for more information.

You can enter a duration in a few different ways. For example, Project recognizes all the following entries as three weeks: 3 w, 3 wks, 3 weeks.

 To assign the same duration to several contiguous tasks, enter the duration once and then use the fill handle in the Duration column to copy the duration to the other tasks.

When you type a duration, Project uses the Change Highlighting feature to show you the other tasks in your project that are affected by the scheduling change you made (see Figure 4.1). In this example, the task I changed — Acquire materials — and the summary task, Phase One Testing, were both affected by the duration I entered. In particular, the finish dates of both tasks were changed by the duration I provided.

FIGURE 4.1

When you change a task's duration, Project highlights other tasks affected by the change.

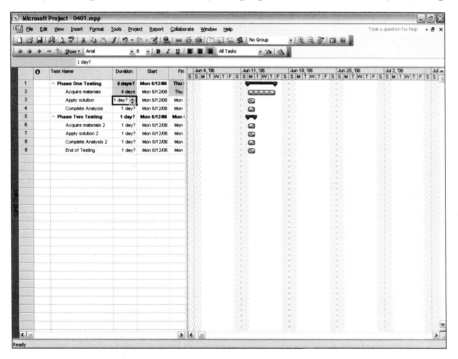

 If the information you enter has results you weren't expecting, you can click the Undo button on the Standard toolbar to reverse the effects. Starting in Project 2007, each time you click the Undo button, Project reverses the effects of each change you made in the order you made them. If you click Undo enough times, Project can return your file to the state that it appeared when you last saved the file.

NEW FEATURE Both Change Highlighting and Multilevel Undo are new to Project 2007.

Start and Finish versus Duration

You can use the Start and Finish fields in the Task Information dialog box to set a start date and finish date for the task rather than enter a duration. However, if you use the Start and Finish dates, Project uses only working days in that date range. If you enter a duration, Project calculates the beginning and end of the task, taking into consideration weekends and holidays. These two methods can have different results.

For example, suppose that you have a four-day task that starts on December 21, 2006. The following table shows how that week and the following week look on a calendar:

Sun	Mon	Tues	Wed	Thurs	Fri	Sat
17	18	19	20	21	22	23
24	25	26	27	28	29	30

December 25, 2006, falls on a Monday. If you entered 12/21/06 as the start date and 12/26/06 as the finish date, Project would calculate that as an estimated three-day task (assuming that your company closes for Christmas), with work on December 21, 22, and 26. However, if you enter four days in the Duration field, the calculated start and finish dates would be 12/21/06 and 12/27/06, respectively, taking into account both the Christmas holiday and a weekend. In this example, the work days are December 21, 22, 26, and 27.

If a task has immutable timing, such as a Christmas celebration on Christmas day, use the Start and Finish fields. If you know how many work days a task will require, but not the days on which the work will occur, use the Duration field to set timing, and let Project calculate the actual work dates based on the calendar.

Using the Task Information dialog box

Follow these steps to assign durations from the Task Information dialog box:

1. Display the Gantt Chart view by choosing View ➪ Gantt Chart.
2. Double-click a task name to open the Task Information dialog box (see Figure 4.2).

FIGURE 4.2

If you double-click an already-entered task name, that name appears in the Name field in this dialog box. If you double-click a blank task name cell, you can fill in the name here.

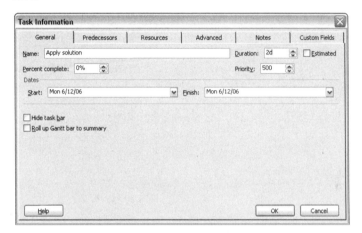

TIP   You can also click the Task Information button on the Standard toolbar, or right-click either the task name or the task's Gantt bar and select Task Information to display this dialog box.

3. Click the arrows in the Duration field to increase or decrease the duration from the default setting of one day. Each click changes the duration by one day.

NOTE   If you change an estimated duration in the Task Information dialog box, Project assumes you want a planned duration and also removes the check from the Estimated box.

To enter a duration in increments other than a day, you can click the Duration field, highlight the current entry, and type a new duration using any of the following abbreviations: *m* for minutes, *h* for hours, *w* for weeks, and *mo* for months.

NOTE   Project uses the Calendar tab of the Options dialog box to determine the number of days in a month.

4. Click OK to establish the task duration. The task's Gantt Chart bar reflects the new task length (see Figure 4.3).

FIGURE 4.3

Task bars become more meaningful after you assign durations.

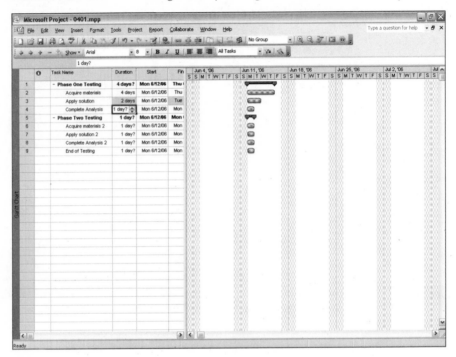

Using your mouse and the task bar

Finally, follow these steps to adjust a task's duration using your mouse and the task bar:

1. Place your mouse pointer on the right edge of a task bar until the pointer becomes a vertical line with an arrow extending to the right of it.

2. Click and drag the bar to the right. As you do, Project displays the proposed new task duration and finish date, as shown in Figure 4.4.

3. Release the mouse button when the duration that you want appears in the information box.

NOTE   When you use the mouse to set a task duration, Project does not make the duration a planned duration; instead, the duration remains an estimated one. To change the duration from estimated to planned, you must make the change using one of the two preceding methods described — the Gantt table or the Task Information dialog box.

FIGURE 4.4

If you're a visually oriented person, dragging task bars to change durations may be the best method for you.

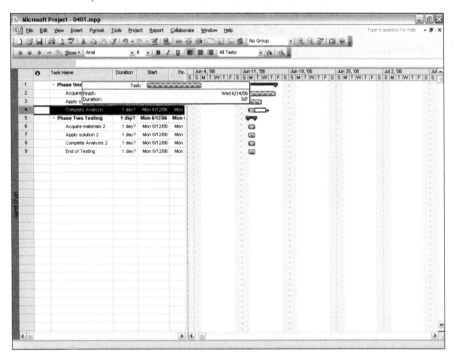

Setting scheduling options

You aren't limited to entering resource-driven tasks or estimated durations on the Gantt table. You can change the default task type and other default scheduling settings for your project. Choose Tools ➪ Options and click the Schedule tab of the Options dialog box to change the default settings for entering tasks, as shown in Figure 4.5.

In this dialog box, you determine the default unit of time for entering task durations (the default is days), the work time (hours), and whether new tasks start on the project start date or the current date. For example, if you are working on a five-year project in which most tasks take months — not days — you may want to change the default setting for the Duration Is Entered In field. If you prefer to have any new tasks begin no earlier than the current date, you can adjust the setting for New tasks. To enter planned durations instead of estimated durations, remove the check mark from the New tasks have estimated durations box on the Schedule tab.

As you gain experience in entering information, you will find ways to customize Project to match your work style. When you are satisfied with the settings in the Schedule tab, click OK to close the Options dialog box.

FIGURE 4.5

Use the Schedule tab of the Options dialog box to change Project's default behavior for scheduling.

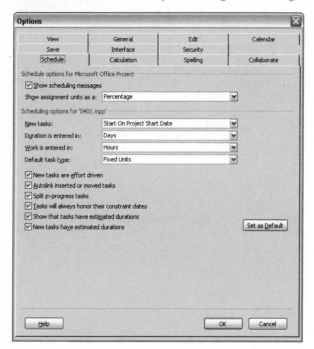

Assigning a calendar to a task

Task calendars became available in Project 2000. You can assign a calendar to a task by using the same steps that you used to create the Press calendar, described in Chapter 3. Choose Tools ➪ Change Working Time to display the Change Working Time dialog box. Click the New button to create the calendar, and provide a name for the new calendar. Then, create the calendar exceptions that apply to the task and click OK to save the calendar.

CROSS-REF For more detailed steps on creating a new calendar and calendar exceptions, see Chapter 3.

To assign a calendar to a task, double-click the task name to open the Task Information dialog box for that task. Click the Advanced tab and open the Calendar list box to assign a special calendar for the task, as shown in Figure 4.6.

FIGURE 4.6

Assign a calendar to a task from the Advanced tab of the Task Information dialog box.

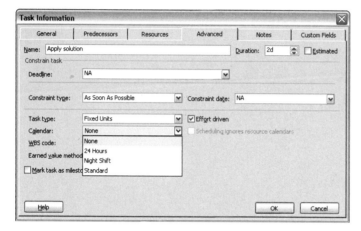

Creating milestones

Managers often use milestones to mark key moments in a project, such as the completion of a phase or the approval of a product or activity. In Project, milestones are tasks that usually have zero duration. The symbol for a milestone on the Gantt Chart is a diamond shape. For example, the diamond in the Gantt Chart shown in Figure 4.7 indicates that the End of Testing task is a milestone.

A task doesn't have to have a zero duration to be a milestone; you can mark any task as a milestone. On the Advanced tab of the Task Information dialog box, place a check mark in the Mark Task As Milestone check box. In this case, the task duration doesn't change to zero. However, the element that represents the task in the Gantt Chart changes from a bar, reflecting the task's duration, to a milestone diamond symbol, representing the task as a moment in time.

 For milestones with durations longer than zero, the diamond appears at the beginning of the duration.

FIGURE 4.7

A milestone typically marks a noteworthy point in your project; a milestone is usually a task of no duration.

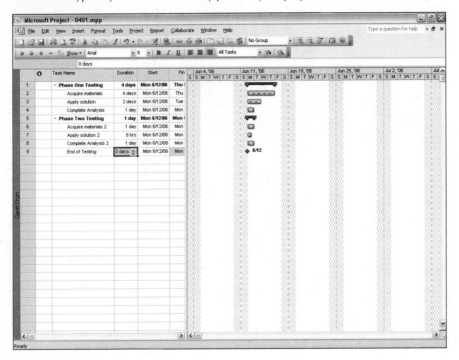

Timing for summary tasks

How do you assign durations for summary tasks? You don't. Remember, summary tasks simply roll up the timing of their subtasks. Therefore, summary tasks don't have any timing of their own. If three subtasks occur one right after the other and each is three days long, the summary task above them takes nine days from beginning to end. If you open the Task Information dialog box for a summary task, most timing settings appear grayed out, indicating that they're not available.

NOTE You can have Project display a summary task for your entire project; the project summary task displays the total time for a project, and, using a project summary task and a cost resource, you can establish a budget for your project. To learn more about cost resources, see Chapter 5. To learn more about project budgets, see Chapter 11.

Using Recurring Tasks

Projects often have tasks that occur on a regular basis. Weekly staff meetings, quarterly reports, or monthly budget reviews are examples of these recurring tasks. Rather than create, for example, 20 or so weekly staff-meeting tasks over the life of a five-month project, you can use Project's Recurring Task feature. This feature enables you to create the meeting task once and assign a frequency and timing to it. Follow these steps to create a recurring task:

1. Because Project inserts tasks above the selected task, select the task that you want to appear below the recurring task and choose Insert ⇨ Recurring Task to open the Recurring Task Information dialog box, as shown in Figure 4.8.

FIGURE 4.8

If a task occurs at regular intervals during the life of a project, you can save time by creating it as a recurring task.

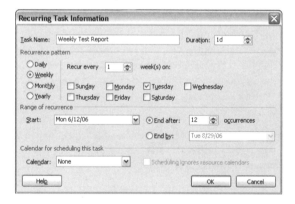

2. Type a name for the recurring task.

3. Set the task duration in the Duration field. For example, does the meeting run for two hours, or does a report take a day to write?

4. Set the occurrence of the task by selecting one of the Recurrence Pattern option buttons: Daily, Weekly, Monthly, or Yearly. Depending on the recurrence that you select, the timing settings to the right of the control buttons change. Figure 4.9 shows the Monthly settings.

FIGURE 4.9

Daily, Weekly, Monthly, and Yearly occurrences require you to make slightly different choices.

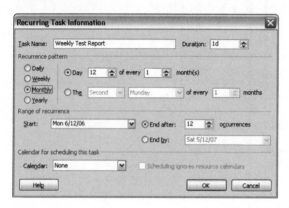

5. Select the appropriate settings for the recurrence frequency. For a Weekly setting, place a check mark next to the day(s) of the week on which you want the task to occur. For example, the task shown in Figure 4.8 occurs every Tuesday. For the Monthly or Yearly setting, select the day of the month on which you want the task to occur. The task in Figure 4.9 occurs on Day 12 of every month.

NOTE For a daily task, you have only one choice: whether you want it to occur every day or only on scheduled workdays. For example, to schedule a computer backup for every day of the week — regardless of whether anyone is at work — you can have the task occur every day. (Ask your IT department how to automate the process so that it occurs even when nobody is at work.)

6. Set the *Range of recurrence* — the period during which the task should recur — by entering Start and End after or End by dates. If you need to repeat a test weekly for only one month of your ten-month project, you can set Start and End after or End by dates that designate a month of time.

TIP If you set the End after number of occurrences, Project calculates the date range that is required to complete that many occurrences of the recurring task and automatically displays the ending date in the End by box. This method can be useful if one of these events falls on a holiday: If one of the occurrences falls on a holiday, Project displays a box that allows you to skip the occurrence or to schedule it on the next working day. For a weekly staff meeting, you can skip that meeting or schedule it on a different day. On the other hand, if you must repeat a test 16 times during the project cycle, you can schedule the test to occur on the next working day to compensate for the holiday. Therefore, set the number of occurrences rather than the time range.

7. Click OK to create the task. Project creates the appropriate number of tasks and displays them as subtasks under a summary task with the name that you supplied in Step 2. In Figure 4.10, I expanded the view of the summary task so that you can see each recurring task; note the recurring task symbol in the Indicators column.

FIGURE 4.10

Task bars appear for each occurrence of the recurring task in the Gantt Chart.

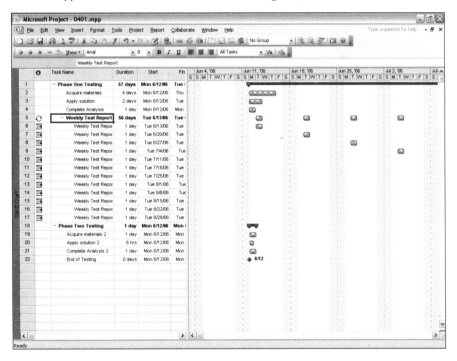

Mysterious Icons in the Indicator Column

The symbol next to each Weekly Test Report task in the schedule shown in Figure 4.10 represents a task with a timing constraint applied. Project applies this constraint automatically as you enter settings for the recurring task.

If you move your mouse pointer over one of these symbols, as I did in the following figure, you can see an explanation of that constraint. For example, each Weekly Test Report task has a Start No Earlier Than constraint, based on the timing that you set in the Recurring Task Information dialog box. The first recurring task can start no earlier than the From date entered there, and each task occurs weekly thereafter. You find out more about setting timing constraints in the next section.

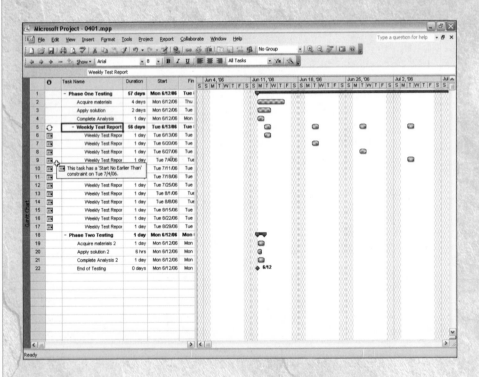

Constraints affect the timing of a task relative to the start or end of your project or to a specific date. Setting a deadline date in Project provides you with a visual reminder if you don't complete a task by the deadline date that you establish.

Establishing Constraints and Deadline Dates

Constraints affect the timing of a task relative to the start or end of your project or to a specific date. Setting a deadline date in Project provides you with a visual reminder if you don't complete a task by the deadline date that you establish.

Understanding constraints

By default, Project sets all tasks that you create to start with an As Soon As Possible constraint. Barring any dependency relationships with other tasks (see the section "Establishing Dependencies Among Tasks," later in this chapter), the task would start on the first day of the project. You can set other constraints as follows:

- **As Late As Possible:** This constraint forces a task to start on a date such that its end occurs no later than the end of the project.

- **Finish No Earlier Than/Finish No Later Than:** This constraint sets the completion of a task to fall no sooner or later than a specific date.

- **Must Finish On/Must Start On:** This constraint forces a task to finish or start on a specific date.

- **Start No Earlier Than/Start No Later Than:** This constraint sets the start of a task to fall no sooner or later than a specific date.

Only the Must Finish On/Must Start On settings constrain a task to start or end on a particular date. All the other settings constrain the task to occur within a certain time frame.

Using deadline dates

You also can establish a deadline date for a task. The deadline date differs from a constraint in that Project doesn't use the deadline date when calculating a project's schedule. Instead, the deadline date behaves as a visual cue to notify you that a deadline date exists (the down-arrow symbol that you see next to the Acquire materials 2 taskbar in Figure 4.11). If you place your mouse over the deadline indicator, Project displays the deadline information. If the task finishes after the deadline date, you also see a symbol in the Indicators column. Be aware that you won't see an indicator if you complete the task prior to the deadline date.

FIGURE 4.11

When you set a deadline date for a task, Project displays an indicator to alert you that you set the deadline.

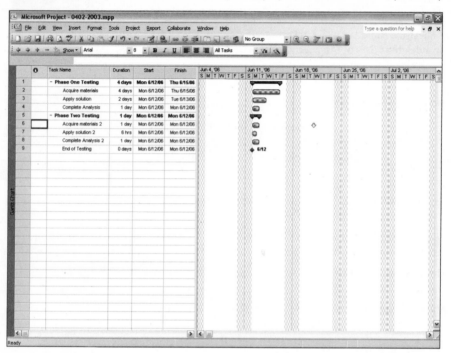

Although deadline dates don't affect the calculation of a project schedule, they do affect a Late Finish date and the calculation of total slack for the project. Also, be aware that you can assign both a deadline date and a constraint to a task. In a project that you schedule from a beginning date, a deadline date has the same effect as a Finish No Later Than constraint in the calculation of slack. If you assign deadline dates to tasks in projects that you schedule from an ending date, those tasks will finish on their deadline dates unless a constraint or a dependency pushes them to an earlier date.

Setting constraints and deadline dates

You set constraints on tasks in your project by using the Advanced tab of the Task Information dialog box (see Figure 4.12). Select a constraint type from the Constraint type drop-down list. For all settings in the type list other than As Late As Possible and As Soon As Possible, designate a date by typing in a date or by clicking the arrow next to the Constraint Date field and choosing a date from the drop-down calendar that appears. Set a deadline date by clicking the arrow next to the Deadline field and choosing a date from the drop-down calendar that appears.

FIGURE 4.12

Click the arrow next to the Constraint Type field to see the various constraints.

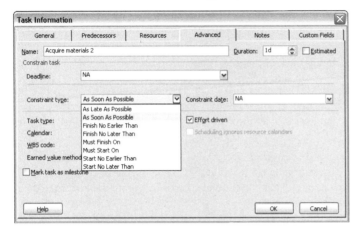

Under what circumstances would constraints be useful? Consider the following situations:

- A project involves preparing a new facility for occupancy, and you want the final inspection of that facility to happen as late as possible.

- The approval of a yearly budget must finish no later than the last day of the fiscal year, ready to begin the new year with the budget in place.

- Billing of a major account must start no sooner than the first day of the next quarter so that the income doesn't accrue on your books this quarter.

- Presentation of all severance packages for laid-off employees must finish on the day that a major takeover of the company is announced.

Deadline dates would be useful in the following situations:

- You need to prepare the annual budget by a deadline date to ensure approval in time to begin the new year with the budget in place.

- You need to prepare severance packages for laid-off employees so that you can present the packages on the day that a major takeover of the company is announced.

You see how constraints and dependencies interact in establishing the timing of tasks in the section "Establishing Dependencies Among Tasks," later in this chapter.

Manipulating the Gantt Chart to View Timing

After you enter several tasks and task durations, you'll probably want to manipulate the timescale in the Gantt Chart to view information about these tasks using different increments of time. Use any of the following methods to modify the appearance of items in your Gantt Chart:

- Adjust the amount of the window that the Gantt table and the Gantt Chart use by moving your mouse pointer over the divider line until it becomes a two-directional arrow pointer. Drag the divider to the right or left to adjust the amount of the window that's taken up by the two panes.

- Modify the width of columns in the Gantt table so that you can see more columns on-screen by moving your mouse pointer over a column heading's right edge until you see the two-directional arrow pointer. Drag the column edge to the right or left to make the column wider or narrower.

- Double-click the column heading, and change the column width in the Column Definition dialog box that appears. You can also use this dialog box to change the column title and the alignment of the column title.

NOTE   You can set the timescale to view three levels.

- Modify the increments of time displayed in the timescale itself either by double-clicking the timescale or by choosing Format ➪ Timescale. The Timescale dialog box appears (see Figure 4.13). You can change the units for the top tier, the middle tier, and the bottom tier. These adjustments enable you to concentrate on a particular period in your project or to view larger increments with less detail. The Count field controls how many instances of the unit Project marks off on your Gantt Chart.

Figure 4.14, for example, shows a top-tier timescale in months, a middle-tier timescale in weeks, and a bottom-tier timescale in days. The count for each tier is 1: one month with each of its four or five weeks shown, and each week's seven days shown.

In the Timescale dialog box, adjust the units to display and set the heading labels and alignment.

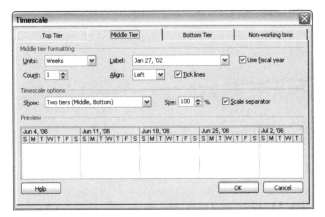

When you specify 1 week in the Count field of the Timescale dialog box, Project marks off every week on the portion of the timescale that displays weeks.

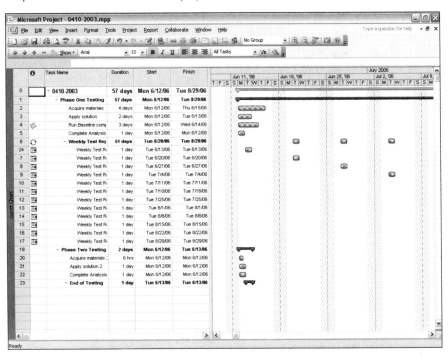

If you change the count for the middle tier — weeks — to 2, the weekly timescale displays two-week increments (see Figure 4.15). To show more of the project on-screen, consider displaying only two tiers of the timescale (see Figure 4.16).

TIP To shrink the timescale even more (that is, to see more of your project on-screen), use the Size setting in the Timescale dialog box. This setting enables you to view the timescale at a percentage of its full size.

You can independently set the use of the fiscal year for any tier of the timescale. To make this feature work, you should set up a fiscal year calendar. Choose Tools ➪ Options and click the Calendar tab of the Options dialog box. Then, change the starting month from January to your fiscal year's starting month.

FIGURE 4.15

Changing the Count field for weeks to 2 causes Project to mark off weeks in two-week chunks.

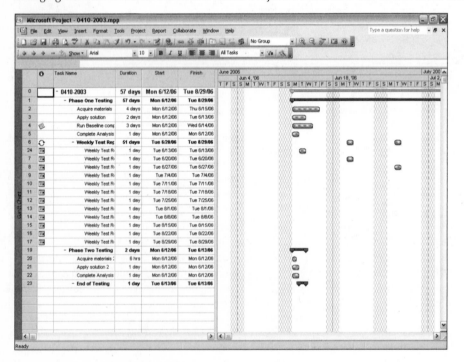

FIGURE 4.16

You can compress the Gantt task bars of your project so that you see more of the project on-screen by adjusting the timescale.

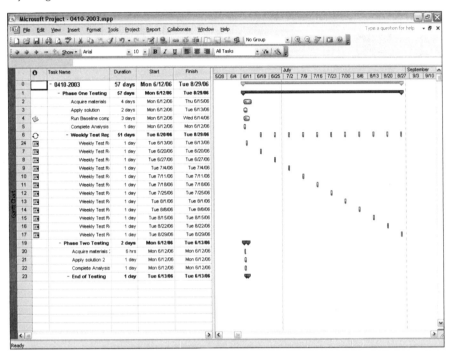

Entering Task Notes

You can attach notes to individual tasks to remind you of certain parameters or details for the task. For example, if a task involves several subcontractors, you may want to list their contact information here so that it's close at hand when you're working on the project schedule. Or, you can use the Notes field to document company regulations that are relative to that type of procedure. When you add a note to a task, you can display the note on-screen and include the note in a printed report.

CROSS-REF You can also attach notes to individual resources and to their assignments, as you find out in Chapter 5.

To enter a note for a task, follow these steps:

1. Double-click a task to open the Task Information dialog box.
2. Click the Notes tab, as shown in Figure 4.17.

FIGURE 4.17

The Notes tab provides simple word processing, such as tools for formatting your notes.

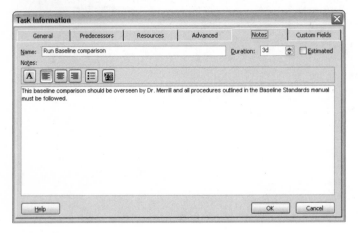

3. Type your note in the area provided. You can use the tools that are above the description box to format your note text.
4. Click OK to attach the note to your task.

A Note icon now appears in the Indicators column of the Gantt table (see Figure 4.18). Move the mouse pointer over this icon to display the note.

You can print notes along with your schedule. To do so, follow these steps:

1. Choose File ➪ Page Setup.
2. Click the View tab to display the settings that are shown in Figure 4.19.
3. Click the Print Notes check box to have Project print notes for tasks.
4. Click OK.

FIGURE 4.18

Project automatically adds an icon for the note to the Indicators column.

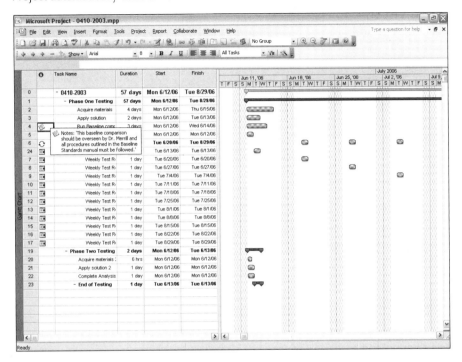

FIGURE 4.19

Notes appear on a separate page after printing your Gantt Chart when you check the Print Notes option.

Establishing Dependencies Among Tasks

Whereas constraints tie tasks to the project start or end or to particular dates, dependencies tie tasks to the timing of other tasks in the project. Dependencies are central to visualizing the true length of a project.

Dependencies exist because all tasks in a project rarely can happen simultaneously; usually, some tasks must start or finish before others can begin. Tasks overlap for many reasons, for example, the inability of resources to do more than one task at a time, the lack of availability of equipment, or the nature of the tasks themselves (you can't start construction until you receive a construction permit). You can't know the total time that you will need to complete a project until you establish durations and dependencies. For example, a project that comprises five 10-day-long tasks with no dependencies among the tasks takes 10 days to complete. But if the tasks must happen one after the other, the project requires 50 days.

Understanding dependencies

A task that must occur before another task is a *predecessor task*. The task that occurs later in the relationship is a *successor task*. A task can have multiple predecessors and successors. Tasks with dependency relationships are *linked*. Gantt Charts show these links as lines running between task bars; an arrow at one end points to the successor task. Some dependency relationships are as simple as one task ending before another can begin. However, some relationships are much more complex. For example, if you're moving into a new office and the first task is assembling cubicles, you don't have to wait until all the cubicles are assembled to begin moving in furniture. You may work in tandem, using the first morning to set up cubicles on the first floor. Then you can begin to move chairs and bookcases into the first-floor cubicles while the setup task continues on the second floor.

Understanding the interactions between constraints and dependencies

Both constraints and dependencies drive the timing of a task. Consider for a moment how constraints and dependencies may interact when you apply one of each to a task. Say that you have a task — to open a new facility — that has a constraint set so that it must start on June 6. You then set up a dependency that indicates that the task should begin after a task — fire inspection — that is scheduled for completion on June 10. When you try to set up such a dependency, Project displays a Planning Wizard dialog box, as shown in Figure 4.20. This dialog box indicates a scheduling conflict. Project displays this dialog box when a conflict exists among dependencies or between constraints and dependencies.

FIGURE 4.20

Multiple dependencies or a combination of dependencies and constraints can cause conflicts in timing.

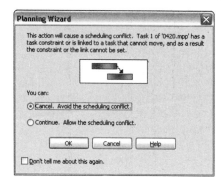

If a conflict exists between a constraint and a dependency, the constraint drives the timing of the task; the task does not move from the constraint-imposed date. You can modify this functionality by choosing Tools ⇨ Options. On the Schedule tab of the Options dialog box, remove the check mark from the Tasks Will Always Honor Their Constraint Dates check box. When you change this option, dependencies — rather than constraints — determine timing.

CROSS-REF See Chapter 9 for more information about resolving timing conflicts.

You can create dependencies in one of the following three ways:

- You can select two tasks and choose Edit ⇨ Link Tasks or use the Link Tasks button on the Standard toolbar. The first task that you select becomes the predecessor in the relationship.

- You can open the successor task's Task Information dialog box and enter predecessor information on the Predecessors tab.

- You can use your mouse button to click the Gantt bar of a predecessor and drag it to the Gantt bar of a successor to create a link to a successor task.

TIP To link a whole range of tasks to be consecutive (one finishes, the next begins, and so on down through the list of tasks), select the range of tasks (drag from the ID number of the first task to the ID of the last task). Then use the Link Tasks button or choose Edit ⇨ Link Tasks to create a string of such relationships at one time.

Allowing for delays and overlap

Although many dependency relationships are relatively clear cut — Task A can begin only when Task B is complete, or Task C can start only after Task B has started — some are more finely delineated. These relationships involve delay and overlap, and these relationships are supported in Microsoft Project by adding lag time or lead time to the dependency relationship.

To understand these two concepts, consider the following examples. Suppose that your project tests a series of metals. In the first task, you apply a solution to the metal, and in the second task, you analyze the results. However, time can be a factor, so you want the analysis to begin only when several days have passed after the application of the solution. You build in a delay between the finish of the first task (the predecessor) and the start of the second (the successor). Figure 4.21 shows a relationship with some lag — delay — between the two tasks. The line between the two tasks indicates the dependency, and the space between the bars indicates the delay in time between the finish of one and the start of the next.

FIGURE 4.21

After you apply the solution, you must wait four days before analyzing the results.

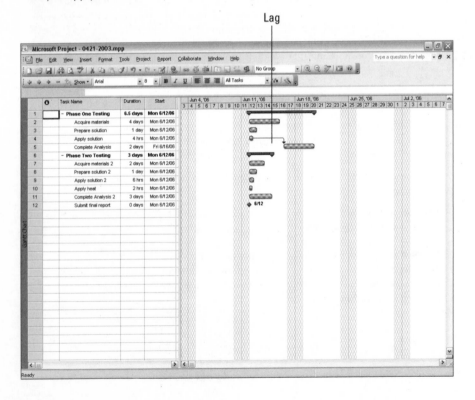

NOTE You create lag or lead time using the Predecessors tab of the Task Information dialog box. You create lag time by entering a positive duration in the Lag field, and you create lead time by entering a negative duration in the Lag field.

NOTE Some people prefer to build a task to represent lag rather than to modify a dependency relationship. For example, instead of placing a dependency between application of the solution and analysis, you can create a three-day-long task called Solution Reaction Period. Then, create a simple dependency relationship between Solution Reaction Period and the analysis so that the analysis task won't begin until Solution Reaction Period is complete. Adding the lag tasks can generate a very long schedule with multiple tasks and relationships to track. But in a simpler schedule, this approach enables you to see relationships as taskbars. You can try both methods and see which works best for you.

Another test in your project involves applying both a solution and heat. You first want to apply the solution for three days, but one day before you finish applying solution, you want to begin to apply heat as well. Notice the overlap between the tasks: the predecessor task — applying the solution — begins on June 12 and runs through June 14. The successor task — applying heat — begins one day before the end of the predecessor task, on June 14. The project shown in Figure 4.22 has some overlap between tasks, created by adding one day of lead time to the successor task.

FIGURE 4.22

Some overlap — lead time — occurs between the application of the solution and the application of the heat in this testing project.

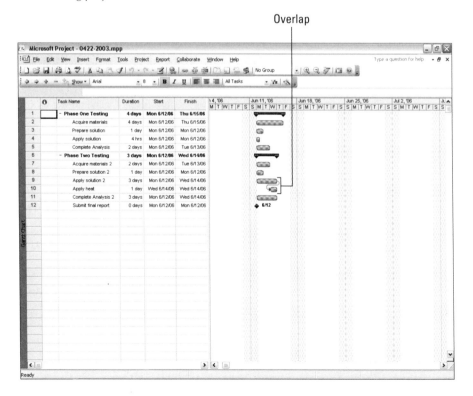

Dependency types

Four basic dependency relationships define the relationship between the start and finish of tasks: start-to-finish, finish-to-start, start-to-start, and finish-to-finish. You can set these dependency relationships on the Predecessors tab of the Task Information dialog box, as shown in Figure 4.23.

FIGURE 4.23

Four types of dependencies enable you to deal with every variable of how tasks can relate to each other's timing.

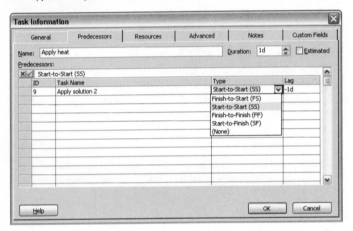

TIP   Use the Lag column on the Predecessors tab of the Task Information dialog box to create lag time between tasks.

The first timing mentioned in each relationship name relates to the predecessor task and the second to the successor. Therefore, a start-to-finish dependency relates the start of the predecessor to the finish of the successor, and a finish-to-start relationship relates the finish of the predecessor to the start of the successor. Project refers to these relationships by their initials, such as *SS* for a start-to-start relationship.

TIP   As you view the figures in the following sections, take note of the direction that the arrow points between tasks. The direction of the arrow provides important visual clues about the type of dependency.

Finish-to-Start (FS)

A finish-to-start relationship is the most common type of dependency and is, in fact, the only relationship that you can create by using your mouse or the Link Tasks tool or command. In the finish-to-start relationship, the successor task can't start until the predecessor task finishes. Examples of this relationship are as follows:

- You must write a report before you can edit it.
- You must have a computer before you can install your software.

In Figure 4.24, you see examples of the FS relationship in which the successor task can start as soon as its predecessor is finished. The following tasks have a finish-to-start relationship:

- Task 2 and Task 3
- Task 3 and Task 4
- Task 4 and Task 5

> **NOTE** The relationship between Tasks 4 and 5 also contains some lag time, as discussed the section "Allowing for delays and overlap," earlier in this chapter.

Start-to-Finish (SF)

With the start-to-finish relationship, the successor task cannot finish until the predecessor task starts. The following are some examples:

- You can finish scheduling production crews only when you start receiving materials.
- Employees can start using a new procedure only when they have finished training for it. If the use of the new procedure is delayed, you also want to delay the training so that it occurs as late as possible before the implementation.

FIGURE 4.24

In the FS relationship, successor tasks can't start until predecessor tasks finish.

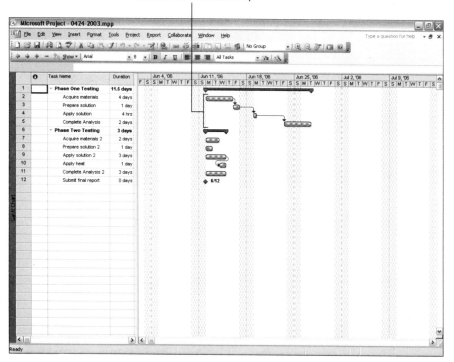

NOTE   Can you set up this start-to-finish example as a finish-to-start relationship? Not really. The idea is to allow no delay between training and implementation. If you set the new procedure to start only when the training finishes, the new procedure can start any time after the training ends, depending on how other relationships may delay it. If the training task has to finish just before the other task starts, delays of the later task (implementation) also delay the earlier task. This fine distinction will become clearer when you see projects in action.

Figure 4.25 shows a start-to-finish relationship between acquiring materials for Phase Two Testing and completing the analysis of Phase One Testing. Assuming that the test results of Phase One determine the materials that you'll need for Phase Two, you can't begin acquiring materials for Phase Two Testing until you have completed the analysis of Phase One Testing. Notice the direction of the arrow that connects the two tasks; it provides a visual clue of the type of dependency that exists between the tasks. In fact, the direction of the arrow in *all* dependencies provides you with valuable information.

FIGURE 4.25

The successor task can't finish until the predecessor task starts.

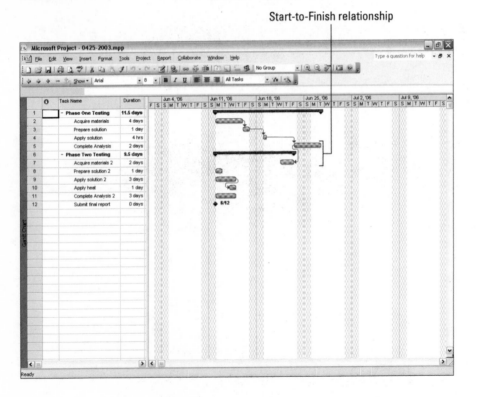

Start-to-Finish relationship

Start-to-Start (SS)

In a start-to-start relationship, the successor can't start until the predecessor starts. Consider the following examples:

- When you start getting results in an election, you can begin to compile them.
- When the drivers start their engines, the flagger can start the race.

In Figure 4.26, Tasks 10 and 11 have a start-to-start relationship. Although you'll need three days to complete the analysis, you can start the analysis as soon as you begin applying heat.

FIGURE 4.26

The successor task can't finish until the predecessor task starts.

Start-to-Start relationship

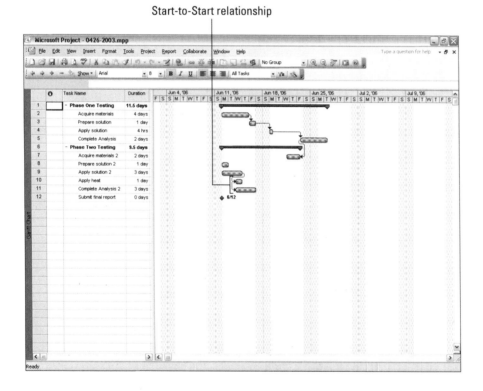

Finish-to-Finish (FF)

In the finish-to-finish dependency, the successor task can't finish until the predecessor task finishes. Consider the following examples:

- You finish installing computers at the same time that you finish moving employees into the building so that the employees can begin using the computers right away.

- Two divisions must finish retooling their production lines on the same day so that the CEO can inspect the lines at the same time.

Suppose that, in Phase Two of the testing in Figure 4.27, you can begin preparing the solution (Prepare solution 2) while you're still acquiring materials (Acquire materials 2). However, you can't finish preparing the solution until you finish acquiring the materials. Therefore, set up a finish-to-finish dependency between the two tasks to make sure that you don't finish preparing the solution if you experience a delay in acquiring materials.

FIGURE 4.27

The successor task can't finish before the predecessor task finishes.

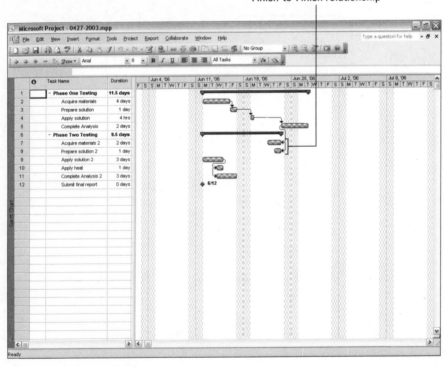

Establishing dependencies

As previously mentioned, you can set dependencies in several different ways. If you use the tasks on the Gantt Chart to set dependencies, you must establish finish-to-start relationships. To establish more complex relationships, including lag and lead, use the Task Information dialog box.

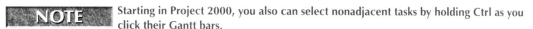

NOTE You can set dependencies between two summary tasks or between a summary task and a subtask in another task group by using a finish-to-start or a start-to-start dependency. You cannot use any other type of dependency, and you cannot set dependencies between a summary task and any of its own subtasks.

Setting finish-to-start dependencies

With the Gantt Chart displayed, you can use your mouse, use the Link Tasks tool, or choose Edit ➪ Link Tasks to set finish-to-start dependencies. Use the following steps to set a simple finish-to-start relationship:

1. Place your mouse pointer over the predecessor task until the pointer turns into four arrows pointing outward.

2. Drag the mouse pointer to the second task. An information box describes the finish-to-start link that you are about to create, as shown in Figure 4.28.

3. Release your mouse button when you're satisfied with the relationship, and Project establishes the link.

To use the Link Tasks tool or the Edit ➪ Link Tasks command, simply follow these steps:

1. Select the tasks that you want to link. To select adjacent tasks, drag through their ID numbers in the Gantt Chart table. To select nonadjacent tasks, hold down Ctrl as you click the ID numbers of the tasks that you want to link.

NOTE Starting in Project 2000, you also can select nonadjacent tasks by holding Ctrl as you click their Gantt bars.

2. Click the Link Tasks tool, or choose Edit ➪ Link Tasks. Project establishes the link.

FIGURE 4.28

The relationship isn't established until you release the mouse button. If you have second thoughts, just drag the pointer back to the predecessor task before releasing your mouse button.

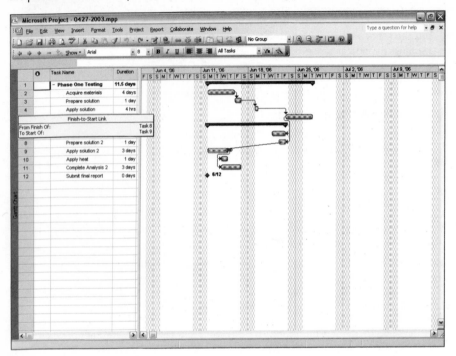

Setting other types of dependencies

You can use either the Task Information dialog box or the Task Dependency dialog box to set any type of dependency. Use the Task Dependency dialog box, as shown in Figure 4.29, to establish dependency types or lag times between tasks. To open the Task Dependency dialog box, double-click the line that connects the tasks that you want to change.

FIGURE 4.29

Use this dialog box to establish task dependencies or lag time.

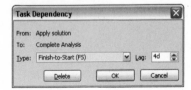

From the Task Information dialog box, in addition to establishing dependencies and lag times, you also can set lead times. If you choose to use the Task Information dialog box, open the dialog box for the successor task and build the relationship on the Predecessors tab.

Follow these steps to create a task dependency:

1. Double-click the task that you want to make a successor. When the Task Information dialog box appears, select the Predecessors tab if it's not already displayed.

2. Click the Task Name column; an arrow appears at its far end.

3. Click the arrow to the right of the column to display the drop-down list of task names, as shown in Figure 4.30.

FIGURE 4.30

Every task that you create for your project appears on this list.

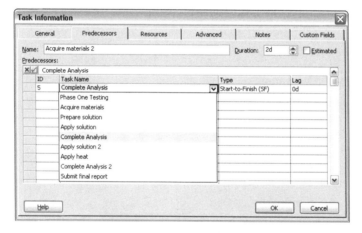

4. Click the task that you want to identify as the predecessor to this task.

5. Click the Type field; a list box arrow appears.

6. Click the arrow to display a list of dependency types.

7. Click the type of dependency that you want to establish, such as start-to-start or start-to-finish.

To establish a dependency with no lag or lead, click OK at this point to create the relationship. To establish a delay, click the Lag column and supply an amount of time for the delay. To establish an overlap, simply enter a negative number in the Lag column. For example, if you want the successor to finish one week before the predecessor finishes, use a finish-to-finish relationship and enter **1 week** in the Lag column.

> **TIP** Here's a quick way to create Finish to Finish, Start to Finish, or Start to Start relationships. Create the default Finish to Start relationship for the tasks. Then, double-click the link line to open the Task Dependency dialog box and change the relationship.

Viewing Dependencies

After you've established several dependencies in a project, you can study them in several ways. You can, of course, open each task's Task Information dialog box and look at the relationships listed on the Predecessor tab. You can also view the lines that are drawn between tasks to see dependencies. You can scroll to the right in the Gantt table, or you can reduce the size of the Gantt Chart to see more of the Gantt table and display the Predecessors column, as shown in Figure 4.31. This column lists any relationships, using the two-letter abbreviations for the dependency type and positive and negative numbers to show lag and overlap.

Or, you can use the Task Drivers pane to explore the relationships of your tasks. You select a task and then choose Project ➪ Task Drivers to display the pane.

FIGURE 4.31

Display the Predecessors column to show all the relationships for a task.

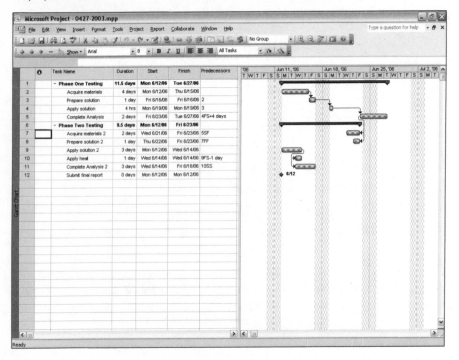

The information that appears in the Task Drivers pane changes, depending on whether you've set a baseline for your project and recorded actual information. If you have not yet set a baseline or recorded any actual information, like the project shown in Figure 4.32, Project displays the selected task's planned start date, predecessor task, type of dependency between the tasks, the amount of lag or lead time between the tasks, the selected task's calendar, and any resource assignments for the selected task. If the selected task is either a summary or subtask, you also see that information in the Task Drivers pane.

You can click any task in the project schedule to see its information in the Task Drivers pane, and, if you click the predecessor task's name in the Task Drivers pane, Project selects the predecessor task and displays its relationship information.

If you have set a baseline and recorded actual information, Project doesn't display relationship information in the Task Drivers pane; instead, you see actual start date information.

NEW FEATURE The Task Drivers pane is new in Project 2007.

CROSS-REF For more information on setting a baseline and recording actual information, see Chapters 11 and 12.

FIGURE 4.32

You can use the Task Drivers pane to explore task relationships.

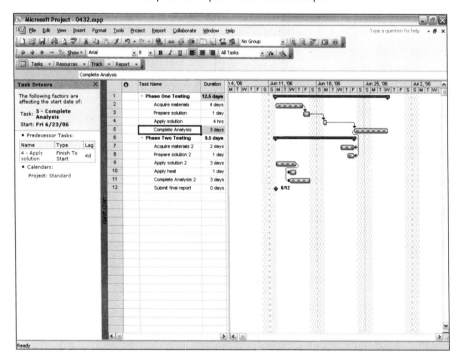

Deleting Dependencies

You can delete dependencies in several ways:

- Open the Task Information dialog box for the successor task, select the Predecessors tab, click the task name for the link that you want to break, and press Delete.

- Display the Predecessors column in the Gantt table, click the Predecessors cell for the successor task, and either press Delete to delete all relationships or edit the predecessor information in the cell or in the entry bar.

- Select the tasks that are involved in the dependency that you want to delete and click the Unlink Tasks tool, or choose Edit ➪ Unlink Tasks.

- Double-click the dependency line, and click the Delete button in the Task Dependency dialog box.

NOTE If you delete a dependency, the task bars may shift accordingly to reflect any new timing.

Summary

In this chapter, you read more about the timing of tasks, including how to set task durations and dependencies. You now should know how to do the following things:

- Differentiate between resource-driven and fixed scheduling

- Establish task durations

- Assign calendars to tasks

- Create recurring tasks

- Establish constraints and deadline dates

- Adjust the timescale to view task durations

- Add and view task notes

- Set, view, and delete dependencies

In Chapter 5, you begin to assign resources to tasks and to find out more about the relationship between resource assignment and task timing.

Chapter 5

Creating Resources and Assigning Costs

The management portion of the term *project management* suggests that you are overseeing and, supposedly, controlling what goes on during the project's lifetime. In the last chapter, you found out how to build the tasks that comprise the project. Now you need to identify the resources for each task. Some tasks require people only; other tasks may also require equipment.

As you create resources, you see that various rates are associated with a resource. As you assign the resource to a task in your project, Microsoft Project automatically begins to calculate the cost of your project.

Understanding Resources

Resources are the people, supplies, and equipment that enable you to complete the tasks in your project. In versions prior to Project 2000, you could define only *work resources* — people or equipment that consume time when working on a task. When you set up work resources, you define the amount of time that the resources have to spend on a project (100 percent is full-time). Similarly, when you assign a work resource to a task, you indicate the amount of time that you want the work resource to spend on the task (100 percent is full-time).

Project 2000 added *material resources* — items that are consumed while working on a project. Material resources use, well, materials such as gasoline or wood — as opposed to time. When you assign a material resource to a task, you specify the amount of the material resource that you intend to use in units that are appropriate for the material resource. You can also indicate whether the amount of material used is based on time. For example, the number of gallons of water that are used when watering a lawn depends on the amount of time that you run the water and the number of gallons per hour that flow from the faucet. Or, you can indicate that the amount of material is fixed. For example, you need five 2×4s to construct a bench — regardless of how long you take to build the bench.

Project 2002 gave you the capability to define *generic resources* — resources (as defined by you) that aren't specific people, equipment, or materials, but rather descriptions of the skills that you need for a task when you don't know what specific resources are available. Although this generic resource feature was designed to work in conjunction with the Resource Substitution Wizard and Enterprise Resources (available in Project Server), you may find generic resources handy even if you don't use Project Server. For example, you can use generic resources when you don't care who does the work — you simply want to track the work that is completed on a project.

CROSS-REF If you're using Project Server, you can also take advantage of three other related features. You can define Enterprise Resources — resources that are available company-wide for projects. You can use the Build Team page to help you select resources for your project from the Enterprise Resource pool, and you can use the Resource Substitution Wizard to replace generic resources with actual resources. Read more about all of these features in Chapter 19.

Project 2007 introduces the *cost resource*. Using a cost resource, you can add a fixed cost to a task without making the cost depend on work performed. If one or more tasks in your project require that you rent a storage unit during part of the project, you can set up the storage unit as a cost resource that you can assign to tasks during the appropriate periods to account for the cost of the storage unit as part of the task. Or, suppose that a resource needs to fly from Salt Lake City to Chicago to complete a task; you can set up the airline tickets as a cost resource and add them to the task.

NEW FEATURE The cost resource is new in Project 2007.

Resources cost money and therefore affect the cost of the project. To manage a project effectively, you should define resources and assign those resources to tasks in the project. Thus, you need to know how Project uses those resource assignments to change the duration and length of your project.

TIP If you are not using Project Server and expect to use the same resources for several projects, consider setting up the resources in a special project that contains no tasks. Then you can use Project's resource pooling feature and the "resource project" to share resources across multiple projects. This approach enables you to set up resources once and then use them repeatedly on many different projects. For more information about resource pooling, see Chapter 15. If you use Project Server, see Chapter 18 for more information about setting up Enterprise Resources.

How resources work

By defining and then assigning resources, you accomplish the following goals:

- You can keep track of the tasks that are being performed by resources — because Project identifies the resources that are assigned to each task.
- You can identify potential resource shortages that may force you to miss scheduled deadlines and possibly extend the duration of your project.

- You can identify underutilized resources. If you reassign these resources, you may be able to shorten the project's schedule.

- You can determine the cost of each task and your project as a whole.

When the tasks that you create are effort driven — Project defines all new tasks as effort driven by default — the resources that you assign to a task affect the duration of the task. For example, if you assign two people to do a job, the job typically gets done in less time than if you assigned only one person to the job. But, you ask, what about the cost? Does the use of additional resources increase the project's cost? Perhaps yes — perhaps no. You may find that completing the project in less time (by using more resources) saves you money because you can accept more projects. Or you may be eligible for a bonus if you complete the project earlier than expected, and the bonus may cover or exceed the cost of the additional resources that you used.

How Project uses resource information to affect the schedule

For effort-driven tasks, Project uses the resource information that you provide to calculate the duration of the task and, consequently, the duration of the project. However, if you set up a task with a fixed duration, Project ignores the resources that are assigned to the task when calculating the duration of the project. Similarly, if you don't assign resources, Project calculates the schedule using only the task duration and task dependency information that you provide.

CROSS-REF See Chapter 4 for information on task durations and task dependencies.

Assigning a resource to a task can affect the duration of the project because work on the task can't begin until the resource is available. Project uses a resource calendar to define the working days and times for a resource, but the resource's availability also depends on other tasks to which you have assigned the resource.

If the work assigned to a resource exceeds the time that is available, Microsoft Project assigns the resource to the task and indicates that the resource is overallocated. This technique enables you to see the problem and decide how to fix it.

How Project gathers cost information

When you assign costs to resources and then assign resources to tasks, Project can calculate the cost of tasks as well as the project. In addition to resource-associated costs, Project also handles fixed costs, which you read more about near the end of this chapter.

CROSS-REF You have the option of assigning costs to resources when you define them, as you see in "Creating a Resource List," later in this chapter.

Assigning costs enables you to monitor and control the money that you're spending on a project. Project shows you where and how you are spending your money. This information enables you to control when a project's costs accrue, which, in turn, helps you to schedule your bill payment. The cost-related information that Project provides helps you to verify the following items:

- The cost of resources and materials for any task
- The cost of any phase of your project as well as the cost of the entire project

TIP Cost information that you gather on one project may help you to calculate bids for future projects.

Creating a Resource List

NOTE If you intend to upload your project into the Project Server database, you may want to assign resources from the Enterprise Resource pool, a company-wide group of resources. See Chapter 18 for details on assigning resources from the Enterprise Resource pool.

Project gives you the option of creating resources one at a time, as you think of them, or entering all (or most) resources by using the Entry table of the Resource Sheet. To display the Resource Sheet, shown in Figure 5.1, click the Resource Sheet button on the View bar or choose View ⇨ Resource Sheet. By default, Project displays the Entry table of the Resource Sheet.

NOTE You can switch tables by choosing View ⇨ Table and then selecting from the submenu that appears. Each table contains columns that are pertinent to its name. For example, the Cost table shows columns that pertain to a resource's cost.

TIP To add resources to your projects that exist elsewhere (such as your company address book or in Microsoft Project Server), click the first link on the Resource page of the Project Guide.

If you use the Resource Sheet to define most of the resources for your project, the process of assigning resources goes much faster because you don't have to stop to create the resource first. Also, using the Resource Sheet is a safe way to define resources; the visual presentation helps you avoid accidentally creating the same resource twice. For example, if you define Vicki and Vickie, Project sees two resources, even though you may have simply misspelled the name the second time.

You can enter the basics for the resource by filling in the Resource Sheet; simply press Tab to move from field to field (cell to cell). The Resource Sheet shown in Figure 5.1 does not show all the fields described in this section. Scroll to the right to see the rest of the Entry table of the Resource Sheet.

TIP You can customize the Resource Sheet to show many additional fields that you may want to set up for each resource. For example, if you need to manually enter e-mail addresses for each resource, you can add the E-mail Address column to the Resource Sheet.

FIGURE 5.1

The Resource Sheet displays a list of the resources that are available to your project.

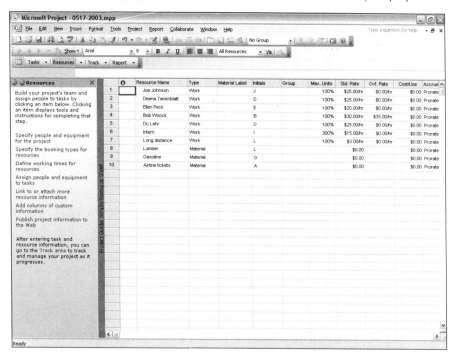

CROSS-REF
See Chapter 7 to find out how to insert a column in a table.

NOTE As part of the Project Guide, you can have Project walk you through the process of creating resources. The Resources page of the Project Guide, visible in Figure 5.1, appears when you display the Resource Sheet view or when you click the Resources button on the Project Guide toolbar. Click a link to walk through the associated steps.

A *field* is a cell in a table into which you type appropriate information. All table and form views contain fields. Each field on the Resource Sheet serves a specific purpose, as follows:

- **Indicators:** Although you can't type in the Indicators field, icons appear here from time to time. Some of the icons appear as Project's response to an action that you've taken. For example, you may see an indicator for an overallocated resource. In other cases, the indicator appears because you entered a note about the resource. See the section "Adding notes to a resource," later in this chapter, for more information.

TIP   If you rest your mouse over an indicator, Project displays the information that is associated with the icon.

- **Resource Name:** Type the name of the resource. For a person, you can type the person's name or you can type a job description, such as Product Analyst 1 or Product Analyst 2.

- **Type:** Use this column to specify whether you're defining a human, material, or cost resource. Project refers to human resources as Work.

- **Material Label:** For material resources, specify the unit of measure. You can set up any label that you want. For example, you can use minutes for long distance, feet for lumber, or miles for gasoline.

- **Initials:** Type initials for the resource, or accept the default that Project provides, which is the first letter of the resource name. This designation appears on any view to which you add the Initials field. Typically, a resource's name appears, but you can customize the view to display initials if you prefer.

- **Group:** Assign resources to groups if they share some common characteristic, such as job function. Then you can use this field as a filtering or sorting mechanism and display information about the group (a particular job function) as opposed to a specific resource. Just type a name to create a group.

TIP   Be sure to spell the group name the same way each time if you want to filter or sort by group.

- **Max. Units:** Project expresses the amount of the work resource that you have available for assignment as a percentage. For example, 100 percent equals one unit, or the equivalent of one full-time resource; 50 percent equals one-half of a unit, or one-half of a full-time resource's time; and 200 percent equals two full-time resources.

- **Std. Rate:** The standard rate is the rate that you charge for regular work for a resource. Project calculates the default rate in hours. However, you can charge a resource's work in other time increments. (For work resources, you can use minutes, days, weeks, months, or years. For material resources, think of the charge as per unit based on the Material Label.) To specify a time increment other than hours, type a forward slash and then the first letter of the word representing the time increment. For example, to charge a resource's use in days, type **/d** after the rate that you specify.

- **Ovt. Rate:** The overtime rate is the rate that you charge for overtime work for a work resource. Again, Project calculates the default rate in hours, but you can change the default unit the same way that you changed it for the standard rate.

- **Cost/Use:** In the Cost/Use column (read as cost per use), supply a rate for costs that are charged for each use of the resource. Resource costs may be based on the Standard rate (which is calculated by multiplying the number of hours times the cost per hour), the Cost/Use rate (a fixed fee for use of the resource), or a combination of the two. Project uses a combination of the Cost/Use field and the Std. Rate field when calculating the cost of a task. If you rented a piece of equipment that costs you $25/hour plus a setup charge of $100, you would assign a Std. Rate of $25/hour and a Cost/Use of $100.

- **Accrue At:** This field specifies how and when Microsoft Project charges resource costs to a task at the standard or overtime rates. The default option is Prorated, but you also can select Start or End. The three are described as follows:

  - If you select Start and assign that resource to a task, Project calculates the cost for a task as soon as the task begins.

  - If you select End and assign that resource to a task, Project calculates the cost for the task when the task is completed.

  - If you select Prorated and assign that resource to a task, Project accrues the cost of the task as you complete scheduled work.

TIP   If you set the cost-per-use rate for a resource and assign that resource to a task, Project will use the Accrue At field to determine whether the cost is applied at the beginning or end of the task. If you set the Accrue At field to Start or Prorated, Project charges the cost at the beginning of the task. If you set the Accrue At field to End, Project charges the cost at the end of the task.

- **Base Calendar:** Base calendar identifies the calendar that Project should use when scheduling the resource. The calendar identifies working and nonworking time. Project assumes that each resource uses the Standard calendar, but as you read later in this chapter, you can create calendars for resource groups (perhaps to handle shift work) or you can modify an individual resource's calendar to reflect vacation or other unavailable time (such as jury duty).

- **Code:** You can use this field as a catchall field to assign any information that you want to a resource, using an abbreviation of some sort. For example, suppose that your company uses cost-center codes. You may want to supply the cost-center code for the resource in the Code field. You can sort and filter information by the abbreviations that you supply in the Code field.

NOTE   After you create a resource, Project displays the resource's ID number on the left edge of the Resource Sheet, to the left of the Indicator column.

Modifying Resource Information

You just learned a quick way to set up a resource — by entering it on the Resource Sheet. In addition, you can use the Resource Information dialog box to fine-tune your resource's definition.

Use the Resource Information dialog box to modify resource information. To display the Resource Information dialog box, double-click any resource on the Resource Sheet or choose Project ➪ Resource Information. Then click the General tab.

You already provided most of the information on this tab on the Resource Sheet, so this section discusses the fields in the dialog box that didn't appear by default on the Entry table of the Resource Sheet.

Assigning a communication method

Use the Email field, shown in Figure 5.2, to supply the e-mail address of a resource.

FIGURE 5.2

Use the General tab of the Resource Information dialog box to add information about a resource, such as an e-mail address or availability.

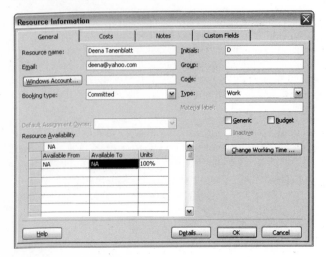

 Project 2007 no longer supports e-mail workgroups.

Specifying resource availability

Suppose that you set up a resource to represent a specific job, such as Intern, as shown in Figure 5.3. And suppose that you have more than one of this resource, but not at all times. Using the Resource Availability table (refer to Figure 5.3), you can specify the time periods for which the resource will be available. Figure 5.3 shows that three interns are available from June 1 through July 31 and only one intern is available from August 1 through August 31.

 Starting in Project 2000, you can contour the availability of resources. See Chapter 10 for more information.

Specifying a booking type

 The Booking Type field became available in Project 2003.

You can specify a booking type for a resource assignment. Booking types are most useful in the Enterprise environment, where you are utilizing the Enterprise Resource Pool.

E-mail and Project

If you're using Outlook and you've stored the resource's e-mail address in your address book, you can click the Details button in the Resource Information dialog box to have Project look up the e-mail address for you. You can then copy the address from the address book, close the address book, and in the Email field, press Ctrl+V to paste the address into the Resource Information dialog box.

However, I suspect that you'll find it faster to use the Specify people and equipment for the project link on the Resources page of the Project Guide to enter e-mail addresses for resources. When you click the link, the page changes and presents you with four options. Select the second one (Add Resources from the Company Address Book), click the Address Book link that appears, as shown in the following figure, and follow the on-screen instructions.

Use the Project Guide to help you enter resource e-mail addresses

The Booking Type field offers you two choices: Committed and Proposed (see Figure 5.4). When you commit a resource, you are officially assigning the resource to the project. When you propose to use a resource, you are indicating that the resource is not yet officially assigned to the project, which essentially leaves the resource's calendar untouched by the proposed assignment to your project. Another project manager could commit the resource to a different project for the same time frame, and Microsoft Project will *not* identify the resource as being overallocated. Project does not consider proposed bookings when calculating resource allocation.

FIGURE 5.3

Use the Resource Availability table to identify when a resource is available.

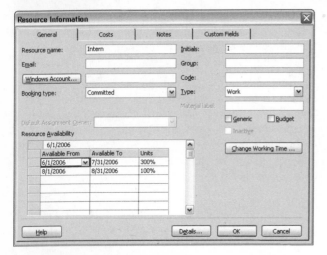

FIGURE 5.4

Specify whether to commit a resource or simply propose its use.

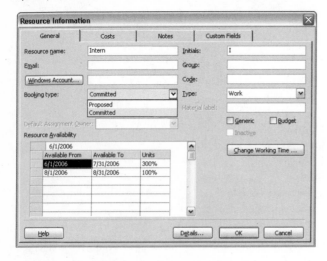

TIP   The Booking type that you choose for a resource applies to *all* tasks in your project to which you assign the resource.

Creating a generic resource and assigning custom fields

The Intern resource that was discussed in the previous section is essentially a generic resource. It's a job description, not a person. To mark a resource as generic, place a check mark in the Generic box on the General tab of the Resource Information dialog box (refer to Figure 5.4). Your company may have set up custom fields in Project that apply to your generic resource. To assign the appropriate custom fields, click the Custom Fields tab and assign any appropriate values to your generic resource, as shown in Figure 5.5.

CROSS-REF See Chapter 18 for more information about creating custom fields.

When you click OK to close the dialog box, you see an icon in the Indicator column like the one shown in Figure 5.6. This icon signifies that the resource is generic.

FIGURE 5.5

You can assign custom fields to generic resources to describe the skills that are required.

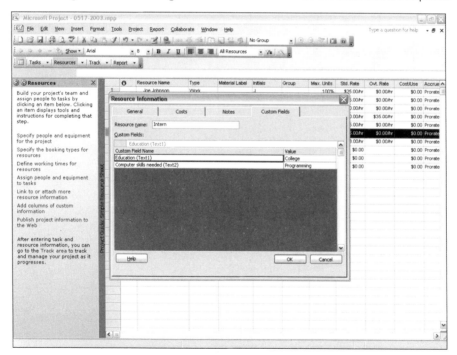

FIGURE 5.6

Identify generic resources by the icon that's shown in the Indicator column.

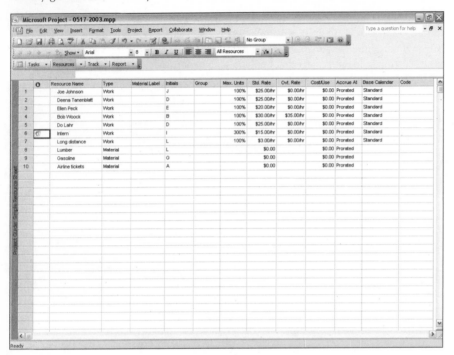

Creating a budget resource

You also can set up a budget resource. Budget resources give you the opportunity to specify how work or costs will be allocated during the project. Suppose, for example, that you want to budget for the cost of a storage unit required during the life of your project. You would create a resource for the storage unit, setting its type as Cost, and then check the Budget check box on the General tab of the Resource Information dialog box to make it a budget resource (see Figure 5.7).

Project doesn't allow you to enter any cost information for a budget resource on the Resource Sheet. To assign a value to the budget resource, you first assign it to the project summary task — and Project won't let you assign a value as you assign the budget resource. Then, you supply a value by adding the Budget Cost field to the table in the Task Usage view or the Resource Usage view.

> **TIP** Project doesn't display the project summary task by default. To display it, start in the Gantt Chart view and choose Tools ➪ Options. At the bottom of the View tab, click Show project summary task and then click OK.

FIGURE 5.7

If you set up a cost resource as a budget resource, you can use it to budget for your project.

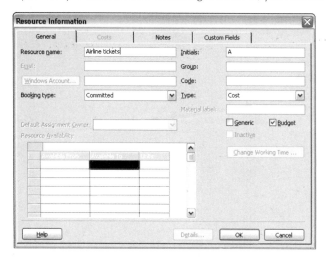

CROSS-REF See Chapter 7 for details on inserting columns to add a field to a view.

You also can set up a work budget resource that you can use to budget for the number of hours of work you intend to perform for the entire project. You then assign the work budget resource to the project summary task. To record the number of hours of work you want to budget for the entire project, add the Budget Work field to the Task Usage view or the Resource Usage view and enter your budget value. As you track the work for your project's tasks, you can compare the work performed with the budgeted work.

Adding notes to a resource

Click the Notes tab of the Resource Information dialog box. The Notes text box, shown in Figure 5.8, is a free-form text box in which you can type any information that you want to store about the resource. For example, you may want to store a reminder about a resource's upcoming vacation or an explanation about resource availability.

After you type text in this box and click OK, a Note indicator icon appears in the Indicator column on the Resource Sheet, as shown in Figure 5.9.

FIGURE 5.8

Use this text box to store information about a resource.

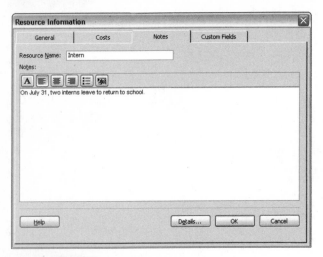

FIGURE 5.9

You don't need to reopen the Resource Information dialog box to read a note. Instead, place your mouse over the icon in the Indicator column, and Project displays the contents of the note.

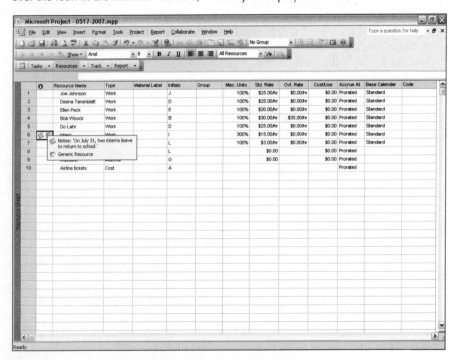

 If more than one indicator appears in the Indicator column, Project displays information about all indicators when you point to the Indicator column.

Calendars and resources

Project uses a base calendar called the Standard calendar to calculate the timing of the project. When you first create a resource for your project, Project uses the Standard base calendar as the default (an eight-hour day and a 40-hour week if you haven't changed this setting in the Project Information dialog box). You can modify working times and create calendar exceptions for resources to accommodate a different work week or planned vacation time.

 The entire project has a Standard calendar, and each resource also has his or her individual Standard calendar.

Modifying a resource's working hours

Suppose that a specific resource won't be available all day on a given day, or even on several specified days. For example, suppose that all the interns work from 1:00 p.m. to 6:00 p.m. You can change the working hours of a resource from the Resource Information dialog box. To change the work week for Interns, follow these steps:

1. Double-click the resource on the Resource Sheet to open the Resource Information dialog box.

2. Click the Change Working Time button. Project displays the resource's calendar with today's date selected.

3. Click the Work Weeks tab (see Figure 5.10).

4. Click the [Default] work week already defined for the calendar by Project.

5. Click Details. Project displays the Details dialog box (see Figure 5.11).

TIP To select multiple days, use Windows selection techniques. To select contiguous days, click Sunday. Then, press and hold the Shift key while clicking Saturday. To select non-contiguous days, press and hold Ctrl as you click each day you want to select.

6. Select the day(s) you want to change on the left side of the dialog box.

7. Select the Set day(s) to These Specific Working Times option.

8. In the Working times section, define the working time for the selected day.

9. Click OK. Project redisplays the Change Working Time dialog box.

When you change the work week, the change you make is not considered an exception; instead, it is considered the normal work week. So, you won't notice any changes to the calendar in the Change Working Time dialog box. However, you can identify the working time for any day by clicking that day on the calendar; the working time appears to the right.

CROSS-REF To avoid overallocating a resource that works part of a day, level the resource on a day-by-day basis. Read more about leveling and handling overallocations in Chapter 10.

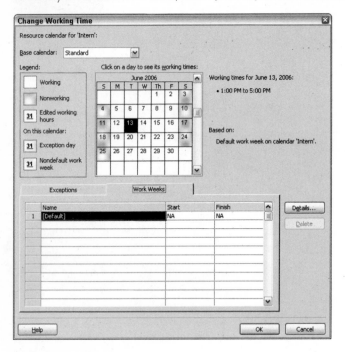

FIGURE 5.10

To modify the default work week, select [Default] on the Work Weeks tab.

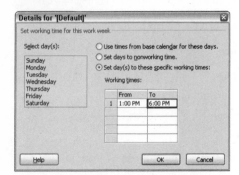

FIGURE 5.11

Use this dialog box to redefine a work week.

Blocking off vacation time

Human resources take time off from work, and to avoid overallocating a person by assigning work during a vacation period, you should mark vacation days as an exception on the resource's calendar. Follow these steps:

Again, by comparing the date to the Legend panel, you can tell the reason for the exception.

1. Double-click the resource on the Resource Sheet to open the Resource Information dialog box.

2. Click the Change Working Time button. Project displays the resource's calendar with today's date selected.

3. In the Name column on the Exceptions tab, type a name that helps you remember the purpose of the exception.

4. In the Start column, select the date on which the exception starts.

5. In the Finish column, select the date on which the exception ends. Project sets every day between the starting and ending dates as an exception on the calendar, and the Details button and the Delete button become available see Figure 5.12.

FIGURE 5.12

To set up a working time exception, type a name for the exception and set dates.

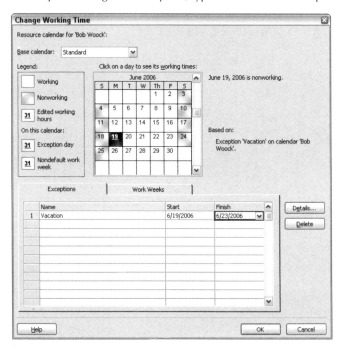

6. Click the Details button. Project displays the Details for dialog box, shown in Figure 5.13.

Use this dialog box to define the working time exception.

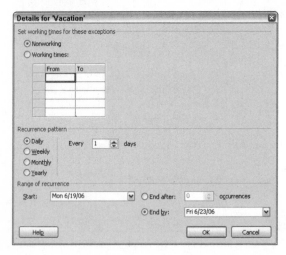

7. In the top section of the dialog box, click the Nonworking option button.

NOTE You can change a resource's working time for a particular day by selecting the Working Times option button and then setting the working times in the From and To boxes.

8. Click OK. When Project redisplays the Change Working Time dialog box, the days you specified between the beginning and ending dates you specified appear as an exception on the calendar (see Figure 5.14).

FIGURE 5.14

Project marks exceptions to the resource's regular calendar with an underscore.

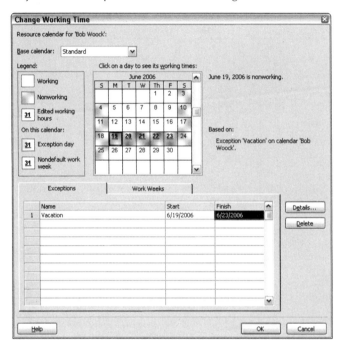

Using Resources and Tasks

You've spent a lot of time in this chapter defining resources and fine-tuning your resource definitions. Now you can finally assign resources to tasks. As noted earlier in this chapter, defining
resources helps you to manage your project more effectively, both in scheduling and in cost.

Assigning resources to tasks

You can easily assign resources to tasks from the Gantt Chart view. Choose View ➪ Gantt Chart or
use the View bar to switch to the Gantt Chart view, and then follow these steps to assign resources
to tasks:

1. Select the task to which you want to assign a resource. You can click the task bar on the
   Gantt Chart, or you can click any column in the Gantt table.

2. Click the Assign Resources button or choose Tools ➪ Assign Resources to open the
   Assign Resources dialog box, as shown in Figure 5.15.

FIGURE 5.15

Use the Assign Resources dialog box to assign a resource to the task that is identified at the top of the box.

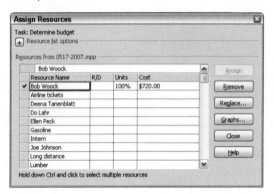

3. Select the resource that you want to assign from the Resource Name list of the Assign Resources dialog box.

TIP Did you forget to define a resource? You don't need to return to the Resource Sheet. Just enter the name of the resource in the Resource Name column of the Assign Resources dialog box.

4. (Optional) If you're using Project Server and you intend to use the Resource Substitution wizard, in the R/D field enter an **R** for Request to indicate that any resource with the required skills can work on the task. Or, enter a **D** for Demand to indicate that the selected resource is specifically required to work on the task.

CROSS-REF For more information about Resource Substitution, see Chapter 19.

5. Do one of the following to assign the amount of a resource:

   ■ To assign any amount other than 100 percent of a resource, type the quantity of the resource as a percentage in the Units column. (Project defines units as percentages, so 100 percent equals one unit of the resource.)

   ■ To assign 100 percent of a resource, leave the Units column blank. Project assigns 100 percent by default.

NOTE You don't need to type the percent sign (%); Project assumes percentages. For example, if you enter 50, Project converts your entry to 50%. However, you can't assign less than 1% of a resource's time.

6. Click Assign. Project places a check mark in the leftmost column of the Assign Resources dialog box to indicate that the resource is assigned to the selected task, and Project calculates the resource's cost using the cost you supplied when you defined the resource.

7. Repeat Steps 3, 4, and 5 to assign additional resources to the selected task, or click Close.

Assigning a budget resource

To assign a budget resource to your project, you must first display the project summary task. Choose Tools ➪ Options and click the View tab. Place a check in the Show Project Summary Task check box (see Figure 5.16). When you click OK, the first task in your project bears the filename of the project.

To assign a budget resource, you must display the project summary task.

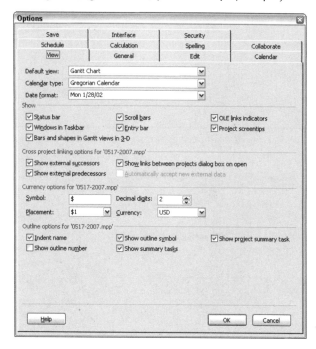

Click the project summary task and then choose Tools ➪ Assign Resources to open the Assign Resources dialog box (see Figure 5.17). Click the budget resource and click Assign. Project places a check in the leftmost column beside the resource to indicate that the resource is assigned to the selected task. You cannot assign any value to the budget resource at this point, so click Close.

NOTE The Assign button will *not* be available for any resource other than a budget resource.

To assign a value to a budget resource, switch to the Task Usage or the Resource Usage view; in Figure 5.18, I'm using the Task Usage view. To add the budget resource value on a specific day, add the Budget Cost or Budget Work fields to the Details section of the view and enter the budget value. To add the budget resource value to the project, regardless of the timeframe, add the Budget Cost and Budget Work fields to the table portion of the view and enter the budget value.

FIGURE 5.17

You use the Assign Resources dialog box to assign a budget resource to the project summary task.

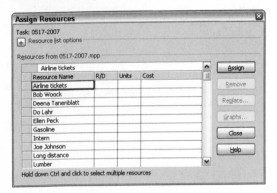

FIGURE 5.18

You can use the Task Usage view or the Resource Usage view to assign budget resource values to the project summary task.

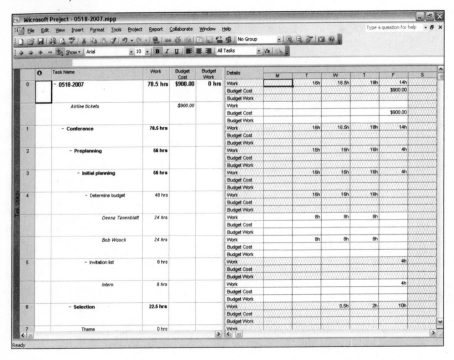

CROSS-REF   See Chapter 7 for details on adding fields to a view.

Getting help while selecting resources to assign

You may have noticed a plus sign (+) next to Resource List options at the top of Figure 5.17. If you click the plus sign, the box expands, as shown in Figure 5.19, to provide you with ways to make selecting resources easier.

FIGURE 5.19

You can narrow your search for resources by filtering, and you can make additional resources available.

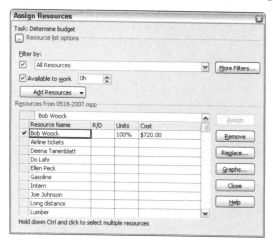

If you check the Filter By check box, Project presents a long list of ways that you can limit the resource list. For example, you can search for only material resources or you can search for resources in a particular group. (Remember that you can assign resources to groups if the resources share a common characteristic.) If you don't find the filter that you want to use, you can create your own filter by clicking the More Filters button and, in the More Filters dialog box that appears, clicking New.

CROSS-REF   See Chapter 7 for information about creating custom filters.

If you check the Available to work box, you can specify the number of hours that you need the resource. Project calculates the remaining available hours of each resource for the duration of the task and compares the results of the calculation with the number of hours that you specified. Resources with available hours equal to or greater than the value that you supplied appear in the list, along with the resources that are already assigned to the selected task.

How Project Calculates Available to Work Time

Project calculates the value for Available to work time by using the resource's calendar, availability contour, and the duration of the task. Based on the resource's calendar, Project calculates the number of working hours for the selected task. Because the resource's availability may be reduced by the availability contour and by other assignments, Project multiplies available working hours by the availability contour value and then subtracts existing assignment work hours to determine Available to work hours.

To see how this works, assume that you have a task to accomplish within a ten-day window and the calendar provides for an eight-hour work day. If Day 3 is a holiday and Days 6 and 7 are the weekend, you have only seven days to complete the task. If you assigned one resource to this task full time, that resource would be allocated for 56 hours. But, if the resource's availability contour were set to 50 percent, the resource's availability would be reduced to 28 hours. And, if the resource were already assigned to another task for 25 percent of the time on Days 1 and 2 (4 hours), the resource's Available to work hours would be 24 hours.

TIP   If you need a resource for 12 days, enter 12d in the Available to work box, and Project converts the value to 96 hours.

You can click the Add Resources button to display a list of sources from which you can select a resource: the active directory, your address book (if you use a MAPI-compliant e-mail program such as Microsoft Outlook or Outlook Express), or Microsoft Project Server — the items that are available in the list depend on your working environment.

NOTE   The Active Directory, one of the options that appears when you click Add Resources, is a Windows network feature. In a Windows network, the administrator can set up an active directory that contains a list of people and the contact information for these people.

The Assign Resources dialog box also contains a Graphs button that shows one of three graphs that you can use to help you select the best resource for the job. Be aware that none of these graphs relates particularly to a task for which you're considering assignment; instead, they focus on the resource.

NOTE   Although you can select multiple resources to graph, this action may not be very useful when you're trying to select resources to assign to a task.

The Work graph, shown in Figure 5.20, shows the amount of work (regardless of the task) that is assigned to the selected resource on a day-by-day basis.

The Assignment Work graph, shown in Figure 5.21, breaks down the total workload of the resource that you're considering, showing you the resource's workload on the selected task, other tasks, and the resource's total availability based on the calendar. Using this graph helps you to see whether you'll overallocate the resource by assigning it to this task.

FIGURE 5.20

On this graph, you see the amount of work that is assigned to the selected resource.

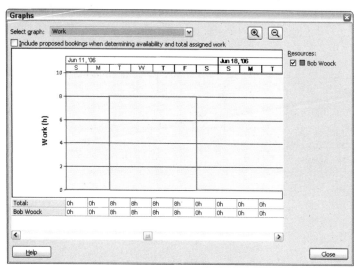

FIGURE 5.21

Use this graph to avoid overallocating a resource.

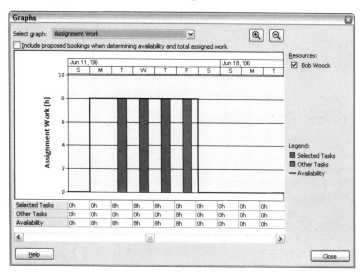

The Remaining Availability graph, shown in Figure 5.22, shows you the resource's unassigned time.

 If you've overallocated a resource, you don't see a negative availability; the resource's availability appears to be 0.

FIGURE 5.22

Use this graph to check a resource's availability.

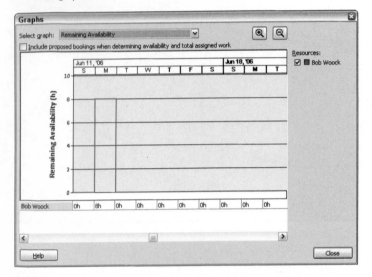

 You also can view the Remaining Availability graph from the Resource Center in Project Web Access.

Some tips about resource assignments

Use the following tips when assigning resources:

- **You can assign several different resources to the same task by simply selecting each resource.** You can select a single resource and immediately click Assign, or you can use standard Windows selection techniques to select several resources and then click Assign only once.

- **You can assign a resource to a task on a part-time basis by assigning less than 100 in the Units column.** The number that you type represents the percentage of working time that you want the resource to spend on the task.

- **You can assign more than one resource by assigning more than 100 in the Units column.**

- **You can consume material resources in two ways: fixed and variable.** When you use fixed consumption, you indicate that — no matter how long the task lasts — you'll use the same quantity of the material. For example, to build a swimming pool, you need 2 tons of concrete — no matter how long it takes you to pour the concrete. When you use variable consumption, you indicate that the length of the task does affect the amount of the material that you will use. For example, when you mow the lawn with a gas mower, the amount of gas that you consume depends on how long you run the mower.

You designate fixed or variable consumption in the Units column of the Assign Resources dialog box. To differentiate between fixed and variable consumption, supply the rate at which you consume a variable resource. In Figure 5.23, gasoline is a material resource that is being consumed at a variable rate because I included the time frame used to measure consumption — the per-hour designation.

FIGURE 5.23

Indicate variable consumption by supplying the rate when you specify the amount that you'll use.

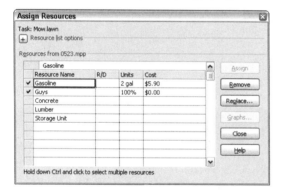

After you assign a resource to a task, the resource name appears next to the task bar on the Gantt Chart by default. Depending on the task type that you set, you may be able to use resource assignments to modify individual task lengths and the entire project schedule. For example, if you assign additional resources to an effort-driven, fixed-unit task, Project shortens the duration of the task. As you read in Chapter 4, the amount of work to be done doesn't change, but the extra concurrent effort shortens the time that's necessary to get the work done. Or, if you assign a resource to work part-time on an effort-driven task, you may find that you can complete several tasks at the same time.

TIP If you overallocate a resource by assigning more of the resource than you have available, Project displays the resource in red on the Resource Sheet view. Chapter 9 explains how to handle these problems.

Removing or replacing a resource assignment

To remove a resource assignment, select the task from which you want to remove the resource assignment using the Gantt Chart view. Then click the Assign Resources button or choose Tools ⇨ Assign Resources to display the Assign Resources dialog box. Highlight the resource that you want to remove from the task. You should see a check mark next to the resource in the leftmost column of the dialog box. Click Remove, as shown in Figure 5.24.

FIGURE 5.24

Remove resources from tasks by selecting them in the Assign Resources dialog box and clicking Remove.

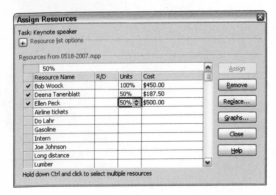

You can be sure that at some point in your project, you will want to change resource assignments. Follow these steps to switch from one resource to another on a particular task:

1. Select the task for which you want to switch resources.

2. Open the Assign Resources dialog box.

3. Highlight the resource that you want to remove from the task; a check mark appears next to the assigned resource.

4. Select Replace. Project displays the Replace Resource dialog box, which enables you to easily select replacement resources, as shown in Figure 5.25.

5. Highlight each resource that you want to assign, and supply units.

6. Click OK.

FIGURE 5.25

The Replace Resource dialog box looks very similar to the Assign Resources dialog box.

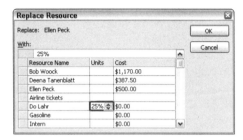

Handling Unusual Cost Situations

Resources go hand in hand with tasks if you're trying to figure out how long it will take to complete a project. If you assign costs to your resources, those costs also affect the cost of your project. Assigning a cost to a resource, however, is not the only way to assign a cost to a project. For example, projects can have fixed costs associated with them. This section starts with a quick look at overall project costs and then focuses on handling unusual cost situations.

Looking at the project's cost

You've seen how to assign costs to resources. You've also seen how to assign resources to tasks — and, by the transitive property of equality (remember that one from high school algebra?), assigning a resource to which you have assigned a cost causes your project to have a cost. Are you wondering what that cost is? From either the Gantt Chart view or the Resource Sheet view, choose Project ➪ Project Information to open the Project Information dialog box. Select Statistics to open the Project Statistics dialog box, as shown in Figure 5.26.

FIGURE 5.26

Check the cost of your project in the Project Statistics dialog box.

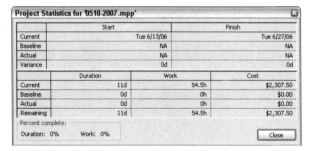

CROSS-REF   Part IV covers tracking, recording work done, and analyzing and reporting on progress. Chapter 14 explains additional ways to view project costs. The following sections consider ways to assign unusual costs to a project.

Assigning fixed costs

This chapter has, to this point, focused on resources, and you have learned how to assign costs to a resource. But the costs of some tasks need to be calculated differently. In Project, you can assign a fixed cost to a task or you can assign a fixed resource cost to a task.

Assigning a fixed cost to a task

Some tasks are fixed-cost tasks, that is, you know that the cost of a particular task stays the same regardless of the duration of the task or the work performed by any resources on the task. For example, your catering service, as part of each job, washes linens. You own the washing machine, and you've done the calculation on the amount of water plus electricity used (plus wear and tear) each time that you run the machine for a wash cycle. Or, you're renting a site for a meeting for a flat fee. In cases like these, you assign the cost directly to the task. If you assign a cost to a task, Project adds the fixed cost of the task to the cost of any resource work that you assign to the task when calculating costs for the project.

NOTE   Remember that assigning a fixed cost to a task does not necessarily make the total cost of the task equal to the fixed cost that you assigned. You can, for example, assign more than one fixed cost as well as variable costs to a task.

To assign a fixed cost to a task, use the Gantt Chart view and apply the Cost table. Follow these steps:

1. Use the View bar or the View menu to switch to the Gantt Chart view.
2. Choose View ➪ Table:Entry ➪ Cost to switch to the Cost table view of the Gantt Chart, as shown in Figure 5.27.
3. Select the task to which you want to assign a fixed cost.
4. Type the cost for that task in the Fixed Cost column and press Enter.

You can control the way that Project accrues the fixed cost for a task from the Fixed Cost Accrual column. Your choices are Start, Prorated, and End. These choices have the same meaning as the accrual choices for resources that were discussed in the section "Creating a Resource List," earlier in this chapter.

TIP   To control the way that Project accrues all fixed costs, use the Calculation tab of the Options dialog box (choose Tools ➪ Options).

FIGURE 5.27

Use the Cost table view of the Gantt Chart to assign costs to tasks.

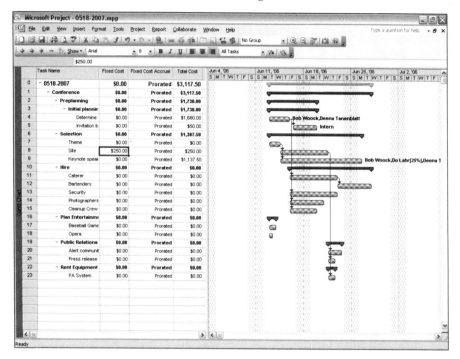

Assigning a fixed resource cost to a task

Suppose that you hire a consultant to perform a task for a fixed amount of money. You can assign the consultant to the task as a fixed-cost resource. I prefer the method described here because it avoids some undesirable side effects. When you use the method I describe and assign only one resource to the task, Project won't turn the task into a Milestone; the duration of the task won't be lost; and Project will apply future resource rate or availability changes to the task to which you assigned the fixed-cost resource.

Follow these steps to assign a fixed resource cost to a task:

1. Set up the resource in the Resource Sheet view. If the resource has some sort of "per unit" cost (an hourly or daily rate), assign that rate in the Std. Rate field. Otherwise, assign a standard rate of $0, as I did in Figure 5.28. Supply the fixed-cost amount in the Cost/Use field.

> **TIP** To keep this example clear, I assigned a Std. Rate of $0 to show you how Project calculates the cost of using the resource as the value you assign in the Cost/Use field, regardless of the amount of time the resource spends working on the task. If your resource has a standard rate, assign it in the Std. Rate field to make Project add the Cost/Use value to the amount of time the resource spends working on the task.

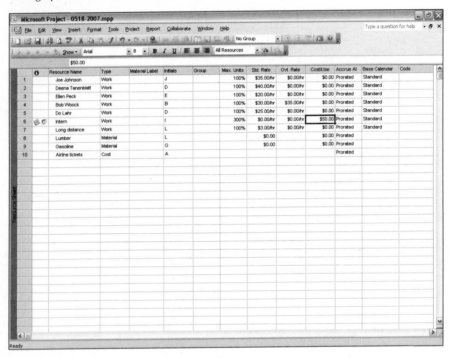

FIGURE 5.28

Setting up a fixed-cost resource.

2. Use the View bar or the View menu to switch to the Gantt Chart view.

3. Choose Window ➪ Split to create a combination view; the Gantt Chart view appears in the top portion of the window and the Task Form view appears in the bottom of the window.

4. Click the top portion of the view and choose View ➪ Table ➪ Costs to switch to the Cost table view of the Gantt Chart.

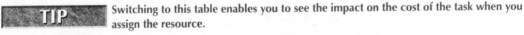

TIP Switching to this table enables you to see the impact on the cost of the task when you assign the resource.

5. Select a task from the Task Name column in the top portion of the view (see Figure 5.29).

6. In the bottom portion of the view, select the resource from the Resource Name column, assign the number of units, and click OK. Project assigns the resource's cost using the rate/hour you supplied in the Std. Rate field *plus* the cost you assigned in the Cost/Use field. The resource's total cost does not depend entirely on the time that a resource spends working on the task.

FIGURE 5.29

Project assigns the cost per use to the task when you assign a resource defined with a cost-per-use value.

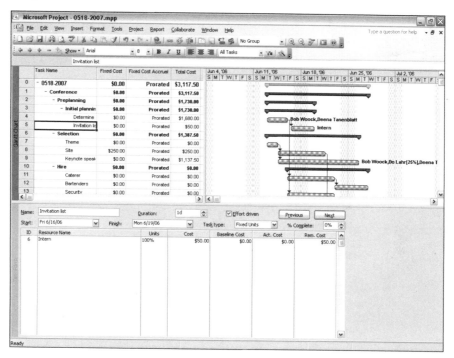

TIP You also can assign the resource to the task by using the steps that were presented in the section "Assigning resources to tasks," earlier in this chapter.

Accounting for resource rate changes

In some situations, you must charge different rates on different tasks for the same resource. Or, you may expect a resource's rate to change during the life of your project. Project uses cost rate tables to accurately reflect resource costs as they change. On cost rate tables, you can identify up to 125 rates for a single resource, and you can identify the effective date of each rate. Cost rate tables help you to account for pay increases or decreases to resources during the life of your project and enable you to charge the same resource at different rates, depending on the task.

To assign multiple rates to a resource, use the Costs tab of the Resource Information dialog box. On the Resource Sheet view, double-click the resource for which you want to assign multiple rates. Click the Costs tab in the Resource Information dialog box, as shown in Figure 5.30.

FIGURE 5.30

Use cost rate tables to assign different rates to a resource.

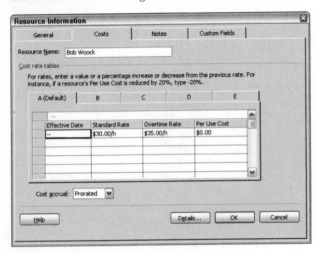

The Costs tab displays five cost rate tables (tabs A through E) that you can use to assign different rates to a resource for use on different dates throughout a project's life. On each cost rate table, you can enter up to 25 rates for the selected resource and indicate an effective date for each rate. Project uses the effective dates that you supply to apply the correct rate to a resource at different times during the project.

If you are specifying a new rate as an increase or decrease of an existing rate, you can specify the new rate in a percentage (such as +10% or −10%); Project calculates the value of the rate for you. You must enter the percent sign.

If you charge different amounts for resources depending on the type of work that they perform, you may want to use each cost rate table tab to represent sets of rates for different kinds of work.

To assign the correct resource cost rate table to a task, follow these steps:

1. Assign the resource to the task by using the Assign Resources dialog box, as discussed in section "Assigning resources to tasks," earlier in this chapter.

2. Choose View ➪ Task Usage or use the View bar to switch to the Task Usage view (see Figure 5.31).

3. In the Task Name column, select the resource for which you want to select a cost table.

4. Click the Assignment Information button on the Standard toolbar to display the Assignment Information dialog box. Click the General tab, shown in Figure 5.32, to select a cost rate table.

5. Select the correct cost rate table from the Cost rate table drop-down list.

6. Click OK.

FIGURE 5.31

The Task Usage view shows you the amount of time that a resource is assigned to a particular task.

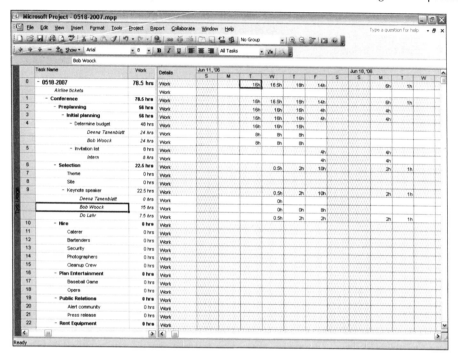

FIGURE 5.32

Use the General tab of the Assignment Information dialog box to select a cost rate table.

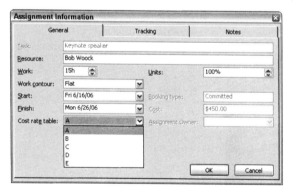

TIP   If you use cost rate tables a great deal, you may want to add the Cost Rate Table column to the table portion of the Task Usage view to easily select a cost rate table without opening the Assignment Information dialog box. See Chapter 7 for details on inserting a column.

Summary

This chapter detailed more about using resources in Project, including how to create and assign resources. The following topics were covered:

- Creating a resource list
- Modifying resource information, including using calendars for resources
- Assigning resources to tasks and removing resource assignments
- Handling fixed costs, both for individual tasks and for resources
- Assigning either a fixed or variable cost to a material resource
- Setting up different rates for resources to account for pay increases or decreases or for charging resources at different rates on different tasks

Chapter 6 presents the basics of using the standard views in Project.

Part III

Refining Your Project

Chapter 6

Understanding the Basics of Views

A project is like a small business. As in any business, different people attend to various aspects of the work. The Accounting department thinks mainly of the costs of doing business. The plant supervisor focuses on deadlines and having enough machinery to get the job done. Your Human Resources department thinks of people — their salaries, hours, benefits, and so on.

As the owner of your project, you are likely to wear all these hats (and more) during the project. Changing views in Project is the practical way of changing hats. You switch to another view to see your work from a different perspective. Each view helps you to focus on a different aspect of your project.

Views in Project enable you to enter, organize, and examine information in various ways. Project provides a variety of views, and this chapter provides you with a basic understanding of the default views. The next chapter covers techniques that you can use to customize views and make them work for you.

What Is a View?

A *view* is a way to examine your project. Different views enable you to focus on different aspects of the project. Project uses three types of views and typically uses them in combination, as follows:

- **Chart or graph views:** Present information by using pictures. You've already seen the Gantt Chart view, which is a chart view.

- **Sheet views:** Present information in rows and columns, similar to the way that a spreadsheet program presents information. The Task

161

Sheet view and the Resource Sheet view are both sheet views, and each row on the sheet contains all the information about an individual task or resource in your project. Each column represents a field that identifies the information that you're storing about the task or resource.

■ **Forms.** Present information in a way that resembles a paper form. You saw the Task Form view in Chapter 5. A form displays information about a single item (or task) in your project.

> **TIP** Shortcut menus are available in many views. Right-click the view to see a shortcut menu.

You can modify the default views by switching what appears on-screen. You can also create custom views. The next two sections describe the following common ways of manipulating views:

■ Switching the table of any view that includes a table

■ Adding or changing the details that appear in any view that contains a Details section

> **CROSS-REF** You can also create a combination view, in which you see one format in one pane of the window and another format in another pane. Read more about creating custom views and combination views in Chapter 7.

Changing a table

If a view contains a table, you can use the Select All button to quickly switch to another table. The Select All button appears in the upper left of the table portion of the view. Right-click the Select All button to open the menu that appears in Figure 6.1.

> **NOTE** Project displays different choices on this menu, and the choices that you see depend on the view that is displayed when you open the menu.

Choose More Tables to open the More Tables dialog box, which displays all the tables that are available in Project (see Figure 6.2). When opened from a Task view, Project shows the tables available in task views; click the Resource option button to see the tables available in resource views.

> **NOTE** The PERT tables won't appear in the More Tables dialog box until you've displayed PERT views. Read more about PERT views in the section "PERT analysis views," later in this chapter.

FIGURE 6.1

Switch tables by choosing from the menu that appears when you right-click the Select All button.

Select All button

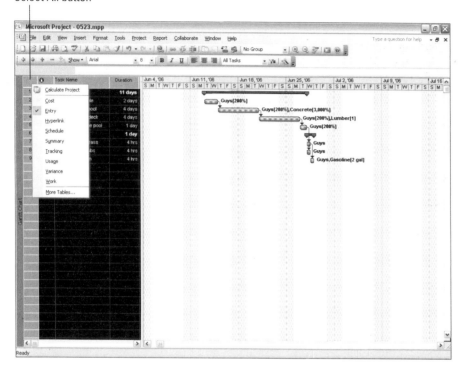

FIGURE 6.2

The More Tables dialog box shows the tables to which you can switch in task views; click the Resource option to view the corresponding tables in resource views.

Changing a Details section

You also can add fields to the Details section of views that displays a Details section — specifically, the Task Usage view and the Resource Usage view. Choose any field from the list that appears when you choose Format ➪ Details, as shown in Figure 6.3.

TIP   You can right-click Details in the upper-left corner of the Details section to see the same menu choices that appear when you choose Format ➪ Details.

FIGURE 6.3

Change the information that appears in the Details section of the view by selecting from this list.

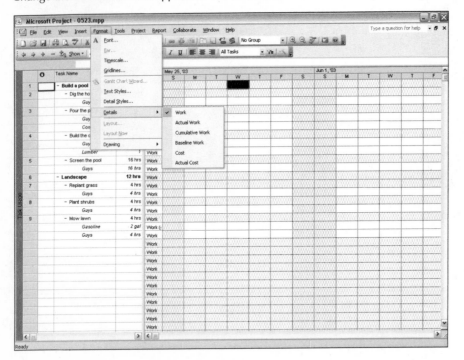

NOTE   Project adds rows to the Details section when you select fields from this menu. To remove a row, repeat the process; that is, choose Format ➪ Details and select the item that you want to remove.

CROSS-REF   Project contains many fields that you can add to the Details section of a usage view; see Chapter 7 for details.

Examining Indicators

Indicators are icons that appear in the Indicator column on table views; the Indicator column appears to the right of the ID column. Indicators represent additional information about the row in which they appear. For example, a Notes indicator appears in the indicator field on the resource sheet if you assign a note to a resource.

CROSS-REF For more information about assigning notes to resources, refer to Chapter 5.

Different icons represent different types of indicators, as follows:

- **Constraint indicators:** These indicators identify the type of constraint that is assigned to a task. For example, a task can have a flexible constraint, such as Finish No Later Than, if the task is scheduled from the finish date. Or, a task can have an inflexible constraint, such as Must Start On, for tasks that are scheduled from the start date. Constraint indicators also show that the task hasn't been completed within the time frame of the constraint.

- **Task type indicators:** These indicators may identify special conditions about a task, such as whether the task is a recurring task or whether the task has been completed. Task type indicators also identify the status of projects that are inserted in a task.

CROSS-REF You can find out more about inserted projects in Chapter 15.

- **Workgroup indicators:** These indicators provide some information about the task and its resources. For example, a workgroup indicator can tell you that a task has been assigned but that the resource hasn't yet confirmed the assignment.

- **Contour indicators:** These indicators identify the type of contouring that is used to distribute the work assigned to the task.

CROSS-REF Read more about contouring in Chapter 10.

- **Miscellaneous indicators:** These indicators identify items, such as a note or a hyperlink, that you created; a calendar that's been assigned to a task; or a resource that needs leveling.

TIP To identify the purpose of an indicator, point at it. Project tells you what the indicator means or displays additional information to remind you of important details. See the Project Help topic, "About Indicators," for a complete list of each indicator icon and its meaning.

Admiring the Views

The following is a list of the default views that are available in Project:

- Bar Rollup
- Calendar
- Descriptive Network Diagram
- Detail Gantt
- Gantt Chart
- Leveling Gantt
- Milestone Date Rollup
- Milestone Rollup
- Multiple Bases Gantt
- Network Diagram
- PA_Expected Gantt
- PA_Optimistic Gantt
- PA_PERT Entry Sheet
- PA_Pessimistic Gantt

- Relationship Diagram
- Resource Allocation
- Resource Form
- Resource Graph
- Resource Name Form
- Resource Sheet
- Resource Usage
- Task Details Form
- Task Entry
- Task Form
- Task Name Form
- Task Sheet
- Task Usage
- Tracking Gantt

NOTE When you initially open the Views window, you see only 24 views listed. The four PERT views don't appear in the window until you use them. After you use these views, they appear in the window.

Deciding which of Project's 28 built-in views (or any of your custom views) suits a particular purpose can be tricky. As you become more familiar with the features of Project and the way that you apply project management concepts and terms to Project, you'll get more comfortable selecting views by name. The View menu and bar list the eight most frequently used views. You can find the other views in the More Views window; simply choose View ⇨ More Views to see these other views.

CROSS-REF Project managers can view related information from Project Server in Project without switching between two windows. See Chapter 19 for more information.

The following sections describe how these views enable you to look at different aspects of your project. Notice the wealth of detail about your project that is available to you.

TIP To display any of these views, choose them from the View bar or right-click the View bar and choose More Views from the menu that appears to select them from the More Views dialog box.

Calendar

The Calendar view in Project 2007 looks more like the calendar view in Outlook 2007, sporting daily, weekly, and monthly views; you can switch to any of these views using the buttons at the top of the calendar. You also can set custom dates to view.

The top selection on the View bar is the Calendar view, as shown in Figure 6.4. The familiar format of the Calendar view makes it easy to use; a black box surrounds "today." Using a monthly calendar format, the Calendar view indicates the length of a task with a bar running across portions of days, or even weeks. In the Calendar view, nonworking days appear shaded. Although a taskbar may extend over nonworking days, such as Saturday and Sunday in this example, the work of the task doesn't progress over those days. Don't forget that every project has a calendar (not to be confused with the Calendar view) that tells Project how to handle events, such as 24-hour shifts, weekends, and holidays off, over the life of your project.

FIGURE 6.4

The Calendar view features a familiar, easy-to-read format.

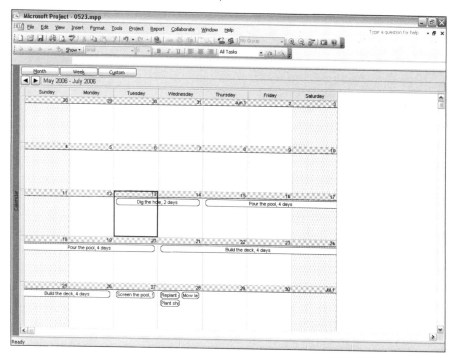

The Calendar view is useful for entering a simple project and for reviewing what needs to be done on a given day. You can move from month to month by using the large arrow buttons in the upper-right corner of the view, next to the current month name. Depending on your screen resolution, you can see slightly more than a month at a time on-screen by using the Zoom Out tool on the Standard toolbar while in Calendar view. Zoom Out shrinks the calendar to accommodate about a month and a half of your schedule.

> **TIP**   To modify the appearance of the Calendar view (for example, to shade working days and leave nonworking days clear), double-click anywhere on the calendar to open the Timescale dialog box and change the corresponding settings.

Detail Gantt

The Detail Gantt view shows a list of tasks and related information, as well as a chart that displays *slippage* as a thin bar between tasks, as shown in Figure 6.5. Choose this view from the More Views dialog box (select View ➪ More Views).

FIGURE 6.5

The Detail Gantt view.

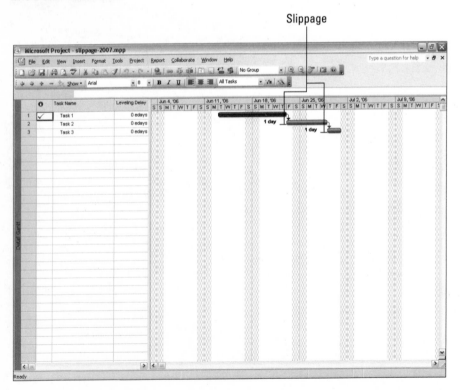

The thin bar that appears at the left edge of the second and third tasks represents slippage. The number of days appears in both cases. Slippage results when you save a baseline on a project initially and then record actual dates or durations for tasks, and the resulting actual finish dates or durations for the task are later than the baseline finish dates or durations. In the figure, the actual start date of the second task was later than the baseline start date; because the third task depends on the second task, both the second and the third tasks are affected.

This view is most useful for evaluating slippage. The default table in the Detail Gantt view is the Delay table. Use the techniques described in the section "Changing a table," earlier in this chapter, to change the table.

You may want to incorporate the Task Details Form view in the bottom pane of the Detail Gantt view so that you can look more closely at the tasks that are associated with slippage or slack. Choose Window ➪ Split, or use the split bar to display the Task Form view in the bottom pane. Then, select a field on the Task Form view, choose View ➪ More Views, and select the Task Details Form view.

NOTE You can create a combination view, with the Detail Gantt view in the top pane and the Task Details Form view in the bottom pane, and save and use this combination view later. See Chapter 7 for more details.

Gantt Chart

Chapter 2 covers the Gantt Chart view, shown in Figure 6.6, in detail. This view makes it easy for you to create a project, link tasks to create sequential dependencies, see how your project is progressing over time, and view tasks graphically while still having access to details.

The Gantt Chart view in Project 2007 has been enhanced; Gantt bars use 256 colors and 3-D texturing. In addition to font color, you now can apply background color and patterns to cells in the table portion of the Gantt view.

FIGURE 6.6

The Gantt Chart view.

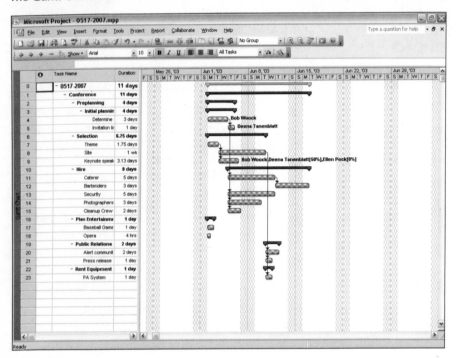

Leveling Gantt

The Leveling Gantt view, shown in Figure 6.7, focuses on task delays. This view provides a graphic representation of delayed tasks while still providing task detail information. The chart portion of the view shows the effects before and after leveling. The default table that appears in the Leveling Gantt view is the Delay table, but you can change the table by using the techniques that are described in the section "Changing a table," earlier in this chapter. You can use the Delay table to add or remove delay time and see the effects of your changes.

FIGURE 6.7

The Leveling Gantt view.

Slack line

Task before leveling   Task after leveling

Leveling delay line

> **NOTE** *Leveling* is the process of resolving resource conflicts or overallocations by delaying or splitting certain tasks. You can read more about resource leveling in Chapter 10.

The top bar represents the task prior to leveling, and the bottom bar represents the task after leveling. The bar to the left of the Keynote speaker task represents delay, and the bar to the right of the Invitation list task and the Site task represents slack.

Tracking Gantt

The Tracking Gantt view is also based on the Gantt Chart view. The Tracking Gantt view provides a great visual way to evaluate the progress of individual tasks and the project as a whole. By using the Tracking Gantt view, you can see how your project has shifted from your original estimates and then decide how to adjust your plans to accommodate delays. Theoretically, if a project ever goes faster than you've anticipated, you can also see the amount of extra time that you've bought yourself as a result of your efficiency. (However, projects so seldom go faster than projected that I won't show that option here!)

Figure 6.8 shows a standard Gantt view of a project that has had some activity. The standard Gantt view shows the progress on tasks as a black bar within the Gantt task bar.

FIGURE 6.8

The standard Gantt view shows you the reality of your project timing at the moment, based on actual work done.

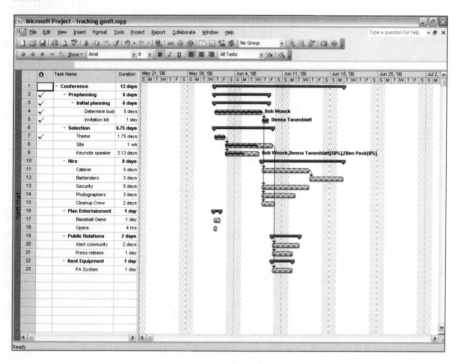

Figure 6.9, on the other hand, shows the same schedule that was displayed using the Tracking Gantt view with the Tracking table (the default table is the Entry table). The Tracking table enables you to update your project by supplying actual information. On the chart portion of the view, you see two bars for every task. The bottom bar reflects baseline settings. The top bar reflects current scheduled start and finish dates if a task has not yet been started. If a task has been started — that is, if you have supplied some amount of work that has been completed — the top bar represents actual information. Project fills in the top bar and makes it solid to represent completed work; a hatching pattern appears in the top bar to represent unstarted work or work in progress (look specifically at Tasks 8 and 9).

In the Tracking Gantt view, you can see that the Determine budget, Invitation list, and Theme tasks have been completed; the Site task is 50 percent complete; and the Keynote speaker task is 20 percent complete. No other tasks have been started, so the top bars on all other tasks represent scheduled start and finish dates, based on progress made so far in the project.

FIGURE 6.9

The Tracking Gantt view shows the discrepancy between your estimates and the real-world activity in your project.

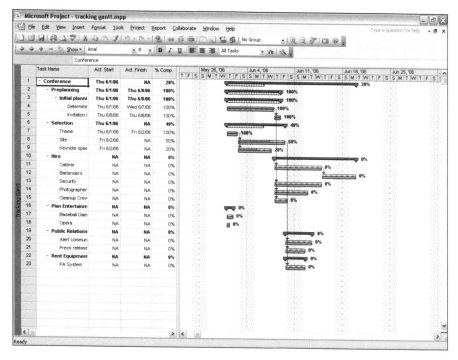

Multiple Baselines Gantt

The Multiple Baselines Gantt view is also based on the Gantt Chart view. The Multiple Baselines Gantt view enables you to see the first three baselines you save for your project. Each baseline is represented by a different color. In Figure 6.10, you see two baselines; two lines represent each task in the chart portion of the view.

The default table for the Multiple Baselines Gantt view is the Entry table, but you can change the table to any table you want using the techniques that are described in the section "Changing a table," earlier in this chapter.

CROSS-REF You can read more about baselines in Chapter 11.

FIGURE 6.10

The Multiple Baselines Gantt view helps you compare the first three baselines you save.

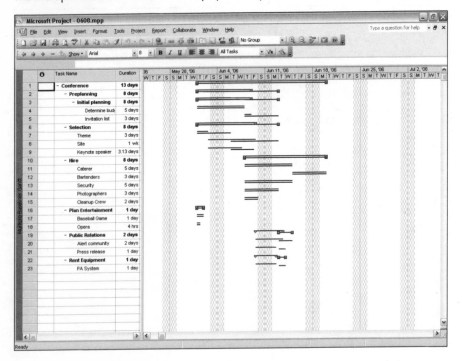

Network Diagram

The Network Diagram became the name for the PERT Chart view that you found in Project 98.

The Network Diagram view, shown in Figure 6.11, has less to do with timing than with the general flow of work and the relationships between tasks in your project. This view makes it easy for you to evaluate the flow of your project and to check task dependencies.

Each node in the Network Diagram view represents a task in your project. For Figure 6.12, I used Project's Zoom command (View ➪ Zoom) to enlarge a node so that you can see the details. A node contains the task name, duration, task ID number in the sequence of the project outline, start date, finish date, and, if assigned, the resource(s). The thickness of the border and color of each node represents different types of tasks — that is, critical tasks are red and their borders are thicker than those of noncritical tasks, which are blue. You can determine (and change) the meaning of node shapes in the Box Styles dialog box (choose Format ➪ Box Styles). The lines that flow between the nodes represent dependencies. A task that must come after another task is completed, called a *successor task*, appears to the right or sometimes below its predecessor.

FIGURE 6.11

The Network Diagram view.

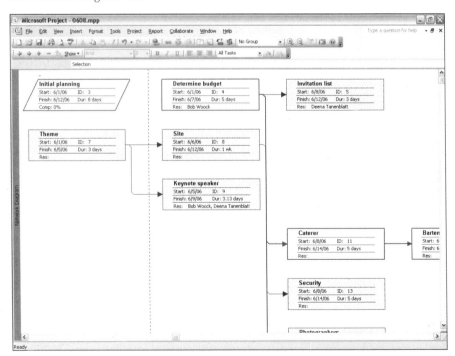

FIGURE 6.12

You can see task details when you examine the nodes of the Network Diagram.

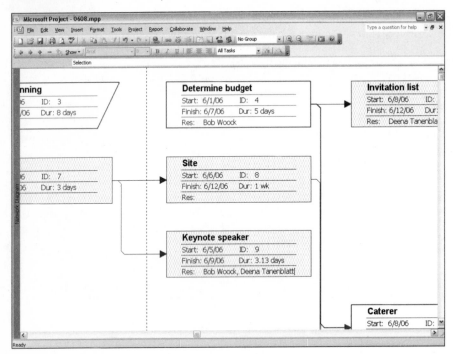

> **TIP** You can right-click anywhere on the Network Diagram view and choose Zoom to set a zoom factor.

You couldn't filter Project 98's PERT Chart view; however, a filtering feature was added in Project 2000. While viewing the Network Diagram, choose Project ➪ Filtered for and select the filter that you want to use.

> **CROSS-REF** You can read more about filtering in Chapter 7.

Starting in Project 2002, you can group tasks in the Network Diagram view; this is similar to the way that you can group tasks in the Gantt view. Colored bands separate the nodes. For example, in Figure 6.13, you see tasks grouped by duration; the group names appear along the left side of the view in the yellow bars that separate each group. Open the Project menu and point to Group to see the groups that are available by default. You also can create your own groups.

FIGURE 6.13

You can group tasks in a variety of ways in the Network Diagram view.

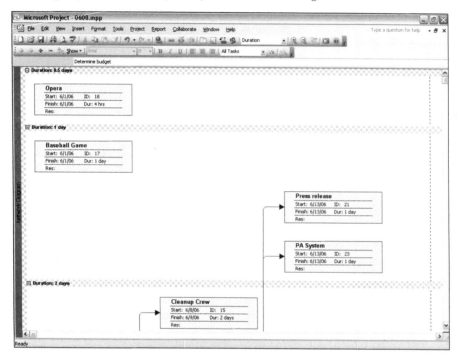

You can also display indicators and custom fields in Network Diagram nodes. You add the node information to an existing node template, or you create a new template. Follow these steps to display indicators or custom fields in nodes:

1. In the Network Diagram view, choose Format ➪ Box Styles. The Box Styles dialog box appears.

2. Click the More Templates button to display the Data Template dialog box (see Figure 6.14).

3. In the Data Template dialog box, you can edit an existing template, make a copy of an existing template and edit the copy, or create a new template. To edit or create a copy of an existing template, select it in the Template in Network Diagram list and choose Copy or Edit. To create a new template, choose New. For this example, I copied the Standard template. In all cases, Project displays the Data Template Definition dialog box, shown in Figure 6.15.

NOTE   You can't edit the Standard template, but you can copy it.

FIGURE 6.14

Add information to a cell of the Network Diagram node.

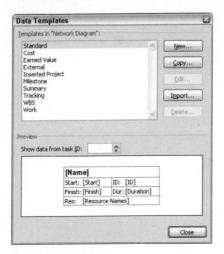

FIGURE 6.15

Use this dialog box to add indicators or a custom field to a Network Diagram node.

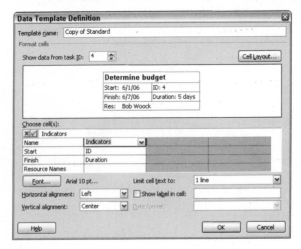

4. Click in the cell where you want either indicators or a custom field to appear, making sure that you click in an empty cell. Project adds a list box indicator to the cell, thus enabling you to open the list and select the information that you want to appear in that cell of the node. In Figure 6.15, I'm adding the Indicators field to the Name cell.

5. Click OK to redisplay the Data Template dialog box.

6. Click Close to redisplay the Box Styles dialog box (see Figure 6.16).

FIGURE 6.16

In this dialog box, select the template you want to apply to selected types of tasks.

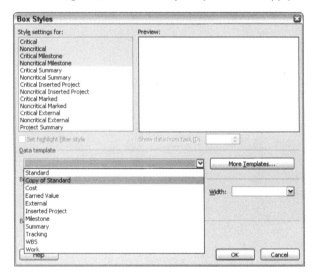

7. In the Style settings for list, select the types of tasks to which you want to apply the template.

TIP You can use Windows selection techniques to select several tasks simultaneously. Click the first task that you want to select. Then, to select contiguous tasks, press Shift and click the last task. Or, to select noncontiguous tasks, press Ctrl and click each task.

8. From the Data template list, select the template that you edited or created.

9. Click OK. You see the new field on appropriate nodes. In Figure 6.17, a Note indicator appears only in the Determine budget task because no other tasks in view have indicators.

FIGURE 6.17

A Network Diagram that displays indicators in the nodes.

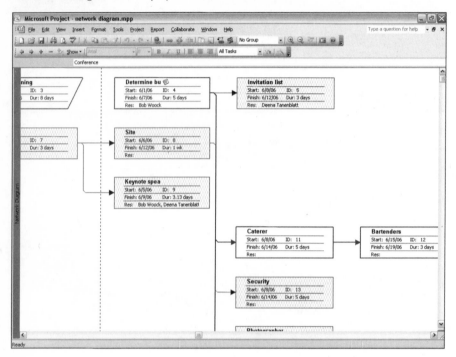

Descriptive Network Diagram

The Descriptive Network Diagram, shown in Figure 6.18, is a cousin of the Network Diagram — and so it focuses on the general flow of work and the relationships among tasks in your project.

Like Network Diagram, each node in the Descriptive Network Diagram view represents a task in your project. If you compare Figures 6-11 and 6-18, you see more detail in the nodes of the Descriptive Network Diagram than you see in the Network Diagram. The Descriptive Network Diagram also indicates whether the task is critical and how complete the task is.

You can filter the Descriptive Network Diagram. Simply choose Project ➪ Filtered for, and select the filter that you want to use.

FIGURE 6.18

The Descriptive Network Diagram view.

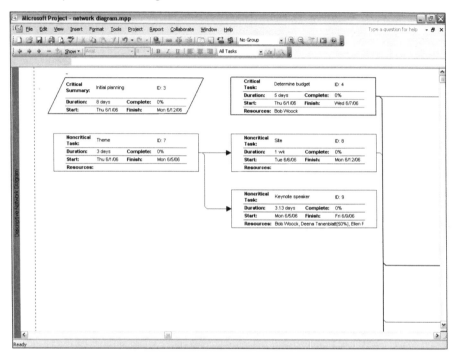

Relationship Diagram

This special version of the Network Diagram view, the Relationship Diagram, shown in Figure 6.19, displays the current task in the center of the pane, with the task's predecessors to the left and successors to the right. When you are working on a large project, this graphic view helps you to focus on one task and the tasks that are linked to it.

FIGURE 6.19

The Relationship Network Diagram view helps you focus on a single task and the tasks linked to it.

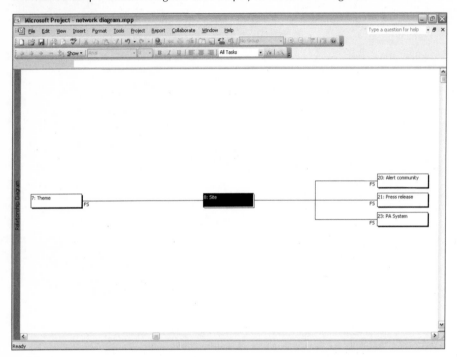

PERT analysis views

PERT analysis is sometimes compared to *what-if analysis*, and many project managers use this approach to estimate a probable outcome. The probable outcome that you estimate may be the duration of a task, its start date, or its end date. As a function of the estimating process, you specify the optimistic, pessimistic, and expected durations of tasks in your project. Then Microsoft Project calculates a weighted average of the three durations.

NOTE PERT stands for *Program Evaluation and Review Technique.* The Special Projects Office of the U.S. Navy devised this method of tracking the flow of tasks in the late 1950s.

You can use the following PERT analysis views in Project to help you make your estimates:

- PA_PERT Entry Sheet
- PA_Optimistic Gantt
- PA_Expected Gantt
- PA_Pessimistic Gantt

You can use the PERT Analysis toolbar, shown in Figure 6.20, to perform PERT analysis. Choose View ➪ Toolbars ➪ PERT Analysis to display the toolbar.

 **You need to use the PERT Analysis toolbar to display the four PERT views the first time. After you've displayed the views, they appear in the More Views window.**

FIGURE 6.20

Use this toolbar to help you with PERT analysis tasks.

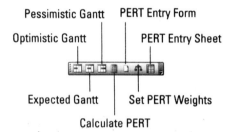

Pessimistic Gantt   PERT Entry Form

Optimistic Gantt   PERT Entry Sheet

Expected Gantt   Set PERT Weights

Calculate PERT

PERT Entry Sheet

The PERT Entry Sheet view, shown in Figure 6.21, focuses PERT analysis entirely on durations. Click the PERT Entry Sheet button on the PERT Analysis toolbar to display this sheet.

Using this sheet, you enter optimistic, expected, and pessimistic durations for each task. When you click the Calculate PERT button on the PERT Analysis toolbar, Project uses a weighted average of the numbers that you supply and calculates the probable duration of the task. Project displays the result in the Duration column for that task. Notice the duration of 1.58 days for the Theme task. Project calculated this duration by using the weighted average of the numbers in the Optimistic Dur., Expected Dur., and Pessimistic Dur. columns for the task.

FIGURE 6.21

Use this view to focus on entering estimated durations for PERT analysis.

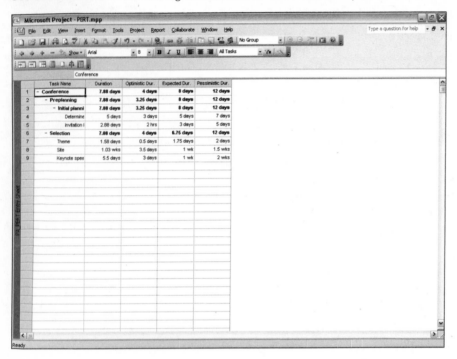

Optimistic Gantt

After you have entered optimistic, expected, and pessimistic durations in the PERT Entry Sheet view and clicked the Calculate PERT button, you can view the optimistic results for your entire project in the Optimistic Gantt view. Click the Optimistic Gantt button on the PERT Analysis toolbar to display the Optimistic Gantt view. As its name implies, the Optimistic Gantt view, shown in Figure 6.22, is a variation of the Gantt Chart view; the Optimistic Case table is on the left side, and Gantt bars are on the right. You can use this view to enter estimated durations and then evaluate the optimistic scenarios for task start dates and end dates.

NOTE   Initially, you may not see bars in any of the PERT Gantt views. While displaying any of these views, click the Calculate PERT button on the PERT Analysis toolbar again, and Project displays the bars.

If you prefer to work with start dates and end dates or to focus entirely on optimistic durations while estimating, you can use this view to enter and evaluate the optimistic scenarios for task durations, start dates, and end dates. If you use this approach, you must also supply the same type of information in the Expected Gantt view and the Pessimistic Gantt view before you click the Calculate button.

FIGURE 6.22

Use the Optimistic Gantt view to analyze optimistic task durations.

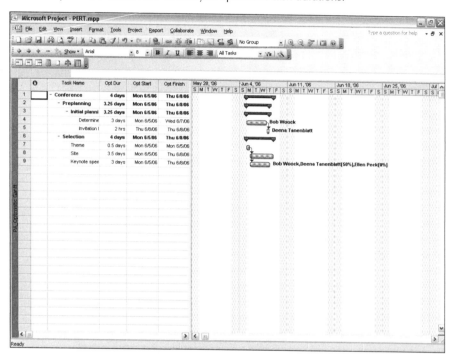

Expected Gantt

After you have entered optimistic, expected, and pessimistic durations on the PERT Entry Sheet and click the Calculate button, you can view the expected results for your entire project in the Expected Gantt view. Click the Expected Gantt button on the PERT Analysis toolbar to display the Expected Gantt view, as shown in Figure 6.23. As are its cousins — the Optimistic and Pessimistic Gantt views — the Expected Gantt view is a variation of the Gantt Chart view. Project displays the Expected Gantt table on the left side and Gantt bars on the right side.

If you prefer to estimate with start dates and end dates or to focus entirely on expected durations, you can use this view to enter estimated durations and then evaluate the expected scenarios for task start dates and end dates. If you use this approach, you also need to supply the same types of information in the Optimistic Gantt view and the Pessimistic Gantt view before you click the Calculate button.

FIGURE 6.23

Use the Expected Gantt view to help create expected task durations.

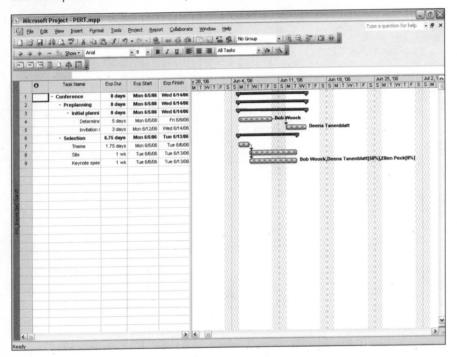

Pessimistic Gantt

After you enter optimistic, expected, and pessimistic durations on the PERT Entry Sheet view and click the Calculate button, you can view the pessimistic results for your entire project in the Pessimistic Gantt view. Click the Pessimistic Gantt button on the PERT Analysis toolbar to display the Pessimistic Gantt view, as shown in Figure 6.24. As are its cousins — the Expected Gantt and the Optimistic Gantt views — the Pessimistic Gantt view is also a variation of the Gantt Chart view. Project displays the Pessimistic Gantt table on the left and Gantt bars on the right. You can use this view to enter estimated durations and then evaluate the pessimistic scenarios for task start dates and end dates.

PERT Weights

Project calculates a weighted average when you use PERT analysis. You can control the weights that Project applies to each scenario from the Set PERT Weights dialog box, as shown in Figure 6.25. Click the PERT Weights button on the PERT Analysis toolbar (the second button from the right on the toolbar). Note that the values you enter must sum to 6.

You can use different weights to change the emphasis that Project applies to its calculation of each scenario.

FIGURE 6.24

Use the Pessimistic Gantt view to help create pessimistic task durations.

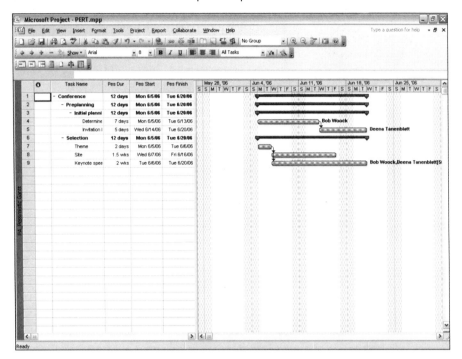

FIGURE 6.25

Use the Set PERT Weights dialog box to adjust the weights that Project applies when making PERT calculations.

Resource Allocation

The Resource Allocation view is a combination view. For example, in Figure 6.26, the Resource Usage view appears in the top pane and the Leveling Gantt Chart view appears in the bottom pane. Note that the names of each view appear in the bar that runs down the left side of the screen.

CROSS-REF See the section "Leveling Gantt," earlier in this chapter, for a discussion of the Leveling Gantt Chart view. Refer to the section "Resource Usage," later in this chapter, for information about the Resource Usage view.

The default table that appears on the Resource Usage view (the upper pane of the combination view) is the Usage table. The default table that appears on the Gantt Chart view (the lower pane of the combination view) is the Entry table. As you scroll down the window, the top and bottom panes move together. You can use the techniques described in the section "Changing a table," earlier in this chapter, to change either table.

FIGURE 6.26

The Resource Allocation view displays resource allocation relative to the project timing.

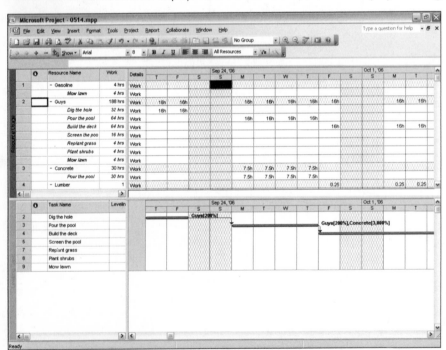

Resource Form

The Resource Form view displays detailed information about one resource at a time, as shown in Figure 6.27.

The Resource Form view.

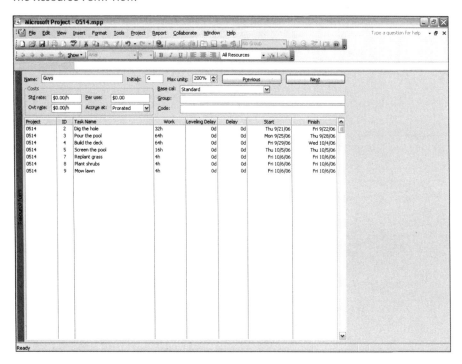

Use the Next and Previous buttons in the upper-right corner of the window to display different resources. If you haven't sorted or filtered resources, Project shows them to you in order of ID number.

Resource Graph

The Resource Graph view shows how a particular resource is being used on a project. You can use the Resource Graph view to spot and correct resources that are inappropriately allocated. Note that the Resource Graph view shows information for one resource at a time. To view a different resource, click the scroll arrows that appear below the left pane in this window. This view works well as part of a combination view.

The Resource Graph view highlights resource conflicts: people, equipment, or other resources that are being overworked or underutilized. Looking at the Resource Graph view as both a single and combination view can show you how assignments on individual tasks are affecting a resource's utilization on a project. Figure 6.28 shows the main Resource Graph view. Figure 6.29 shows the combination view, with details of the tasks being performed shown at the bottom of the Project window. You can create this view by choosing Window ⇨ Split.

FIGURE 6.28

The percentage of a person's available work time is tracked and displayed as overallocated and underallocated.

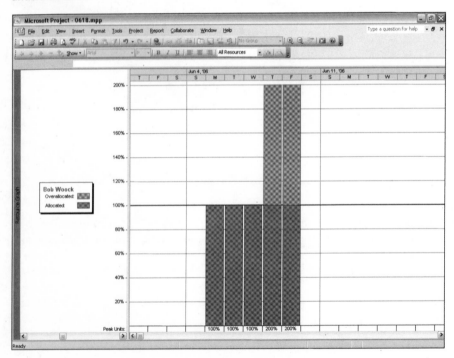

FIGURE 6.29

Displaying task information beneath a Resource Graph can help you to see which work assignments are keeping the resource busy.

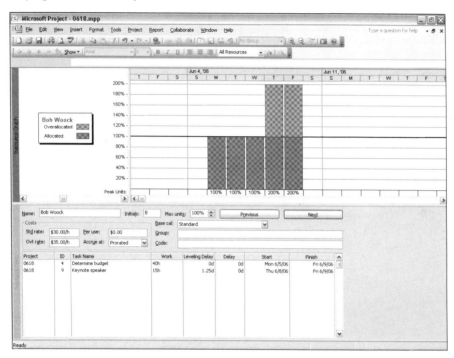

Project displays a resource's total work hours on any particular day as a bar. A bar that falls short of the 100 percent mark indicates that a resource isn't working full-time and may be underutilized. A bar that extends beyond 100 percent indicates that someone is working too many hours in a day. The percentage of the workday that the resource is working appears at the bottom of the usage bars.

NOTE Underutilization may indicate that a resource is busy with other projects the rest of that day, and overutilization may signal occasional and acceptable overtime. See Chapter 8 for more information about interpreting these bars. See Chapter 10 for more details about resolving conflicts in resource time.

Resource Name Form

The Resource Name Form view is a simplified version of the Resource Form view (compare Figure 6.30 with Figure 6.27). None of the cost information appears in this view, nor do you see the resources' maximum units, base calendar, group, or code.

FIGURE 6.30

The Resource Name Form view.

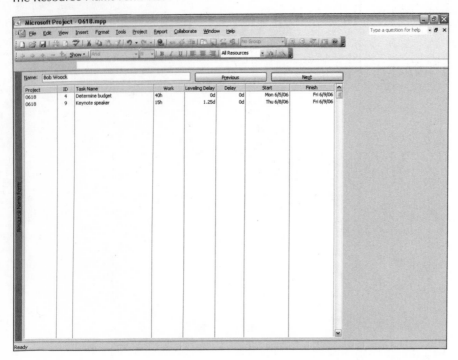

You can use this view to set up basic information about resources for a project—this can give you a good idea about a resource's workload. Use the Previous and Next buttons to view different resources.

Resource Sheet

The Resource Sheet view, shown in Figure 6.31, gives you a wealth of information about the resources that are assigned to your project, including standard and overtime rates, availability for overtime work, and fixed costs.

 By assigning group designations to resources, such as Marketing, Facilities, or Temporary Help, you can use filters to study resource information for just one or two groups at a time.

FIGURE 6.31

You can view both standard and overtime rates in the Resource Sheet view.

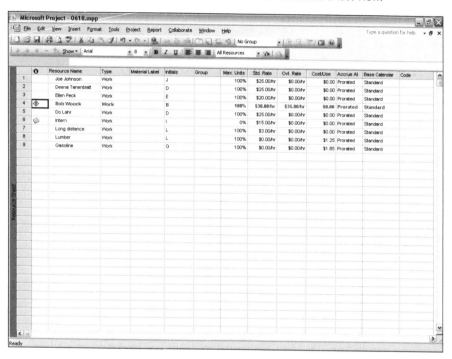

This columnar interface is a great way to prepare to assign resources if, for example, you want to assign lower-cost people to most tasks and higher-cost people to certain mission-critical tasks. This view clearly shows to which group a resource belongs. If overallocations exist, you see a warning flag in the Indicator column in the far left of this view. Switch back to the Resource Graph to get resource-by-resource details on these problems.

TIP The default table that appears on the Resource Sheet view is the Entry table, but you can change this table by using the techniques that are described in the section "Changing a table," earlier in this chapter.

Resource Usage

The Resource Usage view, shown in Figure 6.32, displays each resource and the tasks that are assigned to it. You can use the Resource Usage view to enter and edit resource information, and you can assign or reassign tasks to resources in this view by dragging the tasks among resources.

The Resource Usage view is also useful when you want to do the following:

- Check resource overallocations
- Examine the number of hours or the percentage of capacity at which each resource is scheduled to work
- View a resource's progress or costs
- Determine how much time a particular resource has for additional work assignments

FIGURE 6.32

The Resource Usage view organizes task assignments by resource so that you can easily figure out who's doing what and when it's being done.

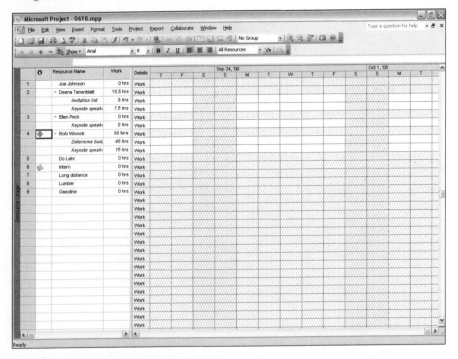

The default table on the left side of this view is the Usage table. You can use the Table Selection button, described in the section "Changing a table," earlier in this chapter, to switch to a different table. Similarly, you can choose either Format ➪ Details or Format ➪ Detail Styles to add to or change the information that appears in the Details section. (Work is the default selection.)

Rollup views

In Project 98, you could display symbols on a summary taskbar that represented subtask dates: Effectively, you "rolled up" the subtasks onto a summary taskbar when you collapsed the outline of the Gantt view. However, rollup wasn't an easy process in Project 98 because you needed to mark each individual task that you wanted to roll up.

Starting in Project 2000, you could allow for rollup behavior at a project level and avoid editing all the tasks. While viewing the Gantt Chart view of your project, choose Format ➪ Layout. Project displays the Layout dialog box, as shown in Figure 6.33.

Use this dialog box to enable rollup behavior for all tasks in your project.

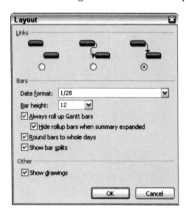

To allow for rollup behavior at a project level and avoid editing all the tasks, select the Always Roll Up Gantt Bars check box. If you don't want see the rollup bars when you expand the project outline to view all tasks, also select the Hide Rollup Bars When Summary Expanded check box.

Using the summary task bar

When you enable rollup behavior and collapse the outline, Project displays a summary task bar that contains symbols that represent subtask dates. Compare Figures 6-34, 6-35, and 6-36, which show various effects of collapsing the outline and rollup behavior. In particular, compare Figures 6-35 and 6-36.

FIGURE 6.34

In this figure, the outline is completely expanded.

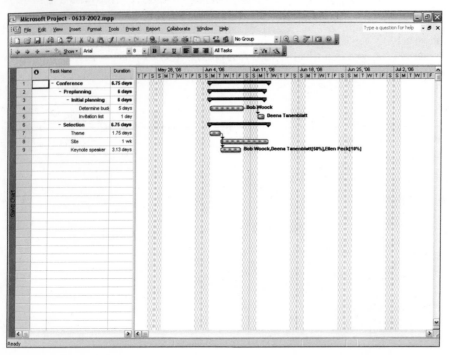

FIGURE 6.35

In this figure, I collapsed the outline for the Selection task, but I didn't enable rollup behavior.

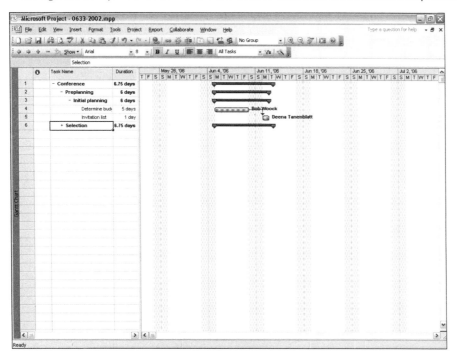

NOTE You can still specify rollup behavior at the task level (using the General tab of the Task Information dialog box) so that Project doesn't roll up all tasks to summary bars when you collapse the outline. Remember that the changes you make in the Layout dialog box don't affect tasks whose rollup behavior you specified at the task level.

FIGURE 6.36

In this figure, I collapsed the outline for the Selection task and enabled rollup behavior.

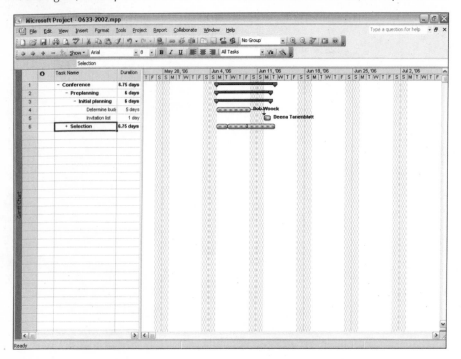

Using the Rollup_Formatting macro

Project contains a special macro called `Rollup_Formatting`. When you run this macro, Project displays, on the Gantt Chart view, a summary bar that contains symbols that represent tasks; you can think of these tasks as being rolled up onto the summary bar. This type of view helps you to create a summarized version of your project and makes important dates visible. The following views help you to see your focus on your project's summary tasks:

- Bar Rollup
- Milestone Date Rollup
- Milestone Rollup

NOTE A rollup view displays only the tasks that you format as rollup tasks in the Task Information dialog box. If you format rollup behavior for tasks in the Task Information dialog box, changing rollup behavior in the Layout dialog box (as discussed in the previous section) doesn't affect the appearance of your Gantt Chart.

This macro doesn't work unless you first mark tasks on the project as tasks that you want to roll up. Follow these steps to mark tasks and run the `Rollup_Formatting` macro:

1. Select tasks in the Gantt Chart view.

You can use Windows selection techniques to select several tasks simultaneously. Click the first task that you want to select. Then, to select contiguous tasks, press Shift and click the last task. Or, to select noncontiguous tasks, press Ctrl and click each task.

2. Click the Task Information button on the Standard toolbar to open the General tab of the Multiple Task Information dialog box, as shown in Figure 6.37.

FIGURE 6.37

Use the General tab of the Multiple Task Information dialog box to mark tasks for rollup.

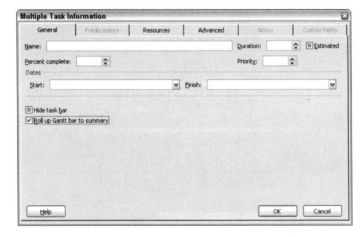

3. Select the Roll Up Gantt Bar to Summary check box.
4. Click OK.
5. Choose Tools ➪ Macros. Then choose Macros from the submenu to open the Macros dialog box, as shown in Figure 6.38.

FIGURE 6.38

Run macros from the Macro dialog box.

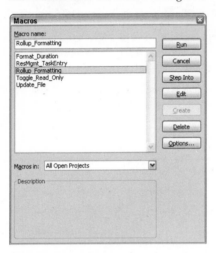

6. Select the `Rollup_Formatting` macro and click Run. Project displays the Rollup Formatting dialog box, as shown in Figure 6.39.

FIGURE 6.39

Choose the style of formatting that you want for your rollup.

7. Select Bars to display rolled up tasks as bars, or select Milestones to display rolled up tasks as milestones, and click OK. Project displays the rolled-up version of your project, as shown in Figure 6.40.

FIGURE 6.40

When you format rollup tasks as milestones, Project displays your project using the Milestone Rollup view.

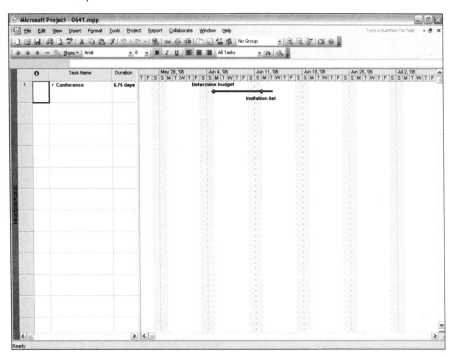

NOTE Using the `Rollup_Formatting` macro can produce unpredictable results if your task start dates are close together. Task names may appear on top of one another — and be unreadable.

Switching rollup views

When you use the `Rollup_Formatting` macro, Project displays only those tasks that you formatted for rollup. The table that you see in the sheet portion of all these views is the Rollup table, but you can switch to another table by using the techniques that are explained in the section "Changing a table," earlier in this chapter. Figure 6.40 showed the Milestone Rollup view that Project displays if you selected Milestones in Step 7. If you select Bars in Step 7, Project displays the Bar Rollup view, as shown in Figure 6.41.

FIGURE 6.41

When you format rollup tasks as bars, Project displays your project using the Bar Rollup view.

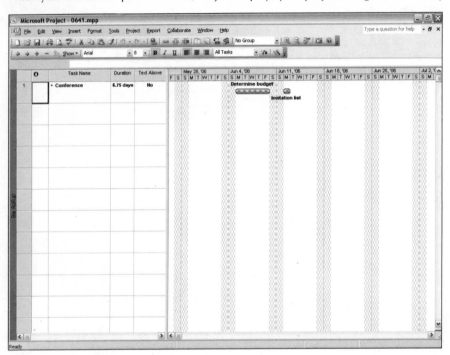

TIP — To redisplay all subtasks in a typical Gantt Chart view, click the Show button on the Formatting toolbar and choose All Subtasks.

But you don't need to rerun the macro to see the Bar Rollup view; using the More Views dialog box (click the More Views button on the View bar or choose View ➪ More Views), you can display the Bar Rollup view or the Milestone Date Rollup view, shown in Figure 6.42.

NOTE — If your start dates are close together, Project overwrites the task names, thus making them difficult or impossible to read.

TIP — To totally remove rollup formatting, perform Steps 1 to 4 in the preceding section, "Using the Rollup_Formatting macro."

FIGURE 6.42

Use this view to see rollup tasks along with their start dates.

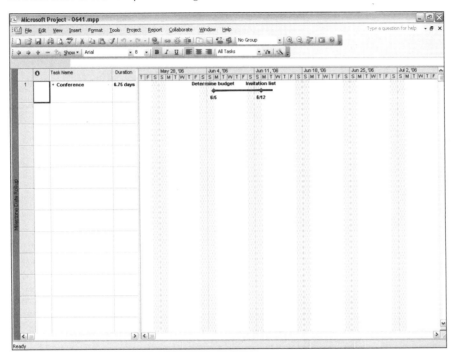

Task Details Form

The Task Details Form view closely resembles the Task Form view and the Task Name Form view. The Task Details Form view, shown in Figure 6.43, enables you to view and edit tracking information about one task at a time.

Use the Previous and Next buttons in the upper-right corner of this view to switch from task to task. If you haven't sorted or filtered tasks, Project displays them in order of ID number. The Task Details Form view is a good choice for part of a combination view.

The Task Details Form view.

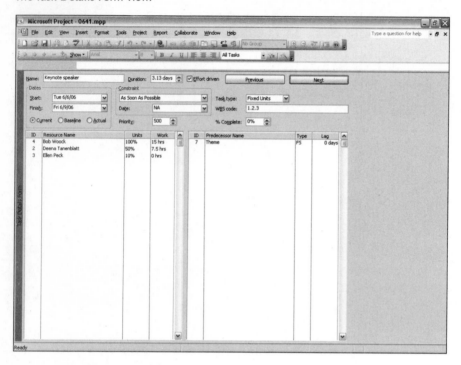

Task Entry

The Task Entry view is a combination view. In Figure 6.44, the Gantt Chart view appears in the top pane, and the Task Form view appears in the bottom pane. To see information about a task in the Task Form view, select the task in the Gantt Chart view. You can see this view easily if you select the Gantt view and then choose Window ⇨ Split.

Only the Gantt Chart view in the top pane uses a table. The default table is the Entry table, but you can use the techniques that are described in the section "Changing a table," earlier in this chapter, to change the table.

FIGURE 6.44

The Task Entry view.

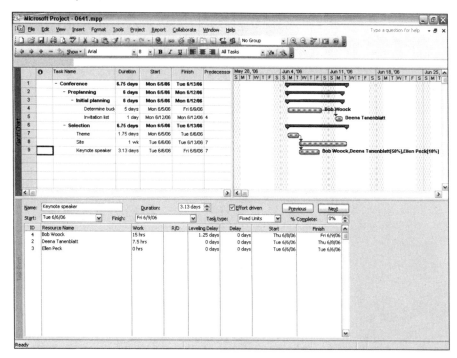

Task Form

The Task Form view appears on the bottom portion of the Task Entry view, as shown previously in Figure 6.44. The Task Form view closely resembles the Task Details Form view, shown previously in Figure 6.43.

The Task Form view provides more resource information (such as costs) than the Task Details Form view, and the Task Details Form view provides more task information (such as predecessors) than the Task Form view. Use the Previous and Next buttons to switch between tasks. The Task Form view also closely resembles the Task Name Form view.

Task Name Form

The Task Name Form view is a cousin to the Task Details Form view and the Task Form view. This simplified version displays the basic characteristics of tasks, one task at a time, as shown in Figure 6.45.

Use the Previous and Next buttons to switch between tasks. Again, if you compare Figures 6-43, the bottom portion of 6-44, and 6-45, you can see how closely these views resemble each other. The Task Name Form view works well as part of a combination view.

FIGURE 6.45

The Task Name Form view

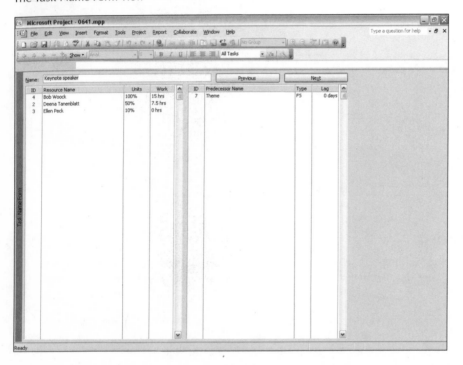

Task Sheet

The Task Sheet view is the counterpart of the Resource Sheet view in that the Task Sheet view displays task information in a spreadsheet-like format. In this view, you can create tasks, link tasks (establishing dependencies), and even assign resources, as shown in Figure 6.46.

This view closely resembles the left portion of the Gantt Chart view and makes it easy to view tasks in chronological order. The default table that appears on the Task Sheet view is the Entry table, but you can use the techniques that are described in the section "Changing a table," earlier in this chapter, to change the table.

FIGURE 6.46

The Task Sheet view helps you to see tasks in chronological order.

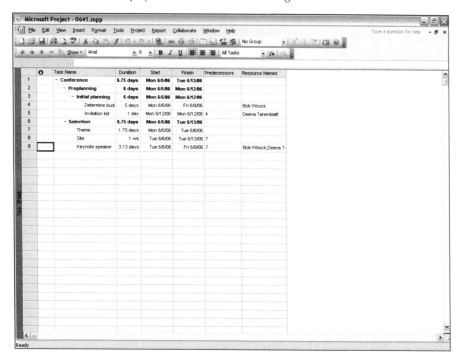

Task Usage

This powerful view, shown in Figure 6.47, enables you to focus on how resources affect the task by showing resource assignments for each task. Use this view to organize resources by task, evaluate work effort and cost by task, and compare scheduled and actual work and costs.

The default table for the left side of the Task Usage view is the Usage table, but you can display other tables by using the Table Selection button, as described in the section "Changing a table," earlier in this chapter. Also, by default, Project shows Work in the Details section on the right. Again, you can select any item from the Format Details menu or in the Details Styles dialog box (choose Format ➪ Detail Styles).

> **NOTE** How can you do 12 hours of work in one eight-hour day, as indicated in the sample project shown in Figure 6.47? Remember that this view shows total resource hours: As the figure shows, two people worked eight hours and four hours, respectively.

FIGURE 6.47

The Task Usage view shows resources grouped under the tasks to which they are assigned.

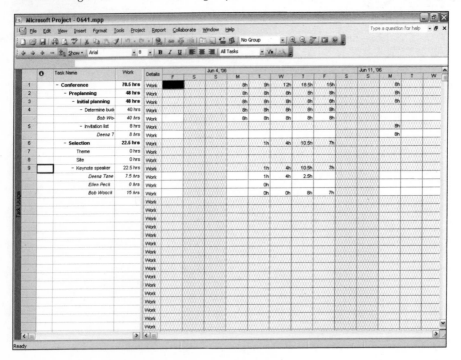

Printing Your Project

When you print a project, you are printing a view. So, before you do anything, select the view that you want to print. If you're printing a sheet view, the number of columns that you see on-screen determines the number of columns that print. If the printed product requires more than one page, Project prints down and across, that is, the entire left side of your project prints before the right side prints.

Printing in Project is similar to printing in any other Microsoft product. You can use the Print button on the Standard toolbar to print using default settings. And what are the default settings? They appear in two dialog boxes that you can view if you don't use the Print button.

NOTE You can also preview before printing, either by clicking the Preview button in the Print dialog box or by clicking the Print Preview button on the Standard toolbar.

Choose File ➪ Print to open the Print dialog box, as shown in Figure 6.48.

FIGURE 6.48

From the Print dialog box, you can control, for example, the printer to which you print and the number of copies that you print.

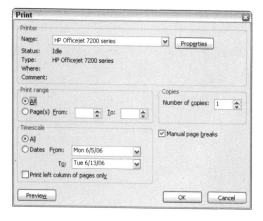

NOTE Starting in Project 2000, when you save the project file, Project retains the settings that you make in this dialog box for the timescale, including whether the Print left column of pages only option is selected and whether the Manual page breaks option is selected.

You can't open the Page Setup dialog box, shown in Figure 6.49, from the Print dialog box, but you can open the Page Setup dialog box either by choosing File ➪ Page Setup or by clicking the Page Setup button that is available in Print Preview. From the Page tab, you can set orientation and scaling. Using scaling, you may be able to fit the printed text onto one page.

FIGURE 6.49

The Page tab of the Page Setup dialog box.

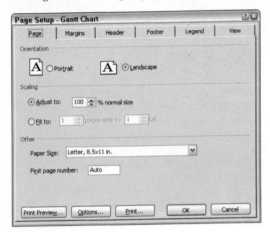

NOTE   Starting in Project 2000, you can set the first page number of the printed product. For example, suppose that your project is 10 pages long but you intend to print only pages 5 and 6. Typically, you would want to number those pages as 1 and 2 — and you can do exactly that by entering 1 in the First page number box.

From the Margins tab, shown in Figure 6.50, you can change the margins for your printed text and determine whether a border should appear.

FIGURE 6.50

The Margins tab of the Page Setup dialog box.

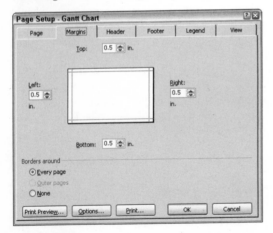

From the Header tab, shown in Figure 6.51, you can define and align header information to appear on the top of every page that you print. Use either the buttons at the bottom of the box or the list box to add information that you want Project to update automatically, such as page numbers.

FIGURE 6.51

The Header tab of the Page Setup dialog box.

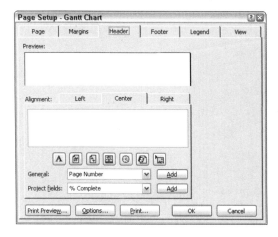

> **TIP** You can include Project level fields in the header, footer, or legend of your printed product. From the appropriate tab of the Page Setup dialog box, use the Project fields list box to select the field that you want to include.

The Footer tab works just as the Header tab does. You can align and include the same kind of updating information in the footer on each page of your printed text.

The Page Setup dialog box changes just slightly, depending on the view that you were using when you opened the dialog box. For example, the Legend tab is available only when you're printing a Calendar, Gantt Chart, or Network Diagram view, as shown in Figure 6.52. The Legend tab works just the same as the Header and Footer tabs, and you can align and include the same kind of updating information.

FIGURE 6.52

The Legend tab of the Page Setup dialog box.

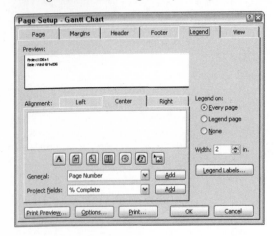

The View tab enables you to control what Project prints, such as all or only some columns, as shown in Figure 6.53.

FIGURE 6.53

The View tab of the Page Setup dialog box.

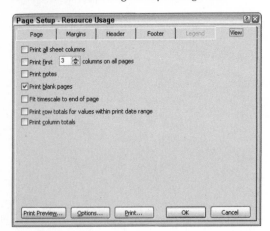

Starting in Project 2003, two options — Print column totals and Print row totals for values within print date range check boxes — appear on the View tab in views where they apply: the Task Usage view and the Resource Usage view (the boxes are unavailable in all other views). When you select the Print Column Totals check box, Project calculates totals in memory and adds a row to the printed page showing totals for time-phased data as well as for sheet data. You can take advantage of the Print row totals for values within print date range check box when you're printing a Usage view. Selecting this box tells Project to add a column to the printed page that shows totals for the time-phased data with the date range that you specify in the Print dialog box. The totals lines print on the same page as the last rows or columns of data, before any Notes pages.

TIP In many cases, you can add a column to a table that gives you the same information that you can get in the row totals. The column prints where you place it, whereas the row totals print on a separate page.

Summary

This chapter covered the standard views that are available in Project. You saw a sample of each view and found out how to print in Project.

Chapter 7 takes you beyond the basics in views. You find out how to customize and filter views and show other available information in views.

Chapter 7

Using Views to Gain Perspective

In Chapter 6, you saw samples of the built-in views that come with Project. And although you may never need any view other than the ones that come with Project, you're not limited to just those views. The potential variations for viewing information about your project are almost mind-boggling. In this chapter, you explore ways to make views work for you.

IN THIS CHAPTER

Customizing views

Filtering views to gain perspective

Customizing Views

You can customize the views in Project so that they show you the information that you need. You can fiddle with the tables in views that contain tables or with the views themselves.

Changing tables

In views containing tables, you can make changes as simple as modifying the height of the rows or switching to a different table. Or, you can modify the appearance of the default table by moving columns around, hiding columns, or adding columns — and save your changes in a new table.

Changing row height and column width

This feature helps you out whenever information is too wide to fit within a column. When you change the height of a row, the data wraps to fit within the taller row.

Notice that the task names for Tasks 5 and 7, shown in Figure 7.1, don't fit within the Task Name column. If I increase the height of those rows, both names wrap so that they are visible, as shown in Figure 7.2.

FIGURE 7.1

You can change the height of a row when the mouse pointer looks like a double-headed arrow.

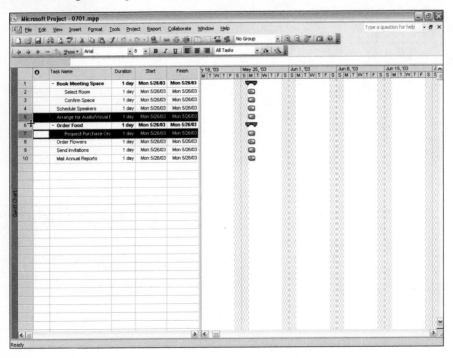

To change the height of a row, select the row and move the mouse pointer into the Task ID number column at the bottom of the selected row. The mouse pointer changes to a pair of arrows pointing up and down (as shown in Figure 7.1). Drag down, and when you release the mouse button, Project increases the height of the selected row and wraps any text in that row that didn't fit within its column.

TIP   To change the height of more than one row, select each row that you want to change. Use Windows selection techniques to select the rows. For example, to select two non-contiguous rows, click the ID of the first row and then press and hold down Ctrl while you click the ID of the second row. When you change multiple rows simultaneously, Project assigns a uniform height to the selected rows.

NOTE   You can change row heights only in full row increments. In other words, you can make a row twice its original size but not one and a half times its original size.

FIGURE 7.2

When you change the height of more than one row at a time, Project assigns a uniform height to all selected rows.

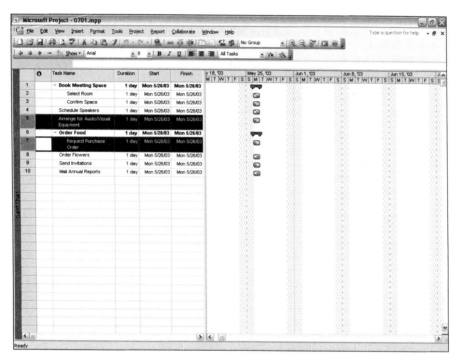

You can make a row wider or narrower by moving the mouse pointer to the right edge of the column heading name. When the mouse pointer changes to a pair of arrows pointing left and right, drag the mouse right to make the column wider and left to make it narrower. Or, double-click to make the column wide enough to accommodate the longest entry in the column.

TIP If you see pound signs (#) in a column, the column isn't wide enough to display the information stored in the field.

Hiding and inserting columns

You can temporarily remove a column from a table by hiding it. Right-click the column heading, and choose Hide Column from the menu that appears. Project doesn't remove the data in the column from the file; instead, the data is hidden from view. To see the column again (or to add a different column to your table), right-click the column heading that you want to appear to the right of the column that you intend to insert. Then, choose Insert Column from the shortcut menu that appears. You see the Column Definition dialog box, as shown in Figure 7.3.

FIGURE 7.3

Use this dialog box to add a column to your table.

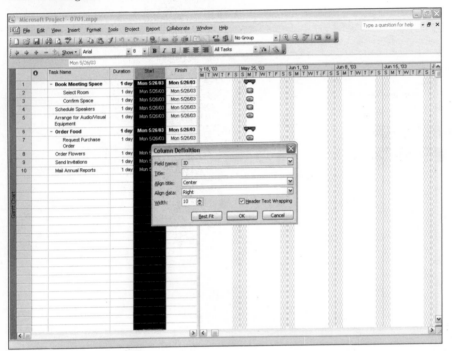

In the Field name list box, select the name of the column that you want to add. You don't need to make any other changes; click the Best Fit button to make sure that Project provides enough space for the column title. Project inserts the column to the left of the selected column.

Adding fields to a usage view

By default, the Work field appears in the Details section of both usage views; you can easily add the Actual Work, Cumulative Work, Overallocation, Cost, and Remaining Availability fields using one of two techniques:

- Choose Format ⇨ Details and then click the appropriate field on the submenu that appears.

- Right-click anywhere in the Details section and then click the appropriate field from the shortcut menu that appears.

But, there are many other fields that you can add to the Details section of a usage view. And, you can use the Detail Styles dialog box shown in Figure 7.4 to add those fields to the Details section. Suppose, for example, that you want to take advantage of the budget resource and enter values for a budget work resource or a budget cost resource. Start in either usage view — the Task Usage view or the Resource Usage view — and choose Format ➪ Detail Styles; Project displays the Detail Styles dialog box.

FIGURE 7.4

The Detail Styles dialog box supplies additional choices that you can display in the Details section of a view.

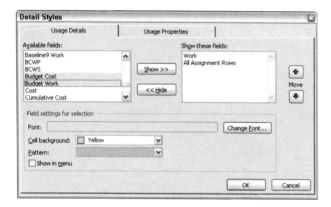

Click a field — such as the Budget Cost field — in the Available fields list (you can use Windows selection techniques to select more than one field simultaneously, as I've done in Figure 7.4). Click the Show button, and the field then appears in the Show These Fields list. When you click OK, Project displays a row for the field in the Details portion of the view.

TIP To select two noncontiguous fields, click the first field and then press and hold Ctrl while you click the second field. To select contiguous fields, click the first field and then press and hold Shift while you click the last field.

You can hide fields in the Details portion of a usage view; right-click anywhere in the Details section, and click the field you want to hide (see Figure 7.5). Project removes the field from the Details portion of the view.

FIGURE 7.5

You can hide fields in a Details section of a usage view by selecting the field from the shortcut menu that appears when you right-click the Details section.

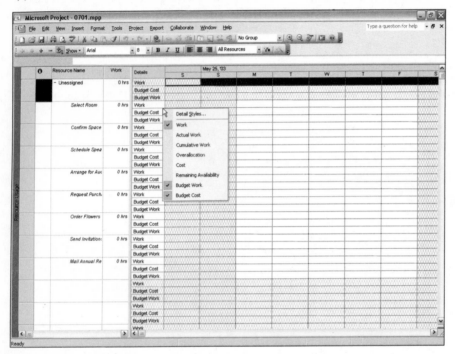

> **NOTE** The Work, Actual Work, Cumulative Work, Overallocation, Cost, and Remaining Availability fields remain available from the submenu or shortcut menu even after you hide them. But if you add a field to the Details portion of a usage view using the Detail Styles dialog box and then subsequently hide that field, it will not appear on a submenu or shortcut menu. To use it again, you must use the Detail Styles dialog box to display it again.

Switching tables

Tables don't appear in every view. For example, neither the Network Diagram view nor the Resource Graph view has a table that displays columns of information. However, views that have tables, such as the Task Usage view or the Gantt view, shown in Figure 7.6, also have a Select All button. Right-click the Select All button to select all the information in the table and list the standard tables that you can display as well as the More Tables option.

> **TIP** Clicking (instead of right-clicking) the Select All button selects all information in the table portion of the view.

FIGURE 7.6

Switch to a different table by selecting it from this shortcut menu.

Select All button

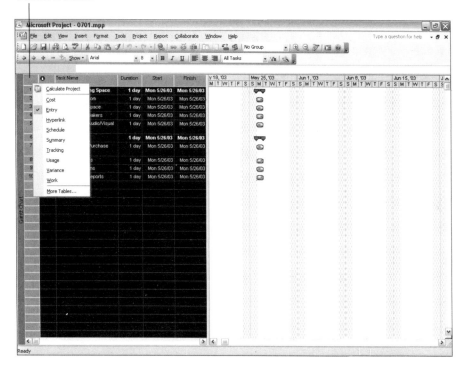

Creating new tables or editing existing tables

As with views, Project has dozens of built-in tables, with a wide variety of information included to help you focus on issues of scheduling, resources, tracking, and so on. The More Tables window enables you to switch to tables that don't appear on the shortcut list of tables. You also can use the More Tables window to modify the fields of information displayed in the columns of tables, and even to create new tables. Creating new tables in Project is remarkably similar to editing existing tables; you use the same dialog box for both operations.

NOTE How do you decide whether to create a new table or modify an existing one? If you can find a predefined table with a similar focus that has several of the fields that you want to include, start with a copy of that table. Then delete, rearrange, modify, or add fields as needed. If you can't find an appropriate model, you may need to create a new table. I suggest using a copy of the table because someone else who is using your schedule will expect to find the default fields in Project's original tables instead of the fields that you establish.

Suppose that the view would be more meaningful if the columns appeared in a different order than the order in which Project shows them. For example, many tables list baseline information first and then list actual information, resulting in this sequence of columns: Baseline Start, Baseline Finish, Actual Start, Actual Finish. Comparing this information may be easier if you create a table that presents the information in this order: Baseline Start, Actual Start, Baseline Finish, Actual Finish—and so on.

Or perhaps you want to add the table to the list of tables on the shortcut menu that appears when you right-click the Select All button. You may even want to add or delete some fields of information (columns) from the table. You can either edit an existing table or make a copy of it and edit the copy.

CAUTION   The More Tables window does not have a Table reset button; consequently, any changes that you make are permanent. I advise you to always make a copy of a table that you want to modify, rather than edit the original table. That way, the original tables remain intact.

Follow these steps to create a new table or edit an existing table:

1. Choose View ⇨ Table ⇨ More Tables. Project displays the More Tables window shown in Figure 7.7.

FIGURE 7.7

Select a table to use, edit, or copy from this dialog box.

2. Click the New button to create a new table, or select a table that you want to edit. You can use the Task or Resource option buttons at the top of the dialog box to display the type of table that you need. Then click either the Edit button to edit the original table or the Copy button to edit a copy of the table. The Table Definition dialog box appears, as shown in Figure 7.8.

NOTE   If you create a copy, you may want to rename it in the Name box instead of using the default "Copy of" name that Project supplies.

3. Enter a name for the table in the Name field. To show this table in the shortcut menu that appears when you right-click the Select All button, select the Show in menu check box.

FIGURE 7.8

Use the Table Definition dialog box to make changes to the appearance of a table. When you create a new table, no information appears in the bottom portion of the dialog box.

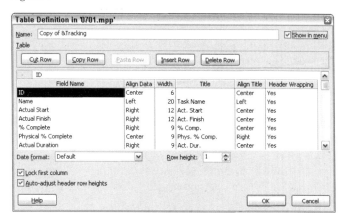

4. To add a field to the table, click a blank space in the area under the Field Name column; an arrow appears on the right side of the field. Click the arrow to display the drop-down list, as shown in Figure 7.9, and select a field name.

TIP Use the Insert Row and Delete Row buttons to add rows in between existing rows or to remove existing rows. To insert a row, click the row below the row you want to add and click Insert Row.

FIGURE 7.9

You can select fields of predefined information to build the columns in your table.

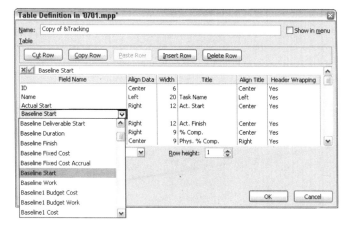

223

5. In the same row, click in the Align Data column. Project displays the default settings for alignment of data and title as well as the width of the column. Click the arrow on the right side of the field; then select Left, Center, or Right alignment for the data in the column.

6. Click the Width column and, if necessary, modify the width of the column to accommodate the type of information that you think will typically go there.

TIP If you aren't sure about the ideal column width, just accept the default. You can easily adjust column widths when the table is on-screen by dragging the edge of the column heading to the right or left.

7. Click the Title field and enter a title for the column if you don't want to use the default field name. Otherwise, skip this step.

8. Click the Align Title column and select a different alignment for the column title if you like.

9. Repeat Steps 4 through 8 to add more fields to your table. To edit your table, use the Cut Row, Copy Row, and Paste Row buttons to reorganize the order of fields in your table.

10. If you have included any columns that include dates, such as Start or Finish information, you can modify the date format by using the drop-down list of choices in the Date Format field. You can also modify the height of all the rows with the Row Height setting.

NOTE The Header Wrapping field — a Yes or No choice — controls whether long titles wrap within the column heading. If you set the Header Wrapping field to No, Project hides that portion of a column title that doesn't fit within the allotted space for the column.

11. If you want the first column of your table to remain on-screen while you scroll across your page, select the Lock first column check box. Typically, the Task ID column is the column that is locked in place in a table.

12. Click OK when you are finished. Then click Apply in the More Tables dialog box to display the new table on your screen.

NOTE By default, changes that you make to tables appear only in the current Project file. If you want new or edited tables to be available to other schedules, you must use the Organizer function in the More Tables dialog box to copy these tables to the `Global.mpt` file. See Chapter 22 for more information.

Working with views

As you discovered in Chapter 6, views display a variety of information: tables with several fields of data, taskbars, network diagram nodes, and so on. Microsoft has provided a plethora of views, meeting just about every information need. Nevertheless, you may want to create a variation on one of those views to look at information from a different perspective. For example, you can create a second Network Diagram view in which you set the nodes to display a different set of information than the standard Network Diagram view. Then, rather than have to modify the nodes in the original Network Diagram view each time to see different information that you call on frequently, you can simply display the new view to use the alternative Network Diagram view. You can base an alternative view on any of the existing views and then change the information that Project displays by default to include only the information that you need.

Adding views

You can select a view from the View bar, or you can choose View ⇨ More Views. Project gives you dozens of alternative views from which to select, as shown in Figure 7.10. When you create a new view, you can include it on the View bar or make it available in the More Views dialog box only.

FIGURE 7.10

A wide selection of built-in views meets most informational needs.

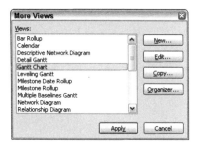

 You can edit an existing view instead of creating a new view. But, as with the More Tables dialog box, the More Views dialog box does not have a View reset button; consequently, any changes that you make are permanent. As I previously suggested, make a copy of a view that you want to modify rather than edit the original view. That way, the original views remain intact.

To add a new view to your copy of Project, follow these steps:

1. Choose View ⇨ More Views.

2. Click the New button in the More Views dialog box (shown in Figure 7.10). The Define New View dialog box appears, as shown in Figure 7.11.

TIP If you can, base your new view on a copy of an existing view by clicking copy after selecting the appropriate view — you'll have less to do to create the view.

FIGURE 7.11

A simple choice awaits you in the Define New View dialog box: a single or combination view.

3. Select the Single view option and click OK. The View Definition dialog box opens, as shown in Figure 7.12.

FIGURE 7.12

Use this dialog box to name and describe your new view.

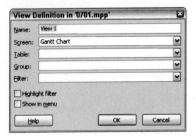

NOTE   If you select the Combination view option, the View Definition dialog box requests slightly different information.

4. Enter the name of the new view in the Name box. Choose a name that describes the information that you'll show in the view.

5. Select a type of view on which to base the new view by clicking the arrow to open the Screen drop-down list. Then choose a view name.

6. Do one of the following:

   ■ If the screen that you chose in Step 5 gives you the option of selecting a table to include with it, select that table from the Table drop-down list shown in Figure 7.13.

   ■ If the screen that you chose in Step 5 does not give you this option, go to Step 7.

FIGURE 7.13

All the built-in tables and new tables that you have created appear on this list.

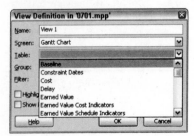

7. Open the Filter list box to choose a filter to apply to the view. By default, Project applies the All Tasks filter; therefore, all tasks appear in the view. To apply a selective filter so that Project highlights only filtered tasks, select the Highlight Filter check box at the bottom of the View Definition dialog box.

NOTE You can set filters to remove tasks from the display that don't meet the filtering criteria, or you can set filters to simply highlight the tasks that meet the criteria. To reformat text that Project highlights as meeting filter criteria, choose Format ⇨ Text Styles.

8. Select the Show in Menu check box to make the new view available as a selection in the View bar and on the View menu. If you don't check this box, you must display the view by selecting it from the More Views dialog box.

9. Click OK and then click Apply in the More Views dialog box to save the new view and display it on-screen.

Creating a combination view

You can manipulate views to see either a single or combination configuration. Combination views display the view that you've selected, as well as a second view that includes information about the selected task. Figure 7.14 shows the Network Diagram view with a combination of visual and textual information.

FIGURE 7.14

A combination view displays information for selected tasks.

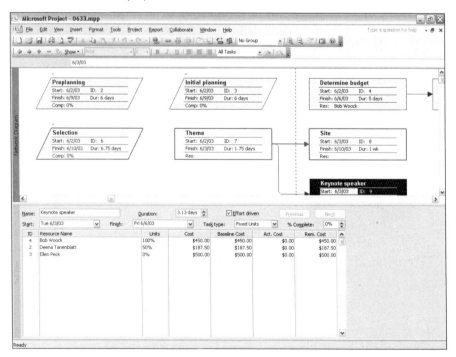

You can display a combination in any view by moving your pointer to the split bar, shown in Figure 7.15, until the pointer becomes two horizontal lines with arrows; then double-click. You can also click and drag the split bar toward the top of your screen, or you can choose Window ⇨ Split. You can return to the simple Network Diagram view by double-clicking the split bar again.

TIP   If you are displaying a combination view and you switch views, the new view also appears as a combination view. To display a new view and have it occupy the full screen, choose Window ⇨ Remove Split. You can always tell which portion of the split view you're in by the active view bar, a dark line that appears along the left edge of the view when you click the upper or lower view.

FIGURE 7.15

When the mouse pointer appears in this shape, you can double-click to create a combination view.

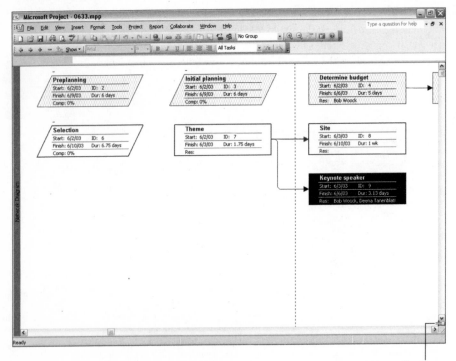

Split bar mouse pointer

Suppose that you want to create a combination view that you can display at any time. Create a new combination view that includes the two views that you want to see together by following these steps:

1. Choose View ⇨ More Views to display the More Views dialog box.

2. Click New to display the Define New View dialog box.

3. Choose the Combination view option to display the dialog box shown in Figure 7.16.

FIGURE 7.16

In the combination view version of the View Definition dialog box, select the two views to place on-screen.

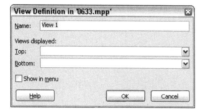

4. Name the view and designate which view should appear at the top of the screen and which view should appear at the bottom.

5. To be able to display the view by choosing it from the View menu, select the Show in Menu check box.

6. Click OK when you finish.

Ordering Tasks in a View

You can think of project management as the attempt to comprehend a large job by breaking the job into progressively smaller pieces — until the job is a collection of tasks. You want to organize the tasks so that you can estimate schedules, resource requirements, and costs. You can sort tasks and assign WBS codes or outline numbers to help you organize the project.

Sorting tasks

Sometimes, sorting information in a different way helps you to see things that you may not have seen otherwise or even to get a better handle on a problem. In Project, you can sort a project from most views in almost any way that you want.

For example, in the Gantt Chart view, Project automatically sorts tasks by ID (see Figure 7.17). But you may find it easier to view your project information if you sort by Finish Date. Choose Project ➪ Sort ➪ by Finish Date, and Project reorders the Gantt Chart view so that tasks are ordered by Finish Date, as shown in Figure 7.18.

When you choose Project ➪ Sort, you see five common sort keys, but if you choose the Sort By command at the bottom of the submenu, the Sort dialog box appears, as shown in Figure 7.19. From this dialog box, you can sort down to three levels. That is, if Project finds a "tie" at the first level, it uses the second sort that you specify to break the tie. And, if Project finds a tie at the second level, it uses the third sort that you specify to break the tie. Using the check boxes at the bottom of the dialog box, you can make your sort choices permanent by reassigning Task IDs, and you can choose to retain the outline structure of the project.

FIGURE 7.17

By default, Project sorts the Gantt view in Task ID order.

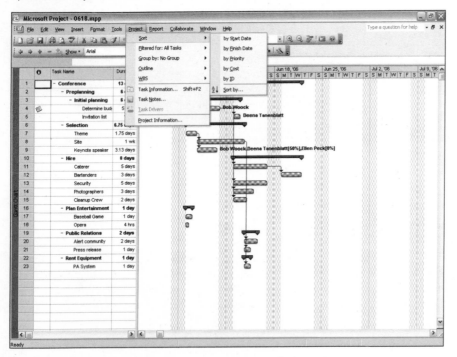

FIGURE 7.18

Using commands from the Sort submenu, you can sort a project by Task Finish Date.

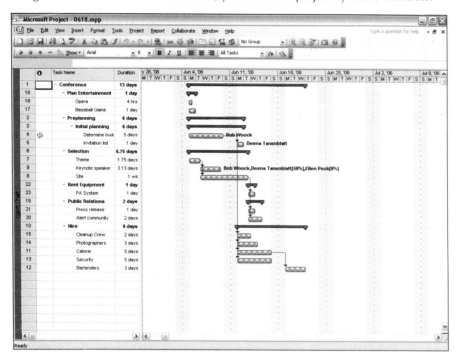

FIGURE 7.19

You can set up a more complex sort structure for Project to use in the Sort dialog box.

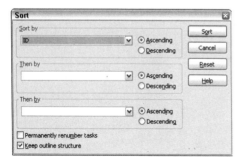

Creating WBS codes

The U.S. defense establishment initially developed the work breakdown structure (WBS), and you find it described in Section 1.6 of MIL-HDBK-881A (30 July 2005) as follows:

- A product-oriented family tree is composed of hardware, software, services, data, and facilities. The family tree structure results from systems engineering efforts during the acquisition of a defense material item.

- A WBS chart displays and defines the product, or products, to be developed and/or produced. It relates the elements of work to be accomplished to each other and to the end product. In other words, the WBS is an organized method to break down a product into subproducts at lower levels of detail.

- WBS can be expressed down to any level of interest. Generally, the top three levels are sufficient unless the items identified are high cost or high risk. Then, is it important to take the WBS to a lower level of definition.

More simply put, a WBS chart shows a numbered list of the tasks that you must complete to finish a project.

In Project 2007, you can't produce a WBS graphic representation of your project that is similar to the one shown in Figure 7.20. You can, however, assign WBS codes to each task. WBS codes can be letters and numbers (or combinations of letters and numbers) that help you identify the relationship among tasks and organize the project.

FIGURE 7.20

The WBS chart is reminiscent of a company organization chart.

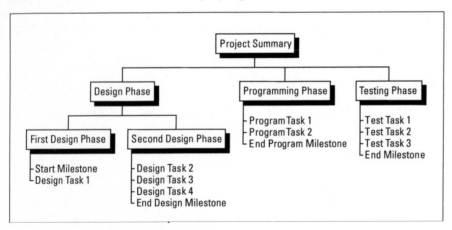

ON the CD-ROM   WBS Chart for Project, an add-on product for Project, creates a WBS chart from a Microsoft Project file. The CD-ROM that accompanies this book includes a sample of the program.

You can use any numbering system that you want for your WBS code structure. Suppose that you assigned codes to your project that are similar to the ones shown in Figure 7.21. The task numbered 1.1.2.3 identifies the first box in Level 2, the second box in Level 3, and the third box on Level 4 of the outline structure of the project. Although Project doesn't produce the graphic representation, it assigns the numbers based on the task's level within the project outline.

To assign WBS numbers to a project, follow these steps:

1. Choose Project ⇨ WBS ⇨ Define Code. Project displays the WBS Code Definition dialog box. The Code preview box shows you the format of the WBS code that you're designing as you design it — and therefore remains blank until you make selections in this dialog box.

2. Use the Project Code Prefix box to apply a prefix to all WBS codes that you assign. For example, you may want to use the initials of the project name.

3. In the Sequence column at the bottom of the box, select the type of character that you want to use for each level of the WBS code. In Figure 7.22, I've selected Numbers (ordered) for both Levels 1 and 2, but you can also include Uppercase Letters or Lowercase Letters. If you choose Characters (unordered), Project inserts an asterisk at that position of the WBS code.

FIGURE 7.21

WBS numbering shows you the hierarchical relationship of tasks in the project.

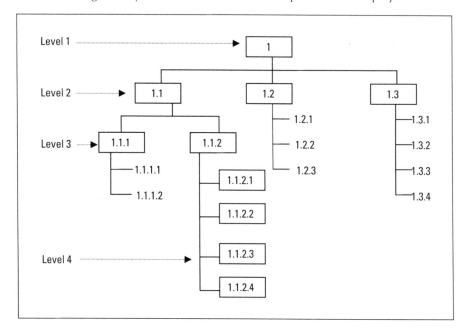

FIGURE 7.22

Use the WBS Code Definition dialog box to define the type of WBS code that you want to use.

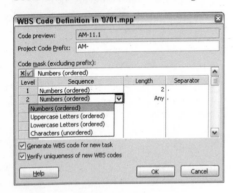

> **NOTE**   If you choose Characters (unordered) in the Sequence column, you can enter any characters that you want into that part of the WBS code. For example, suppose that you use a mask of Numbers (ordered) Length 1, Numbers (ordered) Length 1, Characters (unordered) Length 3. For any third-level task, you can enter any three characters that you want for the third part of the WBS code. In this example, when you enter a third-level task, you initially see a WBS of `1.1.***`. However, you can change it to something like `1.1.a#3`.

4. Open the list box in the Length column and choose the length for the level of the WBS code. In Figure 7.22, I set Level 1 to two digits, but I allowed any number of digits for Level 2. You can choose Any, select from the predefined list of numbers 1–10, or enter any other number.

> **NOTE**   For the technically curious, I tested the number 100, and Project accepted it, but using a 100-digit number in a WBS code isn't particularly practical.

5. In the Separator column, use the list box to select period (.), dash (–), plus (+), or slash (/), or enter any character that is not a number or a letter (such as =).

6. Repeat the previous steps for each level that you want to define.

7. Click OK when you finish.

> **TIP**   You should probably select both check boxes at the bottom of the WBS Code Definition dialog box because doing so ensures that all tasks are assigned WBS codes and that the codes are unique.

The WBS codes don't appear by default in the Gantt Chart view; to view the WBS codes, you must add the WBS column. To add the WBS column to the left of the Task Name column, right-click the Task Name column. Project selects the column and displays a shortcut menu. Choose Insert Column from the shortcut menu, and Project displays the Column Definition dialog box. Open the Field Name list box, and select WBS. If you want, you can change the alignment of data to Left. Then, click Best Fit to add the column to the worksheet portion of the Gantt Chart view, as shown in Figure 7.23.

FIGURE 7.23

When you display the WBS column, Project displays the WBS codes for each task in your project.

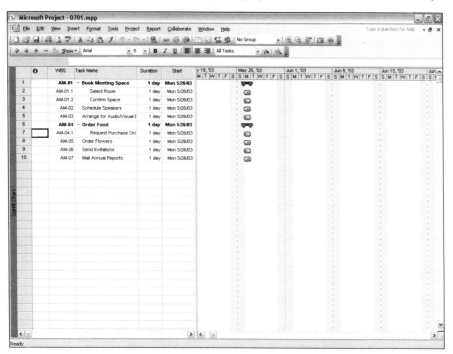

NOTE If you had added the WBS column *before* defining WBS codes, you would have seen outline numbering that corresponded to the task's position in the project outline.

Renumbering WBS codes

WBS codes *don't* automatically renumber themselves in all cases when you change the structure of the project outline. WBS Codes *do* automatically renumber themselves if you change the level of a task within the outline structure of the project. That is, if you promote or demote the task, or if you move it so that it appears at a new level in the outline, or you move a subtask to a new parent task, Project assigns the task a new WBS code. However, if you drag a Level 1 task to a new Level 1 location or if you drag a subtask to a new location beneath its original parent task, both tasks retain their original WBS code number. You can test the premise by dragging Request Purchase Order so that it appears before Order Food. Each task retains its original WBS code, and Project assigns a new WBS Code — AM-08 — to Request Purchase Order (see Figure 7.24). In Figure 7.23, Request Purchase Order had a WBS Code of AM-04.1.

FIGURE 7.24

Because I moved tasks around, the WBS codes are no longer sequential.

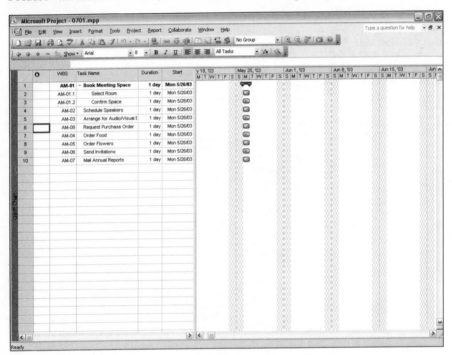

NOTE   If you're working on a government contract for which you and the government have agreed to a numbering scheme and you don't want WBS codes to change, even if you move tasks around, use Outline codes, which are static. You can assign both an Outline code and a WBS code to a task. (You read about Outline codes later in this chapter.)

At times, you'll want to renumber the WBS codes, even though Project didn't renumber them automatically — and you can. In fact, you can renumber the entire project or only selected portions of the project. If you choose to renumber selected portions, you must select the tasks before starting the renumbering process.

CAUTION   You can't undo renumbering WBS codes, so save your project before you start this operation. That way, if you don't like the results, you can close the project without saving it and reopen it in the state before you renumbered it.

To renumber all tasks in the project shown in Figure 7.24, follow these steps:

1. Choose Project ⇨ WBS ⇨ Renumber. Project displays the dialog box shown in Figure 7.25.

FIGURE 7.25

Use this dialog box to renumber the project.

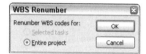

2. Click OK. Project prompts you before renumbering.

3. Click Yes. Project reassigns all WBS numbers, as shown in Figure 7.26.

At this point, I hide the WBS column to keep the display as clean as possible.

FIGURE 7.26

The WBS codes are again sequential after renumbering.

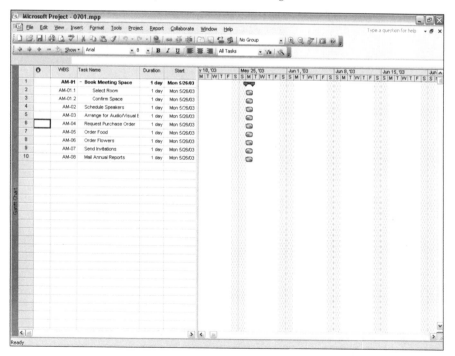

Defining outline numbers

In the preceding section, I offered a scenario in which you're working on a government contract, and you and the government have agreed to a numbering scheme. In a case such as this, you *don't* want WBS codes to change — even if you move tasks around. So, don't rely on WBS codes in Project; instead, use outline codes, which are static.

 You can assign both an outline code and a WBS code to a task.

Outline codes work similarly to the way that WBS codes work. However, outline codes are customizable, and they are not tied to the outline structure of your project. For example, you may want to assign a department code to a task so that you can view the project organized by department. Or, you may want to assign a company cost code to a task so that you can view tasks by cost code.

You can enter outline code information in an ad hoc manner, with no particular rhyme or reason, but most people create a list of valid outline codes for users to enter so that the outline codes assigned are meaningful and consistent.

Outline codes work as you would expect: You define codes at the highest level — we'll call that Level 1 — and then additional codes at various subordinate levels — Level 2, Level 3, and so on. Level 2 codes would appear subordinate to Level 1, Level 3 subordinate to Level 2, and so on.

 Try not to get carried away defining subordinate levels of outline codes; stacking codes deeply makes them harder to use.

To define outline codes, follow these steps:

1. Choose Tools ➪ Customize ➪ Fields. Project displays the Customize Fields dialog box.
2. Open the Type list and choose Outline Code (see Figure 7.27).

FIGURE 7.27

Select an outline code to customize.

CROSS-REF Read more about customizing fields in Chapter 22.

3. Choose an Outline Code to customize.

4. To provide a meaningful name for the code, click the Rename button and enter the new name. Then click OK to redisplay the Customize Fields dialog box.

5. Click the Lookup button; Project displays the Edit Lookup Table dialog box (see Figure 7.28).

Use this dialog box to define the allowable lookup codes.

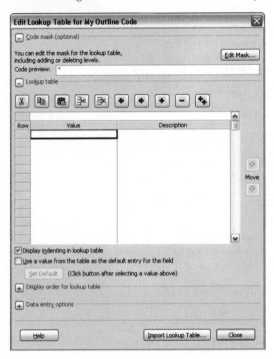

6. To define a mask for the lookup table, click the plus sign (+) beside Code mask; the plus sign (+) changes to a minus sign (–) and displays the top potion of the Edit Lookup Table dialog box. Click the Edit Mask button to display the Code Mask Definition dialog box, shown in Figure 7.29.

The Code Mask Definition dialog box looks and operates like the WBS Code Definition dialog box.

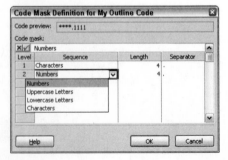

7. In the Sequence column, select the type of character that you want to use for each level of the outline code.

8. In the Length column, use the list to choose the length for the level of the outline code.

9. In the Separator column, use the list box to select period (.), dash (–), plus (+), or slash (/), or enter any character that is not a number or a letter (such as =).

10. Repeat the previous steps for each level of the mask that you want to define.

11. Click OK to redisplay the Edit Lookup Table dialog box.

12. On Row 1 of the Value column, enter a permissible outline code for the first level of your outline — we'll call it Level 1 — and press Enter.

13. On the second line, type an outline code for the second level that is permissible under Level 1 and press Enter; after Project displays the code, move the pointer back into Row 2 and click the Indent button (the right arrow) at the top of the dialog box to indent the code.

14. On the third line, enter another acceptable Level 2 outline code.

If you need a Level 3 outline code under a Level 2 outline code, simply enter the code on a blank line below the Level 2 outline code, press Enter, move the pointer back to the line on which you just typed the code, and click the Indent button again.

To supply another Level 1 code, enter the code, place the pointer on the code's row, and click the Outdent button (the left arrow) as many times as necessary, depending on the last code that you entered.

If you forget to include a code, highlight the code that you want to appear *below* the code that you'll add, and then click the Insert Row button at the top of the dialog box. And, if a code becomes invalid at some later date, reopen this dialog box, highlight the code, and click the Delete Row button.

You can click the plus sign (+) beside Display Order for Lookup Table to control the order in which lookup table codes appear. Similarly, you can click the plus sign (+) beside Data entry options to allow users to add codes to the lookup table or to force entry of only Level 1 codes. In both cases, when you click the plus sign (+), it changes to a minus sign (–) and displays your options.

15. Click Close to redisplay the Custom Fields dialog box.

16. Click OK to save your outline code settings.

Next, you need to insert a column in a table to display outline codes. To do so, you follow the same process that you used to display the column for the WBS code. Right-click the column that you want to appear to the right of the Outline Code column and choose Insert Column. In the Column Definition dialog box, open the Field Name list box and select the outline code that you defined. Click Best Fit, and Project displays the column, empty and waiting for you to assign outline codes to your project's tasks.

Assuming that you followed the preceding steps to create a lookup table of permissible outline codes, you enter codes by clicking in the outline code column; Project displays a list box arrow. When you open the list, the entries from the lookup table appear (see Figure 7.30).

You can enter outline codes using the entries that are listed in the lookup table.

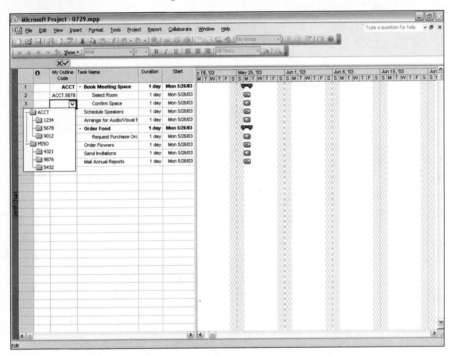

Filtering Views to Gain Perspective

Filters help you to focus on specific aspects of your project. For example, suppose that you want to view the tasks that are assigned to only certain resources or you want to display only the tasks that are on the critical path of your project. You can apply filters to views to limit the information that you see and to help you focus on a particular issue.

Project filters come in two varieties: task filters, which enable you to view specific aspects of tasks, and resource filters, which enable you to view specific aspects of resources. In Table 7.1, you find a description of the default task filters, and in Table 7.2, you find a description of the default resource filters. Many of the filters perform similar functions.

NOTE The Tasks with Deadlines filter and the Tasks with Estimated Durations filter (shown in Table 7.1) first appeared in Project 2000.

TABLE 7.1

Default Task Filters

Filter	Purpose
All Tasks	Displays all the tasks in your project.
Completed Tasks	Displays all finished tasks.
Confirmed	Displays the tasks on which specified resources have agreed to work.
Cost Greater Than	Displays the tasks that exceed the cost you specify.
Cost Overbudget	Calculated filter that displays all tasks with a cost that exceeds the baseline cost.
Created After	Displays all tasks that you created in your project on or after the specified date.
Critical	Displays all tasks on the critical path.
Date Range	Interactive filter that prompts you for two dates and then displays all tasks that start after the earlier date and finish before the later date.
In Progress Tasks	Displays all tasks that have started but haven't finished.
Incomplete Tasks	Displays all tasks that haven't finished.
Late/Overbudget Tasks Assigned To	Prompts you to specify a resource. Then, Project displays tasks that meet either of two conditions: the tasks assigned to that resource that exceed the budget you allocated for them, or the tasks that haven't finished yet and will finish after the baseline finish date. Note that completed tasks do not appear when you apply this filter, even if they are completed after the baseline finish date.
Linked Fields	Displays tasks to which you have linked text from other programs.
Milestones	Displays only milestones.
Resource Group	Displays the tasks that are assigned to resources that belong to the group you specify.
Should Start By	Prompts you for a date and then displays all tasks not yet begun that should have started by that date.
Should Start/Finish By	Prompts you for two dates: a start date and a finish date. Then, Project uses the filter to display those tasks that haven't started by the start date and those tasks that haven't finished by the finish date.
Slipped/Late Progress	Displays two types of tasks: those that have slipped behind their baseline scheduled finish date and those that are not progressing on schedule.
Slipping Tasks	Displays all tasks that are behind schedule.
Summary Tasks	Displays all tasks that have subtasks grouped below them.

continued

TABLE 7.1	(continued)
Filter	**Purpose**
Task Range	Shows all tasks that have ID numbers within the range that you provide.
Tasks with a Task Calendar Assigned	Shows only those tasks to which you've assigned a task calendar.
Tasks with Attachments	Displays tasks that have objects attached or a note in the Notes box.
Tasks with Deadlines	Displays all tasks to which you have assigned deadline dates.
Tasks with Estimated Durations	Displays all tasks that have the estimated duration field checked or tasks for which the default duration estimate has not been changed.
Tasks with Fixed Dates	Displays all tasks that have a start or finish date that has been entered into the start or finish date field directly instead of allowing Project to calculate the Start and Finish dates.
Tasks/Assignments with Overtime	Displays the tasks or assignments that have overtime.
Top Level Tasks	Displays the highest-level summary tasks.
Unconfirmed	Displays the tasks on which specified resources have not agreed to work.
Unstarted Tasks	Displays tasks that haven't started.
Update Needed	Displays tasks that have changes, such as revised start and finish dates or resource reassignments, and that need to be sent to resources for update or confirmation.
Using Resource	Displays all tasks that use the resource that you specify.
Using Resource in Date Range	Displays the tasks that are assigned to a specified resource that start after the first date you specify and finish before the second date you specify.
Work Overbudget	Displays all tasks with scheduled work greater than baseline work.

TABLE 7.2	

Default Resource Filters

Filter	**Purpose**
All Resources	Displays all the resources in your project.
Budget Resources	Displays resources set up as budget resources
Confirmed Assignments	Available only in the Resource Usage view; displays only those tasks for which a resource has confirmed the assignment.
Cost Greater Than	Displays the resources that exceed the cost that you specify.
Cost Overbudget	Calculated filter that displays all resources with a cost that exceeds the baseline cost.

Filter	Purpose
Created After	Displays resources created after a date you specify.
Date Range	Interactive filter that prompts you for two dates and then displays all tasks and resources with assignments that start after the earlier date and finish before the later date.
Group	Prompts you for a group and then displays all resources that belong to that group.
In Progress Assignments	Displays all tasks that have started but haven't finished.
Linked Fields	Displays resources to which you have linked text from other programs.
Non-budget Resources	Displays resources *not* set up as budget resources.
Overallocated Resources	Displays all resources that are scheduled to do more work than they have the capacity to do.
Resource Range	Interactive filter that prompts you for a range of ID numbers and then displays all resources within that range.
Resources – Cost	Displays only those resources with a type of Cost.
Resources – Material	Displays only those resources with a type of Material.
Resources - Work	Displays only those resources with a type of Work.
Resources with Attachments	Displays resources that have objects attached or a note in the Notes box.
Resources/Assignments with Overtime	Displays the resources or assignments that have overtime with Overtime.
Should Start By	Prompts you for a date and then displays all tasks and resources with assignments not yet begun that should have started by that date.
Should Start/Finish By	Prompts you for two dates: a start date and a finish date. Then, Project uses the filter to display those tasks or assignments that haven't started by the start date and those tasks or assignments that haven't finished by the finish date.
Slipped/Late Progress	Displays two types of resources: those that have slipped behind their baseline scheduled finish date and those that are not progressing on schedule.
Slipping Assignments	Displays all resources with uncompleted tasks that are behind schedule because the tasks have been delayed from the original baseline plan.
Unconfirmed Assignments	Displays the assignments for which requested resources have not yet agreed to work.
Unstarted Assignments	Displays confirmed assignments that have not yet started.
Work Complete	Displays resources that have completed all their assigned tasks.
Work Incomplete	Displays all resources with baseline work greater than scheduled work.
Work Overbudget	Displays all resources with scheduled work greater than baseline work.

Applying a filter to a view

By applying a filter to a view, you specify criteria that Project uses to determine what tasks or resources should appear in that view. Project then selects information to display and either high-lights the selected information or hides the rest of the information. To apply a filter and hide all other information, follow these steps:

1. Display the view that you want to filter.

2. Choose Project ➪ Filtered for.

3. Choose the filter that you want from the Filtered for menu.

> **NOTE**   Because Project enables you to apply task filters to task views only and resource filters to resource views only, the Filtered for hierarchical menu shows either All Tasks or All Resources, depending on the view that you displayed before starting these steps.

To apply a filter that doesn't appear on the list, or to apply a highlighting filter, follow these steps:

1. Display the view that you want to filter.

2. Choose Project ➪ Filtered for ➪ More Filters. Project displays the More Filters dialog box, as shown in Figure 7.31.

FIGURE 7.31

Use the More Filters dialog box to apply a filter that doesn't appear on the Filtered For list or to apply a highlighting filter.

3. Click the Task option button to select and apply a task filter; select the Resource option button to apply a resource filter.

> **CAUTION**   Remember that Project doesn't let you apply a task filter to a resource view or a resource filter to a task view.

4. Select a filter name from the list.

5. Click Apply to apply the filter or click Highlight to apply a highlighting filter. If the filter that you want to apply is an interactive filter, type the requested values.

6. Click OK.

 To turn off a filter, choose Project ⇨ Filtered for. Then choose All Tasks or All Resources, as appropriate.

Creating custom filters

If none of Project's default filters meet your needs, you can create a new filter or modify an existing filter by customizing a filter's criteria from the More Filters dialog box. To edit an existing filter, follow these steps:

1. Display the view that you want to filter.

2. Choose Project ⇨ Filtered for ⇨ More Filters to open the More Filters dialog box.

3. Select the option button of the type of filter that you want to use: Task or Resource.

4. Highlight the filter that you want to modify, and click the Copy button. Project displays a Filter Definition dialog box that is similar to the one shown in Figure 7.32.

FIGURE 7.32

The Filter Definition dialog box enables you to edit an existing filter.

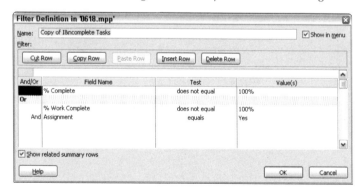

CAUTION The More Filters dialog box does not have a Filter reset button; consequently, any changes that you make are permanent. For this reason, I advise you to click the Copy button to make a copy of a filter that you want to modify, rather than click the Edit button to edit the original filter. That way, the original filters remain intact.

5. Click in the Field Name column; Project displays a list box arrow to the right of the field.

6. Select a field from the list.

7. Repeat Steps 5 and 6 for the Test column and supply a comparison operator.

8. Repeat Steps 5 and 6 in the Value(s) column and supply a filtering value.

9. Repeat Steps 5 through 8 for each criterion that you want to create; also supply an And/Or operator if you supply additional criteria. Remember, *And* means that the filter displays information only if the task or resource meets *all* criteria, whereas *Or* means that the filter displays information if a task or resource meets *any* of the criteria.

10. Click OK to redisplay the More Filters dialog box.

11. Click Apply to apply the filter.

NOTE To create a new filter, click the New button in Step 4. In the Filter Definition dialog box, the name `Filter 1` appears in the Name box and no information appears at the bottom of the box. For the new filter, you need to supply a name and some filtering criteria. To have your new filter appear in the Filtered for list, select the Show in Menu check box.

Each line that you create in the Filter Definition dialog box is called a *statement*. To evaluate certain statements together but separate from other statements in your filter, group the statements into a set of criteria. To group statements, leave a blank line between sets of criteria and select either operator in the And/Or field for the blank row.

If your filter contains three or more statements within one criteria group, Project evaluates all And statements before evaluating Or statements. Across groups, Project evaluates And conditions in the order in which they appear.

Using AutoFilters

AutoFilters are similar to regular Project filters, but you can access them directly on the sheet of any sheet view instead of using a menu or a window. By default, the AutoFilters option is off when you create a project, but you can enable it by clicking the AutoFilter button on the Formatting toolbar.

When you enable AutoFilters, a list box arrow appears at the right edge of every column name in a sheet view. When you open the drop-down list, Project displays filters that are appropriate to the column, as shown in Figure 7.33.

TIP You can turn on AutoFilters automatically for new projects that you create. Choose Tools ➪ Options and click the General tab. Select the Set AutoFilter On for New Projects check box.

FIGURE 7.33

The table of the Gantt Chart view with AutoFilters enabled.

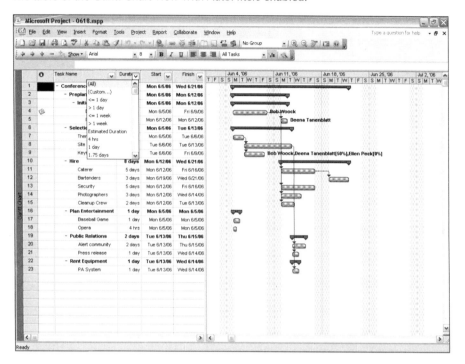

Using grouping

Grouping is another technique that you can use to view information about your project. You may be able to solve a problem if you group tasks by some common denominator. In Figure 7.34, I've grouped tasks by duration to help identify shorter versus longer tasks.

Project contains some predefined groups. To use one of these groups to arrange tasks in a view by the group common denominator, follow these steps:

1. Display the view that you want to use to group tasks.
2. Choose Project ➪ Group By, or use the Group By tool on the Standard toolbar.
3. Choose the group that you want from the Group By menu.

NOTE   Because Project enables you to group tasks only in task views and resources only in resource views, the Group By menu shows either task groupings or resource groupings, depending on the view that you displayed before starting these steps.

FIGURE 7.34

Group tasks in a view to help you identify information about your project.

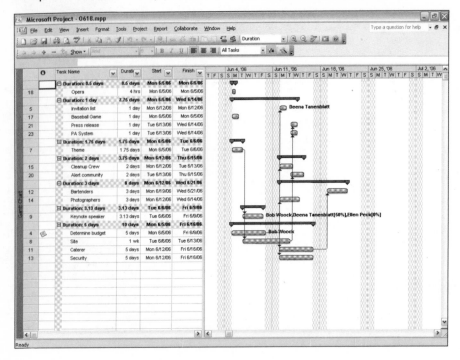

You're not limited to using the groups that appear on the Group By menu; you can group by almost any field. To group in a way that doesn't appear on the menu, follow these steps:

1. Display the view that you want to use to group tasks.

2. Choose Project ⇨ Group by ⇨ More Groups. Project displays the More Groups dialog box, as shown in Figure 7.35.

3. Select the Task option button to apply a task grouping; select the Resource option button to apply a resource grouping.

> **TIP**   Project doesn't let you apply a task group to a resource view or a resource group to a task view.

4. Select a group name from the list.

5. Click Apply to apply the filter or click Edit or Copy to edit a group or make a copy of a group so that you can edit it.

> **CAUTION**   As with its cousins, the More Groups dialog box does not have a Group reset button; consequently, any changes that you make are permanent. I advise you to click the Copy button to make a copy of a group that you want to modify, rather than edit the original group. That way, the original groups remain intact.

FIGURE 7.35

Use the More Groups dialog box to apply a group that doesn't appear on the Group By list or to create a new group by copying and editing an existing group.

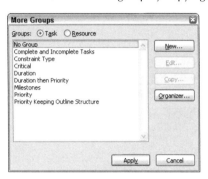

6.   If you simply want to apply a group, click OK. If you are creating a new group by copying an existing group, you see the Group Definition dialog box, as shown in Figure 7.36.

FIGURE 7.36

Use this dialog box to create a custom group based on an existing group.

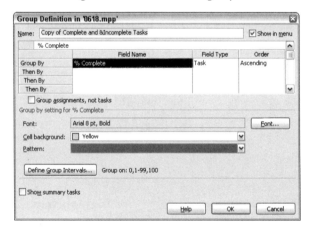

7.   Assign a name to the group that you're creating, and select the Show in Menu box if you want the group to be available from the Group By menu.

8.   Open the Field Name list box, and select a field on which you want Project to group.

9.   In the Order column, choose Ascending or Descending.

10.   (Optional) Select a font for the grouping title information.

11. (Optional) Change the cell background and the pattern that Project displays for the field.

12. (Optional) Click the Define Group Intervals button to display the Define Group Interval dialog box, as shown in Figure 7.37. In this dialog box, you can control the grouping intervals that Project uses. Click OK when you finish to redisplay the Group Definition dialog box.

FIGURE 7.37

Use this dialog box to specify the intervals at which you want Project to group the fields.

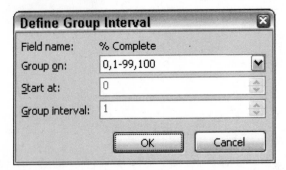

13. Select the Show summary tasks box to include summary tasks in the grouping.

14. Click OK to save your choices and redisplay the More Groups dialog box.

15. Click Apply to apply the group that you just defined.

Working from a usage view, you also can group on assignment fields; follow these steps to do so:

1. Select either the Task Usage view or the Resource Usage view.

2. Choose Project ➪ Group by ➪ Customize Group By. You see the Customize Group By dialog box, as shown in Figure 7.38.

3. Select the fields by which you want to group.

4. Select the Group Assignments, Not Tasks check box.

NOTE In the example, I started working from the Task Usage view. If you start working from the Resource Usage view, the name of the check box changes to refer to resources instead of tasks, and, in the Field Type list, you choose whether to group by assignment or by resource.

FIGURE 7.38

Use this dialog box to group by assignment fields.

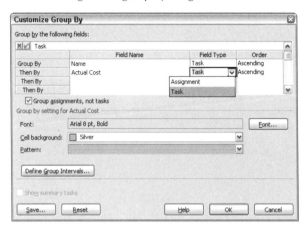

5. In the Field Type column, select whether to group by assignment or by task.

6. Click OK.

 To turn off grouping, choose Project ⇨ Group By. Then choose No Group.

Summary

This chapter covered techniques that you can use to get more information from Project's views. You learned the following:

- How to work with tables
- How to customize views
- How to order tasks in a view
- How to assign WBS codes and outline codes to tasks
- How to filter information while working
- How to group information while working

You can use the skills that you've learned here to make Project work in the way that's most comfortable for you.

Chapter 8 explains how to change the appearance of your project by formatting elements and inserting drawings and objects.

Chapter 8

Modifying the Appearance of Your Project

After you enter the information for your project, you may want to take the time to format the individual elements of the schedule. After all, you may be working with this project for months or even years. Why not get it to look just right?

Project has dozens of ways to format the appearance of elements, from text to taskbars, link lines, and network diagram nodes. Some of these changes are practical; others simply provide shapes or styles that may be more pleasing to you. You can use color and insert drawings or pictures into your schedule to make a visual point. You can also copy pictures of your Project file into other Office documents — for example, to include in a report. So get ready: This chapter is where you can get visually creative!

Changing Project's Looks

Beyond the obvious motivation of making the lines and colors in your schedule more appealing, you may have a practical reason for modifying a schedule's appearance. You may, for example, want to do any of the following to make information about your project more accessible:

- Display information, such as the start and end dates or resources assigned to the task, in text form alongside taskbars. This technique is especially useful for longer schedules in which a taskbar may appear on the printed page far to the right of the task information in the Gantt table.

IN THIS CHAPTER

Changing Project's looks

Using the Gantt Chart Wizard

Formatting elements one by one

Inserting drawings and objects

Consistency Counts

Displaying an abundance of elements on a schedule can be a mixed blessing. For example, high-lighting critical tasks, displaying resource names, and showing baseline, actual lines, and progress lines as well as slack will probably result in a chart that is confusing. Although it may feel good to format to satisfy your penchant for a particular color, remember that you're formatting elements to make project information easier to read.

You'll help everyone in your organization read and understand Project schedules if you make the formatting consistent across your organization. If your coworkers and management see the same formatting in various schedules, they will quickly learn to read the symbols and be less likely to misread a schedule. Set standards for formatting projects in your workgroup and your division (even across your company) and stick to them.

- Use a bolder color for tasks that are on the critical path (tasks that, if delayed, will delay the final completion of the project). This method helps you keep an eye on tasks that are vital to meeting your deadline.

- Modify the display of baseline timing estimates versus actual progress on tasks so that you can more clearly see any divergence.

CROSS-REF You can store multiple baselines. You may want to format your project schedule to more easily distinguish various baselines. See Chapter 11 for more information on multiple baselines.

- Display or hide dependency lines between tasks. In a project with many complex dependency relationships, multiple lines can obscure taskbar elements or network diagram nodes.

In short, beyond mere cosmetics, paying attention to the format of your schedule elements can help you focus on your project. Keep in mind that these changes pertain only to the currently open schedule, and any changes that you make to the format of these elements appear both on-screen and on any corresponding printed versions of the project.

TIP You can change formats whenever you like and then change them back again without changing the data in your project. For example, you may decide not to display dependency lines to print a report of resource assignments for your boss because printing the lines can obscure the list of resources next to each taskbar. You can always redisplay the dependency lines later.

Using the Gantt Chart Wizard

You can make changes to specific elements in several Project views. However, the Gantt Chart view has its own wizard to help you format the various pieces. Running through the Gantt Chart Wizard highlights some of the options.

NOTE A *wizard* is an interactive series of dialog boxes that require you to answer questions or make selections. Project uses your input to create or modify some aspect of your project (in this case, the formatting that is applied to your Gantt Chart). The Microsoft Office family of products uses wizards to automate many functions.

You can use the Gantt Chart Wizard from either the Gantt Chart view or the Tracking Gantt view. Because Gantt Chart Wizard changes apply only to the project file that's open when you run the wizard, start by displaying the project that you want to format. Then follow these steps to run the Gantt Chart Wizard:

NOTE If you don't like the changes you made to the project using the Gantt Chart Wizard, you can Undo the changes that the Gantt Chart Wizard applies to your project if you click Undo before you save your project.

1. Click the Gantt Chart Wizard button on the Formatting toolbar, or choose Format ⇨ Gantt Chart Wizard to start the wizard. A dialog box appears, as shown in Figure 8.1.

FIGURE 8.1

Step 1 of the wizard simply greets you and tells you what the wizard does.

NOTE The four buttons at the bottom of this dialog box appear at the bottom of each wizard dialog box. Click Cancel to leave the wizard without saving any settings, click Back to move back one step, and click Finish to complete the wizard based on the information that you've provided to that point.

2. Click Next to move to the next step. In the second wizard dialog box (see Figure 8.2), indicate the category of information that you want to display. You can select only one item here. Try clicking each of the following choices to see a preview of its style on the left of the dialog box:

   ■ **Standard:** Shows blue taskbars, black summary taskbars, and a black line superimposed over the taskbars to indicate progress on tasks.

   ■ **Critical path:** The Standard layout, with critical-path tasks in red.

   ■ **Baseline:** Displays baseline taskbars and progress taskbars separately rather than superimposed as with the Standard setup, as shown in Figure 8.2.

   ■ **Other:** Displays a drop-down list that contains several alternative, predefined chart styles for the categories of Standard, Critical Path, Baseline, and Status.

   ■ **Custom Gantt Chart:** Displays several additional screens to enable you to create a highly customized Gantt Chart

> **TIP** Highlighting critical tasks in a project helps you to pay special attention to them when reviewing or tracking progress. If you don't want to format the Gantt Chart to treat critical tasks differently, try using a filter to temporarily display only critical tasks, as I discuss in Chapter 7.

FIGURE 8.2

The preview provides an idea of how each option formats your Gantt Chart.

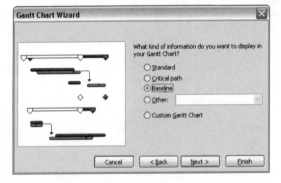

3. Click the option button for Custom Gantt Chart and then click the Next button. The third wizard dialog box appears (see Figure 8.3). In this box, you can choose the type of task information to display with your Gantt bars: Resources and dates (the end date only), Resources, Dates, None (of the choices), or Custom Task Information. When you

choose Dates, as I did in Figure 8.3, Project displays the start date and end date in the taskbar area. If you choose this setting, you don't need to show the corresponding columns for start date and end date in the Gantt table, so this option can help you modify the size of your schedule printout.

FIGURE 8.3

Placing text alongside taskbars can be useful with larger schedules.

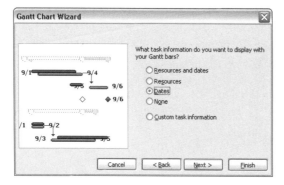

4. Click Next. Using this wizard dialog box (see Figure 8.4), you can decide whether you want to show link lines between dependent tasks.

FIGURE 8.4

Decide whether to display link lines to indicate dependent tasks.

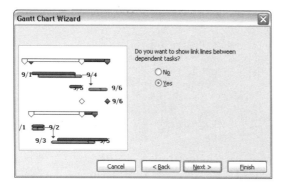

When Enough Is Too Much

If you select the Custom task information option in the Gantt Chart Wizard (refer to Figure 8.3), the wizard opens three consecutive dialog boxes. These three dialog boxes prompt you to display one set of information alongside normal taskbars, another set on summary taskbars, and a third set next to milestone tasks, respectively. The wizard also prompts you to display one set of data to the left of each taskbar, one set to the right, and one set inside the taskbar itself. You could end up with eight pieces of information in and around your various taskbars!

You make your selections from drop-down lists in these three dialog boxes. The information ranges from task name, duration, and priority to percentage of work complete and types of constraints.

If you display nine sets of data in and around taskbars, your Gantt Chart will become unreadable. However, consider this scenario: Put the task name inside both summary and normal taskbars, put the start date to the left and the finish date to the right of normal taskbars, and put the cost of summary tasks to the right of their bars. (The final element is a total of the cost of all tasks beneath the summary tasks.)

You can also modify the information that is available to someone viewing your schedule by changing the columns that appear in the Gantt table pane of the Gantt Chart view.

5. Click Next to preview your formatting options (see Figure 8.5). You can use the Back button to go back and make changes.

FIGURE 8.5

If you don't like what you see, move back to the dialog box in which you made the original setting, change the setting, and then move forward to this dialog box again.

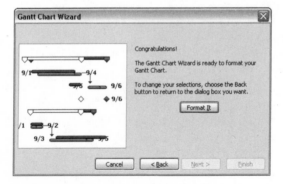

6. Click the Format It button to apply your choices. Project displays a final dialog box to tell you that your formatting is complete.

7. Click the Exit Wizard button to close the dialog box and see your changes.

Formatting Elements One by One

The Gantt Chart Wizard enables you to make changes to several common elements, such as summary taskbars or dependency lines. But Project also enables you to format each of these elements separately and to format them with even more options. You can change the style of many other elements in Project, including the following:

- Text used in your charts
- Boxes used in the Network Diagram Chart view
- Gridlines displayed in various views

Working with text

You may want to change text to be more readable; for example, some people prefer a larger font to make views easy to read. Perhaps you want to use boldface for row and column titles or a distinctive font for summary tasks. Or perhaps you want to change the background color behind text to call attention to certain tasks.

 **Changing the background color of text is new in Project 2007 and particularly useful if you plan to print your project in color or include it in a color slide show.**

NOTE **You format text the same way for any view. You can't format fonts in the Calendar view, but you can format categories of text.**

You can make all these changes and more in Project. You can even change all text in a certain category, or simply change the attributes of a single, selected piece of text in any Project table. For example, you may want to apply boldface to the task name of the milestone Grand Opening, but not to all milestone task names.

NEW FEATURE **Starting in Project 2007, you can undo changes to fonts and other formatting features if you aren't happy with the results.**

Formatting selected text

To format selected text, follow these steps:

1. Move to any view that contains a table of columns (for example, the Gantt Chart, Task Usage, or Resource Sheet views).
2. Click the cell containing the text that you want to format. To format more than one adjacent cell, click the first cell. Then drag your mouse to highlight cells above, below, to the left, or to the right.
3. Choose Format ➪ Font to open the Font dialog box shown in Figure 8.6. From the three lists across the top of this dialog box, you can select a new font, select a font style such as Italic or Bold (Regular is normal text that has neither italic nor bold applied), or change the font size. Select the Underline check box to apply underlining to text, or select a color from the Color and Background Color drop-down palettes. A preview of your selections appears in the Sample area.

NOTE   You can apply a background pattern to a cell, but exercise care, because a background pattern can make text harder to read.

TIP   You can also use a context menu; instead of choosing Format ⇨ Font, right-click and choose Font.

FIGURE 8.6

From the Font dialog box, you can control the style and size of fonts as well as their color and the background appearance of cells.

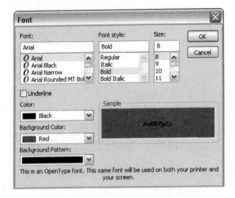

4.   Click OK to save your changes.

If you prefer, you can use buttons on the Formatting toolbar to change font and font size or to apply bold, italic, or underline styles. And you can preview fonts before you select them from the Formatting toolbar (see Figure 8.7).

NOTE   You cannot apply font colors, background colors, or background patterns from the default Formatting toolbar; instead, use the Font dialog box.

CROSS-REF   You can modify the Formatting toolbar to include a button that enables you to open the Font dialog box to show font color, cell background color, and cell background patterns. See Chapter 22 for details on modifying toolbars.

FIGURE 8.7

When you view the fonts in the Font list box, you see a facsimile of the font as it will appear if you choose it.

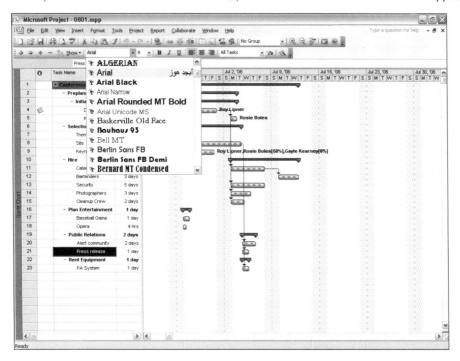

Applying formatting to categories of text

You can use text styles to change the format of text for one cell in a table or to apply a unique format to an entire category of information, such as all task names for milestones. Text styles are identical to the formatting options for text that were described in the preceding section, but you can apply text styles to specific categories of text.

Follow these steps to use text styles to modify text:

1. Choose Format ➪ Text Styles to open the Text Styles dialog box (see Figure 8.8).

2. Click the down arrow next to the Item to Change field to display the options. (This field is the only element that distinguishes the Text Styles dialog box from the Font dialog box that you saw earlier.)

3. Click a category of text to select it. You can format text for categories such as row and column titles, summary tasks, tasks on the critical path, and milestones.

FIGURE 8.8

The default in the Item to Change list box is All (that is, all the text in your project schedule).

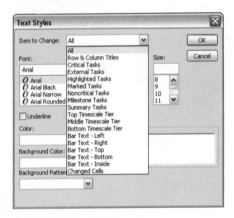

4. Select the settings that you want for the text, including the font, font size, style, color, and script.

5. Click OK to apply the formatting.

Using the Item to Change list box, you can format categories of text to add emphasis to certain key items, such as critical tasks and milestones, or to make your schedule more readable by enlarging text or choosing easy-to-read fonts. Figure 8.9 shows a schedule with separate text styles applied to critical and noncritical tasks. Critical tasks have red backgrounds and italic text, whereas noncritical tasks have pale blue backgrounds.

CAUTION Good advice bears repeating: Don't go overboard with multiple fonts or colors on a single schedule. You can make a project harder to read by using too many fancy fonts. Avoid using more than one or two fonts or colors in your schedule, and vary the text by using bold or italic between categories. Also, try to set up company standards for formatting so that all your project schedules have a consistent, professional look.

FIGURE 8.9

Task names that appear in italics with a red background color indicate critical tasks; noncritical tasks have a pale blue background.

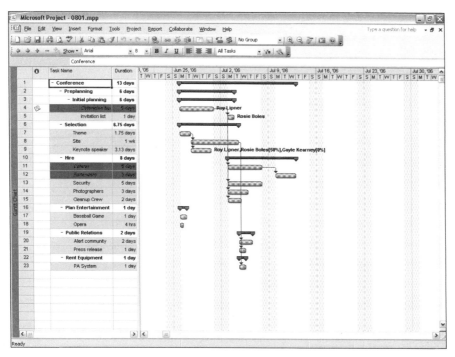

Changing taskbars

In addition to changing text styles in your schedule, you can modify the look of the taskbars. You can make changes to the shape, pattern, and color of bars, as well as to the style of shape that appears on either end of the taskbar.

Formatting taskbars

Formatting taskbars is similar to formatting text. You can format either an individual taskbar or a category of taskbars, such as milestones or critical tasks. Click a particular task and open the dialog box to format just that taskbar by choosing Format ⊃ Bar. Alternatively, you can open the dialog box to format categories of taskbars by choosing Format ⊃ Bar Styles. The settings that you can modify are the same either way.

> **TIP**   You can open the Format Bar dialog box by right-clicking the bar that you want to modify and choosing Format Bar from the shortcut menu that appears. You can open the Bar Styles dialog box by right-clicking a blank spot in the taskbar area of the Gantt Chart and choosing Bar Styles from the shortcut menu that appears.

265

Figure 8.10 shows the Format Bar dialog box; Figure 8.11 shows the Bar Styles dialog box. The bottom half of the Bar Styles dialog box has two tabbed sheets called Text and Bars. Counterparts to these tabbed sheets appear at the top of the Format Bar dialog box and are called Bar Shape and Bar Text. The Bar Styles dialog box has a table from which you can designate the category of taskbar that you want to modify and the changes that you want to make.

FIGURE 8.10

You can modify the appearance of an individual taskbar to draw attention to it.

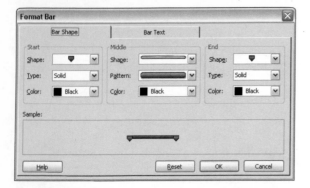

FIGURE 8.11

Use the Bars tab of the Bar Styles dialog box to change the appearance of an entire category of tasks.

Entry bar

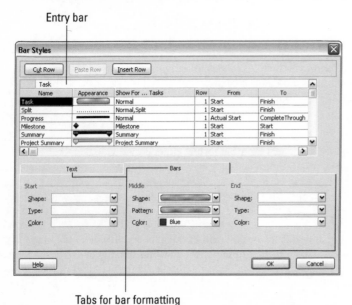

Tabs for bar formatting

You can use the Bars tab at the bottom of the Bar Styles dialog box to set the shape, type or pattern, and color for the bar and its end shapes. Use the Text tab to add text to the chart portion of the Gantt Chart view using the steps that follow.

NEW FEATURE   Starting in Project 2007, you can undo changes that Project applies to your schedule when you use the Bar Styles dialog box.

1. Click the Text tab to select the information that you want to display to the left, to the right, above, below, or inside the selected category of taskbar (see Figure 8.12).

FIGURE 8.12

Be careful not to place too much information around taskbars or you'll create a cluttered, illegible Gantt Chart.

2. Select the Name of the category of taskbar to which you want to add text. If necessary, make changes to the category in the Bar Styles table at the top of the dialog box. Immediately following these steps is an explanation of the type of information that appears in each column of the table.

3. At the bottom of the dialog box, select the location for the text that you want to add. Project displays a list box arrow at the edge of the box.

4. Select the text that you want to appear on the chart portion of the Gantt Chart view for the selected category.

5. Click OK to save your changes.

The columns in the Bar Styles table at the top of the dialog box are as follows:

- **Name:** This column specifies the taskbar category. To create a new taskbar category name, click the Insert Row button at the top of the dialog box and enter a name. This name appears in a legend for your chart when you print it.

- **Appearance:** This column provides a sample of the current formatting settings for the bar.

NOTE   When you click in any of the next four columns, Project displays a list box arrow at the right edge of the column. Open the list box to identify valid choices for these columns.

- **Show For . . . Tasks:** This column defines the types of tasks that the specified formatting affects. You can specify the type of task to affect by selecting the category from a drop-down list or by entering a category name directly in the cell or in the entry bar. To specify more than one category, add a comma (,) after the first type and then select or type a second category. For example, to specify Normal tasks that are critical and in progress as a new category of taskbar style, choose or type in one of the following: Normal, Critical, In Progress.

NOTE   You can type directly in a Bar Styles table cell; you don't need to type in the Entry bar.

- **Row:** The Row column specifies how many rows of bars (as many as four) that you want to display for each task. If you have only one row and you are showing a bar for both the baseline timing and progress, the bars overlap each other. If you want two separate bars, you need two rows. You also can add extra rows to accommodate text above or below taskbars.

TIP   If a task fits in several categories, what happens? Project tries to display multiple formatting settings. (For example, if one category is solid blue and the other is a pattern, you get a blue pattern.) If Project can't display the formats together, the item that is higher in this listing takes over. To modify the formatting precedence, use the Cut Row and Paste Row features to rearrange the rows in the Bar Styles dialog box.

- **From and To:** These columns define the time period that is shown by the bar. The Progress bar, for example, shows the actual date that the task started and the amount of task that was completed through today. Select the time frames from drop-down lists in each of these fields.

Figure 8.13 shows a schedule with expanded rows; the baseline duration is displayed beneath normal taskbars, and resource names appears to the right of taskbars. To display the expanded rows and the baseline duration beneath normal tasks, I used the settings shown in Figure 8.14. In the top of the dialog box, I changed the Row setting for Task from 1 to 2; in the bottom of the dialog box, on the Text tab, I displayed Baseline Duration on the bottom of the tasks and Resource Names to the right of tasks.

FIGURE 8.13

Adding rows to each task can make your schedule easier to read.

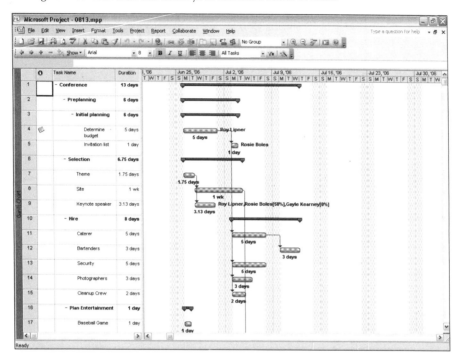

FIGURE 8.14

In the table, I changed the number of rows for Normal tasks. At the bottom of the dialog box, I added Baseline Duration to the bottom row of Normal tasks.

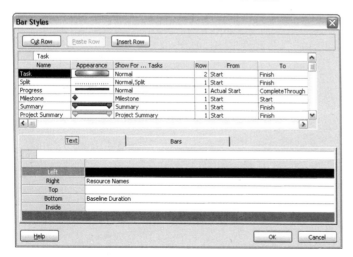

The settings in the Bar Styles dialog box enable you to modify, in great detail, the appearance of your schedule and how Project displays or prints it. If you print a legend along with your schedule, the legend reflects these changes. However, remember that modifying taskbar colors isn't of much use in black-and-white printouts of schedules, and creating too many kinds of formatting with too many variables can make your schedule difficult to read. The advice given previously about standardizing these settings across your organization also holds for changes that you make to taskbar formatting.

Changing the layout of the Gantt Chart

The layout of a Gantt Chart refers to the appearance of link lines, date formats used for information displayed near taskbars, the height of taskbars, and how Project displays certain characteristics of taskbars.

 In views other than the Gantt Chart view, layout affects different elements. For example, in the Calendar view, layout affects the order in which Project lists multiple tasks on one calendar day and how it splits date bars. And, as you'll read in the next section, layout in the Network Diagram Chart view affects link lines and how Project handles page breaks.

To modify the layout, choose Format ➪ Layout. In the Gantt Chart view, the Layout dialog box appears, as shown in Figure 8.15.

FIGURE 8.15

Because layout affects different elements in different views, the Layout dialog box for the Gantt Chart view is different than the Layout dialog box for the Network Diagram and Calendar views.

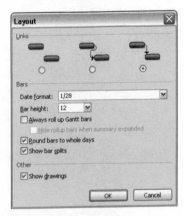

 If you have a short schedule with many tasks running only hours in length, don't round taskbars to whole days.

NEW FEATURE Starting in Project 2007, you can undo changes that Project applies to your schedule when you use the Layout dialog box.

The options that you can set for the Gantt Chart layout are as follows:

- **Links:** Click one of these option buttons to display either no link lines or to use one of the available styles. Remember, link lines graphically display dependency relationships among tasks. To take a quick look at your schedule with no dependency information showing, use the choice of no link lines in this dialog box.

- **Date format:** Use this drop-down list to select a date or time format. Two interesting date formats include a week number (W5/1 and W5/1/02 12:33 PM) of the year and the day of the week. Therefore, W24/3/03 is June 11, 2003 (the third day of the 24th full week of 2003).

NOTE Your nation or industry may use conventions for numbering weeks that may be different than what Project produces.

- **Bar Height:** Select a height in points for the taskbars in your Gantt Chart.

The check boxes in the Layout dialog box have the following effects:

- **Always Roll Up Gantt bars:** This setting gives you the freedom to display your Gantt schedule by rolling up tasks onto summary bars.

- **Hide Rollup Bars when Summary Expanded:** This check box works with the preceding check box to hide rollup behavior if your schedule is completely expanded.

CROSS-REF See Chapter 6 for more on Project's rollup capabilities.

- **Round Bars to Whole Days:** This option works well on longer schedules but not as well on schedules with tasks that tend to run in hourly or half-day increments.

- **Show Bar Splits:** This option provides graphic representation of split tasks on the Gantt Chart.

NOTE *Split tasks* are tasks that start, then stop for a time, and then start again. For example, if you expect to begin hiring employees for the project, but you know that your company imposes a two-week hiring freeze during the last two weeks of the year for accounting purposes, you can create a split task (see Chapter 9). The setting for splits in the Layout dialog box simply enables you to show the split task as separate taskbars or as one continuous taskbar.

- **Show Drawings:** If you select this check box, Project displays drawings that you've inserted on your chart.

Make any choices in the Layout dialog box and click OK to implement them.

Changing gridlines

Gridlines are those lines in the Gantt Chart and the Gantt table that mark off periods of time, rows and columns, pages in your schedule, and regular intervals in the chart. In Figure 8.16, gridlines mark off regular intervals across the chart; this format can help you read across the page on a long schedule. Also, the vertical line that marks the current date appears as a dashed line, rather than as the typical small-dotted line that you've seen in other figures in this chapter.

To modify gridlines, choose Format ➪ Gridlines. The dialog box shown in Figure 8.17 appears. In the Line to Change list, the options Gantt Rows, Sheet Rows, and Sheet Columns enable you to set gridlines at regular intervals. For example, the project in Figure 8.16 has the Gantt Rows set to show at an interval of every four rows. You can change the line type and color only (not the interval) for the other choices in the Line to Change list. To modify these settings, highlight the kind of line that you want to change and then select the desired settings from the Type and Color drop-down lists.

FIGURE 8.16

Displaying additional gridlines can make a schedule easier to read.

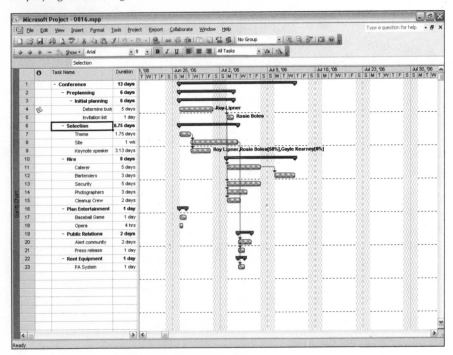

FIGURE 8.17

You can choose gridlines from five different styles.

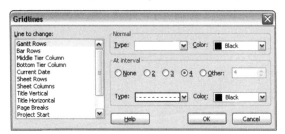

> **TIP** If you make substantial changes in the Gridlines dialog box, consider saving the file as a template for everyone else in your organization to use for their projects. This template not only saves you and your coworkers the effort of repeating the changes but also helps to enforce consistency throughout your organization.

> **NEW FEATURE** Starting in Project 2007, you can undo the effects that you apply in the Gridlines box.

Changing network diagrams

You can format the nodes in a network diagram, and you can control the layout of the network diagram. You can modify the style of text that is placed in network diagram boxes and control the number of fields per node. You can control the size and the shape of the node and adjust the thickness and color of the line that defines the box.

Formatting network diagram nodes

You can modify the boxes that form the various nodes displayed in the Network Diagram Chart view similarly to the way that you can format taskbars in the Gantt Chart. You can format the color and line style of the box itself for each type of task. You can also control the number of fields that appear per node, the shape of the node, the horizontal and vertical alignment of text within the node, and the font that's used in each cell of the node. Use these settings to draw the reader's attention to categories of nodes that you want to emphasize.

> **NOTE** As with task text and taskbars in the Gantt Chart view, you can undo changes that you make here. But be aware that Project has its own color and line scheme for various types of tasks, and you run the risk of formatting one category to look just like another category by mistake. Because interpreting the information in a Project chart is so key to its success, be careful about changing formatting defaults.

Modifying node box styles

You can change the formatting of network diagram boxes individually, or you can change the formatting of a particular category of boxes. To change an individual box, select the box in the network diagram and choose Format ⇨ Box to display the dialog box shown in Figure 8.18.

FIGURE 8.18

To modify the appearance of a single box in the network diagram, use this dialog box.

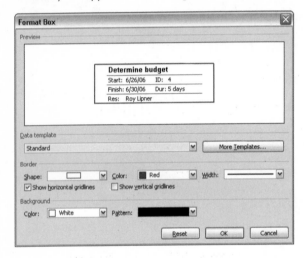

Use the Shape box to select one of ten shapes for the box. Similarly, use the Color box to identify the color for the lines of the box, and use the Width box to specify the width of the box's border. You also can set the Background color and pattern for the node. Project combines the effect of all your changes; watch the Preview to determine their effects. When you finish, click OK to save the changes.

To format a category of box, such as all Critical Milestones, use the Box Styles dialog box, shown in Figure 8.19. You can display this dialog box by choosing Format ⇨ Box Styles.

Select the type of box that you want to format from the Style settings for list. The current settings for the box appear in the Preview window. The rest of the options in this dialog box are the same as the options in the Format Box dialog box, except for the Set Highlight Filter Style check box. You can filter information on the network diagram, as you read in Chapter 7. Selecting the Set Highlight Filter Style check box enables you to set the color that Project uses when filtering tasks on the network diagram.

 **TIP** Make Name one of the pieces of information that you display. Otherwise, the flow of tasks in the network diagram chart is nearly incomprehensible.

FIGURE 8.19

Use this dialog box to select a category of box to format.

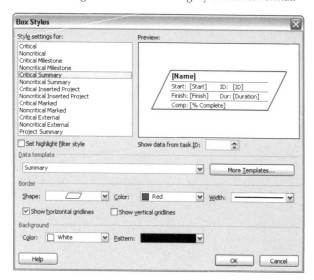

Formatting fields that appear on nodes

Network diagram nodes display the following information by default: Task Name, Duration, ID, Start and Finish Dates, Percent Complete, and Resource Name, if assigned. However, you can display up to 16 fields of information. For example, to focus on costs in today's staff meeting, change the network diagram node information to Task Name, Baseline Cost, Actual Cost, Actual Overtime Cost, and Cost Variance. If your manager wants a network diagram chart report so that he or she can see whether the project schedule is on track, change this information to Task Name, Critical, Free Slack, Early Finish, and Late Finish.

CAUTION Just because you can do something doesn't mean you should do it. Although you can specify up to 16 pieces of information, beware of information overload. Providing too much information in a node makes the network diagram difficult to read and evaluate, and your reader may miss your point.

To modify a node, you can change the information that is included in a node, the font that's used to display the information, and the horizontal and vertical alignment of the information. Follow these steps to modify a node:

1. Open either the Format Box or Box Styles dialog box.

2. Click the More Templates button. Project displays the Data Templates dialog box (see Figure 8.20).

FIGURE 8.20

Select a template to modify or copy, or create a new template.

NOTE A template contains previously established node format settings.

3. Highlight the template that you want to change and click the Edit button. Alternatively, you can create a new template by clicking the New button, or you can copy an existing template and make changes to the copy by clicking the Copy button. For this exercise, I'll copy the Standard template by clicking the Copy button. Regardless of whether you click the New, Edit or Copy button, Project displays the Data Template Definition dialog box (Figure 8.21).

NOTE As you can see in Figure 8.20, you cannot edit the Standard template — the Edit button is not available. To make changes based on the Standard template, you must copy it, as I did in Step 3.

NOTE The picture at the top of the dialog box provides a preview of the current structure of the cell. In this figure, the node contains eight cells — two on each row and four in each column. Blank cells (one each in the top and bottom rows) are merged with nonblank cells.

4. To change the contents of a cell of the node, click the corresponding cell in the middle of the dialog box. A list box arrow appears to the right of the cell. Open the list box to select a new field for the selected cell.

FIGURE 8.21

Use this dialog box to change the information that you show in network diagram nodes.

Click here to change the contents of the cells in the node.

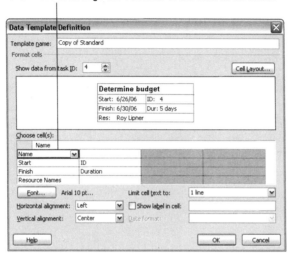

5. To change the font for a particular cell, select that cell and click the Font button. A dialog box appears, from which you can select a new font, the font size, and font attributes, such as boldface or italics.

6. Use the Horizontal alignment and Vertical alignment list boxes to change the alignment of text within its cell.

7. Use the Limit cell text to list box to specify the number of lines for each cell; a cell can have as many as three lines.

8. Select the Show Label in Cell check box to include an identifier in the cell for the type of information. For example, if you select the cell containing Name and then select the Show Label in Cell check box, the title of the task contains Name: followed by the title of the task.

TIP You also can change the label text that appears in the box after you click the Show Label in Cell text box.

9. To increase or decrease the number of cells in the node, click the Cell Layout button to display the dialog box that is shown in Figure 8.22. From this dialog box, specify the number of cells for all nodes. After you click OK, Project redisplays the Data Template Definition dialog box, with the appropriate number of cells available for formatting.

FIGURE 8.22

Use this dialog box to change the number of cells in a node.

10. Click OK to close the Data Template Definition dialog box, click Close to close the Data Templates window, and click OK to close the Box Styles dialog box.

Changing the layout of the network diagram

A significant number of layout controls are available for the network diagram. As Figure 8.23 demonstrates, you can control the layout mode, the box arrangement, the link style and color, and several overall options for the network diagram.

By default, Project automatically positions all boxes on the diagram, but you can choose to manually position the boxes by choosing the Allow Manual Box Positioning option at the top of the Layout box.

Using the Arrangement list box, you can change the order in which Project displays the boxes. Choose from Top Down From Left, Top Down By Day, Top Down By Week, Top Down By Month, Top Down – Critical First, Centered From Left, and Centered From Top. The varying arrangements change the number of pages that are required to print your network diagram.

You also can change the row and column alignment and spacing as well as row height and column width. Using check boxes in the Box Layout section, you can hide or display summary tasks, keep tasks with their summaries, and adjust for page breaks.

FIGURE 8.23

You can control layout mode, box arrangement, and link style for the network diagram.

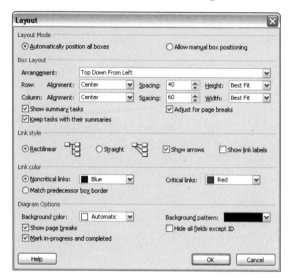

You can control the style of the link lines, and you can choose to show arrows and link labels, which, by default, show the type of link dependency that exists between two tasks (Finish-to-Start, Finish-to-Finish, and so on). And you can select different colors for both critical and noncritical links.

CROSS-REF For more information on types of links, see Chapter 4.

TIP To choose a background color or pattern for individual nodes, use the Format Box or Format Box Styles dialog box; you saw the Format Box Styles dialog box in Figure 8.19.

For the network diagram as a whole (not the individual nodes) you can choose a background color and pattern. You also can mark in-progress tasks with half an X and completed tasks with an entire X. If you hide all information on the nodes except the ID, Project reduces the size of the nodes on your network diagram and therefore reduces the number of pages that will print. You can also choose to show page breaks, which appear as dotted lines on-screen in the Network Diagram view. In Figure 8.24, I've included link labels and hidden all task information except the ID. A page break appears at the right side of the diagram (not shown in the figure).

Remember, creating too many kinds of formatting with too many variables can make your schedule difficult to read. The advice given previously in this chapter about standardizing these settings across your organization also holds for changes that you make to network diagram layouts.

FIGURE 8.24

By adjusting the layout of the network diagram, you can dramatically change its appearance.

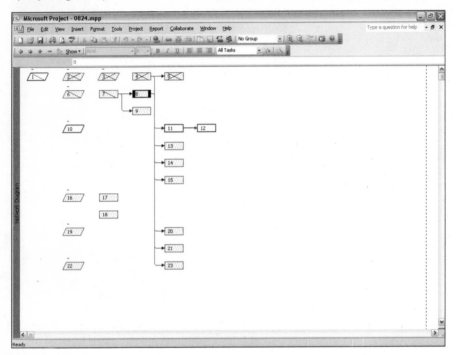

Formatting the Calendar view

The Calendar view in Project 2007 has been enhanced to look and act more like the Calendar view in Outlook. In addition, you now have daily, weekly, and monthly views available, and you can create your own view to help you focus on the tasks for a specific time frame.

As I mention earlier in the chapter, you format text in the Calendar view in the same way that you format text in any other view. Although you can't format the text of individual items in the Calendar view, you can use the Text Styles dialog box as described in the section "Applying formatting to categories of text," earlier in this chapter, to format categories of text.

 **NOTE** You cannot apply background color to the bars on the Calendar, but you can apply color to the text.

In the Calendar view, you can format bar styles and you can change the layout of the calendar. This section explores those types of changes.

Formatting the Calendar entries

By default, when you display the Calendar view, entries appear in boxes that Project calls bars. You can change the style of these bars. For example, you can make all critical tasks appear on the Calendar in red. Choose Format ➪ Bar Styles in the Calendar view to display the dialog box that is shown in Figure 8.25. Select a type of task from the list on the left. As you make changes in the Bar shape area and the Text area, watch the Sample window at the bottom of the box for the effects of your changes.

Use this dialog box to change the appearance of the Calendar view. Assign different font colors to different task types, or use a line instead of a bar to represent the task's duration.

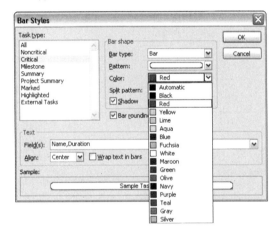

In the Bar shape area, use the Bar type box to display tasks by selecting Line, Bar, or None; choosing None hides the selected task type from the Calendar view. If you choose Bar from the Bar type box, open the Pattern list box and select a pattern, which appears inside the bar for the task type. You can also choose a pattern for Project to display between split tasks from the Split pattern box. Select the Shadow box to display a shadow behind a bar. (This option is available only if you choose Bar from the Bar type box.)

Select the Bar rounding box to tell Project to draw the bar for tasks that take less than one day so that the task's duration is implied. For example, use bar rounding to tell Project to draw a bar that extends three-quarters of the width of the day to represent a task that takes 0.75 days. If you don't use bar rounding, Project doesn't imply the duration of the task by the length of the bar.

In the Text area, you can include Project fields for each task type; to include more than one field, separate fields with a comma (refer to Figure 8.25). Align the text with the bar or line using the Align list box. If you chose Bar as the Bar type, you can select the Wrap Text in Bars check box. When you select this box, Project wraps text so that it fits within the box. For example, if you show the task name and duration in the bar, and the task name is fairly long but the task lasts only one day, Project wraps the text so that the task takes more than one row when it appears on the calendar. You'll be able to read all displayed information about every task. If you don't select the Wrap Text in Bars check box, Project displays only as much information as it can fit in a bar that's sized to match the task's duration. In the example just described, you may not see the entire task name, and you certainly won't see the task duration, because the bar spans only one day.

Changing the Calendar layout

The Calendar view's updated look sports three new buttons that you can use to help you focus on the tasks for a specific timeframe. You can view your project a month at a time or a week at a time, or you can create a custom view. In Figure 8.26, I created a custom view that shows two weeks.

NEW FEATURE The Month, Week, and Custom buttons on the Calendar view are new to Project 2007.

Click the Month button or the Week button to view your project in those increments. You can then use the arrows below the buttons to move forward or backward by the selected increment.

FIGURE 8.26

You can create custom Calendar views to help you focus on a specific time period.

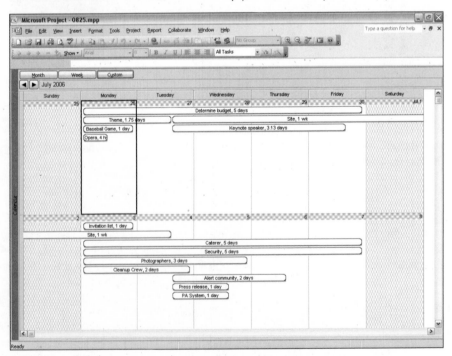

To create a custom view, click the Custom button; the Zoom dialog box appears (see Figure 8.27).

Use this dialog box to specify the time frame to display in the Calendar view.

Use the Layout dialog box, shown in Figure 8.28, to change the layout of tasks in the Calendar view. By default, Project displays tasks in the Calendar view using the currently sorted order of tasks.

Use the Layout dialog box to change the way that Project presents tasks in the Calendar view.

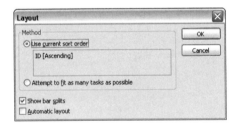

 **CROSS-REF** You can read about sorting tasks in Chapter 7.

If you don't want tasks to appear in the Calendar view using the currently sorted order, select the Attempt to Fit as Many Tasks as Possible option button. Project sorts tasks by Total Slack and then by Duration (longest task first) to try to fit the maximum number of tasks into the rows for a week without overlapping bars.

TIP When multiple tasks fall on the same day, a small down arrow appears in the upper-left corner of the day; you can click the down arrow to see a list of the tasks scheduled for that day.

Deselect the Show Bar Splits check box to hide the designation for split tasks from the Calendar view. Select the Automatic Layout check box to have Project automatically adjust the Calendar view to accommodate new tasks that you add or tasks that you delete.

Inserting Drawings and Objects

We're living in the age of multimedia and MTV. Visual elements have a way of getting a message across that simple text often can't match. Statistics show that 75 percent of the world learns visually. In Project, you can insert graphic images (for example, photos, illustrations, or diagrams) in the following places:

- In a Gantt Chart, in the taskbar area
- In notes (task, resource, or assignment)
- In headers, footers, and chart legends
- In resource or task forms

You also can copy your Project schedule into other Office products.

Copying pictures

Suppose that you've written a report in Microsoft Word and you would *really* like to include your Gantt Chart in the report. You can print it on a separate page, but you can also insert it as a picture in the appropriate place in your Word document. Or, suppose that you want to post a picture of your Project schedule on the Web. You can easily create a picture for either of these purposes using the Copy Picture to Office Wizard or the Copy Picture dialog box.

Using the Copy Picture to Office Wizard, you can send an image and selected fields to Word, PowerPoint, or Visio. To use the Copy Picture to Office Wizard, follow these steps:

1. Right-click on any toolbar to display the available toolbars.
2. Click Analysis. The Analysis toolbar appears.
3. Click the Copy Picture to Office Wizard button. The wizard begins.
4. Click Next to display the Step 1 box of the wizard (see Figure 8.29).
5. Identify the method you want the wizard to use when handling your outline level and click Next.
6. Select the options you want Project to use while creating the image (see Figure 8.30). You can select the rows and portion of the timescale to copy, and you can select the size of the image. Click Next.
7. Select the Office application to which you want to send the picture and the orientation of the picture (see Figure 8.31). Click Next.

FIGURE 8.29

Tell the wizard how to handle your outline level.

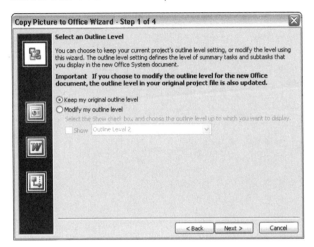

FIGURE 8.30

Set the options for the image.

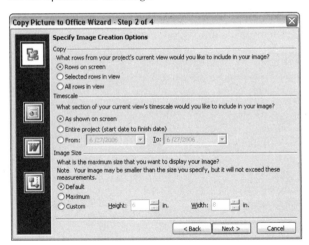

FIGURE 8.31

Select the Office application that should receive the image.

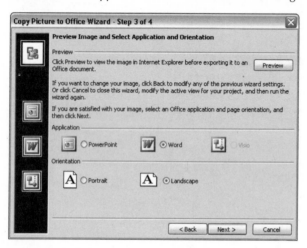

8. Select the Project fields you want to include with the image (see Figure 8.32).

FIGURE 8.32

Identify Project fields to include with the image.

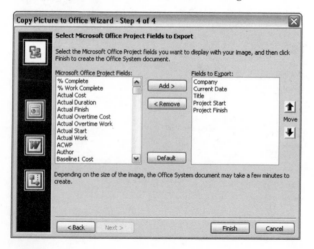

9. Click Finish.

If the Global.mpt file Becomes Damaged. . .

All projects that you create in Project are based on a template; if you don't deliberately select a template, then Project bases your project on the Global.mpt template. If the Global.mpt template becomes damaged, features such as the Copy Picture to Office Wizard can seem to disappear or not function. You correct the problem by forcing Project to recreate the Analysis toolbar. Follow these steps:

1. Click Tools ➪ Customize ➪ Toolbars to display the Customize dialog box.

2. Click the Commands tab.

3. In the Categories list on the left, click "All Commands."

4. In the Commands list on the right, commands appear in alphabetical order; drag COMAddinsDialog to any existing toolbar (see the first figure in this sidebar).

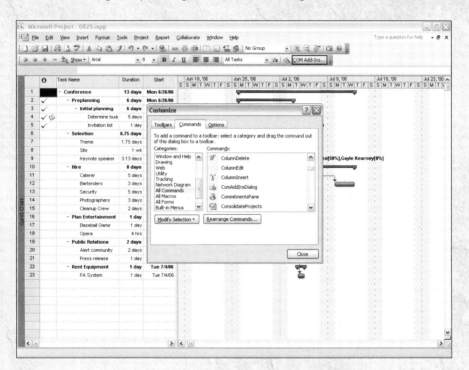

5. Click Close to close the Customize dialog box.

continued

continued

6. Click the COM Add-ins button you just added to a toolbar. The COM Add-ins dialog box appears (see the second figure in this sidebar).

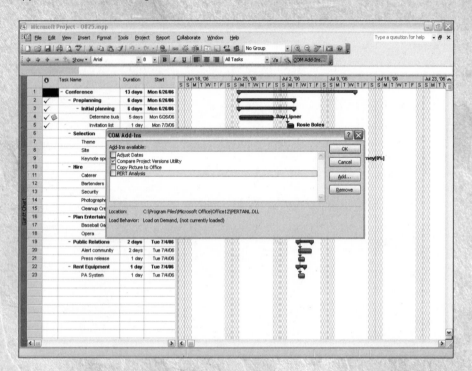

7. Remove the checks beside Adjust Dates, Copy Picture to Office, and PERT Analysis.

8. Click OK.

9. Repeat Steps 6 to 8, but in Step 7, check the boxes you previously unchecked.

Project regenerates the Analysis toolbar and, when you display the toolbar, buttons appear for Adjust Dates, Copy Picture to Office Wizard, and PERT Analysis. If necessary, you can perform the same steps to regenerate the Compare Project Versions toolbar. You may need to close Project and reopen it to make the buttons function properly.

You can remove the COMAddInDialog button from the toolbar by reopening the Customize dialog box and then dragging the button off the toolbar.

Using the Copy Picture command, you copy your Project schedule to the Windows clipboard and then paste it into any application as a graphic image. This technique copies only a picture without Project fields. Switch to the Gantt Chart view and click the Copy Picture button on the Standard toolbar or choose Report ⇨ Copy Picture. The dialog box shown in Figure 8.33 appears.

FIGURE 8.33

Choose the For screen option to copy a Project schedule to the Windows clipboard.

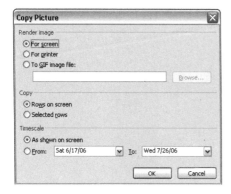

To copy the picture to the clipboard, select the For screen option button in the Render image section and click OK. If the image that you're copying will fit well into another document, Project simply copies the picture to the Windows clipboard. But if the picture that you are copying is particularly large, Project warns you and displays a dialog box that gives you the opportunity to scale the picture before saving or pasting it.

After you've copied the picture, simply switch to the other document in which you want to place the picture and click the Paste button in that document. Figure 8.34 shows a Gantt Chart in Microsoft Word.

When you use the Paste button, you place a graphic in your document. The graphic is not linked to Project in any way, so from the program from which you pasted the chart, you cannot do the following:

- Edit the chart to make scheduling changes
- Double-click the image to open the chart in Project

NOTE Even if you choose the Paste Special command, the image that you copied from Project is exactly that — an image. It is not a Project file that you can link to from another application.

FIGURE 8.34

After you use the Copy Picture command to render an image for the screen, you can paste the image into any document.

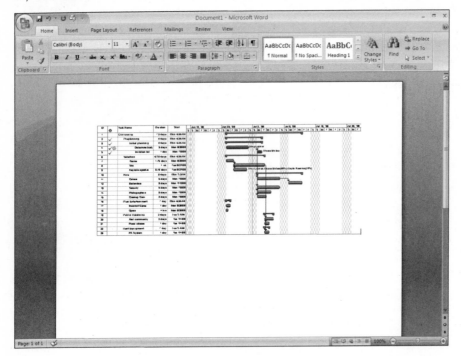

To create a graphic image file that you can use on a Web page or in a document, select the To GIF image file option in the Copy Picture dialog box (shown previously in Figure 8.33).

When you render the image for a printer, Project copies the image to the Windows clipboard but formats the image using your printer driver. If you have a black-and-white printer, the image appears in shades of gray rather than in the colors that you see on-screen. If you have a color printer, the image appears in color, as it looks on-screen. You can view the image by pasting it into another application.

Using visuals in schedules

Because project management is often a serious, information-oriented business, you don't want to overdo the visuals. Remember, both the Gantt Chart and the network diagram are visuals. And, pictures of bunnies and curly doodads aren't likely to sit well with the head of your engineering division. However, used judiciously, images can reinforce the information about your project and lend a professional look to your reports.

Consider using graphics in the following ways:

- Add a company logo to the header of your schedule so that it appears at the top of every page.

- Add a photograph of each of your key resources in his or her resource note. The photo helps you get to know all the team members in a large-scale project so that you can address them by name when you see them.

- If a particular task involves a schematic or diagram of a product, place a copy of the diagram in the task notes for reference.

CAUTION   Placing graphics in a schedule can take up a big chunk of memory, making your file larger and possibly increasing calculation time; for this reason, use graphics only on an as-needed basis.

- If your schedule has a key milestone, place a graphic that suggests success or accomplishment next to the milestone in the Gantt Chart. Every time that you review your schedule with your team, you'll subconsciously focus on that goal and how close you're getting to it, which can boost morale.

NOTE   Graphic objects come in a variety of file formats, depending on the type of graphic and the program in which it was created. You can use scanned images, photo files, illustrations such as clip art, a chart that you've created in Excel, a Word table, and even a video clip. Check the Internet for sources of graphics files, or use the images that are available to the Microsoft Office family of products.

Inserting visual objects

To insert an object into a header, footer, or legend, choose File ➪ Page Setup and click the appropriate tab. Use the Insert Picture button to open a dialog box that enables you to select a picture file to insert (see Figure 8.35).

FIGURE 8.35

You can click this button to open the Insert Picture dialog box and add a picture to a header.

Insert Picture button

To add a picture to a task note, double-click the task to open the Task Information dialog box, select the Notes tab, and use the Insert Object button to insert a file. Suppose that you have an Excel worksheet that provides information that you need for a budgeting task. You can insert a graphic object that shows the worksheet data on the Notes tab of the Task Information dialog box for the budgeting task. Follow these steps to insert the graphic object of worksheet data:

1. Double-click the task with which you want to associate the worksheet.
2. Click the Notes tab.
3. Click the Insert Object button. The Insert Object dialog box appears (see Figure 8.36).

FIGURE 8.36

Select the file that you want to associate with a task.

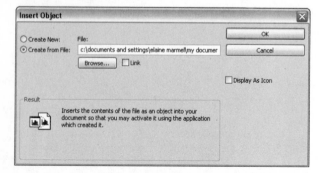

4. Select the Create from File option.

5. Click the Browse button to select the worksheet.

6. Click the OK button. The worksheet information appears as a graphic on the Notes tab, as shown in Figure 8.37.

FIGURE 8.37

The information in the file appears as a graphic object on the Notes tab of the Task Information dialog box.

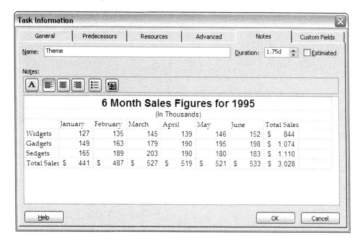

Instead, suppose that you want to see a chart of the information on the Notes tab. Logically, you create the chart in the worksheet and then use the preceding steps — but you get the entire worksheet, both numbers and chart. To place *just* the chart on the Notes tab, follow these steps:

1. Select the chart in Excel and click the Copy button to copy the chart to the clipboard.

2. Switch to Project.

3. Open the Task Information dialog box for the appropriate task.

4. Click the Notes tab.

5. Right-click in the area where the note would appear, and from the submenu that appears, click Paste. The chart alone appears on the Notes tab (see Figure 8.38).

FIGURE 8.38

You can copy any image that you place on the Windows clipboard into Project.

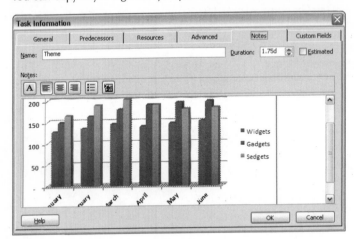

> **TIP** You can place any image directly on the Gantt Chart. Don't open the Task Information dialog box. Instead, copy the image to the clipboard and, after you switch to Project, click the Paste button.

Using the Drawing toolbar

Project has a drawing feature that you can use to build simple diagrams or add shapes or text boxes to the Gantt Chart area of your Project file. For example, you may want to draw a circle around an important taskbar in your schedule to draw attention to it in a presentation. Or, suppose that you want to suggest cutting a task from the project, as shown in Figure 8.39. The formatting methods that I presented in the section "Changing taskbars," earlier in this chapter, enable you to create settings so that predefined information appears next to taskbars in your schedule. However, you must use the Drawing Text Box tool to enter your own text.

To display the Drawing toolbar, shown in Figure 8.40, you can choose either View ➪ Toolbars and select the Drawing toolbar for display, or choose Insert ➪ Drawing.

FIGURE 8.39

Consider using this type of drawing when you display a project on-screen using an LCD panel, or at a trade show.

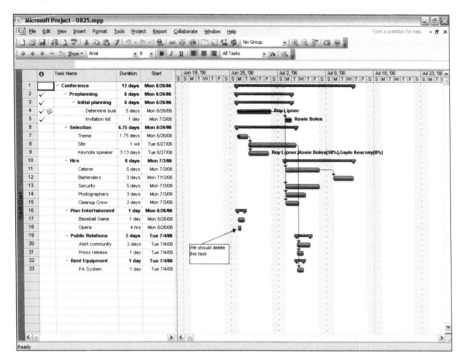

FIGURE 8.40

The Drawing toolbar is a floating toolbar. Drag it up near the Formatting toolbar to dock it at the top of your screen, or click the dark-blue bar at the top and drag to move it around your screen.

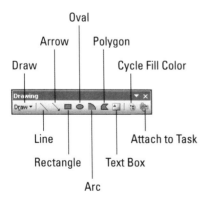

The following points show you how to use the tools on the Drawing toolbar:

- To draw an object, click the Line, Arrow, Rectangle, Oval, Arc, or Polygon button and then click the taskbar area of the Gantt Chart. Hold down your mouse button and drag to draw the shape. When using the Polygon tool, you need to draw several segments to define the multisided shape, clicking at the end of each segment. To complete the polygon, double-click at the end of the last segment. With all the other tools, the shape appears automatically when you drag in one direction and release your mouse button.

- To create text anywhere around your taskbar, click the Text Box button and drag to draw a box. Your insertion point appears in the box whenever you select the box; you can then enter text.

- To fill an object with color, click the Cycle Fill Color button on the Drawing toolbar repeatedly until you see the color that you want.

- By default, Project anchors drawing objects to the timescale. To anchor a drawing object in the Gantt Chart to a particular taskbar — so that if you move the task in the schedule the graphic moves with it — select the object and click the Attach to Task button on the Drawing toolbar. Select the Attach to Task option button in the Format Drawing dialog box, shown in Figure 8.41, enter a task ID number, and enter the settings for the point on the taskbar at which you want to attach the object. Then click OK. You can then drag the drawing to the position where you want to display it. Project adjusts the anchoring position of the drawing in relation to the task but keeps the drawing in the same relative position to the task if you move the task.

FIGURE 8.41

You can attach a graphic to a particular task or position on the timescale.

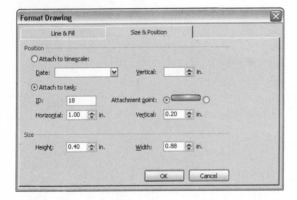

> **TIP** You can also use three tools on the Drawing toolbar with other types of graphic objects that you insert. The Draw, Cycle Fill Color, and Attach to Task buttons work with any selected object, such as clip art.

You can display the Format Drawing dialog box at any time by selecting the drawing and choosing Format ➪ Drawing ➪ Properties. When you no longer need the Drawing toolbar, click the Close button in the upper-right corner to remove it.

Modifying graphics and drawings

You can also use the Format Drawing dialog box to format graphic object styles. To open this dialog box, right-click any drawing object and choose Properties from the shortcut menu that appears. You see the Size & Position tab initially (refer to Figure 8.41). Click the Line & Fill tab to see the choices that are shown in Figure 8.42.

FIGURE 8.42

Rather than cycle through fill colors by using the button on the Drawing toolbar, you can select a fill color from a drop-down palette in the Line & Fill tab of the Format Drawing dialog box.

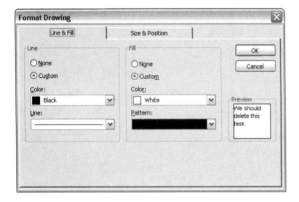

In the Line panel, use the Color and Line drop-down options to assign a style of thickness and color to lines. In the Fill panel, use the Color and Pattern options to place a color and pattern, such as solid or thatched lines, inside an object.

Resizing and moving drawings and other objects are similar to working with objects in other programs. These are described as follows:

- **To resize an object:** Click the object to select it. Click any of the eight selection handles and drag inward to make the object smaller or drag outward to make the object larger.

- **To move an object:** Move your mouse pointer over the object until your cursor changes to four arrows. Click the object, hold down your mouse button, and drag the object anywhere in the Gantt Chart area. Release the mouse button to place the object.

Summary

In this chapter, you discovered many ways to do the following:

- Format text for individual selections or globally by category of task
- Format taskbars and the information that is displayed near them
- Format network diagram boxes and change the information that you display in the Network Diagram view
- Change the layout options for Gantt Chart taskbars and network diagram nodes
- Add gridlines to the Gantt Chart view
- Insert graphic objects and drawings in the Gantt Chart and in notes, or as a header and footer

Chapter 9 explains how to fine-tune timing to resolve scheduling conflicts.

Chapter 9

Resolving Scheduling Problems

Scheduling conflicts are the bane of the project manager's existence. Scheduling conflicts typically fall into the following categories:

- Your project is taking longer than you had planned.
- Your resources are overassigned.

This chapter considers the first problem and focuses on identifying and then resolving scheduling problems; Chapter 10 focuses on the second problem.

Scheduling conflicts announce themselves in a number of ways. Changing views and filtering information by using the techniques that are described in Chapters 6 and 7 may identify some glaring problem that's inherent in your original logic. For example, if you filter your project to view only incomplete tasks or slipping tasks, you may spot some problems. More likely, however, you'll unknowingly create a problem by using a *task constraint,* which is explained in the next section.

IN THIS CHAPTER

Understanding why scheduling conflicts occur

Resolving scheduling conflicts

Using the critical path to shorten a project

Resolving Scheduling Conflicts

Project provides several techniques that you can use to resolve scheduling conflicts. This section covers the following strategies:

- Adding resources
- Using overtime
- Adding time
- Adjusting slack

- Changing constraints
- Adjusting dependencies
- Splitting a task

As you work through the following sections, I suggest that you turn on Change Highlighting if you previously turned it off. Change Highlighting will help you identify the tasks affected by any changes you make as you work. To turn on Change Highlighting, point at the Change Highlighting button on the Standard toolbar or open the View menu. If the ScreenTip or the command reads "Show Change Highlighting," click the tool or the command. If the ScreenTip or the command reads "Hide Change Highlighting," do nothing, because Change Highlighting is turned on.

NEW FEATURE Change Highlighting is a new feature in Project 2007.

Adding resources to tasks

Adding resources to a task can decrease the time that's necessary to complete the task. On the Advanced tab of the Task Information dialog box (see Figure 9.1), set the task type to Fixed Units. In this instance, adding resources to the task reduces the duration of the task. Also, remember that a check mark appears by default in the Effort Driven check box of the Task Information dialog box. When you use the Effort Driven option, Project reallocates the work among the assigned resources.

FIGURE 9.1

The Advanced tab of the Task Information dialog box controls the task type and shows whether the task is effort driven.

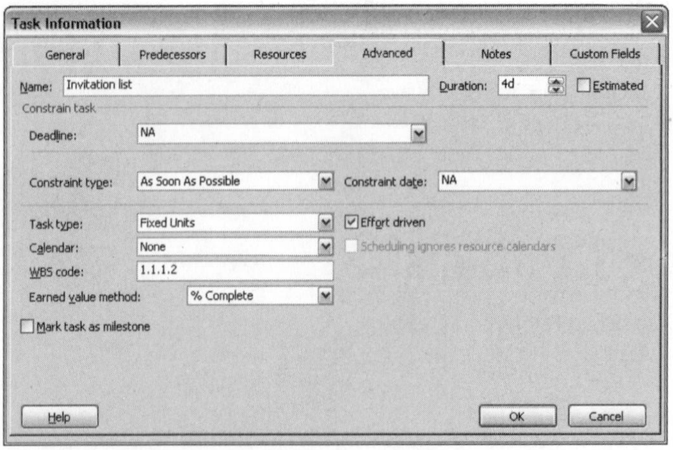

Using overtime

In the best of all worlds, you have unlimited resources and you can add resources to resolve scheduling problems. After performing a reality check, though, you'll discover that you don't have unlimited resources, and adding resources may not be an option. But you may be able to use overtime to shorten a task's duration, which is the next strategy that you can use to resolve scheduling problems.

 For information on resolving resource conflicts, see Chapter 10.

Overtime in Project is defined as the amount of work that is scheduled beyond an assigned resource's regular working hours. Overtime hours are charged at the resource's overtime rate. Overtime work does not represent additional work on a task; instead, it represents the amount of time that's spent on a task outside regular hours. For example, if you assign 30 hours of work and 12 hours of overtime, the total work is still 30 hours. Of the 30 hours, 18 hours are worked during the regular work schedule (and charged to the project at the regular rate), and 12 hours are worked during off hours (and charged to the project at an overtime rate). Therefore, you can use overtime to shorten the time that a resource takes to complete a task.

To enter overtime, follow these steps:

1. Display the Gantt Chart view (choose View ⇨ Gantt Chart or use the View Bar).

2. Choose Window ⇨ Split to reveal the Task Form in the bottom pane.

3. Click the Task Form to make it the active pane.

4. Choose Format ⇨ Details ⇨ Resource Work. Project adds the Ovt. Work column to the Task form (see Figure 9.2).

5. Move to the top pane, and select the task to which you want to assign overtime.

6. Move to the bottom pane and fill in the overtime amount for the appropriate resource.

7. Click OK. Project adjusts the schedule. If you have Change Highlighting enabled, the duration of affected tasks appears highlighted.

TIP **After you finish entering overtime, you can hide the Task form by choosing Window ⇨ Remove Split.**

FIGURE 9.2

Use the Task form and display the Overtime (Ovt. Work) column to add overtime.

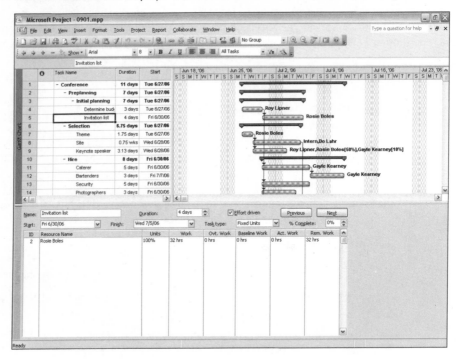

Adding time to tasks

You can also solve scheduling conflicts by increasing the duration of a task. Again, in the best of all worlds, you have this luxury. In reality, you may not. But if you can increase the duration of a task, you may find that once-scarce resources are now available to complete the task — given the task's new timing.

As you know, you can change the duration from several different views, such as the Task Usage view or the Gantt Chart view. You can also use the Task Information dialog box to complete this task (see Figure 9.3). To open the Task Information dialog box, double-click the task; then, use the Duration box to change the duration.

FIGURE 9.3

Change the duration from the Task Information dialog box.

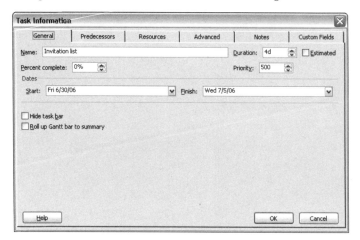

Adjusting slack

Slack time is the amount of time that a task can slip before it affects another task's dates or the finish date of the project. *Free slack* is the amount of time that a task can be delayed without delaying another task. Most projects contain *noncritical tasks with slack* — tasks that can start late without affecting the schedule. If you have slack in your schedule, you may be able to move tasks around to balance phases of the schedule that have no slack with phases that have too much slack. Therefore, you can use tasks with slack to compensate for tasks that take longer than planned or to help resolve overassignment of resources.

NOTE Slack values can also help you identify inconsistencies in the schedule. For example, you see a negative slack value when one task has a finish-to-start dependency with a second task, but the second task has a Must Start On constraint that is earlier than the end of the first task.

Almost by definition, you create slack time if you use the Must Start On constraint when you create your task. You set constraints on the Advanced tab of the Task Information dialog box (see Figure 9.4). To display the Task Information dialog box, double-click the task in your schedule. When the dialog box appears, select the Advanced tab.

FIGURE 9.4

Constraints can often create slack time.

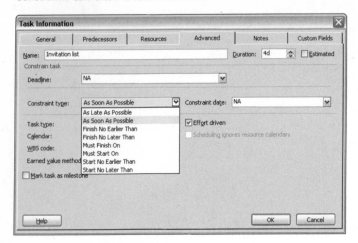

To avoid creating slack time, use the As Soon As Possible constraint whenever possible. To find tasks with slack time, follow these steps:

1. Choose View ➪ More Views to open the More Views dialog box.

2. Select Detail Gantt from the list and click Apply.

TIP You can identify slack on the Gantt bars. Slack appears as thin lines that extend from the regular Gantt bars.

3. Right-click the Select All button and select Schedule from the list of tables.

4. Drag the divider bar to the right to view more of the table. Now you can see the Free Slack and Total Slack fields (see Figure 9.5).

Changing task constraints

Task constraints are the usual culprits when projects fall behind schedule. By default, Project uses the Planning Wizard to warn you when you are about to take an action that is likely to throw your project off schedule. For example, if you impose a Must Start On or Must Finish On task constraint on a task with no slack time and with other tasks linked to it, Project displays the Planning Wizard dialog box (see Figure 9.6).

FIGURE 9.5

You can find slack time in tasks by using the Detail Gantt view and the Schedule table.

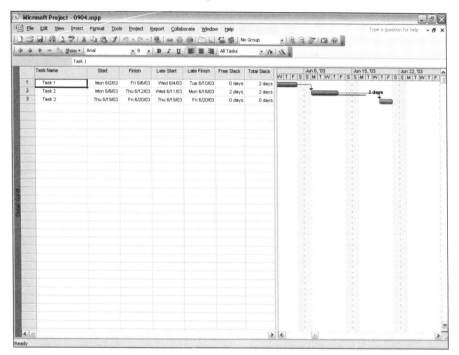

FIGURE 9.6

The Planning Wizard appears by default when you apply a constraint that is likely to lengthen your project schedule.

Similarly, if you impose an illogical start date on a task when recording actual dates, Project displays a Planning Wizard dialog box that resembles the one shown in Figure 9.7. For example, you see a Planning Wizard dialog box if you accidentally enter a start date for Task 2 that is earlier than Task 1, and Task 2 is linked to and succeeds Task 1.

FIGURE 9.7

The Planning Wizard also warns you if you try to record a start date that will cause a scheduling conflict.

Notice that you can turn off the Planning Wizard warnings by placing a check in the Don't Tell Me About This Again check box at the bottom of the Planning Wizard dialog box. (Some people just don't like to have wizards popping up all the time.)

If you turn off the Planning Wizard, Project still warns you if you take actions that cause scheduling problems. Instead of the Planning Wizard, Project displays a more traditional message (see Figure 9.8).

FIGURE 9.8

When you disable the Planning Wizard and take an action that may cause a scheduling problem, Project displays this warning message.

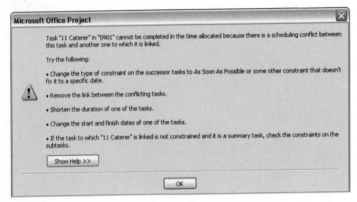

Project makes suggestions concerning actions that you can take to avoid these kinds of conflicts — suggestions that all refer to the predecessor task. Notice also that in contrast to the Planning Wizard, this message box does not give you the option of canceling your action.

So, although you may find the Planning Wizard annoying at some levels, it can actually save you effort at other levels. Sorry that you turned it off? To turn it on again, choose Tools ⇨ Options and click the General tab (see Figure 9.9).

Select the Advice from Planning Wizard check box and then select the Advice About Errors check box. (You also can control the other types of advice that you receive in the same location.)

Adjusting dependencies

By changing task dependencies, you can tighten the schedule and eliminate scheduling conflicts. If you inadvertently link tasks that don't need to be linked, you may create a situation in which you don't have the resources to complete the tasks, and as a result, the project schedule falls behind. If you discover unnecessary links, you can remove them. When you remove the dependencies, you may find holes in the project schedule where work can be performed. After you remove unnecessary dependencies, you may be able to move tasks around and fill those holes.

FIGURE 9.9

You can control whether the Planning Wizard appears from the General tab in the Options dialog box.

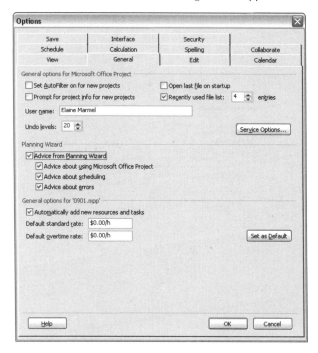

You can use the Task Drivers pane (see Figure 9.10) to identify the task predecessor task that drives the timing of an individual task. Choose Project ➪ Task Drivers to display the pane. Then select a task. Project displays, in the Task Drivers pane, the predecessor task that drives the timing of the selected task.

NEW FEATURE The Task Drivers feature is new in Project 2007.

You can view dependencies graphically if you use the Relationship Diagram view in the bottom pane of the Gantt view (see Figure 9.11). The Relationship Diagram view shows you the selected task and its immediate predecessor and successor. Use the following steps to select the Relationship Diagram view:

1. Choose Window ➪ Split.

2. Click the bottom pane.

3. Choose View ➪ More Views.

4. Select Relationship Diagram from the More Views window and click Apply.

5. In the upper pane, click each task in your project to review its dependencies in the lower pane.

FIGURE 9.10

Use the Task Drivers pane to identify the predecessor task responsible for the timing of a selected task.

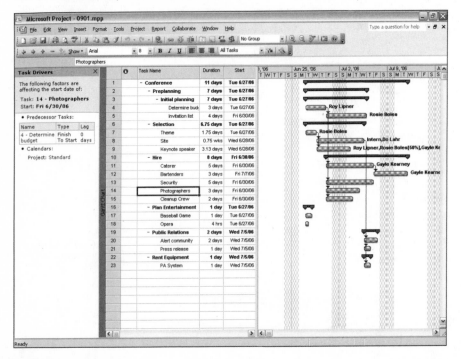

FIGURE 9.11

Use the Relationship Diagram view to review task dependencies.

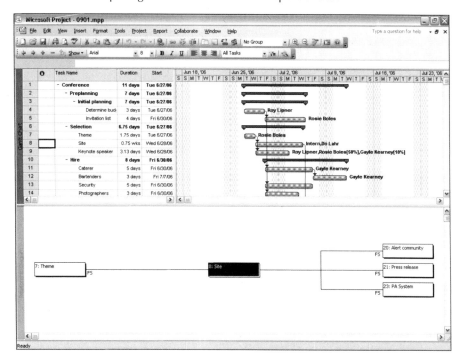

As you review the tasks, ask yourself the following questions:

- Do I really need to complete Task A before Task B begins?
- Can I perform the tasks concurrently?
- Can I do one of the tasks later without harming the project?

Splitting a task

Splitting a task can sometimes be the best way to resolve a scheduling conflict. You may not be able to complete the task on consecutive days, but you can start the task, stop work on it for a period of time, and then come back to the task. Project enables you to split a task anytime you determine that you need to make this type of adjustment. Remember that splitting a task creates a gap, which you see in the task's Gantt bar. Follow these steps to split a task:

1. Switch to the Gantt Chart view.

2. Click the Split Task button on the Standard toolbar. The button appears to be pressed, the mouse pointer changes shape, and a screen tip tells you how to split a task (see Figure 9.12).

3. Move the mouse pointer along the bar of the task that you want to split. As the mouse pointer moves, dates representing the split date appear in the screen tip.

4. Click when the screen tip shows the date on which you want to split the task; Project inserts a one-day split.

 **TIP** If you want the split to last longer than one day, drag to the right instead of clicking.

FIGURE 9.12

Use the Split Task button to divide a task.

Mouse pointer

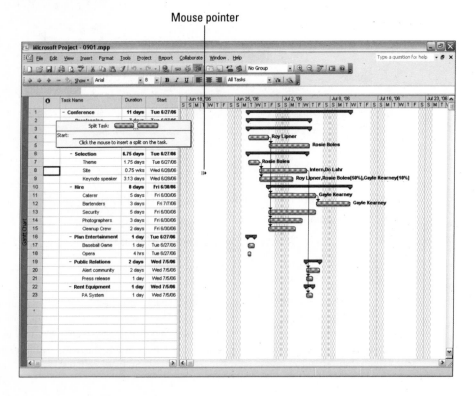

After you split a task, it will look similar to Task 5 in Figure 9.13, with dotted lines appearing between the two portions of the split. If you decide that you want to remove a split, drag the inside portions of the split together so that they touch.

Using the Critical Path to Shorten a Project

Earlier in this chapter, you examined ways to resolve the scheduling conflicts that may develop. But what about simply shortening the time frame that you originally allotted for the entire project, thus becoming a hero? How would you accomplish that goal? You would evaluate — and try to shorten — the critical path.

The *critical path* shows the tasks in your project that must be completed on schedule in order for the entire project to finish on schedule — and these tasks are called *critical tasks*. Most tasks in a project have some slack, and you can delay them some without affecting the project finish date. However, if you delay critical tasks, you affect the project finish date. As you use the techniques described earlier in this chapter in the section "Resolving Scheduling Conflicts" to modify tasks to resolve scheduling problems, be aware that changes to critical tasks will affect your project finish date.

FIGURE 9.13

This Gantt Chart shows a split task.

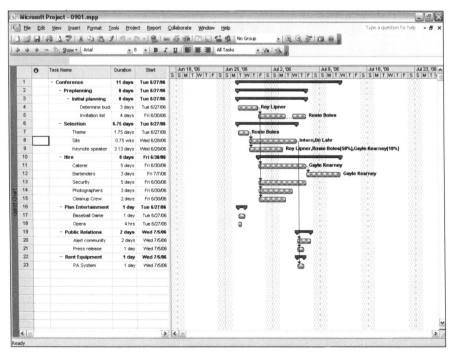

NOTE Noncritical tasks can become critical if they slip too much. You can control how much slack that Project allows for a task before defining the task as a critical task. Choose Tools ➪ Options and then click the Calculation tab. Enter the number of slack days in the Tasks Are Critical If Slack Is Less Than or Equal To box at the bottom of the tab.

Identifying the critical path

You can see the critical path best if you use the Gantt Chart Wizard to display the critical path in red.

CROSS-REF This discussion of the Gantt Chart Wizard focuses on displaying the critical path; see Chapter 8 for a more complete description of that wizard.

Open the View menu and select Gantt Chart. Then click the Gantt Chart Wizard button on the Formatting toolbar (the button at the right edge), or choose Format ➪ Gantt Chart Wizard. The first Gantt Chart Wizard dialog box welcomes you to the Gantt Chart Wizard. Click Next to move on to the next Gantt Chart Wizard dialog box (see Figure 9.14). Select Critical path to describe the kind of information that you want to display on the Gantt Chart.

FIGURE 9.14

Select the Critical Path option button when you run the Gantt Chart Wizard.

Subsequent dialog boxes in the Gantt Chart Wizard enable you to select other types of information to display, such as resources or dates on Gantt bars and links between dependent tasks. These other choices that you can make while running the Gantt Chart Wizard are a matter of personal preference. When you finish, click the Format It button and then click the Exit Wizard button.

When you view the Gantt Chart, all tasks in the project still appear, but tasks on the critical path appear in red.

NOTE After you use the Gantt Chart Wizard, you can switch to any view and the critical tasks appear in red. Try the Network Diagram view, for example; the critical tasks appear in red boxes.

You can use formatting to identify critical tasks. When you apply formatting to critical and noncritical tasks, this formatting appears in all views in which you can see task bars. The formatting identifies critical tasks with a Yes in the bar of the tasks and noncritical tasks with a No.

To apply formatting, follow these steps:

1. Display the Gantt Chart view.

2. Choose Format ➪ Bar Styles; Project displays the Bar Styles dialog box.

3. Select Task from the list at the top of the Bar Styles dialog box to apply formatting to noncritical tasks.

4. Click the Text tab at the bottom of the dialog box.

5. Select a position for the formatting: Left, Right, Top, Bottom, or Inside. When you click a position, a list box arrow appears.

6. Click the list box arrow and scroll to select Critical (see Figure 9.15).

FIGURE 9.15

Use the Text tab of the Bar Styles dialog box to apply formatting that distinguishes critical from noncritical tasks.

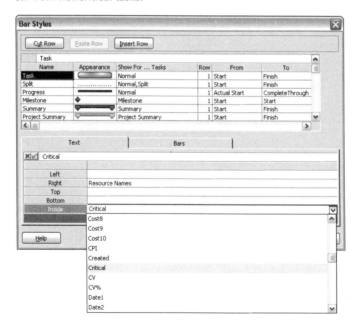

7. Click OK.

After you apply the formatting, the Gantt Chart shows critical and noncritical tasks (see Figure 9.16). Because I placed critical information inside task bars, No appears inside noncritical tasks and Yes appears inside critical tasks.

Even with formatting, this approach to identifying the critical path can be cumbersome if your project contains many tasks. Alternatively, you can identify the critical path by filtering for it. As Chapter 7 explains, you can apply the Critical filter to any task view to display only critical tasks (see Figure 9.17). To apply the filter, display the view that you want to filter and choose Project ➪ Filtered for ➪ Critical or choose Critical from the Filter list box on the Formatting toolbar.

FIGURE 9.16

The formatting in this Gantt Chart identifies critical and noncritical tasks.

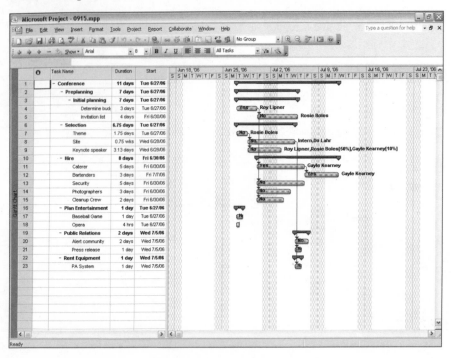

FIGURE 9.17

Filter to display only critical tasks.

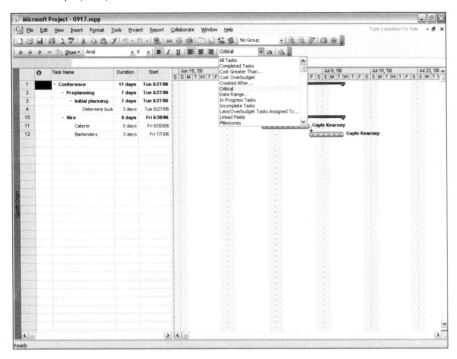

TIP   Filtering is an effective tool to display only certain aspects of the project, but sometimes you need to view all the tasks in your project and still identify the critical ones. If you use formatting (your own or the formatting that is supplied by the Gantt Chart Wizard), you can always identify critical and noncritical tasks — even if you are viewing all the tasks in your project.

Shortening the critical path

Shortening the time that is allotted on the critical path shortens your project's duration. The converse is also true: Lengthening the time that's allotted on the critical path lengthens the project. In all probability, you, as the project manager, are also responsible (at least to some extent) for the cost of a project. Typically, the longer a project goes on, the more it costs. Therefore, shortening the critical path is often the project manager's goal.

Shortening a project's duration can result in an earlier finish. But it also can mean starting later. Obviously, the second alternative is riskier, particularly if you are not confident in your estimates. If you are new to project management, you probably should not plan to start later; instead, use project management tools to help you evaluate the accuracy of your estimating skills. Over time (and multiple projects), you'll know how accurate your estimates are and then you can take the risk of starting a project later than initially planned.

To reduce the time that is allotted on the critical path, you can do one or both of the following:

- Reduce the duration of critical tasks
- Overlap critical tasks to reduce the overall project duration

To reduce the duration of critical tasks, you can do any of the following:

- Reassess estimates and use a more optimistic task time. The PERT Analysis views can help you here.
- Add resources to a critical task. Remember, however, that the task must not be a fixed-duration task; adding resources to a fixed-duration task does not reduce the time needed to complete the task.
- Add overtime to a critical task.

To overlap critical tasks, you can do one or both of the following:

- Adjust dependencies and task date constraints
- Redefine a finish-to-start relationship to either a start-to-start or a finish-to-finish relationship

After you know the techniques that you can apply to adjust the critical path, you need to ask the important question: What's the best way to identify tasks that you want to change and then make the changes? The answer: Select a view, and filter it for critical tasks only. I prefer the Task Entry view, which is a combination view of the Gantt Chart and the Task Form view, because the top pane displays a graphic representation of the project and the bottom pane displays most of the fields that you may want to change (see Figure 9.18).

To set up this view, select the Gantt Chart view. The table that you apply to the Gantt Chart is a matter of personal preference; you may consider the Schedule table because it shows slack information. After you select the Gantt Chart view, choose Window ⇨ Split. The Task Form appears in the bottom pane.

 **TIP** If you don't see the Predecessor information in the Task Form, right-click the Task Form window and choose Resources & Predecessors from the menu that appears.

To filter for critical tasks, click in the Gantt Chart in the top pane of the view and choose Project ⇨ Filtered for ⇨ Critical. Click each critical task to evaluate it, and make changes in the Task Form in the bottom pane of the screen.

 **TIP** You also can sort your critical tasks by duration. That way, the critical tasks are in order from the longest to the shortest, and you can focus on trying to shorten longer tasks.

The Task Entry view, filtered for critical tasks, is probably the easiest view in which to work if you're trying to adjust the critical path.

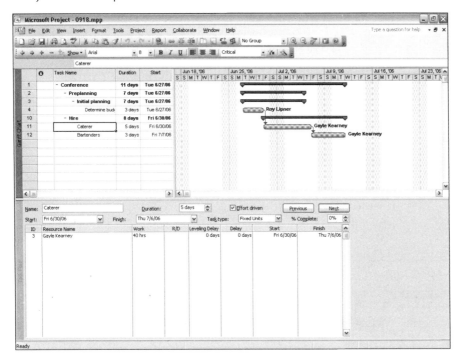

Using Multiple Critical Paths

Project enables you to view more than one critical path in a project. This feature comes in handy when you have lots of tasks that are driving other tasks and you want to find out which ones are truly critical to finishing the network of tasks on time.

By default, when you view only one critical path, you're viewing the tasks that must be completed to finish the project on time. These tasks have no total slack. (*Total slack* is the amount of time that you can delay a task without delaying the completion of the project.)

Suppose, however, that your project contains many subtasks, and within the subtasks you have dependencies. You may start wondering, within a given network of tasks, which ones are really critical. In this case, view your project with multiple critical paths, where Project displays a separate critical path for each network of tasks.

Consider the project that appears in Figure 9.19. In this figure, you see the following four networks of tasks:

- Network 1: Task IDs 2, 3, and 4
- Network 2: Task IDs 6 and 7
- Network 3: Task IDs 9 through 13
- Network 4: Task IDs 15 through 18

The critical path for the project appears with a cross-hatched pattern (on-screen, it's also red) and revolves around the tasks in the first two networks.

When you display multiple critical paths, you see a critical path for each network of tasks (see Figure 9.20). For each unique task, Project sets its late finish date equal to its early finish date. When a task has no links, it is critical because its late finish is equal to its early finish. If a network of tasks contains slack, such as Network 3, some tasks are not critical whereas others are critical. When you view multiple critical paths, you can determine which tasks within a network of tasks must be completed on time to avoid delaying the network.

FIGURE 9.19

This project contains four networks of tasks.

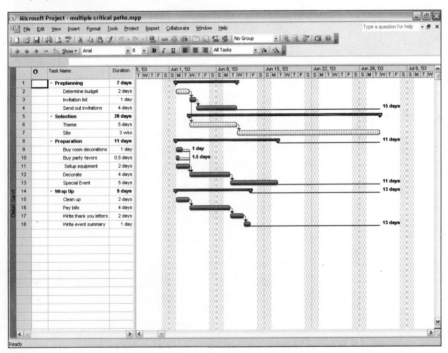

FIGURE 9.20

When you view multiple critical paths, you see the critical tasks within each network of tasks in your project.

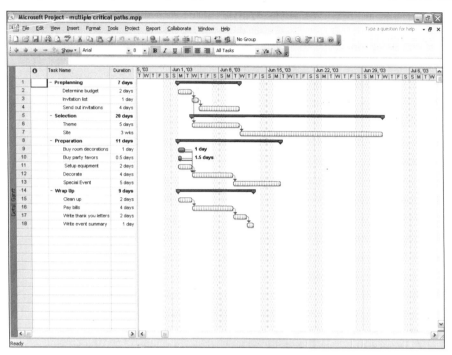

By default, Project displays only one critical path, but you can change this default. Choose Tools ⇨ Options and click the Calculation tab to display the dialog box that appears in Figure 9.21. Select the Calculate Multiple Critical Paths check box and click OK.

Over time, the critical path of your project may change as tasks on the critical path are completed either ahead of schedule or behind schedule. If your schedule contains slack — the amount of time you can delay tasks before affecting other tasks or the project end date — you may be able to adjust your schedule to get it back on track. Use the Detail Gantt view with the Schedule table to help evaluate the slack in your schedule. On the Gantt Chart, slack appears as thin bars on the right side of task bars. In the Schedule table, you'll find fields for Free Slack and Total Slack.

Display multiple critical paths within a project from the Calculation tab of the Options dialog box.

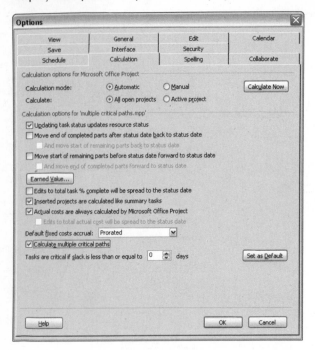

Summary

This chapter described the following techniques that you can use to resolve scheduling conflicts and shorten the length of your project:

- Adding resources to tasks
- Using overtime
- Adjusting slack
- Changing task constraints and dependencies
- Adjusting the length of the critical path

In Chapter 10, you find out how to resolve conflicts that occur with resources.

Chapter 10

Resolving Resource Problems

*R*esource allocation is the process of assigning resources to tasks in a project. Because the potential for resource overallocation always accompanies resource assignment, this chapter explores the causes of resource overallocation and suggests methods to resolve the conflicts.

Understanding How Resource Conflicts Occur

As you assign resources to tasks, Project checks the resource's calendar to make sure that the resource is working. However, Project doesn't assess whether the resource is already obligated when you assign the resource to a new task; Project enables you to make the assignment. Be aware, though, that the additional assignment may lead to overallocating the resource. Overallocation occurs when you assign more work to a resource than the resource can accomplish in the time that you've allotted for the work to be completed.

For example, if you assign Gayle to work full-time on two tasks that start on the same day, you actually assign Gayle to 16 hours of work in an 8-hour day — not possible unless Gayle is a really dedicated employee who has no life outside work. On the other hand, if you have a group of three mechanics and you assign two mechanics to work on two tasks that start on the same day, you still have one spare mechanic and no overallocation.

Figure 10.1 shows a series of tasks under the Plan Entertainment and Public Relations tasks that begin on the same day. By assigning the same resource to them, an overallocation is inevitable. And overallocations can cause delays in the project schedule.

FIGURE 10.1

Assigning the same resource to tasks that run simultaneously causes an overallocation.

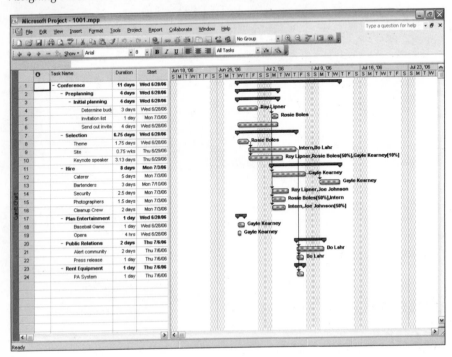

To calculate the scheduled start date for a task, Project checks factors such as the task's dependencies and constraints. Project then checks the resource's calendar to identify the next regular workday and assigns that date as the start date for the task. If you haven't assigned resources to the task, Project uses the project's calendar to calculate the next regular workday. But when Project calculates the task start date, it does not consider other commitments that the resource may have.

Spotting Resource Conflicts

Before you can resolve resource conflicts, you need to spot them. You can use views or filters to help you identify resource overallocation problems.

Using views to spot resource conflicts

Use a resource view, such as the Resource Sheet view or the Resource Usage view, to find resource conflicts. In these views, overallocated resources appear in red. In addition, a Caution icon appears in the Indicator column to signal an overassigned resource. You can see a message about the over-allocation if you point at the icon with your mouse. For information on addressing overallocations, see "Delaying tasks by leveling resource workloads," later in this chapter.

To display the Resource Usage view that appears in Figure 10.2, select Resource Usage from the View bar or choose View ➪ Resource Usage.

You also can see a graphic representation of a resource's allocation by switching to the Resource Graph view. To display the view that appears in Figure 10.3, select Resource Graph from the View bar or choose View ➪ Resource Graph.

The Resource Usage view displays overallocated resources in red, and an icon appears in the Indicator column.

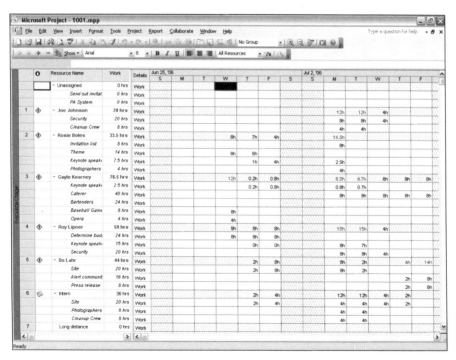

FIGURE 10.3

The Resource Graph view provides a picture of a resource's allocation.

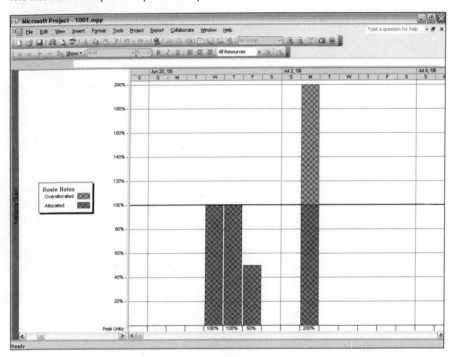

The Resource Allocation view is useful for working with overallocations; a Gantt Chart in the lower pane shows the tasks assigned to the resource that you select in the top pane. Tasks that start at the same time overlap in the Gantt Chart pane. This view helps you pinpoint the tasks that are causing the resource's overallocation. The top portion of the view in Figure 10.4 shows that Gayle Kearney is overallocated on Wednesday, June 28. If you examine that day more closely, you'll notice that Gayle is scheduled to work 12 hours that day. In the bottom portion of the view, the two tasks to which she's assigned 100 percent of the time are Baseball Game and Opera — and the Gantt view makes it easy to see the overlap of the two tasks on that Wednesday.

FIGURE 10.4

The Resource Allocation view uses the Gantt Chart format to show the tasks assigned to the resource selected in the top pane.

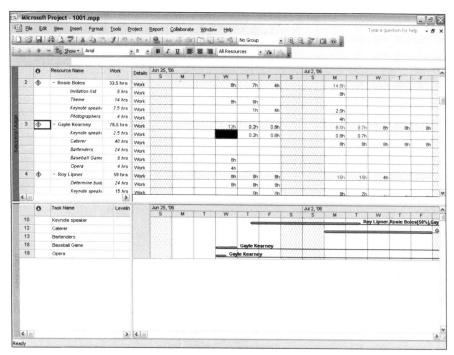

To switch to the Resource Allocation view, choose View ➪ More Views and then select Resource Allocation.

Using filters to spot resource conflicts

Filtering is another simple technique that you can use to resolve resource conflict problems. If you filter the Resource Usage view to display only overallocated resources (see Figure 10.5), the problems become even more apparent. To filter the view, switch to it first by choosing View ➪ Resource Usage. Then open the Filter list box on the Formatting toolbar and choose Overallocated Resources, or choose Project ➪ Filtered ➪ Overallocated Resources.

FIGURE 10.5

You can filter the Resource Usage view to show overallocated resources only.

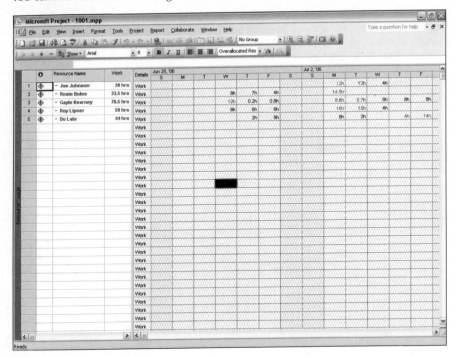

Next, add the Overallocation field to the view to identify the extent of the resource's overallocation. Choose Format ⇨ Details ⇨ Overallocation. As Figure 10.6 shows, Project adds a row to the timescale portion of the view to show you the number of hours that you need to eliminate to correct the overallocation.

FIGURE 10.6

Add the Overallocation field to the Resource Usage view.

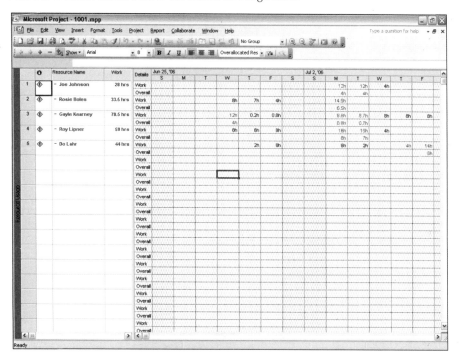

Resolving Conflicts

After you find the overallocations, you need to resolve the conflicts. Project managers use several methods to resolve conflicts.

Changing resource allocations

If you play around with resource allocations, you may be able to resolve a resource conflict. Adding a resource is one obvious way to resolve an overallocation. For example, suppose that Task 3 is an effort-driven task that has a resource conflict with Task 4. The two tasks don't run concurrently, but Task 3 is continuing when Task 4 is supposed to start. Suppose also that you need the same resource, Rosie Boles, to work on both tasks. Adding a resource (Do Lahr) to Task 3 reduces the amount of time that it takes to finish Task 3, which can eliminate Rosie's conflict between Tasks 3 and 4.

CROSS-REF You can add a resource by using the techniques that are described in Chapter 5, or you can add a resource to a task by using the Resource Usage view (described in the section "Adding a task assignment to a resource," later in this chapter).

Switching resources

You also can resolve resource conflicts by switching resources. You can use this technique when one resource is overallocated but you have another resource available that's capable of doing the job. You switch resources by replacing resources on the task in question.

Start in the Resource Usage view, where you can focus on resource conflicts (refer to Figure 10.2; Figures 10-5 and 10-6 are also based on the Resource Usage view). When you are ready to switch resources, I suggest that you create a combination view that shows the Gantt Chart in the top of the view and the Resource Usage view in the bottom of the view (see Figure 10.7).

FIGURE 10.7

Using a combination of the Gantt view and the Resource Usage view helps focus on correcting resource overallocations.

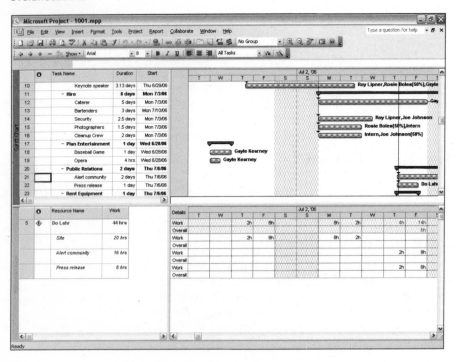

CROSS-REF See Chapter 6 to learn how to create a combination view.

Then, follow these steps:

1. In the upper pane, find and click the task on which you want to switch resources. In the bottom of the window, Project displays all the tasks assignments for each resource assigned to the selected task.

2. Click the Assign Resources button to open the Assign Resources window.

3. Highlight the resource you want to switch.

4. Click the Replace button. The Replace Resource dialog box appears (see Figure 10.8).

5. Select the resource you want to use on the task.

6. Fill in the Units column.

FIGURE 10.8

Use the Replace Resource dialog box to substitute one resource for another.

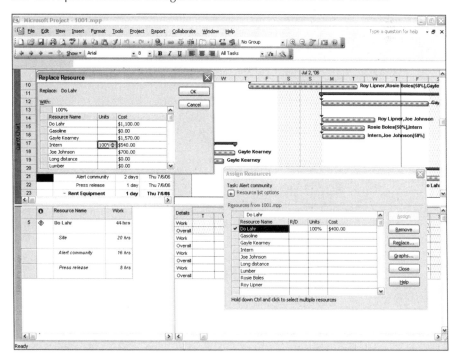

7. Click OK in the Replace Resource dialog box.

NOTE Depending on your option settings, you may see a message from the Planning Wizard. Read the message and click OK to continue.

8. Click Close in the Assign Resources window.

Project will change the assignment without affecting historical actuals, and no resources are affected other than the ones involved in the switch.

CROSS-REF If you're using Project Server, you can take advantage of the Resource Substitution Wizard to substitute generic resources automatically. See Chapter 19 for more details.

Adding a task assignment to a resource

You add a task assignment to a resource using essentially the same process as I describe in the preceding section, "Switching resources" — except that you don't replace a resource. Set up the combination view where the Gantt Chart appears in the top pane and the Resource Usage view appears in the bottom pane. In the upper pane, find and click the task to which you want to add a resource. In the bottom of the window, Project displays all the tasks assignments for each resource assigned to the selected task. Click the Assign Resources button to open the Assign Resources window. Highlight the resource you want to add, fill in the Units column, and click Close. Project will add the resource to the task.

Adding or deleting a resource assignment

You can add or delete a resource assignment using a number of techniques. For example, you can use the Assign Resources window, or you can work in the Gantt Chart view and then split the view (choose Window ➪ Split) to display the Task Entry view — a combination of the Gantt Chart view in the top pane and the Task Form view in the bottom pane (see Figure 10.9).

Select a task in the Gantt Chart view and then do the following:

- To add a resource assignment, select the resource from the list box that appears when you click the Resource Name column of the Task Entry view.

- To delete a resource assignment, select the resource's ID number in the Task Entry view and press Delete.

- To switch resources, use the Replace Resource dialog box (see "Switching resources," earlier in this chapter, for more details).

TIP Working in the Gantt Chart view is effective, but the Resource Usage view helps you to focus on resource conflicts.

CAUTION You shouldn't delete a resource assignment that contains actual work. If you do, you will see misleading information about the task. Suppose, for example, that you assign one resource to a task, the resource completes the task, and then you delete the resource assignment. Project shows the task as completed, but you won't complete any work or actual work at the task level.

FIGURE 10.9

You can work in the Task Entry view to add or delete resource assignments.

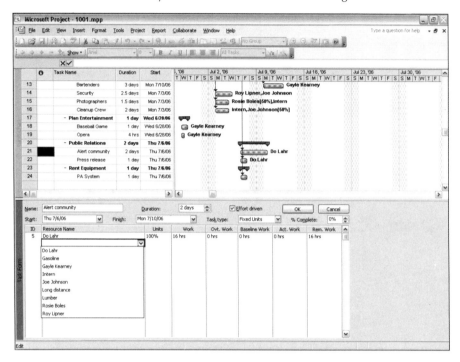

Scheduling overtime

You also can resolve a resource conflict by scheduling overtime for the resource. *Overtime* in Project is the amount of work that is scheduled beyond an assigned resource's regular working hours, and overtime hours are charged at the resource's overtime rate. Overtime work does not represent additional work on a task; instead, it represents the amount of time that's spent on a task during nonregular hours. By scheduling overtime, the resource may finish the task faster and therefore eliminate the conflict. As you read in the last chapter, you assign overtime from the Gantt Chart view. Use the following steps to schedule overtime:

1. Display the Task Entry view (choose View ➪ More Views ➪ Task Entry and select Apply).

2. Click the Task Form to make it the active pane.

3. Choose Format ➪ Details ➪ Resource Work. Project displays the Ovt. Work column in the Task Form pane (see Figure 10.10). In this column, 0h means that you have not yet assigned overtime.

FIGURE 10.10

Use the Task Form, and display the Overtime column to add overtime.

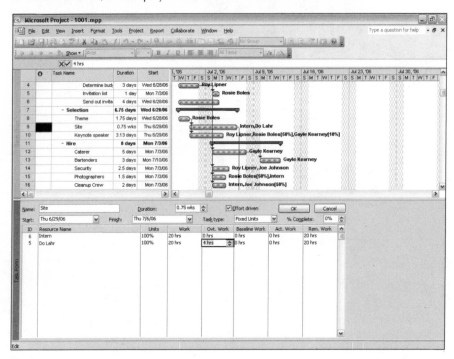

4. Select the task in the top pane to which you want to assign overtime.

5. Go to the bottom pane, and fill in the overtime amount for the appropriate resource.

> **TIP** When you finish entering overtime, you can hide the Task Form by choosing Window ▷ Remove Split.

Redefining a resource's calendar

If your resource is a salaried resource, you may have the option of redefining a resource's calendar so that hours typically considered nonworking (and therefore charged at an overtime rate if worked) become working hours. If a resource has a conflict and the number of hours in conflict on a given day is low enough, you can eliminate the conflict by increasing the working hours for the resource for that day.

> **NOTE** You can make this kind of change to any resource — Project won't stop you. But you need to consider the effects on the cost of your project. If you are paying a resource at an overtime rate for working during nonworking hours, you don't want to change nonworking hours to working hours in Project. If you do, you will understate the cost of your project.

To change a resource's working calendar, go to the Resource Usage view. Identify the resource that has a conflict and note the number of hours that the conflict involves. Double-click the resource that has a conflict to open the Resource Information dialog box for that resource. Click Change Working Time to view that resource's calendar (see Figure 10.11).

To change the standard working hours for a resource, follow these steps:

1. Click the Exceptions tab.

2. Click the first date on which the resource is overallocated.

3. In the Name column, type a name for the exception you're about to create and click outside the Name column. Project displays the date you clicked in Step 2 in both the Start and Finish columns.

4. Click the Details button.

5. Click the Working times option button and use the From and To boxes to set up nonstandard working hours for the resource.

FIGURE 10.11

Open the Change Working Time dialog box from the Resource Information dialog box to change the standard working hours for a resource.

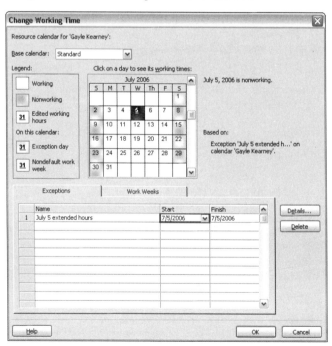

333

6. If you want to change the resource's standard working hours for more than one day, select an option in the Recurrence pattern section and then set a date range in the Range of recurrence section. In Figure 10.12, I set the workday to last 10.5 hours for three days: July 5, July 6, and July 7.

FIGURE 10.12

Set nonstandard working hours during a specified time period for a particular resource.

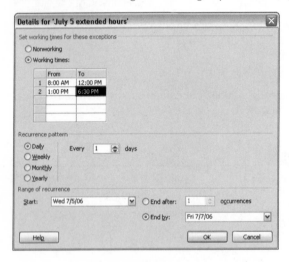

7. Click OK to redisplay the Change Working Time dialog box; the working hours for the specified dates will appear if you click those dates on the calendar.

8. Click OK to save the exception to standard working hours for the resource.

9. Click OK to close the Resource Information dialog box.

Assigning part-time work

Suppose that a resource is assigned to several concurrent tasks and is also overallocated. Suppose also that you don't want to add other resources, switch to a different resource, or add overtime. You can assign the resource to work part-time on each of the tasks to solve the conflict, although the tasks may take longer to complete by using this method. Or, you may want to use this method in conjunction with additional resources to make sure that you can complete the task on time.

To assign a resource to work part-time, you can change the number of units of the resource that you apply to the task. By default, Project sets task types to Fixed Units. Therefore, if you change the amount of time that a resource works on a task, Project changes the duration of the task accordingly.

NOTE To retain the duration and assign a resource to work part-time on a task, change the task type to Fixed Duration. By making this change, however, you are indicating that the task can be completed by the resource in the allotted amount of time — effectively, you are shortening the amount of time that it takes to complete the task because you're applying less effort during the same time frame.

To change a task's type to Fixed Duration and then assign a resource to work on the task part-time without changing the task's duration, follow these steps:

1. Display the Resource Allocation view by using the More Views window (choose View ➪ More Views).

2. In the upper pane, click the task that you want to change. In the lower pane, Project displays that task in Gantt format.

3. In the lower pane, double-click the task that you want to change. Project displays the Task Information dialog box. Click the Advanced tab (see Figure 10.13).

FIGURE 10.13

Use the Advanced tab of the Task Information dialog box to change the task type.

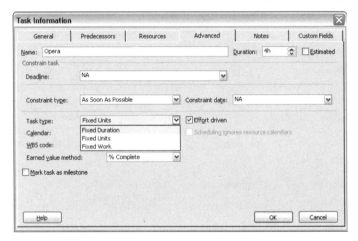

4. Open the Task type list box and select Fixed Duration.

5. Click OK.

6. Click the task in the top pane.

7. Click the Assignment Information button on the Standard toolbar, or double-click the task to open the Assignment Information dialog box. Figure 10.14 shows the General tab.

FIGURE 10.14

Use the Assignment Information dialog box to change a resource's workload to part-time.

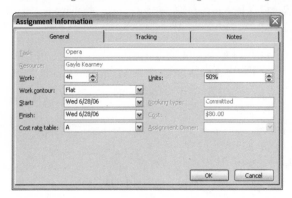

8. Change the default value in the Units box (100%) to reflect the percentage of time that you want the resource to spend on the task — in this case, the value should be less than 100%.

9. Click OK.

Controlling when resources start working on a task

For cases in which you've assigned more than one resource to a task, consider staggering the times that the resources begin working on the task to resolve resource conflicts. When you delay a resource's start on a task, Project recalculates the start date and time for that resource's work on the task. To stagger start times for resources, work in the Task Usage view and follow these steps:

 This technique can extend the duration of the task, which may not be a viable option for you.

1. Choose View ➪ Task Usage.

2. Select the resource whose work time you want to delay in the Task Name column.

3. Click the Assignment Information button or double-click the resource. Project displays the General tab of the Assignment Information dialog box (as shown previously in Figure 10.11).

4. Change the dates in the Start or Finish boxes.

5. Click OK.

 You also can alter the assignment start and finish dates directly in the Task Usage table.

Delaying tasks by leveling resource workloads

If you have scheduled several tasks to run concurrently and you now find resource conflicts in your project, you can delay some of these tasks to *level* — or, spread out — the demands that you're making on your resources. Leveling is the process of resolving resource conflicts by delaying or splitting tasks to accommodate the schedules of assigned resources. You can ask Project to select the tasks to delay or split by using its leveling feature, or you can control the process manually by examining the project to identify tasks that you are willing to delay or split.

Letting Project level resource loads

When Project does the leveling for you, it redistributes a resource's assignments and reschedules them according to the resource's working capacity, assignment units, and calendar. Project also considers the task's duration, constraints, and priority.

What is a task's *priority*? Well, leveling typically results in Project's delaying some tasks, and you can use the task's priority to control the order in which Project levels tasks to try to avoid delaying certain tasks. By default, Project assigns all tasks a priority of 500. When you assign different priorities to tasks, Project considers the priorities of each task when you level and attempts to avoid delaying tasks in order of their priority, from highest to lowest — the higher the number, the higher the priority. Effectively, Project delays tasks with lower priorities before delaying tasks with higher priorities; if everything else is equal, Project will delay a task with a priority of 5 before it will delay a task with a priority of 15. So, before you start to use the automatic-leveling feature, consider how you want to prioritize tasks.

 The priority of 1000 is treated in a special way; Project will not consider delaying any task to which you assign a priority of 1000.

To set a priority, follow these steps:

1. Choose View ➪ Gantt Chart.

2. Double-click the task for which you want to set a priority, or select the task and click the Task Information button on the Standard toolbar. Project displays the Task Information dialog box.

3. Use the General tab to set a priority (see Figure 10.15).

 You might prefer to set priorities from the table portion of the Gantt Chart view or the Task Usage, where you can easily see the priorities of neighboring tasks.

 After you prioritize tasks — but before you level — you can sort tasks by priority to view the tasks that Project is most likely to level.

FIGURE 10.15

Set a priority for the task.

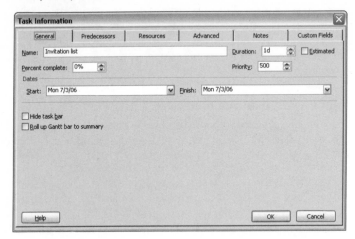

To level tasks automatically, follow these steps:

1. Choose Tools ⇨ Level Resources to open the Resource Leveling dialog box (see Figure 10.16).

FIGURE 10.16

From the Resource Leveling dialog box, you can set resource leveling options.

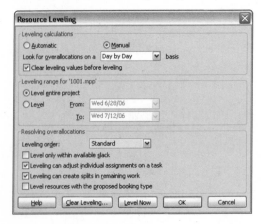

2. Select the Automatic option button to have Project automatically level resources, if necessary, whenever you make a change to your schedule. Select Manual to perform leveling
   only when you click the Level Now button in this dialog box.

3. Use the Look for Overallocations on a . . . Basis list box to select a basis. The *basis* is a
   time frame, such as Day by Day or Week by Week. (The Indicator box in the Resource
   Usage view may contain a note that suggests the appropriate basis.)

4. Select the Clear Leveling Values before Leveling check box to make Project 2007 reset all
   leveling delay values to 0 before leveling. If you don't check this box, Project 2007 does
   not reset leveling values but builds upon the values. During leveling, the scheduling for
   previously leveled tasks will probably not change.

5. In the Leveling Range For panel, select either to level the entire project or to level only for
   specified dates.

6. In the Leveling Order list box, select the order that you want Project to consider when
   leveling your project. If you choose ID Only, Project delays or splits the task with the
   highest ID number. If you choose Standard, Project looks at predecessor dependencies,
   slack, dates, and priorities when selecting the best task to split or delay. If you choose
   Priority, Standard, Project looks first at task priority and then at all the items that are
   listed for the Standard leveling order.

7. Select any of the following options:

   ▪ Level Only Within Available Slack: This avoids changing the end date of your project.

   ▪ Leveling Can Adjust Individual Assignments on a Task: In this case, leveling adjusts
     one resource's work schedule on a task independent of other resources that are work-
     ing on the same task.

   ▪ Leveling Can Create Splits in Remaining Work: This allows leveling to split tasks to
     resolve resource conflicts.

   ▪ Level Resources with the Proposed Booking Type: Check this box to have Project
     include tasks containing proposed resources during the leveling process.

8. Click Level Now to apply leveling.

You can review the effects of leveling from the Leveling Gantt Chart view, as shown in Figure 10.17.
Choose Views ➪ More Views ➪ Leveling Gantt and then click Apply. Project adds green bars to
your Gantt Chart, which represent the duration of tasks before leveling. Depending on the nature
of your project, Project may build more slack into your tasks.

FIGURE 10.17

The Leveling Gantt Chart view shows how leveling affects your project.

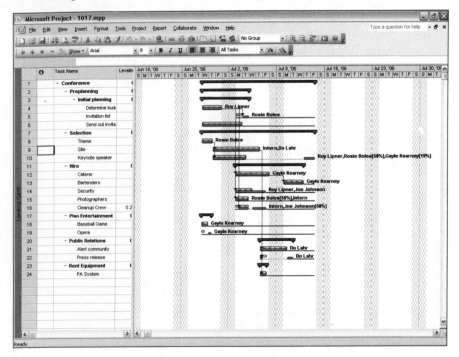

To remove the effects of leveling, reopen the Resource Leveling dialog box (choose Tools ⇨ Level Resources) and click the Clear Leveling button. A subsequent dialog box enables you to clear leveling for the entire project or for selected tasks only.

NOTE If you are scheduling from a finish date, you still can level to resolve resource conflicts. Project calculates the delay by subtracting it from a task's or assignment's finish date, causing the finish date to occur earlier.

Making adjustments to leveling

You can adjust leveling when automatic leveling doesn't provide acceptable results or when you have just a few resource conflicts to resolve. To make leveling adjustments to resources in Project, use the Resource Allocation view and follow these steps:

1. Choose View ⇨ More Views. From the More Views dialog box, highlight Resource Allocation and click Apply.

2. Highlight the task that you want to delay in the top pane.

3. In the bottom pane, enter an amount in the Leveling Delay field. Project delays the task accordingly and reduces the resource's conflict.

Figures 10-18 and 10-19 show "before" and "after" pictures for manual leveling. I used a simple situation to demonstrate the effects of manual leveling: I set up a project with only two tasks and one resource, and I assigned the same resource full-time to both tasks. Notice that manually leveling the second task delays the second task so that it starts when the first task finishes.

FIGURE 10.18

The Resource Allocation view before manual leveling.

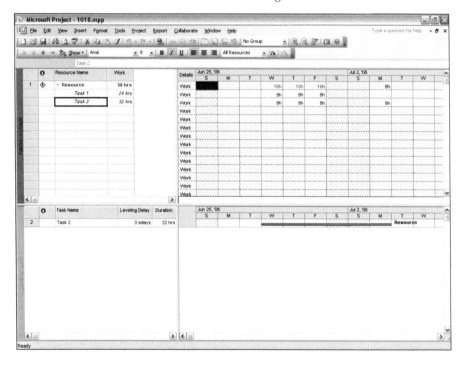

FIGURE 10.19

The Resource Allocation view after manually leveling the second task.

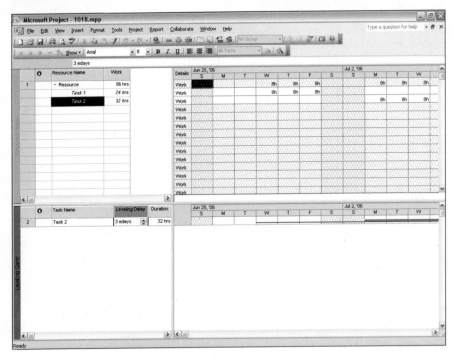

Contouring resources

Contour is the term that Project uses to refer to the shape of a resource's work assignment over time. Contours come in several flavors; the most common are Flat, Back Loaded, Front Loaded, and Bell. The default contour is Flat, which means that a resource works on a task for the maximum number of hours that he or she is assigned to a task for the duration of the assignment. You can use different contours to control how much a resource is scheduled to work on a task at a given time — and possibly resolve a conflict.

> **TIP** Add the Peak Units field to the Resource Usage view to display the maximum effort — as distributed over time — that a resource is expected to work. This field is particularly useful when you have selected a contour other than the default (Flat).

The Flat contour assigns a resource to work the maximum number of hours per time period throughout the duration of the task. By changing the contour, you can more accurately reflect the actual work pattern for the resource while working on a task.

To better understand contours, think of dividing each task into 10 equal timeslots. By using the various contours, Project assigns percentages of work to be done in each timeslot. Contours help you to assign work to a task, based on when the task requires the effort. For example, if a task requires less effort initially, consider using a Back Loaded contour. If a task requires most effort in the middle of the task, consider using a Bell, Turtle, or even an Early Peak contour.

CAUTION If you start changing contours from the default Flat contour, you may inadvertently create a resource conflict. Therefore, viewing the contours that you set can help you resolve resource conflicts.

Setting a contour pattern

To set a contour pattern, follow these steps:

1. Choose View ⇨ Task Usage. In the sheet portion of the view, Project displays each task in your project with the resources that are assigned to it listed below the task, showing the number of hours per day that a resource is assigned to a task.

2. In the Task Name column, double-click the resource whose contour you want to change, or select the resource and click the Assignment Information button on the Standard toolbar. Then click the General tab of the Assignment Information dialog box (see Figure 10.20).

FIGURE 10.20

Use the General tab of the Assignment Information dialog box to select a contour.

3. Open the Work contour list box and select a contour.

4. Click OK.

TIP To change the start and end dates for the resource's work on the task, use the Start and Finish list boxes.

When you select a contour other than Flat, an indicator showing the type of contour appears next to the resource in the Indicator column. If you pass the mouse pointer over the indicator, Project identifies the contour that was applied to the resource (see Figure 10.21).

FIGURE 10.21

Project displays an icon in the Indicator column next to a resource for which you have chosen a contour other than Flat.

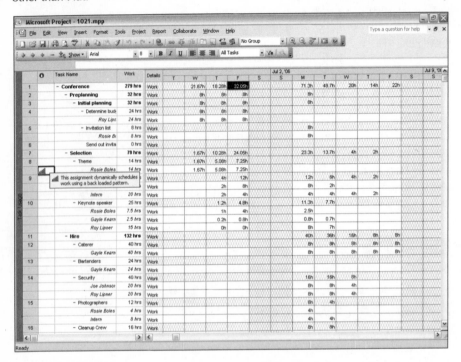

 **TIP** The same icon appears in the Indicator column in the Resource Usage view.

Keep the following points in mind when working with contours:

■ Suppose that you apply a contour other than the default Flat contour to a task, and later you add new total work values to the task. Project automatically reapplies the contour pattern to the task and the resources first by distributing the new task work values across the affected time span and then by assigning new work values to the resources that are working on the task.

■ If you set a contour and then change the start date of the task or the start date of a resource's work on the task, Project automatically shifts the contour and reapplies it to include the new date, thus preserving the pattern of the original contour.

■ If you increase the duration of a task, Project stretches the contour to include the new duration.

- Suppose that you apply a contour other than the default contour to a task. If you manually edit a work value on the portion of a view that displays the contour, Project no longer applies the contour pattern automatically. However, you can reapply the contour to redistribute the new values.

- If you enter actual work and then change the task's total work or total remaining work, Project automatically redistributes the changes to the remaining work values and not to the actual work.

Contouring a resource's availability

You can contour a resource's availability using the General tab of the Resource Information dialog box (see Figure 10.22). In the Resource Availability list box, set Available From and Available To dates for the selected resource. When would you use this feature? A particular resource may be available to work on your project only part-time for a specified time frame. Or, suppose that you have five computer programmers, but only three are available in August and one retires in September. Use the Resource Availability section to specify the availability of your resources, which will influence your project's schedule.

FIGURE 10.22

Set dates that represent the resource's availability so that you can assign the resource to a task by using only the dates that the resource is available.

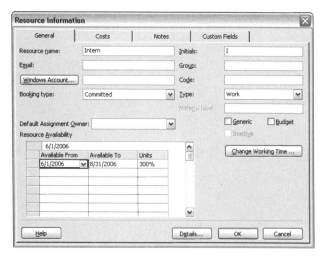

Pooling resources

Finally, you can try to solve resource conflicts by using a resource pool. A *resource pool* is a set of resources that are available to any project. You can use resources exclusively on one project, or you can share the resources among several projects.

Typically, resource pooling is useful only if you work with the same resources on multiple projects and you don't use Project Server. Different project managers can share the same resources. Because resource pooling is so closely tied to the topic of managing multiple projects, I postpone further discussion until Chapter 15; in that context, you'll better understand the application of resource pooling to resolving resource conflicts.

If you're using Project Server, you don't need to use resource pooling. Instead, you'll be more interested in using Enterprise resources and the Resource Substitution Wizard to resolve resource conflicts. See Chapters 18 and 19 for more information.

Summary

This chapter explained how to identify and resolve resource conflicts that can delay a project. The techniques involved include the following:

- Changing resource allocations
- Scheduling overtime
- Redefining a resource calendar
- Assigning part-time work
- Controlling resource start times
- Leveling resource workloads
- Contouring resources

In the next chapter, you discover the art of tracking your progress by comparing your project to its baseline.

Part IV

Tracking Your Progress

Chapter 11

Understanding Tracking

T his chapter marks something of a turning point in this book and in your use of Project. Up to this point, you've been in the planning phase: building a project schedule, entering tasks, adding resources, and shifting things around so that resource assignments don't conflict and so that tasks have the proper relationships to each other. You've even tweaked details such as text formatting and the appearance of taskbars. You now have a workable, good-looking project in hand—and now you are ready to start the project.

Tracking is the process of comparing what actually happens during your project to your estimates of what would happen. To track, you need to take a picture of your project schedule at the moment your planning is complete; this moment is called a *baseline*. But you also have to understand what steps are involved in tracking and how to set up efficient procedures to handle these steps.

NOTE   You can store up to 11 baselines for any project.

Understanding the Principles of Tracking

A good plan is only half the battle. How you execute that plan is the key. Think of yourself as the quarterback in a football game. If you run straight down the field toward the goalpost, never swerving to avoid an oncoming opponent, you won't get very far. Project tracking is similar: If you don't swerve and make adjustments for the changes in costs and timing that are virtually inevitable in any human endeavor, you're not playing the game correctly.

Project management software greatly enhances your ability to quickly see problems and revise the plan to minimize any damage. Project enables you to compare what you thought would happen to what actually happens over the course of the project.

Estimates versus actuals

The plan that you've been building is an estimate of what can occur. It's your best guess (an educated one, I hope) about how long tasks may take, how one task affects another, how many resources you need to complete the work, and what costs you expect your project to incur. Good project managers keep good records of their estimates and actuals to become better project managers. By comparing these two sets of data, you can see where your estimates were off and then use this information to make your next plan more realistic. You can also use data on actual costs and timing to make the changes in your strategy that are necessary to keep you on track and meet your current project's goals.

Tracking in Project consists of entering information about actuals, such as the actual start date, the actual finish date, and the actual duration of a task. You enter actual time that is worked by resources and actual costs that are incurred. When you enter information about actuals, Project shows you a revised schedule with projections of how the rest of the schedule is likely to play out, based on your actual activity.

Project managers usually track activity on a regular basis, such as once a week or every two weeks. This tracking includes information about tasks in progress as well as about tasks that have been completed.

This tracking activity also enables you to generate reports that show management where your efforts stand at any given point in time. By showing managers the hard data on your project's status — rather than your best guess — you can make persuasive bids for more time, more resources, or a shift in strategy if things aren't going as you expected. Figure 11.1 shows a Tracking Gantt view using the Tracking table.

 Chapter 12 explains the specific steps for updating a project to reflect actual progress.

Making adjustments as you go

Tracking isn't something that you leave to the end of the project, or even to the end of individual tasks. Tracking tasks in progress on a regular basis helps you to detect any deviation from your estimates. The earlier you spot a delay, the more time you have to make up for it.

 If Project determines that you're running late on a task, it automatically moves dependent tasks into the future.

FIGURE 11.1

Use the Tracking Gantt view to display the progress of your project.

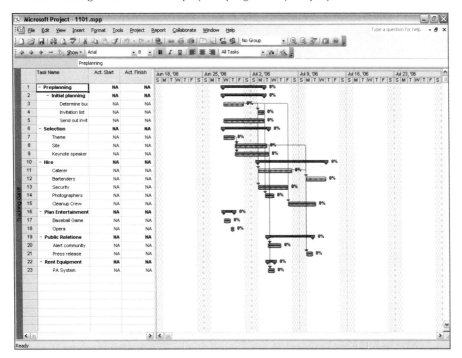

For example, suppose that you estimated that a task would take three days. However, you have already put four days of effort into it, and it's still not complete. Project not only tells you that you're running late but also moves future tasks that depend on this task farther out in the schedule. Project also shows any resource conflicts that result when resources have to put in more work than you estimated in resource views, such as the Resource Sheet and Resource Graph view. Project clearly shows how one delay ripples through your schedule.

TIP Project adjusts your project's cost as you track to reflect the effect of higher-than-expected costs.

Project also shows the effect of unanticipated costs on the total budget. If the costs that you track on early tasks are higher than anticipated, Project displays your projected total costs, based on a combination of actual costs and the remaining estimates. Project shows you exactly how much of your budget you have used and how much you have remaining, so you can revise your resource allocations to stay within your overall budget.

How Much Have You Accomplished?

As I describe in Chapter 12, you record activity on a task by entering an estimate of the percentage of the task that's complete, actual resource time spent on the task, or actual costs incurred (such as fees or equipment rentals paid), or by entering the hours of work done per time period. Estimating "the completeness" of a task is not an exact science, and different people use different methods.

With something concrete, such as a building under construction, you can look at the actual building and estimate fairly accurately how far along the project has progressed. Most projects aren't so straightforward, however. How do you estimate how far along you are in more creative tasks, such as coming up with an advertising concept? You can sit in meetings for five weeks and still not find the right concept. Is your project 50 percent complete? Completion is hard to gauge from other, similar projects on which you've worked—perhaps on the last project, you came up with the perfect concept in your very first meeting.

Don't fall into the trap of using money or time spent as a gauge. It's (unfortunately) easy to spend $10,000 on a task that is estimated to cost $8,000 and still be only 25 percent to completion. You probably have to use the same gut instincts that put you in charge of this project to estimate the progress of individual tasks. Hint: If your project has individual deliverables that you can track, document them and use them consistently when you make your estimate.

Using Baselines

You complete the planning phase of your project by setting a baseline. You have seen this term in previous chapters, but take a moment to grasp its significance in the tracking process.

What is a baseline?

A *baseline* is a snapshot of your project when you complete the planning phase, or sometimes at the end of some other critical phase. The baseline is one set of data that is saved in the same file where you track actual progress data. Project enables you to save up to 11 baselines and an equal number of interim plans during your project. You can show a wide variety of information about your baseline(s), or you can choose not to display baseline information.

Some projects, particularly shorter ones that run only a few weeks or even a couple of months, may have one baseline set at the outset and may proceed close enough to your estimates that they can run their course against that single baseline. Other projects, especially longer ones, may require you to set several baselines along the way, particularly if the original estimate is so out of line with what has transpired in the project that the original is no longer useful. You can modify the entire baseline if changes are drastic and occur early in the project, or you can modify the baseline estimates only going forward from a particular point in the project.

For example, if your project is put on hold shortly after you complete the schedule and you actually start work three months later than you had planned, you would be wise to set a new baseline schedule before restarting. If, however, you're six months into your project and it is put on hold for three months, you may want to modify the timing of future tasks and reset the baseline only for tasks going forward to help you retain the ability to accurately assess how well you estimated.

Costs can change a baseline, too. For example, what if you save a baseline that is set to fit within a $50,000 budget and, before you start work, cost-cutting measures hit your company and your budget is cut to $35,000? You would be wise to make the changes to your resources and costs, and then reset your baseline. Setting interim baselines keeps your projects from varying wildly from your estimates when mitigating circumstances come into play.

Setting a baseline

In most cases, you need to save the project file — without setting the baseline — several times during the planning phase.

When you're ready, you can use the Set Baseline dialog box to save up to 11 baselines and 10 interim plans for your project. Each baseline is a picture of your project at the time that you save it, and each baseline that you set includes information about tasks, resources, and assignments. For tasks, Project saves duration, start and finish dates, work, timephased work, cost, and timephased cost. For resources, Project saves work, timephased work, cost, timephased cost, budget work, timephased budget work, budget cost, and timephased budget cost information with the baseline. For assignments, Project saves start and finish dates, work, timephased work, costs, and timephased costs.

When you save interim plans, Project saves a set of task start and finish dates that you can compare with another interim plan or with a baseline plan, thus helping you to keep an eye on progress or slippage. Saving baselines and interim plans can help you compare current information (found in the start and finish fields) with baseline information (found in the baseline fields). The distinction between baselines and interim plans in Project is the amount and type of information that Project saves.

To control the settings when you set a baseline, follow these steps:

1. Set up the baseline project that you want to save.
2. Choose Tools ➪ Tracking ➪ Set Baseline to open the Set Baseline dialog box, as shown in Figure 11.2.
3. Open the Set baseline list box and select the baseline that you want to set.
4. Click OK.

FIGURE 11.2

Use this dialog box to save a baseline or interim plan.

When you set baselines for selected tasks, you can choose to roll up baselines to all summary tasks and from subtasks into their parent summary task(s) — thus helping to maintain accurate baseline information, as shown in Figure 11.3. The relationship between the tasks in the project and the task(s) that you select prior to opening the dialog box determine the effect of these check boxes.

FIGURE 11.3

You can control Project's behavior when rolling up baseline information for selected tasks.

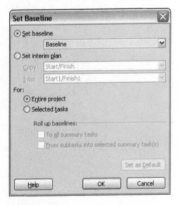

For example, suppose that you have a project set up like the one shown in Figure 11.4. Furthermore, suppose that you select Task 6, a child of Task 1 and the parent of Tasks 7 and 8, before you open the Set Baseline dialog box. If you select only the From Subtasks into Selected Summary Task(s) check box, Project rolls up the information from Tasks 7 and 8 to Task 6. If you select only the To All Summary Tasks check box, Project rolls up baseline information from Task 6 without regard to the baseline information that is stored for Tasks 7 and 8. If you select both check boxes, Project rolls up baseline information from Tasks 7 and 8 to Task 6 and then rolls up that information to Task 1.

Suppose that you want to update the baseline to reflect approved changes to the project, such as added tasks, or changes to existing tasks that affect the cost or schedule of the tasks. Highlight the added or changed tasks and the parent summary task and then set the baseline. In the Set Baseline box (refer to Figure 11.3), choose the Selected Tasks option and check both boxes in the Roll Up Baselines section. Project will update the baseline for the changed tasks and then change all the summary levels to reflect the change.

FIGURE 11.4

Ancestry determines baseline information rollup behavior. In this sample project, Tasks 3 and 6 are children of Task 1, and Task 6 is the parent of Tasks 7 and 8.

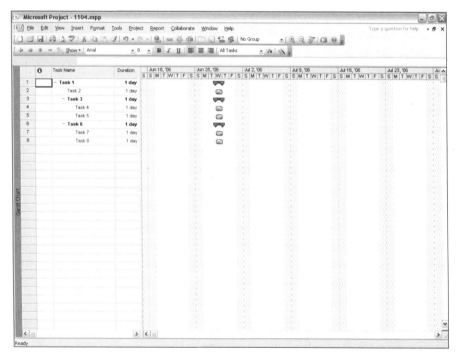

Changing the Baseline

Most of the time, you *don't* want to make changes to a baseline. It's a moment that's frozen in time, a record against which you can compare your progress. If you change a baseline on a regular basis, you are defeating its purpose.

That said, you will encounter some circumstances in which, for strategic reasons, you need to modify a baseline project and reset the baseline or set a second or third baseline to document major shifts in the project. However, if you are overriding the original baseline, you must do so in a thoughtful and efficient way. This section discusses some of the times when changes to a baseline are necessary and explains how you can make those changes.

Adding a task to a baseline

It is fairly common to set your baseline plan and then realize that you left out a step, or then decide to break one step into two steps. Perhaps your company institutes a new requirement or process, and you have to modify a task to deal with the change. You don't want to reset your whole project baseline, but you want to save that one task along with the original baseline. You can make this change after you set the original baseline.

To add a task to your baseline so that you can track its progress, follow these steps:

1. Do one of the following:
    - To add a new task to the schedule and then incorporate it into the baseline, first add the task in the Task Name column on your Gantt Chart and then select it.
    - To save modifications to an existing task, first make the changes and then select the task.
2. Choose Tools ➪ Tracking ➪ Save Baseline. The Save Baseline dialog box appears.
3. Select the baseline that you want to modify from the Save baseline list.
4. Choose the Selected tasks option button, as shown in Figure 11.5.
5. Choose the appropriate Roll Up Baselines settings (see the preceding section for details on these options).
6. Click OK to save the baseline, which now includes the new task.

NOTE You can add tasks to the baseline by entering them in the Gantt table, using columns such as Baseline Duration and Baseline Start or Finish. However, adding baseline data this way does not enable all baseline calculations. For example, adding a task at the end of the project with this method doesn't affect a change in the baseline finish date.

FIGURE 11.5

Make modifications to tasks and save them in an already established baseline.

Using interim plans

You can use the baseline in different ways. You can refer to it as your original estimate and compare it with actual results at the end of the project to see how well you guessed, and to learn to make better guesses on future projects. But the baseline also has an important practical use during the project: It alerts you to shifts so that you can make changes to accommodate them. The second use may prompt you to save interim plans.

The initial baseline(s) may quickly take on more historical than practical interest. You should not change the initial baseline(s) because that record of your original planning process is important to retain. However, if timing shifts dramatically away from the baseline plan, all the little warning signs that Project gives you about being off schedule become useless. A project that starts six months later than expected will show every task as late and every task as critical. To continue generating useful project information, you need to revise the schedule to better reflect reality. Only by setting interim plans can you see how well you're meeting your revised goals.

NOTE Remember that interim plans contain a set of task start and finish dates that you can compare with another interim plan or with a baseline plan, thus helping you to keep an eye on progress or slippage. A baseline includes much more information — duration, start and finish dates, work, and cost information about tasks, resources, and assignments. Setting baselines and interim plans helps you to compare current information, found in the start and finish fields, with baseline information, found in the baseline fields.

You can set interim plans for all the tasks in the project. However, you should usually set an interim plan only for tasks going forward. For example, if a labor strike pushes out a manufacturing project by two months, you should keep the baseline intact for all the tasks that were completed at the time the strike started and save an interim plan for all the tasks that must still be performed when the strike ends.

> **NOTE** You also can use interim plans to copy baseline information from one baseline to another.

You can set an interim plan by following these steps:

1. Select various tasks to include in the interim plan.

2. Choose Tools ⇨ Tracking ⇨ Set Baseline to open the Set Baseline dialog box.

3. Select the Set interim plan option button. Project makes the Copy and Into fields available.

4. Open the Copy list. In Figure 11.6, I've opened the Into list, which contains the same choices as you'll find in the Copy list.

The choices in the Copy and Into lists enable you to save several sets of start and finish dates in interim plans.

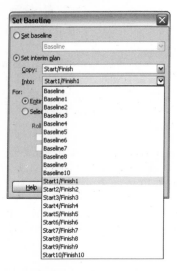

5. Select Start/Finish from the Copy drop-down list to copy the current start and finish dates.

6. Open the drop-down list for the Into field and select a numbered item, such as Start1/Finish1, to copy the dates into new fields, thus creating an interim plan.

7. Select the Entire project option button to create an interim plan for the whole project, or choose the Selected tasks option button to create an interim plan that retains the original interim plan or baseline information for any tasks that you didn't select, yet saves new baseline information for the tasks that you have selected.

8. Click OK to save the interim plan.

Remember that you can use the various numbered Start/Finish items to set up to 10 interim plans plus the original, for a total of 11 interim plans over the life of your project.

Clearing a baseline or interim plan

Inevitably, you set a baseline or an interim baseline and then find a reason to clear it. Suppose, for example, that you thought you finished the planning stage of the project. The project hasn't yet started, and you attend a meeting in which you inform everyone that you're "good to go" for next Monday. Naturally, your announcement triggers discussion and, by the time the discussion ends, the scope of the project has expanded (or contracted) considerably. You now need to work again on the planning phase of your schedule — and you really don't want to adjust the baseline. Instead, you want to get rid of it. After you make all your changes, you can set the correct baseline.

To clear a baseline, choose Tools ➪ Tracking ➪ Clear Baseline. Project displays the Clear Baseline dialog box (see Figure 11.7). In this dialog box, you can choose to clear a baseline plan or an interim plan for the entire project or for selected tasks.

FIGURE 11.7

Set the baseline too soon? Clear it from this dialog box so that you can make adjustments and set the baseline correctly.

Viewing Progress with the Tracking Gantt View

Baselines help you to see how your estimates differ from actual activity in the project. Project enables you to see this variance both graphically, with baseline and actual taskbars, and through data that is displayed in tables in various views. The next section briefly explains how to display baseline and actual data and how you can use this feature to understand the status of your project.

CROSS-REF   In Chapter 12, you find out how to enter tracking data.

Interpreting the Tracking Gantt view

The Tracking Gantt view is most useful in viewing progress against your baseline estimates. To display the Tracking Gantt view, click its icon in the View bar or choose View ➪ Tracking Gantt. This view shows the Entry table by default. However, you can add or remove fields (columns), or you can display other tables of information. In Figure 11.8, I chose to display the Tracking table, and I added columns to include baseline information.

CROSS-REF   **Review Chapter 7 for more information about changing and modifying tables.**

Notice the Baseline Duration and Baseline Cost fields that I added to the table, as well as the Actual Duration and the Actual Cost fields, which appear in the default Tracking table. These fields help you to compare estimated versus actual timing and costs.

FIGURE 11.8

The Tracking Gantt table can display a wealth of information.

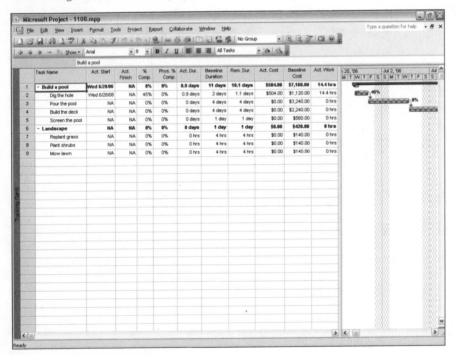

The default Tracking table also contains the following information:

- **% Complete:** This field shows the progress of various tasks in the schedule. Figure 11.9 shows that one task is complete.

- **Physical % Complete:** A field that you can use to calculate BCWP (budgeted cost of work performed). Project calculates the % Complete field for you based on Total Duration or Actual Duration values you enter, but Project allows you to enter a value for the Physical % Complete field. Use this field to calculate BCWP when the % Complete value would not accurately represent the real work performed on a task.

- **Remaining Duration:** This field reflects the amount of time needed to complete an unfinished task. You can enter a value into this field or you can allow Project to calculate it for you by entering a value into either the Actual Duration field or the % Complete field. If you enter a value for Remaining Duration, Project calculates a new % Complete value and a new Duration value; Project changes the Duration value to equal the sum of Actual Duration and Remaining Duration, leaving Actual Duration untouched.

- **Actual Work:** In the Actual Work field, you'll see the amount of work that has been performed by resources. There are Actual Work fields for tasks, resources, and assignments, as well as timephased Actual Work fields for tasks, resources, and assignments.

The Tracking Gantt view displays both a table and taskbars to give you a graphic view of progress on the project. The bars on the Tracking Gantt vary in appearance slightly from the taskbars on the standard Gantt Chart view; the Tracking Gantt bars indicate progress on tasks in the project. At the top of the Tracking Gantt, you see the summary task for the project, and below it, you see a black-and-white hatched bar. That bar represents progress on the summary task. The noncritical tasks appear in blue, and critical tasks appear in red.

On all tasks that aren't summary tasks, you see two bars: The top bar represents expected duration; the bottom bar represents baseline duration.

The percentage indicator at the edge of a task reflects the percentage complete for that task. The top bars of completed tasks, such as the Dig the Hole task, are solid in color, whereas the top bars of incomplete tasks, such as the Build the Deck task, are patterned and appear lighter in color. The bars of partially completed tasks, such as the Pour the Pool task, are solid on the left and patterned on the right; the solid part represents the completed part of the task whereas the patterned part represents the incomplete part of the task.

FIGURE 11.9

Various taskbar styles and color codes display the project's progress and variances.

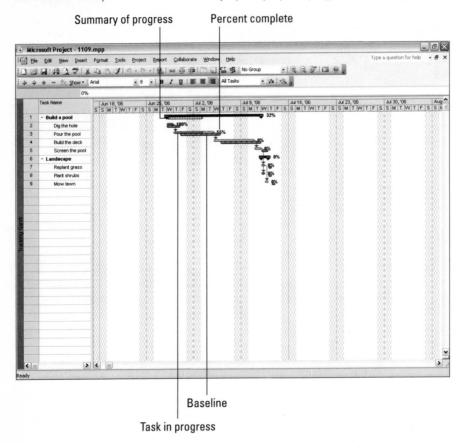

Summary of progress   Percent complete

Baseline

Task in progress

You also can tell at a glance whether a task completed earlier or later than estimated. Look at the Dig the Hole task: The top bar (actual duration) is shorter than the bottom bar (baseline duration).

The Task Variance table

As you change the table displayed in the Tracking Gantt view, you see different information about your progress in the project. The Variance table, for example, highlights the variance in task timing between the baselines and actuals. To display this table, shown in Figure 11.10, right-click the Select All button in the upper-left corner of the table where the row containing column headings and the task number column meet. Choose Variance from the list of tables that appears.

FIGURE 11.10

If you're behind schedule, you can easily see the awful truth in the Variance table.

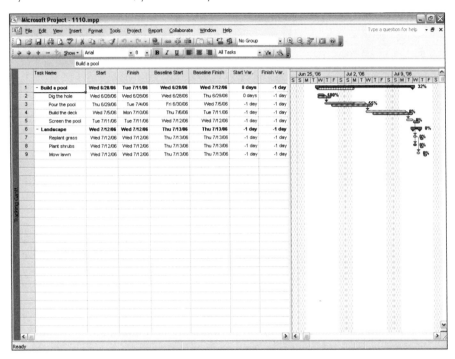

You can easily compare the Baseline Start and Baseline Finish and the actual Start and Finish columns that show actual data for tasks on which you have tracked progress as well as baseline data for tasks with no progress. This table also contains fields to show you the Start Variance (how many days late or early the task started) and the Finish Variance (how many days late or early the task ended).

The Task Cost table

The Task Cost table is most useful for pointing out variations in money spent on the project. Figure 11.11 shows a Task Cost table for a project in progress, with some costs incurred and others yet to be expended. At this point, the Pour the Pool task is exceeding its projected cost by $1,000. Project takes the following factors into account when calculating cost variations:

- Actual resource time worked

- The estimate of days of resource time still to be expended to complete the task

- Actual costs (such as fees and permits) that have been tracked on the task

FIGURE 11.11

The Task Cost table shows where you've spent too much and where you have a lot more money to spend.

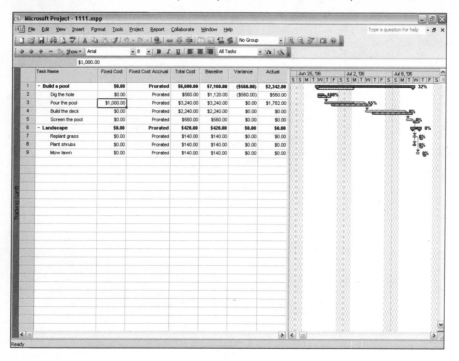

Compared to a baseline estimate of $2,240.00, the Pour the Pool task is over budget.

The Task Work table

The Work table of the Tracking Gantt view, shown in Figure 11.12, focuses on the number of work hours put in by resources that are working on tasks. For example, the Baseline work for the Pour the Pool task was 64 hours. However, the task is only partially complete and has taken 94 hours. Therefore, the Variance field (the difference between the baseline hours of work and the actual hours spent) shows a loss of 30 hours. On the other hand, the Baseline estimate for the Dig the Hole task was 32 hours, and the task was completed in 14 hours. The Variance column shows a saving of 18 hours; the negative value indicates that fewer hours were used than were estimated in the baseline.

You'll see many of these tables and more tracking views as you work through the next few chapters. At this point, you should have a good idea of the types of information that you can get by tracking progress on your project.

FIGURE 11.12

To determine whether a task is taking much more effort than you estimated, check the Task Work table.

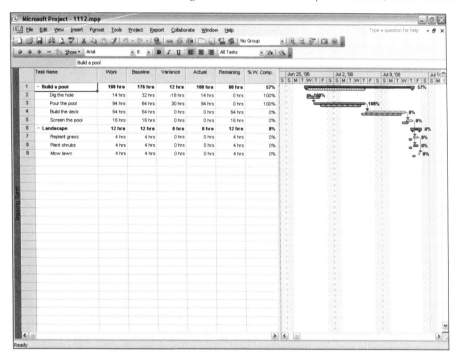

Understanding Tracking Strategies

As you use Microsoft Project on real projects, your tracking skills will improve. However, if you follow certain basic principles of tracking from the start, you can save yourself a lot of aggravation in your first few projects.

Tackling the work of tracking

First, update your project schedule frequently and at regular intervals. Many people see tracking as a monumental task: All the details of each task's progress and duration, as well as all the resources and costs that are associated with each task, must be entered one by one. You have to gather that data through resource timecards, reports from other project participants, and vendor invoices. You must type in all the information that you gather. I won't kid you: Tracking can be hard work. However, the more often you track, the less the tracking data will pile up and the less likely it is to overwhelm you.

Help yourself with the tracking task by assigning pieces of the updating to various people in your project. If a particular resource is in charge of one phase of the project, have him or her track the activity on just that phase. You can use various methods of compiling those smaller schedules into a master schedule.

CROSS-REF   Part V of this book provides ideas for compiling several schedules and managing schedules with workgroups.

If you have a resource available, such as an administrative assistant who can handle the tracking details, all the better. Make sure that you provide this assistant with appropriate training (and a copy of this book) so that he or she understands the tracking process well enough to be accurate and productive. However, this resource probably does not need to be a Project expert to take on some of the work.

TIP   To help you remember to track, enter tracking as a recurring task, occurring once every week or two, within your project file. And don't forget to include required meetings (such as progress meetings and performance reviews) in your schedule.

Keeping track of tracking

Using task notes to record progress and changes can be another good strategy for effective tracking. If an important change occurs that doesn't merit changing your baseline, use the task notes to record it. When you reach the end of the project, these notes help you to document and justify everything from missed deadlines to cost overruns.

TIP   Try to set some standards for tracking in your organization. For example, how do you determine when a task is complete? How do you measure costs, and what is the source of information on resource time spent on a task? Project becomes a much more effective management tool if each project manager uses identical methods of gauging progress and expenditures, just as your company's accounting department uses standards in tracking costs.

Setting multiple baselines is useful, but how do you decide when to save each iteration? You may want to consider setting a different baseline for each major milestone in your project. Even long projects usually have only four or five significant milestones, and they are likely to occur after you have accomplished a sizeable chunk of work.

Summary

This chapter explored some of the fundamental concepts of tracking activity on a project. You became familiar with the following:

- How to set, modify, and clear baselines
- How to view your baseline estimates against actual progress

Chapter 12 covers the mechanics of tracking, recording the actuals, and streamlining the entry of this data.

Chapter 12

Recording Actuals

Actuals represent what has, in fact, occurred during your project. In Microsoft Project, you can record actual information about the cost of a task and about the time that was spent completing the task. By recording actual information, you accomplish the following things:

- You let Project automatically reschedule the remainder of your project.

- You provide management with a way to measure how well your project is going.

- You provide yourself with valuable information on your estimating skills — information that you can apply to the remainder of the current project and to your next project.

Organizing the Updating Process

Before you launch into the mechanics of updating a project, you should take a moment to examine the updating process. Updating a project can become complicated, particularly for large projects with many resources assigned to them. You need to establish efficient manual procedures for collecting information in a timely fashion, and then you need to determine the best ways to enter that information into Project.

Individuals working on tasks should answer the following questions regularly:

- Is the task on schedule?

- How much is done?

- Is a revised estimate available on the duration of the task?

- Is a revised estimate available on the work that is required to complete the task?

> **TIP** If your organization has forms and processes in place to capture actuals and status information, use those forms and processes as much as possible. Although the organization's forms and processes may not currently capture project information, sometimes it is easier to ask for a little more information using current forms than it is to create new forms and processes.

You may want to create a form for participants to use for their regular reports. Their reports should provide the information that you need to update your project plan in Project. You may be able to use one of the reports in Project (or customize one of Project's reports) to provide the necessary information.

> **CROSS-REF** If you use Project Server, you can take advantage of electronic tracking and reporting capabilities. See Chapters 19 and 20 for more information.

You also should decide how often you need to receive the collection forms. If you request the reports too frequently, your staff may spend more time reporting than working. On the other hand, if you don't receive the reports often enough, you won't be able to identify a trouble spot early enough to resolve it before it becomes a major crisis. As the manager, you must decide on the correct frequency for collecting actual information for your project.

> **TIP** You can use the timephased fields in Project to track actual work and costs on a daily or weekly basis. Read more about timephased cost tracking in the section "Tracking work or costs regularly," later in this chapter.

When you receive the reports, you should evaluate them to identify unfinished tasks for which you need to adjust the planned duration, work, and costs. You'll find that these adjustments are easiest to make if you make them before you record a task's actual dates or percentage of completion.

Also, remember that recording actual information enables you to compare estimates to actuals; this comparison often proves to be quite valuable. To make this comparison, make sure that you set a baseline for your project.

> **CROSS-REF** See Chapter 11 for more information on setting baselines.

Understanding Calculation Options

You need to understand the calculation options that you can set in Project; they affect the "bottom line" of both the project's cost and schedule. You can review and change calculation options on the Calculation tab of the Options dialog box. Choose Tools ➪ Options to display the Options dialog box and then click the Calculation tab (see Figure 12.1). In the paragraphs that follow, I describe the various options that you see in this figure.

FIGURE 12.1

Use this dialog box to set the options that Project will use to calculate your project's schedule and cost.

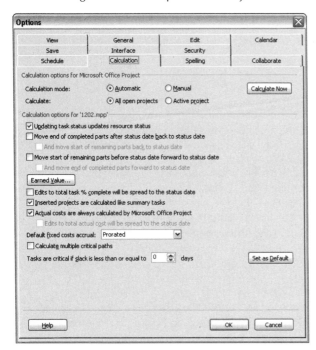

Calculation Mode and Calculate options: You can control when Project calculates changes that you make to the project; if you choose Automatic, Project updates your project as you make changes. If you choose Manual, you must reopen the Options dialog box and you can click the Calculate Now button to update your project. You also can choose to apply the calculation mode to all open projects or only to the active project. Automatic calculation is the default, but if your project is very large, calculating can take quite a while; under these circumstances, you may want to switch to manual calculation to save time. When your project is set to manual calculation and you make a change that requires recalculation, you see `Calculate` in the status bar — a reminder to calculate the project when you finish making changes.

Updating Task Status Updates Resource Status check box: Select this box to have Project update resource status to correspond with any updated task status. (This option works in reverse, too. If you update a resource's status, Project also updates task status accordingly.) Suppose, for example, that you update the percentage of completion for a task. When you select this box, Project also updates the % Complete field for the resource and the assignment.

 **NOTE** You can set calculation options that make Project change task start dates and adjust remaining portions of tasks when tasks begin early or late.

Adjusting for late or early starts: By default, when tasks begin late or early, Project doesn't change the task start dates or adjust the remaining portions of tasks. The following four check boxes were introduced in Project 2003 and enable you to change this default behavior so that Project updates the tasks in relation to the Status Date:

- Move End of Completed Parts after Status Date Back to Status Date
- And Move Start of Remaining Parts Back to Status Date
- Move Start of Remaining Parts before Status Date Forward to Status Date
- And Move End of Completed Parts Forward to Status Date

 You can find the project's status date in the Project Information dialog box (choose Project ⇨ Project Information). If the status date isn't set, Project uses the current date.

The check boxes work in pairs — that is, the first two check boxes work together and the second two check boxes work together. To better understand Project's behavior and the first pair of check boxes, suppose that the Status Date is December 9 and you have a task with a Start Date of December 14 and a duration of four days. Furthermore, suppose that the task actually starts on December 7. If you select the first check box, Project moves the task start date to 12/7, sets the percent complete to 50%, and schedules the start of the remaining work for 12/16 — thus creating a split task. If you also select the second check box, Project makes the changes that I just described *and* moves the start of the remaining work to 12/9.

Now consider the second pair of check boxes. Again, suppose that the Status Date is December 9 and you have a task with a Start Date of December 1 and a duration of four days. Furthermore, suppose that the task actually starts on December 7. If you select the third check box, Project leaves the task start date at 12/1, sets the percent complete to 50%, and schedules the start of the remaining work for 12/9 — again creating a split task. If you also select the fourth check box, Project makes the changes that I just described but also moves the task's actual start date to 12/7.

Note that these options don't apply when you record actual information on Summary tasks. These options apply only when you make total actual value edits, including task total actual work, task actual duration, total percent complete, and percent work complete. The settings of these check boxes don't apply if you use timesheet information from Project Server to update your project.

- **Earned Value button:** Click this button to set earned value options for the project.

CROSS-REF See Chapter 14 for more information about earned value.

- **Edits to Total Task % Complete Will Be Spread to the Status Date check box:** By default, this box is not selected, which makes Project distribute changes to the task percentage of completion to the end of the actual duration of the task. If you select this check box, Project instead distributes the changes evenly across the schedule to the project status date.
- **Inserted Projects Are Calculated Like Summary Tasks check box:** When this box is selected (as it is by default), Project treats inserted projects like summary tasks when calculating the project schedule, instead of treating them like a separate project.

CROSS-REF See Chapter 15 for more information about inserting projects.

■ **Actual Costs Are Always Calculated by Microsoft Office Project check box.** When you select this check box, Project calculates actual costs. You can't enter actual costs until a task is 100% complete; Project will overwrite any costs that you enter prior to 100% completion as it recalculates costs. You also can't import actual cost values.

■ **Default Fixed Costs Accrual list box:** Use this list box to choose a method for Project to accrue fixed costs for new tasks. You can have Project accrue fixed costs at the start of a task or at the end of a task, or you can prorate the costs throughout the duration of the task.

■ **Calculate Multiple Critical Paths check box:** When you select this check box, Project calculates and displays separate critical paths in the project — and sets the late finish date for tasks without successors or constraints to their early finish date. By changing the finish dates of these tasks, Project makes these tasks critical. When you deselect this box, Project sets the late finish date for these tasks to the project finish date, which leaves these tasks off the critical path.

■ **Tasks Are Critical If Slack Is Less Than or Equal to *x* Days list box:** By default, Project sets this value to 0; only tasks with no slack appear on the critical path. You can force tasks in your project onto the critical path by increasing this value.

■ **Set as Default button:** The calculation options listed at the top of the box apply to all projects. Although all the other options shown in Figure 12.1 apply only to the project you are currently viewing, you can make them apply to all projects by clicking the Set as Default button.

Throughout the rest of this chapter, I use the default settings in Project to demonstrate the effects of updating a project.

Updating Tasks to Reflect Actual Information

You can record actual information for a project by filling in the following fields for each task that tracks the progress of your project:

■ Actual start date

■ Actual finish date

■ Actual duration

■ Remaining duration

■ Percentage complete

NOTE The fields mentioned above are one possible set of fields that you can use to record actual information; there are other alternatives. For example, some people focus on updating only Actual Work and Remaining Work; in this case, Project updates the fields listed above.

In some cases, when you enter information into one of these fields, Project calculates the values for the other fields. For example, if you enter a percentage complete for a task, Project calculates and supplies a start date, an actual duration, a remaining duration, and an actual work value.

Setting actual start and finish dates

The Gantt Chart view displays projected start and finish dates for tasks. In this section, you find out how to enter and view actual start and finish dates (and compare current, baseline, and actual dates) in the Task Details view, as shown in Figure 12.2.

Starting from the Gantt Chart view, follow these steps to set up your screen:

1. Choose Window ➪ Split to display the Task Form view.
2. Click the bottom pane.
3. Choose View ➪ More Views to open the More Views dialog box.
4. Select Task Details Form and click Apply.
5. In the top pane, select the task for which you want to record actuals.

FIGURE 12.2

Use the Task Details form to enter actual information.

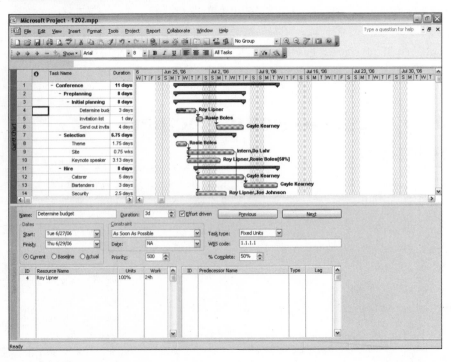

6. In the Dates section of the bottom pane, select the Actual option button to identify the type of dates that you want to enter.

   The three option buttons (Current, Baseline, and Actual) refer only to the dates that you can view and set. In other words, you don't see baseline assignments at the bottom of the view if you click Baseline.

7. Record either a Start or a Finish date and click OK.

Project initially sets the Actual Start Date and Actual Finish Date fields to NA to indicate that you have not yet entered a date. When you update your project to provide actual start and finish dates, Project changes the projected start and finish dates to the actual dates that you enter. When you enter an actual start date, Project changes only one other field — the projected start date. However, when you enter an actual finish date, Project changes several other fields: the Percent Complete field, the Actual Duration field, the Remaining Duration field, the Actual Work field, and the Actual Cost field. If you didn't set an actual start date, Project also changes that field.

Recording actual durations

The actual duration of a task is the amount of time that was needed to complete the task. To record an actual duration, you can use the Update Tasks dialog box. Choose Tools ➪ Tracking ➪ Update Tasks or click the Update Tasks button on the Tracking toolbar to display the Update Tasks dialog box (see Figure 12.3).

FIGURE 12.3

Use the Update Tasks dialog box to set the actual duration for a task by filling in the Actual Dur field.

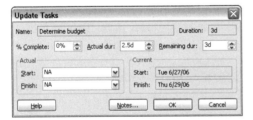

 You can display the Tracking toolbar by choosing View ➪ Toolbars ➪ Tracking.

When you set an actual duration that is less than or equal to the planned duration, Project assumes that the task is progressing on schedule. Therefore, when you click OK, Project sets the actual start date to the planned start date — unless you previously set the actual start date. In that case, Project leaves the actual start date alone. In either case, Project calculates the percentage complete and the remaining duration for the task.

NOTE   To see the updated remaining duration, reopen the Update Tasks dialog box.

If you set an actual duration that is greater than the planned duration, Project assumes that the task is finished but that it took longer than expected to complete. Project adjusts the planned duration to match the actual duration and changes the Percent Complete field to 100% and the Remaining Duration field to 0%.

You can use the Calculation tab in the Options dialog box (choose Tools ➪ Options) to set Project to update the status of resources when you update a task's status. If you set this option and then supply an actual duration, Project also updates the work and cost figures for the resources.

CROSS-REF   You find out more about this option in the section "Overriding resource cost valuations," later in this chapter.

NOTE   Don't change the actual duration of a task if you use effort-driven scheduling. Instead, change the number of resource units that are assigned or the amount of the resource assignment. Remember that the duration of effort-driven tasks is affected by resource assignments.

Setting the Percent Complete value

Before I dive into a discussion of the Remaining Duration field, take a look at the Tracking table, which contains, in table form, all the fields into which you can enter actual information. In the two preceding sections, you saw that you can use the Task Form Details view and the Update Tasks dialog box to record and view actual information. The Task Form Details view provides a limited way to update tasks. Although the Update Tasks dialog box provides a complete way to enter actual information, I find that it's easiest to enter all actual information into Project by using the Tracking Table view (see Figure 12.4).

To display the Tracking Table view, start in the Gantt Chart view and follow these steps:

1. Click the top pane of the Gantt Chart.
2. Choose Window ➪ Remove Split to display the standard Gantt Chart.
3. Right-click the Select All button and choose Tracking from the menu that appears. Project displays the Tracking Table view in the left portion of the Gantt Chart view.

TIP   To see all the columns that are available on the Tracking Table view, narrow the chart portion of the window.

CROSS-REF   For information on creating custom fields, see Chapter 22.

   On the CD, look for the Status Date Field and Current Date Field Example.mpp file.

FIGURE 12.4

The Tracking Table view helps you view and enter actual values for tasks.

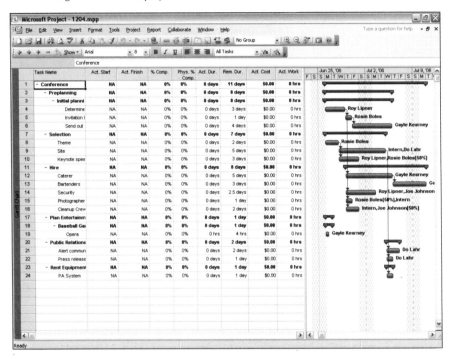

You can establish the progress of work performed on a task by assigning a Percent Complete value to the task. Any value less than 100 indicates that the task is not complete. You can set Percent Complete value from the Task Details form, from the Update Tasks dialog box, or from the Tracking table. Or, you can select the task from any task view and use the percentage buttons on the Tracking toolbar (see Figure 12.5). Right-click any toolbar and choose Tracking to display the Tracking toolbar.

FIGURE 12.5

Use these buttons to set a task's actual progress at 0%, 25%, 50%, 75%, or 100% complete.

Percentage buttons

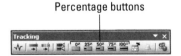

Customize the Tracking Table

Project calculates some of the fields that store actuals when you enter information in other fields that store actuals. For this reason, I recommend that you create your own version of the Tracking table that displays the fields into which you will enter information in contiguous columns. Placing the fields together on a customized Tracking table will make your data entry much easier — and provide an easy way for someone other than you to enter the data. (See Chapter 6 for details on customizing a table.) You might want to consider including the project's status date and the current date on your Tracking table to help you easily find any tasks not completed prior to the status date, identifying work that needs to be rescheduled. To include this information, you need to create custom fields. This book's CD contains a file called Status Date Field and Current Date Field Example.mpp. In this file, you'll find a sample Tracking table that also contains the Status Date and Current Date fields and the formulas you need to create these fields. To view and use the formulas, follow these steps:

1. On each field's column heading, right-click and choose Customize Fields. Project displays the Customize Fields dialog box with the highlighted field selected.

2. Click the Formula button to view the formula for that field.

3. In your own project file, create custom fields using these formulas.

If you enter a Percent Complete value, Project assigns an Actual Start Date (unless you had entered one previously). Project also calculates the Actual Duration and Remaining Duration values. If you set your options to update resources when you update tasks, Project also calculates the Actual Cost and Actual Work values. If you enter 100 in the Percent Complete column, Project assigns the planned finish date to the Actual Finish Date column. If this value is not correct, don't enter a Percent Complete value; instead, enter an Actual Finish Date.

Setting work completed

Sometimes, you must schedule tasks based on the availability of certain resources. In these cases, tracking progress on a task is easiest if you update the work completed. Updating this value also updates the work that each resource is performing.

In the same way that Project calculates duration information when you fill in a duration field, Project updates the work remaining by subtracting the work performed from the total work scheduled.

Use the Tracking Table view to enter information into the Act. Work (Actual Work) column, but start in the Task Usage view so that you can enter actual work performed for specific resources. Choose View ➪ Task Usage, right-click the Select All button, and choose Tracking from the short-cut menu that appears. Then, drag the divider bar almost completely to the right edge of the screen to reveal the Act. Work column (see Figure 12.6).

NOTE If you are scheduling tasks based on the availability of resources in general instead of the availability of specific resources, you can still use this view to record actual work. However, you need to enter the value on the same row as the task, rather than on the individual rows for the resources. Project divides the actual and remaining work among the resources.

Setting remaining durations

The Rem. Dur. (Remaining Duration) column shows how much more time you need to complete a task. If you change only the value in the Remaining Duration column so that it is higher or lower than the existing figure, Project assumes that you are changing the planned duration of the task instead of tracking actual progress for the task. In this case, Project adjusts the schedule based on the new planned duration.

But if you enter a value into the Rem. Dur. (Remaining Duration) column after entering an Act. Dur. value, Project assumes that the work for the task will be completed based on the remaining duration value. Therefore, Project sets the % Comp. (Percent Complete) value based on a combination of the remaining duration value that you supplied and the original planned duration.

FIGURE 12.6

The Tracking Table view with resources displayed.

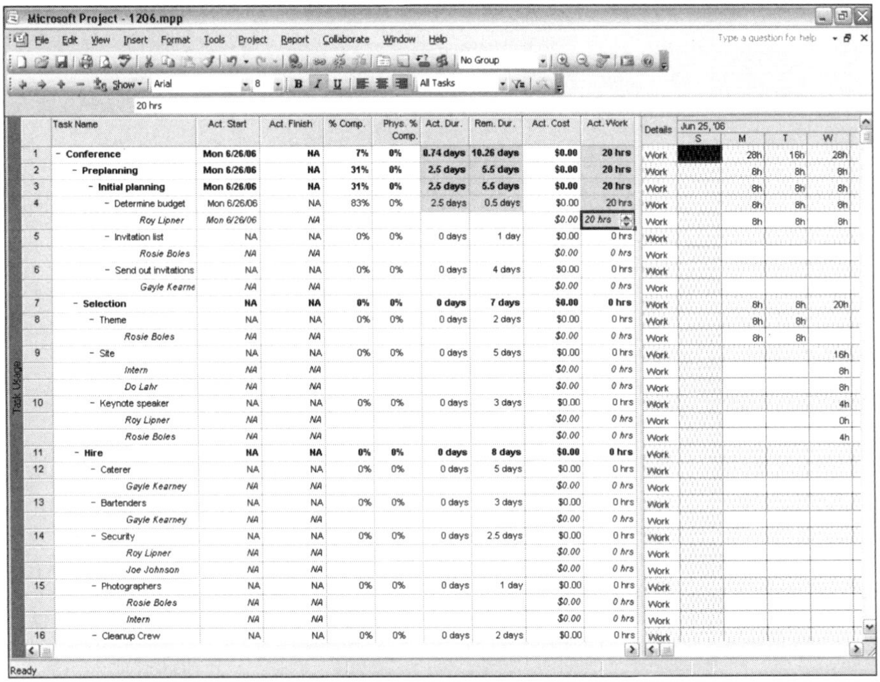

In Figure 12.7, the planned duration for Task 4 was originally three days. I recorded an actual duration value of 1½ days, and Project updated the % Comp. field to reflect that the task was half complete. I then recorded a remaining duration of 1 day, and Project adjusted the % Comp. field from 50% complete to 64% complete; recording the remaining duration value adjusted the project schedule.

Similarly, if you enter information into the % Comp. field and the Rem. Dur. field, Project adjusts the Act. Dur. field using a combination of the remaining duration value and the original planned duration.

If you have entered actual duration information or percent complete information, entering 0 in the Rem. Dur. (Remaining Duration) column is the same as entering 100% in the Percent Complete column; that is, Project assigns the planned finish date to the Actual Finish Date column. If this value is not correct, change the Actual Finish Date.

FIGURE 12.7

When you set the remaining duration value after setting an actual duration, Project updates the task's percent complete field.

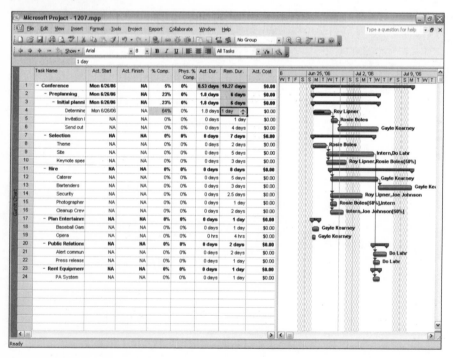

Using Actuals and Costs

Except for fixed-cost tasks, Project uses the cost of the resources that are assigned to the task over the duration of the task to calculate a task's cost. Costs are accrued, and total project costs are the sum of all resource and fixed costs. Therefore, if you previously set up and assigned resources to your tasks, Project has been calculating and accruing the costs for you; all you need to do is review and analyze the costs.

Alternatively, you may have chosen not to assign resources to your tasks, or you may have changed your default options so that Project wouldn't calculate costs. How can you do that? Choose Tools ➪ Options to display the Options dialog box. On the Calculation tab, look at the Calculation options for your project (see Figure 12.8). If the Updating Task Status Updates Resource Status check box is not selected, Project has not been calculating your project's costs. Remember, however, that this check box is selected by default, as you see in the figure.

FIGURE 12.8

From the Calculation tab of the Options dialog box, you can tell whether Project has been calculating your project's costs.

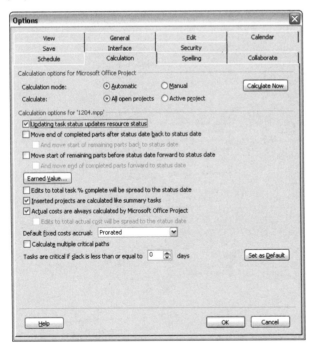

If you did not assign resources or you changed the defaults, Project can't calculate the cost of your project unless you provide additional information after the task is completed. You can review and update your project's costs from one of two cost tables: the Cost table for tasks or the Cost table for resources. You can also override the costs that Project assigns.

Using the Cost table for tasks

The Cost table for tasks, shown in Figure 12.9, displays cost information based on each task in your project. This table shows you the baseline cost (the planned cost), the actual cost, the variance between planned and actual costs, and the remaining cost of the task.

If you assign a fixed cost to a task in this table, Project adds the fixed cost to the calculated cost for the task. To display this table, start in the Gantt Chart view. Then right-click the Select All button to display the shortcut menu of tables and choose Cost. You may also need to slide the chart pane all the way to the right to see all the fields on the Cost table for tasks.

The Cost table for tasks is most useful if you saved a baseline view of your project, because it enables you to compare baseline costs with actual costs.

FIGURE 12.9

The Cost table for tasks.

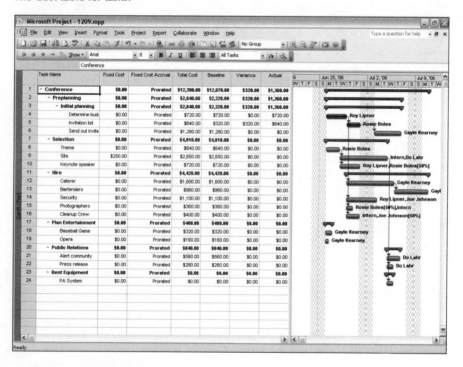

Using the Cost table for resources

The Cost table for resources is similar to the Cost table for tasks, with the breakdown of costs being displayed by resource rather than by task, as shown in Figure 12.10.

To display this table, begin with a resource view such as the Resource Sheet view. Then, right-click the Select All button and choose Cost from the shortcut menu that appears.

As is the Cost table for tasks, the Cost table for resources is useful if you saved a baseline view of your project, because it enables you to compare baseline costs with actual costs.

Overriding resource cost valuations

Project's default settings automatically update costs as you record progress on a task. Project uses the accrual method that you selected for the resource when you created the resource.

CROSS-REF For more information about setting a resource's accrual method, see Chapter 5.

FIGURE 12.10

The Cost table for resources.

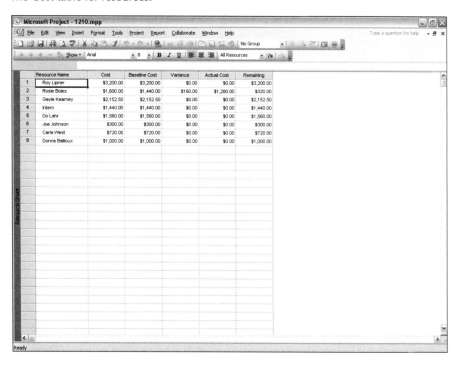

	Resource Name	Cost	Baseline Cost	Variance	Actual Cost	Remaining
1	Roy Lipner	$3,200.00	$3,200.00	$0.00	$0.00	$3,200.00
2	Rosie Boles	$1,600.00	$1,440.00	$160.00	$1,280.00	$320.00
3	Gayle Kearney	$2,152.50	$2,152.50	$0.00	$0.00	$2,152.50
4	Intern	$1,440.00	$1,440.00	$0.00	$0.00	$1,440.00
5	Do Lahr	$1,560.00	$1,560.00	$0.00	$0.00	$1,560.00
6	Joe Johnson	$300.00	$300.00	$0.00	$0.00	$300.00
7	Carla West	$720.00	$720.00	$0.00	$0.00	$720.00
8	Donna Ballioux	$1,000.00	$1,000.00	$0.00	$0.00	$1,000.00

Alternatively, you can enter the actual costs for a resource assignment, or you can track actual costs separately from the actual work on a task. To do so, after the task is completed, you must enter costs manually to override Project's calculated costs. Before you can override the costs that Project calculated, however, you must turn off one of the default options. Follow these steps to adjust Project's default settings so that you can override calculated costs:

1. Choose Tools ➪ Options to display the Options dialog box.

2. Click the Calculation tab.

3. Remove the check from the Actual Costs Are Always Calculated by Microsoft Office Project check box (see Figure 12.11).

NOTE The Edits to Total Actual Cost Will Be Spread to the Status Date check box becomes available. Check this box if you want Project to distribute the edits that you intend to make through the Status Date. If you don't check the box, Project distributes the edits to the end of the actual duration of the task.

FIGURE 12.11

Revise the default settings to override Project's calculated costs.

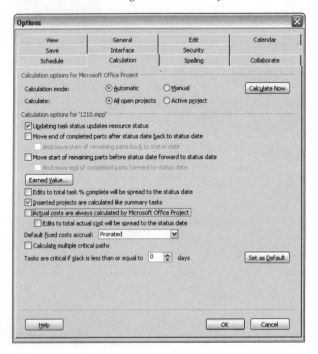

4. Click OK.

5. Choose View ⇨ Task Usage.

6. Right-click the Select All button to display the table shortcut menu and choose Tracking. Project displays the Tracking Table view (see Figure 12.12).

7. Drag the divider bar to the right so that you can see all the columns.

8. Select the task or resource to which you want to assign a cost.

9. Enter the cost in the Act. Cost (Actual Cost) column.

TIP If you change your mind and want Project to calculate costs as it originally did, repeat Steps 1 and 2 to display the Calculations tab of the Options box and select the Actual Costs Are Always Calculated by Microsoft Office Project check box to restore the default calculation method. Project warns you that it will overwrite any manually entered costs when you click OK.

FIGURE 12.12

The Tracking Table view with the Act. Cost (Actual Cost) column visible.

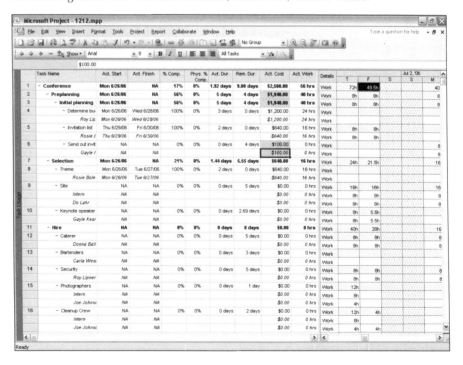

Techniques and Tips for Updating

Project users can find ways to accelerate the updating process. For example, you can do the following:

- Use Project's timephased fields to easily update your project on a regular basis

- Update the progress of several tasks simultaneously

- Reschedule incomplete work so that it starts on the current date

NOTE You can speed the data entry process if you create a custom Tracking table that groups the fields into which you enter actual information. You might want to consider including the project's status date and the current date on your tracking table to help you easily find any tasks not completed prior to the status date, identifying work that needs to be rescheduled. To include this information, you need to create custom fields.

CROSS-REF See Chapter 6 for details on creating customized tables. For information on creating custom fields, see Chapter 22.

ON the CD-ROM On the CD, you'll find the Status Date Field and Current Date Field Example.mpp file, which contains the formulas you need to create these fields. On each field's column heading, right-click and choose Customize Fields to open the Customize Fields dialog box; then, click the Formula button to view the formula for that field.

Tracking work or costs regularly

Project's timephased fields enable you to update the progress of your project on a regular basis, such as daily or weekly. To use timephased fields to record progress information for resources, start by displaying the Resource Usage view (choose View ➪ Resource Usage). Then right-click the Select All button and select Work from the shortcut menu that appears to change the table. Your screen should resemble Figure 12.13.

You'll to want to use most of the right side of the view, but on the left side of the view, you really need only the Actual Work column, which is hidden by the right side of the view. You can slide the divider bar over to the right, but then you would lose the right side of the view. Or, after sliding the divider bar, you can hide all the columns between the Resource Name column and the Actual Work column. To redisplay them, you need to insert each of them.

FIGURE 12.13

Preparing to use timephased fields.

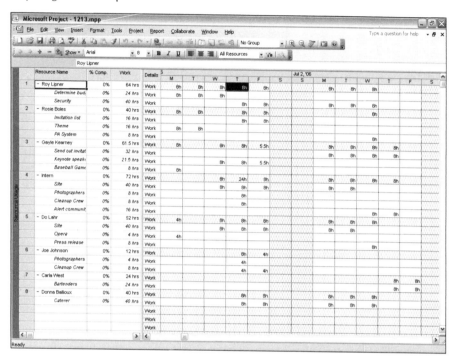

To set up the left side of the view so that you can see the Actual Work column, insert that column between the Resource Name column and the % Comp. (Percent Complete) column. To insert the column, follow these steps:

1. Click the title of the Percent Complete column to select the entire column.
2. Choose Insert ⇨ Column to open the Column Definition dialog box (see Figure 12.14).

FIGURE 12.14

Add the Actual Work column from the Column Definition dialog box.

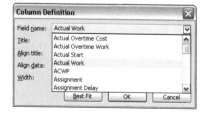

3. Open the Field Name drop-down list and select Actual Work.

4. Click OK.

Project inserts the Actual Work column to the left of the % Comp. column and to the right of the Resource Name column.

Next, you should decide how often you want to update your project. To update daily, you don't need to make any changes to the timescale on the right side of the window. But if you want to update weekly (or with some other frequency), you need to change the timescale. To change the timescale, choose Format ⇨ Timescale. Project opens the Timescale dialog box (see Figure 12.15). This example doesn't require any timescale changes, but if you wanted to change the timescale to weekly (for example), choose the middle tier, open the Units list box, and select Weeks. Then hide the other tiers using the One tier (Middle) option in the Show list box in the Timescale options section.

FIGURE 12.15

Use the Timescale dialog box to change the increments that appear on the right side of the Resource Usage view.

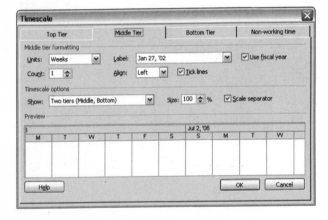

When you add a timephased field for Actual Work, you can see the results as you update the schedule. Choose Format ⇨ Details ⇨ Actual Work. Project adds a row for every task on the right side of the view. To enter hours worked for a particular day, click the letter of the column representing that day to select the entire day (see Figure 12.16). Then enter the hours for the correct resource and task in the Actual Work column that you added on the left side of the view.

NOTE   Remember, however, that you can't add costs to override Project's automatically calculated costs unless you open the Options dialog box (choose Tools ⇨ Options), select the Calculation tab, and remove the check from the Actual Costs Are Always Calculated by Microsoft Office Project check box.

FIGURE 12.16

Add actual work information for a specific day.

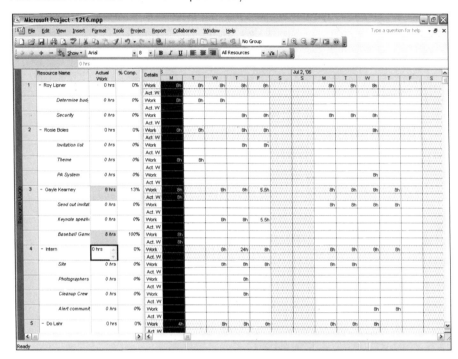

This entire process also works if you are updating costs on a daily basis, with the following minor changes:

- Begin in the Task Usage view instead of the Resource Usage view.
- Add the Tracking table instead of the Work table.

TIP To hide the Actual Work column that you added to the left side of the view, select the entire column and then choose Edit ➪ Hide Column. The left side of the view returns to its default appearance. To hide the Actual Work row that you added to the right side of the view, choose Format ➪ Details ➪ Actual Work again and remove the check mark from Actual Work.

Accelerating the updating process

If you have several tasks that are on schedule or were completed on schedule, you can update these tasks simultaneously by following these steps:

1. Select the Gantt Chart view.

If you want to update the entire project, don't select any tasks.

2. In the Task Name column, select the tasks that you want to update. For example, Figure 12.17 shows three tasks selected for updating.

FIGURE 12.17

Selecting tasks to update.

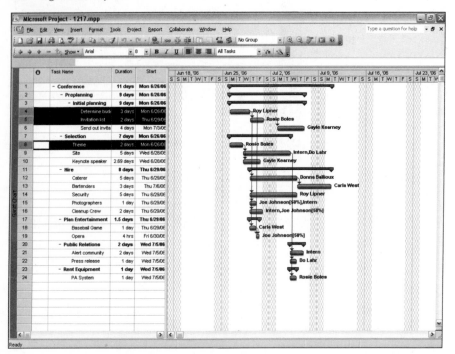

You can select tasks by using the same techniques that you use in Windows Explorer. To select two or more contiguous tasks, click the first task, hold down Shift, and click the last task. To select two or more noncontiguous tasks, hold down Ctrl as you click each task that you want to select.

3. Choose Tools ➪ Tracking ➪ Update Project to display the Update Project dialog box (see Figure 12.18).

FIGURE 12.18

Use the Update Project dialog box to update your project.

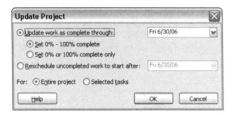

4. Make sure that the correct date appears in the list box next to the Update Work As Complete Through option button.

5. Select one of the following:

   ■ **Set 0% – 100% Complete:** This option tells Project to calculate the Percent Complete for each task.

   ■ **Set 0% or 100% Complete Only:** Select this option to have Project mark completed tasks with 100% and leave incomplete tasks at 0%.

6. Specify whether to update the entire project or selected tasks by selecting the appropriate option.

7. Click OK.

 When you select the Entire project option in Step 6 and update your project, Project sets the project status date to the date that you selected in Step 4.

Letting Project reschedule uncompleted work

If you updated your project and you had partially completed tasks, you can guarantee that no remaining work is scheduled for dates that have already passed. You can make sure that all remaining work is scheduled for future dates by rescheduling the work to start on the current date.

 In Project 2000 and earlier, if you rescheduled work by using the technique that I describe in this section, Project would remove task constraints that you applied. For example, suppose that you rescheduled the work of a task that had a Must Finish On constraint, and rescheduling moved the finish date beyond the constraint date. Project 2000 and earlier did not honor the constraint date; instead, these versions changed the constraint to As Soon As Possible. To preserve a task's constraints, you had to reschedule the remaining work manually.

Starting in Project 2002, Project does not remove constraints and reschedule tasks without progress. However, be aware that this behavior may leave your project in an infeasible situation. Project displays a message if this situation occurs, and you can manually make changes as needed.

Follow these steps to tell Project to reschedule remaining work for future dates:

1. Select the Gantt Chart view.

2. Go to the Task Name column and select the tasks that you want to update. See the previous section for techniques that you can use to select tasks.

3. Choose Tools ➪ Tracking ➪ Update Project to open the Update Project dialog box (see Figure 12.19).

FIGURE 12.19

Use this dialog box to reschedule incomplete work to start today.

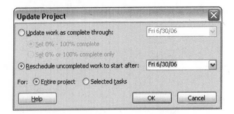

4. Select the Reschedule Uncompleted Work To Start After option button and choose the date from which you want to reschedule all unfinished work.

> **NOTE** Project 2000 introduced the ability to set a date from which you wanted to reschedule uncompleted work. However, if you rescheduled work *twice*, Project 2000 ignored all dates except the first rescheduling date that you supplied. Starting in Project 2002, Project reschedules selected tasks for your project each time that you change the date.

5. Specify whether to update the entire project or selected tasks by selecting the appropriate option button.

6. Click OK.

> **NOTE** When you reschedule a partially completed task by using the technique just described, Project automatically splits the task between the completed portion and the remaining portion. Therefore, the Gantt Chart may display a split task that has a gap between its two parts because the completed portion may have finished sometime before the remaining portion is scheduled to start.

Reviewing Progress

When you start recording actuals, you'll want to review the progress of your project — and Project can help you.

Using the Tracking Gantt view

The Tracking Gantt view, shown in Figure 12.20, uses the Entry table and probably provides the most effective picture of your project's progress. The bottom bar on the chart portion of the view (black hatching on your screen) represents the baseline dates for each task. The top bar spans either the scheduled start and finish dates or (if a task has been completed) the actual start and finish dates for each task.

 **TIP** If a task is finished, a check mark appears in the Indicator column on the left side of the view next to the task.

Project formats the task bar to indicate the task's status as follows:

- The top bar of tasks not on the critical path appears blue; the top bar of tasks on the critical path appears red. The percent complete appears on the right side of all tasks.

- For partially completed tasks not on the critical path, if you look closely you can see that the completed portion appears darker blue than the uncompleted portion.

- For partially completed tasks on the critical path, the completed portion appears darker red than the uncompleted portion and the distinction between the completed and uncompleted portion is easy to see.

FIGURE 12.20

The Tracking Gantt view helps you understand the progress of your project.

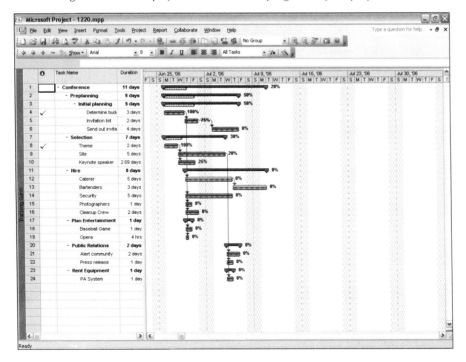

Using the Work table for tasks

The Work table for tasks, shown in Figure 12.21, shows the total time that is required from all resources to complete the task. Work differs from task duration because:

- Work measures how many hours of effort are needed to complete a task.
- Task duration measures the amount of time (number of days) that is allotted to the task.

If the total work for a task is 16 hours but the task duration is only one day, you either need to add another resource (meaning that two people can complete the task in one day) or extend the task's duration.

The Work table for tasks includes baseline information so that you can compare your progress to your original estimate. For this table to be meaningful, therefore, you must have saved a baseline for your project. And as you may have guessed, you can enter information in the Work table for tasks.

You can apply the Work table for tasks to any task sheet view. In Figure 12.21, the Work table appears on the left side of the Task Usage view. Choose View ➪ Task Usage; then, right-click the Select All button and choose Work from the shortcut menu that appears.

FIGURE 12.21

The Work table for tasks.

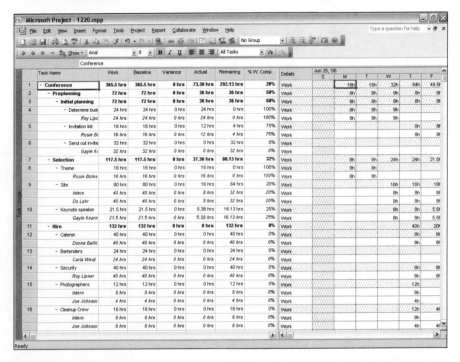

Using the Work table for resources

The Work table for resources displays work information for resources. Again, work represents the total time that is required from all resources to complete the task. The Work table for resources also includes baseline information so that you can compare your progress to your original estimate.

You can apply the Work table for resources to any resource sheet view. In Figure 12.22, for example, the Work table for resources appears on the left side of the Resource Usage view. Select the Resource Usage view from the View bar; then, right-click the Select All button and choose Work from the shortcut menu that appears.

Viewing progress lines

Project contains another tool that you can use to show the progress that you're making on your project — if you have saved a baseline of your project. If you add progress lines to the Gantt Chart of your project, as I did in Figure 12.23, Project draws a line that connects in-progress tasks. The progress line creates a graph of your project with peaks pointing to the right for work that is ahead of schedule and peaks pointing to the left for work that is behind schedule. The distance between the peaks and the line indicates the degree to which the task is ahead of or behind schedule.

The Work table for resources.

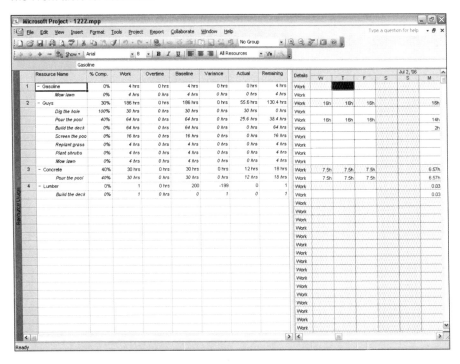

FIGURE 12.23

A Gantt Chart with a progress line added.

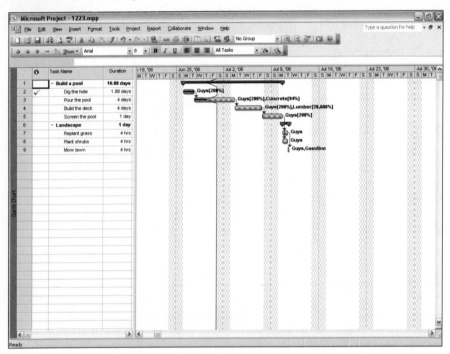

To add a progress line, follow these steps:

1. Choose View ➪ Gantt Chart.
2. Choose Tools ➪ Tracking ➪ Progress Lines to open the Progress Lines dialog box and display the Dates and Intervals tab.
3. Select the Display Selected Progress Lines check box to activate the Progress Line Dates list.
4. Click once in the Progress Line Dates list. Project displays a list box arrow.
5. Click the list box arrow, and a small calendar appears (see Figure 12.24).
6. Select a date for the progress line.
7. Select either Actual plan or Baseline plan in the Display progress lines in relation to panel.
8. Click OK.

    Project adds the progress line to your Gantt Chart, which looks like the progress line shown previously in Figure 12.23.

FIGURE 12.24

The Dates and Intervals tab of the Progress Lines dialog box.

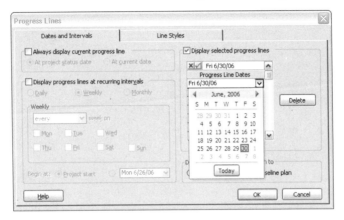

As you can imagine, a progress line on a project with a large number of tasks can begin to look messy. But if you decide that you like progress lines, you can display them at varying intervals, as shown previously in Figure 12.23. You also can add specific dates to the Progress Line Dates list on the right side of the Progress Lines dialog box to display multiple progress lines on the Gantt Chart. If you decide to display more than one progress line, you may want to use the Line Styles tab of the Progress Lines dialog box to format the lines so that you can tell them apart (for example, you can change their colors).

To stop displaying progress lines, reopen the Progress Lines dialog box and deselect any check boxes on the Dates and Intervals tab.

Summary

In this chapter, you found out how to record actual information about tasks and resources. For example, you should now be able to do the following:

- Set actual start and finish dates
- Set actual and remaining durations
- Set the percent complete for a task
- Set the work completed for a task
- Use cost tables for tasks and resources
- Review the progress of your project

Chapter 13 shows you how to report on a project's progress.

Chapter 13

Reporting on Progress

As you saw in Chapters 6 and 7, Project contains various views that help you to evaluate the progress of your project, identify areas with problems, and even resolve problems. Although you can print views, sometimes you need to present information in a format that is not available in any view. This chapter examines the use of reports for presenting your Project information.

You can create two kinds of reports using your project's data:

■ Traditional text reports, typically in row and column format. These types of reports have long been available in Project.

■ Visual reports, which present pictures of your project's data in the form of charts and diagrams. Visual reports export your project data to either Excel or Visio.

Visual reporting is new to Project 2007.

In this chapter, I present the traditional text reports first and then introduce the new visual reports.

Creating Text Reports

All text reports in Project have certain common characteristics. For example, you can print any report or you can review the report on-screen.

 NOTE Project organizes text reports into categories of reports that are related to the same subject; for example, all the cost reports fall into the Costs category.

Follow these steps to display the reports that are available in a particular category:

1. Choose Report ➪ Reports to open the Reports dialog box (see Figure 13.1).

FIGURE 13.1

Select a report category from the Reports dialog box.

2. Click the category of report that you want.

3. Click Select. Project displays the reports that are available in that category.

4. Select a report.

5. Click Select. Project displays the report on-screen in Print Preview mode (see Figure 13.2).

Use the scroll arrows on the toolbar at the top of the screen to move around the report. The Zoom button enlarges the image so that you can read the report's content on-screen. Or, if you prefer, click the portion of the report that you want to enlarge; the shape of the mouse pointer indicates that it will zoom in on the area that you click. To zoom out again, click the Full Page button or click again on the report. To display more than one page at a time, click the Multiple Pages button.

If you decide to print the report, you can review the page settings first. Click the Page Setup button to display the Page Setup dialog box, shown in Figure 13.3.

FIGURE 13.2

A report in Print Preview mode.

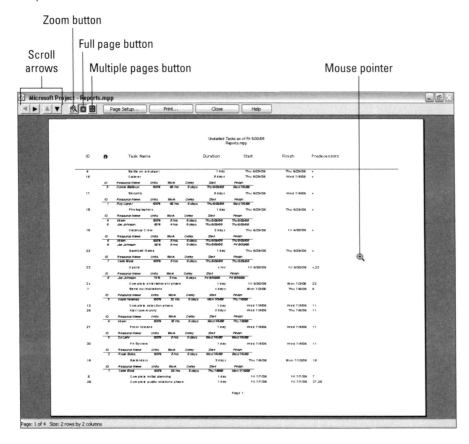

CROSS-REF Chapter 6 describes the tabs of the Page Setup dialog box.

To print a report, click the Print button. Project displays the Print dialog box (see Figure 13.4). Alternatively, you can return to Project by clicking the Close button.

FIGURE 13.3

Use the Page Setup dialog box to set orientation, scaling, margins, and — if appropriate — header and footer information.

FIGURE 13.4

In the Print dialog box, select a print range for the report.

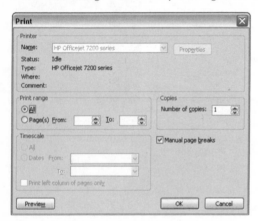

Looking at the big picture

When you select Overview in the Reports dialog box, Project displays the top-level, summary-type reports (see Figure 13.5).

NOTE You can use the Edit button to change the information that appears on the report. You can also use the Edit button to customize the report, which I discuss near the end of the discussion of text reports.

FIGURE 13.5

The reports that are available in the Overview category.

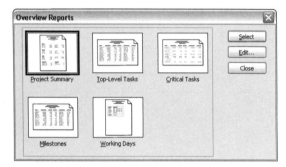

Project Summary

The Project Summary report (see Figure 13.6) shows top-level information about your project. This report presents summarized information about dates, duration, work, costs, task status, and resource status.

Top Level Tasks

The Top Level Tasks report (see Figure 13.7), shows — as of today's date — the summary tasks at the highest level in your project. You can see scheduled start and finish dates, the percentage complete for each task, the cost, and the work required to complete the task.

Critical Tasks

The Critical Tasks report (see Figure 13.8) shows the status of the tasks on the critical path of your project — those tasks that make the project late if you don't complete them on time. This report displays each task's planned duration, start and finish dates, the resources that are assigned to the task, and the predecessors and successors of the task.

FIGURE 13.6

The Project Summary report.

Reports.mpp

as of Fri 6/30/06

Dates

Start:	Mon 6/26/06	Finish:	Mon 7/10/06
Baseline Start:	Mon 6/26/06	Baseline Finish:	Mon 7/10/06
Actual Start:	Mon 6/26/06	Actual Finish:	NA
Start Variance:	0 days	Finish Variance:	0 days

Duration

Scheduled:	11 days	Remaining:	8.82 days
Baseline:	11 days	Actual:	2.18 days
Variance:	0 days	Percent Complete:	20%

Work

Scheduled:	362.5 hrs	Remaining:	289.13 hrs
Baseline:	362.5 hrs	Actual:	73.38 hrs
Variance:	0 hrs	Percent Complete:	20%

Costs

Scheduled:	$12,087.50	Remaining:	$9,129.38
Baseline:	$12,087.50	Actual:	$2,958.13
Variance:	$0.00		

Task Status

Tasks not yet started:	16
Tasks in progress:	7
Tasks completed:	2
Total Tasks:	25

Resource Status

Work Resources:	8
Overallocated Work Resources:	0
Material Resources:	0
Total Resources:	8

FIGURE 13.7

The Top Level Tasks report.

Top Level Tasks as of Fri 6/30/06
Reports

ID	Task Name	Duration	Start	Finish	% Comp.	Cost	Work
1	Conference	11 days	Mon 6/26/06	Mon 7/10/06	18%	$0.00	0 hrs
2	Preplanning	9 days	Mon 6/26/06	Thu 7/6/06	45%	$2,960.00	72 hrs
8	Selection	7 days	Mon 6/26/06	Tue 7/4/06	38%	$3,642.50	117.5 hrs
12	Hire	8 days	Thu 6/29/06	Mon 7/10/06	0%	$4,290.00	130 hrs
18	Plan Entertainment	1.5 days	Thu 6/29/06	Fri 6/30/06	0%	$315.00	11 hrs
21	Public Relations	2 days	Wed 7/5/06	Thu 7/6/06	0%	$560.00	24 hrs
24	Rent Equipment	1 day	Wed 7/5/06	Wed 7/5/06	0%	$320.00	8 hrs

Milestones

The Milestones report (see Figure 13.9) shows information about each milestone in your project. If you marked summary tasks to appear as milestones in the Task Information dialog box, summary tasks also appear on this report as milestones. For each milestone or summary task, Project displays the planned duration, start and finish dates, predecessors, and the resources that are assigned to the milestone.

FIGURE 13.8

The Critical Tasks report.

Critical Tasks as of Fri 6/30/06
1213.mpp

ID	❶	Task Name			Duration	Start	Finish	Predecessors
1		**Conference**			**11 days**	**Mon 6/26/06**	**Mon 7/10/06**	
2		**Preplanning**			**9 days**	**Mon 6/26/06**	**Thu 7/6/06**	
3		**Initial planning**			**9 days**	**Mon 6/26/06**	**Thu 7/6/06**	
4		Determine budget			3 days	Mon 6/26/06	Wed 6/28/06	
	ID	*Successor Name*	*Type*	*Lag*				
	5	*Invitation list*	*FS*	*0 days*				
	12	*Caterer*	*FS*	*0 days*				
	14	*Security*	*FS*	*0 days*				
	15	*Photographers*	*FS*	*0 days*				
	16	*Cleanup Crew*	*FS*	*0 days*				
11		**Hire**			**8 days**	**Thu 6/29/06**	**Mon 7/10/06**	
12		Caterer			5 days	Thu 6/29/06	Wed 7/5/06	4
	ID	*Successor Name*	*Type*	*Lag*				
	13	*Bartenders*	*FS*	*0 days*				
13		Bartenders			3 days	Thu 7/6/06	Mon 7/10/06	12

FIGURE 13.9

The Milestones report.

Milestones as of Fri 6/30/06
Reports

ID	❶	Task Name	Duration	Start	Finish	Predecessors
2		Preplanning	10 days	Mon 6/26/06	Fri 7/7/06	
3		Initial planning	10 days	Mon 6/26/06	Fri 7/7/06	
9		Selection	8 days	Mon 6/26/06	Wed 7/5/06	
5		Settle on a budget	1 day	Thu 6/29/06	Thu 6/29/06	
14		Hire	9 days	Thu 6/29/06	Tue 7/11/06	4
21		Plan Entertainment	2.5 days	Thu 6/29/06	Mon 7/3/06	
24		Complete entertainment phase	1 day	Fri 6/30/06	Mon 7/3/06	23
13		Complete selection phase	1 day	Wed 7/5/06	Wed 7/5/06	11
25		Public Relations	3 days	Wed 7/5/06	Fri 7/7/06	
8		Complete initial planning	1 day	Fri 7/7/06	Fri 7/7/06	7
28		Complete public relations phase	1 day	Fri 7/7/06	Fri 7/7/06	27,26
20		Complete hiring phase	1 day	Tue 7/11/06	Tue 7/11/06	16

Working Days

As Figure 13.10 demonstrates, the Working Days report shows the base calendar information for your project. You can see the name of the base calendar for the project and the working hours that are established for each day of the week, along with any exceptions that you defined.

FIGURE 13.10

The Working Days report.

Base Calendar as of Fri 6/30/06
Reports

BASE CALENDAR:	Standard
Day	Hours
Sunday	Nonworking
Monday	8:00 AM – 12:00 PM, 1:00 PM – 5:00 PM
Tuesday	8:00 AM – 12:00 PM, 1:00 PM – 5:00 PM
Wednesday	8:00 AM – 12:00 PM, 1:00 PM – 5:00 PM
Thursday	8:00 AM – 12:00 PM, 1:00 PM – 5:00 PM
Friday	8:00 AM – 12:00 PM, 1:00 PM – 5:00 PM
Saturday	Nonworking
Exceptions:	None

Generating reports on costs

When you select Costs in the Reports dialog box, Project displays thumbnail sketches of the reports that describe the costs that are associated with your project (see Figure 13.11).

FIGURE 13.11

The reports that are available in the Cost category.

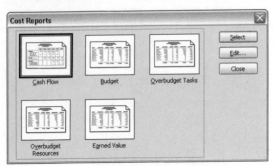

NOTE You can use the Edit button to change the information that appears on the report. You can also use the Edit button to customize the report, which I discuss near the end of the discussion of text reports.

Cash Flow

The Cash Flow report (see Figure 13.12) is a tabular report that shows, by task, the costs for weekly time increments.

The Cash Flow report.

Cash Flow as of Fri 6/30/06
Reports

	6/25/06	7/2/06	7/9/06	6/25/06		Total
Conference						
Preplanning						
Initial planning						
Determine budget	$1,200.00					$1,200.00
Settle on a budget						
Invitation list	$640.00					$640.00
Send out invitations		$1,120.00				$1,120.00
Complete initial planning						
Selection						
Theme	$640.00					$640.00
Site	$1,350.00	$900.00				$2,250.00
Keynote speaker	$752.50					$752.50
Complete selection phase						
Hire						
Caterer	$400.00	$600.00				$1,000.00
Bartenders		$480.00	$240.00			$720.00
Security	$800.00	$1,200.00				$2,000.00
Photographers	$260.00					$260.00
Cleanup Crew	$310.00					$310.00
Complete hiring phase						
Plan Entertainment						
Baseball Game	$240.00					$240.00
Opera	$75.00					$75.00
Complete entertainment phase						
Public Relations						
Alert community		$320.00				$320.00
Press release		$240.00				$240.00
Complete public relations phase						
Rent Equipment						
PA System		$320.00				
Total	$6,667.50	$5,180.00	$240.00			$12,087.50

If you click Cash Flow in the Cost Reports dialog box (previously shown in Figure 13.11) and then select Edit before you choose Select ⇨ Project, the Crosstab Report dialog box opens (see Figure 13.13). On the Definition tab, you can change the time increments.

FIGURE 13.13

Use the Crosstab Report dialog box to change the default settings for the report.

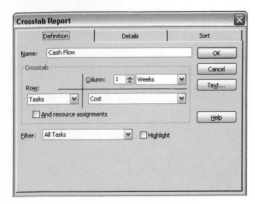

See the section "Customizing reports," later in this chapter, for more information about the Crosstab Report dialog box.

Earned Value

The Earned Value report (see Figure 13.14) shows you the status of each task's costs when you compare planned to actual costs. Some column headings in this report may seem cryptic; see Table 13.1 for translations.

 **NOTE** Even printed in landscape format, the columns of this report don't fit on one page. The BAC and the VAC columns are missing from the figure; they are printed on Page 2 of the report.

CROSS-REF For more information about how Project handles earned value, see Chapter 14.

Project calculates BCWS, BCWP, ACWP, SV, and CV through the project status date. SV represents the cost difference between current progress and the baseline plan, and Project calculates this value as BCWP minus BCWS. CV represents the cost difference between actual costs and planned costs at the current level of completion, and Project calculates this value as BCWP minus ACWP. EAC shows the planned costs based on costs that are already incurred plus additional planned costs. VAC represents the variance between the baseline cost and the combination of actual plus planned costs for a task.

FIGURE 13.14

The Earned Value report.

Earned Value as of Fri 6/30/06
Reports

ID	Task Name	Planned Value - PV (BCWS)	Earned Value - EV (BCWP)	AC (ACWP)	SV
1	Conference	$6,657.50	$1,440.00	$0.00	($5,227.50)
4	Determine budget	$1,200.00	$1,200.00	$1,200.00	$0.00
5	Settle on a budget	$0.00	$0.00	$0.00	$0.00
6	Invitation list	$640.00	$480.00	$480.00	($160.00)
7	Send out invitations	$0.00	$0.00	$0.00	$0.00
8	Complete initial planning	$0.00	$0.00	$0.00	$0.00
10	Theme	$640.00	$640.00	$640.00	$0.00
11	Site	$1,350.00	$450.00	$450.00	($900.00)
12	Keynote speaker	$752.50	$188.13	$188.13	($564.38)
13	Complete selection phase	$0.00	$0.00	$0.00	$0.00
15	Caterer	$400.00	$0.00	$0.00	($400.00)
16	Bartenders	$0.00	$0.00	$0.00	$0.00
17	Security	$800.00	$0.00	$0.00	($800.00)
18	Photographers	$260.00	$0.00	$0.00	($260.00)
19	Cleanup Crew	$310.00	$0.00	$0.00	($310.00)
20	Complete hiring phase	$0.00	$0.00	$0.00	$0.00
22	Baseball Game	$240.00	$0.00	$0.00	($240.00)
23	Opera	$75.00	$0.00	$0.00	($75.00)
24	Complete entertainment phase	$0.00	$0.00	$0.00	$0.00
26	Alert community	$0.00	$0.00	$0.00	$0.00
27	Press release	$0.00	$0.00	$0.00	$0.00
28	Complete public relations phase	$0.00	$0.00	$0.00	$0.00
30	PA System	$0.00	$0.00	$0.00	$0.00
		$13,335.00	$4,398.13	$2,958.13	($8,936.88)

TABLE 13.1

Headings in the Earned Value Report

Heading	Translation
BCWS	Budgeted Cost of Work Scheduled
BCWP	Budgeted Cost of Work Performed
ACWP	Actual Cost of Work Performed
SV	Schedule Variance
CV	Cost Variance
BAC	Budgeted at Completion
EAC	Estimate at Completion
VAC	Variance at Completion

Budget

The Budget report (see Figure 13.15) lists all tasks and shows the budgeted costs as well as the variance between budgeted and actual costs.

> **NOTE** This report doesn't have much meaning unless you have saved a baseline of your project; the values in the variance column change from $0.00 as you complete tasks. Also, the report includes Actual and Remaining columns that wouldn't fit on the same page as the other columns in the figure.

FIGURE 13.15

The Budget report.

Budget Report as of Fri 6/30/06
Reports

ID	Task Name	Fixed Cost	Fixed Cost Accrual	Total Cost	Baseline	Variance
11	Site	$250.00	Prorated	$2,250.00	$2,250.00	$0.00
17	Security	$0.00	Prorated	$2,000.00	$2,000.00	$0.00
4	Determine budget	$0.00	Prorated	$1,200.00	$1,200.00	$0.00
7	Send out invitations	$0.00	Prorated	$1,120.00	$1,120.00	$0.00
15	Caterer	$0.00	Prorated	$1,000.00	$1,000.00	$0.00
12	Keynote speaker	$0.00	Prorated	$752.50	$752.50	$0.00
16	Bartenders	$0.00	Prorated	$720.00	$720.00	$0.00
6	Invitation list	$0.00	Prorated	$640.00	$640.00	$0.00
10	Theme	$0.00	Prorated	$640.00	$640.00	$0.00
26	Alert community	$0.00	Prorated	$320.00	$320.00	$0.00
30	PA System	$0.00	Prorated	$320.00	$320.00	$0.00
19	Cleanup Crew	$0.00	Prorated	$310.00	$310.00	$0.00
18	Photographers	$0.00	Prorated	$260.00	$260.00	$0.00
22	Baseball Game	$0.00	Prorated	$240.00	$240.00	$0.00
27	Press release	$0.00	Prorated	$240.00	$240.00	$0.00
23	Opera	$0.00	Prorated	$75.00	$75.00	$0.00
1	Conference	$0.00	Prorated	$0.00	$12,087.50	($12,087.50)
5	Settle on a budget	$0.00	Prorated	$0.00	$0.00	$0.00
8	Complete initial planning	$0.00	Prorated	$0.00	$0.00	$0.00
13	Complete selection phase	$0.00	Prorated	$0.00	$0.00	$0.00
20	Complete hiring phase	$0.00	Prorated	$0.00	$0.00	$0.00
24	Complete entertainment phase	$0.00	Prorated	$0.00	$0.00	$0.00
28	Complete public relations phase	$0.00	Prorated	$0.00	$0.00	$0.00
		$250.00		$12,087.50	$24,175.00	($12,087.50)

Overbudget reports

Project contains two Overbudget reports: one for tasks and one for resources. Neither report prints if you haven't yet indicated that some tasks are at least partially completed. Instead, you see the message that appears in Figure 13.16. Overbudget tasks and overbudget resources are described as follows:

FIGURE 13.16

This message appears when you attempt to print an Overbudget report before you mark any tasks as being at least partially complete.

■ **Overbudget Tasks:** This report (see Figure 13.17) shows cost, baseline, variance, and actual information about tasks that exceed their budgeted amounts. In the figure, the Actuals and Remaining columns are missing because they wouldn't fit on the first page of the report.

FIGURE 13.17

The Overbudget Tasks report.

Overbudget Tasks as of Fri 6/30/06
Reports

ID	Task Name	Fixed Cost	Fixed Cost Accrual	Total Cost	Baseline	Variance
5	Invitation list	$0.00	Prorated	$600.00	$200.00	$400.00
9	Site	$250.00	Prorated	$1,350.00	$1,050.00	$300.00
4	Determine budget	$0.00	Prorated	$960.00	$720.00	$240.00
10	Keynote speaker	$0.00	Prorated	$1,257.50	$1,137.50	$120.00
		$250.00		$4,167.50	$4,167.50	$1,060.00

■ **Overbudget Resources:** This report (see Figure 13.18) displays resources whose costs will exceed baseline estimates, based on the current progress of the project.

FIGURE 13.18

The Overbudget Resources report.

Overbudget Resources as of Fri 6/30/06
Reports

ID	Task Name	Cost	Baseline Cost	Variance	Actual Cost	Remaining
5	Do Lahr	$1,400.00	$1,100.00	$300.00	$0.00	$1,400.00
4	Roy Lipner	$2,130.00	$1,770.00	$360.00	$960.00	$1,170.00
2	Rosie Boles	$1,237.50	$837.50	$400.00	$600.00	$637.50
		$4,767.50	$3,707.50	$1,060.00	$1,560.00	$3,207.50

Producing reports on time

By using the Current Activities reporting category, you can produce reports on the timing of your project. Click Current Activities in the Reports dialog box. Choose Select to open the Current Activity Reports dialog box (see Figure 13.19) and view the reports that are available in this category.

FIGURE 13.19

The reports that are available in the Current Activities category.

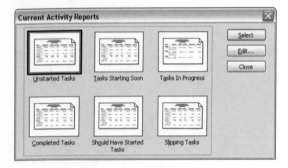

Unstarted Tasks

The Unstarted Tasks report (see Figure 13.20) lists the tasks that have not yet started, sorted by the scheduled start date. For each task, Project displays the duration, predecessor, and resource information (if you assigned resources).

Tasks Starting Soon

When you print the Tasks Starting Soon report (see Figure 13.21) Project displays the Date Range dialog boxes. The information that you provide in these two dialog boxes tells Project the date range to use when selecting tasks for this report. In the first dialog box, specify the earlier date; in the second dialog box, specify the later date, using the mm/dd/yy format. On the report, Project includes tasks that start or finish between the two dates that you specify.

The information that appears on the report is similar to the information that you find on the Unstarted Tasks report: the duration, start and finish dates, predecessors, and resource information (if you assigned resources). Completed tasks also appear on this report; the check mark that appears in the Indicator column on the report identifies them.

FIGURE 13.20

The Unstarted Tasks report.

Unstarted Tasks as of Fri 6/30/06
Reports

ID ⓘ	Task Name	Duration	Start	Finish	Predecessors
5	Settle on a budget	1 day	Thu 6/29/06	Thur 6/29/06	4
15	Caterer	5 days	Thu 6/29/06	Wed 7/5/06	4

ID	Resource Name	Units	Work	Delay	Start	Finish
8	Donna Ballioux	100%	40 hrs	0 days	Thu 6/29/06	Wed 7/5/06

ID ⓘ	Task Name	Duration	Start	Finish	Predecessors
17	Security	5 days	Thu 6/29/03	Wed 7/5/06	4

ID	Resource Name	Units	Work	Delay	Start	Finish
1	Roy Lipner	100%	40 hrs	0 days	Thu 6/29/06	Wed 7/5/06

ID ⓘ	Task Name	Duration	Start	Finish	Predecessors
18	Photographers	1 day	Thu 6/29/06	Thu 6/29/06	4

ID	Resource Name	Units	Work	Delay	Start	Finish
4	Intern	100%	8 hrs	0 days	Thu 6/29/06	Thu 6/29/06
6	Joe Johnson	50%	4 hrs	0 days	Thu 6/29/06	Thu 6/29/06

ID ⓘ	Task Name	Duration	Start	Finish	Predecessors
19	Cleanup Crew	2 days	Thu 6/29/06	Fri 6/30/06	4

ID	Resource Name	Units	Work	Delay	Start	Finish
4	Intern	100%	8 hrs	0 days	Thu 6/29/06	Thu 6/29/06
6	Joe Johnson	50%	6 hrs	0 days	Thu 6/29/06	Fri 6/30/06

ID ⓘ	Task Name	Duration	Start	Finish	Predecessors
22	Baseball Game	1 day	Thu 6/29/06	Thu 6/29/06	4

ID	Resource Name	Units	Work	Delay	Start	Finish
7	Carla West	100%	8 hrs	0 days	Thu 6/29/06	Thu 6/29/06

ID ⓘ	Task Name	Duration	Start	Finish	Predecessors
23	Opera	4 days	Fri 6/30/06	Fri 6/30/06	4,22

ID	Resource Name	Units	Work	Delay	Start	Finish
6	Joe Johnson	75%	3 hrs	0 days	Fri 6/30/06	Fri 6/30/06

ID ⓘ	Task Name	Duration	Start	Finish	Predecessors
24	Complete entertainment phase	1 day	Fri 6/30/06	Mon 7/3/06	23
7	Send out invitations	4 days	Mon 7/3/06	Thu 6/29/06	6

ID	Resource Name	Units	Work	Delay	Start	Finish
3	Gayle Kearney	100%	32 hrs	0 days	Mon 7/3/06	Thu 7/6/06

ID ⓘ	Task Name	Duration	Start	Finish	Predecessors
13	Complete selection phase	1 day	Wed 7/5/06	Wed 7/5/06	11
26	Alert community	2 days	Wed 7/5/06	Thur7/6/06	11

ID	Resource Name	Units	Work	Delay	Start	Finish
4	Intern	100%	16 hrs	0 days	Wed 7/5/06	Thu 7/6/06

ID ⓘ	Task Name	Duration	Start	Finish	Predecessors
27	Press release	1 day	Wed 7/5/06	Wed 7/5/06	11

ID	Resource Name	Units	Work	Delay	Start	Finish
5	Do Lahr	100%	8 hrs	0 days	Wed 7/5/06	Wed 7/5/06

ID ⓘ	Task Name	Duration	Start	Finish	Predecessors
30	PA System	1 day	Wed 7/5/06	Wed 7/5/06	11

ID	Resource Name	Units	Work	Delay	Start	Finish
2	Rosie Boles	100%	8 hrs	0 days	Wed 7/5/06	Wed 7/5/06

ID ⓘ	Task Name	Duration	Start	Finish	Predecessors
16	Bartenders	3 days	Thu 7/6/06	Mon 7/10/06	15

ID	Resource Name	Units	Work	Delay	Start	Finish
7	Carla West	100%	24 hrs	0 days	Thu 7/6/06	Mon 7/10/06

ID ⓘ	Task Name	Duration	Start	Finish	Predecessors
8	Complete initial planning	1 day	Fri 7/7/06	Fri 7/7/06	7
28	Complete public relations phase	1 day	Fri 7/7/06	Fri 7/7/06	27,26

FIGURE 13.21

The Tasks Starting Soon report.

Tasks Starting Soon as of Fri 6/30/06
Reports

ID ❶		Task Name			Duration	Start	Finish	Predecessors
1		Conference			11 days	Mon 6/26/06	Mon 7/10/06	
11		Site			5 days	Wed 6/28/06	Tue 7/4/06	10

	ID	Resource Name	Units	Work	Delay	Start	Finish
	4	Intern	100%	40 hrs	0 days	Wed 6/28/06	Tue 7/4/06
	5	Do Lahr	100%	40 hrs	0 days	Wed 6/28/06	Tue 7/4/06

| 12 | | Keynote speaker | | | 2.69 days | Wed 6/28/06 | Fri 6/30/06 | 10 |

	ID	Resource Name	Units	Work	Delay	Start	Finish
	3	Gayle Kearney	100%	21.5 hrs	0 days	Wed 6/28/06	Fri 6/30/06

| 6 | | Invitation list | | | 2 days | Thu 6/29/03 | Fri 6/30/06 | 5 |

	ID	Resource Name	Units	Work	Delay	Start	Finish
	2	Rosie boles	100%	16 hrs	0 days	Thu 6/29/06	Fri 6/30/06

| 15 | | Caterer | | | 5 days | Thu 6/29/03 | Wed 7/5/06 | 4 |

	ID	Resource Name	Units	Work	Delay	Start	Finish
	8	Donna Ballioux	100%	40 hrs	0 days	Thu 6/29/06	Wed 7/5/06

| 17 | | Security | | | 5 days | Thu 6/29/03 | Wed 7/5/06 | 4 |

	ID	Resource Name	Units	Work	Delay	Start	Finish
	1	Roy Lipner	100%	40 hrs	0 days	Thu 6/29/06	Wed 7/5/06

| 19 | | Cleanup Crew | | | 2 days | Thu 6/29/06 | Fri 6/30/06 | 4 |

	ID	Resource Name	Units	Work	Delay	Start	Finish
	4	Intern	100%	8 hrs	0 days	Thu 6/29/06	Thu 6/29/06
	6	Joe Johnson	50%	6 hrs	0 days	Thu 6/29/06	Fri 6/30/06

| 23 | | Opera | | | 4 days | Fri 6/30/06 | Fri 6/30/06 | 4,22 |

	ID	Resource Name	Units	Work	Delay	Start	Finish
	6	Joe Johnson	75%	3 hrs	0 days	Fri 6/30/06	Fri 6/30/06

| 24 | | Complete entertainment phase | | | 1 day | Fri 6/30/06 | Mon 7/3/06 | 23 |
| 7 | | Send out invitations | | | 4 days | Mon 7/3/06 | Thu 6/29/06 | 6 |

	ID	Resource Name	Units	Work	Delay	Start	Finish
	3	Gayle Kearney	100%	32 hrs	0 days	Mon 7/3/06	Thu 7/6/06

| 13 | | Complete selection phase | | | 1 day | Wed 7/5/06 | Wed 7/5/06 | 11 |
| 26 | | Alert community | | | 2 days | Wed 7/5/06 | Thur7/6/06 | 11 |

	ID	Resource Name	Units	Work	Delay	Start	Finish
	4	Intern	100%	16 hrs	0 days	Wed 7/5/06	Thu 7/6/06

| 27 | | Press release | | | 1 day | Wed 7/5/06 | Wed 7/5/06 | 11 |

	ID	Resource Name	Units	Work	Delay	Start	Finish
	5	Do Lahr	100%	8 hrs	0 days	Wed 7/5/06	Wed 7/5/06

| 30 | | PA System | | | 1 day | Wed 7/5/06 | Wed 7/5/06 | 11 |

	ID	Resource Name	Units	Work	Delay	Start	Finish
	2	Rosie Boles	100%	8 hrs	0 days	Wed 7/5/06	Wed 7/5/06

Tasks in Progress

As Figure 13.22 shows, the Tasks in Progress report lists tasks that have started but not yet finished. You see the tasks' duration, start and planned finish dates, predecessors, and resource information (if you assigned resources).

Completed Tasks

The Completed Tasks report (see Figure 13.23) lists tasks that have completed. You can see the actual duration, the actual start and finish dates, the percent complete (always 100 percent — if a task is only partially complete, it won't appear on this report), the cost, and the work hours.

FIGURE 13.22

The Tasks in Progress report.

Tasks Starting Soon as of Fri 6/30/06
Reports

ID ❶		Task Name			Duration	Start	Finish	Predecessors
June 2006								
1		Conference			11 days	Mon 6/26/06	Mon 7/10/06	
11		Site			5 days	Wed 6/28/06	Tue 7/4/06	10
	ID	*Resource Name*	*Units*	*Work*	*Delay*	*Start*	*Finish*	
	4	*Intern*	*100%*	*40 hrs*	*0 days*	*Wed 6/28/06*	*Tue 7/4/06*	
	5	*Do Lahr*	*100%*	*40 hrs*	*0 days*	*Wed 6/28/06*	*Tue 7/4/06*	
12		Keynote speaker			2.69 days	Wed 6/28/06	Fri 6/30/06	10
	ID	*Resource Name*	*Units*	*Work*	*Delay*	*Start*	*Finish*	
	3	*Gayle Kearney*	*100%*	*21.5 hrs*	*0 days*	*Wed 6/28/06*	*Fri 6/30/06*	
6		Invitation list			2 days	Thu 6/29/03	Fri 6/30/06	5
	ID	*Resource Name*	*Units*	*Work*	*Delay*	*Start*	*Finish*	
	2	*Rosie boles*	*100%*	*16 hrs*	*0 days*	*Thu 6/29/06*	*Fri 6/30/06*	
July 2006								
1		Conference			11 days	Mon 6/26/06	Mon 7/10/06	
11		Site			5 days	Wed 6/28/06	Tue 7/4/06	10
	ID	*Resource Name*	*Units*	*Work*	*Delay*	*Start*	*Finish*	
	4	*Intern*	*100%*	*40 hrs*	*0 days*	*Wed 6/28/06*	*Tue 7/4/06*	
	5	*Do Lahr*	*100%*	*40 hrs*	*0 days*	*Wed 6/28/06*	*Tue 7/4/06*	

FIGURE 13.23

The Completed Tasks report.

Completed Tasks as of Fri 6/30/06
Reports

ID	Task Name	Duration	Start	Finish	%Comp.	Cost
June 2006						
4	Determine budget	3 days	Mon 6/26/06	Wed 6/28/06	100%	$1,200.00
10	Theme	2 days	Mon 6/26/06	Tues 6/27/06	100%	$640.00

Should Have Started Tasks

When you print the Should Have Started Tasks report (see Figure 13.24), you must supply a date by which tasks should have started. Project uses this date to determine which tasks appear on the report.

FIGURE 13.24

The Should Have Started Tasks report.

Should Have Started Tasks as of Fri 6/30/06
Reports

ID	o	Task Name	Start	Finish	Baseline Start	Baseline Finish	Start Var.
2		**Preplanning**	**Mon 6/26/06**	**Fri 7/7/06**	**Mon 6/26/06**	**Thu 7/6/06**	**0 days**
3		**Initial planning**	**Mon 6/26/06**	**Fri 7/7/06**	**Mon 6/26/06**	**Thu 7/6/06**	**0 days**
5		Settle on a budget	Thu 6/29/06	Thu 6/29/06	NA	NA	0 days

	ID	Successor Name	Type	Lag			
	6	Invitation list	FS	0 days			

ID	o	Task Name	Start	Finish	Baseline Start	Baseline Finish	Start Var.
14		**Hire**	**Thu 6/29/06**	**Tue 7/11/06**	**Thu 6/29/06**	**Mon 7/10/06**	**0 days**
15		Caterer	Thu 6/29/06	Wed 7/5/06	Thu 6/29/06	Wed 7/5/06	0 days

	ID	Successor Name	Type	Lag			
	16	IBartenders	FS	0 days			

ID	o	Task Name	Start	Finish	Baseline Start	Baseline Finish	Start Var.
17		Security	Thu 6/29/06	Wed 7/5/06	Thu 6/29/06	Wed 7/5/06	0 days
18		Photographers	Thu 6/29/06	Thu 6/29/06	Thu 6/29/06	Thu 6/29/06	0 days
19		Cleanup Crew	Thu 6/29/06	Fri 6/30/06	Thu 6/29/06	Fri 6/30/06	0 days
21		**Plan Entertainment**	**Thu 6/29/06**	**Mon 7/3/06**	**Thu 6/29/06**	**Fri 6/30/06**	**0 days**
22		Baseball Game	Thu 6/29/06	Thu 6/29/06	Thu 6/29/06	Thu 6/29/06	0 days

	ID	Successor Name	Type	Lag			
	23	Opera	FS	0 days			

For each task on the report, Project displays planned start and finish dates, baseline start and finish dates, and variances for start and finish dates. Successor task information appears when a task on the report has a successor defined. In the figure, the Finish Variance column is missing because it wouldn't fit on the first page of the report.

Slipping Tasks

The Slipping Tasks report (see Figure 13.25) lists the tasks that have been rescheduled from their baseline start dates.

This report displays the same information as the information that you saw on the Should Have Started Tasks report, but the presentation of the information changes the focus of your attention. In the figure, the Finish Variance column is missing because it wouldn't fit on the first page of the report.

FIGURE 13.25

The Slipping Tasks report.

Slipping Tasks as of Fri 6/30/06
Reports

ID	Task Name	Start	Finish	Baseline Start	Baseline Finish	Start Var.
2	Preplanning	Mon 6/26/06	Fri 7/7/06	Mon 6/26/06	Thu 7/6/06	0 days
3	Initial planning	Mon 6/26/06	Fri 7/7/06	Mon 6/26/06	Thu 7/6/06	0 days
9	Selection	Mon 6/26/06	Wed 7/5/06	Mon 6/26/06	Tue 7/4/06	0 days
14	Hire	Thu 6/29/06	Tue 7/11/06	Thu 6/29/06	Mon 7/10/06	0 days
21	Plan Entertainment	Thu 6/29/06	Mon 7/3/06	Thu 6/29/06	Fri 6/30/06	0 days
25	Public Relations	Wed 7/5/06	Fri 7/7/06	Wed 7/5/06	Thu 7/6/06	0 days

Preparing reports on work assignments

Using the Assignments reporting category of the Reports dialog box, you can produce reports on the resource assignments in your project. Click the Assignments category. Choose Select to open the Assignment Reports dialog box (see Figure 13.26) and view the reports that are available in this category.

FIGURE 13.26

The reports that are available in the Assignments category.

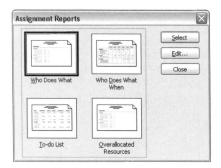

Who Does What

The Who Does What report (see Figure 13.27) lists resources and the tasks to which they are assigned, the amount of work planned for each task, the planned start and finish dates, and any resource notes.

Who Does What When

The Who Does What When report (see Figure 13.28) also lists resources and the tasks to which they are assigned. This report, however, focuses your attention on the daily work that is scheduled for each resource on each task.

FIGURE 13.27

The Who Does What report.

Who Does What as of Fri 6/30/06
Reports

ID ❶		Resource Name				Work	
1		Roy Lipner				64 hrs	
	ID	*Task Name*	*Units*	*Work*	*Delay*	*Start*	*Finish*
	4	Determine budget	100%	24 hrs	0 days	Mon 6/26/06	Wed 6/28/06
	17	Security	100%	40 hrs	0 days	Thu 6/29/06	Wed 7/5/06
2		Rosie Boles				40 hrs	
	ID	*Task Name*	*Units*	*Work*	*Delay*	*Start*	*Finish*
	6	Invitation list	100%	16 hrs	0 days	Thu 6/29/06	Fri 6/30/06
	10	Theme	100%	16 hrs	0 days	Mon 6/26/06	Tue 6/27/06
	30	PA System	100%	8 hrs	0 days	Wed 7/5/06	Wed 7/5/06
3		Gayle Kearney				53.5 hrs	
	ID	*Task Name*	*Units*	*Work*	*Delay*	*Start*	*Finish*
	7	Send out invitations	100%	32 hrs	0 days	Mon 7/3/06	Thu 7/6/06
	12	Keynote speaker	100%	21.5 hrs	0 days	Wed 6/28/06	Fri 6/30/06
4		Intern				72 hrs	
	ID	*Task Name*	*Units*	*Work*	*Delay*	*Start*	*Finish*
	11	Site	100%	40 hrs	0 days	Wed 6/28/06	Tue 7/4/06
	18	Photographers	100%	8 hrs	0 days	Thu 6/29/06	Thu 6/29/06
	19	Cleanup Crew	100%	8 hrs	0 days	Thu 6/29/06	Thu 6/29/06
	26	Alert community	100%	16 hrs	0 days	Wed 7/5/06	Thu 7/6/06
5		Do Lahr				48 hrs	
	ID	*Task Name*	*Units*	*Work*	*Delay*	*Start*	*Finish*
	11	Site	100%	40 hrs	0 days	Wed 6/28/06	Tue 7/4/06
	27	Press release	100%	8 hrs	0 days	Wed 7/5/06	Wed 7/5/06
6		Joe Johnson				13 hrs	
	ID	*Task Name*	*Units*	*Work*	*Delay*	*Start*	*Finish*
	18	Photographers	50%	4 hrs	0 days	Thu 6/29/06	Thu 6/29/06
	19	Cleanup Crew	50%	6 hrs	0 days	Thu 6/29/06	Fri 6/30/06
	23	Opera	75%	3 hrs	0 days	Fri 6/30/06	Fri 6/30/06
7		Carla West				32 hrs	
	ID	*Task Name*	*Units*	*Work*	*Delay*	*Start*	*Finish*
	16	Bartenders	100%	24 hrs	0 days	Thu 7/6/06	Mon 7/10/06
	22	Baseball Game	100%	8 hrs	0 days	Thu 6/29/06	Thu 6/29/06
8		Donna Ballioux				40 hrs	
	ID	*Task Name*	*Units*	*Work*	*Delay*	*Start*	*Finish*
	15	Caterer	100%	40 hrs	0 days	Thu 6/29/06	Wed 7/5/06

FIGURE 13.28

The Who Does What When report.

Who Does What When Usage as of Fri 6/30/06 Reports

	6/1	6/2	6/3	6/4	6/5	6/6	6/7	6/8	6/9	6/10	6/11	6/12	6/13	6/14	6/15	6/16	6/17	6/18	6/19
Joe Johnson									12 hrs	12 hrs	4 hrs								
Security									8 hrs	8 hrs	4 hrs								
Cleanup Crew									4 hrs	4 hrs									
Rosie Boles		8 hrs	7 hrs	4 hrs	####	8 hrs			12 hrs	8 hrs									
Invitation list		8 hrs	6 hrs						8 hrs	8 hrs									
Theme			1 hr	4 hrs	####	8 hrs													
Keynote Speaker									4 hrs										
Photographers																			
Gayle Kearney		12 hrs							8 hrs	8 hrs	8 hrs	8 hrs	8 hrs			8 hrs	8 hrs	8 hrs	
Keynote Speaker									8 hrs	8 hrs	8 hrs	8 hrs	8 hrs						
Caterer																8 hrs	8 hrs	8 hrs	
Bartenders		8 hrs																	
Baseball Game		4 hrs																	
Opera																			
Roy Lipner		8 hrs	8 hrs	8 hrs	12 hrs	8 hrs			8 hrs	12 hrs	4 hrs								
Determine budget		8 hrs	8 hrs	8 hrs	4 hrs	8 hrs													
Keynote speaker					8 hrs					4 hrs									
Security									8 hrs	8 hrs	4 hrs								
Do Lahr			2 hrs	8 hrs	8 hrs				8 hrs	8 hrs	14 hrs	6 hrs							
Site			2 hrs	8 hrs	8 hrs				8 hrs	4 hrs	8 hrs	6 hrs							
Alert community										2 hrs	6 hrs								
Press release										2 hrs									
Intern			2 hrs	4 hrs	4 hrs				12 hrs	10 hrs									
Site			2 hrs	4 hrs	4 hrs				4 hrs	2 hrs									
Photographers									4 hrs	4 hrs									
Cleanup Crew									4 hrs	4 hrs									
Long distance																			
Lumber																			
Gasoline																			

417

> **TIP** You can use the Edit button in the Assignment Reports dialog box to change the timescale on the report from daily to some other increment, such as weekly. Also, you may want to change the date format on the Details tab to a wider format (as I did in Figure 13.28) if you see pound signs (###) in your report. See the section "Customizing reports," later in this chapter, for more information.

To Do List

The To Do List report (see Figure 13.29) lists, on a weekly basis, the tasks that are assigned to a resource that you select. When you are ready to print this report, Project first displays the Using Resource dialog box, which contains the Show Tasks Using list box. When you open the list box, you see a list of your resources. Select a resource, and click OK. The To Do List report shows the task ID number, duration, start and finish dates, predecessors, and a list of all of the resources that are assigned to each task.

FIGURE 13.29

The To Do List report.

To Do List as of Fri 6/30/06
Reports

ID	❶	Task Name	Duration	Start	Finish	Predecessors	Resource Names
Week of June 1							
5	✓	Invitation list	3 days	Fri 6/6/03	Tue 6/10/03	4	Rosie Boles
8		Theme	1.75 days	Mon 6/2/03	Tue 6/3/03		Rosie Boles
10		Keynote speaker	4.13 days	Tue 6/3/03	Tue 6/10/03	8	Roy Lipner, Rosie Boles[50%]
Week of June 8							
5	✓	Invitation list	3 days	Fri 6/6/03	Tue 6/10/03	4	Rosie Boles
10		Keynote speaker	4.13 days	Tue 6/3/03	Tue 6/10/03	8	Roy Lipner, Rosie Boles[50%]
15		Photographers	1.5 days	Mon 6/9/03	Tue 6/10/03	4	Rosie Boles[50%], Intern

Overallocated Resources

The Overallocated Resources report (see Figure 13.30) shows the overallocated resources, the tasks to which they are assigned, and the total hours of work that are assigned to them. You can also see the details of each task, such as the allocation, the amount of work, any delay, and the start and finish dates.

FIGURE 13.30

The Overallocated Resources report.

Overallocated Resources as of Fri 6/30/06
Reports

ID ❶		Resource Name				Work	
1 ◇		Joe Johnson				28 hrs	
	ID	Task Name	Units	Work	Delay	Start	Finish
	14	Security	100%	20 hrs	0 days	Mon 6/9/03	Wed 6/11/03
	16	Cleanup Crew	50%	8 hrs	0 days	Mon 6/9/03	Tue 6/10/06
2 ◇		Rosie Boles				49.5 hrs	
	ID	Task Name	Units	Work	Delay	Start	Finish
	5	Invitation list	100%	24 hrs	0 days	Fri 6/6/03	Tue 6/10/03
	10	Keynote speaker	50%	7.5 hrs	0 days	Tue 6/3/03	Thu 6/5/03
	8	Theme	100%	14 hrs	0 days	Mon 6/2/03	Tue 6/3/03
	15	Photographers	50%	4 hrs	0 days	Mon 6/9/03	Mon 6/9/03
3 ◇		Gayle Kearney				76 hrs	
	ID	Task Name	Units	Work	Delay	Start	Finish
	10	Keynote speaker	0%	0 hrs	0 days	Tue6/3/03	Tue 6/3/03
	12	Caterer	100%	40 hrs	0 days	Mon 6/9/03	Fri 6/13/03
	13	Bartenders	100%	24 hrs	0 days	Mon 6/16/03	Wed 6/18/03
	18	Baseball Game	100%	8 hrs	0 days	Mon 6/2/03	Mon 6/2/06
	19	Opera	100%	4 hrs	0 days	Mon 6/2/03	Mon 6/2/06
4 ◇		Roy Lipner				71 hrs	
	ID	Task Name	Units	Work	Delay	Start	Finish
	4	Determine budget	100%	32 hrs	0 days	Mon 6/2/03	Fri 6/6/03
	10	Keynote speaker	100%	19 hrs	0 days	Thu 6/5/03	Tue 6/10/03
	14	Security	100%	20 hrs	0 days	Mon 6/9/03	Wed 6/11/03
5 ◇		Do Lahr				56 hrs	
	ID	Task Name	Units	Work	Delay	Start	Finish
	9	Site	100%	32 hrs	0 days	Tue 6/3/03	Tue 6/10/03
	21	Alert community	100%	16 hrs	0 days	Tue 6/10/03	Thu 6/12/03
	22	Press release	100%	8 hrs	0 days	Tue 6/10/03	Wed 6/11/03
						280.5 hrs	

Reporting on workloads

You can use the Workload category to produce reports on task and resource usage in your project. Click Workload in the Reports dialog box and choose Select to open the Workload Reports dialog box (see Figure 13.31).

FIGURE 13.31

The Workload Reports dialog box.

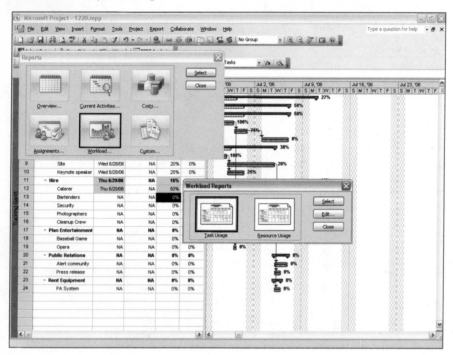

Task Usage

The Task Usage report (see Figure 13.32) lists tasks and the resources that are assigned to each task. It also displays the amount of work that's assigned to each resource in weekly time increments.

> **TIP** You can change the time increment by clicking Edit in the Workload Reports dialog box. See the section "Customizing reports," later in this chapter, for more information about editing reports.

Resource Usage

The Resource Usage report (see Figure 13.33) lists resources and the tasks to which they are assigned. As does the Task Usage report, this report shows the amount of work that is assigned to each resource for each task in weekly time increments, but this report focuses your attention on the resource.

FIGURE 13.32

The Task Usage report.

Task Usage as of Fri 6/30/06
Reports

	6/25/06	7/2/06	7/9/06	7/16/06	Total
Conference					
Preplanning					
Initial planning					
Determine budget	24 hrs				24 hrs
Roy Lipner	24 hrs				24 hrs
Settle on a budget					
Invitation list	16 hrs				16 hrs
Rosie Boles	16 hrs				16 hrs
Send out invitations		32 hrs			32 hrs
Gayle Kearney		32 hrs			32 hrs
Complete initial planning					
Selection					
Theme	16 hrs				16 hrs
Rosie Boles	16 hrs				16 hrs
Site	48 hrs	32 hrs			80 hrs
Intern	24 hrs	16 hrs			40 hrs
Do Lahr	24 hrs	16 hrs			40 hrs
Keynote speaker	21.5 hrs				21.5 hrs
Gayle Kearney	21.5 hrs				21.5 hrs
Complete selection phase					
Hire					
Caterer	16 hrs	24 hrs			40 hrs
Donna Ballioux	16 hrs	24 hrs			40 hrs
Bartenders		16 hrs	8 hrs		24 hrs
Carla West		16 hrs	8 hrs		24 hrs
Security	16 hrs	24 hrs			40 hrs
Roy Lipner	16 hrs	24 hrs			40 hrs
Photographers	12 hrs				12 hrs
Intern	8 hrs				8 hrs
Joe Johnson	4 hrs				4 hrs
Cleanup Crew	14 hrs				14 hrs
Intern	8 hrs				8 hrs
Joe Johnson	6 hrs				6 hrs
Complete hiring phase					
Plan Entertainment					
Baseball Game	8 hrs				8 hrs
Carla West	8 hrs				8 hrs
Opera	3 hrs				3 hrs
Joe Johnson	3 hrs				3 hrs
Complete entertainment phase					
Public Relations					

FIGURE 13.33

The Resource Usage report.

Resource Usage as of Fri 6/30/06
Reports

	6/25/06	7/2/06	7/9/06	7/16/06		Total
Roy Lipner	40 hrs	24 hrs				64 hrs
Determine budget	24 hrs					24 hrs
Security	16 hrs	24 hrs				40 hrs
Rosie Boles	32 hrs	8 hrs				40 hrs
Invitation list	16 hrs					16 hrs
Theme	16 hrs					16 hrs
PA System		8 hrs				8 hrs
Gayle Kearney	21.5 hrs	32 hrs				53.5 hrs
Send out invitations		32 hrs				32 hrs
Keynote speaker	21.5 hrs					53.5 hrs
Intern	40 hrs	32 hrs				72 hrs
Site	24 hrs	16 hrs				40 hrs
Photographers	8 hrs					8 hrs
Cleanup Crew	8 hrs					8 hrs
Alert community		16 hrs				16 hrs
Do Lahr	24 hrs	24 hrs				48 hrs
Site	24 hrs	16 hrs				40 hrs
Press release		8 hrs				8 hrs
Joe Johnson	13 hrs					13 hrs
Photographers	4 hrs					4 hrs
Cleanup Crew	6 hrs					6 hrs
Opera	3 hrs					3 hrs
Carla West	8 hrs	16 hrs	8 hrs			32 hrs
Bartenders		16 hrs	8 hrs			24 hrs
Baseball Game	8 hrs					8 hrs
Donna Ballioux	16 hrs	24 hrs				40 hrs
Caterer	16 hrs	24 hrs				40 hrs
Total	194.5 hrs	160 hrs	8 hrs			362.5 hrs

NOTE Project 2000 introduced two variations of the Resource Usage report — the Resource Usage (material) and Resource Usage (work) reports. Both reports look identical to the Resource Usage report but, as you would expect, one shows only material resources whereas the other shows only work resources. Both reports are custom reports; to print them, follow the instructions in the next section.

Customizing reports

Project contains some custom reports. In addition to printing these custom reports, you can customize any of the other reports that are described in this chapter. Click the Custom category in the Reports dialog box and choose Select to open the Custom Reports dialog box (see Figure 13.34).

FIGURE 13.34

The Custom Reports dialog box.

Not all the reports listed in the Custom Reports dialog box are custom reports. However, you can print any of the standard reports either from this dialog box or as described earlier in this chapter. Remember, though, that you must use this dialog box to print the three custom reports.

NOTE You can create your own reports by clicking the New button in the Custom Reports dialog box (refer to Figure 13.34). When you define a new custom report, Project offers you four formats. Three formats are based on the reports that are discussed in this section: the Task report format, the Resource report format, and the Crosstab report format. The fourth format, the Monthly Calendar format, functions just like the Working Days report that I discussed earlier in this chapter.

Custom reports

Project contains the following custom reports:

- The Task report
- The Resource report
- The Crosstab report

Task report

The Task report (see Figure 13.35) shows task information, such as the ID number, task name, indicator icons, task duration, planned start and finish dates, predecessors, and (if resources have been assigned) resource names.

The Task report.

Task as of Fri 6/30/06
Reports

ID	❶	Task Name	Duration	Start	Finish	Predecessors
1	✓	Conference	11 days	Mon 6/26/06	Mon 7/10/06	
4		Determine budget	3 days	Mon 6/26/06	Wed 6/28/06	
5		Settle on a budget	1 day	Thu 6/29/06	Thu 6/29/06	4
6		Invitation list	2 days	Thu 6/29/06	Fri 6/30/06	5
7		Send out invitations	4 days	Mon 7/3/06	Thu 7/6/06	6
8		Complete initial planning	1 day	Fri 7/7/06	Fri 7/7/06	7
10	✓	Theme	2 days	Mon 6/26/06	Tue 6/27/06	
11		Site	5 days	Wed 6/28/06	Tue 7/4/06	10
12		Keynote speaker	2.69 days	Wed 6/28/06	Fri 6/30/06	10
13		Complete selection phase	1 day	Wed 7/5/06	Wed 7/5/06	11
15		Caterer	5 days	Thu 6/29/06	Wed 7/5/06	4
16		Bartender	3 days	Thu 7/6/06	Mon 7/10/06	15
17		Security	5 days	Thu 6/29/06	Wed 7/5/06	4
18		Photographers	1 day	Thu 6/29/06	Thu 6/29/06	4
19		Cleanup Crew	2 days	Thu 6/29/06	Fri 6/30/06	4
20		Complete hiring phase	1 day	Tue 7/11/06	Tue 7/11/06	16
22		Baseball Game	1 day	Thu 6/29/06	Thu 6/29/06	4
23		Opera	4 hrs	Fri 6/30/06	Fri 6/30/06	4,22
24		Complete entertainment phase	1 day	Fri 6/30/06	Mon 7/3/06	23
26		Alert community	2 days	Wed 7/5/06	Thu 7/6/06	11
27		Press release	1 day	Wed 7/5/06	Wed 7/5/06	11
28		Complete public relations phase	1 day	Fri 7/7/06	Fri 7/7/06	27,26
30		PA System	1 day	Wed 7/5/06	Wed 7/5/06	11

Resource report

As you can see from the report sample shown in Figure 13.36, the Resource report shows resource information. On Page 1, you find the resource ID number; indicator icons; the resource name, type, initials, material label, group, and maximum units. On the second page of the report (not shown), Project displays rate information; accrual information; base calendar information; and code information.

 In this figure, you can't see the columns that printed on Page 2 of the report: Overtime Rate, Cost/Use, Accrue At, Base Calendar, and Code.

FIGURE 13.36

The Resource report.

Resource as of Fri 6/30/06
Reports

ID	❶	Task Name	Type	Material Label	Initials	Group	Max. Units
1		Roy Lipner	Work		R		100%
2		Rosie Boles	Work		R		100%
3		Gayle Kearney	Work		G		100%
4		Intern	Work		I		100%
5		Do Lahr	Work		D		100%
6		Joe Johnson	Work		J		100%
7		Carla West	Work		C		100%
8		Donna Ballioux	Work		D		100%

Project 2003 introduced two variations of the Resource report: the Resource (material) and Resource (work) reports. Both reports look identical to the Resource report but, as you would expect, one shows only material resources whereas the other shows only work resources.

Crosstab report

The Crosstab report (see Figure 13.37) is a tabular report that shows task and resource information in rows and time increments in columns.

TIP Much of the information on the Crosstab report also appears on the Task Usage report and the Resource Usage report. These reports give you more formatting options, such as the period that's covered by the report and the table that's used in the report.

Customizing an existing report

You can customize almost every report that you've seen in this chapter. For a few reports, such as the Working Days report, the only item that you can change is the font information that Project uses to print the report. For other reports, however, you can change the table or the task or resource filter to change the content of the report. Click the Edit button when preparing to print the report to make any of these changes. When you click the Edit button, Project opens the dialog box that relates to the report that you selected. For example, if you select the Working Days report in the Overview Reports dialog box (choose Report ➪ Reports ➪ Overview) and then click Edit, Project opens the Report Text dialog box (see Figure 13.38).

FIGURE 13.37

The Crosstab report.

Crosstab as of Fri 6/30/06
Reports

	6/25/06	7/2/06	7/9/06	7/16/06
Conference				
Preplanning				
Initial planning				
Determine budget	$1,200.00			
Roy Lipner	$1,200.00			
Settle on a budget				
Invitation list	$640.00			
Rosie Boles	$640.00			
Send out invitations		$1,120.00		
Gayle Kearney		$1,120.00		
Complete initial planning				
Selection				
Theme	$640.00			
Rosie Boles	$640.00			
Site	$1,350.00	$900.00		
Intern	$480.00	$320.00		
Do Lahr	$720.00	$480.00		
Keynote speaker	$752.50			
Gayle Kearney	$752.50			
Complete selection phase				
Hire				
Caterer	$400.00	$600.00		
Donna Ballioux	$400.00	$600.00		
Bartenders		$480.00	$240.00	
Carla West		$480.00	$240.00	
Security	$800.00	$1,200.00		
Roy Lipner	$800.00	$1,200.00		
Photographers	$260.00			
Intern	$160.00			
Joe Johnson	$100.00			
Cleanup Crew	$310.00			
Intern	$160.00			
Joe Johnson	$150.00			
Complete hiring phase				
Plan Entertainment				
Baseball Game	$240.00			
Carla West	$240.00			
Opera	$75.00			
Joe Johnson	$75.00			
Complete entertainment phase				
Public Relations				
Alert community		$320.00		
Intern		$320.00		

FIGURE 13.38

Use the Report Text dialog box to change the font of the report items.

Similarly, if you select the Tasks Starting Soon report from the Current Activities dialog box and then click Edit, Project opens the Definition tab of the Task Report dialog box (see Figure 13.39).

FIGURE 13.39

Use the Definition tab to change the report's filter or table.

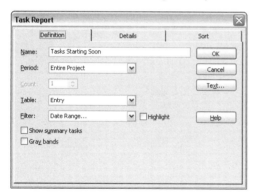

From the Details tab (see Figure 13.40), select the information that you want to have included on the report. You may want to display predecessors for tasks or place a gridline between details.

FIGURE 13.40

Use the Details tab to specify the information that you want to include on the report.

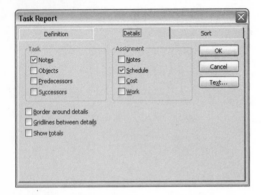

 The options on the Details tab change from report to report.

From the Sort tab, shown in Figure 13.41, select the sort orders for the report.

FIGURE 13.41

Select a sort order for the report.

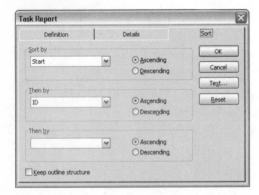

Editing Reports: The Type Determines the Dialog Box

Remember that the type of report that you select initially determines the dialog box that you see when you click Edit in the report's category dialog box (for example, the Overview Reports dialog box or the Cost Reports dialog box). In addition to the dialog boxes that you've seen in this chapter, you may also see the Resource Report dialog box or the Crosstab Report dialog box, both of which contain slightly different options (primarily on the Definitions tab) than the Task Report dialog box.

For example, when you edit the Who Does What report before printing it, Project opens a Resource Report dialog box. On the Definitions tab of this dialog box, you can select filters that are related to resources, whereas the filters in the Task Report dialog box pertain to tasks. Or, if you edit the Cash Flow report before printing it, Project opens a Crosstab Report dialog box from which you can select the information that you want to appear on each row; the default information is Tasks and Cost.

Visual Reporting

NEW FEATURE Visual reporting is new to Project 2007.

Project 2007 introduces a new kind of reporting called *visual reporting*. The visual reports you create use Project data to build PivotTables in Excel and PivotDiagrams in Visio. After you produce a report, you can manipulate it in Excel or Visio using the techniques in those programs that you use to manipulate any Excel PivotTable or Visio PivotDiagram.

You produce visual reports from the Visual Reports – Create Report window (see Figure 13.42). You can open this window by choosing Report ➪ Visual Reports.

You'll find the reports broken into six categories:

- Task Usage
- Resource Usage
- Assignment Usage
- Task Summary
- Resource Summary
- Assignment Summary

FIGURE 13.42

Use this window to create visual reports.

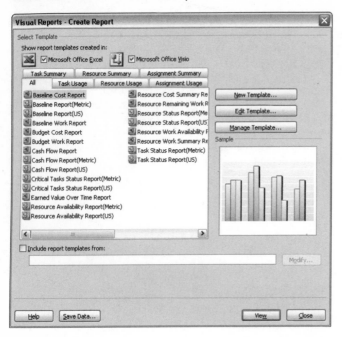

The reports that appear in the Visual Reports – Create Report window are the templates that come with Project, but you also can create your own reports if you don't find a report that suits your needs.

In this section, I describe each of the report templates that come with Project. Then, at the end of this section, I walk you through creating your own visual report.

Task Usage reports

Two reports appear in the Task Usage category of reports: the Cash Flow Report and the Earned Value Over Time Report. Both reports are based on timephased data.

Cash Flow Report

The Cash Flow report, an Excel PivotTable, uses timephased data to produce a bar graph similar to the one shown in Figure 13.43.

Earned Value Over Time Report

The Earned Value Over Time Report, an Excel PivotTable, uses timephased data to produce a chart that plots actual cost of work performed (ACWP), Planned Value – PV (BCWS), and Earned Value – EV (BCWP) over time, similar to the one shown in Figure 13.44.

 This report replaces the Analyze Timescaled Data Wizard.

FIGURE 13.43

The Cash Flow Report.

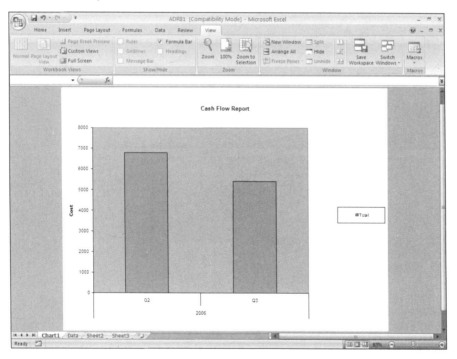

FIGURE 13.44

The Earned Value Over Time Report.

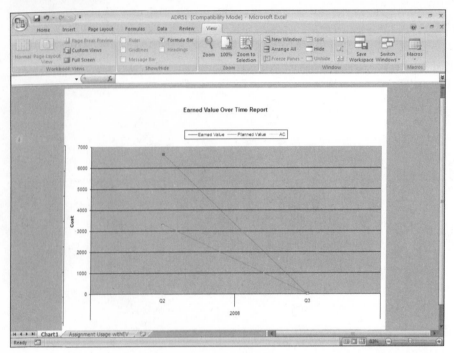

Resource usage reports

The Resource Usage visual report category contains five reports. For two of the reports, the Cash Flow Report and the Resource Availability Report, you'll find both Metric and US versions.

Cash Flow Report

You'll find a Metric and a US version of the Cash Flow Report, a Visio PivotDiagram. Using your project data, this report produces a diagram (see Figure 13.45) that shows planned and actual costs for your project over time and breaks the information down by resource type, showing work, material, and cost information.

FIGURE 13.45

The Cash Flow Report.

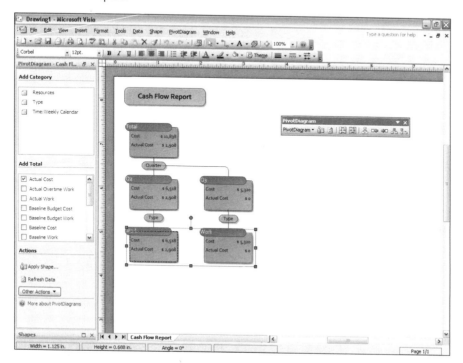

Resource Availability Report

You'll find a Metric and a US version of the Resource Availability Report, a Visio PivotDiagram. Using your project data, this report produces a diagram (see Figure 13.46) that shows total capacity, work, and remaining availability for work resources.

FIGURE 13.46

The Resource Availability Report.

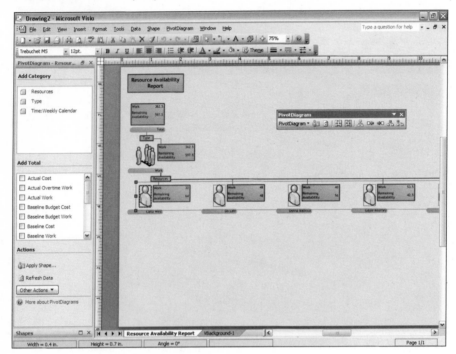

Resource Cost Summary Report

The Resource Cost Summary Report, an Excel PivotTable, produces a pie chart (see Figure 13.47) that divides resource costs between resource types.

FIGURE 13.47

The Resource Cost Summary Report.

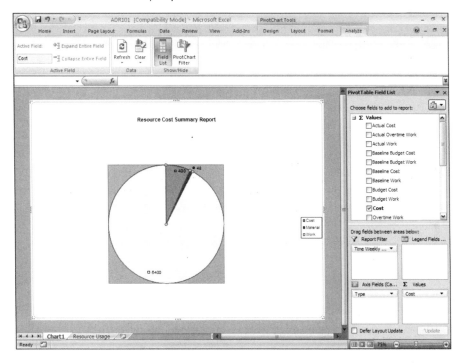

Resource Work Availability Report

The Resource Work Availability Report is an Excel PivotTable that produces a column chart (see Figure 13.48) showing work and remaining availability over time.

FIGURE 13.48

The Resource Work Availability Report.

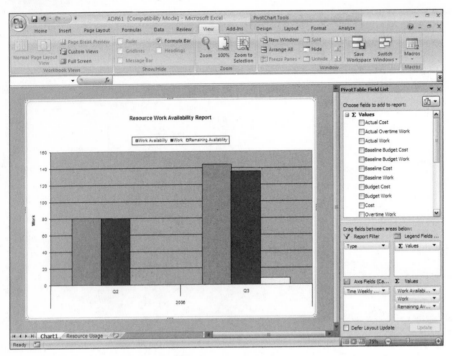

Resource Work Summary Report

The Resource Work Summary Report is an Excel PivotTable that produces a column chart (see Figure 13.49) showing work, remaining availability, and actual work for each work resource in your project.

FIGURE 13.49

The Resource Work Summary Report.

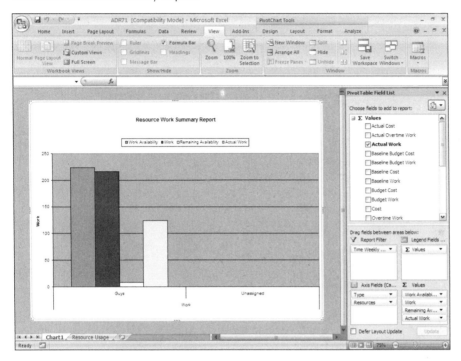

Assignment Usage reports

The Assignment Usage visual report category contains five reports. For one of the reports, the Baseline Report, you'll find both Metric and US versions.

Baseline Cost Report

The Baseline Cost Report is an Excel PivotTable that produces a column chart (see Figure 13.50) that compares baseline cost, planned cost, and actual cost.

FIGURE 13.50

The Baseline Cost Report.

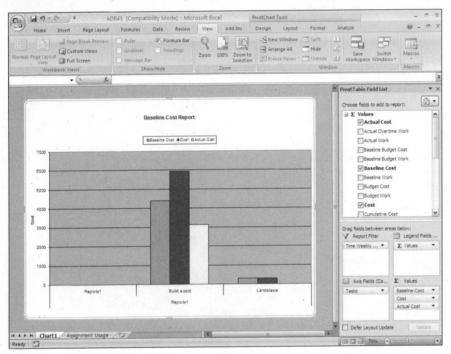

Baseline Report

You'll find a Metric and a US version of the Baseline Report, a Visio PivotDiagram. Using your project data, this report produces a diagram (see Figure 13.51) that shows baseline and actual work and costs for your project over time. The report flags instances in which planned work exceeds baseline work and planned cost exceeds baseline cost.

FIGURE 13.51

The Baseline Report.

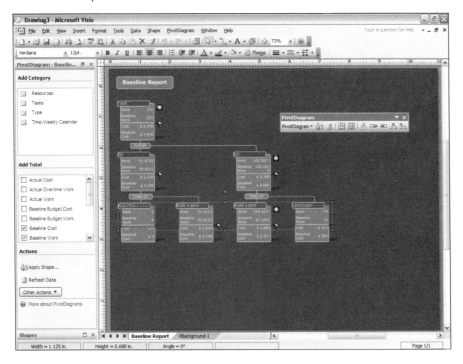

Baseline Work Report

As is its cousin the Baseline Cost Report, the Baseline Work Report is an Excel PivotTable that produces a column chart (see Figure 13.52) that compares baseline work, planned work, and actual work.

FIGURE 13.52

The Baseline Work Report.

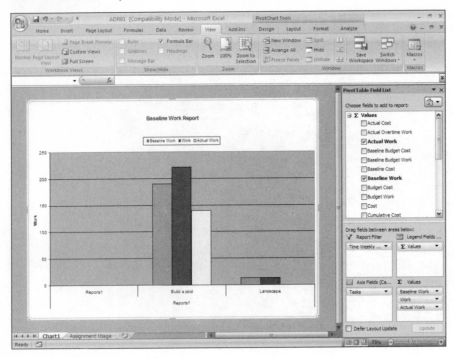

Budget Cost Report

The Budget Cost Report is an Excel PivotTable that produces a column chart (see Figure 13.53) that compares budget cost, baseline cost, planned cost, and actual cost.

FIGURE 13.53

The Budget Cost Report.

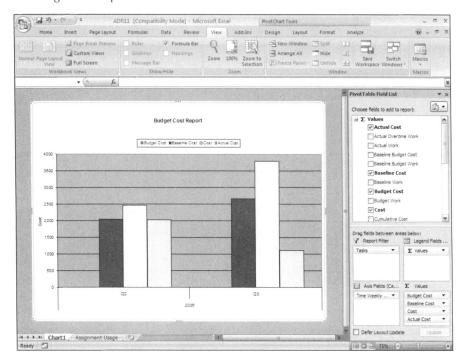

Budget Work Report

Similar to its cousin the Budget Cost Report, the Budget Work Report is an Excel PivotTable that produces a column chart (see Figure 13.54) that compares budget work, baseline work, planned work, and actual work.

FIGURE 13.54

The Budget Work Report.

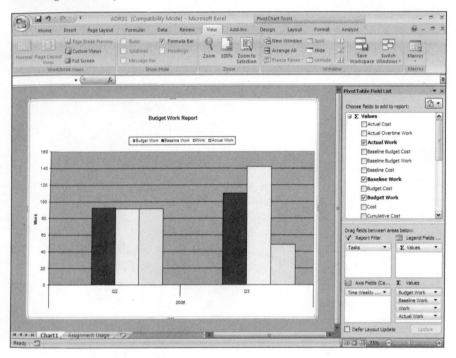

Summary reports

Finally, you'll find two task summary visual reports, one resource summary visual report, and one assignment summary visual report. US and Metric versions exist for both task summary reports and the assignment summary report.

Critical Tasks Status Report

This task summary report comes in a Metric version and a US version. A Visio PivotDiagram, the Critical Tasks Status Report (see Figure 13.55) shows the work and remaining work for both critical and noncritical tasks, along with the percent of work complete.

The Critical Tasks Status Report.

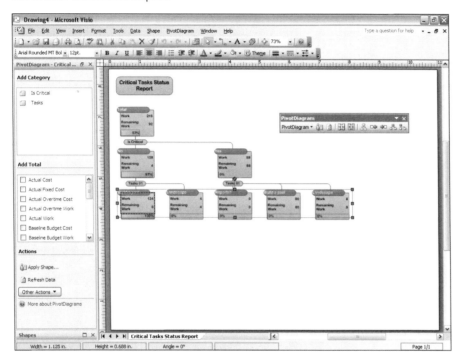

Task Status Report

This task summary report also comes in a Metric version and a US version. A Visio PivotDiagram, the Task Status Report (see Figure 13.56) shows work and percent of work complete for tasks at the highest level in your project outline.

FIGURE 13.56

The Task Status Report.

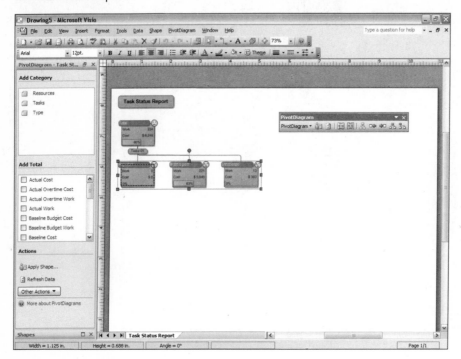

Resource Remaining Work Report

A resource summary report, the Resource Remaining Work Report is an Excel PivotTable that produces a column chart (see Figure 13.57) that shows work, remaining work, and total work for each work resource on your project.

FIGURE 13.57

The Resource Remaining Work Report.

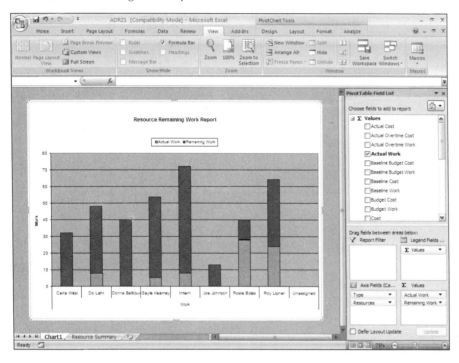

Resource Status Report

This assignment summary report also comes in a Metric version and a US version. A Visio PivotDiagram, the Resource Status Report (see Figure 13.58) shows work and cost values for each of your project's resources.

FIGURE 13.58

The Resource Status Report.

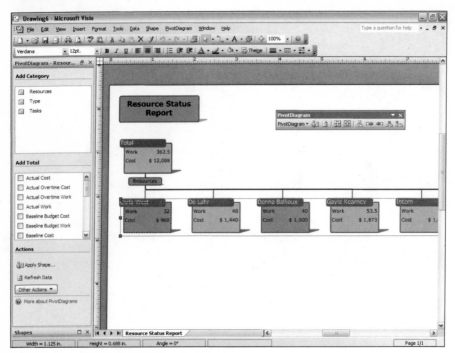

Customizing visual report templates

Because of the variety of available report templates, the odds are good that you won't need to create your own template. But you can create a new template or edit an existing template to suit your needs.

When you create a new template, Project bases it on an existing template. To create a new custom visual report template, follow these steps:

1. Choose Reports ⇨ Visual Reports to display the Visual Reports – Create Report dialog box.

2. Click the New Template button. Project displays the Visual Reports – New Template dialog box (see Figure 13.59).

3. Choose Excel or Visio as the application that will display the report. If you select Visio, choose between Visio (Metric) or Visio (US Units).

4. Open the Choose the data on which you want to report list box and select an existing visual report to act as the foundation for your new report.

FIGURE 13.59

Use this dialog box to describe the new template you want to create.

 To include timephased data on your report, select Task Usage, Resource Usage, or Assignment Usage.

5. Click the Field Picker button. Project displays the Visual Reports – Field Picker dialog box (see Figure 13.60).

FIGURE 13.60

Use this dialog box to select the fields you want to include in your visual report template.

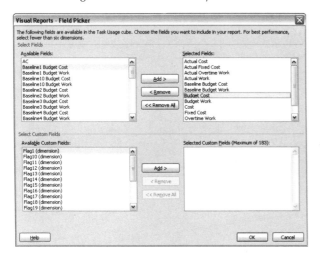

The fields that appear in this dialog box change depending on the report template you selected in Step 4. But the dialog box functions the same, regardless of the choice you make in Step 4. The columns on the right show the fields currently included in the report template, and the columns on the left show the fields available to add to the template. To include a new field, click it in one of the columns on the left and click the Add button. To remove an existing field from the report, click it in one of the columns on the right and click Remove. When you finish selecting fields, click OK twice.

Project begins to go through the process of building the report that you described. Either an Excel window or a Visio window appears to enable you to establish the PivotTable or PivotDiagram. Figure 13.61 shows an empty Excel PivotTable with fields on the right so that I can drag and drop the fields into the appropriate places on the PivotTable.

FIGURE 13.61

A blank PivotTable or PivotDiagram appears so that you can format your report.

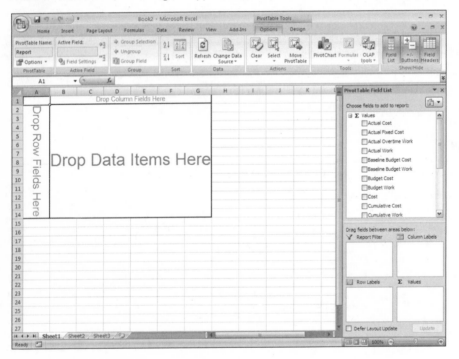

When you finish setting up the template, click Office ➪ Save As. In the Save As dialog box, the default location for templates appears automatically. Provide a name for the template and click Save.

 If you save your template in the default location, it will appear automatically in the Visual Reports window along with other visual report templates.

You also can export data as an OLAP cube or as a reporting database; see Chapter 25 for details.

Summary

In this chapter, you found out how to produce text reports and visual report in Project, and you examined samples of the text and visual reports available in Project.

In addition, you should now know how to customize any standard text report or visual report in Project. The next chapter shows you how to analyze your project's progress.

Chapter 14

Analyzing Financial Progress

W hen you analyze the progress of your project, you must measure not only the progress of the schedule but also the progress based on the costs that you incur. In Microsoft Project, you measure the earned value of your project.

Understanding Earned Value

Earned value is the measurement that project managers use to evaluate the progress of a project based on the cost of work performed up to the project status date. When Project calculates earned value, by default it compares your original cost estimates to the actual work performed to show whether your project is on budget. You can think of earned value as a measurement that indicates how much of the budget should have been spent in comparison to the cost of the work performed thus far to the baseline cost for the task, resource, or assignment.

NOTE You can calculate earned value by manually recording the Physical % Complete instead of letting Project calculate % Complete, which is actual duration divided by total duration.

To work with and use earned value information effectively, you must first perform the following tasks:

- Save a baseline for your project
- Assign resources with costs to tasks in your project
- Complete some work on your project

451

Understanding earned value fields

The fields that appear as headings in the Earned Value report you saw in Chapter 13 also appear on various earned value tables. *Earned value fields* are currency fields that measure various aspects of earned value. The following table translates the acronyms that Project uses to represent the earned value fields.

Acronyms	Earned Value Fields
BCWS	Budgeted Cost of Work Scheduled
BCWP	Budgeted Cost of Work Performed
ACWP	Actual Cost of Work Performed
SV	Schedule Variance
CV	Cost Variance
BAC	Budgeted at Completion
EAC	Estimate at Completion
VAC	Variance at Completion

Three of the preceding fields are really at the heart of earned value analysis:

- BCWS measures the budgeted cost of individual tasks based on the resources and fixed costs that are assigned to the tasks when you schedule them.

- BCWP indicates how much of a task's budget should have been spent given the actual duration of the task. For example, suppose that you have a task budgeted at $100 and work has been performed for one day. You find that, after one day, 40 percent of the work has been completed. You would expect that 40 percent of the cost of the task, or $40, would also be incurred. Therefore, the BCWP for the task is $40.

- ACWP measures the actual cost that is incurred to complete a task. During the completion process, ACWP represents the actual costs for work performed through the project's status date.

BCWS, BCWP, ACWP, SV, and CV are all calculated through today or through the project status date. SV represents the cost difference between current progress and the baseline plan, and Project calculates this value as BCWP minus BCWS. CV represents the cost difference between actual costs and planned costs at the current level of completion, and Project calculates this value as BCWP minus ACWP. EAC shows the planned costs based on costs that are already incurred plus additional planned costs. VAC represents the variance between the baseline cost and the combination of actual costs plus planned costs for a task.

> **NOTE** Project calculates BCWP at the task level differently from the way it calculates BCWP at the assignment level. Because Project rolls the task-level BCWP values into summary tasks and the project summary task, I suggest that you use the task-level BCWP values.

Project uses BCWS, BCWP, ACWP, SV, and CV as task fields, resource fields, and assignment fields; Project also uses timephased versions of each field. BAC, EAC, and VAC, however, are task fields only.

Project 2003 introduced some earned value fields, some of which appear by default on earned value tables. And, using the techniques described in Chapter 7, you can add any of these fields to any table:

- **Physical % Complete:** This field represents your estimate of the progress of a task, regardless of actual work or time, and is not a timephased field. Project uses Physical % Complete to calculate BCWP on subtasks and rolls up BCWP to associated summary tasks. See the next section for details on having Project use Physical % Complete as the method for calculating earned value.

> **NOTE** You may be wondering about the difference between the % Complete field and the Physical % Complete field. Project calculates % Complete by dividing actual task duration by total duration. Physical % Complete is *your* estimate of where a task stands and has no connection to duration.

- **CPI:** CPI stands for *Cost Performance Index,* and Project calculates CPI by dividing BCWP by ACWP. This field appears by default in the Earned Value Cost Indicators table and is a timephased field.

- **SPI:** SPI stands for *Schedule Performance Index,* and Project calculates SPI by dividing BCWP by BCWS. This field appears by default in the Earned Value Schedule Indicators table and is a timephased field.

- **CV%:** CV% stands for *Cost Variance %,* and Project calculates this field by dividing CV by BCWP and multiplying the result by 100. This field appears by default in the Earned Value Cost Indicators table and is a timephased field.

- **SV%:** SV% stands for *Schedule Variance %,* and Project calculates this field by dividing SV by BCWS and multiplying the result by 100. This field appears by default in the Earned Value Schedule Indicators table and is a timephased field.

- **EAC:** EAC stands for *Estimate at Completion,* and although this field isn't new (it existed in Project 2000), it was improved in Project 2003. Project calculates this field by using the following formula: ACWP + (BAC – BCWP) / CPI. This field appears by default in the Earned Value for Tasks and the Earned Value Cost Indicators tables and is not a timephased field.

> **NOTE** The meaning of EAC changed in Project 2003. In Project 2000, EAC was simply the cost of the task, retitled to "EAC." In Project 2003, the field became a separate field with a formula behind it.

- **TCPI:** TCPI stands for *To Complete Performance Index,* and Project calculates this field by using the following formula: (BAC – BCWP) / (EAC – ACWP). This field appears by default in the Earned Value Cost Indicators table and is not a timephased field.

Using the Physical % Complete method to calculate earned value

Project can use the % Complete method or the Physical % Complete method to calculate earned value. Unless you specify otherwise, Project uses the % Complete method.

You can set Physical % Complete as the default earned value calculation method for your project by following these steps:

1. Choose Tools ⇨ Options.

2. Click the Calculation tab.

3. Click the Earned Value button. The Earned Value dialog box appears (see Figure 14.1).

FIGURE 14.1

Choose the method of earned value calculation that you want Project to use.

4. From the Default task Earned Value method list box, choose Physical % Complete.

5. From the Baseline for Earned Value calculations list box, choose a baseline (Project stores 11 baselines for earned value).

 Clearing a baseline *after* entering Physical % Complete values does *not* clear those values.

6. Click OK twice to save the settings.

The preceding steps set the default for all new tasks that you enter in your project. If your project already contains tasks (or if you want to use the Physical % Complete method for some but not all tasks), set the earned value calculation method on a task-by-task basis. Follow these steps to do so:

1. Select the task(s) for which you want to set the earned value calculation method to Physical % Complete.

2. Click the Task Information button on the Standard toolbar.

3. Click the Advanced tab.

4. From the Earned value method list box, choose Physical % Complete (see Figure 14.2).

Assign the Physical % Complete method as appropriate to tasks in the Task Information dialog box.

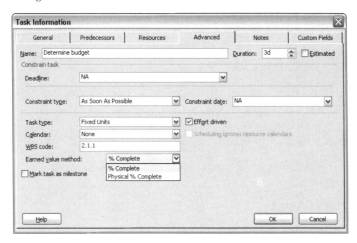

To record Physical % Complete, add the field as a column on a table view (in Figure 14.3, I've added it to the Earned Value for Tasks table) and then enter appropriate amounts for tasks. You'll see other earned value fields update accordingly.

 To insert a column, click the heading of the column to the right of the column that you are inserting. Then choose Insert ⇨ Column.

Setting the date for earned-value calculations

By default, Project uses today's date to calculate earned-value information. However, you can set a project status date for Project to use instead of today's date when it calculates earned value. From any view, choose Project ⇨ Project Information to open the Project Information dialog box (see Figure 14.4).

FIGURE 14.3

Record Physical % Complete values by adding the field to a table and then entering the information.

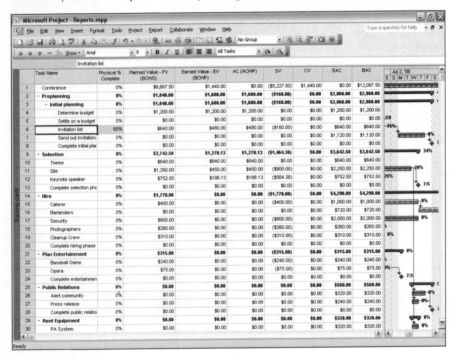

FIGURE 14.4

Use this dialog box to set a date for Project to use when calculating earned value.

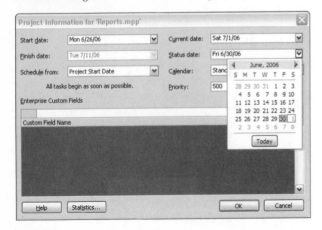

From the Status Date list box, select the date that you want Project to use when it calculates earned value and click OK.

Using earned value tables

Project contains four earned-value tables that you can use to compare your expected costs with your actual costs. The four earned-value tables — Earned Value for Tasks, Earned Value Cost Indicators, Earned Value Schedule Indicators, and Earned Value for Resources — help you evaluate the relationship between work and costs. You can use the earned-value tables to forecast whether a task will finish within the budget based on the comparison of the actual costs incurred for the task to date and the baseline cost of the task.

Using the Earned Value table for tasks

When you use the Earned Value table for tasks, you can compare the relationship between work and costs for tasks. This table helps you evaluate your budget to estimate future budget needs and prepare an accounting statement of your project. You can use the information in the table to determine whether sufficient work is getting done for the money that you're paying or whether tasks need more money or less money, or perhaps should be cut. That is, the information in the Earned Value for tasks table helps you assess whether the money that you're spending on a task is enough money, too much money, too little money, or perhaps wasted money.

To display the Earned Value table for tasks, follow these steps:

1. Start in any task view, such as the Task Usage view.

2. Right-click the Select All button and choose More Tables from the shortcut menu that appears.

3. In the More Tables dialog box that appears, select Earned Value.

4. Click Apply. Project applies the Earned Value table for tasks to the view (see Figure 14.5).

All the fields on this sheet except BAC are calculated. You can type values in the field to change information in the table.

FIGURE 14.5

The Earned Value table for tasks.

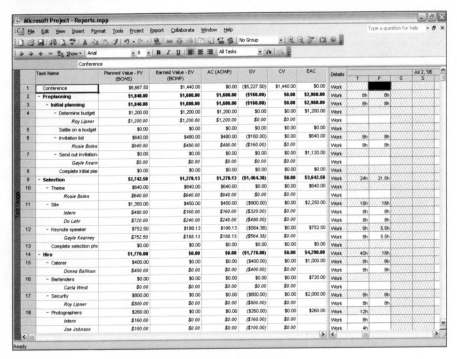

Using the Earned Value table for resources

When you use the Earned Value table for resources, you can compare the relationship between work and costs for resources. This table also helps you to evaluate your budget to estimate future budget needs and prepare an accounting statement of your project. You can use the information in the table to determine whether the work is getting done for the money that you're paying or whether you need more or less of a particular resource.

To display the Earned Value table for resources (see Figure 14.6), follow the same steps you used in the preceding section to display the Earned Value table for tasks, but start in any resource view, such as the Resource Sheet view.

All the fields in this sheet except BAC are calculated. You can enter values in this field to change information in the table.

FIGURE 14.6

The Earned Value table for resources.

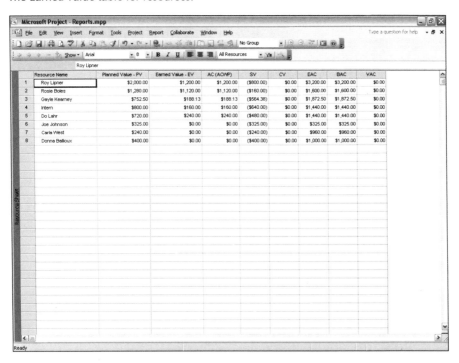

Using the Earned Value Cost Indicators and Earned Value Schedule Indicators tables

Project 2003 introduced two tables that are similar to their cousin, the Earned Value for Tasks table. The Earned Value Cost Indicators table enables you to compare the various cost factors related to tasks in your project (see Figure 14.7). The Earned Value Schedule Indicators table for tasks enables you to focus on the effects of scheduling variances on the cost of your project (see Figure 14.8).

FIGURE 14.7

The Earned Value Cost Indicators table closely resembles the Earned Value for Tasks table but focuses on different earned-value fields.

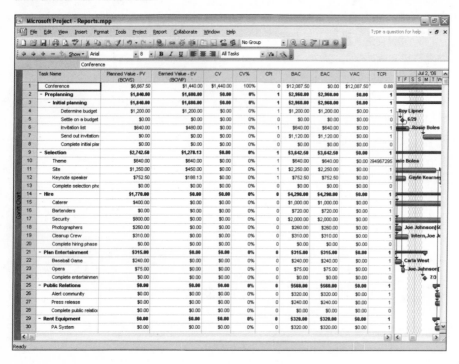

To display the Earned Value Cost Indicators table, start in any task view that contains a table. Then, right-click the Select All button and choose More Tables from the shortcut menu that appears. In the More Tables dialog box, select Earned Value Cost Indicators and click Apply.

To display the Earned Value Schedule Indicators table, start in any task view that contains a table. Then, right-click the Select All button and choose More Tables from the shortcut menu that appears. In the More Tables dialog box, select Earned Value Schedule Indicators and click Apply.

The Earned Value Schedule Indicators table closely resembles the Earned Value for Tasks table but focuses on different earned-value fields.

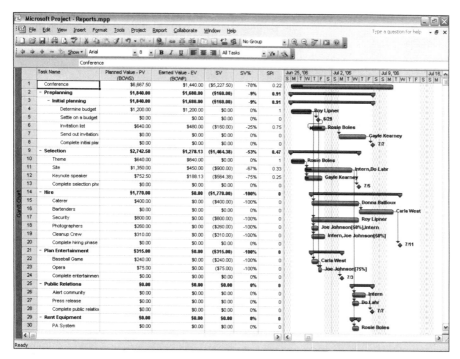

Evaluating Cost Information

If you own Microsoft Excel, you can use it to assist you in evaluating cost information. By exporting information to Excel, you can chart earned value, analyze timescaled information, or create PivotTables.

Charting earned value

The saying goes, "A picture is worth a thousand words." And when looking at earned-value information, you may find it easier to understand the information if you use a picture rather than study Project's earned-value tables. You can export the earned-value information to Microsoft Excel (you must be using Excel version 5.0 or later) and then use Excel's Chart Wizard to create charts of earned-value information.

CROSS-REF   To find out more about Project's capabilities to export and import data, see Chapter 25.

When you export earned values from Project to Excel, you create an Excel workbook that contains a task ID, a name, and the various earned values for each task (see Figure 14.9).

FIGURE 14.9

An Excel workbook that was created by exporting earned-value information from Project to Excel.

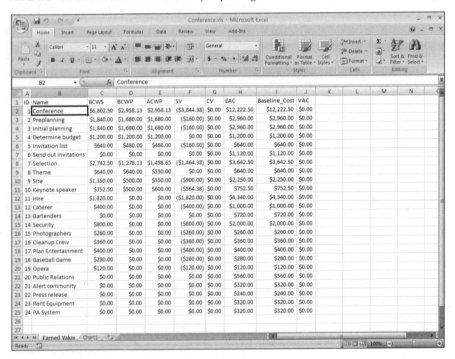

To create an Excel workbook like the one shown in Figure 14.9, follow these steps:

1. In the Project file containing the information that you want to use in Excel, choose File ⇨ Save As to open the Save As dialog box.

2. Type a name for the Excel workbook in the File Name list box. Don't worry about the extension; Project supplies it.

3. Open the Save as type list box and select Microsoft Excel Workbook. The Save As dialog box should resemble the one that is shown in Figure 14.10.

FIGURE 14.10

The Save As dialog box as it appears after you choose to save an Excel workbook file.

4. Click Save to start the Export Mapping wizard.

5. Click Next.

6. Choose Selected Data in the next box of the wizard and then click Next.

7. Choose Use existing map in the next box of the wizard and then click Next.

8. Choose Earned Value information from the list of available maps in the Export Wizard dialog box (see Figure 14.11) and click Finish.

FIGURE 14.11

Choose Earned value information as the map from the Export Wizard dialog box.

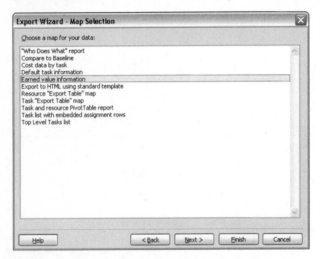

You can continue clicking Next in the wizard, but to chart earned value in Excel, you usually don't need to make any changes in the remaining dialog boxes that the wizard presents.

Open Microsoft Excel and then choose Office ⇨ Open. In the Open dialog box that appears, navigate to open the workbook that you just created. You can use Excel's Chart Wizard to create as many charts from this data as you want. For example, the chart in Figure 14.12 compares budgeted cost of work performed with actual cost of work performed for three tasks.

FIGURE 14.12

An Excel chart comparing two earned values for selected tasks.

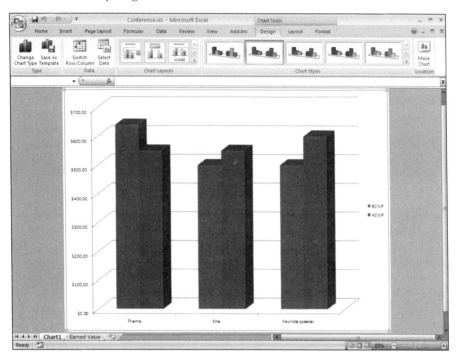

To create a chart like the one shown in Figure 14.12, follow these steps:

1. Select the cells you want to chart. For the example chart, I selected the cells D9.E11.

2. Click Insert and then click Column to open the Column gallery (see Figure 14.13).

FIGURE 14.13

Select a column chart style for the selected data.

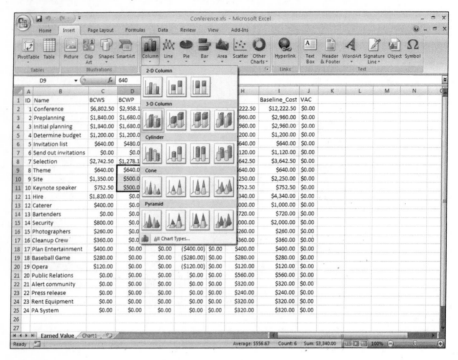

3. Select a column style. Excel inserts the chart in your spreadsheet; the chart is selected. Chart Tools appear on the Ribbon.

4. Click Select Data on the Ribbon to display the Select Data Source dialog box (see Figure 14.14).

5. Click an entry in the Legend Entries list; in the example, I clicked Series1.

6. Click Edit. Excel displays the Edit Series dialog box (see Figure 14.15).

7. Click the Series Name Collapse Dialog button at the right edge of the Series Name box. Excel collapses the dialog box so that you can select a cell in the spreadsheet.

8. Click the column heading for the value represented by the leftmost bar; in the example, I clicked D1, which contains the label for BCWP. Excel changes the information in the collapsed Edit Series dialog box to match your selection (see Figure 14.16).

FIGURE 14.14

Use this dialog box to assign meaning labels to the data in the chart.

Edit button   Select Data button

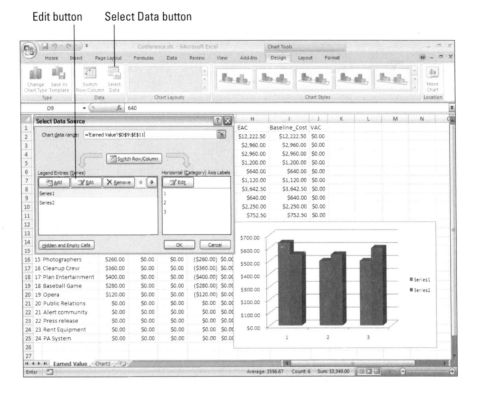

FIGURE 14.15

Use this dialog box to select a legend label.

Collapse Dialog button

FIGURE 14.16

The collapsed Edit Series dialog box containing a legend label selection.

9. Click the Collapse Dialog button to redisplay Edit Series dialog box; then, click OK to redisplay the Edit Data Source dialog box. Excel shows the name change in the Legend Entries list in the dialog box and on your chart (see Figure 14.17).

FIGURE 14.17

The legend for the first set of values now displays a name instead of the generic title "Series1" that Excel assigns.

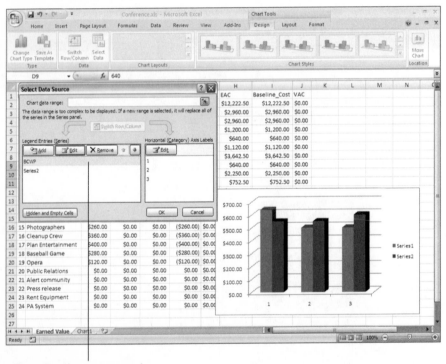

The name change appears here.

10. Repeat Steps 5 to 9 for Series2.

11. For the entries in the Horizontal Axis Labels list, repeat Steps 5 to 9 to select row headings to use as X-axis labels, *with one exception:* Select all row labels simultaneously. In the example, when I repeated Step 8, I selected cells B9.B11 to replace the numbers 1, 2, and 3 that Excel assigned to the X axis of the chart. You complete Step 11 only *once;* this step assigns labels to all three entries in the Horizontal Axis Labels list simultaneously. When you complete this step, the Edit Data Source dialog box will resemble the one shown in Figure 14.18.

FIGURE 14.18

The Edit Data Source dialog box after you have assigned labels to the horizontal axis and the legend.

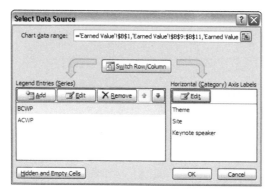

12. Click OK.

In the chart shown previously in Figure 14.12, I placed the chart in its own sheet by making sure that the chart was selected and clicking Move Chart Location at the right edge of the Design tab on the Ribbon. In the Move Chart dialog box that appeared, I clicked the New sheet option.

Using PivotTables for analysis

Excel PivotTables can be interesting and useful when you want to analyze Project earned-value data. The PivotTable is an interactive table that summarizes large amounts of data in a cross-tabular format. When you use Project to create a PivotTable in Excel, you get two PivotTables in the same workbook: a Task PivotTable and a Resource PivotTable. The Task PivotTable shows resources, tasks to which the resources are assigned, and costs for the resource per task. The Resource PivotTable summarizes resources by showing work that is assigned to each resource and the total cost of each resource. In addition to the PivotTable worksheets, the same Excel workbook also includes two worksheets—Tasks and Resources—that Excel uses to create these two PivotTables.

To export Project information to create PivotTables in Excel, follow these steps:

1. Start in any view of your project.

2. Choose File ⇨ Save As to open the Save As dialog box.

3. Type a name for the Excel workbook that you want to create in the File Name box. Don't worry about the extension — Project supplies it.

4. Select Microsoft Excel PivotTable from the Save As Type list box.

5. Click Save to start the Export Mapping Wizard.

6. Click Next.

7. Choose Use Existing Map and click Next.

8. Select Task and resource PivotTable and then click Finish (see Figure 14.19). The hourglass icon for the mouse pointer appears, indicating that you should wait while action takes place. You'll also hear action on your hard drive.

FIGURE 14.19

The Map Selection portion of the Export Wizard dialog box.

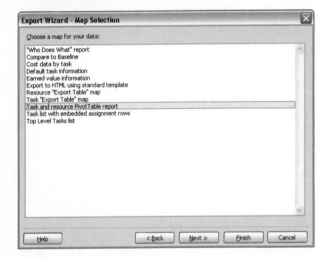

   You can continue clicking Next in the wizard, but to chart earned value in Excel, you usually don't need to make any changes in the remaining dialog boxes that the wizard presents.

To view the PivotTables and their source data, start Excel and open the file that you just created. The workbook contains four sheets that should resemble the sheets that appear in Figures 14-20, 14-21, 14-22, and 14-23.

FIGURE 14.20

The Resource PivotTable.

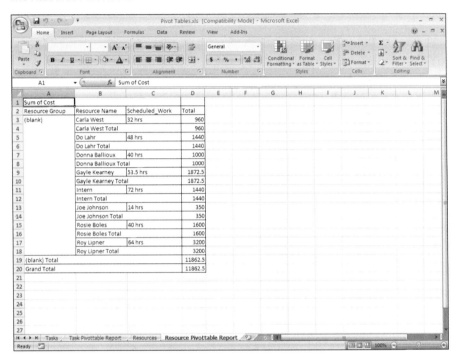

FIGURE 14.21

The Resources sheet that Excel used to create the Resource PivotTable.

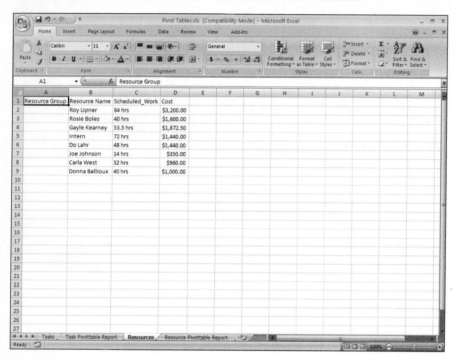

FIGURE 14.22

The Task PivotTable.

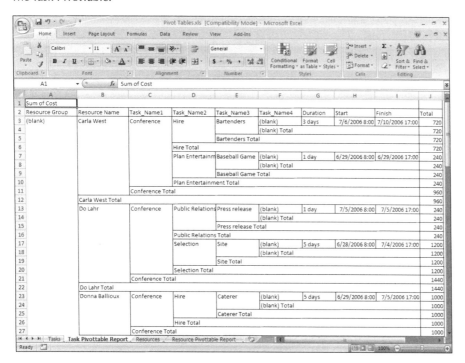

FIGURE 14.23

The Tasks sheet that Excel used to create the Task PivotTable.

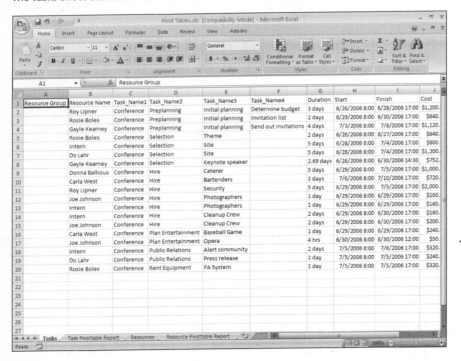

> **TIP** You may need to widen columns in Excel to see all the data. Double-click the right border of the column letter to do so.

Making Adjustments During the Project

Now that you've seen the various ways you can collect and analyze financial data about your project, you need to use that information to make improvements to your project. You can use many of the techniques that you used to implement changes to your project because of scheduling problems or resource conflicts.

> **CROSS-REF** Find out how to deal with scheduling problems by using the techniques that are discussed in Chapter 9. You'll find help resolving resource problems in Chapter 10.

Changing the schedule

After evaluating earned value information, you may want to change the schedule. For example, you may want to do the following:

- Add resources to tasks
- Use overtime
- Increase task duration
- Adjust slack
- Change task constraints
- Adjust dependencies
- Split tasks
- Adjust the critical path

You may also need to make changes to the baseline project that you saved.

CROSS-REF For more information on adjusting the baseline, see Chapter 11.

Modifying resource assignments

Your evaluation of earned value information may prompt you to make changes to resource assignments on your project. For example, you may need to do the following:

- Change resource allocations
- Schedule overtime
- Redefine a resource's calendar
- Assign part-time work
- Control when resources start working on a task
- Level workloads
- Contour resources
- Pool resources

TIP When you're working on an unusually large project, you may find it easier to break your project into smaller, more manageable portions called *subprojects*. In Project, you can create subprojects and then consolidate them into the larger project to see the bigger picture (see Chapter 15).

Summary

This chapter explained how to analyze the costs in your project. After reading this chapter, you should know the following:

■ How to use Project's earned value tables

■ How to chart earned value information, analyze timescaled information, and use Microsoft Excel PivotTables

■ How to make adjustments to your project

In Chapters 15 through 21, you discover how Project helps you work in groups.

Part V

Working in Groups

Chapter 15

Coordinating Multiple Projects Outside Project Server

arge projects are the most difficult to manage. Organization is a corner-stone to good project management, and in a large project, the sheer number of tasks makes the job more difficult than usual. In Microsoft Project, you can use the concept of consolidated projects to break projects into smaller, "bite-sized" pieces and then combine the smaller projects to view the bigger picture.

Consolidating Projects

When you're faced with a complex problem, finding the solution typically becomes easier if you can simplify the problem. Similarly, when you need to manage a complex project with many tasks, you may find it easier to organize the process if you deal with a limited number of tasks at one time.

Microsoft Project makes it easy for you to take this approach to planning large, complex projects. By using Project's consolidation features, you can create subprojects, which you can think of as the tasks that constitute one portion of your large project. When you create a subproject, you save it as a separate project file. You can assign resources and set up each subproject with links and constraints — just as if it were the entire project. When you need to view the bigger picture, you can consolidate the subprojects into one large project. When you consolidate, you insert one project into another project; therefore, subprojects are also called *inserted projects*.

Consolidation Concepts

Consolidation changed from Project 95 to Project 98. In Project 95, many project tools, such as copying and pasting, didn't work in consolidated projects. Project 95 used two techniques to work with multiple projects: *consolidation,* and *master projects* and *subprojects.* By using the second technique, you created a link between a placeholder task in the master project and the subproject.

In Project 98, you no longer needed to think about master projects versus subprojects. Subprojects still existed as separate projects, but you included subprojects in a consolidated project. In addition, Project 98 provided much greater flexibility in the consolidated project, but sacrificed performance. Project 2000, Project 2003, and Project 2007 all handle consolidation in the same way as Project 98, but you'll find improved consolidation performance in the later editions of Project. You can think of the consolidated project as the host project into which you insert subprojects.

NOTE   If you're a Project Professional user who also uses Project Server, you may be wondering whether consolidation applies to you. Although views in Project Server can "roll up" project information, you still need consolidation techniques if you want to see one critical path across all consolidated projects. Also, I describe resource pooling in this chapter. This concept applies more to Project Standard users than Project Professional users using Project Server. Project Professional users using Project Server can use the Enterprise Resource Pool in Project Server.

When you work in a consolidated project, you can focus on just the desired portion of the project. Subprojects appear as summary tasks in the consolidated project, and you can use Project's outlining tools to hide all tasks that are associated with any subproject.

CROSS-REF   See Chapter 3 for more information on outlining.

From the consolidated project, you can view, print, and change information for any subproject — just as if you were working with a single project.

Setting up to use consolidation

Consolidation can help you achieve the following objectives:

- Tasks in projects that are managed by different people may be interdependent. Through consolidation, you can create the correct dependencies to accurately display the project's schedule and necessary resources while still allowing independent project management.

- A project may be so large that breaking it into smaller pieces can help you to organize it. You can use consolidation to combine the smaller pieces to view the big picture.

■ You may be pooling the resources of several projects and find that you need to level the resources. Consolidating enables you to link the projects sharing the resources so that you can level the resources.

NOTE If you're using Project Standard, you can't take advantage of the Enterprise Resource Pool that's available in Project Server; therefore, the resource pooling techniques that I describe in this chapter apply to you. If you're using Project Professional and Project Server, you may want to consider using the Enterprise Resource Pool instead of using resource pooling as described in this chapter. To do so, see Chapter 18.

When should you decide to use consolidation? It doesn't really matter. You may realize right away that the project is too large to handle in a traditional way, or you may discover that the project is bigger than you originally thought as you work on it. Suppose, for example, that the Marketing department of a software company decides midway through the development cycle to bundle various products under development. Doing so introduces dependencies where none originally existed — and provides an interesting opportunity for using consolidation.

If you decide to use consolidation before you start your project, simply create separate Microsoft Project files for various portions of the project. These files act as subprojects when you consolidate. You need to set up each subproject file so that it is independently complete, and you need to create links within each subproject file, as necessary. This chapter explains techniques for consolidating the subprojects and linking them.

If you start a project and then decide that you want to use consolidation, you can create subprojects by following these steps:

1. Save your large project file.

2. Select all the tasks that you want to save in your first subproject file and click the Copy button.

3. Click the New button to start a new project; use the Project Information dialog box (see Figure 15.1) to set basic project information, such as the project's start date and scheduling method.

TIP If the Project Information dialog box doesn't appear automatically when you start a new project, choose Project ➪ Project Information to display it. To make the Project Information dialog box appear each time you start a new project, choose Tools ➪ Options, click the General tab, and check the Prompt for Project Info for New Projects check box.

4. Click the Paste button.

FIGURE 15.1

Use the Project Information dialog box to set basic project information.

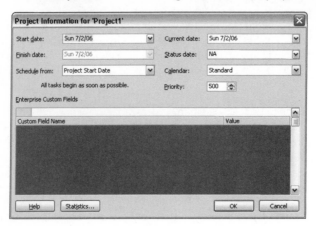

5. Save the subproject, and close it.

6. Repeat Steps 2 through 5 until you have saved several separate files that contain portions of your larger project.

Edit each subproject file that you create to make it an independently complete project. Then, you can use the techniques that are explained in the following section to consolidate the subprojects and link them.

Inserting a project

To consolidate project files into one large project, you insert projects into a host project file, often referred to as the *consolidated project file*. Each project that you insert appears as a summary task in the consolidated project file, and Project calculates inserted projects the same way as summary tasks. An icon in the Indicator field identifies an inserted project (see Figure 15.2).

FIGURE 15.2

A special icon in the Indicator field identifies inserted projects.

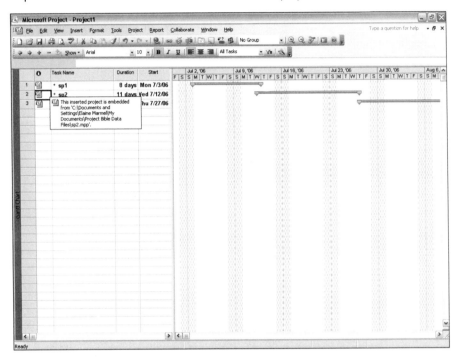

You can insert projects at any outline level. The level at which an inserted project appears depends on the outline level that appears at the location where you intend to insert a project. To insert a project, simply select the task that you want to appear below the inserted project; Project then inserts the project above the selected task. Typically, an inserted project appears at the same level as the selected task. However, if the task that is above the selected task is indented farther than the selected task, the inserted project appears at the same level as that indented task. Or, if the task that's above the selected task is at the same level or outdented farther than the selected task, the inserted project appears in the outline at the same level as the selected task. Compare Figures 15-3, 15-4, and 15-5.

FIGURE 15.3

I expanded the Initial Planning Meeting task and then chose the Selection task when I inserted subproject2. This subproject appears at the same outline level as the Send Out Invitation task that's above it.

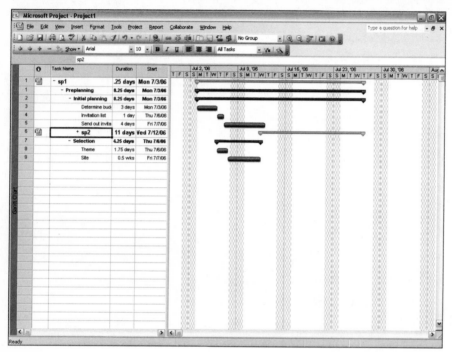

FIGURE 15.4

I collapsed the Initial Planning Meeting task and then chose the Selection task when I inserted subproject2. This subproject appears at the same outline level as the Initial Planning Meeting task.

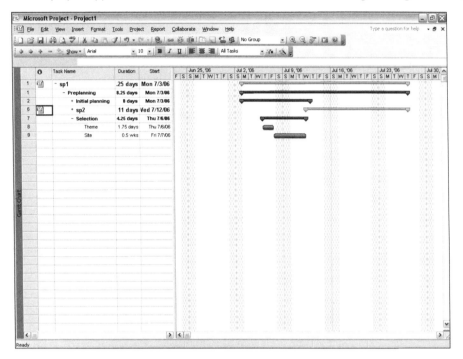

FIGURE 15.5

I selected the Determine Budget task and then inserted subproject2. This subproject appears at the same outline level as Determine Budget because the task above — Initial Planning Meeting — is outdented farther than Determine Budget (the selected task).

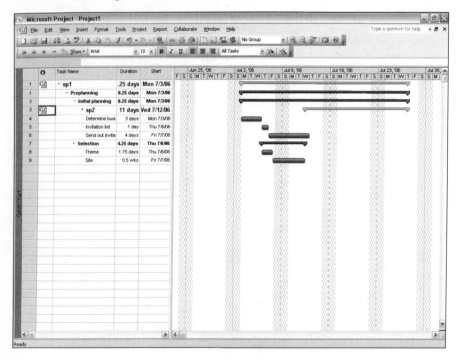

To produce a consolidated project in which the inserted projects line up at the highest outline level the same way as those of the project that appears in Figure 15.6, make sure that you collapse the preceding inserted project so that you can't see its tasks when you insert the next subproject.

TIP   You can hide or show tasks after you insert the project by clicking the summary task's outline symbol — the plus or minus sign next to the task name.

FIGURE 15.6

When subproject3 was inserted, subproject2 was selected and its subordinate tasks were visible, but the subordinate tasks of subproject1 were not visible.

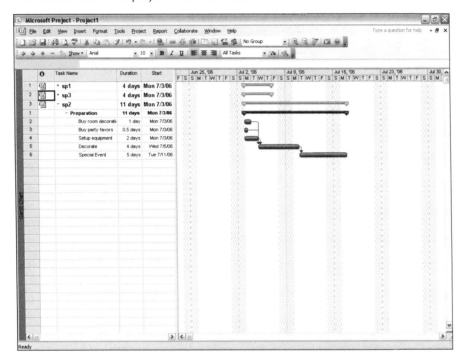

To insert a project, follow these steps:

1. Open the project in which you want to store the consolidated project.

2. Switch to the Gantt Chart view.

3. Click the Task Name column in the row where you want the inserted project to begin.

> **NOTE** When you insert a project, Project places the project immediately above the selected row. Therefore, if your consolidated project already contains tasks, click the task in the Task Name column that you want to appear below the subproject.

4. Choose Insert ⇨ Project to open the Insert Project dialog box (see Figure 15.7).

487

The Insert Project dialog box works the same as the Open dialog box.

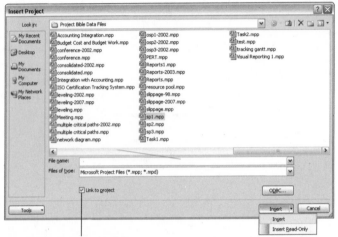

Link to project check box

5. Use the Look In list box to navigate to the folder that contains the project that you want to insert.

6. Highlight the file that you want to insert.

7. Change any insert project options as follows:

    ■ If you remove the check from the Link to Project check box, Project doesn't link the inserted project to its source project.

    ■ If you choose Insert Read-Only from the Insert drop-down menu, Project doesn't change the source project when you change the inserted project.

8. Click Insert (or Insert Read-Only). Project inserts the selected file into the open project. The inserted file appears as a summary task, with its subordinate tasks hidden.

Using inserted projects and their source files

You can link an inserted project to its source file, as you saw in Figure 15.7. If you don't link an inserted project to its source file, any changes that you make to the inserted project while working in the consolidated project file don't affect the source file. Similarly, any changes that you make to the source file don't affect the consolidated project file that contains the subproject. Therefore, why wouldn't you want to link the files? You may want to create a consolidated file just so that you can generate a report quickly.

In many circumstances, linking the files makes updating easier. Linking ensures that any changes that you make in either the consolidated project or the subproject file affect the other file. When you insert a project and link it to its source file, you create a link between two files that works like any link that you create between two files in the Windows environment. For example, if you rename the subproject file or move it to a different folder than the one in which you originally saved it, you need to update the link to the consolidated project; otherwise, the link does not work. If you move a file that you have linked, you can update the link on the Advanced tab of the Inserted Project Information dialog box for the inserted project (see Figure 15.8).

FIGURE 15.8

The Advanced tab of the Inserted Project Information dialog box.

> **TIP** You also can unlink subprojects from their source files by using the Advanced tab of the Inserted Project Information dialog box. To do so, deselect the Link to Project check box.

Or you can simply attempt to expand the inserted project in the consolidated project file. When you click the plus sign next to the subproject, Project automatically displays a dialog box that looks like the Open dialog box. Use this dialog box to navigate to the new location of the file and click OK after you finish, reestablishing the link between the files.

Consolidating all open projects: A shortcut

Follow these steps to consolidate several subprojects at the same time:

1. Open all the subprojects that you want to consolidate.
2. Choose Window ➪ New Window to open the New Window dialog box (see Figure 15.9).

FIGURE 15.9

Use the New Window dialog box to quickly consolidate open projects.

3. Press and hold down Ctrl, and click each project that you want to consolidate.

4. Click OK.

Project creates a new consolidated project that contains the projects that you selected in the New Window dialog box. Project inserts the subprojects into the consolidated project in the order in which the subprojects appear in the New Window dialog box.

Moving subprojects within a consolidated project

You can move subprojects around in the consolidated project by cutting a subproject row to delete it and then pasting the row where you want it to appear. When you select a summary row that represents a subproject and click the Cut button on the Standard toolbar, Project opens the Planning Wizard dialog box (see Figure 15.10).

FIGURE 15.10

The Planning Wizard dialog box appears when you try to delete a summary task.

Select the Continue option button and click OK. The summary task that represents the subproject and all its subordinate tasks disappears. When you paste the subproject, Project places the subproject immediately above the selected row. Therefore, in the Task Name column, you must click the task that you want to appear below the subproject. Then click the Paste button on the Standard toolbar. Project reinserts the subproject at its new location.

 If you intend to move many tasks, you may want to select the Don't Tell Me About This Again check box to avoid viewing the Planning Wizard dialog box.

Understanding Consolidated Projects and Dependencies

In a consolidated project, you typically have tasks — either in the consolidated project or in one subproject — that are dependent on tasks in another subproject. You can create links between projects in a consolidated file, and if necessary you can change the links that you create.

Linking tasks across projects

You can create four different types of dependencies: finish-to-start, start-to-start, finish-to-finish, and start-to finish. In addition, these types support lead and lag time. The process of linking tasks with dependencies across projects is much the same as the process of creating dependencies for tasks within the same project. Starting in the consolidated project file, follow these steps:

1. Click the Gantt Chart on the View bar.
2. Select the tasks that you want to link.

 To select noncontiguous tasks, press and hold down Ctrl as you click each task name in the order you want to link the tasks.

3. Click the Link Tasks button on the Standard toolbar. Project creates a finish-to-start link between the two tasks.

 You can create the link in the consolidated project file by dragging from the Gantt bar of the predecessor task to the Gantt bar of the successor task.

You also can link tasks by typing in the Predecessors field, using the format `project name\ID#`. The project name should include the path to the location of the file as well as the filename, and the ID# should be the ID number of the task in that file. In Figure 15.11, the Buy room decorations task, Task 2 in a Project file called SP2.MPP, is linked to the Site task, which is Task 8 in a Project file called `SP1.MPP`. You can see the complete pathname of a linked task in the Entry bar (just below the toolbars) when you highlight the task.

FIGURE 15.11

You can type in the Predecessors field to create a link between tasks across Project files.

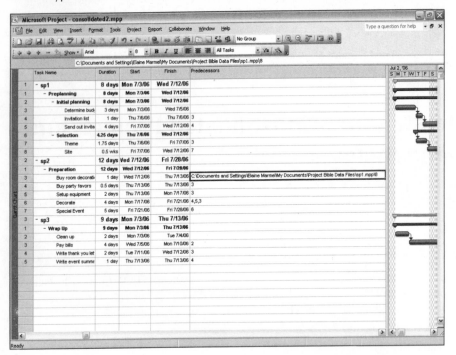

When you link tasks between projects, the task links look like standard links in the consolidated project. However, when you open either of the subproject files, you see that Project has inserted an external link (see Figure 15.12). The name and the Gantt Chart bar of each externally linked task appear gray. If you point at the Gantt Chart bar, Project displays information about the task, including the fact that it is an external task.

If you double-click the task name of the external task, Project opens the subproject that contains the task to which the external task is linked.

FIGURE 15.12

FIGURE 15.12

When you link tasks across files, Project inserts an external link in the subproject file.

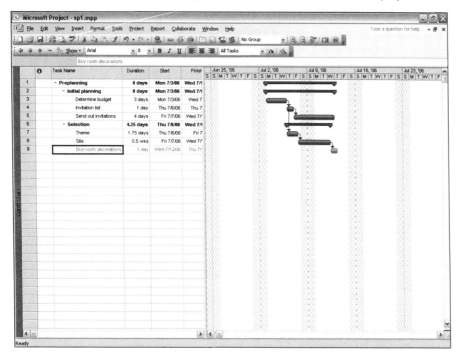

Changing links across projects

After you link tasks across projects, you may need to change information about the link. For example, you may want to change the type of dependency from the default finish-to-start link, or you may want to create lag time.

You can modify a link between tasks in different subprojects from the subproject or from the consolidated project. In the subproject, double-click the line that links an internal task to the external task (see Figure 15.13). In the consolidated project, double-click the line that links the two tasks (see Figure 15.14). In both cases, Project displays the Task Dependency dialog box.

FIGURE 15.13

In a subproject, double-click the link line between the internal task and the external task to display the Task Dependency dialog box.

Double-click this arrow

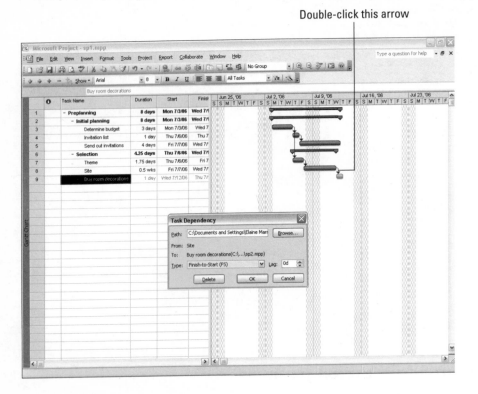

The two versions of the dialog boxes differ slightly. If you work from within the subproject, you can update the path of the link and use the Type list box to change the type of link and the Lag box to change the amount of lag time between the linked tasks. If you work from within the consolidated project, you can't update the path of the link, but you can change the type of link and the amount of lag time.

Consolidated projects — to save or not to save

You don't need to save consolidated project files unless you want them. You can create the consolidated project file by choosing either Window ➪ New Window or Insert ➪ Project—both are described earlier in this chapter. You can use the consolidated project to create links and even reports, and then close the consolidated project file without saving it. For example, suppose that you created the consolidated project by inserting projects and the inserted projects are not open. When you close the consolidated project, Project first asks whether you want to save the consolidated project. Whether you choose to save the consolidated project doesn't change Project's behavior; Project next asks whether you want to save changes that you made to inserted projects (see Figure 15.15).

FIGURE 15.14

In a consolidated project, double-click the line that links the tasks to display the Task Dependency dialog box and change the dependency information about tasks that are linked across projects.

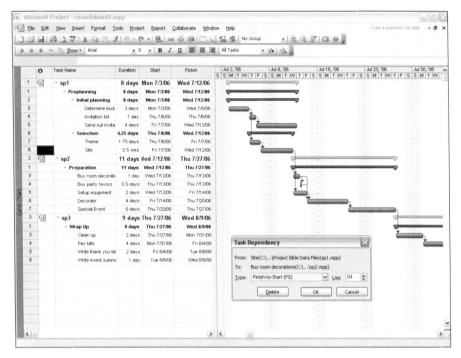

FIGURE 15.15

When you close a consolidated project that you created by inserting projects, Project asks whether you want to save changes — including links — that you made to each subproject.

Project treats a subproject file the same as any other Project file; when you close a subproject, Project asks whether you want to save changes to the file.

If you save the changes to the subprojects — even if you don't save the consolidated project — external tasks, such as the one that you saw previously in Figure 15.12, appear in the subproject files when you open them.

Viewing Multiple Projects

Creating a consolidated project makes your work easier because you can display and hide selected portions of your project. The consolidated project that appears in Figure 15.16 contains three inserted projects. As you can tell from the outline symbols, you can't see all the tasks in this consolidated project in the figure; the tasks for subproject3 are hidden.

Suppose that you need to focus on the middle portion of the project. As Figure 15.17 demonstrates, you can easily focus on the portion of the project that currently needs your attention by clicking the outline symbols to the left of each summary task to expand only the portion of the project that you want to view. Notice that task numbering within each subproject begins with Task ID 1.

FIGURE 15.16

This consolidated project contains three inserted projects.

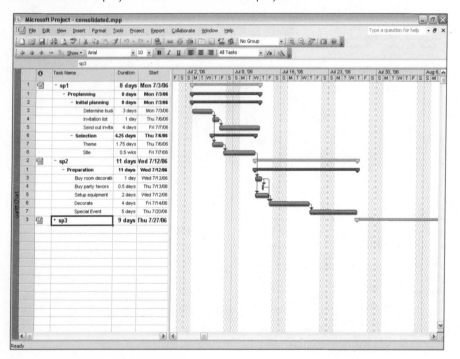

FIGURE 15.17

Close inserted projects so that just their summary tasks appear when you want to focus on a portion of a consolidated project.

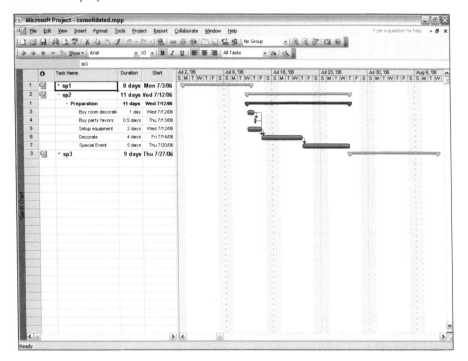

Viewing the Critical Path across Projects

When you consolidate projects, by default Project calculates inserted projects such as summary tasks, effectively showing you the overall critical path across all the projects by using the late finish date of the master project to make calculations. This behavior can make subprojects within the master project look as though they don't have critical paths of their own (see Figure 15.18).

FIGURE 15.18

By default, Project treats inserted projects as summary tasks, and you don't see critical paths for individual inserted projects.

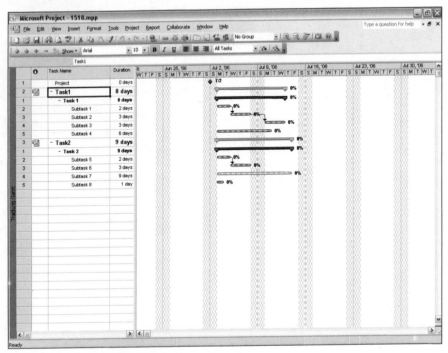

Suppose that you want to see each subproject's critical path while viewing the master project. To do so, you think, "I'll turn on multiple critical paths in the master project." That's the right idea, but because multiple critical paths apply only to tasks that are owned by the project, nothing will change. In this example, the tasks (Task 1 and Task 2) in Figure 15.18 are owned by subprojects, so turning on multiple critical paths in the master project won't have any effect.

You can, however, tell Project to *stop* treating subprojects as summary tasks. If you do, Project uses the late finish dates that the subprojects pass along to the consolidated project to determine the critical path — and you're likely to see each subproject's critical path (see Figure 15.19). When you turn off this setting, you see critical paths in the consolidated project as they appear in each subproject.

FIGURE 15.19

When Project doesn't treat inserted projects as summary tasks, you're likely to see multiple critical paths in a master project.

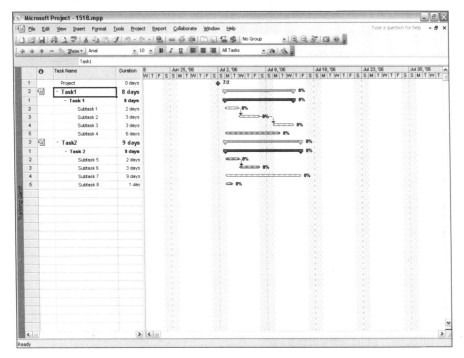

To change Project's behavior in the master project, choose Tools ⇨ Options and click the Calculation tab. Then, remove the check from the Inserted Projects Are Calculated Like Summary Tasks check box (see Figure 15.20).

FIGURE 15.20

The Inserted Projects Are Calculated Like Summary Tasks check box controls whether Project uses the subprojects' late finish dates or the master project's late finish date for calculations.

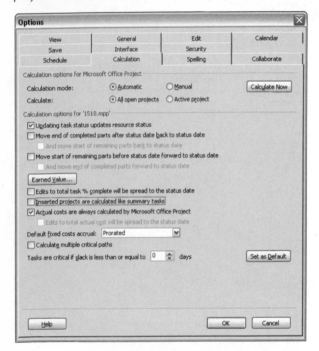

Sharing Resources Among Projects

Creating a resource pool can be useful if you don't use Project Server and you work with the same resources on multiple projects. A *resource pool* is a set of resources that are available to any project. You can use resources exclusively on one project, or you can share the resources among several projects.

If you work in an environment in which several project managers use the same set of resources on various projects, consider using a resource pool. Setting up a resource pool in Project can be a good way to schedule resources and resolve resource conflicts.

CROSS-REF   See Chapter 10 for more information on other techniques that you can employ to resolve resource conflicts. See Chapter 18 for information about using the Enterprise Resource Pool feature of Project Server.

Creating a resource pool and sharing the resources

Setting up a resource pool in Project can facilitate resource management, especially for resources that are shared on several projects. To create a resource pool, you simply set up a project file that contains only resource information.

If you have already set up a project that contains all the resources that are available, you can use that project as a model. After you identify a project that can serve as the resource pool, you designate it as the resource pool project by using the following steps:

 You don't need to delete all the tasks in the project that will serve as the model for the resource pool. You just need the resource information in the file.

1. Open the project that contains the resources and that will serve as the resource pool file.

2. Open the project that is to use the resource pool (that is, the project on which you want to work).

3. Choose Tools ➪ Resource Sharing ➪ Share Resources. Project displays the Share Resources dialog box (see Figure 15.21).

FIGURE 15.21

The Share Resources dialog box.

4. Click the Use resources option button and then use the From list box to select the resource pool project. Doing so indicates that you want to use the resources that are defined in that project.

 If you open only the project on which you want to work, the Use Own Resources option button is the only choice available, and you can't share resources with the resource pool. The first time that you want to enable resource sharing, you must open both the project that you determined would serve as the resource pool and the project on which you want to work. In addition, if you have any other projects open, they appear as candidates for the resource pool project when you open the From list box, because Project enables you to select from any open project when you identify the resource pool.

5. Select an option to tell Project how to handle calendar conflicts. If you select the Pool Takes Precedence option button, the resource calendars in the resource pool file take precedence when conflicts arise. If, however, you select the Sharer Takes Precedence option button, the resource calendars in the file that you're updating take precedence over the resource calendars in the resource pool file when conflicts arise.

6. Click OK.

If you switch to the Resource Sheet view of the file that you want to update, Project displays all the resources that are contained in the resource pool file, along with any resources that you may have set up in your project file.

You can now continue working in your project, or you can save your project and close it. You can also close the resource pool file.

Opening a project that uses a resource pool

At some point, you will save and close your file and then come back to work on it at a later time. You don't need to open the resource pool file at that time. Instead, when you open your file after you have set it up to share resources, the Open Resource Pool Information dialog box appears (see Figure 15.22).

FIGURE 15.22

The Open Resource Pool Information dialog box.

When you select the first option, Project opens the resource pool in addition to your file. If you select the second option, Project opens only your file, and Project does not transfer to the resource pool any changes that you make to the resources in your file because the resource pool file isn't open.

NOTE   When you select the first option in the Open Resource Pool Information dialog box, Project automatically opens the resource pool file as a read-only file. This action enables you to make changes to your project without tying up the resource pool file; therefore, multiple users can use the resource pool simultaneously.

Updating information in the resource pool

If you make changes to resource information while you're working on your project, you must update the resource pool file so that others who are using the resource pool have the most up-to-date information. To update the resource pool, make sure that the resource pool file is open, even in read-only mode. Then choose Tools ➪ Resource Sharing ➪ Update Resource Pool (see Figure 15.23).

When you open only your project and make changes to the resources, this command is not available. Furthermore, if you open only your project, save and close your project, and then open the resource pool file, this command is still not available. To ensure that Project incorporates the changes in the resource pool that you make to resources in your project, be sure to open the resource pool file when you open your file.

 **TIP** To ensure consistency and avoid arguments in the workplace, it's best to make one group or person responsible for updating the resource pool.

FIGURE 15.23

The Update Resource Pool command is available if you set up resource sharing and you make a change in your project while the resource pool file is open.

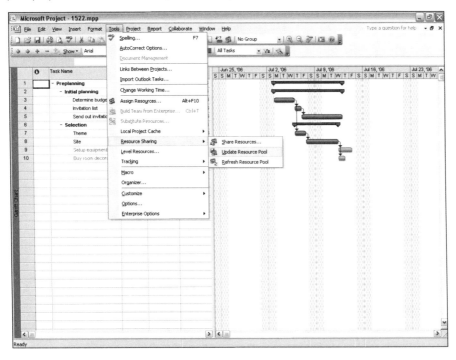

If you forget to update the resource pool after you make a change in your project that affects the resource pool, Project displays a message, shown in Figure 15.24, when you save your project.

FIGURE 15.24

If you forget to update the resource pool, Project alerts you when you save your project.

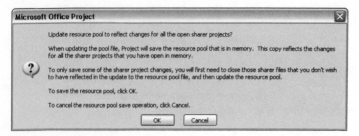

NOTE   Project stores the relative path to projects that are linked to resource pools. If you move one or the other, Project is still able to open the files.

Quit sharing resources

Suppose you decide that you no longer want to use the resource pool file. Follow these steps to disable the resource pool for a specific project:

1. Open that project.
2. Choose Tools ➪ Resource Sharing ➪ Share Resources.
3. Select the Use Own Resources option button in the Share Resources dialog box (refer to Figure 15.21).

However, suppose you decide that you want to disable the resource pool in general for all files that are sharing the resources of one resource pool. Do you need to open each file and disable resource sharing? No. Follow these steps to disable the resource pool file in general:

1. Open the resource pool file in read-write mode by using the Open dialog box — the same way that you would open any file. Project displays the Open Resource Pool box (see Figure 15.25). Choose the middle option or the last option in this dialog box; either option enables you to disable the pool because both options open the file as a read-write file.
2. Choose Tools ➪ Resource Sharing ➪ Share Resources. Project displays the Share Resources dialog box (see Figure 15.26).

FIGURE 15.25

Use this dialog box to determine whether you open the resource pool file as a read-only file or a read-write file.

FIGURE 15.26

The Share Resources dialog box.

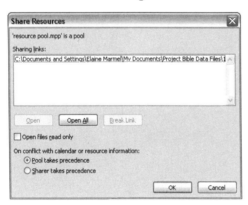

3. Select the project(s) that you want to exclude from the resource pool. You can select multiple noncontiguous projects by pressing and holding down Ctrl when you click the mouse, or you can select contiguous projects by pressing and holding down Shift when you click the mouse.

4. Click Break Link.

5. Click OK.

Summary

This chapter described how to consolidate projects and pool resources. You should now know how to do the following:

- Insert projects
- Understand and work with consolidated projects and dependencies
- Manage the view of a consolidated project
- Display multiple critical paths
- Share resources

Chapter 16 introduces Project Server.

Chapter 16

Preparing to Use Project Server

You'll be tempted, but please don't skip this chapter. I know it sounds like a pun when talking about project management software, but planning the implementation of Project Server (a project) is the single most important action that you can take to ensure a successful venture.

Implementing Project Server isn't only about hardware configurations and installing software. It's about planning for the needs of your organization so that you can correctly configure Project Server. It's about assessing where your organization is today and where it plans to go. It's about identifying the players, their needs, and their roles in the process. It's about figuring out what needs to be done, who has the skills and availability to do it, when it needs to be done, and what else depends on it getting done.

In this chapter, you review the process that you need to follow for your organization to accept the changes that using Project Server will bring and make the changing process successful and as painless as possible.

IN THIS CHAPTER

Understanding Project Server and Project Web Access

Assessing requirements

Designing the system

Outlining an implementation strategy

Avoiding traps

Understanding Project Server and Project Web Access

The concept behind Project Server is that all the projects that your organization manages affect each other, and the need for collaboration on projects is greater than it has ever been. As the number of projects and the size of your organization grow, so does the need to manage the management of projects. Project Server enables you to store all projects and all resources for the organization in one central database on your company's local-area network (LAN) or intranet so that limited resources can be matched to projects. Only the project manager, the resource manager, and the administrator must actually install and use Project Professional. All other resources on the project use Project Web Access, a browser-based product, to view project data that is stored in the Project Server database. Using Project Server and Project Web Access (and without using Project Professional), team members, managers, and executives can accomplish the following:

- Enter and view time sheet information
- View a project's Gantt Chart
- Receive, refuse, and delegate work assignments
- Update assignments with progress and completion information
- Attach supporting documentation, such as budget estimates or feasibility studies, to a project
- Receive notices about task status
- Perform analysis and produce organization-wide reports
- Carry out basic issue and risk management
- Send status reports to the project manager

CROSS-REF For more detail about the roles of managers, team members, and executives, see Chapters 19, 20, and 21, respectively.

Here's how the process works in general. The network administrator (or someone with similar skills and network privileges) installs Project Server on a Web server or in a server farm. The project manager creates a project in Project Professional. When the project manager is ready to store the project in Project Server, he or she publishes the project information. At this point, anyone with Internet Explorer 6.0 (or a later version), access to Project Server, and proper viewing rights can view the project information as it appears in Project Professional by using Project Web Access, the browser-based client side of Project Server.

CROSS-REF For details on the hardware and software that are needed for Project Server see Chapter 17.

Using a variety of tools, the project manager can assign resources to the project using a company-wide pool of available resources that are stored in the Project Server database. Team members can see, in Project Web Access, the assignments that they have received and use Project Web Access to update work assignments, send status reports to the project manager, and even set up to-do lists.

NOTE The project manager uses both Project Professional and Project Web Access, but other project resources typically use only Project Web Access.

TIP Using the Outlook add-in that's available in Project Web Access, resources can import tasks from Project Server and export work information from Outlook to Project Server.

CROSS-REF For more information on using Outlook with Project Web Access, see Chapter 20.

The Project Server Database

Each Project Server database actually consists of four databases:

- The Draft database
- The Published database
- The Archive database
- The Reporting database

The Draft database is a "holding tank" area where project managers using Project Professional can store projects that they don't yet want the general public to view. Only users of Project Professional can view draft projects.

The Published database is the location where projects are available to users of Project Web Access (PWA). Using PWA, team members can update time sheets, update project information, and view reports, based on their PWA credentials.

The Archive database contains older and backed-up versions of published projects.

The Reporting database holds the data used in reports; in this database, Project Server generates reports and OLAP cubes. This database is optimized to generate reports, and Project Server updates the information in the Reporting database almost as soon as information changes.

Project Server enables you to create consistent projects that use the same custom settings. Using the Enterprise Global template, each project that you create contains all the same fields, maps, views, tables, reports, filters, forms, toolbars, groups, and calendars that are stored in the global template file that's included in Project Professional, along with additional enterprise-only fields. Project Server administrators can define whether fields are required and can create look-up tables and value lists for fields. Because the settings are stored in the Enterprise Global template, they can be used repeatedly without having to re-create information.

Does your organization need Project Server? The following is a list of scenarios for which Project Server would work well:

- You manage many different projects using the same resources.
- Your organization is growing and has identified a need for tracking projects more accurately or using resources more efficiently.
- Your organization has determined that the time of project managers *and* resources time would be used more efficiently if resources could record their time directly in the project schedule rather than provide it to the project manager, who then updates the schedule.
- Your executives want better organization-wide reporting and analysis tools than you can currently provide.

- Your managers need to model what-if scenarios.

- Your users need access to project data anywhere in the world.

Project Server was originally designed as a LAN-based product. If your organization uses a LAN and wants one central database to store both projects and resources, Project Server should meet your needs.

Suppose that your organization uses a wide-area network (WAN). You can use Project Server configured in a server farm; to improve performance, you may want to use additional software such as Terminal Services or Citrix, although the implementation of active cache in Project 2007 may diminish this need. Active cache is a local cache that Office Project Professional 2007 uses to interact with Office Project Server 2007. Active cache manages updates to project and enterprise global resource pool information. In addition, active cache uses message-based updates that transfer only the differences between files rather than the whole files to Office Project Server 2007.

 Active cache is new to Project Server 2007.

What's New in Project Server 2007

In Table 16.1, I've summarized the new features in Project Server 2007.

TABLE 16.1

New Features in Project Server 2007

Feature	Description
Active Cache	A local cache that Project Professional 2007 uses to interact with Project Server 2007. The Active cache manages updates to project and enterprise global resource pool information. In addition, active cache uses message-based updates that transfer only the differences between files rather than the whole files to Office Project Server 2007.
Assignment Owner	The individual who is responsible for entering actual work or reporting progress against an assignment. In Office Project Server 2003, named enterprise resources could use Project Web Access to report their own time. In Office Project Server 2007, you can track time and assignments for named enterprise resources and generic, cost, or material resources using Project Web Access.
Cube Building Service	Building the Project Server OLAP cube has improved; you use a graphical interface to specify the cube settings, including the custom fields to include in the cube. The cube building service uses the data generated by the Reporting Data Service and metadata from the Reporting database to build cubes for end-user reporting.

Feature	Description
Deliverables	Project managers can create a Windows SharePoint Services list of deliverable products similar to milestones and assign a date to each deliverable. Other project managers can then use these deliverables to create dependencies that link projects.
Event Model	An event, triggered by program logic or a user action, signals the occurrence of an action. Events can trigger processes in the Windows Workflow Foundation. Using the server-side Event Model, developers can extend the Office Project 2007 functionality by developing custom event handlers and associating them with events that occur in Office Project Server 2007.
Multi-currency support	Project Server 2007 enables you to define an exchange rate table for each project. This exchange rate table supports conversion on task or assignment cost fields. Resources may have rates in multiple currencies, but reports, the Project Center, and data cubes use only one currency.
Programs	Programs are collections of projects to accomplish a large objective. You can analyze, report, and use key performance indicators on programs.
Project Server Interface	Project Server 2003 used the Project Data Service (PDS) application programming interface; in Project Server 2007, the Project Server Interface (PSI) replaces the PDS. Office Project Web Access, Office Project Professional 2007, and third-party applications interact with Project Server 2007 solely through the PSI.
Queuing Service	To provide better use of server resources, Project Server 2007 uses the Queuing Service, a server-side service that queues work requests pending server availability.
Reporting Data Service	This service pulls data from the Project Server Draft, Publish, , and Archive databases and converts the data to a format that the cube building service can use to build an OLAP cube. The report data service then loads the converted data into the Reporting database.
Server-side scheduling	Project Server 2007 uses a server-side scheduling engine, which reduces the licensing needs for Project Professional 2007 to a client access license (CAL). Essentially, because of the server-based scheduling engine, third-party providers can build front-end applications that won't require installing Project Professional in each client machine.
Time sheets	The behavior of time sheets in Project Server 2007 has changed significantly from Project Server 2003. In Project Server 2003, you used the timesheet mainly to report on task status. In Project 2007, you can enter times for Project 2007 activities, nonproject time, and project tasks. In addition, you can enter time independently; you no longer need an assignment. In Project Server 2003, you recorded time for individual tasks. In Project Server 2007, you can record time against the summary task, project, or account code level. You can enable timesheet auditing to log changes to saved time sheets. Time sheets can display billable, nonbillable, overtime, and scheduled hours and can support fiscal periods. Project managers can approve or reject time sheets independently from project status updates. Additionally, Project Server 2007 can lock tasks and projects against further time tracking.

Planning the Project

If you think about the implementation of Project Server the same way that you think about planning other information technology projects, you won't be surprised to find out that you need to take the same actions:

- Assess requirements
- Design the system
- Develop an implementation strategy

Assessing requirements

Determining your organization's direction and needs may be the most important phase of the implementation process, because the Project Server design ultimately depends on the information that you gather.

Start by setting up a team to implement the system. You'll need people who are good at gathering information, making design decisions, and managing implementation. Be sure to include people who are experienced in using enterprise project management systems. You'll need a mix of business people and technical people to address the various facets of implementing Project Server. The business people should include senior project managers and staff with experience using Project. The technical people should include those who are experienced in your company's network architecture and hardware configuration. To customize or automate Project Server functions, you should include a technical person with skills in developing object models for Project. Everyone on the team should be familiar with your company's standards.

> **TIP** If you find yourself missing key team members, check the CD that comes with this book. It contains the Microsoft Office Project 2007 Bible Web page, on which you'll find links to the sites of many Project Partners — companies that are experienced in project management and in using and implementing project management systems, Microsoft Office Project Professional, and Project Server.

The team needs to set milestone dates and task durations for each of the activities in the next five sections.

Identify the people who will approve the Project Server design

As with any project, it is important to identify the decision-makers as soon as you start. If possible, include one or more of them on the team so that they are a part of the process and they feel ownership for the system that you ultimately design.

Identify staff members to interview

Identify people who fill the following roles:

- **Team members:** People to whom work is assigned.
- **Resource managers:** People who delegate work to team members and monitor project progress and resource utilization.

- **Project managers:** People who prepare project plans.

- **Portfolio managers:** People who are familiar with company standards and can manage the Enterprise Global template as well as other enterprise templates. The portfolio manager may also manage enterprise resources.

- **Executives:** People who view reports on projects and resources.

- **Administrators:** People who manage changes and access to the Project Server database. The people who start the administrator job may ultimately phase out of the job because the job changes over time. Initially, the administrator installs and sets up Project Professional, Project Server, and SQL Server and may use both Project Server and SQL Server tools to meet the needs of users. Eventually, the administrator role becomes a maintenance function, for which knowledge of Project Server administrative functions is the only prerequisite.

 In some environments, the resource manager, project manager, and portfolio manager may all be the same person.

Create a requirements definition questionnaire

To effectively interview, the team should create a questionnaire to obtain information about how people work. To gather information for your questionnaire, use the reports that your company currently uses to record project performance. Evaluate each report to identify the resources and projects that are (or should be) included on the report; how tasks, projects, and resources are categorized; and who uses each report. To help you produce your questionnaire, you may want to download Microsoft's Enterprise Information Framework (EIF), a series of documents that describe implementing Project Server from the perspective of project managers, not IT professionals. In particular, the EIF Interview spreadsheet contains sample questions and codes them based on who should answer the question. Then, the Requirements Specification document assigns the question to a category that helps you identify how each question can help you with some aspect of the implementation. You can download the EIF (eif.exe) at the following Web site:

```
http://www.microsoft.com/downloads/details.aspx?FamilyId=6CC5B2D6
-FBB6-4BE0-8046-21B57590F465&displaylang=en
```

The EIF was originally created for Project 2002. Although portions of the EIF no longer apply, the concepts it uses to help you determine requirements are still valid.

TIP Some of the Project Partners have developed their own questionnaires to help define requirements and design the system. For example, Project Server Support, Inc. has created the EWQ (Enterprise Web Questionnaire), which is role based and customizable and includes reports.

Conduct interviews

When you conduct interviews, make sure that you include more than one person in each role. Because no two people are identical, two people filling the same role do things differently and potentially have different needs.

Calculate ROI

As part of your organization's consideration of using Project Server, you should calculate your return on investment (ROI). Implementing Project Server requires software and role-based training for resources, and it may also require investments in hardware. Don't skip this important step; use whatever technique your organization has developed to calculate ROI to assess the costs and benefits of implementing Project Server.

Designing the system

You design your Project Server database using the information that you gathered while defining requirements. This information should help you identify which features in Project Server you want to implement. The System Design workbook in the EIF applies to Project 2002; you can use it as a reference point to help you transfer your requirements information into Project Server database elements, but it will require updating since Project 2007 contains features not available in Project 2002.

As a part of the design process, the implementation team must also address issues that are not directly related to the construction of the Project Server database.

Assessing the technology environment

As you find out in Chapter 17, Project Server requires certain software, and the hardware that you use affects the performance of Project Server. You must evaluate the software and hardware that you have, as well as your network architecture, and factor in costs and timelines for upgrading as necessary.

Addressing special needs

From the requirements definition, you need to identify whether your organization wants to construct a document library and deal with issues in a collaborative way. To use these Project Server features, you also need Windows Sharepoint Services, which comes with Project 2007 Server.

Project Server comes with some standard e-mail notifications that it can send when certain conditions are met. Your organization may want to add to these notifications; if so, the implementation team needs to create these special e-mail notifications.

The implementation team also needs to customize the Project Guide, which was introduced in Project 2002, if the requirements definition indicates that customization would benefit your organization.

Establishing and enforcing organizational standards

To use an organization-wide project management tool, you need shared terminology across projects that all project managers use. All managers need to apply the same processes and procedures to their projects. If your organization doesn't already have standardized language, processes, and procedures in place, you'll need to develop them. If your organization has established standards, your standards may or may not work within the framework of Project Server.

Project Server contains several features that can help you establish and enforce standards in your organization's project management efforts. The Enterprise Global template — comparable to the Global template in Project Professional — contains a collection of all default settings that are used by projects across your organization. Someone with administrative privileges in your company should customize the Enterprise Global template so that it contains the custom fields, look-up tables for outline codes, views, and calendars that meet the needs of your organization. That way, as project managers create new projects, basing them on the Enterprise Global template enforces standard usage across all the organization's projects. The Enterprise Resource Pool helps you ensure that resource names, definitions, contact information, and calendars are consistent across all projects.

Custom fields

You create and use custom fields to meet some specific need concerning the data that your organization uses in its projects. Project enables you to create custom fields to assign to either resources or tasks. Because Project Server stores custom fields in the Enterprise Global template, you can enforce standards across projects by setting up custom fields for all project managers to use on all projects.

CROSS-REF In Chapter 18, you find out about creating custom fields.

Outline codes

You can use outline codes to produce work breakdown structures or organization breakdown structures to provide different ways of looking at tasks, resources, and projects. Project uses outline codes to help create these different structures. You can standardize outline codes, also stored in the Enterprise Global template, by using look-up tables for the values that are available for the outline codes. In this way, projects remain standardized because everyone uses the same set of outline codes.

CROSS-REF In Chapter 7, you find out about outline codes.

Views

The administrator creates views in the Project Server database to control the information that is seen by various Project Web Access users. For each view, the administrator specifies the format of the view, grouping of information on the view, any filters for the view, and the categories to which the view belongs.

CROSS-REF In Chapter 18, you find out about creating views.

NOTE Views that the project manager creates and uses in Project Professional are based on the Global template. The fields that are used to create views in Project Web Access are stored in the Publish database and are unique to Project Web Access. Creating a view in Project Professional does not duplicate the view in Project Web Access.

Calendars

Project makes use of the following four types of calendars:

- **Base calendar:** Provides the source information for the other three types of calendars.

  Project provides the following types of base calendars (you can customize others):

  - Standard (Monday through Friday, 8 a.m. to 5 p.m., with an hour break)
  - 24-hour
  - Night-shift

CROSS-REF Chapter 3 covers base calendars.

- **Project calendar:** The base calendar that is assigned to a specific project.

CROSS-REF Chapter 3 covers project calendars.

- **Resource calendar:** Assumes the working and nonworking times of the project calendar for a resource and can be customized to show the following resource data:

  - Nonstandard working times
  - Planned time off

CROSS-REF Chapter 10 covers resource calendars.

- **Task calendar:** Assumes the working and nonworking times of the project calendar for a task and can be customized to show nonstandard working time.

  The task calendar is useful for situations such as shutting down a server for maintenance during nonbusiness hours.

CROSS-REF Chapter 4 covers task calendars.

Enterprise resource pool

By using an enterprise resource pool, you can share resources between projects and identify conflicts between assignments in different projects. An enterprise resource pool is simply a central repository of all available resources. By storing information about all resources, their calendars, and their assignments in one place, you can manage resource utilization and sharing more easily because resource information across your company is standardized; every project manager knows the skills and availability of every resource.

CROSS-REF You find out more about the enterprise resource pool in Chapter 18.

Training

Chapters 18 through 21 describe the ways that various organizational members may use Project Server. Each role player requires training to successfully fill his or her role. Factor both the time and the cost of training into your project plan.

Developing a strategy for implementation and configuration

Project Server isn't the type of software that you install and then immediately start using. To make your implementation successful, you should plan it as a phased process.

Consider first creating a prototype of the system, and from your requirements document, identify a few projects and project teams to participate in the prototype test. Make sure that you select users who represent all the various roles that were identified earlier so that you can fully test the system. Also, select projects that don't depend on other projects that won't be a part of the prototype. Design and develop the prototype system, and demonstrate it to the implementation team. Make modifications to the prototype design based on input from the implementation team, and demonstrate the prototype to senior management. Again, make changes as needed.

CAUTION Don't assume that project managers who have been using Project Professional for years can build plans that are suitable for the enterprise. For portfolio analysis and resource management to have meaning across the enterprise, plans and resource management must be consistent and standard across projects.

After you complete the prototype, you need to develop training materials and, once again, select projects and project teams that represent each of the roles that were identified earlier to participate in the pilot phase. Reset the Project Server database and load the pilot projects. At this stage, you should include at least one project that has external dependencies to another project to test that aspect of usage, and then make adjustments as needed. Train the pilot group and allow its members to use Project Server for at least four reporting cycles. Be sure to solicit feedback so that you can address all the issues that arise.

Identify groups to which you can open the system, and plan the timing of each group's introduction to the system. As you introduce each group, you need to add that group's projects to the Project Server database and provide training to the group. Allow enough time for each group to get up and running before introducing the next group.

When you're satisfied that you've ironed out any kinks that were identified during the prototype and pilot phases, expand the user base of the system again, adding projects to the Project Server database based on the groups that you identified, and train the new group that is to begin using the system. Allow each group to work through at least three reporting cycles before you add additional groups. Remember, as you add new groups, you must provide training to users.

Avoiding the Pitfalls

You need to consider one last subject: avoiding the pitfalls that are associated with implementing Project Server.

When you define requirements, be sure that you ask how many projects each project manager expects to be managing at any one time and determine the average size of the project. You may discover that some project managers define a project differently than others. This presents a problem only if you find that project managers tend to manage many projects and each project has only one or two tasks. In cases like these, defining these projects as separate entities in Project 2007 will make maintenance difficult. You may instead want to combine these smaller projects into one larger Project 2007 file.

Also ask both project managers and team members about the current reporting process. Ask whether the organization has one, and determine whether it works or whether people regularly bypass it. If people bypass the reporting process, try to determine why. The process may need to be changed to better suit the needs of those who are using it. If you expect to produce accurate reports and forecasts, the information that you provide to Project 2007 needs to be accurate and timely.

Determine whether the organization considers available resources when it accepts projects. If it does not, it will probably experience changes to project scope, costs, and resources regularly, and Project 2007 won't provide accurate information about resource requirements. Try to get senior management to agree to new methods that include the evaluation of resource needs when considering new projects.

Ask different role players how they deal with problems that arise on projects. If you get different answers from different people, then you don't have a company-wide mechanism in place that deals with resolving problems. In such cases, only some projects will be accurately reporting status, and any comparison or forecasting that you do will be inaccurate. To solve this problem, find a method that you can standardize across the organization. Define the tools to use to look for problems, when to use these tools, the options available to solve problems, and who needs to be in the loop to resolve problems.

NOTE   Don't forget to establish a method to deal with problems while implementing Project Server — that is, make sure that the implementation project has a mechanism to address problems.

Ask project managers about the methods they use to analyze performance. Determine whether they use earned value, and identify the method of earned value. Project supports only the Percent Complete and Physical Percent Complete methods. If the organization is using some other method or uses methods inconsistently throughout the organization, you can't accurately analyze performance across the organization.

Identify the types of costs that the organization wants to track, because Project tracks costs by calculating the cost of resources using rate tables or fixed costs. Many projects have sizeable costs that are not resource related. The implementation team must make it clear to the organization exactly what Project can and cannot calculate.

Phase the introduction of Project Server into your environment to avoid disrupting your regular business process, but don't let more than six months pass without introducing a new group to Project Server. In this way, you interrupt your business only minimally, but you don't lose the momentum of the implementation.

Identify the criteria that the implementation team needs to meet to have the system accepted by management as well as by team members. Keep those criteria in mind through all phases of the process.

Summary

To successfully implement Project Server, you must think of the process as a project that needs to be managed. By its nature, this project is an information technology project that affects the majority of your organization.

In this chapter, you reviewed the following items:

- Understanding the basic functioning of Project Server and Project Web Access
- Defining requirements
- Using requirements to identify elements that are needed for the Project Server database
- Developing a strategy to implement the Project Server database
- Avoiding pitfalls while implementing Project Server

In Chapter 17, you find out about installing Project Server.

Chapter 17

Installing and Configuring Project Server

T his chapter is aimed at IT administrators — the people who handle the hardware and software setup. If you're an everyday user or a project manager, you probably won't enjoy this chapter very much and you're welcome to skip it.

To install and use Project Server, you must install certain software — and, in some cases, the software that you install depends on the features of Project Server that you decide to use. The hardware that you use must also meet some basic specifications. And you need to consider the user and network environment in which you will run Project Server to maximize performance.

In this chapter, you read about the software that you need, the basic hardware specifications, and the network issues that affect Project Server performance. You also find some sample hardware configurations that you may consider, given your user and network environment. You work through installing peripheral software; at that point, you're ready to install Project Server and Windows SharePoint Services and configure farm services. And finally, a troubleshooting section appears at the end of this chapter that addresses some of the techniques you can use to address performance issues.

Reviewing Requirements

You can install Project Professional 2003 and Project Professional 2007 side by side on the same computer and Project Server 2007 on the same hardware where you have installed Project Server 2003.

However, only Project Professional 2007 can connect to Project Server 2007. Project Professional 2003 cannot connect to Project Server 2007, and Project Professional 2007 cannot connect to Project Server 2003. Read the next three sections completely before you install anything to get a complete picture of the process.

Meeting software requirements

As you would expect, the software requirements for servers differ from those for client computers.

Software requirements for servers

For basic use of Project Server, you need, at a minimum, Windows Server 2003, Standard or Enterprise Edition, 32-bit or 64-bit, with Service Pack 1 or later. You'll need to enable Microsoft Internet Information Server (IIS) 6.0 or above and .NET Framework. You'll also need Windows Workflow Foundation.

For your database engine, you need SQL Server 2000 with Service Pack 3 or higher or SQL Server 2005. If you want to use the portfolio modeling features that are available in Project Web Access, you need SQL Server Analysis Services and SQL Server Reporting Services, which are included with SQL Server but must be installed separately.

Project Server depends on the Windows SharePoint Services 3.0 (WSS) platform, which comes on the Project Server 2007 CD and installs automatically when you install Project Server.

NOTE The version of WSS that ships with Project Server will give you what you need to run Project Server, but it doesn't include some of the more advanced features available in Microsoft Office SharePoint Server, such as automated document lifecycle processing. If you need those features, get and use a separate copy of Microsoft Office SharePoint Server.

To use e-mail notifications, both the server and client machines need Internet SMTP/POP3, IMAP4, or MAPI-compliant messaging software.

Software requirements for client computers

On the client side, the project manager needs Project Professional, but other resources need Internet Explorer 6.0 or higher.

If you plan to import and export tasks between Project and Outlook, the client machine also needs Outlook 2007 or Outlook 2003. You may experience some functionality limitations if you use Outlook 2003.

Meeting hardware requirements

The recommendations in this section come from Microsoft and depend largely on the number of services that you intend to install.

Hardware requirements for servers

Typically, you install Project Server on the company's server or in a server farm. If you're planning to use the bare-minimum hardware, you should load only Project Server on that computer. Other components, such as SQL Server, should run on separate computers.

CROSS-REF See the sections "Considering software/hardware scenarios" and "Troubleshooting Your Installation," later in this chapter, for more information on load balancing and improving performance.

Microsoft recommends that you install Project Server on a computer with a minimum Pentium III processor that runs at 700 MHz and has 1GB of RAM. If necessary, you can run Project Server on a Pentium III, 550 MHz machine with only 512MB of RAM. This computer must also have a DVD-ROM drive, a Super VGA (800 × 600) or higher resolution monitor, and a Microsoft Mouse–compatible pointing device.

For the computer on which you install Project Server, you need 200MB of available hard drive space. To install WSS, you need another 70MB of hard drive space and a minimum of 256MB of RAM — 512MB of RAM is recommended.

To install SQL Server 2000, you need 250MB of hard drive space and 64MB of RAM — 128MB is recommended. If you also intend to install SQL Analysis Services, you need another 130MB of hard drive space and another 64MB of RAM — another 128MB is recommended.

Hardware requirements for client computers

Microsoft recommends that each client machine have, at a minimum, a 300 MHz processor, have 192MB of RAM, and use Windows XP Professional as the operating system. The minimum processor on a client machine is a Pentium 133 MHz. Each client machine should have a Super VGA (800 × 600) or higher resolution monitor with 256 colors and a Microsoft Mouse–compatible pointing device.

You can check the Microsoft Office Project home page for more information:

```
Project Home Page
http://office.microsoft.com/project/
```

Assessing the network environment

The total number of users, the number of concurrent users updating the Project Server databases, and the number of projects that you store in the Project Server databases are directly related to the amount of traffic that you can expect on your network. Using older network architecture (10Base-T) in a heavily trafficked environment will undoubtedly result in complaints that the system is slow. You may want to plan to upgrade your network infrastructure.

Project Server is designed as a local-area network–based product that can provide one central location to store projects and resources. To use Project Server across a wide-area network (WAN), you may need to use Terminal Services or Citrix software to improve performance. However, Project Professional 2007 connects to Project Server 2007 in a much more efficient manner than Project Professional 2003 connected to Project Server 2003, diminishing, if you're lucky, the need to use Terminal Services or Citrix.

Considering software/hardware scenarios

The hardware/software configuration that works most effectively in your environment is influenced by the following factors, which contribute to the overall performance of Project Server:

- The total number of users
- The number of concurrent users
- The number of assignments per project
- The number of projects that you want to store in the Project Server databases
- The features of Project Server that you want to use

NOTE   To improve performance, Project Professional 2007 interacts with Project Server 2007 through a local active cache that manages replicating the enterprise global resource pool information and updating projects. When you make changes in Project Professional and upload them to Project Server 2007, the active cache delivers message-based differences between files rather than entire files.

As you already know, you must install IIS, SQL Server, and Windows SharePoint Services. Optionally, you can install SQL Analysis Services and SQL Reporting Services. And, of course, you load Project Server and, at a minimum, Windows SharePoint Services. Succinctly stated, you're loading a lot of software.

Because Project Server 2007 depends on Windows SharePoint Services 3.0, you have some choices about how you configure the hardware on which you will load the software, and your choices will affect the performance of Project Server. You can use a single server or you can use a server farm.

In the server farm, you can place various components and services on several networked computers to balance the load. The server farm also improves your ability to gracefully handle or expand to meet growing needs. And when you use a server farm, you limit the impact created when a single component or service faults.

You can set up Project Server 2007 in one of three server farm configurations: small, medium or large. There are many ways that you can set up each server farm size, and Microsoft makes some recommendations about the various server farm configurations, which I review here. These configurations focus primarily on the Web front-end servers, application servers, and SQL servers used in a Project Server environment.

In the Project Server environment, you typically place Windows SharePoint Services farms and Project Web Access, the browser-based tool used to access Project Server on Web front end servers, applications such as the Project Server Interface, Project Server business objects, and Project Server reporting and queuing services on application servers, and Project Server SQL databases, SQL Analysis Services and SQL Reporting Services on SQL servers.

Using WSS, you can configure server farms in tiers so that you can improve performance by balancing loads.

The Small Server Farm

In a small server farm, you load everything on one or two servers.

In the single-tier configuration, referred to as "standalone installation mode," you load everything onto one server. If you're working in a very small company, this approach may work for you, but it has fault tolerance, load balancing, and scalability limitations.

In the two-tier configuration, you dedicate one computer as the SQL Server, placing SQL 2000 or SQL 2005 and SQL Analysis Services and SQL Reporting Services on that computer. Then use another computer as both a Web front-end server and an application server, where you install Project Server and Windows SharePoint Services. This configuration separates database processing from other processing, which typically improves performance.

The Medium Server Farm

In a medium server farm, you use three tiers, installing each component in a separate tier.

This approach works well when you need to accommodate more users because you can add additional Web front-end servers and application servers. And if necessary, you can add additional database servers.

The Large Server Farm

This configuration closely resembles the medium server farm in that you still use three tiers and install each component in a separate tier. In the large server farm configuration, you may also be using other services available through SharePoint Server 2007 such as Search, Index, or Excel Calculation Services. In this case, you set up each of these services on its own server.

When you're ready to set up Project Server, review the guidelines that Microsoft will be publishing to help you decide whether to use a server farm and, if so — the likely case for Project Server installations — the size of the server farm to set up. The guidelines will consider factors such as the number of tasks, resources, and assignments in your projects, the number of projects you have and whether most of your projects are small, medium, or large in nature. The beauty of the server farm concept lies in the ease with which you can expand any tier within the farm to improve performance.

Installing Peripheral Software

Let me state upfront that this is a lengthy process. For those of you who have installed Project Server in the past, you'll find that the process of installing Project Server 2007 is easier than the installation process was for prior versions.

Before you install Project Server, you need to install Windows Server 2003 Standard or Enterprise Edition, 32 bit or 64 bit. You also need to install SQL Server 2000 with Service Pack 3 or later or SQL Server 2005 and, if you plan to use the Portfolio Management feature of Project Server, SQL Analysis Services. If you expect to use the document and risk management features of Project Server, you also need to enable Microsoft Internet Information Server (IIS) 6.0 or above. You have a lot of software to install and configure before you ever get to installing Project Server and Windows SharePoint Services.

NOTE   Windows SharePoint Services 3.0 comes on the CD with Project Server 2007 and installs as part of the installation process for Project Server 2007. But you may want to install Microsoft Office SharePoint Server to take advantage of some of its more advanced features, such as automated document lifecycle processing.

As you saw from the preceding section, you don't need to install all products on one machine, but you *must* install all products before you install Project Server. Also, you may need to adjust some of the settings for most of these products.

NOTE   Please don't try skipping anything. You will not be a happy camper. A successful installation for Project Server depends on first installing and configuring the peripheral software.

SQL Server and Analysis Services

After installing SQL Server and Analysis Services following the instructions that are provided by Microsoft, verify that you are using the correct SQL version.

Checking the SQL version

To confirm that you are using SQL Server 2000 with Service Pack 3 or higher, use the Query Analyzer. In Windows Server 2003, choose Start ➪ All Programs ➪ Microsoft SQL Server ➪ Query Analyzer.

NOTE   Depending on the mode in which SQL is operating, you may be prompted to log on to the Query Analyzer when you open the Query Analyzer window.

In the top portion of the SQL Query Analyzer window, enter the following query and press F5 (see Figure 17.1).

```
Select @@version
```

In the bottom of the window, you see the version of SQL that you have installed. Any version of SQL Server 2000 equal to or higher than 8.00.760 is acceptable.

You can download SQL 2000 from the following URL:

```
http://www.microsoft.com/technet/prodtechnol/sql/2000/downloads/d
efault.mspx
```

FIGURE 17.1

Use this query to check the version of SQL.

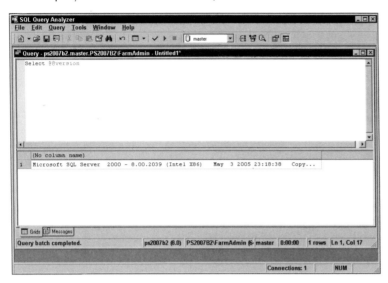

You can download SQL 2005 from the following URL:

```
http://www.microsoft.com/technet/prodtechnol/sql/2005/downloads/
default.mspx
```

Internet Information Services (IIS)

IIS is a Windows component and is *not* enabled by default when you install Windows Server 2003. You need IIS to use Windows SharePoint Services. If you've already enabled IIS, skip to the next section.

Enabling IIS

In the Control Panel, choose Add or Remove Programs. In the Add or Remove Programs window that appears, click Add/Remove Windows Components. Then, follow these steps to enable IIS:

1. In the Windows Components window, highlight Application Server and click the Details button.

2. Select the Application Server Console check box.

3. Select the Internet Information Services (IIS) option (see Figure 17.2) and click the Details button.

FIGURE 17.2

After selecting the ASP.NET check box, highlight Internet Information Services (IIS) so that you can click Details.

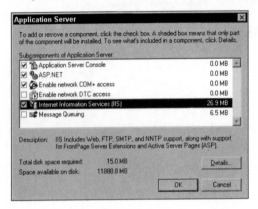

4. In the Internet Information Services (IIS) dialog box, select the Internet Information Services Manager check box.

 **If the FrontPage 2002 Server Extensions check box is selected, click to deselect it.**

5. Select the World Wide Web Service check box and click Details (see Figure 17.3).

FIGURE 17.3

After selecting the Internet Information Services (IIS) check box, highlight World Wide Web Service so that you can click Details.

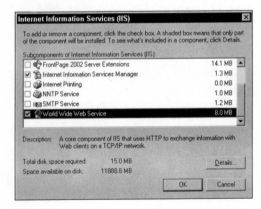

6. In the World Wide Web Service dialog box, make sure that the World Wide Web Service check box is selected.

7. Click OK three times to redisplay the Windows Components Wizard dialog box.

8. Click Next. Windows installs the selected components.

9. Click Finish.

Checking the IIS mode

For Project Server components to function properly, IIS cannot run in Isolation mode. Windows Server 2003 automatically sets up IIS so that it doesn't run in isolation mode. If you upgraded from Windows Server 2000 to Windows Server 2003, you should confirm or change the IIS mode by following these steps:

1. Choose Start ➪ Administrative Tools.

2. Click Internet Information Services (IIS) Manager to display the Internet Information Services (IIS) Manager window, as shown in Figure 17.4.

FIGURE 17.4

Use this window to check the mode in which IIS is running.

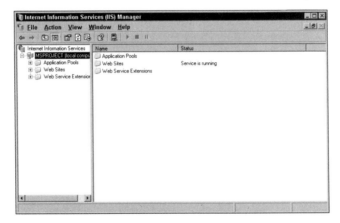

3. In the left pane, expand the tree to view the Web Sites folder.

4. Right-click the Web Sites folder and choose Properties from the shortcut menu that appears.

5. In the Web Sites Properties dialog box that appears, click the Service tab (see Figure 17.5).

FIGURE 17.5

Confirm that IIS is not running in Isolation mode.

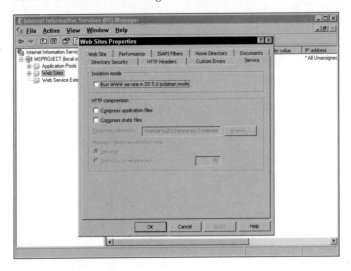

6. If the Run WWW Service in IIS 5.0 Isolation Mode check box is selected, click to deselect it.

7. Click OK and close the Internet Information Services (IIS) Manager window.

Installing .NET Framework 3.0

Next in the process, you need to install .NET Framework 3.0. You'll need to download .NET Framework; visit http://www.microsoft.com/downloads/search.aspx?display lang=en and enter **.NET Framework 3.0** in the Search box to find the file.

After you download the executable file, double-click it and follow the on-screen instructions to install it.

Setting Up Windows Security Accounts

The installation wizard for Project Server 2007 asks you for Windows security account information. The Project Server Deployment Guide describes five user accounts, but you can combine these accounts to meet the requirements of your organization. Most organizations will set up separate accounts for the Windows SharePoint Services Service Account, the Shared Service Provider Administrator, and the Project Server Instance Administrator. If one person manages all of the roles

I'm about to describe, you can set up only one account. If your organization is large enough to separate functions from a security perspective, then set up the number of accounts you need.

Windows SharePoint Services Service account

This account serves as the administrator for all Windows SharePoint Services activity. You establish this unique domain user account to create the Windows SharePoint Services Configuration database in SQL Server. Using this account, you configure the farm from the Windows SharePoint Services Central Administration page. This account also acts as the application pool identity for the SharePoint Central Administration application pool and the Windows SharePoint Services Timer service runs under this account. When you configure Windows SharePoint Services after installing Project Server, the wizard adds this account to the SQL Server Logins, the SQL Server Database Creator server role, and the SQL Server Security Administrators server role. If you separate security functions within your organization, follow the principle of least privilege and do not make this user account a member of any particular security group on your front-end servers or your back-end servers.

The Application Pool security account

Application pools are a feature of Internet Information Services 6.0. Using application pools, you can use an isolated process to run Web applications. You use the Application Pool security account, a domain user account, to run an application pool. During the process of provisioning Windows SharePoint Services, you'll be asked for an Application Pool security account twice: once when you create an unextended Web site to host the Shared Service Provider and once when you create an extended Web site to host the Project Web Access SharePoint Team site. In the first case, the account you supply will be granted rights to the Project Server databases. In the second case, the account you supply will be granted access to the Project Web Access sites and project workspaces on the computer on which the Web front end is running.

You don't need to make this account a member of any particular security group. If you separate security functions within your organization, follow the principle of least privilege and select a unique user account that does not have administrative rights on your front-end servers or on your back-end database servers. Many organizations use the Windows SharePoint Services service account for the Application Pool Security account.

Site Collection Owner account

A site collection is a group of sites built on Microsoft Windows SharePoint Services that all exist under a top-level site. During the Windows SharePoint Services provisioning process, after you create the extended Web site to host the SharePoint Team Site, you create a new Windows SharePoint Services site collection and supply this account to designate a primary site collection owner. The Site Collection Owner account has administrative rights over the Windows SharePoint Services site collection. Many organizations use the Windows SharePoint Services service account for the Site Collection Owner account.

Shared Service Provider Administrator account

Using Microsoft Office SharePoint Server 2007, you can share services such as the Project Server Interface Web services, Excel Calculation Services, and Enterprise Search Web services. These shared services use an application pool that you can specify during the initial configuration of Microsoft Office Project Server 2007; at that time, you specify an account to use to administer shared Web services. This account is called the Shared Service Provider (SSP) account and must have Database Creator and Security Administrator permissions on SQL Server.

Project Server Instance Administrator account

Use this account to administer Microsoft Office Project Server 2007. This account must be a valid domain user unless you are using forms authentication. When you install Microsoft Office Project Server 2007 to the farm, you'll be prompted to enter this account information.

Creating an account

You create all accounts the same way, assigning privileges to each account in accordance with the guidelines provided above and the security structure of your organization. Follow these steps to set up an account in Windows Server 2003:

1. Choose Start ➪ Administrative Tools.

2. Click Computer Management to display the Computer Management window (see Figure 17.6).

FIGURE 17.6

Use this window to create new Windows accounts.

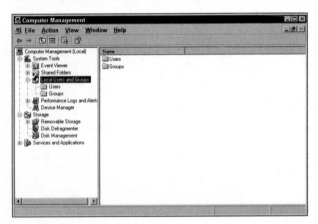

3. Click the plus sign (+) next to Local Users and Groups to expand the folder.

4. Right-click the Users folder and choose New User from the menu that appears. The New User dialog box opens.

5. In the User name box, enter a name for the account you're creating. In this example, I called my account **WSSAdmin** (see Figure 17.7).

FIGURE 17.7

Create a Windows account.

6. In the Password box, enter a password and reenter it in the Confirm password box.

CAUTION   **Don't forget to write down the password.**

7. Deselect the User Must Change Password At Next Logon check box.

8. Select the User Cannot Change Password check box and the Password Never Expires check box.

9. Click the Create button.

Repeat these steps to create each of the accounts you intend to use to administer the various components of Project Server.

When you finish creating the accounts, add each account to the appropriate security group. Click the Groups folder in the left pane of the Computer Management window. In the right pane, click each account and choose Action ⇨ Add to Group. In the Properties box that appears, click the Add button to display the Select Users dialog box (see Figure 17.8).

FIGURE 17.8

FIGURE 17.8

Supply the path for the selected administrative account.

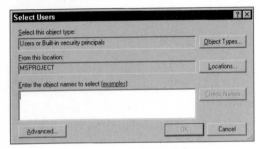

In the Enter the object names to select box, enter ***servername\account***, where *account* is the account for which you are setting privileges and *servername* is the name of the computer associated with the account. Click OK twice to redisplay the Computer Management window.

Repeat this process for each account to assign it to the appropriate security groups. When you finish, you can close the Computer Management window.

Installing Project Server and Windows SharePoint Services

NOTE   If you are upgrading from Project Server 2003 to Project Server 2007, you can find documents on online at `http://office.microsoft.com/project/` that describe the process for you. Follow those documents; in this chapter, the information applies to new installations.

Just to review: Make sure that you have installed Windows Server 2003, enabled Microsoft Internet Information Server (IIS) 6.0 or above, and installed SQL Server 2000 with Service Pack 3 or SQL Server 2005 and, if appropriate, SQL Analysis Services and SQL Reporting Services using the same level and service pack as SQL. As noted earlier in this chapter, you don't need to install all products on one machine, but you *must* install all products before you install Project Server. Also make sure that you've established the Windows accounts described in the preceding section.

CAUTION   I can't stress strongly enough how important it is for you to follow all the steps of the installation process in order. If you skipped something earlier, please go back and do it now. You'll be much happier if you do.

As you would expect, a wizard walks you through the process of installing Project Server and Windows SharePoint Services. Initially, the wizard asks for the type of installation you want: Basic or Advanced (see Figure 17.9).

Choose the type of installation you want.

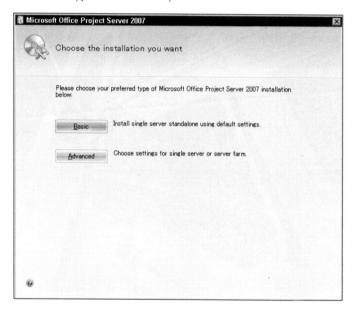

The Basic installation is a single-box installation that uses default settings. This installation suits a very small company or someone who wants to evaluate Project Server. If you select this type of installation, you get to sit back and watch. Choose Advanced for any installation other than a one-box installation or if you want to change the default settings for a single-box installation — and I assume, in the rest of this section, that you chose Advanced.

You next select the type of installation you want: a complete installation, which installs all components; a Web front-end installation only; or a stand-alone installation that installs all components on one box using settings you specify. I assume here that you are creating a new installation for Project Server 2007.

You now sit back while the installation wizard works; when it finishes, it prompts you to complete the configuration of your server by running the SharePoint Products and Technologies Configuration Wizard (see Figure 17.10).

FIGURE 17.10

After the installation finishes, the wizard prompts you to configure Project Server 2007.

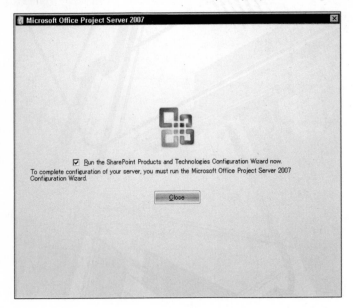

To configure Windows SharePoint Services, you need to know the name of the database and database server where you intend to store server farm configuration data. You also need to know the username and password for the database account that will administer the server farm.

The wizard prompts you to specify whether you want to connect to an existing server farm or create a new server farm. Because I'm assuming that this is a new installation, select the option to create a new farm.

Next, you specify configuration database settings (see Figure 17.11). You specify the name of the database server and the database, along with the username and password of the account that will administer the farm.

Next, the wizard prompts you to supply a port number for the first server in the server farm; this server will host the server farm Web site. You can specify a port number, but in most cases, you should simply let the wizard select one for you. In addition, you need to select a security configuration for the server farm; you choose between NTLM and Kerberos (see Figure 17.12).

FIGURE 17.11

Specify Windows SharePoint Services configuration database settings.

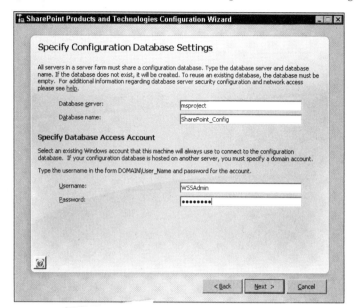

FIGURE 17.12

Specify a port for the first server in the farm and a security configuration.

The wizard summarizes your selections, and when you click Next, the wizard begins the configuration process. When the wizard finishes, you see a screen like the one shown in Figure 17.13, which lists your configuration choices and indicates that configuration was successful.

FIGURE 17.13

The final screen of the Windows SharePoint Services Installation and Configuration Wizard.

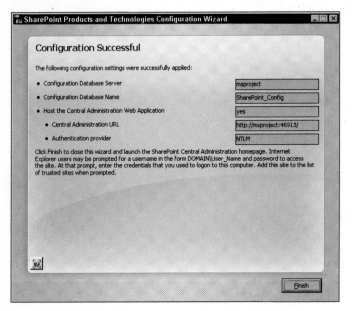

When you click Finish, the wizard opens Internet Explorer and displays the SharePoint Central Administration home page (see Figure 17.14). You may be prompted for a username and password; specify the username in the format domain\username. When prompted, add the site to your trusted sites.

 Add this site to your Favorites list.

You use SharePoint Central Administration to perform several actions:

- Configure farm services
- Create a Web application for the Shared Services Provider
- Create and extend the Project Web Access Web application
- Use the Shared Services Provider Web application to create the Shared Services Provider
- Install Office Project Server 2007 to the farm

FIGURE 17.14

The SharePoint Central Administration home page.

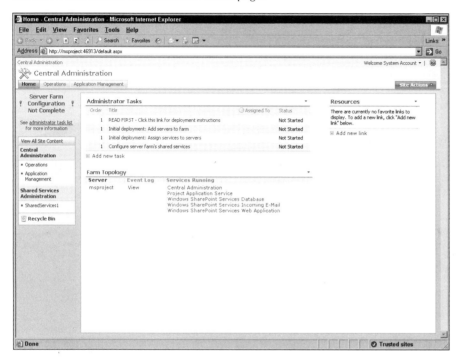

Once again, you need to complete the steps in the order listed; the installation documents that you can find online at http://office.microsoft.com/project/ provide detailed steps to walk you through performing each action.

When you configure farm services, you start the Project Application Service and the Windows SharePoint Services Web application, enabling the Project Server Application and the Web Front End tiers on the server.

You then create an unextended Web site to host the Shared Services Provider.

Next, you create an extended Web site to host the SharePoint team site; when you finish this process, you will have a new top-level site for the site collection that contains no data.

Using the Shared Service Provider Web application you created, you next create the Share Service Provider.

Last, when you create the Project Web Access instance on the farm, you specify the Project Server Administrator account, identify the database server that will host your Project Server 2007 databases, and name the Project Server databases.

You're now ready to open Project Web Access.

Connecting to Project Server through Project Web Access

Okay, now for the fun part — finally seeing what you installed! Open Internet Explorer and, in the address bar, enter the following text:

```
http://servername/psinstance
```

You replace *servername* with the name of your server and *psinstance* with the name you used to create your instance of Project Server. If you accepted defaults during installation, the default instance of Project Server is named pwa.

You are then automatically directed to the home page for the Windows account logged on to your computer (see Figure 17.15).

FIGURE 17.15

The opening page in Project Web Access.

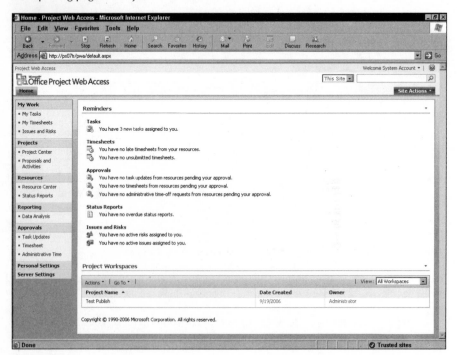

> **NOTE** If your organization uses Project Server authentication instead of Windows authentication, you are automatically directed to a logon page, where you supply your username and password. To log on as the Administrator, enter **Administrator** for the username and provide the password that you supplied when you installed Project Server.

Troubleshooting Your Installation

If you follow the installation steps in order, your installation should be problem free. After all the software is installed, the most common problem is system performance. You can improve system performance by balancing the load on your system.

What techniques should you try so that you can balance the load? You need to approach this problem by determining the cause of the problem, because the solution that you choose is dictated by the cause of the problem. For example, it would be a waste of money to upgrade all your CPUs if network traffic is the source of the problem.

Make use of the Windows System Monitor to determine where you have bottlenecks. If you find that you are fully using your CPU, you can try upgrading the CPU, adding another CPU, or off-loading services to reduce the load on the CPU. You can also use clustering to help balance the load; all Project Server components can be clustered.

> **NOTE** Although you can cluster SQL, you don't cluster SQL to balance a load; instead, you cluster it to provide a fail-safe mechanism. If you cluster SQL and a server goes down, the event will be invisible to the end user.

If you determine that network traffic is the source of the problem, balance the load by installing additional NICs. For example, you may install a second NIC in the computer where SQL is stored and then tie Project Professional traffic to one NIC and Project Server traffic to the other NIC. You can also make use of switches and routers to help balance network traffic.

Summary

In this chapter, you explored the software and hardware requirements for Project Server. You found out about the order in which you need to install the other software packages before you install Project Server and the basic configuration settings for those packages. You installed and configured Project Server so that the database was ready to be customized for your organization's needs.

You read about potential performance issues and saw some sample hardware configurations to help you improve performance. In Chapter 18, you explore the administrative tasks that are associated with customizing the Project Server database to support your organization.

Chapter 18

Project Server and the Administrator

In Chapter 16, you reviewed design issues and approaches to successfully implementing Project Server. In Chapter 17, you went through the process of installing and configuring the software that is necessary to use Project Server database. In this chapter, you explore setting up and customizing the Project Server environment to meet your organization's needs.

During this stage where you set up and customize the Project Server environment, you need the skills of the following types of people:

- An information technology (IT) person with background in hardware, networking, and connectivity

- A project management (PM) person with extensive knowledge of your organization's needs while managing Projects

After the design and implementation team has identified certain components that your organization will use, the IT person can work independently on some tasks while, at the same time, the PM person works independently on other tasks. To complete the setup, these two individuals will probably work together. As you read the tasks in this chapter, you can decide who should perform each task.

This chapter is organized to present tasks in the order that they need to be done. Doing things in order when setting up and customizing the Project Server environment to meet your organization's needs is not as critical as doing things in order was when installing the software, but doing some tasks before other tasks can make the implementation run smoother. And you'll find that some of the tasks overlap. For example, you add users to groups and groups to users. In most of these cases, it really doesn't matter which you do first, because you'll complete one task when you complete the other task.

When you have Project Server up and running, you will need to make occasional changes to the environment. For these types of changes, the Project Server administrator needs to be someone with project management background rather than someone with an information technology background. The role of administrator for the Project Server environment over time will fall to someone who is more intimately involved with project management and will become a maintenance job.

Double-Checking Settings

> **NOTE** Throughout the rest of my discussion of Project Server, I use the sample database.

The Project Server environment contains many useful default values and settings. You should double-check these values and settings to make sure that they will work within the framework of your organization. Use Project Web Access to check settings.

> **NOTE** On all the pages that you see in this section, you can make changes if necessary. Usually, it is not necessary to change the information.

Launch Project Web Access by starting Internet Explorer and entering the URL for your Project Server environment. If your organization uses Windows authentication and you are logged onto the computer using the Windows account of the Project Server administrator, you see the Project Web Access home page for the Project Server administrator (see Figure 18.1).

If you aren't logged onto the computer using the Windows account of the Project Server administrator, you can switch to the Project Server administrator's account using the menu in the upper-right corner of the screen. When you click Sign In as Different User, a prompt appears, asking you for a username and password. Enter the username and password of the Project Server administrator and click OK.

Project Web Access Home page for the administrator, which contains an additional link in the Quick Launch pane that runs down the left side of the screen: the Server Settings link. From the Server Settings link, the Project Server administrator can manage and customize the Project Server environment and Project Web Access by using the links on the Server Settings page (see Figure 18.2).

The Project Web Access home page of the Project Server administrator.

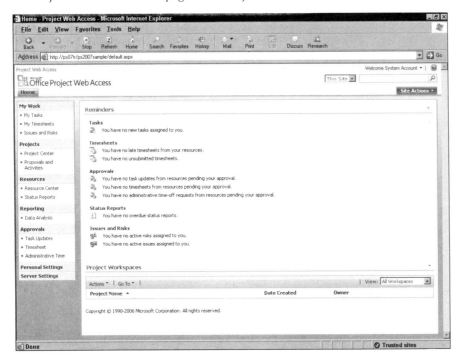

Forms Authentication versus Windows Authentication

As you'd expect, if your organization uses Windows authentication, you aren't prompted for a username and password when you navigate to the URL for Project Web Access; instead, you are automatically logged in to the Project Server environment with the credentials associated with the username and password you used when you logged on to your computer.

If your organization uses Project Server Forms authentication instead of Windows authentication and you navigate to the URL for your Project Server database, you are automatically directed to a logon page, where you supply your Project Server username and password. To log on as the Administrator, enter **Administrator** for the username and provide the password that you supplied when you installed Project Server.

Throughout this chapter, I use Windows Authentication.

FIGURE 18.2

The Project Server Administrator manages most settings in the Project Server environment from the Server Settings page.

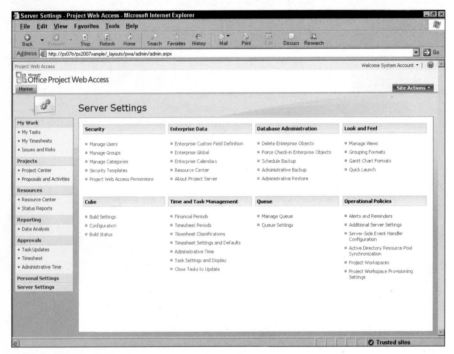

NOTE   Unless otherwise specified, all tasks that I describe in the following sections assume that you begin by logging on to Project Web Access as administrator and clicking the Server Settings link in the Quick Launch pane.

Specifying Project Server features for your organization

The Server configuration page appears in Figure 18.3; you display this page by clicking the Additional Server Settings link in the Operational Policies section of the Server Settings page. On the Additional Server Settings page, the administrator confirms whether your organization will do the following:

- Allow master projects in the Project Server environment.
- Allow projects to use the local base calendar instead of the Enterprise base calendar.

■ Set a default currency and decide whether to enforce a uniform, single currency in the Project Server environment (you specify the currency in the Enterprise global template) or permit projects to be published in a variety of currencies.

■ Establish resource capacity settings that specify the number of months behind and ahead that the report database maintains data for resources. You also set a schedule for maintaining forward-looking data. This setting helps you manage the size of the reporting database, which affects the speed of producing reports.

■ Specify the basis for the resource plan work week; choose to calculate resource full-time equivalent from resource base calendars or by setting a number of hours per week.

■ Specify the URL for Microsoft Reporting service — typically a machine name.

■ Indicate whether the Project "state" field is governed by an external workflow. The state field works with proposal projects and, if you've installed Microsoft Office Server System, you can enable the auto workflow feature, which then updates the value in the state field automatically as the project goes through the proposal process. Without Microsoft Office Server System, you can update the state field manually.

FIGURE 18.3

The features on this page control some basic enterprise features in the Project Server environment.

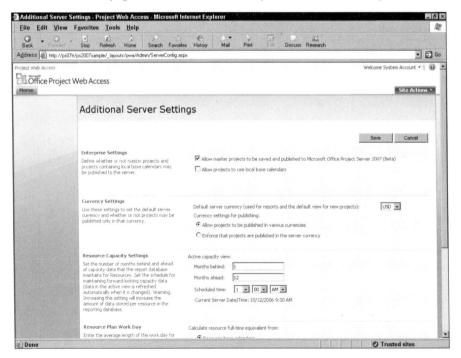

Managing Windows SharePoint Services

As its foundation, Project Server uses Windows SharePoint Services technology. And there are a number of settings in the Project Server environment that you control through Windows SharePoint Services. To manage these settings, click the Site Actions tab in the upper-right corner of the Project Web Access window and choose Site Settings to display the Site Settings page shown in Figure 18.4. You'll make your Project Server environment easier for users to use if you preset these settings to match the ones your organization uses.

FIGURE 18.4

Use the links on this page to manage Windows SharePoint Services settings.

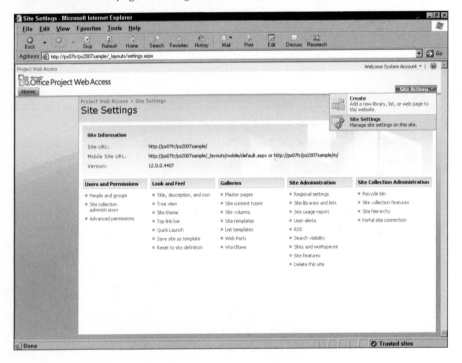

For example, you can click the Regional settings link to set your time zone, select a calendar type, define your work week, and select a time format (see Figure 18.5).

When you click the Quick Launch link in the Look and Feel section of the Site Settings page, you find that you can control the Windows SharePoint Services links that appear in the Quick Launch pane that runs down the left side of Project Web Access; you also can control the order of those links (see Figure 18.6).

From the Regional Settings page, you can define your work week.

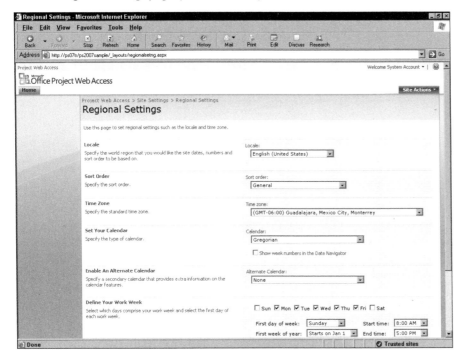

FIGURE 18.6

Control the elements that appear on the Quick Launch pane, along with their order.

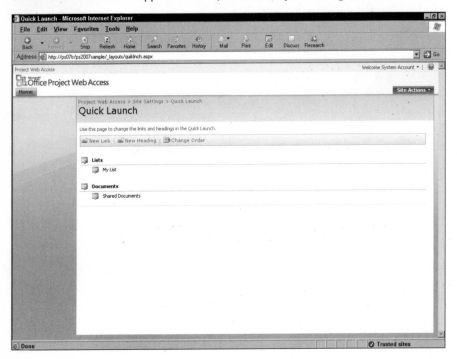

Managing Security Settings

To manage security settings, Project Server uses security templates, groups, and categories.

Managing security templates

The Project Server environment contains some default security templates, which are sets of permissions. You use security templates to assign a set of permissions to a user or a group of users.

The Project Server environment contains security templates for each of the predefined groups that you find in the Project Server environment. You can modify the default security templates or create your own; click the Server Settings link in the Quick Launch pane and then click Security Templates in the Security section of the Server Settings page. On the Manage Templates page that appears, click the name of the template that you want to modify or click New Template at the top of the page. As you can see in Figures 18.7 and 18.8, security templates contain a long list of information; the list of Global Permissions extends even further down the page than you see in Figure 18.5. You include or exclude permissions in a template by selecting the Allow or Deny check box for that right.

 Typically, you don't "deny" a feature; instead, you either select or deselect the Allow box.

 Read more about categories later in this chapter.

FIGURE 18.7

Use security templates to create sets of permissions.

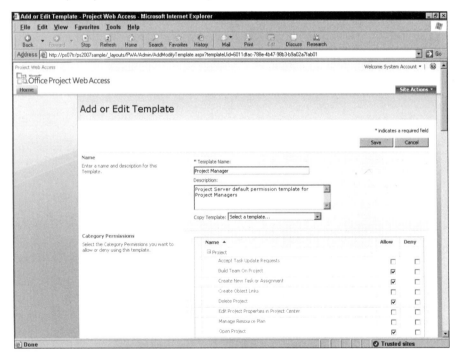

FIGURE 18.8

You set category permissions and global permissions.

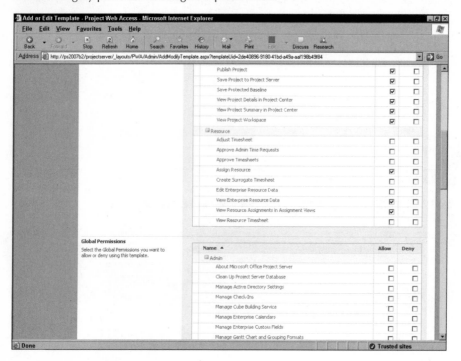

Managing groups

Groups are collections of users. Project Server enables you to group users in some fashion that is logical in your organization. Grouping users makes it easier to assign security permissions, and you can assign one user to more than one group. You find the following predefined groups in the database:

- Administrators
- Executives
- Portfolio Managers
- Project Managers
- Proposal Reviewers
- Resource Managers
- Team Leads
- Team Members

Double-check the predefined groups and make sure that you have groups that accurately reflect the structure of your organization. Display the page that appears in Figure 18.9 by clicking the Server Settings link in the Quick Launch pane on the left side of the Project Web Access window. Then, click the Manage Groups link in the Security section of the Server Settings page.

When you create or modify a group by clicking the group name, you can add users to the group, assign categories and category permissions to the group, assign global permissions to the group, and assign a Digital Dashboard to the group. In Figure 18.10, you see the Global Permissions portion of the Add Groups page. Notice that you can set permissions using a template and that all the available templates appear in a list box next to the Set Permissions with Template button.

NOTE I realize that you're double-checking the groups before adding users to the Project Server environment, so you can't add users to groups. Don't worry, though. When you add users, you get the opportunity to assign them to groups, so you don't need to assign users to groups when you create or modify groups.

FIGURE 18.9

The groups defined by default in a new Project Server environment.

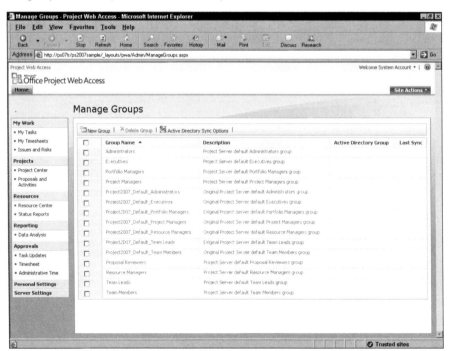

FIGURE 18.10

You can assign users and categories to groups.

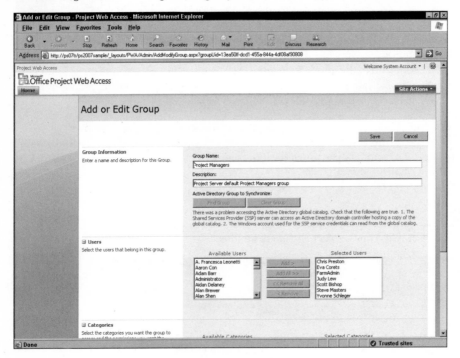

Working with categories

Categories are security tools you use to map users and groups to the projects, resources, views, and custom fields the users and groups can see in Project Web Access. In other words, in a category, you identify the users, projects, project views, Project Center views, Portfolio Analyzer views, Resource Center views, and Resource Assignments views to include in the category. The Project Server environment includes, by default, the following categories that are tied to the default groups that were identified in the section "Managing groups," earlier in this chapter:

- **My Direct Reports:** Includes all projects and views that are worked on or managed by a user and resources that are managed by a user. This category includes the Resource Managers group.

- **My Organization:** Includes all projects, all views, and the following groups: administrators, executives, portfolio managers, project managers, proposal reviewers, and resource managers.

- **My Personal Projects:** Includes all projects for which the user is the Project Owner or Status Manager and all views that are defined for those projects. This category includes the executive, portfolio manager, project manager, resource manager, team leads, and team members groups.

- **My Projects:** Includes all projects that are worked on or managed by a particular user, all views that are defined for those projects, and the Project Managers, Resource Managers, and Team Leads groups.

- **My Resources:** Includes the projects that are worked on by resources who report to a specific user as well as views for those projects. Resource Managers belong to this group.

- **My Tasks:** Includes all projects to which a user is assigned, a view of the assignments for those projects, and the Team Members group.

To create a new category or edit an existing category, click the Server Settings link in the Quick Launch pane on the left side of the Project Web Access window. Then, click the Manage Categories link in the Security section of the Server Settings page. On the Manage Categories page that lists the categories I just described, click New Category to create your own category or click any category name to edit that category.

If you click an existing category, you see the Add or Edit Category page (the top of the page appears in Figure 18.11), where you select the users and groups that you want to include in this category and the projects that users in this category can view.

FIGURE 18.11

Use this page to define the users and groups that you want to include in the category and the projects that users in this category can view.

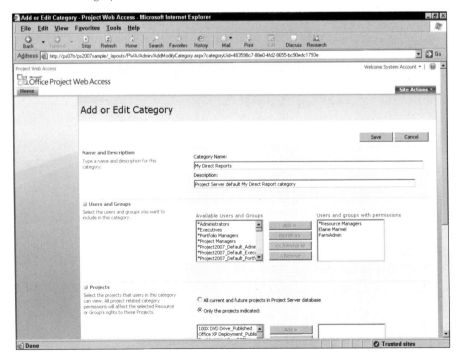

Scroll down and identify the resources whose information will be visible by users included in the category and specify the resource security permissions that Project Server should apply to the resources you select (see Figure 18.12).

NOTE   I realize that you haven't added users yet, so specifying resources for a category may seem to pose a problem. However, when you add users in the next section, you see that you can assign a user to a category. So, you get the opportunity to "double back" and connect the category with the user.

In the next section of the page, specify the views that you want to include in the category; in this section, the views are broken down by Project, Project Center, Resource Assignments, Resource Center, My Work, Resource Plans, Team Tasks, Team Builder, and Timesheet. In Figure 18.13, I've shown you only a portion of the views you can select to include in the category.

FIGURE 18.12

Identify resources that users in this category can view.

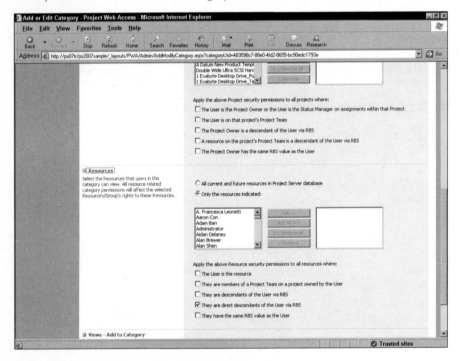

FIGURE 18.13

Specify the views that you want to include in the category.

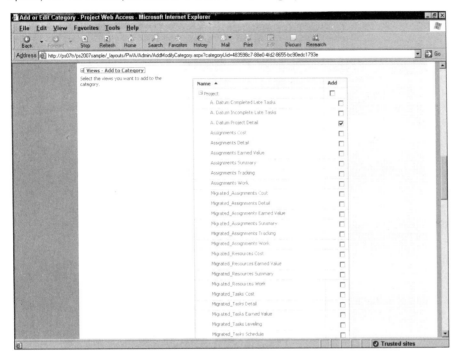

In the last portion of the page, shown in Figure 18.14, identify the type of custom field access you want to provide in the Project Center, Portfolio Resource Center, Status, and Build Team views when accessed by users included in the category.

Managing Users

Okay, "double-checking" is over. Now you're doing "new stuff." To enable people to use Project Web Access, you need to add users. Click the Server Settings link in the Quick Launch pane on the left side of the Project Web Access window. Then, click the Manage Users link in the Security section of the Server Settings page to display the Manage Users page (see Figure 18.14).

FIGURE 18.14

Use this page to add or modify users.

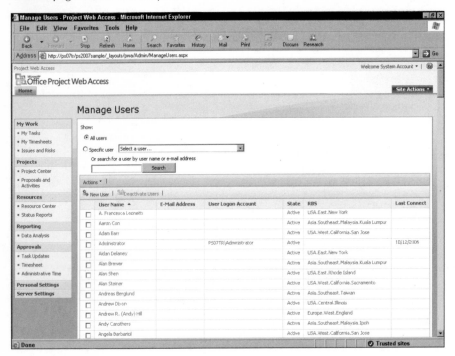

From this page, the Project Server administrator can add, modify, or deactivate user accounts. In addition, the administrator can merge two usernames into one account if a user appears twice in the Log On list under two different names.

> **TIP** You can print the list of users or export the list to Excel if you click the Actions button above the list of usernames.

To add a user, click New User at the top of the list of users. To edit a user, click the user's name. When you add or edit a user, you see a page on which you specify the user's name and other identification information, the type of authentication to use (Windows Authentication or Forms authentication), the user's assignment attributes, resource custom fields, security groups, security categories, global permissions, group fields, team details, and system identification data. In Figure 18.15, you see the top of the Edit User page.

FIGURE 18.15

At the top of the page, supply basic user identification information.

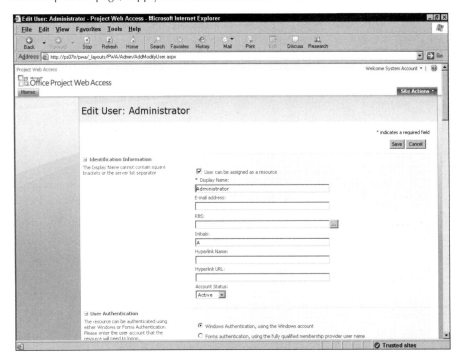

Assignment attributes and resource custom fields will be specific to your organization, but typically they include information that indicates whether the resource can be leveled and the resource's base calendar and default booking type. Similarly, group fields, team details, and system identification data will be specific to your organization.

Security groups and categories include the information discussed previously in this chapter in the sections, "Managing groups" and "Working with categories." You can read about global permissions in the section "Managing security templates."

TIP   To manage security effectively, don't set permissions for a user. Instead, set permissions in security templates and assign the security templates to categories and groups. Then, assign users to groups; in this way, users will inherit the permissions set for a category and group.

Working with Views

A *view* contains a set of fields and filters that Project Web Access uses when displaying project information. Through views, the administrator controls what you see in Project Web Access because views enable users to examine project information in different ways.

The Project Server database contains many default views. The administrator uses the Manage Views page, shown in Figure 18.16, to create new views and modify or delete existing views. Display this page by clicking the Server Settings link in the Quick Launch pane on the left side of the Project Web Access window. Then, click the Manage Views link in the Look and Feel section of the Server Settings page.

Before you make changes here — either to create a view or to modify an existing view — I suggest that you continue customizing until you can load a project into the Project Server environment. With a project in the database, you can view that project using each default view that's available in the Project Server environment. You may find that Microsoft has already created the view that you want or a view that is close enough to the one you want that you can modify an existing view.

FIGURE 18.16

On this page, you can create a new view or modify or delete an existing view.

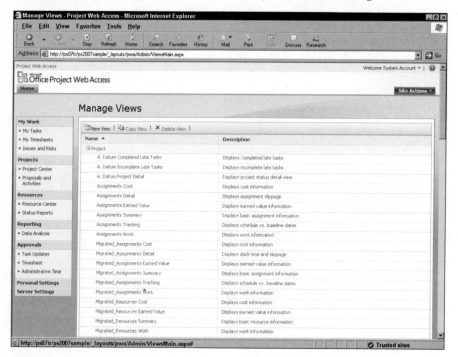

To add a view, click the New View link at the top of the Manage Views page. And, although you can directly edit an existing view by clicking its name, I suggest that you click Copy View at the top of the page to duplicate the view and then edit the copy.

In Figure 18.17, you see the top of the Edit View page when editing a Project view. When you edit a view, you can't change the View Type at the top of the page, but this field is available when you create a new view, and you can select Project, Project Center, Resource Assignments, Resource Center, Data Analysis, My Work, Resource Plan, Team Tasks, Team Builder, or Timesheet for the type for the view.

The type of view that you select determines the choices that appear as you scroll down the page to create the view. For example, for Project, Project Center and Resource Assignments views, you can choose a Gantt Chart format that is not available for other views. In Figure 18.18, you see the bottom of the Edit View page when modifying a Project view.

FIGURE 18.17

At the top of the page, specify the type of view, the view name, the tables and fields that you want to appear in the view, and some of the view format options.

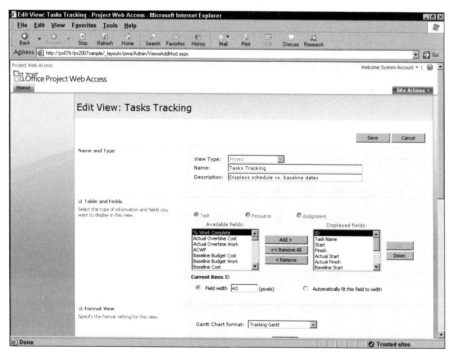

FIGURE 18.18

At the bottom of the page, select other view format options, including outline levels, grouping and sorting options, filter options, and security categories.

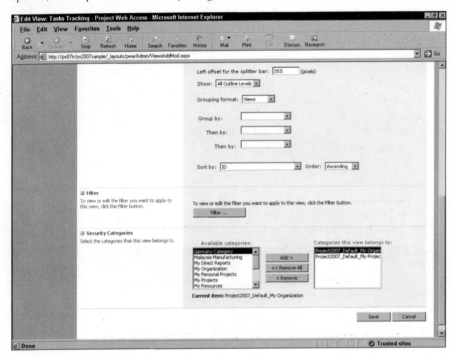

Working with the Enterprise Global Template

You can compare the Enterprise Global template to the Global template in Project Professional. Both serve the same purpose — to store a collection of all default settings that are used by projects across your organization. Each new project is based on the Enterprise Global template, enforcing standard usage across all the organization's projects.

Working with the Enterprise Global

Someone with administrative privileges in your company customizes the Enterprise Global template so that it contains the custom fields and calendars that meet the needs of your organization. When you customize the Enterprise Global template, it opens in Project Professional (note the title bar in Figure 18.19), where you can customize fields, groups, and filters, just to name a few elements.

NOTE A complete list of the elements that you can customize in the Enterprise Global appears on the Configure Project Professional page in Project Web Access, which appears when you click the Enterprise Global link in the Enterprise Data section of the Server Settings page.

To open the Enterprise Global in Project Professional, click the Server Settings link in the Quick Launch pane on the left side of the Project Web Access window. Then, click the Enterprise Global link in the Enterprise Data section of the Server Settings page; the Configure Project Professional page appears. Click the Configure Project Professional button.

When you finish, choose File ➪ Close. You'll be prompted to check in the Enterprise Global. Click Yes to save your settings and make the Enterprise Global available in Project Web Access.

FIGURE 18.19

You can customize the Enterprise Global using Project Professional.

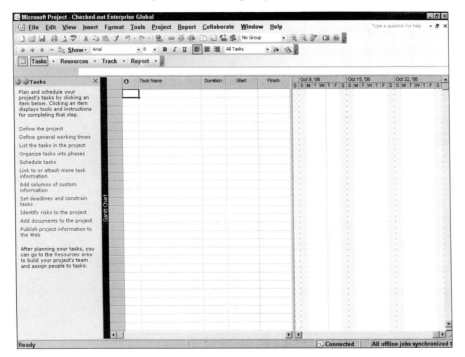

Defining Enterprise custom fields

Custom fields can be used for many purposes. For example, your organization may want to set up a custom field for Project Status and assign values such as Active, Approved, Closed, and Opportunity. Or, if your organization opts to use generic resources and wants to be able to match the skills of a generic resource with a real resource that possesses those skills, you can create a custom field and establish a value list for the field where each value represents a set of skills. After you assign the appropriate value to each resource by using the custom field, you can use the code to match skills that are required by generic resources with skills that are possessed by real people when project managers run the Team Builder.

CROSS-REF   In Chapter 19, you can find an example in which I used an enterprise resource custom outline code with the Team Builder to substitute real resources for generic ones.

You set up enterprise custom fields and outline codes essentially the same way that you set up custom fields, as I describe in Chapter 22, and custom outline codes, as I described in Chapter 7, but you use Project Web Access.

Click the Server Settings link in the Quick Launch pane on the left side of the Project Web Access window. Then, click the Enterprise Custom Field Definition link in the Enterprise Data section of the Server Settings page. The Custom Fields and Lookup Tables page appears (see Figure 18.20), listing all custom fields that currently exist in the Enterprise Global. Below the list of custom fields, you also see a list of defined lookup tables; you can identify the lookup table assigned to a given custom field in the Lookup Table field on the right side of the Enterprise Custom Fields table.

TIP   When you create a custom field and a lookup table, give them the same name so that you can easily identify what goes with what.

You can edit an existing field by clicking its name; if you want to create a new custom field based on the definition of an existing custom field, click anywhere on the row of the existing custom field and then click the Copy Field button above the list of fields. Or, you can click the New Field button to create a new custom field (see Figure 18.21).

FIGURE 18.20

The list of existing custom fields.

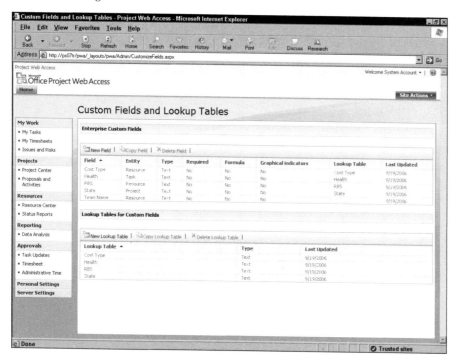

For all custom fields, you supply a name. For the Entity, you can select Project, Resource, or Task, and, for the Type, you can select Text, Cost, Date, Duration, Flag, or Number. In the Custom Attributes section, you can assign a look-up table or a formula to the custom field. In the Values to Display section, you specify whether you want to see data or graphical indicators, and in the Required section, you can specify whether the user must supply data for the field.

FIGURE 18.21

Defining attributes for a new enterprise custom field.

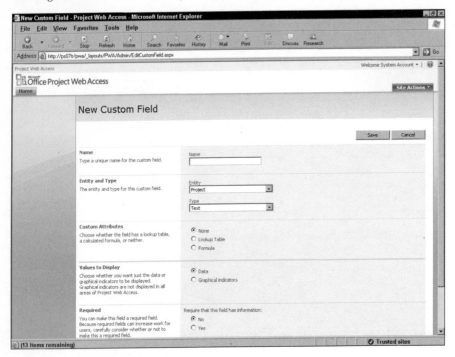

If you select Resource as the Entity, you also specify calculation methods for assignment rows. If you select Task as the Entity, you specify calculation methods for both assignment rows and summary rows.

You can click the New Lookup Table button to define a look-up table; the process is the same as the one described in Chapter 22.

If you've already stored resources in the Enterprise Resource Pool, you need to edit the resources to assign a value to each of them for the new custom field. Follow the steps described in the section "Creating the Enterprise Resource Pool," later in this chapter, to assign values for the custom field to resources that are stored in the Enterprise Resource Pool.

If you have not yet stored resources in the Enterprise Resource Pool, edit the resources in the usual way. When you import the resources to the Enterprise Resource Pool, you have the option of including the custom fields.

Creating Enterprise calendars

Assign a calendar to the Enterprise Global template to enforce common workdays and work times across all projects. Resources in the Enterprise Resource Pool can use the calendar in the Enterprise Global template unless you override that calendar by assigning a resource-specific calendar.

You set up the calendar for the Enterprise Global template the same way that you set up a calendar for a project, but you start in Project Web Access. Click the Server Settings link in the Quick Launch pane on the left side of the Project Web Access window. Then, click the Enterprise Calendars link in the Enterprise Data section of the Server Settings page. The Enterprise Calendars page appears (see Figure 18.22).

You can edit an existing calendar by clicking anywhere on the line where its name appears and then clicking the Edit Calendar button above the list of calendars. If you want to create a new calendar based on an existing calendar, click anywhere on the row of the existing custom field and then click the Copy Calendar button. Or, you can click the New Calendar button to create a new calendar. When you edit or create a calendar, Project Web Access opens the Change Working Time dialog box in Project Professional (see Figure 18.23).

FIGURE 18.22

This page lists the calendars defined in the Enterprise Global.

FIGURE 18.23

You work in Project Professional to create or edit an enterprise calendar.

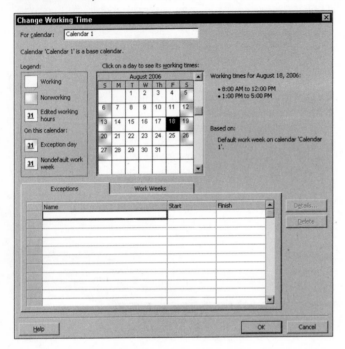

CROSS-REF   For details on making calendar changes, see Chapter 3.

Setting Up and Editing Enterprise Resources

The Enterprise Resource Pool is a single repository that project and resource managers can use when assigning resources to their projects. The Enterprise Resource Pool includes summary resource assignments, resource base calendars, and any enterprise resource fields that you defined in the Enterprise Global template. Project managers borrow resources from the Enterprise Resource Pool to assign them to a project. The Project Server administrator can set the permissions for others to add, edit, and delete resources from the Enterprise Resource Pool. Project Server manages the check-out/check-in operations.

To improve performance, Project Professional interacts with Office Project Server 2007 through a local cache that manages replication of the enterprise global resource pool information, delivering changes only instead of entire files.

Creating the Enterprise Resource Pool

The easiest way to create the Enterprise Resource Pool is to use a project that contains the resources that you want to store in the Enterprise Resource Pool. Then, a wizard in the Project Guide walks you through setting up the Enterprise Resource Pool. Make sure that the project containing the resources is closed or checked in and then follow these steps to create the Enterprise Resource Pool:

1. Open Project Professional and make sure that you connect to the Project Server environment; you'll see the Login dialog box, where you enter your username and password and click OK.

2. Choose Tools ➪ Enterprise Options ➪ Import Resources to Enterprise. The Open dialog box appears.

3. Select the project that contains the resources and click Open.

4. If you've set up any custom fields for resources, click the Map Resource Fields link in the Project Guide pane to display the Map Custom Fields dialog box and match custom fields that you've set up for resources to enterprise resource fields.

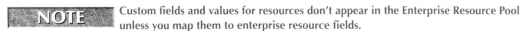 Custom fields and values for resources don't appear in the Enterprise Resource Pool unless you map them to enterprise resource fields.

5. Click Continue to Step 2 in the Project Guide and identify the resources that you want to upload to the Enterprise Resource Pool by choosing Yes in the Import column (see Figure 18.24).

TIP You can view and change the information for any displayed resource by selecting that resource and clicking the Resource Information button. Project displays the Resource Information dialog box for the selected resource. Errors appear in red.

6. Click Validate Resources in the Project Guide pane. Project compares the selected resources to those in the Enterprise Resource Pool and displays any errors.

7. Correct the errors and click Save and Finish in the Project Guide pane. Project sends the resources to the Enterprise Resource Pool in the Project Server environment. In the Project Guide pane, Project Professional gives you the opportunity to optionally set booking types of either Proposed or Committed for selected resources.

8. Click Done.

FIGURE 18.24

Identify resources that you want to store in the Enterprise Resource Pool.

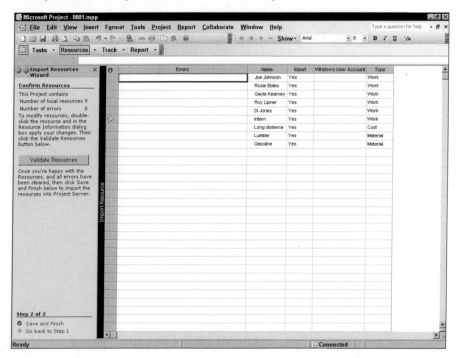

Editing resources in the Enterprise Resource Pool

After you have stored a resource in the Enterprise Resource Pool, what happens if you find out that you need to make a change to that resource? Suppose, for example, that you create a new custom field and you need to assign a value for the field to a resource in the Enterprise Resource Pool. You can edit the resource by checking it out, making the change, and then checking it back in. While resources are checked out, others can't make and save changes to the resources.

Follow these steps to check out resources from the Enterprise Resource Pool:

1. Open Project Professional and connect to the Project Server environment.
2. Choose Tools ⇨ Enterprise Options ⇨ Open Enterprise Resource Pool. Project displays a temporary project called Checked-out Enterprise Resources that lists the resource pool; notice the title bar in Figure 18.25.

FIGURE 18.25

Checked-out enterprise resources appear in Project Professional.

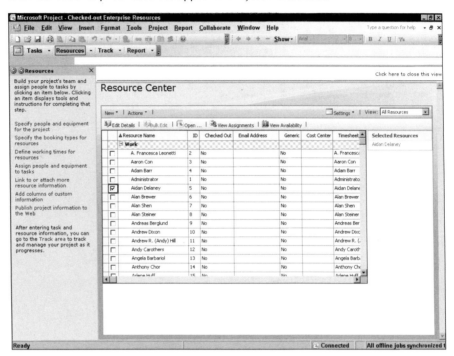

3. Place a check mark next to the resource(s) that you want to edit.

TIP When you want to edit multiple resources, check each of them and then click Open in Step 4 instead of Edit Details. The resources appear in the Resource Sheet view in Project Professional.

4. Click the Edit Details button above the list of resources. The Edit Resource window appears (see Figure 18.26).

5. Make changes to the resource.

6. Click Save and Continue to save your changes to the Enterprise Resource Pool.

FIGURE 18.26

Make changes to the resource in this window.

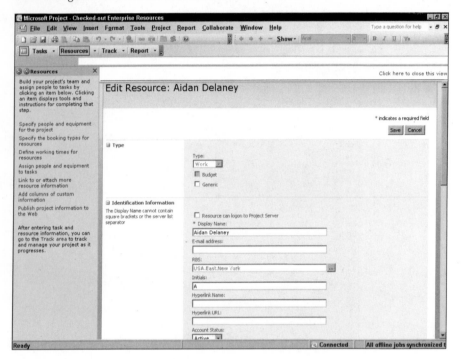

7. Click Save to check the resource back in to the Enterprise Resource Pool; Project closes the Edit Resource window and redisplays the Resource Center window in Project Professional (refer to Figure 18.25).

8. Choose File ➪ Exit to close Project Professional.

Importing Projects

You will, no doubt, have projects already created and in progress that you want to load into the Project Server environment. You can use the Project Guide in Project Professional to walk you through loading these projects. Follow these steps:

1. Open Project Professional and log on to Project Server.

2. Choose Tools ➪ Enterprise Options ➪ Import Project to Enterprise. The Open dialog box appears.

3. Navigate to the .mpp file that you want to import into the Project Server environment and click Open. Project opens the project and displays the Import Project Wizard, a five-step process, in the Project Guide pane.

4. Click Map Resources to match resources in the project to resources in the Enterprise Resource Pool. Project displays the Map Project Resources onto Enterprise Resources dialog box (see Figure 18.27). To map resources, click in the Action on Import column, and a list box appears. Select an action for each resource — you can select Map to enterprise resource or Keep local with base calendar. If you choose Map to an enterprise resource, click in the Calendar or Enterprise Resource column and select the enterprise resource. If you chose Keep local with base calendar, select a valid calendar in the Calendar or Enterprise Resource column. When you finish, click OK.

FIGURE 18.27

Map project resources to enterprise resources.

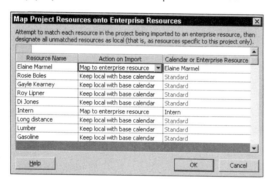

5. Click Continue to Step 2 in the Project Guide pane, where you validate the resources in the project. See "Creating the Enterprise Resource Pool," earlier in this chapter, for details on completing this step.

6. Click Continue to Step 3 in the Project Guide pane, where you can match local task custom fields to Enterprise task custom fields. Click the Map Task Fields link to display the Map Custom Fields dialog box. Place a check mark in the column of the field that you want to map. Click in the From: Task Field column and a list box appears; select the field to map. Then, click in the To: Enterprise Task Field column and another list box appears; select the Enterprise task field that corresponds to the local task field. Repeat this process for each local custom field you want to map to an Enterprise custom field. When you finish, click OK.

7. Click Continue to Step 4 in the Project Guide pane, where you confirm the tasks that Project will import to Project Server. If any errors appear, correct them.

8. Click Continue to Step 5 in the Project Guide pane, where you click the Save As link to save the project to Project Server (see Figure 18.28).

FIGURE 18.28

When you click Save As in the Project Guide pane, the Save to Project Server dialog box appears.

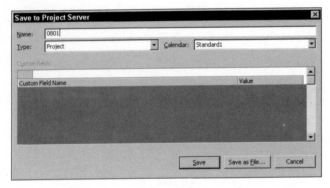

9. Enter a name for the project in Project Server and click Save. Project imports your project into Project Server.

10. Click Save and Finish in the Project Guide pane.

When you close the project in Project Professional, you'll see a dialog box that asks you whether you want to save changes to the project and whether you want to check the project in to Project Server. Save the changes and check in the project so that others can use it.

Managing Timesheet and Task Settings

Project Server contains a variety of timesheet and task settings that you can manage through Project Web Access.

Financial Periods

Use the Fiscal Periods page to establish fiscal periods that match your business's fiscal periods.

To display the Fiscal Periods page (see Figure 18.29), click the Server Settings link in the Quick Launch pane on the left side of the Project Web Access window. Then, click the Financial Periods link in the Time and Task Management section of the Server Settings page.

FIGURE 18.29

Use this page to establish fiscal periods that match those of your company.

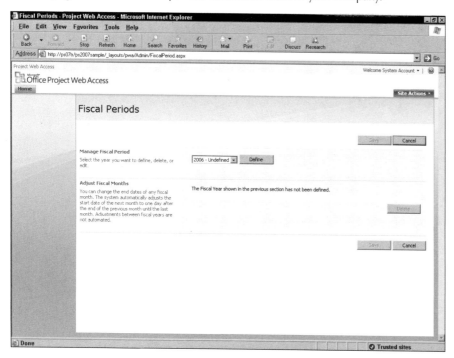

When you change an ending date of a fiscal month, Project Server automatically adjusts the start date of the next month.

Timesheet Periods

Use the Timesheet Periods page to create reporting periods for timesheet entries. When users want to record time spent on project tasks, they will select a time period. You can create 52 weekly time periods, 26 biweekly periods, and 12 monthly periods. You should create periods that match the way project managers want users to report time spent.

To display the Timesheet Periods page (see Figure 18.30), click the Server Settings link in the Quick Launch pane on the left side of the Project Web Access window. Then, click the Timesheet Classifications link in the Time and Task Management section of the Server Settings page.

FIGURE 18.30

Create timesheet periods.

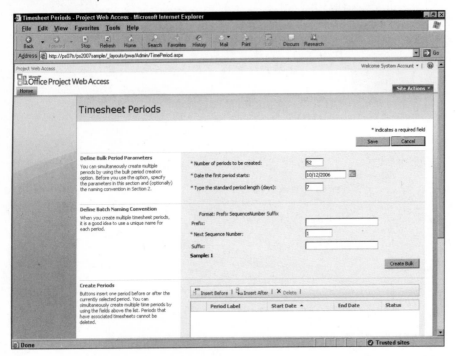

In the top portion of the page, define the type of periods you want to create. Use the center portion of the page to help you create several periods simultaneously instead of creating periods one at a time. In the bottom portion of the page, you can insert a single period before or after an existing period, and you can delete any period that doesn't have any timesheets associated with it. Note that you can't leave gaps in dates when you set up time periods.

Timesheet classifications

Use this page to set up classifications that match account codes or cost codes that your company uses in its general ledger. On timesheets, Project Server assigns each timesheet line to a classification; in this way, you can match lines that appear on timesheets with account codes or cost codes in your general ledger to help you track project costs.

To display the Edit or Create Line Classifications page (see Figure 18.31), click the Server Settings link in the Quick Launch pane on the left side of the Project Web Access window. Then, click the Timesheet Classifications link in the Time and Task Management section of the Server Settings page.

FIGURE 18.31

Use this page to create or edit classifications that can be assigned to timesheet lines.

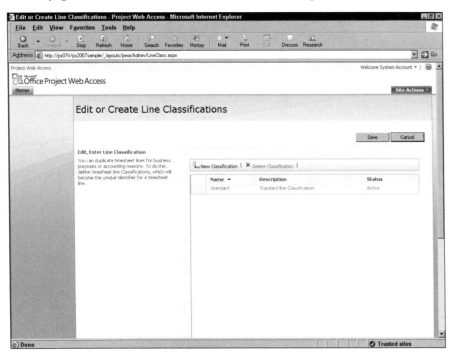

Timesheet Settings and Defaults

Using the Settings and Defaults page, the administrator can set a variety of default settings related to timesheets. To display this page, click the Server Settings link in the Quick Launch pane on the left side of the Project Web Access window. Then, click the Timesheet Settings and Defaults link in the Time and Task Management section of the Server Settings page.

Using the settings at the top of the page (see Figure 18.32), you can control the information timesheets display both in Outlook and in Project Web Access. You also can control whether users enter data against projects or against assignments, and you can set the default timesheet unit.

FIGURE 18.32

Control the way timesheet data appears.

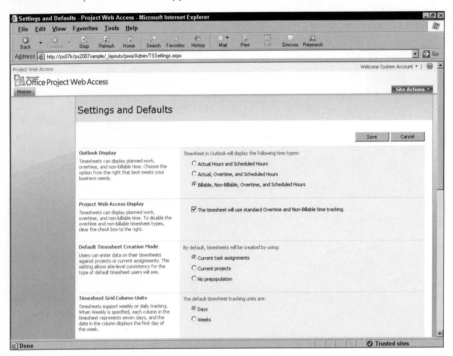

Using the settings at the bottom of the page (see Figure 18.33), you can set the default reporting units, set reporting limits per timesheet if appropriate for your organization, set policies regarding reporting of future time or unverified timesheet lines, enable or disable timesheet auditing, and established fixed approval routing, which requires that the same person approve each timesheet.

FIGURE 18.33

Set reporting defaults.

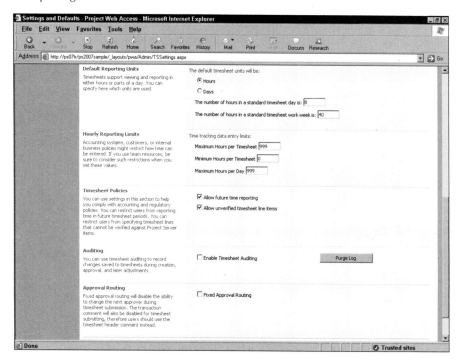

Task Settings and Display

From the Task Settings and Display page, you can set a variety of options that control the way tasks function and display in Project Web Access. To display this page, click the Server Settings link in the Quick Launch pane on the left side of the Project Web Access window. Then, click the Task Settings and Display link in the Time and Task Management section of the Server Settings page.

At the top of the page (see Figure 18.34), you can set the default tracking method for projects that are published to the Project Server environment and permit project managers to select different tracking methods when creating their projects. Project offers three possible ways for users to record actual work in Project Server. The advantages and disadvantages of each are as follows:

■ **Percent of Work Complete:** This method is the fastest way for resources to record time, but it is also the least accurate because it is based on the resource's estimate of the total amount of work to be done, along with the amount that is actually completed. Resources enter the percentage amount.

■ **Actual Work Done and Work Remaining:** This method is the middle-of-the-road method. It is both moderately accurate and moderately fast. Resources enter the hours, days, weeks, and so on of the amount of work done and the amount of work remaining to be completed.

■ **Hours of Work Done per Time Period:** This method is the most accurate method but also the most time consuming. Resources enter the actual hours worked on each task for a specified time — typically, a day.

You also can specify whether project managers can change actual time worked and whether users can update task progress using timesheet information. And, you can specify how often users should report their hours.

FIGURE 18.34

The administrator can select a default tracking method for published projects and allow managers to choose a different method.

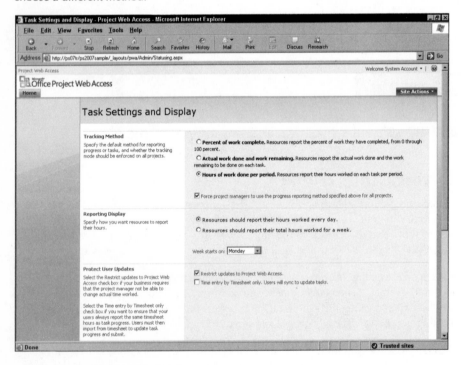

At the bottom of the page (see Figure 18.35), you can define the parameters of a "current task" that will determine the tasks users see when they view current tasks. And, you can specify whether to permit users to view the Gantt Chart view.

Close Tasks to Update

On the Close Tasks to Update page (see Figure 18.36), you can lock down tasks so that resources cannot report time for those tasks.

FIGURE 18.35

Define the parameters of a current task.

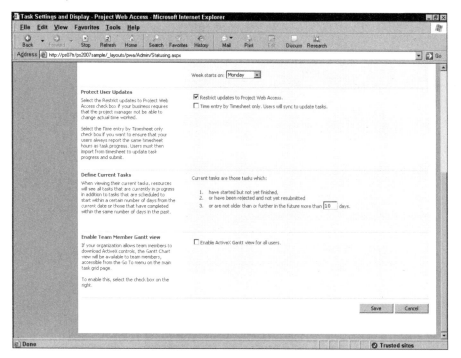

FIGURE 18.36

Use this page to identify tasks to which users can no longer record time.

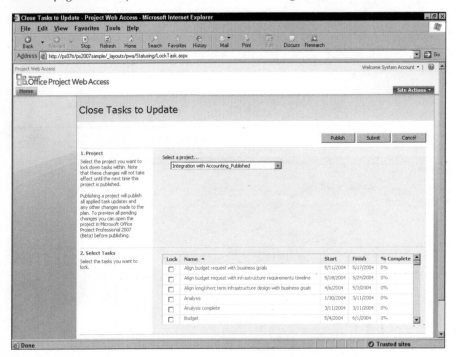

Setting Up Administrative Time

Administrative time is a fact of life, and you use the Edit or Create Administrative Time (see Figure 18.37) page to set up administrative time categories that users can use to record administrative time on timesheets.

To display this page, click the Server Settings link in the Quick Launch pane on the left side of the Project Web Access window. Then, click the Administrative Time link in the Time and Task Management section of the Server Settings page.

These categories represent reasons that a resource may not be available for work — for example, vacation, sickness, jury duty, or bereavement. When you check the Always Display box, the administrative time category appears on each resource's timesheet with a work assignment of 0 hours. The resource can fill in time as needed.

FIGURE 18.37

From this page, you can create administrative time categories.

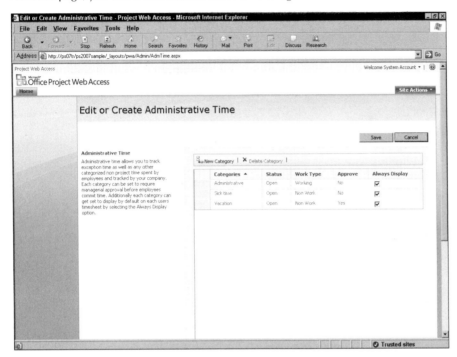

Customizing Project Web Access

The administrator can customize Project Web Access in the following ways:

- Control the appearance of the Quick Launch pane
- Control the formatting of Gantt task bar styles and the timescale
- Establish grouping formats for the timesheet and views in the Project Center and the Resource Center

Control the appearance of the Quick Launch pane

From the Edit Quick Launch page (see Figure 18.38), you can control the appearance of the Quick Launch pane. To display this page, click the Server Settings link in the Quick Launch pane on the left side of the Project Web Access window. Then, click the Quick Launch link in the Look and Feel section of the Server Settings page.

FIGURE 18.38

Use this page to customize the appearance of the Quick Launch pane.

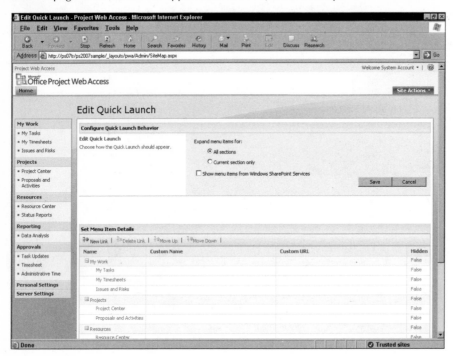

By default, all choices appear in each section of the Quick Launch pane, but you can choose to display only the main headings; then, if you click a main heading, the subordinate headings for that section appear. You also can choose to hide or display menu items from Windows SharePoint Services in the Quick Launch pane.

In addition, you can reorganize or hide default menu items in the Quick Launch pane and, if you click the New Link button, you can add a new menu item to the Quick Launch pane.

Selecting the Gantt taskbar styles and timescales

Using the Gantt Chart Formats page (see Figure 18.39), the administrator can control the appearance of Gantt taskbars on the timescale of Gantt Charts for some or all Gantt Charts that team members and managers view in Project Web Access. To display this page, click the Server Settings link in the Quick Launch pane on the left side of the Project Web Access window. Then, click the Gantt Chart Formats link in the Look and Feel section of the Server Settings page.

FIGURE 18.39

The administrator can modify the appearance of Gantt taskbars on timescales in Project Web Access.

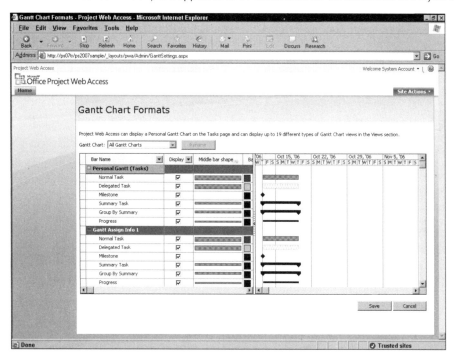

Selecting grouping formats

Using the Grouping Formats page (see Figure 18.40), the administrator can format the appearance of grouped information on the timesheet. The administrator can also define the appearance of up to ten groups for views in the Projects Center and the Resource Center. To display this page, click the Server Settings link in the Quick Launch pane on the left side of the Project Web Access window. Then, click the Grouping Formats link in the Look and Feel section of the Server Settings page.

FIGURE 18.40

Establish grouping formats for the timesheet and for views that appear in the Project Center and the Resource Center.

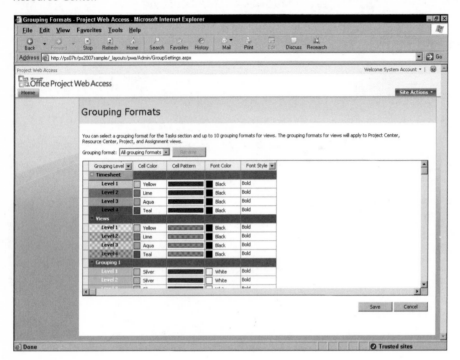

Housekeeping Chores

As you would expect, some housekeeping tasks need to be done to keep the Project Server environment in good working order. You need to do the following tasks:

- Periodically check in projects and resources
- Delete information from the Project Server databases
- Back up and restore the Project Server databases

Checking in enterprise projects and resources

Occasionally, as administrator, you may need to check in projects or resources. For example, after hours, you may be planning maintenance to the Project Server environment and someone may have left work without closing a project.

Instead of tracking down the machine of the person who checked out the project, you can use the Force Check-in Enterprise Objects page (see Figure 18.41). To display this page, click the Server Settings link in the Quick Launch pane on the left side of the Project Web Access window. Then, click the Force Check-in Enterprise Objects link in the Database Administration section of the Server Settings page.

 When you force check-in, none of the edits made by the person who checked out the project will be saved.

From this page, you can check in Enterprise projects, resources, custom fields, calendars, look-up tables for Enterprise custom fields, and resource plans. Use the list box at the top of the page to select the type of object you want to check in. Then, check the object and click the Check-In link.

FIGURE 18.41

Check in Enterprise objects from this page.

Managing information in the Project Server databases

The administrator can (and should) periodically delete old information from the Project Server environment, because response time from the database increases as the database grows in size. To help maintain speed for team members when they work in Project Web Access, the administrator can delete old, unnecessary information by using the Delete Enterprise Objects page (see Figure 18.42). To display this page, click the Server Settings link in the Quick Launch pane on the left side of the Project Web Access window. Then, click the Delete Enterprise Objects link in the Database Administration section of the Server Settings page.

Click the option buttons next to the type of items that you want to delete; then, select the objects you want to delete and click the Delete button.

 **TIP** If a project workspace exists for a project you are deleting, you probably want to delete both the project and the workspace.

FIGURE 18.42

Use this page to reduce the size of the database and speed the processing in the database.

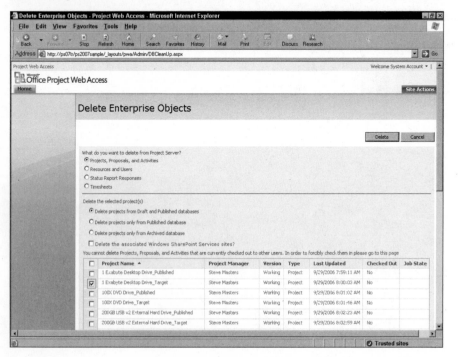

Backing up and restoring

Backing up and restoring the Project Server database is one of the most important actions you can take to protect your data. The backups you create in Project Web Access are item-level backups designed to work with SQL Server database backups — not in place of SQL Server database backups.

Schedule backups

From the Daily Backup Schedule page (see Figure 18.43) you can set up a schedule for backing up items in the Project Server environment, and you can specify the number of versions of the backup that you want to keep. Project Server stores the backups in the Archive database, and the more versions you keep, the larger the Archive database becomes.

FIGURE 18.43

Use this page to identify the items to back up and the number of backups to retain.

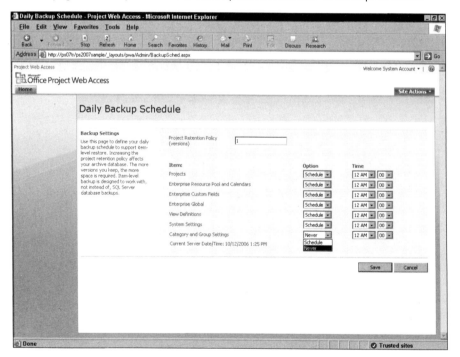

To display this page, click the Server Settings link in the Quick Launch pane on the left side of the Project Web Access window. Then, click the Schedule Backup link in the Database Administration section of the Server Settings page.

Make a backup

The administrator can back up items in the Project Server databases outside of the daily schedule using the Backup page (see Figure 18.44).

To display this page, click the Server Settings link in the Quick Launch pane on the left side of the Project Web Access window. Then, click the Administrative Backup link in the Database Administration section of the Server Settings page.

Restore a backup

When you need to restore a backup, use the Restore page (see Figure 18.45). To display this page, click the Server Settings link in the Quick Launch pane on the left side of the Project Web Access window. Then, click the Administrative Restore link in the Database Administration section of the Server Settings page.

FIGURE 18.44

Use this page to back up items in the Project Server databases on demand.

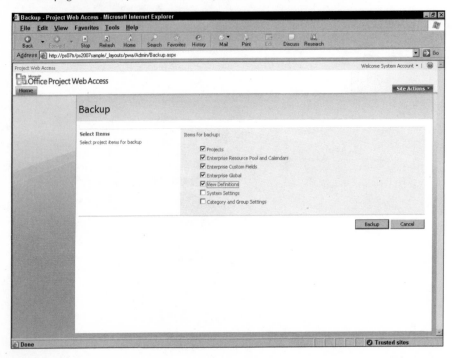

Project Server and the Administrator 18

FIGURE 18.45

Restore a backup from this page.

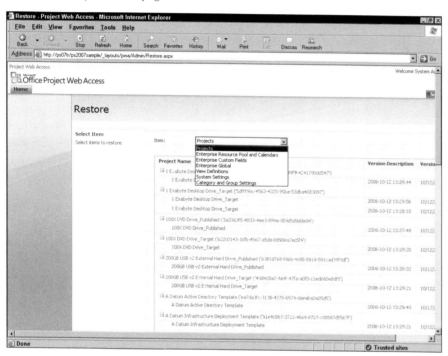

Use the Item list box to select the type of object you want to restore. You can selectively restore projects; to do so, click a project and then click the Restore button.

Managing the Queue

Project Server uses a service to queue work requests until the server becomes available to act on the request. This functionality works very much the way a print queue works and improves the performance of Project Server.

You can control the behavior of the queue. Using the Queue Settings page (see Figure 18.46), you can establish or change settings for the Project queue or the Timesheet queue. You can set the maximum number of job processor threads, the polling interval, the subjob retry interval, the subjob retry limit, the SQL retry interval, and the SQL retry limit for both types of queues.

FIGURE 18.46

Establish or modify queue settings.

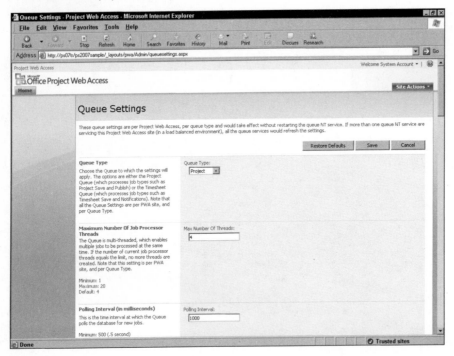

To display this page, click the Server Settings link in the Quick Launch pane on the left side of the Project Web Access window. Then, click the Queue Settings link in the Queue section of the Server Settings page.

Using the Manage Queue Jobs page (see Figure 18.47), you can view the current status of queued jobs and, if you want, retry or cancel jobs. To display this page, click the Server Settings link in the Quick Launch pane on the left side of the Project Web Access window. Then, click the Manage Queue link in the Queue section of the Server Settings page.

FIGURE 18.47

Use this page to manage queued jobs.

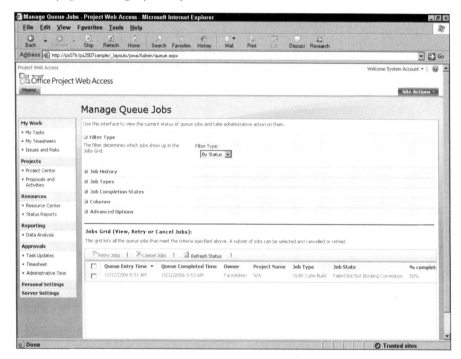

Managing the OLAP cube

Project Server 2007 uses the Cube Building service to build portfolio analyzer cubes. You can establish cube building settings, configure the cube's dimensions, measures, and calculated members, and monitor the cube building status. The cube building service uses data and metadata generated from the Reporting database to build cubes for end-user reporting.

Migrating the Analysis Services Repository

 The following is a one-time-only procedure.

The information that is stored in the Analysis Services Repository is used to build the OLAP cube. Initially, this information is stored in the format of an Access database. If you leave the information in this format, permissions for using the cube are difficult to control. Therefore, before you build the cube, you should migrate the Analysis Services Repository to an SQL Server database. This two-part process involves first creating an empty SQL database and then migrating the Analysis Services data into it. To create the SQL database, follow these steps:

1. Choose Start ➪ All Programs ➪ Microsoft SQL Server ➪ Enterprise Manager. You see the SQL Server Enterprise Manager window (see Figure 18.48).

FIGURE 18.48

Use this window to create a new SQL database.

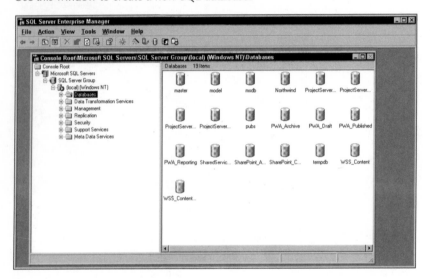

2. Expand the tree in the left pane until you see the Databases folder.

3. Right-click the Databases folder and choose New Database from the shortcut menu that appears. You see the Database Properties dialog box.

4. In the Name text box, type a name for the database that is to hold the OLAP information (I called mine OLAPRepository) and click OK.

5. Close the SQL Server Enterprise Manager window.

To migrate the Analysis Services information into the SQL database that you just created, follow these steps:

1. Choose Start ➪ All Programs ➪ Microsoft SQL Server ➪ Analysis Services ➪ Analysis Manager. You see the Analysis Manager window, as shown in Figure 18.49.

FIGURE 18.49

Use this window to migrate the Analysis Services Repository.

2. Expand the tree in the left pane until you see the name of the server on which Analysis Services is installed.

3. Right-click the name of the Analysis Services server and choose Migrate Repository from the shortcut menu that appears to start the Migrate Repository Wizard.

4. On the first screen, choose Analysis Services native format and click Next.

5. On the next screen, enter the name of the server on which SQL Server is installed; then click Next.

6. On the next screen, choose the authentication method that you use to connect to the SQL server — either Windows Authentication or SQL Server authentication. If you use SQL Server authentication, enter your login ID and password.

7. Click Next, select the database that you created in the preceding set of steps (see Figure 18.50), and click Finish.

FIGURE 18.50

Select the SQL database that you created.

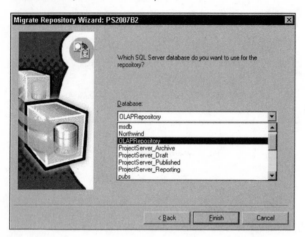

8. When the process finishes, close the Analysis Manager window.

Configuring the cube

You can use the Cube Configuration page (see Figure 18.51) to customize the OLAP cubes Project Server builds by adding custom fields as dimensions, measures, or calculated members. To display this page, click the Server Settings link in the Quick Launch pane on the left side of the Project Web Access window. Then, click the Configuration link in the Cube section of the Server Settings page.

FIGURE 18.51

Add custom fields to OLAP cubes.

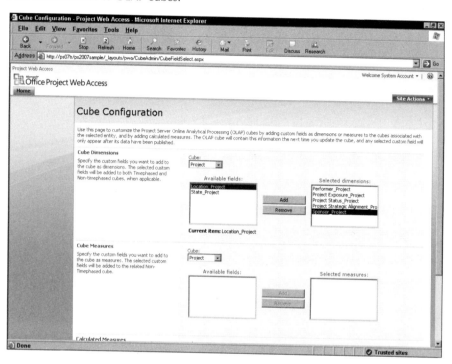

Establish cube building settings

Building the OLAP cube can be a time-consuming process, so plan to do it during a period when people don't need to be using the Project Server environment. Use the Cube Build Settings page (see Figure 18.52) to establish cube building settings and build the cube. To display this page, click the Server Settings link in the Quick Launch pane on the left side of the Project Web Access window. Then, click the Building Settings link in the Cube section of the Server Settings page.

FIGURE 18.52

Use this page to provide the information that is needed to build the OLAP cube.

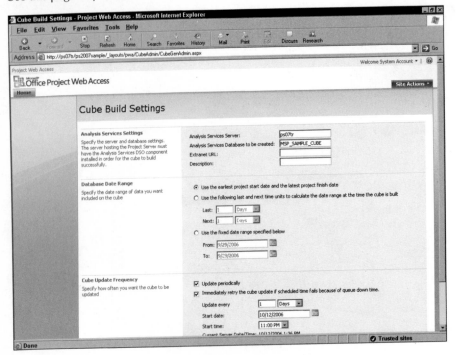

In the Analysis Services Settings section, enter the name of the server on which Analysis Services is installed, the name that you want to assign to the OLAP cube, and, optionally, a description.

In the Database Date Range section, choose the date range for the data that you want to include when building the cube.

In the Cube Update Frequency section, specify how often you want Project Server to update the cube. Then, click Save and Build Now to build the cube or Save to simply save the settings.

Checking cube building status

You can use the Cube Build Status page (see Figure 18.53) to monitor the progress of building the cube; you can also build the cube from the Cube Building Status page. To display this page, click the Server Settings link in the Quick Launch pane on the left side of the Project Web Access window. Then, click the Building Status link in the Cube section of the Server Settings page.

FIGURE 18.53

Use this page to monitor the cube construction process.

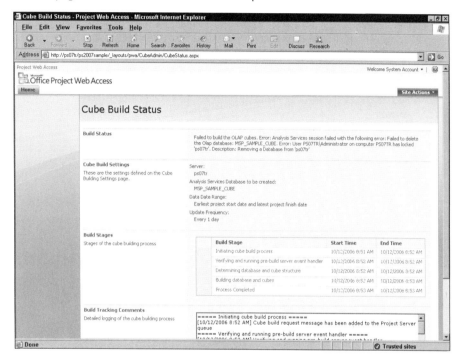

Enabling users to view the cube

After you've created the OLAP cube, you need to give users access to it so that they can use it with the Portfolio Analyzer feature in Project Web Access. Follow these steps to provide access to the OLAP cube:

1. Choose Start ➪ All Programs ➪ Microsoft SQL Server ➪ Analysis Services ➪ Analysis Manager to open the Analysis Manager window.

2. Expand the tree in the left pane until you open the OLAP cube to which you want to give permissions (see Figure 18.54).

FIGURE 18.54

Find the OLAP cube to which you want to assign permissions.

3. Right-click Database Roles and choose Manage Roles from the shortcut menu that appears to display the Database Role Manager dialog box.

4. Click New to open the Create a Database Role dialog box (see Figure 18.55).

5. Enter the name of the role in the Role name box and then click Add on the Membership tab to open the Add Users and Groups dialog box (see Figure 18.56).

FIGURE 18.55

Use this box to enable additional users to use the OLAP cube.

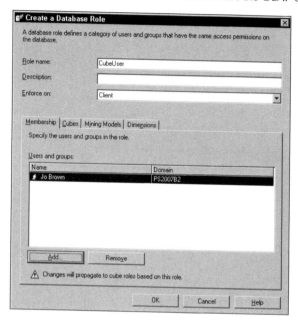

FIGURE 18.56

Select users to add to a role.

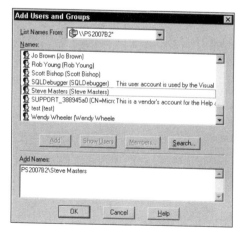

6. In the List Names From list box, select the *servername/machinename* or domain name as appropriate.

7. Click Show Users and select a user who you want to be able to use the cube. Click Add.

8. Repeat Step 7 for each user who should have access to the cube. Then click OK.

9. Click the Cubes tab of the Create a Database Role dialog box (see Figure 18.57) and select the MSP_PORTFOLIO_ANALYZER check box. Then click OK.

FIGURE 18.57

Select the cube to which you want to add the role.

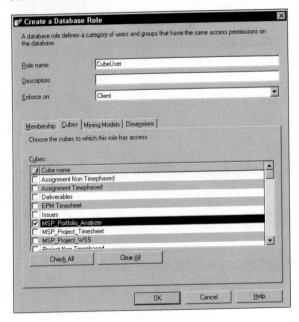

10. When you finish, close the Database Role Manager dialog box and the Analysis Manager window.

Managing operations

The Project Server administrator also can control over a variety of operational policies. I covered some of these earlier in this chapter; in this section, I review the operational policies associated with:

- Alerts and reminders
- Managing customer server event handlers

■ Synchronizing the Active Directory Group with the Enterprise Resource Pool

■ Working with project workspaces

Alerts and reminders

Using the Alerts and Reminders page (see Figure 18.58) the administrator can set up the SMTP mail server that is used in the E-mail Notifications and Reminder feature of Project Server and customize the default e-mail message that is sent.

To display this page, click the Server Settings link in the Quick Launch pane on the left side of the Project Web Access window. Then, click the Alerts and Reminders link in the Operational Policies section of the Server Settings page.

FIGURE 18.58

Establish the e-mail server and default e-mail message from this page.

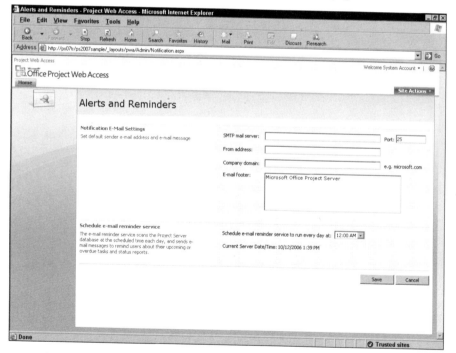

Configuring the server-side event handler

Using the Events page (see Figure 18.59), the Project Server administrator can configure the server-side event handler to create, modify, and delete event handlers. To display this page, click the Server Settings link in the Quick Launch pane on the left side of the Project Web Access window. Then, click the Server-Side Event Handler Configuration link in the Operational Policies section of the Server Settings page.

To create a new event handler, click an event source link and then click the New Event Handler button. The Event Handler page (see Figure 18.60) appears, in which you can associate an event handler with a Project Server event. An event signals that a particular action occurred because of some user interaction such as a mouse click or some program logic.

FIGURE 18.59

Use this page to manage custom server event handlers.

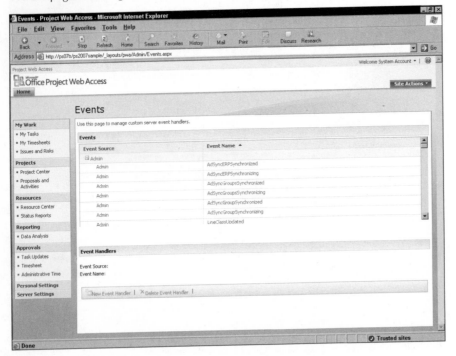

FIGURE 18.60

Use this page to associate an event handler with a Project Server event.

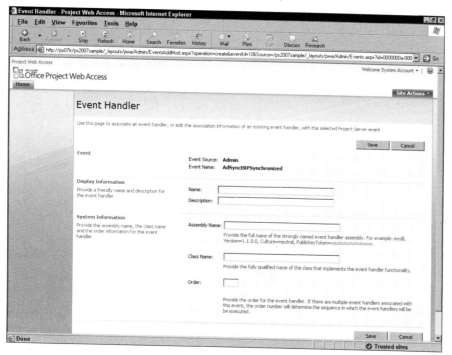

Synchronizing the Enterprise Resource Pool with an Active Directory Group

Using the Active Directory Enterprise Resource Pool Synchronization page (see Figure 18.61), you can select an Active Directory Group with which to synchronize the Enterprise Resource Pool, check the status of the synchronization, schedule synchronization, and choose to reactivate inactive users. To display this page, click the Server Settings link in the Quick Launch pane on the left side of the Project Web Access window. Then, click the Active Directory Resource Pool Synchronization link in the Operational Policies section of the Server Settings page.

FIGURE 18.61

Use this page to establish synchronization settings for the Enterprise Resource Pool and an Active Directory Group.

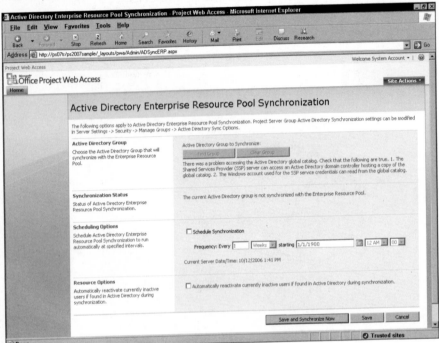

Working with Project Workspaces

Using the Project Workspaces page (see Figure 18.62), the Project Server administrator can create a Windows SharePoint Services site, change the address of a site, delete a site, and synchronize access to sites. To display this page, click the Server Settings link in the Quick Launch pane on the left side of the Project Web Access window. Then, click the Project Workspaces link in the Operational Policies section of the Server Settings page.

FIGURE 18.62

Use this page to make changes to Windows SharePoint Services sites.

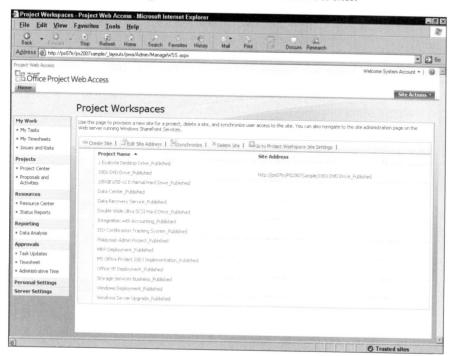

On the Project Workspace Provisioning Settings page (see Figure 18.63), the Project Server administrator can select the default Web application and site URL under which Windows SharePoint Services project workspaces are provisioned, establish default workspace properties, select a provisioning mode when projects are published, and identify the way Project Server grants access to project workspaces.

FIGURE 18.63

Synchronize administrators from this page.

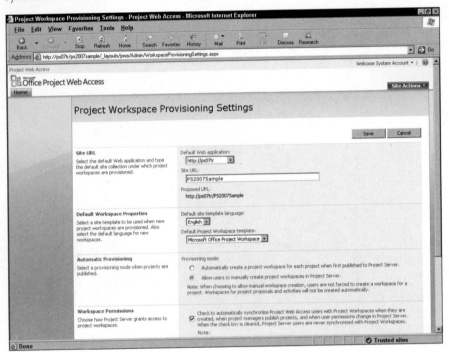

To display the Project Workspace Provisioning Settings page, click the Server Settings link in the Quick Launch pane on the left side of the Project Web Access window. Then, click the Project Workspace Provisioning Settings link in the Operational Policies section of the Server Settings page.

Summary

Customizing the Project Server environment to meet your organization's needs is a task that initially requires the joint efforts of a person with project management background and a person with information technology background. Some of the customization tasks are performed in Project Professional and the rest are performed in Project Web Access. When the database is set up, the Project Server administrator's role becomes mostly occasional maintenance.

In this chapter, you completed tasks that were needed to customize the Project Server environment to meet the needs of your organization. Specifically, you did the following:

- Double-checked settings
- Set up users
- Set up the Enterprise Global template
- Set up the Enterprise Resource Pool
- Imported projects into the Project Server database
- Customized Project Web Access
- Reviewed housekeeping tasks

In Chapter 19, you see how the Project/Resource Manager works with Project Professional and Project Web Access.

Chapter 19

Project Server and the Project/Resource Manager

Project Server offers a wide variety of tools to project managers to help them manage projects more effectively. In this section, you learn how to connect to Project Server, create a Web-based project, use the Enterprise Resource Pool to assign resources to your project, track project progress, and take advantage of Project Server's management tools to use resources and manage projects more effectively.

NOTE The information in Chapters 19 through 21 applies to Project Professional. If you are using Project Standard, you can't use Project Server and Project Web Access.

Connecting to Project Server

If you plan to use Project with Project Server (as opposed to using Project in a stand-alone environment), you need a Project Server account, which enables you to log on to Project Server.

Creating a Project Server logon account

You can easily create your own Project Server account from within Project after you know the URL for your Project Server environment; your Project Server administrator will most likely give you this URL.

To create a Project Server Account, follow these steps:

1. Start Project Professional.
2. Choose Tools ➪ Enterprise Options ➪ Microsoft Project Server Accounts. You see the Project Server Accounts dialog box (see Figure 19.1).

FIGURE 19.1

Use this dialog box to add a Project Server logon account and to specify connection state detection options.

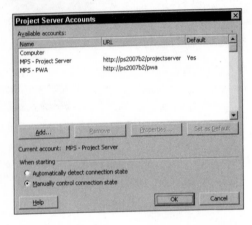

3. Click the Add button. You see the Account Properties dialog box (see Figure 19.2).

FIGURE 19.2

Use this dialog box to create a new Project Server account.

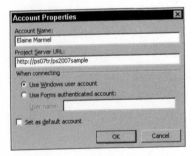

4. In the Account Name box, enter a name for the account. You must use a name that no other user is already using — such as your own name.

5. In the Project Server URL box, enter the URL for the location of your Project Server database.

6. In the When Connecting section, choose the type of connection that your organization uses, as follows:

   ▪ Use your Windows logon information by selecting the Use Windows user account option button.

   ▪ Use Forms authentication and supply your account name in the User Name box.

NOTE Windows user account authentication is generally more stringent than Project Server authentication.

7. (Optional) If you intend to create more than one account and you want the current account to be your default logon account, select the Set as default account check box.

NOTE Why create another account? If your company uses more than one instance of Project Server, you need more than one account to access the correct database.

8. Click OK. You see the Project Server Accounts dialog box again.

9. At the bottom of the box, choose whether you want to log on automatically or manually control the connection state. If you choose the Automatically Detect Connection State option button, Project attempts to detect the Project Server when you open Project in the future. If you choose the Manually Control Connection State option button, the dialog box shown in Figure 19.3 appears when you open Project in the future, giving you the opportunity to choose the account that you want to use to log on to Project Server.

FIGURE 19.3

You see this box if you choose to manually control the connection state.

TIP You may also see the Project Server Accounts dialog box if you've lost your connection with the Project Server.

Logging on to Project Server

You have the option of working with a project while connected to Project Server or working with the project in a stand-alone environment — and you make that choice when you start Project Professional.

For example, suppose that you use Project from a notebook computer while traveling. During your time away from the office, you want to keep track of the time that you spend working. If you manually control the connection state, as described in the previous section, select your profile in the Project Server Accounts dialog box (shown previously in Figure 19.3) and then click the Work Offline button. If you chose to automatically detect the connection state, you won't connect to Project Server when you start Project if your computer isn't connected to the network.

> **TIP** If you are connected to the Project Server environment and you see a message that indicates that you're not allowed to log on because the environment is unavailable, double-check with the Project Server administrator and make sure that you have been set up as a user in Project Server who belongs to the Project Managers (or higher) group.

Creating a Web-Based Project

The project manager is the person who builds and maintains the project schedule and makes task assignments. The "boss" uses Project to create the schedule and make assignments to team members to track their activities. When setting up the project schedule, the project manager must set up the project so that it can be uploaded (published) to the Project Server database. To successfully establish a Web-based project, the project manager should complete the following tasks in Project:

- Review the project's options to use Web communications
- Publish project information to the Project Server database

Understanding the structure of the Project Server database

The Project Server database I keep referring to is actually a collection of databases. As a project manager, you interact with several of these databases and most of the interaction is invisible to you. However, you'll work better if you understand the interaction that deals with draft projects versus published projects.

Whenever you create a project in Project Professional, you can — and should — save a copy of it to your local hard disk as described in Chapter 3. At some point, you'll want to place the project in the Project Server database, but you won't be ready for the world at large to have access to the project because you really haven't finished working with it. At this point, you save a draft project in the Project Server database. You can continue to work with the draft project that is stored in the Project Server database and modify it, and the project won't be visible to other users.

When you are ready to let the world see your project, you publish it. At this point, two versions of your project reside in the Project Server database — the draft version and the published version. You can continue to work with your project in Project Professional; typically, you'll work with the draft version and ultimately republish it to update the version that everyone else sees.

When you work with draft or published projects in Project Professional, you take advantage of the local cache introduced in Project 2007; the local cache speeds up the interaction of Project Professional and the Project Server database. Later in this chapter, you'll read more about managing the local cache so that you work efficiently.

Reviewing a project's Web-based options

While logged on to the Project Server database, follow these steps to set the options of a project to use Web communications:

1. Open the project for which you want to set Web-based options.

2. Choose Collaborate ⇨ Collaboration Options. Project displays the Collaborate tab of the Options dialog box (see Figure 19.4).

FIGURE 19.4

To review a project's options for Web communication, use the Collaborate tab in the Options dialog box.

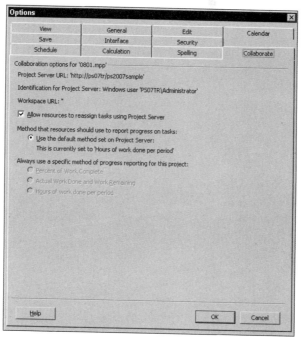

NOTE   After you store the project in the Project Server environment, the Workspace URL will appear if you establish a Windows SharePoint Services project workspace for the project.

3.   Choose whether resources can delegate tasks in Project Web Access.

4.   Click OK to save your settings.

Storing a draft project in the Project Server database

You can store draft projects in the Project Server database before you're ready for the world of Project Web Access users to view those projects. You must first create this draft version before Project Professional will let you publish your project, which is the state assigned to a project that the world of Project Web Access users can view.

Open Project Professional and log on to Project Server (refer to the section "Logging on to Project Server," earlier in this chapter). Then, open the project that you want to store in the Project Server database and choose File ⇨ Save As. The Save to Project Server dialog box appears (see Figure 19.5); any custom fields stored in the Enterprise Global template appear at the bottom of the box.

FIGURE 19.5

When the Enterprise Global template contains custom fields, the Save to Project Server dialog box looks like this.

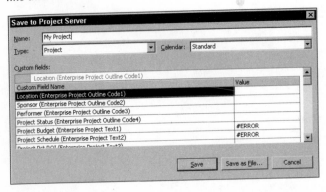

TIP   If you prefer wizards, you can use the Import Project Wizard to save your project to the Project Server database. Don't open your project; instead, choose Tools ⇨ Enterprise Options ⇨ Import Project to Enterprise. Then, follow the steps that appear in the Project Guide; see Chapter 18 for details. Using the Import Wizard, you can map local fields to enterprise fields and import resources.

When you send updates — like the draft project we just uploaded — from Project Professional to Project Server, Project updates Project Server using a local cache that manages the updating process. The local cache helps improve performance. You can read more about managing the local cache later in this chapter.

Watch the status bar after you click Save; you'll see information that describes the progress of the updating process.

Publishing project information

When you're ready for the world to see your project, you publish it.

Choose File ➪ Publish; the Publish Project dialog box appears (see Figure 19.6). You can choose to create a Windows SharePoint Services project workspace for the project at the same time that you publish the project. If your organization uses the Windows SharePoint Services features that help manage documents, issues, and risks associated with projects, you may want to check the Create a workspace for this project option button. Project fills in all the information for you, and there really isn't any reason to change any of it. If you choose not to create the project workspace, the Project Server administrator can create it later.

FIGURE 19.6

When you publish a project, you can choose to create a Windows SharePoint Services project workspace for it.

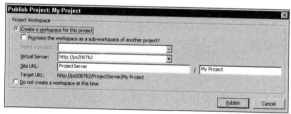

Click Publish and you can watch the status bar to monitor progress while Project updates Project Server.

Working with Web-Based Projects

In many ways, working with a Web-based project is no different from the ways I've described working with projects throughout the rest of this book. You still perform the same tasks, but the way you perform them may be different. In this section, you learn how to open a project stored in the Project Server database in Project Professional. You also can view Project Web Access pages that display project information without leaving Project Professional.

Opening a project stored in the Project Server database

Even if you're connected to the Project Server database, in Project Professional you have the option of opening the original project schedule stored on your hard disk, or you can open either the draft version or the published version stored in the Project Server database. Click the Open button on the Standard toolbar. You see the Open dialog box (see Figure 19.7).

FIGURE 19.7

In this dialog box, open an original .mpp file or open the draft or published project stored in the Project Server database.

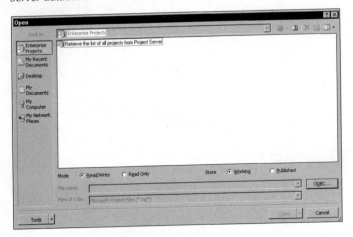

To open the original Project .mpp file, use the buttons on the left side of the dialog box to navigate to the location where you stored the .mpp file on your hard disk, click the file, and then click Open.

Opening a project stored in the Project Server database takes a bit more thought because you need to decide whether you want to open the draft version or the published version of the project. But before I discuss those choices, I need to address the fact that the first time you display the Open dialog box, no projects appear at all.

Understanding the Open dialog box

The first time you display the Open dialog box, no projects appear in it; instead, you see only one item — the Retrieve the List Of All Projects from Project Server item. Don't panic: This condition exists only because you haven't opened a project stored in the Project Server database yet. The situation I'm about to describe reminds me of the age-old question: "Which came first, the chicken or the egg?" (and makes my head hurt, I might add).

When you are connected to the Project Server database and you open a project in Project Professional, Project Professional stores a copy of the project in the local cache; the local cache is new to Project 2007 and serves the purpose of improving performance when exchanging information between Project Professional and the Project Server database. Read more about the local cache in the next section.

The Open dialog box lists projects stored in the local cache. So, you won't see any projects listed in the Open dialog box until you've opened a project; the *next* time you display the Open dialog box, that project will appear in the list, along with the Retrieve the List of All Projects from Project Server item. If you see only one item — the Retrieve the List of All Projects from Project Server item — in the Open dialog box, you simply don't have any projects stored in your local cache.

You can easily view all the available draft or published projects by double-clicking the Retrieve the List of All Projects from Project Server item.

Opening a draft project or a published project

The Mode options and the Store options at the bottom of the dialog box impact both the projects you can open and the way in which you can work with those projects. These options work together.

The Store options determine whether you select a draft version of a project or a published version of a project. Working represents the projects stored in the draft database, whereas Published represents the projects stored in the published database. So, to view and open projects in the draft database, you click the Working option, and to view and open published projects, you click the Published option. By default, Project displays draft projects in the Open dialog box; you can view published projects by switching the Store option. And yes, if you don't see any difference between the two lists, all draft projects have been published.

The Mode options determine whether you can save changes to a project you open; however, the Mode options work with the Store options. When you select Working as the Store option, you'll notice that you can choose either Read/Write or Read Only as the Mode option. But when you select Published as the Store option, you can select, for the Mode option, only the Read Only option. By implication, you can make changes only to a project stored in the draft database, which is the default database from which to open projects.

If you open a draft project, you can save changes that you make to it in the Project Server database by saving and then publishing the project as described earlier in this chapter.

NEW FEATURE Project 2007 sends only the changes back to the Project Server database, which speeds up the updating process significantly.

If you open a published project, you cannot save changes to it directly, but you can save them in a roundabout fashion. You might want to use a published version to create a draft version with which to work. Open the published version, which will be a read-only copy, and then follow the steps provided earlier in this chapter to save a draft version; when you supply the filename, use the same name as that of the published version. You'll see a prompt that indicates that you'll be overwriting an existing project. If you choose to proceed, your draft copy will be the same as the published copy.

TIP You can use the same technique to create a local `.mpp` version of a draft or published project. Open a project from the Project Server database and then choose File ➪ Save As. In the Save to Project Server dialog box, click the Save as File button.

Closing a project stored in the Project Server database

When you close the project, Project prompts you to check in the project. When you opened the project, you checked it out, and while a project is checked out, nobody else can open it in Project Professional and work on it. So, when you close the project, Project Professional prompts you to check the project in, and you should check it in.

If the project remains checked out, you can check it in from Project Web Access. In the Quick Launch pane of Project Web Access, click the Project Center link. Then, click the Go To button and choose Check in My Projects. Project displays the Force Check-in Enterprise Objects page, where you place a check beside the project you want to check in and click the Check In button.

CROSS-REF See Chapter 18 for more information on using the Force Check-in Enterprise Objects page.

Managing the local cache

NEW FEATURE The local cache is new to Project 2007.

The local cache helps streamline the process of updating the Project Server database with changes from Project Professional. You can manage the local cache from Project Professional.

You can view and change the cache settings, which include the size and location of the local cache, from the Cache Settings dialog box (see Figure 19.8). Choose Tools ➪ Local Project Cache ➪ Cache Settings to display this dialog box.

FIGURE 19.8

Establish the size and location of the local cache from this dialog box.

From the Status tab of the Active Cache Status dialog box (see Figure 19.9), you can view the status of updates you sent to the Project Server database. If errors occur, they'll appear on the Errors tab. To view this dialog box, choose Tools ➪ Local Project Cache ➪ View Status.

FIGURE 19.9

You can see the status of updates you send from Project Professional to the Project Server database from this dialog box.

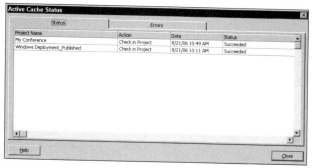

Finally, you can remove projects from the local cache to free cache space and improve performance between Project Professional and the Project Server database. Choose Tools ➪ Local Project Cache ➪ Clean Up Cache to display the Clean Up Cache dialog box, shown in Figure 19.10.

FIGURE 19.10

Use this dialog box to clean up the local cache.

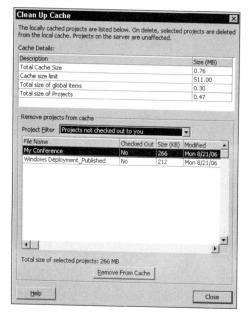

By default, Project displays projects in the local cache that are not checked out to you; you can open the Project Filter list box and change the view to projects that are checked out to you. To remove a project from the cache, click it in the bottom portion of the window and click Remove From Cache. When you finish, click the Close button.

Viewing Project Server pages in Project Professional

One of the neat features available in Project 2007 is the ability to display Project Server pages in Project. Choose Collaborate ➪ Project Center to see the Project Center while working in Project Professional (see Figure 19.11), or choose Collaborate ➪ Resource Center to see the Resource Center (see Figure 19.12). To return to Project, click the <u>Click here to close this view</u> link in the upper-right corner of the page.

FIGURE 19.11

View the Project Center while working in Project.

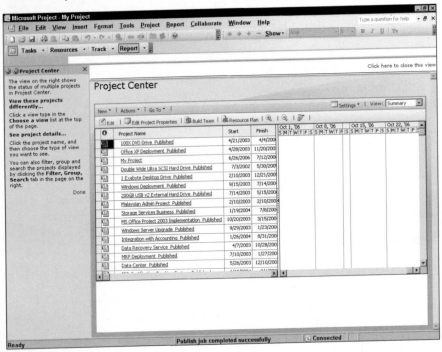

FIGURE 19.12

View the Resource Center while working in Project.

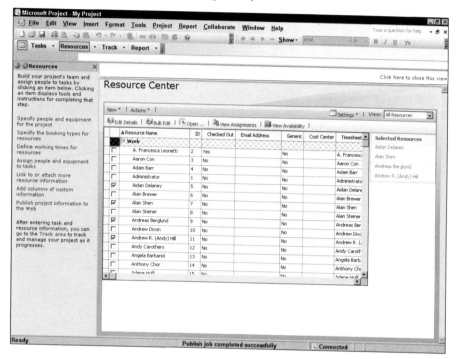

> **TIP**
>
> If you don't see any projects or resources (or projects or resources that you think you should see) in the Project Center and Resource Center views, check with the Project Server administrator and make sure that you have the proper security permissions.

Using activity plans and proposals

Suppose that you're using Project Web Access and you'd like to set up a work list—a simple list of tasks. At the moment, you don't need the capabilities of Project Professional but you might in the future. You can set up an activity plan.

> **NOTE**
>
> Activity plans replace To Do Lists found in Project Web Access 2003.

Suppose that you need to set up a work list, but you would really like to tie your list of tasks to the workflows available in Windows SharePoint Services. You don't need the capabilities of Project Professional at the moment, but again, you might in the future. In this case, you can set up a proposal. In addition to tying a proposal to the workflows in Windows SharePoint Services, you can set the state of a proposal to manage its approval process.

NOTE If your organization has installed Microsoft Office Server System (MOSS), then the state field of a project can be updated automatically based on the workflow. If your organization doesn't use MOSS, you can manually update the state of a proposal in Project Web Access.

You can convert both activity plans and proposals into projects.

NOTE You can create as many activity plans and proposals as you want. Think of each as the task list for a potential new project.

To set up a new activity plan or proposal, click the Proposals and Activity Plans link in the Quick Launch pane. Project Web Access displays the Proposals and Activity Plans page (see Figure 19.13). Click the New button and choose either Activity Plan or Proposal.

For this example, I discuss a proposal. The only visual difference between an activity plan and a proposal appears on the Summary Information page (see Figure 19.14); the proposal contains a workflow state field that you can set manually or, if your organization uses MOSS, can be set automatically. You won't see this field on the Summary Information page of an activity plan.

FIGURE 19.13

Creating a proposal or activity plan

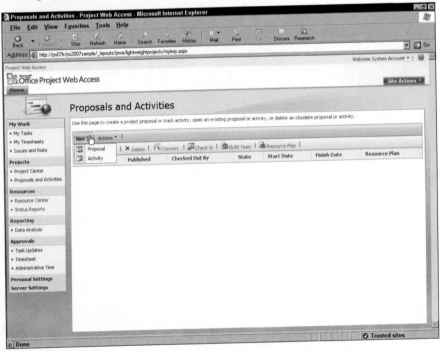

FIGURE 19.14

Provide the summary information needed to set up a proposal; you'd supply the same information except for the Workflow Status field if you were setting up an activity plan.

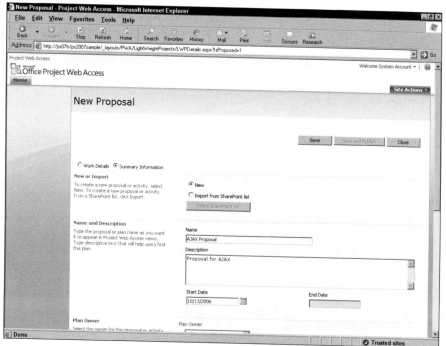

Click the Work Details option at the top of the page. On this page, shown in Figure 19.15, you can set up tasks, identify them as milestones if appropriate, and link the tasks to each other. You also can click the Link Documents button to attach a document to the proposal and even assign resources (use the Build Team button to add resources to the proposal or activity plan; then, click them in the Resource Name list).

When you finish, you can click Save to save the proposal or activity plan, or you can click Save and Publish to both save the proposal or activity plan and publish it for others to see.

FIGURE 19.15

Create tasks to place on your to-do list.

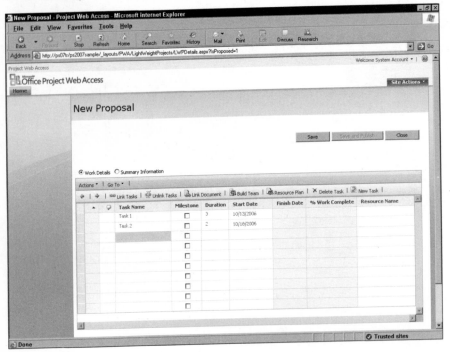

Assigning Resources to Projects

If your organization uses Project Server, project and resource managers have some additional powerful tools at your disposal to assign resources and manage resource use. Your organization will probably use the Enterprise Resource Pool that's available in Project Server; this provides a list of all resources that are owned by your organization. The administrator initially builds the Enterprise Resource Pool and imports existing projects to Project Server. If you have appropriate permissions, you can add resources to the Enterprise Resource Pool.

CROSS-REF See Chapter 18 for more information on adding resources to the Enterprise Resource Pool and importing projects to Project Server.

You can use the Team Builder feature and the Enterprise Resource Pool to select resources for a project. You also can assign generic resources to your project and then use the Team Builder feature to help you replace the generic resources with real resources.

CROSS-REF Typically, the Project Server administrator sets up the Enterprise Resource Pool. See Chapter 18 for more information.

CROSS-REF See Chapter 5 for information on creating generic resources.

In addition, if you manage more than one project at a time, you can take advantage of the Resource Substitution Wizard to identify the best possible use of limited resources.

CROSS-REF You can assign resources to Web-based projects the same way that you assign them to stand-alone projects — see Chapter 5 for details.

Adding enterprise resources to your project

You can use the Build Team dialog box to view the resources in the Enterprise Resource Pool and assign them to your project. Choose Tools ➪ Build Team from Enterprise. Project displays the Build Team dialog box (see Figure 19.16).

FIGURE 19.16

Use this dialog box to select resources to assign to your project.

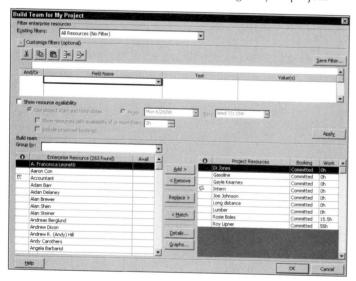

By default, you see all resources, but you can limit the resources that you see by applying filters. Use the Existing filters drop-down list and click the plus sign (+) that appears next to Customize filters to choose fields by which to filter. In Figure 19.16, I've already clicked the plus sign, so it appears as a minus sign (–), and you can see the additional space for specifying filters. You also can filter by available hours to work for a given time period.

You can filter by RBS (Resource Breakdown Structure) code, and you can set as many filters as you want. By using the And choice, you reduce the number of possible resources that Project displays.

After you select resources and click OK, the resources appear on the Resource Sheet of your project and you can assign tasks to them. When you republish your project, the Enterprise Resource Pool is updated to reflect the assignments.

Replacing generic resources with real resources

If your organization uses generic resources, you can use the Team Builder to match a generic resource in your project to a real resource that has the same skill set that you defined for the generic resource. Project Server matches generic resources to real resources by using an enterprise resource custom outline code with a value list for the field, where each value represents a set of skills. After you assign the appropriate value to each resource by using the custom field, you can use the code to match skills that are required by generic resources with skills that are possessed by real people when project managers run the Team Builder.

You'll find one enterprise resource custom outline code that the staff at Microsoft pre-named — the RBS code. Conceptually, you can compare this code for resources to a WBS code for tasks. Your organization may want to use the RBS code to establish a skill set, or your organization may want to use the RBS code for a different purpose, such as assigning a resource's geographic location. Regardless of the enterprise custom outline code that you choose, the concept I'm about to describe is the same.

The Project Server administrator typically creates the enterprise custom fields and outline codes in Project Server. Anyone who has security rights to update the Enterprise Resource Pool can assign the appropriate RBS code to each resource. To find out how to set up and assign enterprise custom fields and outline codes, see Chapter 18.

To use the Team Builder to replace generic resources with real resources, filter the Enterprise Resource Pool so that it displays only those that match the generic resource. Follow these steps to filter the Enterprise Resource Pool:

1. In Project, open the published version of the project containing generic resources that you want to replace.
2. Choose Tools ➪ Build Team from Enterprise. Project displays the Build Team dialog box.
3. In the list on the right side of the dialog box, click the generic resource for which you want to search for a replacement.
4. Click the Match button. Project displays, in the left side of the dialog box, those resources that match the selected generic resource (see Figure 19.17).

FIGURE 19.17

Replace a generic resource in your project with a real resource from the filtered Enterprise Resource Pool list.

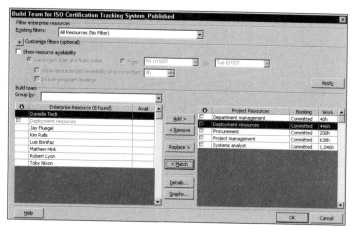

5. To assign a real resource in place of a generic resource, click the resource that you want to use in your project from the list on the left.

6. Click the Replace button. Project replaces the resource in the Team Resource list with the Enterprise resource that you selected. When you click OK, Project also updates the project by replacing the generic resource with the one that you selected.

Notifying resources of assignments

The project manager assigns work to resources. To notify the resources of the work assignments, the project manager publishes the assignments. At a minimum, the team members receive notifications of new or updated assignments on the Home page in Project Web Access. If your organization chooses, team members may also receive e-mail notifications.

Using the Resource Substitution Wizard

Suppose that you manage multiple projects with the same set of resources and you want to try to smooth work assignments and reduce overallocations across one or more projects. You can use the Resource Substitution Wizard to help you find resources to fill your needs.

The Resource Substitution Wizard can use different criteria to substitute resources. For example, the wizard can simply consider the resources in the projects that you select and reallocate them to better use their time. Or, the wizard can use the RBS (Resource Breakdown Structure) code that is assigned to resources to match skills required by resources that are already assigned to tasks and then substitute other resources with the same RBS code.

NOTE The Project Server administrator typically creates the RBS custom field code; the creator of the resource (often the Project Server administrator) assigns the custom field to the resource. To find out how to set up and assign custom fields, see Chapter 18.

Follow these steps to run the Resource Substitution Wizard:

1. Open the project(s) for which you want to substitute resources.

2. Choose Tools ⇨ Substitute Resources. The first screen of the Resource Substitution Wizard appears.

3. Click Next. Check the project(s) that you want the wizard to consider while substituting resources (see Figure 19.18).

FIGURE 19.18

Each project that you have open is listed and selected.

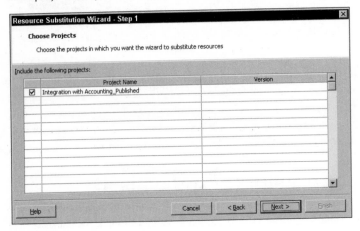

4. Click Next. Choose resources for the wizard to consider when rescheduling projects (see Figure 19.19).

5. Click Next. Choose related projects to consider when rescheduling.

6. Click Next. Specify options for the wizard to use when rescheduling (see Figure 19.20). You can set the priority or choose to use resources from the pool or from the project.

FIGURE 19.19

Use this screen to identify the resources that the wizard should consider when making substitutions.

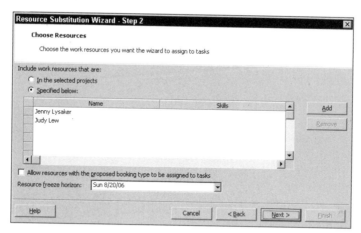

FIGURE 19.20

Specify options for rescheduling.

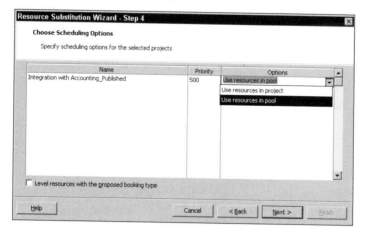

TIP By selecting the check box at the bottom of Figure 19.20, you can also level resources set up with a booking type of "proposed."

7. Click Next. You see a summary of the options that you've selected (see Figure 19.21).

FIGURE 19.21

After you set up your options, the wizard displays a summary.

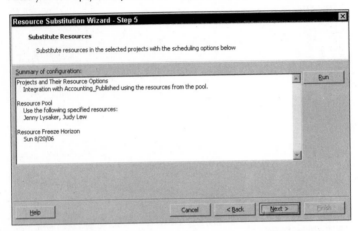

8. Click the Run button to run the wizard with the options that you've selected. The Run button changes to the Stop button while the wizard runs

9. When the Run button reappears, click Next. The wizard displays a grid of assignments that it has changed (see Figure 19.22) so that you can do the following:

   ▪ Review the results

   ▪ Back up and change the wizard's options to try again

   After you make your decision(s), click Next.

10. You see the Update Options screen of the wizard, where you can choose to have Project update the projects considered by the wizard based on the results of the wizard. You also can choose to save the results of the wizard to a file. When you click Next, a final page appears.

11. If you aren't satisfied with the results of the wizard, simply close the affected projects without saving them.

FIGURE 19.22

The wizard's suggested changes.

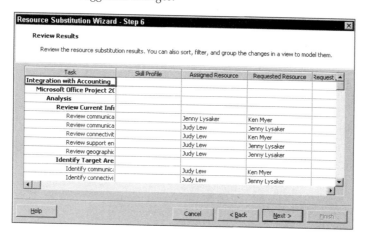

The Resource Substitution Wizard can also help you to select resources for more than one project at a time, so you can quickly develop staffing models. As Step 3 demonstrated, you can select the open projects that you want the Resource Substitution Wizard to consider; simply open each project before you start the wizard. After the wizard has finished, don't forget to level the projects to see how the wizard's resource assignments change project finish dates and resource use. If you aren't satisfied with the results of the wizard, simply close the affected projects without saving them.

Assigning resources using Project Web Access

Are you a resource manager but you don't have Project Professional? You can manage resources, including building a team for your project, using Project Web Access. Follow these steps to assign and manage resources:

1. Log on to Project Web Access.

TIP The Home page that appears in Project Web Access is customizable; see Chapter 20 for details.

2. Display the Project Center page by clicking Project Center in the Quick Launch pane on the left side of the page (see Figure 19.23).

Start the team-building process from the Project Center.

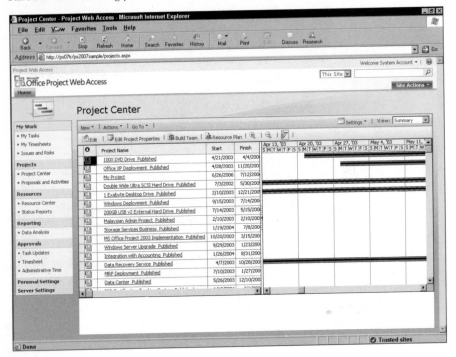

3. Click the link of the project for which you want to build a team. Project Web Access displays the Project Details page for the project in the Project Center (see Figure 19.24).

The Project Details page for a project in Project Web Access closely resembles the Gantt Chart view in Project Professional.

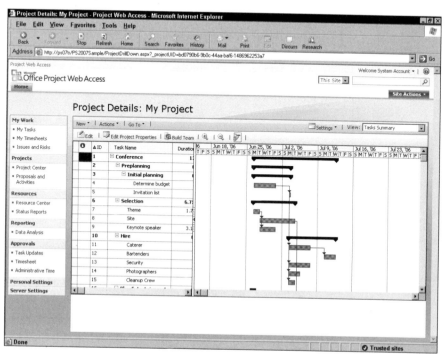

4. Click the Build Team button above the list of tasks. Project Web Access displays a list of resources on the left side of the Build Team page (see Figure 19.25). You see only those resources for which you have permission to view within your RBS code. On the right side of this page, you the see resources that already work on your project.

FIGURE 19.25

Build a team for a project using Project Web Access.

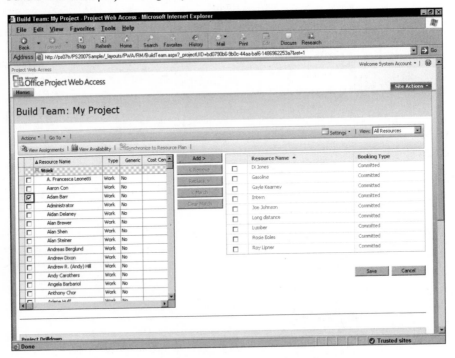

5. In the list on the left, select the resources that you want to add to the project.

6. Click the Add button.

7. To assign the resource, click the Save button on the Build Team page. But before you assign the resource, read on.

You can create a filter to find resources with specified skills. Click the Settings button at the top of the page and choose Filter to display the area where you can use enterprise outline codes to define and apply a filter.

You can replace generic resources easily. Select the generic resource on the right and then click the Match button. Project Web Access displays, on the left, real resources with the same skills as the selected generic resource. To replace the generic resource, select it on the right side of the window and select the real resource that you want to use on the left side of the window. Then click the Replace button.

By clicking a resource in the list on the right and then clicking in the Booking Type column, you also can specify whether you want the resources to be committed to the project or only proposed for the project.

You can view an availability graph of a resource before you add it to your project. Place a check beside the resource in the list on the left, and then click the View Availability button (refer to Figure 19.25). Project opens a separate page to display the Resource Availability graph (see Figure 19.26).

You also can view the resource's assignments by placing a check beside the resource in the list on the left and then clicking the View Assignments button. Once again, Project Web Access opens a separate page that shows all the selected resource assignments (see Figure 19.27).

FIGURE 19.26

The View Resource Availability graph that you see when you click the Availability button

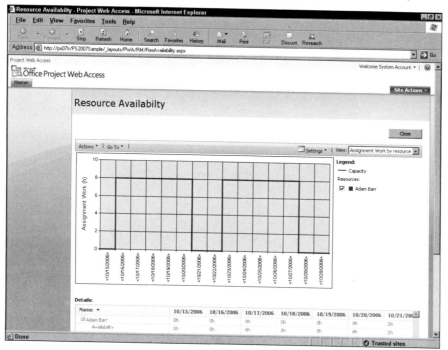

FIGURE 19.27

FIGURE 19.27

View assignments for a selected resource.

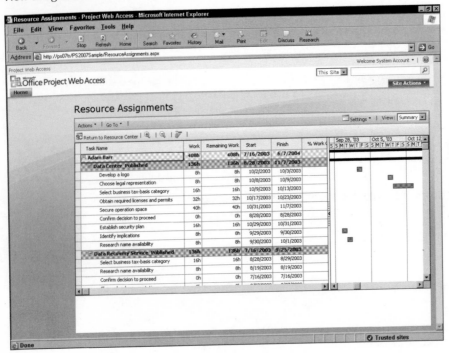

Tracking Progress

After you've set up a project and uploaded it to Project Server, you need to track the progress of your project. To effectively track progress, you need to do the following:

- Establish a tracking method
- Set up a status report form for team members to complete
- Receive updates from team members as they update the project in Project Web Access
- As appropriate, adjust actual work

Establishing a tracking method

Your organization may have selected a tracking method for you. If so, you can't select a tracking method. If you can select a different tracking method, you'll see the available methods on the Collaborate tab of the Options dialog box in Project Professional. Choose Collaborate ➪ Collaboration Options. Project displays the Collaborate tab of the Options dialog box, with options for specifying a method of reporting progress at the bottom of the dialog box (see Figure 19.28).

FIGURE 19.28

Use this dialog box to select the tracking method if your organization permits you to use a method other than the default method.

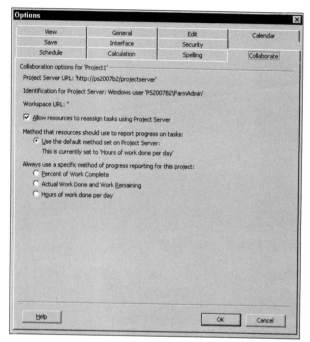

You can choose one of three possible ways for users to record actual work in Project Server:

- **Percent of Work Complete:** This method is the fastest way for resources to record time, but it is also the least accurate because it is based on the resource's estimate of the total amount of work to be done, along with the amount that is actually completed. Resources enter the percentage amount.

- **Actual Work Done and Work Remaining:** This method is the middle-of-the-road method. It is both moderately accurate and moderately fast. Resources enter the hours, days, weeks, and so on of the amount of work done and the amount of work remaining to be completed.

- **Hours of Work Done per Time Period:** This method is the most accurate method but also the most time consuming. Resources enter the actual hours worked on each task for a specified time — typically, a day.

If your organization has locked down the tracking method in Project Server, none of the options at the bottom of Figure 19.28 will be available. If the options are available, you can choose to use the Project Server method or select a method for the current project.

Setting up status reports

As a manager, you can create the layout for the status report that you want to view from your team members. When you create a status report layout, you specify how often you want status reports, when reporting should begin, which resources should report, and the section you want included in the report.

To create a standard layout for a status report, click the Status Reports link in the Quick Launch pane to display the Status Reports page (see Figure 19.29). The Status Reports page lists existing status report layouts and status reports you need to submit.

To create a status report layout, you set up a request. Click the New button and then click New Request. The Status Report Request page appears. On the top of the page, you assign a name to the status report, establish a frequency and a start date, and identify the resources you want to submit the report (see Figure 19.30).

FIGURE 19.29

The Status Reports page lists all information concerning status reports.

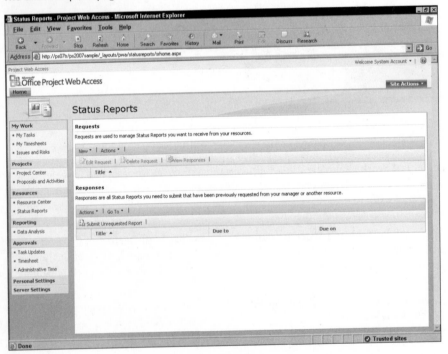

FIGURE 19.30

Identify the users who should submit the status report.

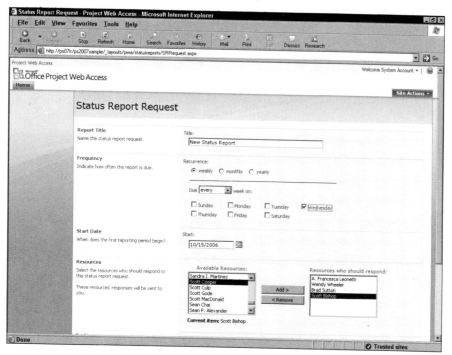

At the bottom of the page (see Figure 19.31), establish the sections that should appear in the report. You can add a section by clicking the Insert Section button. Project Web Access adds blank lines in which you enter the section names. Click Send when you finish; Project Web Access creates the status report and sends a skeleton of the status report to the selected team members, requesting a status report. The team members can then use the skeleton to fill in the information that you want to see.

FIGURE 19.31

Identify the information that should appear in the report.

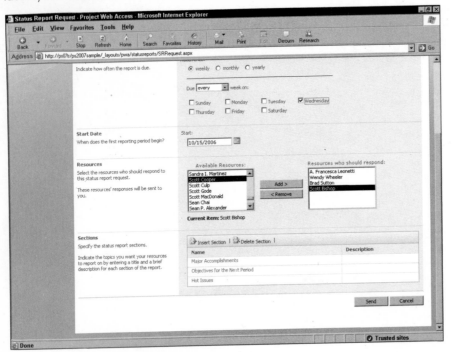

Receiving updates from team members

NOTE In Project 2003, resources reported administrative time using administrative projects. This behavior has changed in Project 2007; resources now use pre-established tasks that appear on the time sheet to report administrative time so that there is no need to set up administrative projects.

If you manage resources and approve their time, when you log on to Project Web Access your home page indicates in the Approvals section how many task updates from resources are pending your approval (see Figure 19.32).

FIGURE 19.32

In the Approvals section, Project Web Access indicates the number of task updates that await your approval.

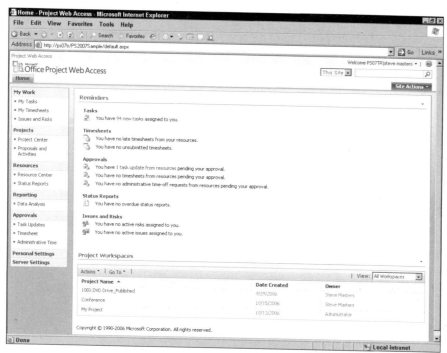

To view the task updates, you can click the link in the Approvals section or you can click Task Updates in the Approvals section of the Quick Launch pane. The Task Updates page appears (see Figure 19.33).

Accept or reject any update by clicking in the leftmost column to select an update. Then, click the Accept button or the Reject button. If, after reviewing updates, you want to accept all updates received, you can click the Select All button and then click the Accept button. Project Web Access gives you the opportunity to preview the project plan to see the effects of the updates on the plan.

FIGURE 19.33

From this page, you can view and accept or reject the task updates.

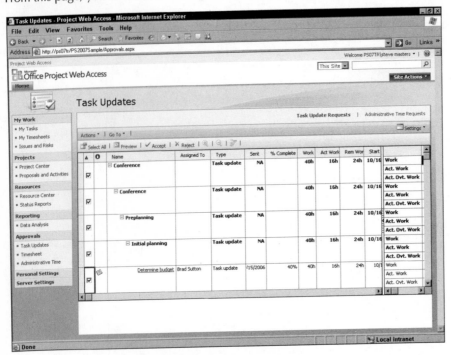

TIP	You can set up rules to automatically accept changes from selected users for selected projects. Click Task Update in the Quick Launch pane. Then, click the Actions button and choose Manage Rules.

Project managers can view updates and approve them in Project Web Access, using the technique just described, or in Project Professional. When you open the project in Project Professional, you'll see a message like the one shown in Figure 19.34.

FIGURE 19.34

When a team member has submitted an approved update to a plan, Project Professional displays this message when you open the project.

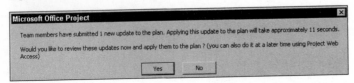

If you choose Yes, Project opens the project and displays the updates using the same Task Updates window that appears in Project Web Access (see Figure 19.35). Using the buttons that appear above the updates, you can preview the updates, and accept or reject the updates.

Working with issues and risks

Using Windows SharePoint Services features, you can create and track issues and risks that are associated with a project in general or with specific tasks in a project. Issues and risks can be initiated by anyone with proper permissions, and the concept behind them is to promote collaboration on the project team.

CROSS-REF You also can attach documents to tasks, activity plans, or proposals. See Chapter 20 for more information about document tracking.

FIGURE 19.35

The project manager can review and approve plan updates in Project Professional.

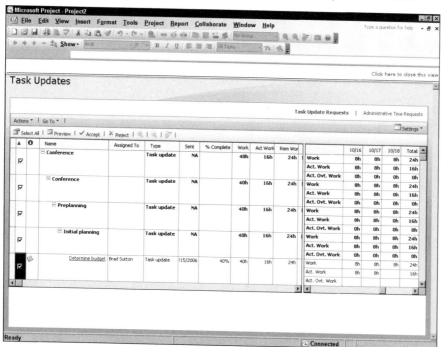

Tracking issues

Issues are unexpected things that occur on projects. They may be problems or they may be opportunities. When they arise, you can create an issue, let others on the team review the issue, assign the issue to someone to address, and monitor the progress of the issue.

You set up an issue for tracking from the project's workspace. Project workspaces appear at the bottom of your Home page. Click the link to the appropriate project's workspace to display the Home page of the project's workspace in Windows SharePoint Services (see Figure 19.36).

To find the Issues list, click View All Site Content at the top of the Quick Launch pane. Windows SharePoint Services displays the All Site Content page, where you'll see the Issues in the Lists section (see Figure 19.37).

FIGURE 19.36

The Home page for a project's workspace in Windows SharePoint Services

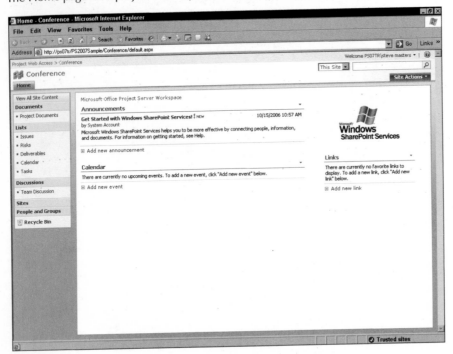

FIGURE 19.37

From the All Site Content page, you can open the Issues list.

Click Issues to open the Issues list page. Any previously defined issues appear on this page, along with summary information about the issue. To define a new issue, click the New button, and Windows SharePoint Services displays the Issues page, where you can define an issue (see Figure 19.38).

FIGURE 19.38

Defining an issue for the Issues list of a project.

Assign a title, status, and priority to the issue; assign the issue to someone; identify the issue owner; set a due date; describe the issue; and (if possible) provide a resolution for it. At the top of the page, you can attach files to the issue or link it to tasks within the project. Attached files and links appear at the bottom of the Issues page, which doesn't appear in Figure 19.38. Click OK when you finish filling in the screen. Project redisplays the Issues list where all issues for the project appear (see Figure 19.39).

NOTE You edit an issue by clicking its link. You can filter issues by clicking the View button at the top-right edge of the Issues list.

FIGURE 19.39

On the Issues list, you see issues for the selected project.

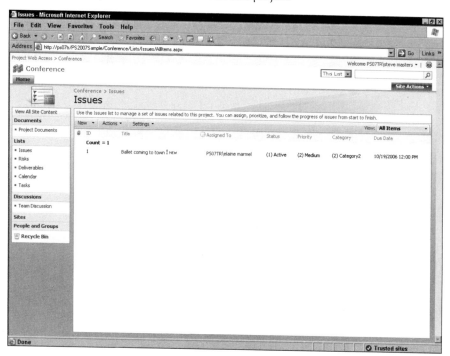

If someone assigns an issue to you, you'll see a notification on your Home page when you log into Project Web Access. You can click the Issues/Risk Center link in the Quick Launch pane to view the issues and risks assigned to you (see Figure 19.40). Click the project name to navigate to the Issues list page of the project's workspace in Windows SharePoint Services — the page shown previously in Figure 19.39 — and click the issue to read the details.

FIGURE 19.40

All issues and risks assigned to you appear on this page, organized by project.

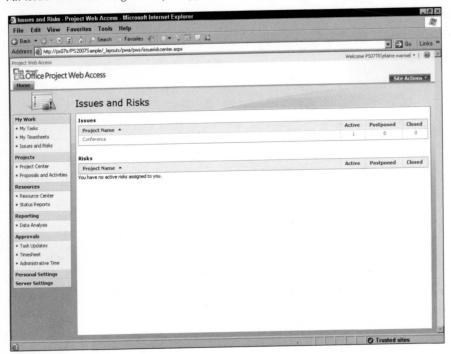

> **TIP** Windows SharePoint Services opens as a separate browser instance. To return to Project Web Access, close the browser instance displaying Windows SharePoint Services or use the Windows taskbar to switch between the two browser instances.

Tracking risks

Risks are possible events or conditions that could negatively impact a project. Risks are events that have not yet occurred but that *could occur*. Essentially, a risk is an issue before it happens.

You create a risk the same way that you create an issue — click the project on your Home page that you want to associate with the risk. In Windows SharePoint Services, click the View All Site Content link at the top of the Quick Launch pane in Windows SharePoint Services. Then, click the Risks list icon to display the Risks list. Click the New icon to display the Risks page, where you describe the risk and, if appropriate, attach files or link the risk to a project task. Click OK to save the risk.

You view risks assigned to you from the Issues/Risks Center that appeared Figure 19.40.

Managing deliverables

NEW FEATURE Deliverables are a new feature in Project 2007.

Deliverables are, typically, work products that you deliver as a function of completing a task or a project. Deliverables can be documents such as financial reports or the birthday cake for the CEO's retirement party.

It's certainly possible that the deliverables of one project will affect another project — and that deliverables therefore need to be tracked and possibly even linked to tasks.

After you have published a project and created a workspace for it, you can set up its associated deliverables in Project Professional and manage their dependencies. Deliverables are stored in Windows SharePoint Services in the Deliverables folder.

To set up a deliverable, open the draft version of the project in Project Professional. Then, choose Collaborate ➪ Manage Deliverables. In the Project Guide pane, click the Add new deliverable link. The pane changes to resemble what you see in Figure 19.41.

FIGURE 19.41

Define the deliverable in the Project Guide pane.

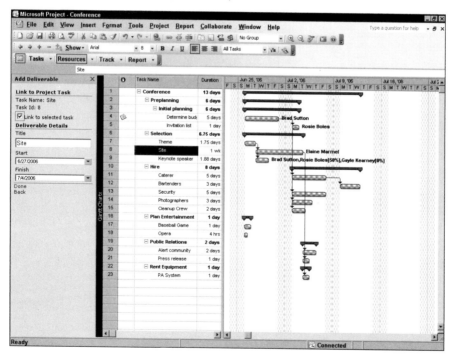

You can link the deliverable to a task and assign start and finish dates, but those are not requirements of setting up a deliverable. Project treats deliverable dates as it treats deadline dates; the project won't slip if you miss a deliverable date, but you'll see a visual cue for a missed deliverable date.

When you finish, click Done. The Project Guide pane updates, and if you click the Open deliverables in browser link in the Project Guide, your project's deliverables appear in a Windows SharePoint Services window (see Figure 19.42).

After you create deliverables in your project, you can use Project Professional to link the deliverables to tasks in other projects. In Project Professional, open the draft versions of the project that contains the deliverable that you want to link and the project that contains the task to which you want to link the deliverable. Then, choose Collaborate ➪ Manage Dependencies on Deliverables.

In the Project Guide pane, click the Add new dependency link. Then, when prompted to select a dependent project, select the project containing the deliverables. The Project Guide pane then displays available deliverables in the project you selected.

FIGURE 19.42

Deliverables stored in Windows SharePoint Services.

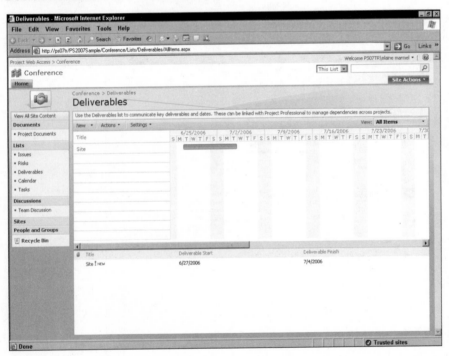

TIP   Point the mouse at a deliverable to see the details of that deliverable.

Click the deliverable that you want to link in the Project Guide pane and select the task to which you want to link the deliverable in the task list. Then, check the Link to Selected Task box at the bottom of the Project Guide pane (see Figure 19.43). Click Done, and Project establishes the dependency between the deliverable and the selected task. An indicator appears in the Indicators column.

FIGURE 19.43

Deliverables you can link to tasks appear in the Project Guide pane.

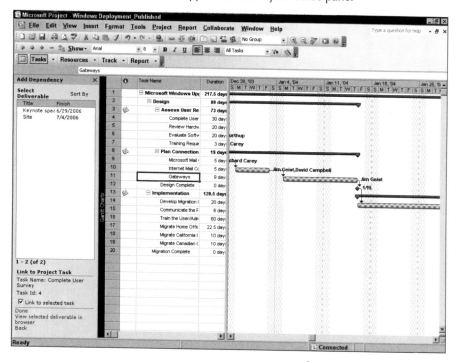

Summary

In this chapter, you read about how to address your primary concerns as a project or resource manager who deals with Web-based projects. You found out how to do the following:

- Log on to Project Server
- Create a Web-based project
- Manage resource assignments for Web-based projects
- Track the progress of Web-based projects
- Manage issues and risks associated with projects

For information about the behind-the-scenes tasks that helped create your Project Server environment, read Chapter 18. For more information on the day-to-day tasks that your team members can perform, see Chapter 20. To see how an executive can take advantage of Project Web Access, see Chapter 21.

Chapter 20

Project Server and the Day-to-Day User

At this point in the book, you have probably realized that the world of project management has moved beyond the traditional pencil-and-ruler war room and into the world of technology. Nowhere is this shift more evident than in the many ways that project managers can take advantage of the Internet to communicate with others, present information, and gather data.

If your organization uses Project Server, then you, as a team member, should read this chapter to find out how you can make use of Project Web Access — the browser-based interface that connects to the Project Server database — to view the tasks that you need to accomplish, update the schedule with work completed, and even enter new tasks that may arise.

In this chapter, you read about how the average team member can connect to Project Server, update timesheets and task status, and report to the project manager. Project Web Access also interacts with Outlook, and in this chapter, you find out how to use those tools together.

IN THIS CHAPTER

Logging on to Project Web Access

Reviewing the Home page

Customizing the Home Page

Viewing information for tasks and timesheets

Project Web Access and Outlook

Viewing and uploading project-related documents

Reporting status

Logging on to Project Web Access

To log on to Project Server by using Project Web Access, a resource needs to know the URL for the Web database. The project manager should notify the resource of the URL. To log on to Project Server, open Internet Explorer and, in the Address box, enter the URL of the Web database.

> **TIP**   Save the URL in your Favorites list, or if you use Project Web Access more than any other Web page, set it up as your Home page so that Project Web Access appears when you open Internet Explorer. To set Project Web Access as your Home page, enter the address into the Address box. Then choose Tools ⇨ Internet Options. On the first page, click the Use Current button in the Home Page section and click OK.

The window that appears next depends on the method that you use to log on to Project Server. If you aren't using Windows user accounts, you see a page that you use to log on to Project Web Access; supply your username and password. If your organization set up Project Server to use Windows user account logons, you don't see the logon page; instead, you bypass this page and see your Project Web Access Home page.

Reviewing the Home Page

The Project Web Access Home page serves the same function as most home pages on the Web (see Figure 20.1). It introduces you to Project Web Access; in the Reminders section, you'll see summary information such as the number of new tasks that you have, the number of unsubmitted timesheets you have, the number of overdue status reports you have, and the number of issues and risks assigned to you.

You can use the Quick Launch pane that appears on the left side of the screen to navigate to other areas of Project Web Access and to Windows SharePoint Services.

> **NOTE**   You can set the Quick Launch pane to display links related to Windows SharePoint Services; throughout this chapter, I've hidden those links.

If your organization has set up Windows SharePoint Services workspaces for projects, you'll see any project workspaces that you have permission to view below the Reminders pane.

The Home tab and the Quick Launch pane remain visible at all times.

A typical Project Web Access Home page, from which you can navigate to other areas of Project Web Access.

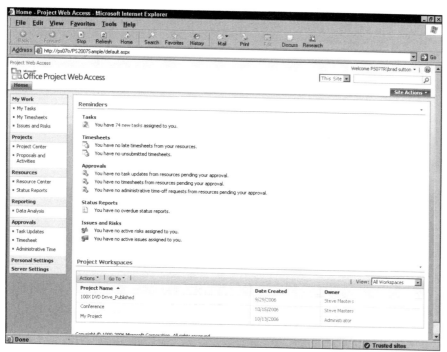

Customizing the Home Page

You can customize the appearance of your Project Web Access Home page either temporarily or permanently using the Web Part menu that appears on the Home page beside each part. Each Web Part menu is a small, downward-pointing carat at the right edge of a section on the Home page; in Figure 20.2, the mouse pointer is pointing at a Web Part menu.

You can temporarily close a section of the Home page; click the Web Part menu and choose Minimize. In Figure 20.2, I've minimized the Project Workspaces section. To redisplay the information, click the Web Part menu and choose Restore.

FIGURE 20.2

You can minimize sections on the Home page to temporarily hide the information.

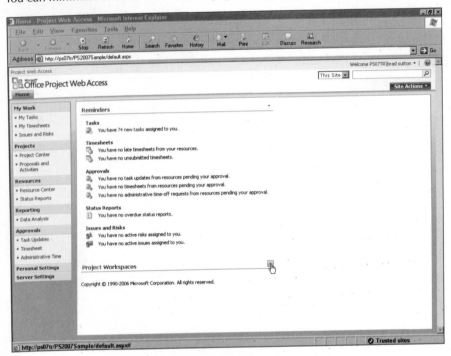

If you want to remove a section from the Home page on a more permanent basis, click the Web Part menu and choose Close. Project Web Access removes the section from your Home page entirely.

You can add sections to the Home page; for example, suppose that you close the Project Workspaces and then change your mind. You can add it back. Click any Web Part menu and choose Modify My Web Part. Project Web Access displays the Home page in Edit mode (see Figure 20.3).

TIP You also can click your name in the upper-right corner of the Project Web Access screen and choose Personalize this Page to add, remove, or reorganize your Home page information.

FIGURE 20.3

The Home page in Edit mode after I closed the Project Workspaces section.

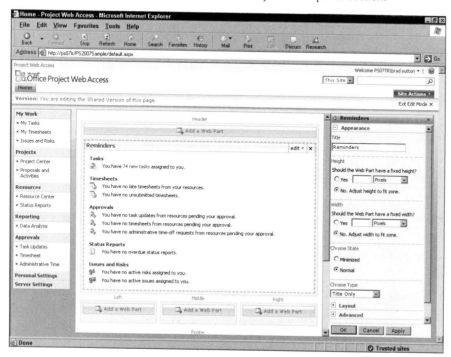

Click an Add a Web Part button (in Figure 20.3, I clicked the Middle Add a Web Part button) and Project Web Access displays the Add Web Parts dialog box (see Figure 20.4).

Scroll down and place a check beside the element(s) you want to display on the Home page. Then, click the Add button. Project Web Access redisplays the Home page, still in Edit mode; the Home page now includes the element(s) you added.

FIGURE 20.4

Use this dialog box to add a Web part to the Home page.

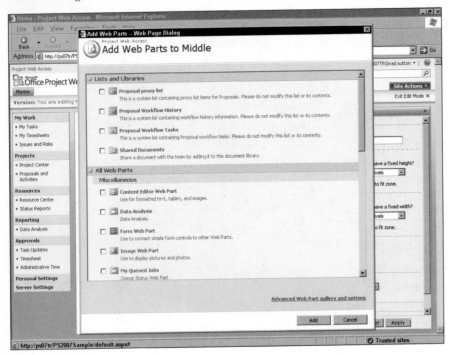

If you want to reorganize Home page elements, drag the title of a section to a new location.

Click Exit Edit Mode in the upper-right corner of the page to display your new Home page.

 **TIP**   You can use the techniques described in the section to modify the appearance of most pages in Project Web Access.

Viewing Information

The Project Center displays individual projects — typically, those on which you have assigned work (see Figure 20.5). On each line, you see a Gantt taskbar that shows you the duration of the project and progress that's been made on the project so far.

 **NOTE**   You must have appropriate permissions from the Project Server administrator to the Project Center.

FIGURE 20.5

In the Project Center, you see one-line entries representing projects that are stored in the Project Server database.

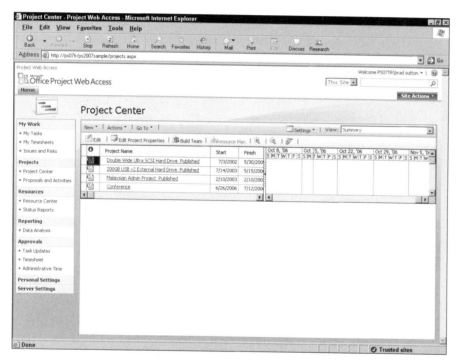

You can organize the projects by using the Filter, Group, and Search options, which you can display by clicking the Settings button. You can open a particular project in Project Web Access by clicking the link that appears in the Project Name column.

NOTE If you have proper permissions, you can view and edit resources and resource assignments from the Resource Center; typically, project managers and resource managers have permission to view the Resource Center, but team members don't have permission.

Working with your tasks

Work assignments go from Project Professional to team members via Project Web Access. If your organization chooses, the Project Server administrator can set up e-mail notifications so that Project Server generates e-mail notices and reminders of events, such as past due tasks. These e-mail notices and reminders appear in your regular e-mail client inbox.

But as you saw, when you log on to Project Web Access, the Home page also indicates whether you have new task assignments. You can view your task assignments from the My Tasks page (see Figure 20.6).

As life would have it, you may not work on only one project at a time. The My Tasks page lists the project and, indented, each task assigned to you on the project. Beside each project, you'll see either a plus or a minus sign; you can click the symbol to toggle between the plus and minus sign. When you see a plus sign, your tasks on the project are hidden; click the symbol to change it to a minus sign and view your tasks on the project.

TIP   On the upper-right side of the My Tasks page, the View list box enables you to view assignments or timesheets. In Figure 20.6, you're viewing assignments. Later in this chapter, you'll see the results of viewing Timesheets.

FIGURE 20.6

The My Tasks page lists your task assignments, both new and existing.

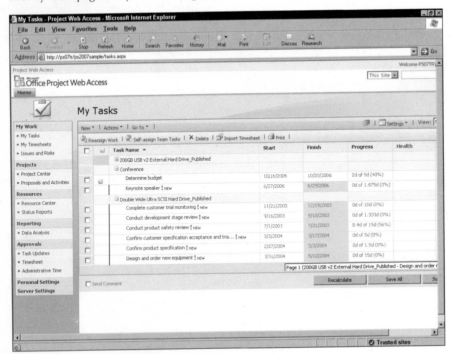

Entering time on tasks

If you click a task name, Project Web Access displays the Assignment Details page (see Figure 20.7). From this page, you can see the details of the task, including the planned work, and, if you scroll down the screen, any transaction comments and task history, attachments, contacts, related assignments, and notes.

 **TIP**   Use the Attachments section to attach a document, issue, or risk to a task.

You also can report time spent on the assignment. Above the grid that displays planned, work, and overtime hours, you see a set of dates with arrows pointing in either direction. Click the arrows to display the time frame that you want to update. Then, click in the cell that represents the intersection of the date that you worked and the type of hours you want to record — typically, work hours. Click the Recalculate button to refresh the page. When you click Save, Project Web Access saves your updates and redisplays the My Tasks page.

FIGURE 20.7

The Assignment details page in Project Web Access.

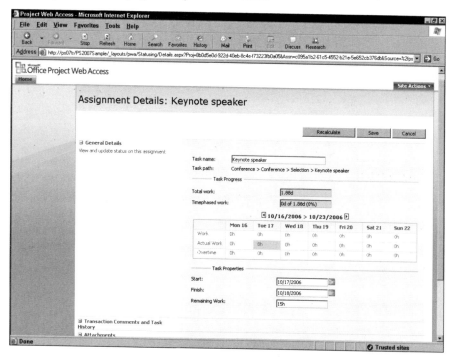

If you recorded time on the task using the My Timesheet page, you can import work values you entered on your timesheet. On the My Tasks page, click the Import Timesheet button. Project Web Access displays the Import Timesheet page (see Figure 20.8). Select the timesheet on which you recorded work values and click the Import button. A message appears, asking you to confirm that you want to import the values. When you click Yes, Project Web Access imports any work values you recorded on the My Tasks page for the selected task.

Submitting task updates

Saving a task update doesn't send it to the project manager. The My Tasks page provides a visual cue when you've recorded work but haven't yet submitted the update; an exclamation point appears beside the task title (see Figure 20.9). If you point the mouse at the exclamation point, a tip appears, indicating that you have not yet submitted the update.

FIGURE 20.8

Use this page to import work values from your timesheet to the appropriate task on the My Tasks page.

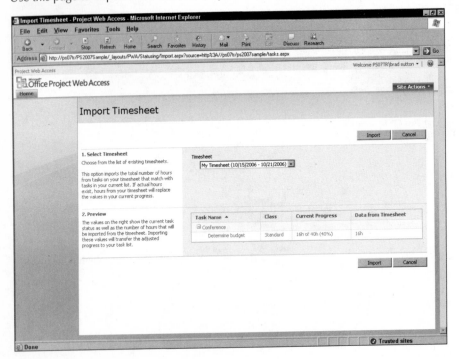

FIGURE 20.9

You can identify updates you haven't submitted by the exclamation point that appears beside the task name.

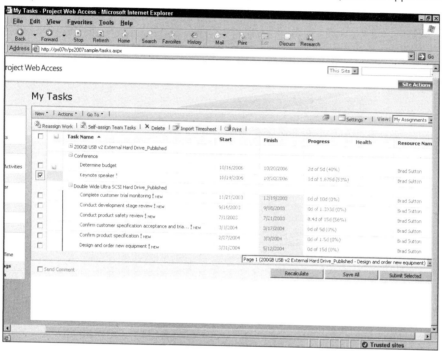

When you're ready to submit an update, click in the leftmost column beside the task to select it and then click the Submit Selected button. If you checked the Send Comment box at the bottom of the My Tasks page, the Submit Changes dialog box appears; you can use it to enter a comment to the project manager. Click OK, and Project Web Access submits your updates. A message appears at the bottom of the My Tasks page, indicating that your changes have been submitted.

 You can enter several task updates and save them without submitting them if you click the Save All button.

Adding tasks

As a team member, you may realize that what you're doing requires more work than the manager anticipated — and may even call for tasks that the manager didn't assign to you. If your Project Web Access privileges permit, you can add a task from the My Tasks page. Click the New button and choose Task. Project Web Access displays the New Task page (see Figure 20.10).

FIGURE 20.10

Add tasks to the project from this page.

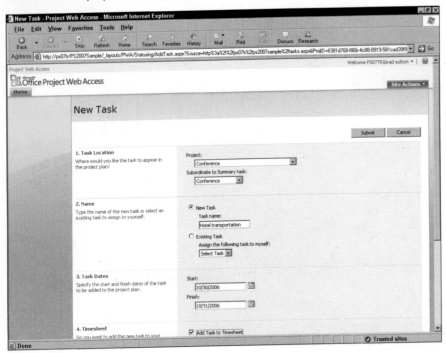

Select the project to which you need to add the task from the Project drop-down list and then select the task's level in the outline. Supply a task name and estimated start and end dates. Check the Add Task to Timesheet box to make the task appear on your timesheet; for more information on using your timesheet, see "Working with your timesheet," later in this chapter. Scroll down to optionally provide a comment about the task.

TIP   You can use this page to assign an existing project task to yourself. You also can click the Self-assign Team Tasks button on the My Tasks page to assign an existing task to yourself.

Click the Submit button, and Project Web Access adds the task to your My Tasks page (and to your timesheet, if appropriate).

To notify the project manager about the additional work, you need to select the task on the My Tasks page and click the Submit Selected button.

To notify your manager of the new task, click the Update All button or the Update Selected Rows button. Project Web Access sends the notice of the new task to the manager and changes the icon to reflect the task's new status—that you've notified your manager but your manager hasn't yet updated the project. Your manager has the option to add the task to the project or to reject the task.

Reassigning a task

You're overloaded with work and you can't possibly complete everything that you've been assigned. But—luckily for you—management just approved your request to hire an intern to help you. Now you need to reassign some of your tasks—and keep your project manager informed of the change in assignments.

 You can reassign tasks only if you have the correct permissions.

To reassign tasks, click the My Tasks link in the Quick Launch pane. Then, click the Reassign Work button. The Task Reassignment page appears (see Figure 20.11).

On the line of the task you want to reassign, select a resource in the last column. Provide a start date for the new task and, if you want, any comments about the assignment. Then, click the Submit button.

FIGURE 20.11

Select a resource for the appropriate task.

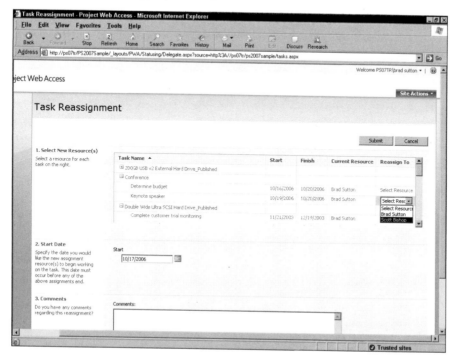

Project Web Access redisplays the My Tasks page; the task you reassigned still appears in your task list. Select the task and click Submit Selected; after the project manager approves the reassignment, the reassigned task appears on the Microsoft Project Web Access My Tasks page of the affected recipient. The reassigned task remains on the My Tasks page of the person who reassigned it; that person can delete the task.

Select the task and click Submit Selected or simply click Save All. After the project manager approves the reassignment, the reassigned task appears in the Microsoft Project Web Access Task Center of the affected recipient. The reassigned task remains in the Task Center of the person who reassigned it; that person can delete the task.

Working with your timesheet

Some organizations prefer that you record the time you work on tasks using a timesheet. Typically, these organizations set up Project Web Access so that timesheets for appropriate periods appear on the My Timesheets page; click the My Timesheet link in the Quick Launch pane to display the My Timesheets page (see Figure 20.12), which displays summary information about each timesheet.

FIGURE 20.12

The timesheet periods for which you can create or update timesheets appear in the Timesheet List.

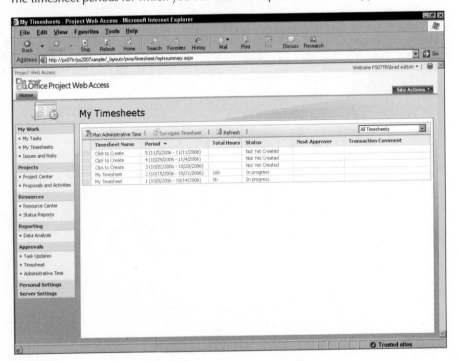

Click in the Timesheet Name column beside the timesheet you want to display. Project Web Access displays the timesheet for the period you selected (see Figure 20.13). If you don't have any timesheets in progress, click the Click to Create link beside the appropriate timesheet period.

 **TIP** To see timesheets for specified periods, use the View list box.

If your organization set up administrative time for you, it appears on the timesheet, as do any tasks planned for the timesheet working period. Depending on your organization's defaults, you can view planned time for the task. If you click the task name, you see the Assignment Details page, shown earlier in Figure 20.7.

FIGURE 20.13

The timesheet for the selected period.

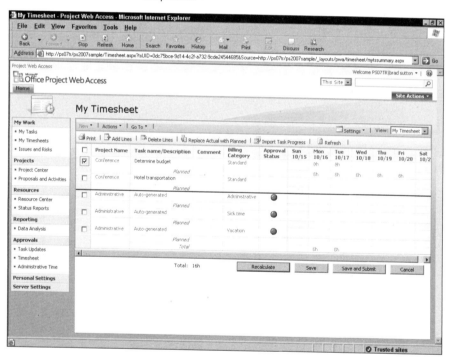

Entering time

You can enter time in a number of ways:

- Manually
- Replacing actual with planned time
- Importing task progress

To record time manually, click in the box that represents the intersection of the date for which you want to record work and the task on which you want to record work. Then, type the number of hours you want to record.

NOTE The numbers that you can enter depend on the settings that your project manager or your organization has selected. You may be able to fill in the % work complete, actual work done and work remaining, or the hours of work done per day.

You can replace actual work values with planned work values for an entire row. Select the task by clicking in the leftmost column; the Replace Actual with Planned button becomes available. When you click the button, Project Web Access notifies you that you're about to replace regular time you have already reported with planned values from the assignment's scheduled tasks. If you click Yes, Project Web Access replaces all existing work values with the assignment's planned work values.

Finally, you can import work values you entered on the My Tasks page. With the appropriate timesheet displayed on the My Timesheet page, select the task for which you want to import work values and click the Import Task Progress button. A message appears, asking you to confirm that you want to import the values. When you click Yes, Project Web Access imports any work values you recorded on the My Tasks page for the selected task.

TIP If tasks on which you need to report don't appear on your timesheet, click the Add Lines button. Project Web Access displays a dialog box that you can use to create a new line for your timesheet. You can choose from among tasks assigned to you or you can type a title for the line.

Saving timesheet entries

You don't typically finish recording all information on a timesheet at one time. You can click the Save button on the Timesheet page to save your entries but keep the timesheet available for further updating; you'll want to take this approach as long as your working dates fall in the period covered by the timesheet.

When the timesheet period no longer covers your working period, click the Save and Submit button to save your work and submit your timesheet for approval.

TIP You can print your timesheet at any time; view it and click the Print icon.

If your organization permits you to select the person who approves your timesheet, a dialog box appears in which you can select the person who approves your timesheet and supply any appropriate comments; click OK, and Project Web Access displays the Timesheet List page. You can identify the timesheet you submitted using the Status column (see Figure 20.14).

Reporting administrative time

Suppose that you were just selected for jury duty. And, of course, you're scheduled to work on a project at the same time. It happens — something comes up, and you are not available to work during the time that you had been scheduled to work. From the My Timesheet page, you can report actual administrative time using the preestablished administrative time tasks that appear on your timesheet, and you fill in these tasks in the same way that you report work you performed on a task.

FIGURE 20.14

You can identify submitted timesheets by looking at the Status column.

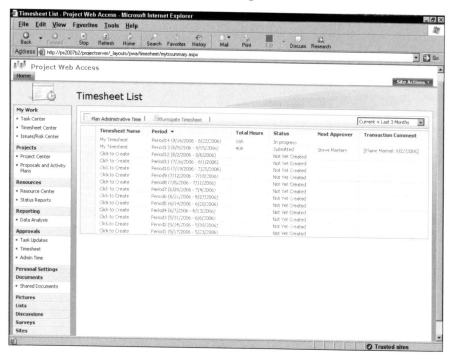

Project Web Access and Microsoft Outlook

Do you use Outlook? Would you like to be able to get a better handle on *all* the things you need to do by viewing them all in one place? If your Project Server administrator has enabled Outlook integration, you can synchronize Outlook with Project Web Access.

NOTE   If you want Project Web Access to display in Outlook, you need Outlook 2003 or a later version.

Integrating the Outlook Calendar with Project Web Access

Using Outlook 2003, you can import assignments from Project Web Access to your Outlook Calendar. You can choose to import assignments automatically at regular intervals, or you can import them when you choose. And, you can work on tasks, record the information in Outlook, and then upload the information to Project Web Access.

NEW FEATURE   You can choose to exchange information between Project Web Access and either the Outlook Task List or the Outlook Calendar.

If Outlook integration is set up, the appearance of Outlook changes. The Project Web Access toolbar appears in the main window, and on the Tools menu, you see a menu for Project Web Access. In Figure 20.15, I've moved the Project Web Access toolbar so that you can see it; it typically appears anchored below the Standard toolbar.

Setting up integration

To enable integration between Project Web Access and Outlook, open Project Web Access. Then, click the Personal Settings link in the Quick Launch pane; when the Personal Settings page appears, click Set Up Outlook Sync. Project Web Access displays the Synchronize Your Tasks with Outlook page (see Figure 20.16). Click the Download Now button. When the File Download dialog box appears, click Run. If an Internet Explorer security warning dialog box appears, click Run. When prompted to proceed with the installation, click Yes. Then, click the Install button, and when the integration finishes, click OK.

FIGURE 20.15

When Outlook is integrated with Project Web Access, you'll notice changes in Outlook.

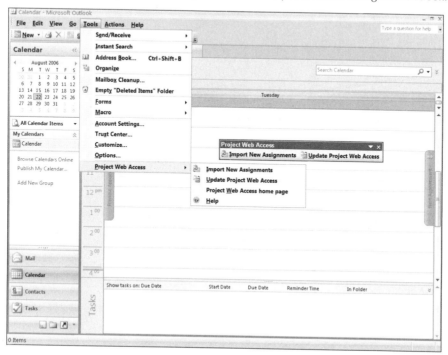

You may need to edit your logon information in Outlook. In Outlook, choose Tools ➪ Options. On the Project Web Access tab, click the Advanced Options button. In the Advanced Options dialog box that appears, click the Enter login information button to display the Enter Login Information dialog box. Supply the URL for your Project Server database and select a connection method.

FIGURE 20.16

Use this page to establish integration between Outlook and Project Web Access.

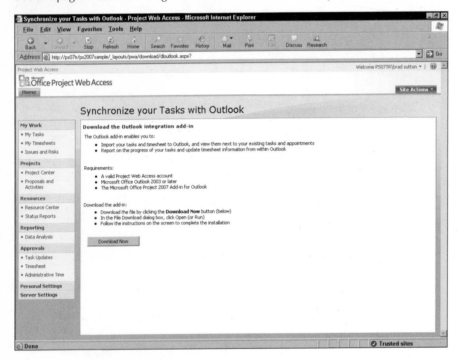

Setting integration options

You have some choices about the way that updating occurs. By default, you manually import all assignments from Project Web Access to the Outlook To-Do List and all updates from Outlook to Project Web Access. You can import assignments to the Outlook Calendar, choose to import for a specific time period, and set up the updating process to occur automatically by changing your Assignment Import settings. In Outlook, choose Tools ➪ Options and then click the Project Web Access tab (see Figure 20.17).

First, choose whether to import Project Web Access assignments to the Outlook To-Do List or to the Outlook Calendar.

To import assignments for a specify time period, use the Date Range section; select the Next option button and specify the time frame.

FIGURE 20.17

Set the options for exchanging information between Outlook and Project Web Access.

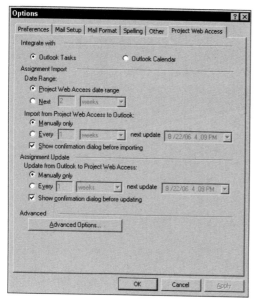

You can choose to import assignments from Project Web Access to Outlook automatically based on a time frame. You can make similar choices about updating Project Web Access with information that you record in Outlook. When you click the Advanced Options button, you can set your Project Web Access URL, as you saw in the preceding section; you also can determine Project Web Access's behavior in Outlook for creating reminders.

Importing Project Web Access assignments into Outlook

While working in Outlook, you can launch Project Web Access and view your Home page. In Outlook, choose Tools ➪ Project Web Access ➪ Project Web Access home page.

When you have assignments in Project Web Access and you click the Import New Assignments button on the Project Web Access taskbar in Outlook, you see a window similar to the one shown in Figure 20.18.

Click OK to add your PWA assignments to your Outlook Calendar or your Outlook task list. If you import the assignments to your calendar, they appear on your calendar on the start date of the assignment, but not associated with a particular time. If you import the assignments to the Outlook task list, they appear as dated list items; if you view the task in the Outlook To-Do List, you see both the start and due dates of the assignment (see Figure 20.19).

FIGURE 20.18

This window appears when you import assignment information from PWA to your Outlook Calendar.

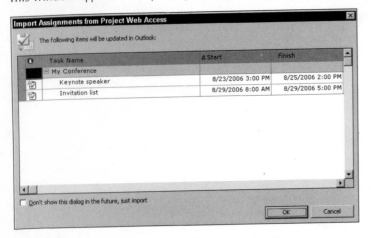

FIGURE 20.19

Project Web Access assignments as they appear on your Outlook To-Do list after you import them.

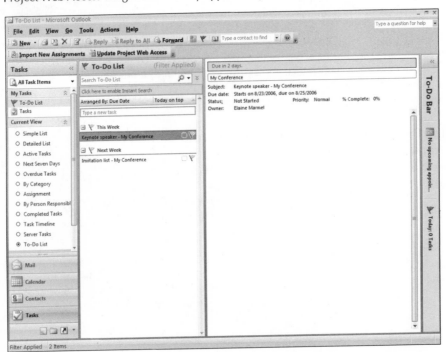

Updating Project Web Access with Outlook information

When you work on a task that you imported to Outlook from Project Web Access, you record your work by double-clicking the task in Outlook to view a window similar to the one shown in Figure 20.20.

As you fill in time worked in the grid, Outlook saves the updates and updates the status of the task, but you need to click the Save to Project Web Access button to transfer your updates to Project Web Access. You can simultaneously submit the updates to the project manager if you leave the And Submit to Project Manager box checked. If you uncheck this box, Outlook transfers the updates to your Project Web Access timesheet; from there, you can submit it to the project manager.

FIGURE 20.20

When you open a task imported from Project Web Access, you see a window like this one.

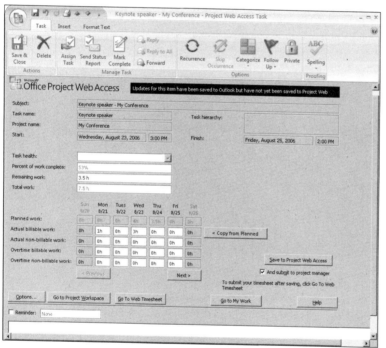

Working with Documents

Using Windows SharePoint Services features, project managers or the Project Server administrator can create a workspace for a project. In this workspace, anyone with proper privileges can store project-related material, such as supporting documents or pictures. This feature comes in handy when you have a budget justification or a feasibility study or some other supporting document that you want to be able to "grab" whenever the need arises.

NOTE   Windows SharePoint Services is a feature-rich product that supports a wide variety of team-oriented functions to facilitate document sharing and team communication. You can post documents in the `Shared Documents` folder, available from the Project Web Access Home page; the `Shared Documents` is a public, company-wide space that anyone in the organization can access.

CROSS-REF   You also can link supporting documents directly to issues, risks, tasks, activity plans, or proposals. See Chapter 19 for details on attaching documents to issues, risks, activity plans, and proposals, and see "Working with your tasks," in this chapter, for details on attaching documents to tasks.

To post documents related to a specific project, the project must have a workspace. By default, in the project's workspace you'll find the `Project Documents` folder; only those with access to the project workspace also have access to the documents in this folder.

To attach and view the documents for a particular project, click the link on your Home page to the project workspace for that project. The Windows SharePoint Services Home page appears in a separate browser instance. Click the <u>View All Site Content</u> link at the top of the Quick Launch pane on the left to view the All Site Content page (see Figure 20.21).

In the Document Libraries section or using the Quick Launch pane that runs down the left side of the screen, click the `Project Documents` folder to view the list of documents that are shared by the team (see Figure 20.22).

FIGURE 20.21

From this page, you have access to Windows SharePoint Services features associated with your project.

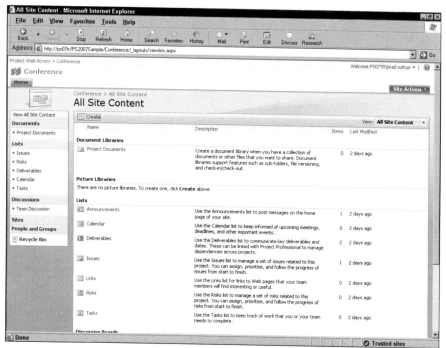

You can add a document to the Project Documents folder. First, click the Upload button. On the Upload Document: Project Documents page that appears (see Figure 20.23), click the Browse button and use the Choose File dialog box that appears to navigate to the document you want to upload. Click OK, and Windows SharePoint Services uploads the document. A window appears that enables you to update the properties of the document you uploaded by supplying a title, owner, and status. You also can link project tasks, risks or issues to the document you upload.

FIGURE 20.22

The contents of the Project Documents library.

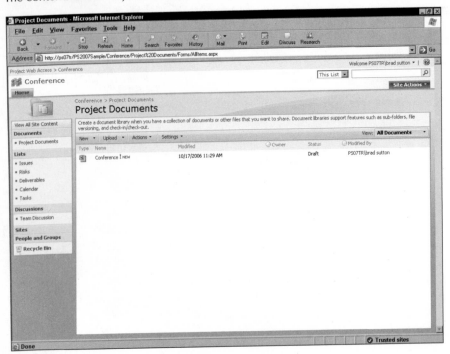

TIP   To upload multiple documents click the <u>Upload Multiple Files</u> link and use the Windows Explorer–like view to select multiple documents.

To view a document, click its link. The program that created the document opens it and you see the contents of the document.

TIP   To return to Project Web Access, click the Project Web Access link in the upper left corner of the Windows SharePoint Services page.

FIGURE 20.23

FIGURE 20.23

Use this page to upload a document.

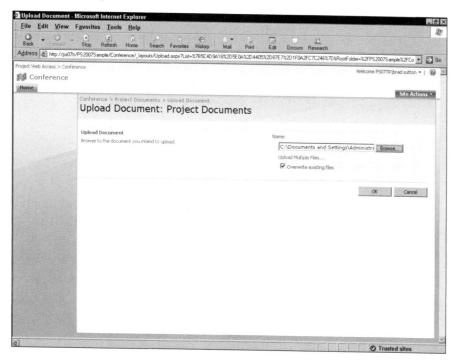

Reporting Status

Project Web Access provides you with status reports that you can send to your project manager.

> **TIP** Don't forget: You can create an issue or a risk if you've run into something unexpected that you want to report; other team members, as well as your project manager, can see and comment on the issue or risk. You can attach the issue to a specific task or to the project in general.

You've already seen how Project Web Access enables you to send work assignment updates from the My Tasks page or the My Timesheet page. But you can also send both solicited and unsolicited status reports to your project manager. Click the Status Reports link in the Quick Launch pane. If your project manager has requested a status report, the Status Reports page looks similar to the one shown in Figure 20.24.

FIGURE 20.24

Status reports requested by your project manager appear on the Status Reports page.

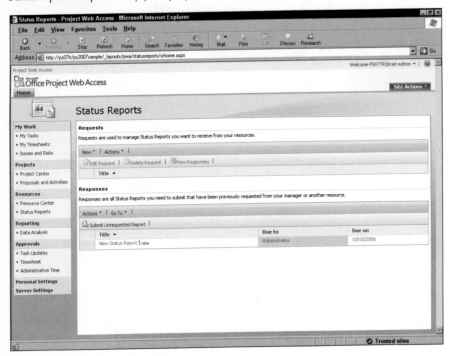

You can click the status report link to open the status report; the Status Report Response page looks like the page shown in Figure 20.25 and displays information that your manager requested. Fill in the report. If you need to include information that doesn't fit in any of the existing sections, you can add a section at the bottom of the report. When you're ready to submit the report, click the Send button at the bottom of the page.

If the project manager didn't request a status report but you want to submit one, click the Submit Unrequested Report button on the Status Reports page; Project Web Access displays the Unrequested Status Report page, which strongly resembles a requested status report except that you select the report recipients and you define the report sections. You can use an unsolicited status report as a simple way to communicate with other members of your team.

FIGURE 20.25

A typical status report page.

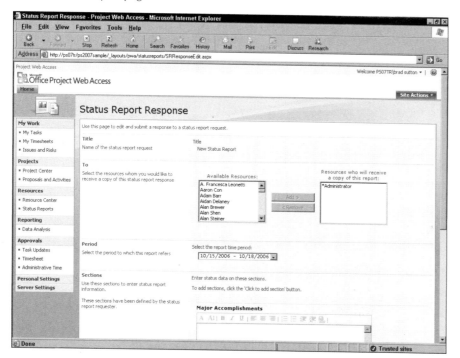

Summary

In this chapter, you read about how the day-to-day user interacts with Project Server using Project Web Access. The user can view and update tasks, fill in timesheets, provide status reports, and create documents. The user can synchronize Outlook with Project Web Access and exchange information seamlessly between the two programs.

In Chapter 21, you see how executives use Project Web Access.

Chapter 21

Project Server and the Executive

Executives use Project Web Access to evaluate the portfolio of work that is happening across the organization. They make use of the Project and Resource Centers to gain high-level views of the work and drill down to get details. Using analysis tools, executives can identify trends in schedule, resource, and cost information and proactively address problem areas. In this chapter, you review the areas of Project Web Access that are of interest to an executive.

Reviewing Your Portfolio

You open Project Web Access the same way other users open it; use Internet Explorer and navigate to the IP address supplied by your Project Server administrator. If your organization uses Forms authentication, you see a logon page where you provide a username and password and then Project Web Access displays your Home page. If your organization uses Windows authentication, you see your Home page immediately (see Figure 21.1). You navigate in Project Web Access using the Quick Launch pane that appears down the left side of the screen, and you can control and customize the information that appears in the pane to the right of the Quick Launch pane using the techniques described in Chapter 20.

FIGURE 21.1

The Project Web Access Home page.

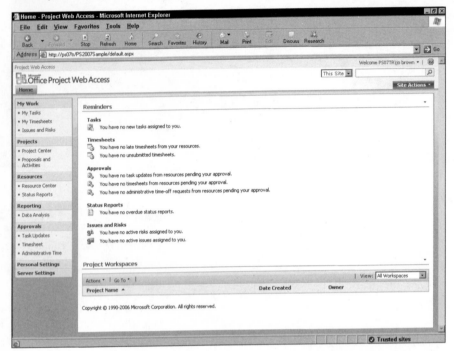

When you click the Project Center link in the Quick Launch pane, you see the Project Center (see Figure 21.2). The Project Center provides a high-level picture of all the projects that you have security permissions to view. Your organization can create custom views for the Project Center, each providing you with different kinds of detail. Use the View list box to see the views that are available to you.

CROSS-REF You can use activity plans or proposals in Project Web Access to keep track of things that may turn into projects in the future. If you create either activity plans or proposals, the items in the list can be converted into a project in Project Professional. For more information on activity plans and proposals in Project Web Access, see Chapter 19.

FIGURE 21.2

In the Project Center, you see projects for which you have security permissions to view, and you can switch views to see information in different ways.

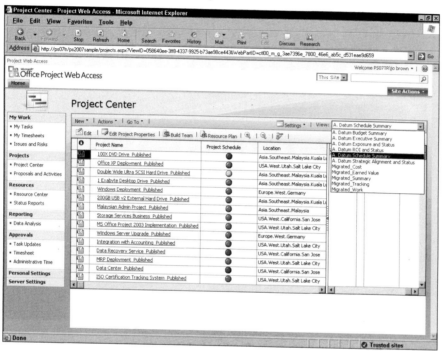

Each view of the Project Center shows you both a table and a Gantt Chart view. You can drag the double-line divider to view more of the table and less of the Gantt Chart or vice versa (see Figure 21.3); as you pause the mouse pointer over the vertical double line that divides the table from the chart portion of the view, the mouse pointer shape changes.

You can click the Settings button next to the View list to display menu options that enable you to sort, filter, and group information in any view; you also can choose the Search command from the Settings menu to look for information. You also can use the options on the Go To menu to view the issues, risks, documents, and deliverables associated with any project.

FIGURE 21.3

You can display more or less of the table in each view.

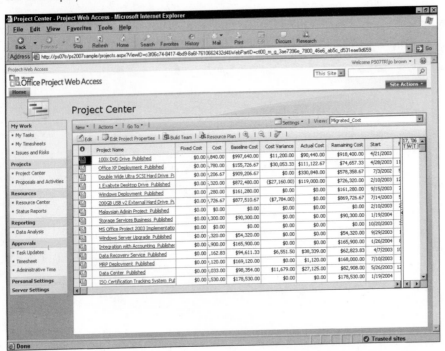

The information displayed in both the table and the Gantt Chart portion of each view differs, helping to provide you with a different perspective while analyzing your business. To give you a taste of the kinds of things you can do with views in Project Web Access, the A. Datum Executive Summary view in the sample Project Server database for A. Datum Corporation has been customized to include color indicators that help a viewer determine, at a glance, projects that pose potential problems (don't you love that alliteration?). As you move the mouse pointer over an indicator, you see a tip that describes the meaning of that indicator (see Figure 21.4).

FIGURE 21.4

The red indicator in the Project Schedule column of this view identifies a project that exceeds its schedule by more than five days; the same red indicator in the Project Budget column identifies a project that exceeds its budget by more than 20%.

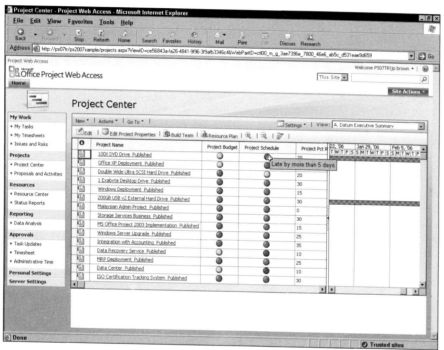

You can drill down in any project and use additional views to see different kinds of detail. In Figure 21.5, I drilled down in the Data Recover Service project in the sample database because the project is slightly over budget and running behind schedule, and I wanted to try to determine why. After the project appeared on-screen, I selected the A. Datum Project Detail view. Other views in the View list box provide different kinds of detail for the selected project.

FIGURE 21.5

Drill down in a project to view details.

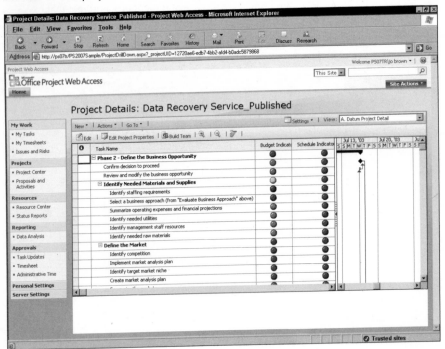

After viewing the project, I noticed that the first task in the project, "confirm decision to proceed," has a red indicator in the Schedule Indicator column, indicating that the task is behind schedule. Since the Gantt portion of the view indicates that the first task is on the critical path, that's not a good sign.

Identifying Trends and Potential Problems

NOTE   To use the analysis tools described in this chapter, the Project Server administrator must build an OLAP (Online Analytical Processing) cube. Periodically, the cube must be rebuilt to keep the information that is being analyzed and modeled up to date. If you get an error message when trying to use the Portfolio Analyzer or you suspect that the information that you're seeing is out of date, contact your Project Server administrator, who can set up cube building in such a way that the cube should never really be out of date.

CROSS-REF   Chapter 18 describes how to build the OLAP cube and give rights to use it.

From the Data Analysis page, executives can analyze project data to identify trends and potential problem areas.

Click the Data Analysis link in the Quick Launch pane to display the Data Analysis page (see Figure 21.6). On the Data Analysis page you find both the table and chart portions of a PivotTable. And, as with the Project Center, you can work with different views on the Data Analysis page.

FIGURE 21.6

The Data Analysis page.

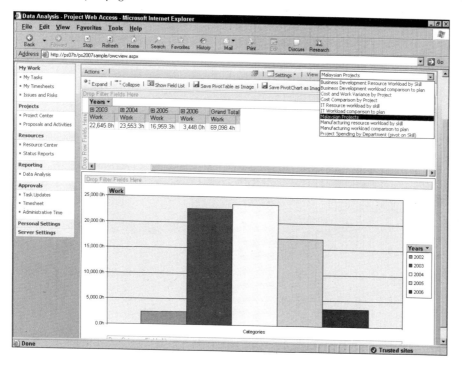

> **TIP** You can save the chart, the PivotTable, or both as a `.gif` file using the buttons that appear toward the top of the Data Analysis page.

The Malaysian Projects view in the sample database shows Work over a four-year period. I can use the Field List, shown in Figure 21.7, to add fields to the view to obtain more information. You display the Field List by clicking the Show Field List button above the PivotTable.

FIGURE 21.7

Use the PivotTable Field List to add or reorganize chart information.

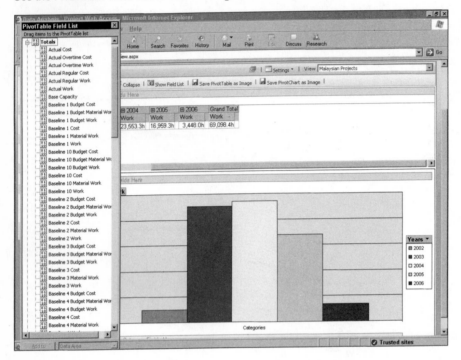

For example, I dragged Actual Work and Remaining Work onto the PivotTable, placing each of them alongside Work to create the graph shown in Figure 21.8. I then opted to use the Years dropdown list in the PivotTable to limit the years on the chart.

You can draw attention to anything you find using the collaboration tools that are provided by Windows SharePoint Services (WSS). You can create and monitor an issue or a risk. You also can respond to issues and risks. And you can attach documents to projects, tasks, or to-do lists.

CROSS-REF   See Chapter 20 for more information on issues and risks as well as more information on document sharing.

FIGURE 21.8

Add fields to change the information that appears on the chart.

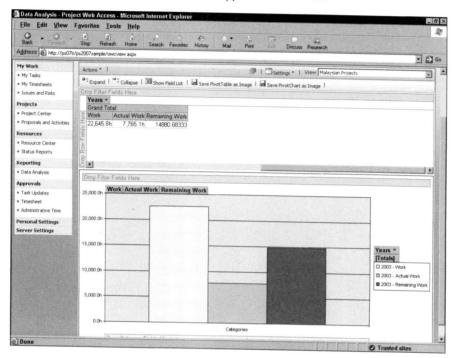

Summary

In this chapter, you've seen how executives can use Project Web Access to evaluate the portfolio of work that is happening across the organization. They can use the Project Center to view work at a high level and drill down to get details. Using the Data Analysis page, executives can evaluate resource utilization and determine whether the organization has enough resources available to take on a particular project.

Part VI

Advanced Microsoft Project

Chapter 22

Customizing Microsoft Project

IN THIS CHAPTER

Using custom fields

Customizing the interface

You can customize the Project working environment in several ways. For example, you can use custom fields to store and manipulate custom data in a project file. And you can change the way that various elements appear on-screen and how you use Project's tools and commands. Suppose that you use a particular command for sharing resources all the time. You can perform that action quickly if you can access the command from a tool on the standard toolbar. Or, maybe you never use the Task Note tool and prefer to get it off the toolbar and place its command on a menu. Perhaps none of Project's built-in views or tables contains quite the combination of information that you use most often.

Microsoft Project enables you to customize most of its elements. This chapter shows you how to create and use custom fields, make changes to the behavior of the Project interface, and create and modify toolbars and menus to make Project work the way that's best for you.

CROSS-REF This chapter focuses on customizing Project. See Chapter 19 for information about customizing Project Server.

Using Custom Fields

In Chapter 7, you read about outline codes, which are custom fields in Project. Starting in Project 2000, custom fields enable you to create pick lists to use to ensure accurate data entry, create formulas to perform calculations on custom data, and insert icons that indicate graphically that a field contains custom data.

> **TIP**   Consider customizing fields to help create standardization within your organization. If all projects in your organization use the same standards, you avoid problems when you merge or consolidate projects or move them into Project Server.

Customizing data entry

Suppose that your boss wants your best guess about whether you'll keep to the schedule on a task-by-task basis. You can set up a custom field and provide the information on any sheet view of Project. I show you this process in two phases:

- Create a custom field
- Use the custom field

Creating a custom field

In this section, I show you how to create a custom field, which you do by following these steps:

1. Choose Tools ➪ Customize ➪ Fields. Project displays the Custom Fields dialog box (see Figure 22.1).

FIGURE 22.1

Select a custom field type.

698

2. Select either Task or Resource. Then, open the Type list box and choose the type of field that you want to customize. The type that you choose determines the values that you can include in the pick list. Choose Text to include only alphanumeric characters in the pick list. If you choose Date, Start, or Finish, you must include date-formatted numbers in the pick list. If you choose Number or Cost, you can include only numbers in the pick list. If you choose Flag, you can include only Yes or No in the Value List dialog box. For this example, I chose Text because I want to set up a value list that contains Yes, No, and Maybe.

3. To provide a meaningful name for the code or custom field, click the Rename button and type the new name. You can't use any name that Project is already using. (In this example, I named the field Best Guess.) Then, click OK to redisplay the Customize Fields dialog box.

4. Click the Lookup button to display the Edit Lookup Table for Field Name dialog box (see Figure 22.2).

FIGURE 22.2

Use this dialog box to define the values that you want Project to display in the pick list during data entry.

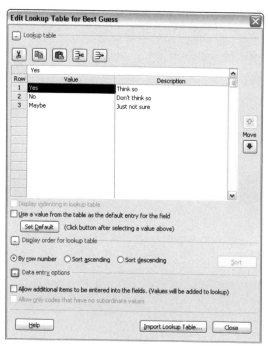

5. In the Value column, type the first value that you want to appear in the list. The values that Project lets you include in the value list depend on the field type that you chose in Step 2. If you chose Text, you can include only combinations of letters and numbers. If you chose Date, Start, or Finish, you must include date-formatted entries. If you chose Number or Cost, you can include only numbers in the value list. If you chose Flag, you can include only Yes or No in the value list.

> **NOTE**   If you chose Flag, you need to substitute Yes or No for standard flag choices, such as True and False or On and Off.

6. (Optional) In the Description column, provide a description of the value.

7. Repeat Steps 5 and 6 for each list value that you want to define.

8. You can set a default value to appear as the entry for the field. Click the value in the list that you want selected by default and click the Set Default button. Project checks the Use a Value from the List as the Default Entry for the Field check box and displays the selected value and its description in blue, bold text.

9. You can specify the order for the value list in the Display Order for Lookup Table section; click the plus sign (+), which changes to a minus sign (–) to display sort options.

10. In the Data Entry options panel of the dialog box, you can permit the user to enter values other than those in the list and add those values to the value list.

> **NOTE**   Although you can allow users to enter information not stored in the value list, using that information can be troublesome. If users misspell entries or don't use entries consistently, you won't be able to filter or group effectively.

11. Click Close to save the value list and redisplay the Customize Fields dialog box.

12. Click OK to redisplay your project.

Using a custom field for data entry

Now that you've created a custom field, let's walk through the process of using it for data entry.

To use the custom field, you need to display it as a column in a sheet view. If you defined a task field, you can use any task sheet view; if you defined a resource field, use any resource sheet view.

To display the custom field in a column on a sheet view, right-click the title of the column that you want to appear to the right of the custom field. Project selects the column and displays a shortcut menu from which you can choose Insert Column. In the Column Definition dialog box (see Figure 22.3), open the Field Name list box and select the custom field that you defined, using the name that you supplied when you defined the field. Optionally, change the rest of the information in the dialog box and click OK. The custom field appears on-screen.

FIGURE 22.3

Select the custom field that you created.

When you click in the field, a list box arrow appears. When you open the list box, the value list that you established appears (see Figure 22.4). Select values from the list, or simply type them. In my example, if you try to enter a value that doesn't exist in the list, Project displays an error message instructing you to use a value from the list.

FIGURE 22.4

As you fill in the field, select from the pick list.

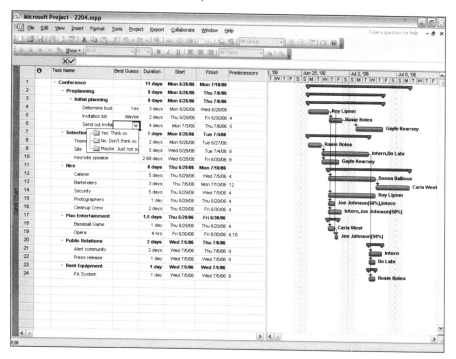

CAUTION You can't use custom fields to create value lists for regular Project fields. For example, suppose that you've decided that you don't want to use all 1,000 of Project's priorities. In fact, you want your people to use only five possible priorities: 100, 200, 300, 400, and 500 (100 being the lowest priority and 500 being the highest priority). You can create a Number custom field (called Priority Lvl, for example) that allows the entry of only these five values in a sheet view. However, users can open the Task Information dialog box and assign any priority value in the Priority field — and Project permits the assignment. The custom field Priority Lvl is not substituting for the actual field Priority, and users can circumvent the custom value list.

Using formulas in custom fields

Suppose that your manager tells you that part of your evaluation in project management depends on the accuracy of your cost estimates. Under these circumstances, you may want to monitor the tasks for which cost exceeds baseline cost. You can set up a custom field to help you easily identify those tasks. Follow these steps to do so:

1. Choose Tools ⇨ Customize ⇨ Fields. Project displays the Custom Fields dialog box, shown previously in Figure 22.1.

2. Select either Task or Resource and then open the Type list box and choose the type of field that you want to customize. For this example, I choose Task and Cost because I want to compare task cost values.

TIP The type of field that you select from the Type list matters in a different way when you're creating a formula instead of a value list. If you select the wrong type when creating a value list, you can't set up the appropriate values for the list. However, if you select a type that doesn't match what you're trying to calculate in a formula, Project lets you create the formula but displays ERROR in the custom field column on the sheet. For example, suppose that you want to calculate a cost and you select Date from the Type list. Project still permits you to create the formula, but because the formula doesn't make sense, you see the message ERROR when you display the custom field column.

3. To provide a meaningful name for the field, click the Rename button and type the new name. You can't use any name that Project is already using; in the example, I named the field Difference. Then, click OK to redisplay the Customize Fields dialog box.

4. Click the Formula button to display the Formula for dialog box. Figure 22.5 shows the formula that I set up for this example.

5. Create a formula in the text box by selecting fields or functions. To select a field, click the Field button; Project displays a list of field categories. Select the appropriate field category, and Project displays a list of the available fields (see Figure 22.6). To select a function, follow the same process by clicking the Function button.

FIGURE 22.5

This dialog box lets you define the values that you want Project to display in the pick list during data entry.

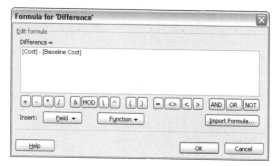

FIGURE 22.6

Select a field or a function to include in the formula.

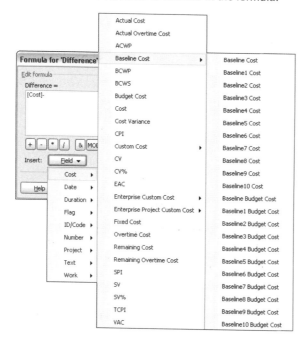

CROSS-REF In Appendix C, you find three tables. Table C-1 contains a list of all available Task fields, and Table C-2 contains the same information for Resource fields. Table C-3 lists the functions that you can include in a formula as well as a description of each function's purpose.

6. To make a calculation, use the operators that appear above the Field and Function buttons.

TIP If you've created this formula in another project, you can import the formula from the Global template (assuming that you saved the formula in the Global template), or you can open the project that contains the formula before you create the formula in the new project. When you click the Import Formula button, Project displays a list of available templates or open Project files. Select the appropriate location, field type, and field name. Then click OK.

7. In the Formula for dialog box, click OK. Project warns you that it will discard any information that was previously stored in the custom field and replace the information with the calculated values based on the formula.

8. In the Customize Fields box, click OK to save the formula and redisplay the Customize Fields dialog box.

9. (Optional) Assign the formula to summary rows.

If you click OK at this point, Project calculates a value for the formula. You can see the value if you display the column for the custom field, as I did in Figure 22.7. Based on the formula that I created, positive values represent tasks where Actual Cost exceeded BCWP (budgeted cost of work performed) — and technically, my Difference column is nothing more than the Variance column of the Cost table.

Suppose that you don't want to eyeball figures to find the problem tasks. You can insert icons to represent positive and negative values (and make the job of identifying the problem tasks much easier) by following these steps:

1. In the Custom Fields dialog box, highlight the custom field that you created and click the Graphical Indicators button (refer back to Figure 22.1). Project displays the Graphical Indicators dialog box (see Figure 22.8).

FIGURE 22.7

When you display the column for a custom field containing a formula, you see the result of the formula.

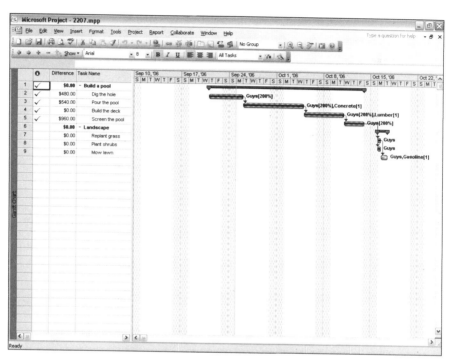

2. Choose the type of row to which you want to assign an indicator: Nonsummary, Summary, or Project summary.

3. In the Test For section, set up the test that Project should use. In each column, you can choose from lists. In the Value(s) column, you can compare the formula result to the value of another field or to a numeric value. In my example, if the result of the formula is greater than 0, I want to see a red flag, because the actual cost of the task exceeds the baseline cost. If, however, the actual cost is less than or equal to the baseline cost, things are fine, so I want to see a happy face (you can find other indicator choices in the Image list).

FIGURE 22.8

Set up the test that Project should perform on the formula's result and the indicator to display, based on the test results.

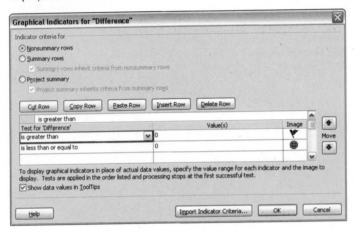

If you've set up graphical indicators in another project, you can import the criteria from either the Global template (assuming that you saved the formula in the Global template) or from another open project. When you click the Import Indicator Criteria button, Project displays a list of available templates or open Project files. Select the appropriate location, field type, and field name. Then click OK.

4. To see the mathematical results of the formula in a ToolTip when you point the mouse at the indicator, select the Show Data Values in ToolTips check box.

5. Click OK to redisplay the Customize Fields dialog box.

6. Click OK again to redisplay your project.

If necessary, display the column for the custom field. Right-click the column that you want to appear to the right of the custom field column and choose Insert Column. Then, select the custom field. When Project displays the column, it will contain an indicator (see Figure 22.9). If you selected the Show Data Values in ToolTips check box, you can point the mouse at an indicator to see the results of the formula. (The ToolTip hides the icon on-screen; otherwise, I would show you the ToolTip.)

FIGURE 22.9

The custom field column contains an indicator.

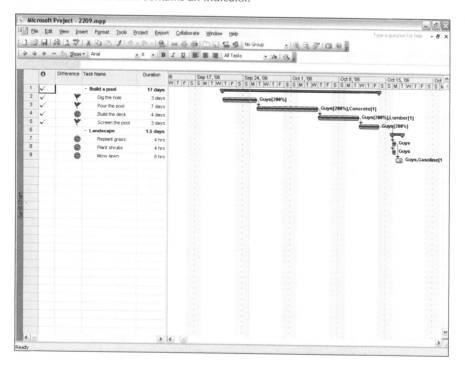

Modifying the Interface

In addition to using custom fields to customize data entry and make calculations, you can customize Project's interface. For example, you can control the number of times you can click the Undo button before Project stops undoing your actions or the number of icons that appear in the Windows taskbar when you open multiple projects. Use Project's Organizer to move tables and views among project files. And you can modify toolbars and customize menus to make them work the way that you work.

Setting levels of Undo

Project allows you to undo actions you take while working in a Project file. Prior to Project 2007, you could undo only the last action you took. Starting in Project 2007, you can set the number of times you can click Undo anywhere between 1 and 99.

NEW FEATURE   Starting in Project 2007, you can undo as many as the last 99 actions you took.

By default, Project lets you undo your last 20 actions, but you can change that number. Choose Tools ➪ Options and click the General tab. Then, change the number in the Undo levels box (see Figure 22.10).

Windows taskbar icons

In Project 98 and earlier versions of Project, you saw only one icon on the Windows taskbar while Project was open — regardless of the number of Project files that you opened. Starting in Project 2000, by default, you see an icon on the Windows taskbar for every open Project file (see Figure 22.11).

FIGURE 22.10

Use this field to control the number of times the Undo button will work.

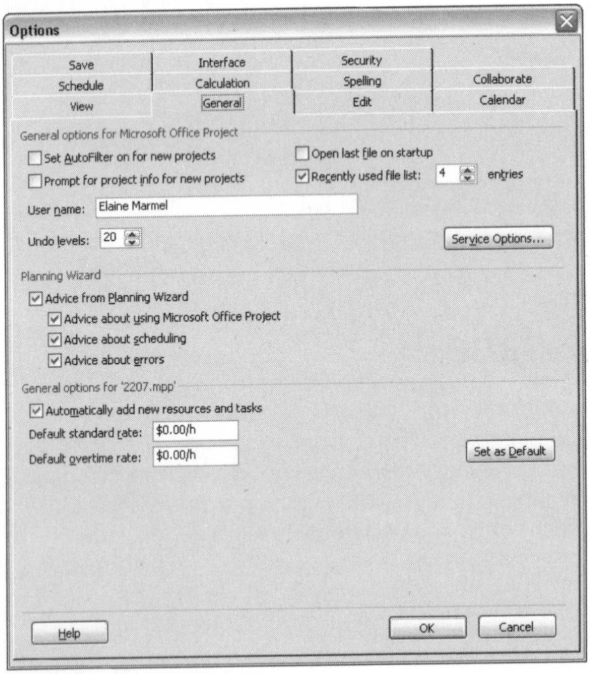

FIGURE 22.11

By default, you see multiple icons for Project on the Windows taskbar when you open multiple projects.

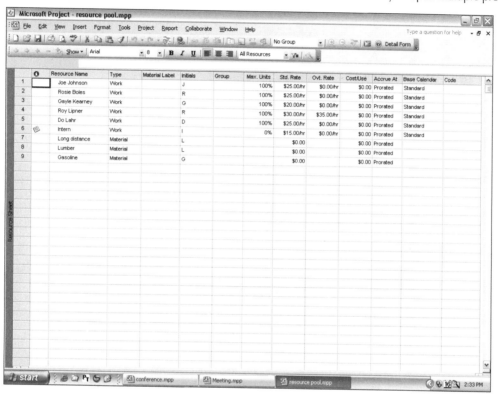

Depending on the number of open files, you may not necessarily be able to identify the file from the icon on the Windows taskbar, but you can see a few letters of the filename on the icon. In addition, if you point the mouse at the icon, you see a ToolTip that shows the entire path and filename.

Suppose that you belong to the school of users who don't *want* an icon on the Windows taskbar for each open file; you believe that makes working harder, not easier. You can reinstate the behavior of Project 98 and earlier versions by deselecting the Windows in Taskbar check box on the View tab of the Options dialog box (see Figure 22.12).

FIGURE 22.12

To reintroduce the behavior of Project 98 and earlier versions, deselect the Windows in Taskbar check box.

Remove the check from this box.

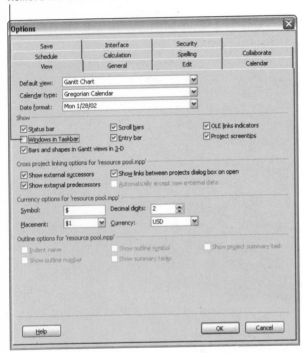

NOTE Regardless of the behavior that you choose in the Options dialog box, all open Project files appear at the bottom of the Window menu. You can switch among Project files by using the Windows menu in Project or the Windows taskbar.

Saving Project files

Using the Save tab of the Options dialog box (see Figure 22.13), you can set the following defaults:

■ By opening the Save Microsoft Office Project Files As list box, you can specify the default file format for each new Project file that you save. For example, you might want to save all Project 2007 files in Project 2000 – 2003 format if you regularly share files with someone who uses one of those versions of Project.

CAUTION If you save files that were created in Project 2007 in the format of Project 2000 – 2003, you may lose information. For example, background cell formatting doesn't exist in any version of Project prior to Project 2007. If you apply background formatting to cells in a file and then save the file in Project 2000 – 2003 format, you'll lose the formatting.

FIGURE 22.13

Project has several features that are associated with saving files.

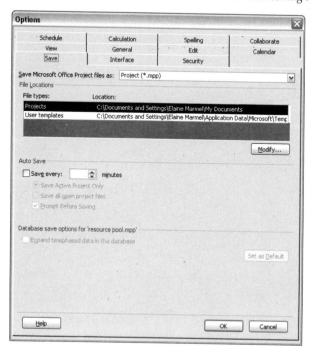

NOTE   By default, the projects you save use the Project 2007 format, which is not the same format as any earlier version of Project. Project 2003, Project 2002, and Project 2000 share one file format, and you can no longer save a file in Project 98 format.

- You can set a default file location to save all files and user templates. By setting these locations, you don't need to navigate to the correct folder each time that you want to save a new file or template.

- Use the Auto Save feature to save project files on a regular basis. The Auto Save feature is particularly valuable to people who tend to work extensively, forget to save regularly, and become victims of power failures or server crashes. If you use Auto Save, you can open your file as of the last automatic save.

- You can choose to expand timephased data in a database; this setting only applies when you save Project data to a database such as SQL or Access. If you check this box, your SQL programmer will be able to create a report directly from the database (without going through Project) that analyzes timephased data. If you deselect this box (the default), Project stores timephased data in binary format, which you can't read (unless you're a computer guru or a VB programmer), but using binary format for this data speeds Project's reading and writing to the database.

Using the Organizer

Project uses the Organizer to help you share views, tables, forms, reports, and more among projects. To display the Organizer box shown in Figure 22.14, choose Tools ➪ Organizer. You also can .open the Organizer box from the More Views box shown in Figure 22.15.

FIGURE 22.14

All views in the Global template (Global.mpt) file are available to every file that is based on the Global.mpt file.

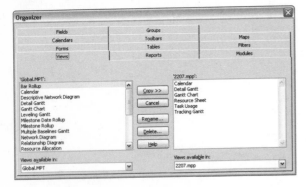

FIGURE 22.15

You can display the Organizer by clicking the Organizer button in the More Views dialog box.

Use the various tabs in the Organizer dialog box to copy elements from the Global template (Global.mpt) to the current project. You also can copy elements from the current project to the Global template or simply between projects. First, open the Project file that contains the element you want to copy and the Project file into which you want to copy the information. Then, in the Organizer box, use the list boxes at the bottom of each tab to select the file containing the information and the file that should receive the information.

> **NOTE** When you copy an element to the Global template, that element becomes available to all files that were created with your copy of Project.

Making changes to toolbars

Toolbars are to Windows software what remote controls are to television: effortless, high-tech ways to take action. Toolbars are easy to use and always right at hand. However, you and Microsoft may not agree on which tools you use most often.

You can easily modify the arrangement of tools in Project. You can add or remove tools from a toolbar, change the function of a tool, create your own set of tools, or even edit the look of tools.

> **NOTE** You can make changes to your Project environment effective for your copy of Project alone, for those in a group, or across your company. Project saves your changes to the Global.mpt file and opens new projects based on this Global template file by default. To share changes, share the Global.mpt; otherwise, your changes affect only your copy of Project.

Combining or separating toolbars

Throughout this book, you've seen the Standard toolbar on a separate row from the Formatting toolbar — much as they appeared in Project 98 and earlier versions. If screen real estate is vital to you, consider placing the toolbars on the same row, as they appear in Figure 22.16. When you use this feature, Project initially displays the tools that Microsoft thinks users use most often. If you need a tool that you don't see, click the Toolbar Options button to display a hidden palette of additional available buttons. After you select a tool from the hidden palette, that tool appears on the toolbar, replacing the least-used tool, if necessary. As you work, the toolbars become personalized to your work habits, displaying the tools that you use most often.

FIGURE 22.16

You can make the Standard and Formatting toolbars share a row on-screen and select a button that you don't see initially by opening the hidden palette.

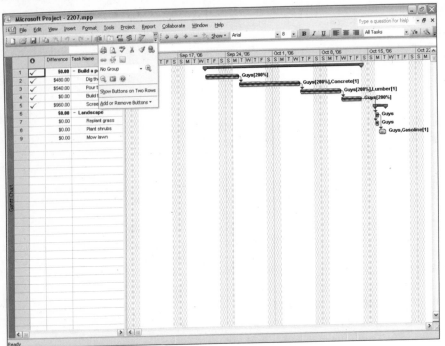

In a similar fashion, you can personalize the menus in Project to display the commands that you use most frequently. When you enable this behavior and open a menu, you see a limited set of commands. At the bottom of the menu, you see the expand arrows pointing down (see Figure 22.17). When you click the expand arrows, the rest of the commands on the menu appear. The gray bar that runs down the left side of the menu is lighter for hidden commands than for the more frequently used commands (see Figure 22.18). As with the tools that are on the toolbars, if you select a hidden command, it becomes a frequently used command and appears on the abbreviated menu the next time that you open the menu.

FIGURE 22.17

Initially, only some commands appear on the menu.

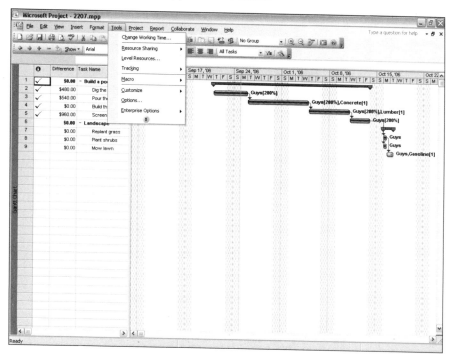

You control this toolbar and menu behavior by using the first three check boxes on the Options tab of the Customize dialog box, as shown in Figure 22.19.

TIP By checking the Show Full Menus After a Short Delay check box, you tell Project to automatically show all commands on the menu after a short delay so that you don't have to click the Expand arrows.

FIGURE 22.18

Click the expand arrows to display the entire menu.

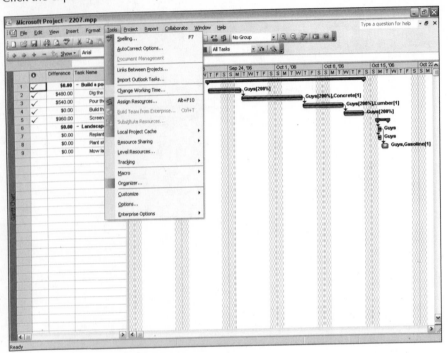

FIGURE 22.19

Use the Personalized Menus and Toolbars section to control the behavior of Project's menus and toolbars.

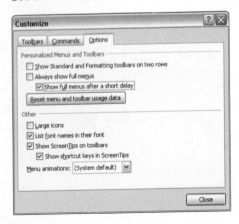

Adding and deleting tools from a toolbar

Although toolbars include many commonly used functions, they aren't all-inclusive. For example, the Formatting toolbar includes commands to change the font and font size; apply bold, italic, and underline effects; and align tasks. But it doesn't include any tools to add background formatting to cells. If you apply background formatting often, you may want to add a button to the Formatting toolbar to open the Text Styles dialog box so that you can quickly and easily apply background formatting to cells.

To add tools to any toolbar, locate the tool in the appropriate category and then drag it onto the toolbar where you want it to appear. Follow these steps to add a tool to a toolbar:

1. Choose View ⇨ Toolbars ⇨ Customize to open the Customize dialog box and click the Toolbars tab (see Figure 22.20).

FIGURE 22.20

The toolbars that have a check mark here are currently displayed on-screen.

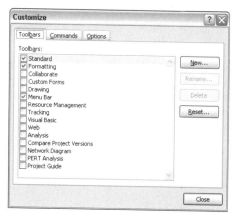

2. Select the check box for the toolbar on which you want to place the tool so that Project displays that toolbar. For example, if you want to add the Paste as Hyperlink button to the Web toolbar, make sure that you display the Web toolbar.

3. Click the Commands tab (see Figure 22.21).

4. Click the category of command that contains the tool that you want to add to a toolbar. For example, the Text Styles tool appears in the Format category.

> **TIP** If you don't know the category to which a tool command belongs, use the scroll bar in the Categories list and select All Commands at the bottom of the list. The Commands list then displays every available command in predominantly alphabetical order.

FIGURE 22.21

These categories of commands contain all the possible tools that are built into Project.

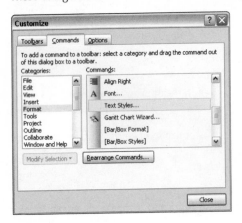

5. Click the item in the Commands list, drag it from the dialog box onto your screen, and place it anywhere on the toolbar of your choice.

You also can easily remove a tool from a toolbar. With the Customize dialog box open, display the toolbar that contains the tool that you want to remove and drag the tool off the toolbar.

NOTE To restore a toolbar's original settings, open the Customize dialog box, select the Toolbars tab, click the toolbar name in the list of toolbars, and click Reset. Project restores the default tools.

Creating custom toolbars

Rather than modify some of Project's toolbars, you may prefer to create a custom toolbar that contains all the tools that you use most often. You create custom toolbars from the Customize dialog box by following these steps:

1. Display the Toolbars tab of the Customize dialog box.
2. Click the New button. The New Toolbar dialog box appears (see Figure 22.22).

FIGURE 22.22

Name your toolbar anything you like—perhaps after your spouse, your pet, or your favorite movie star.

3. Type a toolbar name and click OK. A small toolbar, devoid of tools at the moment, appears. You can drag this floating toolbar to any location on the screen that's convenient for you.

4. Click the Commands tab.

5. Click tools in any category and drag them onto the new toolbar. Figure 22.23 shows the new toolbar that I created.

FIGURE 22.23

Place tools in any order that you like. To move a tool, drag it to its new position on the toolbar.

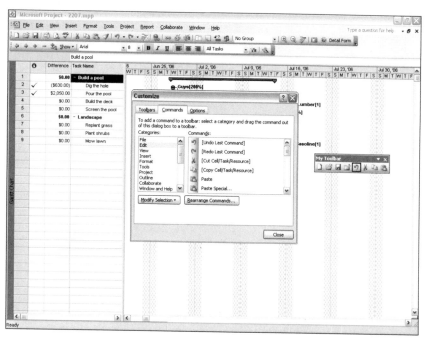

6. You can add dividers (thin gray lines) to separate groups of tools on your new toolbar. Select the tool that you want to place to the right of the divider and then click the Modify Selection button on the Commands tab. The menu shown in Figure 22.24 appears.

7. Select the Begin a Group command from this menu to insert a divider in your toolbar (see Figure 22.25).

FIGURE 22.24

This menu offers options to work with button images as well as options to modify other toolbar features.

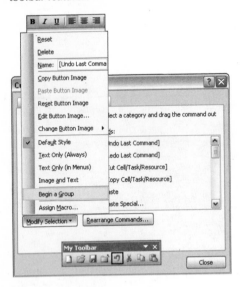

FIGURE 22.25

Place a divider on a toolbar to make logical groupings of tools that perform certain types of functions.

Divider

To delete a divider, select the tool to the divider's right and, using the Modify Selection pop-up menu, select Begin a Group again to deselect that command.

Changing and editing button images

Don't like the little pictures that Microsoft assigned to its tools? No image appears for the tool you added to your toolbar? Feeling creative? Project enables you to select from a whole set of other button designs, from smiling faces to musical notes, or to edit a button image with picture and color tools.

If anyone else uses your copy of Project, be cautious about changing tool images. Someone who is accustomed to Project's standard tool images may press a button and, unaware of its true function, not be able to function with your copy of Project.

To change the images that appear on tools, follow these steps:

1. Choose Views ⇨ Toolbars ⇨ Customize to open the Customize dialog box.

2. Click the Commands tab.

3. Click a tool on any toolbar that you have displayed. (To display a toolbar, select it on the Toolbars tab of this dialog box.)

4. Click the Modify Selection button and select Change Button Image. The pop-up palette of images appears (see Figure 22.26).

FIGURE 22.26

From an hourglass to an eight ball, these images are both clever and descriptive.

5. Click an image that you want to use.

NOTE To return an image to its original setting, choose Modify Selection ⇨ Reset Button Image.

6. Click Close to close the Customize dialog box after you finish.

TIP ToolTips still work with modified buttons and are a great help in remembering what function a button performs. Just pause your mouse pointer on any tool and its original name appears.

Rather than replace the button image with a predefined picture, you can edit the existing picture by modifying the pattern and colors on it. For example, if two tools seem similar to you, you can differentiate them by applying a bright-red color to either one. Button images comprise many tiny squares called *pixels*. By coloring in the pixels, you can form an image. You can use a color palette and the individual pixels to modify button images or even draw an entirely new image.

To edit a button image, follow these steps, starting from the Customize dialog box Commands tab:

1. Click a tool on any displayed toolbar and then click Modify Selection.

2. Select the Edit Button Image command to open the Button Editor dialog box (see Figure 22.27).

FIGURE 22.27

The small Preview window helps you see how changes to individual picture pixels will appear on the button image.

3. Try the following techniques:

   ■ To make changes to an image, click a color block in the Colors palette and then click an individual pixel.

   ■ To remove color from a pixel, click the Erase block in the Colors palette and then click the pixel.

> **TIP** To color in or erase a large area of pixels, click a color in the palette or the Erase block, click a pixel, and then drag your cursor in any direction to color or erase multiple pixels in one motion. Release your cursor to stop painting or erasing the pixels.

   ■ To see more of a large button that doesn't fit in the Picture box, use the Move arrows to move up and down or from side to side to display the image's edges.

4. Click OK to save your changes and to return to the Customize dialog box. Click Close to return to your Project screen.

Customizing project menus

Toolbars aren't the only way to get things done in Project, and toolbars aren't the only elements in Project that you can customize. You also can create new menus and modify existing menus to your heart's content. For example, you can add a command to the File menu that changes the current view to the Network Diagram view and prints a report. You can add these functions because menu commands are like *macros* in that recorded series of keystrokes or programming commands.

> **NOTE** Macros are really a form of computer program. Visual Basic is the macro-programming language that you use in Microsoft products. In a macro, you save a string of commands that instruct the software to perform one or more actions. Project provides an easy method for selecting commands to associate with a macro and for saving the macro as a custom menu command. See Chapter 23 for more on macros.

When you select a menu command, you are actually running a macro, telling Project to repeat the sequence of events that copies a selected piece of text, causes a dialog box to appear, and so on.

You can use your own macros and Project's built-in commands to customize Project by building new menus and changing the function of existing commands. Or, you can delete menus or commands on menus that you don't need.

Adding menus

To add a new menu to your Project menu bar, you follow a process that is similar to that used to add a new toolbar. First, you drag a new, blank menu to the menu bar, then you assign it a name, and finally you drag commands onto it.

> **NOTE** As with toolbars, Project adds new menus to your Global template file, the default file on which all project files are based. Therefore, changes that you make to menus or the menu bar are, in effect, changes for all files that you create with this copy of Project.

Follow these steps to add a new menu to Project:

1. Choose View ➪ Toolbars ➪ Customize to open the Customize dialog box.
2. Make sure that the menu bar is showing on your screen. If it's not, click the menu bar item on the Toolbars tab of the Customize dialog box.
3. Click the Commands tab.
4. Scroll to the bottom of the list of Categories and click the New Menu category. The single selection, New Menu, appears in the list of commands (see Figure 22.28).

FIGURE 22.28

The New Menu category has only one command in it.

5. Click the New Menu item in the Commands list and drag it up to the menu bar. When the dark vertical line of your mouse pointer appears where you want to place the new menu, release the mouse button. Project places the New Menu on the menu bar.

6. Select the New Menu and then click the Modify Selection button. From the pop-up menu, highlight New Menu and type a specific menu name (see Figure 22.29). Then click outside the Modify Selection menu to close it.

7. Select a category of commands that you want to place on the new menu. If you have created a macro and want to place it on the menu, select the All Macros category, which includes standard menu-command macros as well as macros that you've created.

8. Drag an item in the Commands list up to the New Menu on the menu bar. A small, blank box appears under the menu heading.

9. Place the mouse pointer in that blank area and release the mouse button to place the command on the menu.

10. Click Close to close the Customize dialog box.

FIGURE 22.29

The menu name should help you remember the commands that the menu contains.

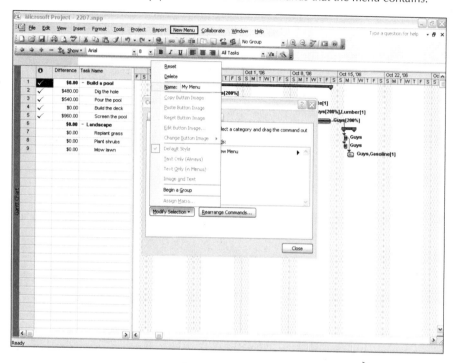

You can repeat Steps 7 through 9 to build the new menu. To divide the menu into groups of commands, you can choose Modify Selection ⇨ Begin a Group to add dividing lines.

Assigning new commands

You may also want to modify the function of an existing menu command. For example, if you create a macro that invokes the Print command and accepts all the Print dialog box defaults for you, you can assign that macro to the Print command. That way, you don't have the extra step of clicking OK to accept print defaults every time you print. As always, be careful about replacing the function of one command with another if other people will be using your copy of Project.

 **TIP**   You can reinstate all the menu defaults by clicking the Toolbars tab in the Customize dialog box, clicking the Menu Bar item, and clicking Reset.

To change the macro that is associated with a command, follow these steps:

1. Display the Customize dialog box (choose View ➪ Toolbars ➪ Customize).

2. Open the menu on which you want to edit a command.

3. Right-click the command that you want to change; the menu shown in Figure 22.30 appears.

FIGURE 22.30

You can use this menu to add a button image next to a menu command.

4. Select the Assign Macro command from this menu to open the Customize Tool dialog box, as shown in Figure 22.31.

5. Click the Command drop-down list and select the command that you want to associate with the menu item.

6. (Optional) Type a description of what this command does.

7. Click OK to return to the Customize dialog box and then click Close to save the new command with the menu item.

FIGURE 22.31

The Command entry in the Customize Tool dialog box is the name of the macro that Project invokes.

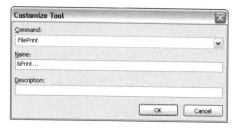

Deleting commands and menus

Is your screen getting cluttered with custom commands and menus? To remove a particular command or a whole menu without resetting all the menu changes that you've made, follow these steps:

1. Open the Customize dialog box.

2. Click a menu name or open the menu and click a particular command.

3. Drag the item off the menu bar, and close the Customize dialog box.

That's all there is to it!

Summary

In this chapter, you found out how to do the following:

- Work with custom fields to create data entry value lists and formulas
- Modify Project's behavior to display only one icon on the Windows taskbar or to display an icon for each open project
- Take advantage of the new features for saving your projects
- Display the Standard and Formatting toolbars on the same row or on separate rows
- Customize the features (toolbars and menus) that you use to get things done

In the next chapter, I discuss details about creating your own macros, which can form the basis for new tools and menus and streamline the repetitive tasks that you perform to create and track a schedule.

Chapter 23

Using Macros to Speed Your Work

Macros are small programs that carry out repetitive tasks that you perform frequently. You may have used macros in a word processing program. Macros work the same way in Project as they do in your word processor.

Don't let the word *program* in the preceding paragraph deter you from getting to know macros. Although you can work with the macro programming code, Project provides an easier way for you to write a macro, which I present in this chapter.

IN THIS CHAPTER

Using macros

Recording macros

Running macros

Using shortcuts to run macros

Using Macros

Macros are most useful when you need to perform any repetitive task. In particular, you can use Project macros to do the following:

- Display or hide frequently used toolbars
- Display frequently used tables
- Display frequently used views
- Switch to a custom view
- Generate standard reports

As you become comfortable using Project, you'll identify the steps that you take over and over again; these tasks are excellent candidates for macros.

Recording Macros

Project stores macros in the Visual Basic for Applications (VBA) programming language. And if you're adept at programming, you can write your macro directly in the VBA programming language. Figure 23.1 shows a sample of the instructions that are stored in a macro in Visual Basic.

Most people prefer to record a macro. When you record a macro, you have Project memorize the steps that you want to take and then store those steps. That is, you do whatever it is you want Project to do. Project then converts those actions into Visual Basic statements and stores the statements in a macro. Later, when you want to take that action again, you run your macro, which I discuss in the next section.

Before you record a macro, you should run through the steps that you want to take. You may even want to write down the steps. That way, you are less likely to make (and record) mistakes.

FIGURE 23.1

A sample set of instructions that are stored in a macro.

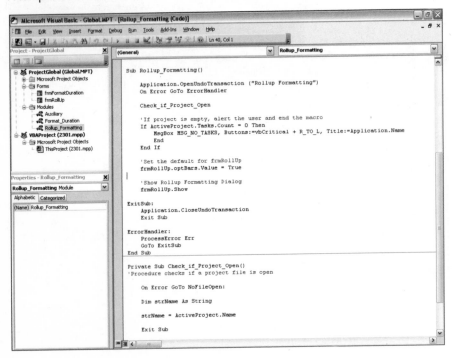

Suppose that you find yourself often displaying a split view with the Gantt Chart on top and the Task Details Form below. Because you do this often, it would make a useful macro. First, walk through the process to create the view so that you know what steps you take:

1. Open the View menu and click Gantt Chart.

TIP By selecting the view first, you force Project to start your macro from the Gantt Chart view, regardless of the view that you were using before you ran your macro.

2. Choose Window ⇨ Split to open the bottom pane that shows, by default, the Task Form view.

3. Click the bottom pane and choose View ⇨ More Views to open the More Views dialog box.

4. Select the Task Details Form.

5. Click Apply.

Now that you know what you intend to record, use the following steps to record the macro:

1. Choose Tools ⇨ Macro ⇨ Record New Macro to open the Record Macro dialog box (see Figure 23.2).

FIGURE 23.2

The Record Macro dialog box.

2. Enter a name for the macro in the Macro name box.

The first character of the macro name must be a letter, but the other characters can be letters, numbers, or underscore characters. You can't include a space in a macro name, so try using an underscore character as a word separator, or capitalize the first letter of each word.

3. (Optional) To assign the macro to a keyboard shortcut, type a letter in the Shortcut key box. The letter that you assign can be any letter key on your keyboard, but it can't be a number or a special character. You also can't assign a key combination that is already used by Microsoft Project. If you select a reserved letter, Project displays the warning message that appears in Figure 23.3 when you click OK.

FIGURE 23.3

Project displays this warning message if you select a keyboard shortcut that's already in use.

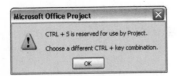

Keyboard shortcuts are only one of the ways that you can run a macro. In the section "Using Shortcuts to Run Macros," later in this chapter, you discover other methods to play back a macro as well as how to assign a keyboard shortcut after you've recorded and stored your macro.

4. In the Record Macro dialog box, open the Store Macro In list box and click the location where you want to store the macro. You can store the macro in the Global File or in the current project. To make a macro available to all projects, select Global File.

The Global File is also called the *Global template file* and it acts the same as the Normal template in Word or the Book1 template in Excel. Any customized features (such as macros, toolbars, or menus) that you store in the Global File are available to any project file. On the other hand, customized features that you store in an individual project file are available only to that file.

5. Type a description of the macro or the function that it performs in the Description box. This description appears whenever you run the macro from the Macros dialog box.

6. Use the options that are in the Row references and Column references sections to control the way that the macro selects rows and columns if you select cells while running a macro. For rows, the macro always selects rows — regardless of the position of the active cell — because it records relative references to rows. If you want a macro to always select the same row, regardless of which cell is first selected, select Absolute (ID).

> **NOTE** For columns, the macro always selects the same column each time that you run the macro — regardless of which cell is selected first — because the macro records absolute references to columns. If you want a macro to select columns, regardless of the position of the active cell when you run the macro, select Relative in the Column references section.

7. Click OK, and Project redisplays your project. You don't notice any differences, but Project is now recording each action that you take.

8. Take all the actions that you want to record.

9. Choose Tools ⇨ Macro ⇨ Stop Recorder (see Figure 23.4) to stop recording your macro.

FIGURE 23.4

When you're finished recording a macro, use the Stop Recorder command.

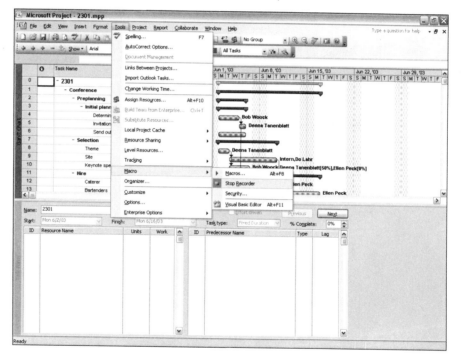

Running Macros

To use a macro that you have recorded, simply run the macro. Some people refer to this action as "playing back" the macro because they associate recording and playing back with the process of recording a TV program on a VCR and then playing back the recording.

If your macro makes substantial changes to your project, you should save the project before you run the macro. With unlimited Undo capabilities, you could undo its effects, but I doubt you'd find that fun. Just closing the project and reopening it would be much easier. To run a macro, follow these steps:

1. Open the project that contains the macro. If you stored the macro in the Global template file, you can open any project.

2. Choose Tools ➪ Macro ➪ Macros to open the Macros dialog box (see Figure 23.5).

FIGURE 23.5

The Macros dialog box.

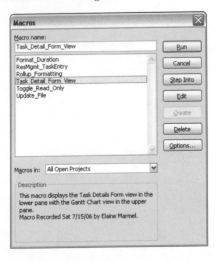

3. Select the macro that you want to run from the Macro name list.

4. Click Run. Project performs the steps that you recorded in the macro.

 **TIP** If your macro is long and you want to stop it while it's still running, press Ctrl+Break. If your macro is short, it will probably finish before you can stop it.

Using Shortcuts to Run Macros

Although you can run macros by selecting them from the Macros dialog box, if you use a macro on a regular basis you may want to shorten the method for running the macro. You can create one of the following to do so:

- A toolbar button that runs the macro
- A menu command that runs the macro
- A keyboard shortcut that runs the macro

Assigning a macro to a toolbar button

Suppose that you're a fan of toolbar buttons and you create a macro that you use a lot. You find yourself wanting a toolbar button that you can click to make your macro run. Well, you can get your wish by adding a button to a toolbar and assigning your macro to that button.

CAUTION **Adding buttons to the toolbars that come with Project isn't always a good idea. If you add a toolbar button to one of the toolbars that comes with Project and you reset that toolbar, the button that you added disappears.**

The following steps explain how to add a button that's assigned to a macro to the Standard toolbar, but you can also add toolbar buttons for macros to a custom toolbar that you create.

CROSS-REF Chapter 22 explains how to create a custom toolbar.

1. Check to see whether the toolbar to which you want to add a button appears on-screen. If it does, go to Step 2. Otherwise, display the toolbar by right-clicking any toolbar button and choosing the toolbar from the shortcut menu that appears.
2. Choose View ➪ Toolbars ➪ Customize to open the Customize dialog box.

TIP You can also open the Customize dialog box by choosing Tools ➪ Customize ➪ Toolbars.

3. Click the Commands tab (see Figure 23.6).
4. Scroll down the Categories list and select All Macros. Project displays a list of macros in the Commands list on the right side of the dialog box.
5. Drag the macro that you want to add onto the desired toolbar (see Figure 23.7). As you drag, the mouse pointer image changes to include a small button and a plus sign. As you move the mouse pointer over a toolbar, a large insertion point marks the location where the button will appear when you release the mouse button.

FIGURE 23.6

From the Commands tab of the Customize dialog box, you can add macros as buttons to toolbars.

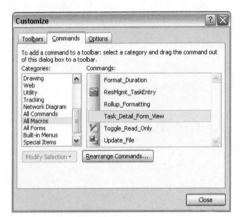

FIGURE 23.7

The image of the mouse pointer icon changes as you drag a macro onto the Standard toolbar.

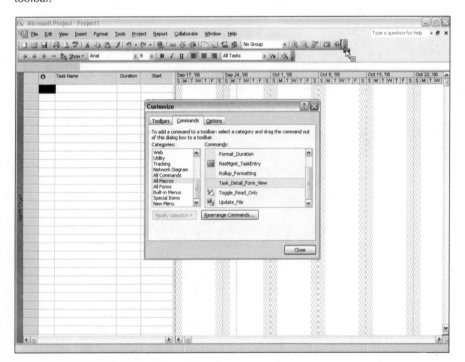

6. Release the mouse button and a new button appears on the toolbar (see Figure 23.8).

TIP If you're concerned about using excessive screen real estate, you may want to take advantage of the feature in Project that permits the Standard toolbar and the Formatting toolbar to share the same row. Buttons that are not used frequently reside on a hidden palette. See Chapter 22 for more information about customizing Project.

7. To change the name of the toolbar button, click Modify Selection in the Customize dialog box to open the pop-up menu that appears in Figure 23.9.

FIGURE 23.8

The new button after dropping it on the toolbar.

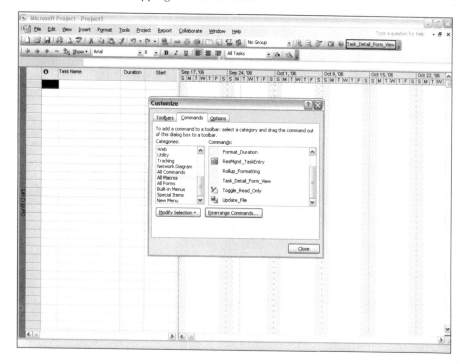

FIGURE 23.9

The menu that appears when you click the Modify Selection button to change a macro button's name.

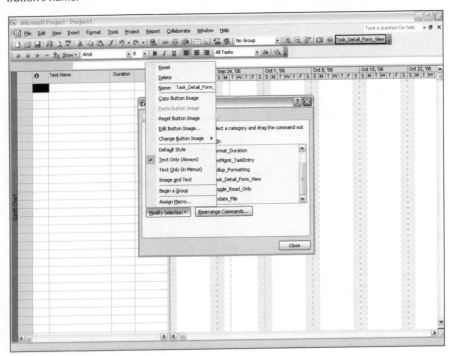

8. Type the name, exactly as you want it to appear on the toolbar button, into the Name box. You can include spaces.

 If you prefer to use an image instead of text, click Default Style on the Modify Selection pop-up menu and then click Change Button Image to select a button image.

9. Press Enter. The pop-up menu disappears, and Project renames the macro toolbar button (see Figure 23.10).

10. Close the Customize dialog box.

FIGURE 23.10

I renamed the toolbar button Detail Form.

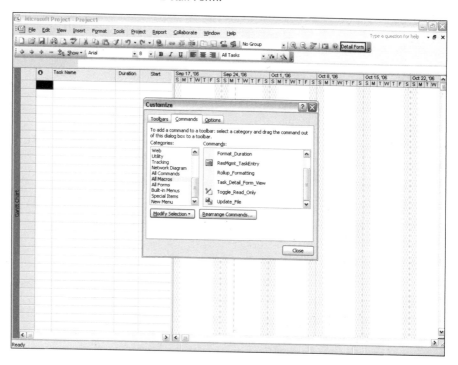

When you add a toolbar button to an existing toolbar, Project saves it in your Global template file. Any other project files that you open on your computer using that Global template file contain the new toolbar button.

> **TIP** If you change your mind and don't want the button on the toolbar, you can remove it by opening the Customize dialog box and then simply dragging the button off the toolbar and dropping it anywhere on your project. The button disappears but the macro is still available.

Assigning a macro to a menu command

Maybe you're not a toolbar person, or maybe you just prefer to use menu commands. This section shows you how to add a command that's assigned to a macro to the Tools menu.

CAUTION As with toolbars, be aware that adding commands to the menus that come with Project isn't always a good idea. If you add a command to one of the standard menus and you reset that menu, the command that you added will disappear.

You can also add commands for macros to custom menus that you create, and if you don't want your custom menu to appear all the time, you can create a custom toolbar and drag menus onto it. Then you can hide or display the toolbar as needed.

CROSS-REF See Chapter 22 for more information about creating custom menus and toolbars.

Follow these steps to add a command that runs your macro to a menu:

1. Choose View ➪ Toolbars ➪ Customize to open the Customize dialog box.

TIP You also can open the Customize dialog box by choosing Tools ➪ Customize ➪ Toolbars.

2. Click the Commands tab (see Figure 23.11).

FIGURE 23.11

You can add macros as commands on menus by using the Commands tab of the Customize dialog box.

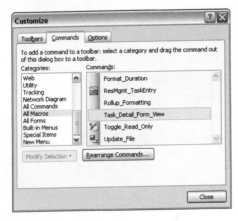

---

3. Scroll down the Categories list and select All Macros. Project displays a list of macros in the Commands list on the right.

4. Drag the macro that you want to add to the desired menu (see Figure 23.12). As you drag, the mouse pointer image changes to include a small button and a plus sign (+). As you move the mouse pointer over a menu, the menu opens; a large horizontal insertion point marks the location where the button will appear when you release the mouse button.

5. Release the mouse button. The macro appears on the menu (see Figure 23.13).

FIGURE 23.12

The image of the mouse pointer icon changes as you drag a macro onto a menu.

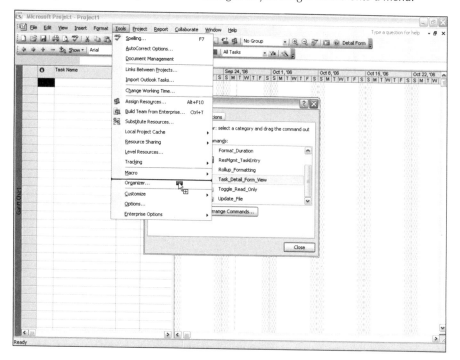

FIGURE 23.13

A macro has been placed on the Tools menu.

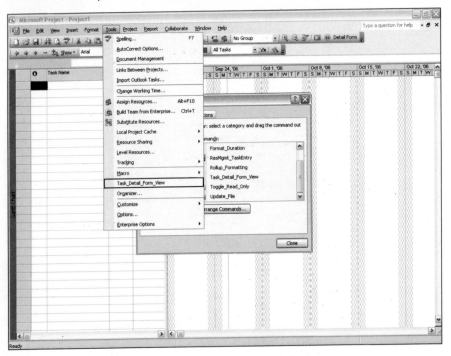

6. To change the name of the macro on the menu, click Modify Selection in the Customize dialog box to open the pop-up menu (see Figure 23.14).

7. Type the name (including spaces, if you want) in the Name box, exactly as you want it to appear on the toolbar button.

FIGURE 23.14

Modifying the command name on the menu.

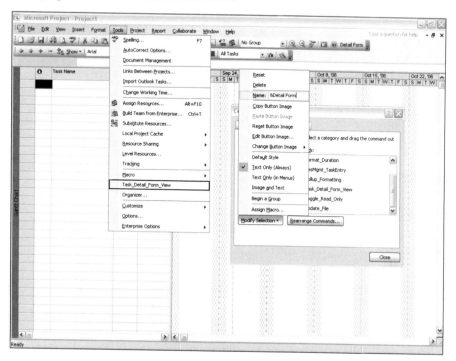

NOTE To provide a hotkey character for your macro name, place an ampersand (&) immediately before the character that you want to be the hotkey — as I did before the *D* of Detail in Figure 23.14. If your macro name contains a number, you can make it the hotkey character using the same technique. Make sure that the letter you select is not already in use by some other command on the same menu. When the command appears on the menu, the hotkey character will be underscored, enabling you to choose the command from the menu by pressing the hotkey character combination. For example, I can choose the Detail Form command by pressing Alt+T+D. Alt-T opens the Tools menu, and D selects Detail Form, the item in that menu with D as the hot key.

8. Press Enter. The pop-up menu disappears and Project renames the menu command. As Figure 23.15 shows, the command includes your hotkey if you added an ampersand.

9. Close the Customize dialog box.

When you add a command to one of the default menus, Microsoft Project saves the command and the menu in your Global template file. Any other project file that you open on your computer using that Global template file contains the new menu command.

TIP If you change your mind and don't want the command on the menu, you can remove it by opening the Customize dialog box and then simply dragging the command off the menu and dropping it anywhere on your project. The command disappears but the macro is still available.

FIGURE 23.15

The command after renaming it and assigning it a hotkey.

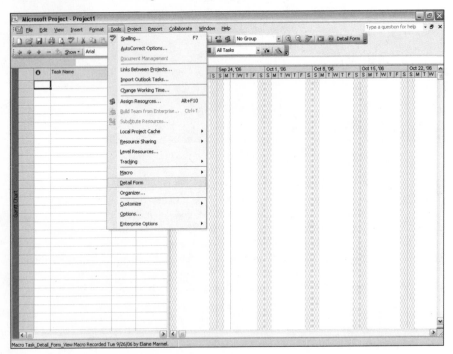

Assigning a keyboard shortcut to a macro

Suppose that after you experiment, you decide that you really want to run your macro from a keyboard shortcut. Furthermore, suppose that you didn't set a shortcut when you created the macro. Follow these steps to add a keyboard shortcut to the macro after you create it:

1. Open the project that contains the macro.

2. Choose Tools ➪ Macro ➪ Macros to open the Macros dialog box (see Figure 23.16).

FIGURE 23.16

The Macros dialog box.

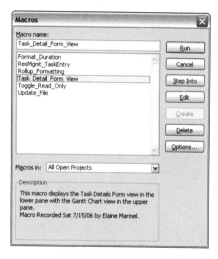

 You can also press Alt+F8 to display the Macros dialog box.

3. Highlight the macro to which you want to add a keyboard shortcut.

4. Click Options to open the Macro Options dialog box that appears in Figure 23.17.

5. Place the insertion point in the Shortcut key box and type a letter.

FIGURE 23.17

Set a keyboard shortcut for a macro from the Macro Options dialog box.

6. Click OK. If the combination that you selected (Ctrl plus the letter that you typed) is not in use by Project, Project displays the Macros dialog box again. If Project is using the combination that you selected, even for another macro, Project asks you to try a different combination.

7. Close the Macros dialog box.

To run your macro, press the keyboard combination that you assigned. If you decide that you don't want to run your macro by using this keyboard combination, you can change the combination by using the preceding steps, or you can remove the keyboard combination that you assigned by reopening the Macro Options dialog box and deleting the letter from the Shortcut key box.

Summary

In this chapter, you found out how to use macros in Project. In particular, you now know how to do the following:

■ Create macros

■ Use macros

■ Assign shortcuts to macros to make them easy to run

Chapter 24 explains how to customize Project using VBA.

Chapter 24

Customizing Microsoft Project Using VBA and Active Scripting

A s you saw in Chapter 23, a macro is an automated set of instructions that can help you accomplish a specific task in Project. Macros are especially useful for completing tedious, repetitive tasks. You can record a macro in Project, or you can produce even more powerful automation by writing your own Visual Basic for Applications, or VBA, code.

For example, suppose that you need to increase the work for every task in your project that is assigned to a new, less-experienced resource. If you had to accomplish this manually, you could edit every task to which this resource is assigned in your project and modify the assignment's work field. If this were a large project with several hundred tasks, you see how this could take you hours to accomplish. It is easier to write some VBA code and then take just a few seconds to run the code. Furthermore, after you write your code, you can reuse it as many times as you like. If this idea appeals to you, customizing Project using VBA code is definitely worth exploring.

In this chapter, you find the following three case studies, which show the benefits of customizing Project 2007 using code:

- Writing VBA code to filter all tasks on the project's critical path that should have finished by the current date, but have not.

- Increasing the work value for a particular resource in the project for all tasks that have not yet completed.

- Customizing the Project Guide to incorporate your company standards into the project initiation process.

This chapter is not intended to be a comprehensive VBA reference guide for Project. Instead, its purpose is to introduce you to many concepts of automating Project and to help you get your feet wet in the world of writing custom code.

IN THIS CHAPTER
Filtering to see critical tasks and resource assignments
Adjusting work using code
Customizing the Project Guide

Example One: Creating a Filter to See Critical Tasks and Resource Assignments

As a project manager, you must be able to easily identify the tasks in your project that are falling behind schedule. In particular, if a late task is on the project's critical path, the late task is having a direct impact on your ability to complete the project on schedule.

In this first example, you see how you can use VBA to easily identify the tasks on your project's critical path that should have finished by the current date, but have not. After you have identified these tasks, you can filter the list of tasks for a particular resource — you can identify late, critical tasks by person.

Recording a macro to create a filter for critical tasks

Recording a macro that captures the basic steps of the process is an excellent technique for producing the foundation for the VBA code that you will ultimately need. After you've recorded the basic VBA code in a macro, you can customize the code to accomplish your exact requirements. In Figure 24.1, you see a project with all of its tasks visible.

FIGURE 24.1

A project with all its tasks visible.

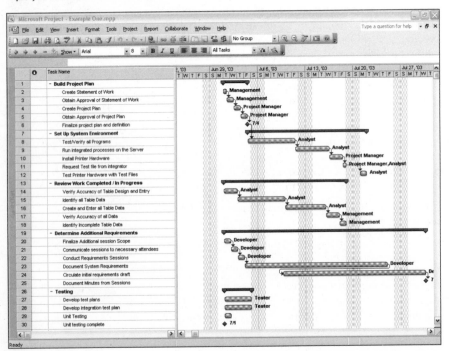

Use the following steps to create a filter that shows only the tasks in the project that should have finished by the current date and are on the critical path:

1. Start Project and open the `Example One.mpp` file.

ON the CD-ROM You can find `Example One.mpp` on the CD that accompanies this book.

2. Choose Tools ⇨ Macro ⇨ Record New Macro. The Record Macro dialog box appears.
3. In the Macro name box, enter **FilterCriticalTasksByDateAndResource**, as shown in Figure 24.2, and click OK. The macro recorder will now capture all your actions.

FIGURE 24.2

The Record Macro dialog box.

4. Choose Project ⇨ Filtered for ⇨ More Filters to open the More Filters window.
5. Click the New button to open the Filter Definition dialog box.
6. Complete the Filter Definition dialog box, shown in Figure 24.3, and click OK. Project redisplays the More Filters window.

NOTE The text in the Value field `Today` is automatically translated to the current date when you run the macro.

7. Click the Apply button in the More Filters window.
8. Choose Tools ⇨ Macro ⇨ Stop Recorder to stop recording the macro. At this point, your recorded keystrokes have filtered the project to show only critical tasks that have not yet been completed.

Compare Figure 24.4 with Figure 24.1. Notice that only the tasks that are on the critical path are now visible.

FIGURE 24.3

In this figure, you're using the Filter Definition dialog box to set up the macro to filter for critical tasks for the Analyst resource.

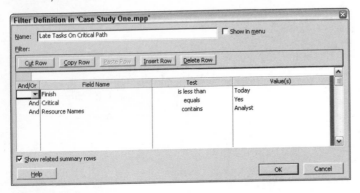

FIGURE 24.4

The project has been filtered to show only the critical tasks.

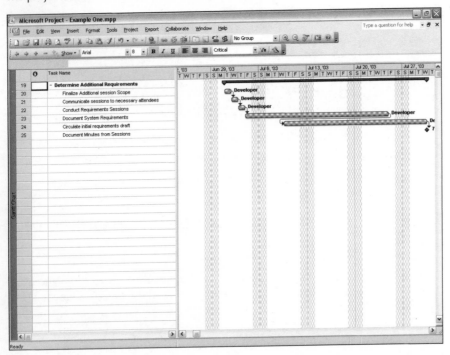

Editing the macro to show only specified resources

The macro that you just recorded works fine for the Analyst resource, but you would really like to be able to run this same code for any resource in your project. To add this flexibility to the code, you must add a few additional lines to the macro to prompt the user to enter the name of a resource to include in the filter. Use the following steps:

1. Choose Tools ➪ Macro ➪ Macros to open the Macros dialog box.

2. Select the `FilterCriticalTasksByDateAndResource` macro and click the Edit button to open the Visual Basic Editor. See the sidebar "Key Components of the Visual Basic Editor" for a description of the window and its elements.

NOTE The terminology may seem a bit confusing: You use the Visual Basic UserForm window to create dialog boxes or windows that will be a part of your user interface. The windows or dialog boxes that you create in the UserForm window are known as UserForm objects and are usually called simply UserForms. In this chapter, whenever you see UserForm by itself, the term refers to a UserForm object. All references to the window will appear as UserForm window.

3. Close the Project Explorer window and the Properties window (if open) by clicking the X in the upper-right corner of each window. The Code window now occupies the full screen, as shown in Figure 24.5.

FIGURE 24.5

The Code window displays the VBA code that was generated by recording a macro.

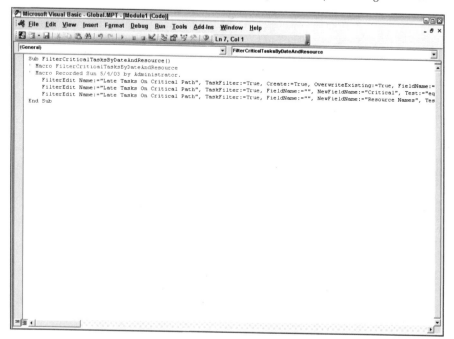

NOTE The Code window contains the VBA code that was generated when you recorded your macro. The macro code is known as a sub procedure. A sub procedure is a set of instructions in your program that is executed as a unit. The code between the lines `Sub FilterByCurrent DateAndCritical()` and `End Sub` are the instructions that create a filter programmatically. The lines with the green text (it really is green, even though you can't tell because the book is black and white) that begin with an apostrophe are comments that are used to document the code.

4. In the Code window, modify the sub procedure by adding the following lines and changes that appear in boldface:

```
Sub FilterCriticalTasksByDateAndResource()

Dim strResourceName As String
' Macro FilterCriticalTasksByDateAndResource
' Macro Recorded Sun 5/4/03 by Administrator.
    strResourceName = InputBox("Please enter the resource
name:")
    FilterEdit Name:="Late Tasks On Critical Path",
TaskFilter:=True, Create:=True, OverwriteExisting:=True,
FieldName:="Finish", Test:="is less than", Value:="Today",
ShowInMenu:=False, ShowSummaryTasks:=True
    FilterEdit Name:="Late Tasks On Critical Path",
TaskFilter:=True, FieldName:="", NewFieldName:="Critical",
Test:="equals", Value:="Yes", Operation:="And",
ShowSummaryTasks:=True
    FilterEdit Name:="Late Tasks On Critical Path",
TaskFilter:=True, FieldName:="", NewFieldName:="Resource
Names", Test:="contains", Value:= strResourceName,
Operation:="And", ShowSummaryTasks:=True
End Sub
```

ON the CD-ROM This module is available on the CD that accompanies this book. To add the module from the CD instead of creating it manually, display the Code window and choose File ➪ Import File. Then, browse the CD for the file `module1.bas`.

Testing the code

Now you can run the modified code to test the changes that you made. Use the following steps to do so:

1. Click the Run Sub/UserForm button in the toolbar at the top of the Visual Basic window shown in Figure 24.6.

Key Components of the Visual Basic Editor

The Visual Basic Editor is the common programming environment that is used in all Microsoft Office applications, including Project 2007. Some of the key components of the Visual Basic Editor, shown in this figure, are as follows:

Project explorer window

Code window

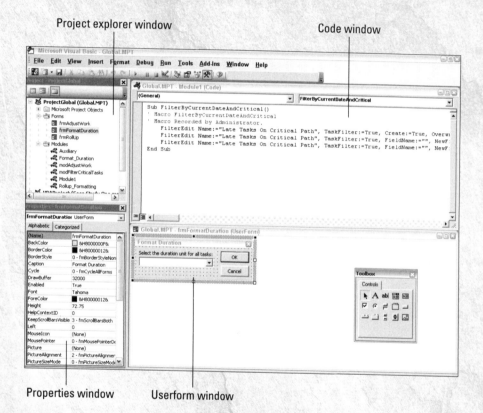

Properties window   Userform window

- **Project Explorer window:** The Project Explorer window displays a hierarchical list of the projects and all the items that are contained in and referenced by each of the projects.

- **Properties window:** The Properties window lists design-time properties for selected objects and their current settings. An *object* is a piece of the application that can be manipulated. In Project, entities such as a task, resource, or assignment are objects. In fact, the entire application of Project is considered to be an object. A *property* is a value that you can set to determine the object's appearance or behavior. For example, the Start date and Name are properties of a task object.

continued

continued

- **Toolbox:** The Toolbox displays the standard Visual Basic controls, such as list boxes, text boxes, and labels that can be added to a dialog box.

- **Code window:** Use the Code window to write, display, and edit Visual Basic code. The Code window occupies the same screen area as a UserForm.

- **UserForm window:** In the UserForm window, you create the windows or dialog boxes (called UserForm objects) in your project.

FIGURE 24.6

Click the Run Sub/UserForm button to run the VBA sub procedure.

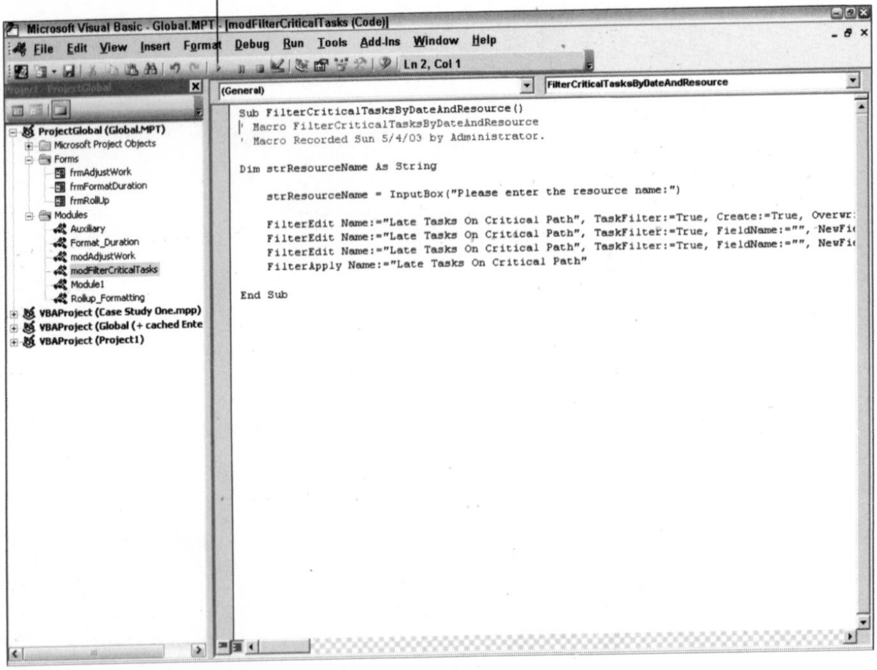

Run Sub/Userform button

2. The Microsoft Project dialog box opens (see Figure 24.7). At the prompt to enter the resource name, enter **Project Manager** and click OK.

FIGURE 24.7

Select a resource whose tasks you want to view.

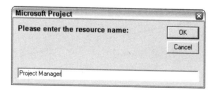

Project applies the filter so that you can view only the tasks in the project that are late, on the critical path, and assigned to the resource called Project Manager (see Figure 24.8).

FIGURE 24.8

After adding the filter, you can view tasks that are on the critical path for the specified resource.

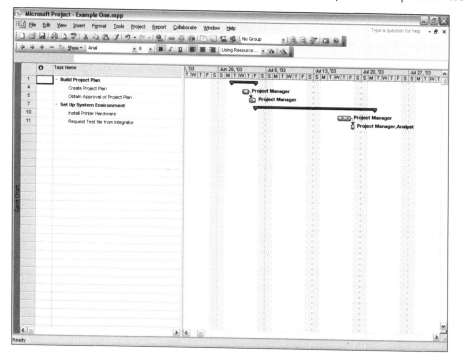

Let's review the changes that you made to the code so that you can understand the purpose of each change. The line that begins with `Dim` declares a variable that VBA uses to store the resource name that the user types into the dialog box. The variable that you created is known as a *string variable*, which is designed to store text.

The line `strResourceName = InputBox("Please enter the resource name:")` displays a dialog box known as an InputBox; the InputBox prompts the user to type in the resource name, and VBA stores the name that the user enters in the variable `strResourceName`.

On the last line, which begins with `FilterEdit`, you substituted the text `Analyst` with the variable `strResourceName`. VBA uses the name that the user entered in the InputBox as the filter value for the `Resource Names` field.

 To run your macro without having to choose Tools ⇨ Macro ⇨ Macros, you can assign your macro to a toolbar button or add it to a custom menu.

 See Chapter 23 for detailed instructions on assigning macros to toolbars or menus.

Example Two: Creating a UserForm Object to Adjust Work

To use Project effectively and consistently in an organization, you should begin each new project using a template. A template may contain items such as standard tasks that have been defined within your organization as well as generic resources such as Programmer, Systems Analyst, and so on. In addition, a template is often created so that generic resources are assigned to standard tasks with the typical amount of work that it takes for that resource to complete each task in the project.

 Information about templates that come with Project and creating a new project using a template appears in Chapter 3.

For example, the resource Programmer may typically need 16 hours of work on the Write Design Document task. But suppose that your organization has just hired a new programmer with little experience in writing design documents in your organization's format. In this case, you would increase the work for each task to which you assign the programmer by a factor of 50 percent. If the programmer is assigned to a lot of tasks in your project, it would be time consuming to manually adjust the work for each task.

In the following example, you will see how to create a UserForm Object to automate the process of adjusting the work for a selected resource in your project.

Designing the UserForm

A UserForm is a window or a dialog box that you design based on the requirements of your application. When you design a UserForm, try to make it appear the same as other Project dialog boxes. The more familiar you can make a UserForm, the more likely someone will use it.

ON the CD-ROM This completed UserForm is available on the CD that accompanies this book. To add the UserForm from the CD instead of creating it manually, choose File ⇨ Import File and browse for the file `frmAdjustWork.frm`. A new folder called Forms will appear in the Project Explorer window. In this folder, you'll see `frmAdjustWork`; double-click it to open it.

Creating a UserForm

You need to insert a new UserForm so that you can create a custom interface for your application. Follow these steps to create a UserForm:

1. Start Project and open the `Example Two.mpp` file.

2. Choose Tools ⇨ Macro ⇨ Visual Basic Editor to open the Visual Basic Editor (VBE), as shown in Figure 24.9.

3. Choose Insert ⇨ UserForm. You see a screen similar to that shown in Figure 24.10.

FIGURE 24.9

You will insert the UserForm on the CD into the Visual Basic Editor window.

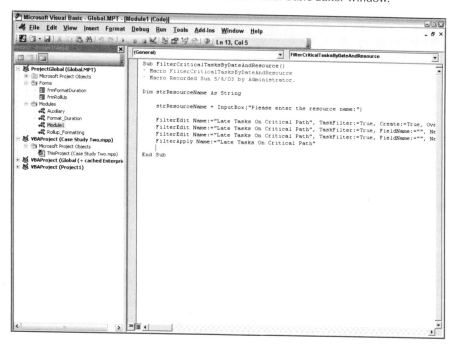

FIGURE 24.10

A UserForm for designing a custom dialog box.

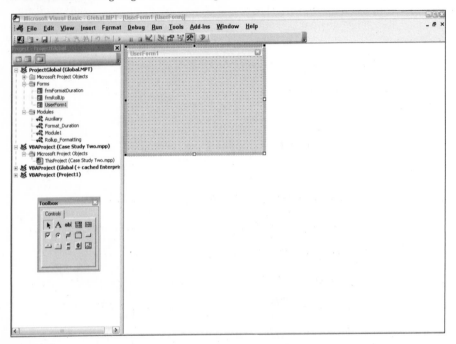

Adjusting the size of the UserForm

Now that you have inserted a UserForm, you need to adjust the size of the UserForm to accommodate the controls that you will place on the form. To change the size of the form, adjust the UserForm's properties. Properties include attributes such as height, width, position, font, color, text, and so on.

Click anywhere on the UserForm and choose View ➪ Properties Window to open the Properties window, as shown in Figure 24.11.

 **NOTE** The Properties window was probably already displayed in the Visual Basic Editor window. This window typically appears in the lower-left corner of your screen.

FIGURE 24.11

The Properties window allows you to set the attributes of the UserForm.

In the Properties window, set each of the properties for the UserForm, as shown in the following table.

Property	Enter the Following
(Name)	FrmAdjustWork
Caption	Adjust Work
Height	145
Width	240

Adding controls to the UserForm

To make the form useful, you need to add controls. For this UserForm, you need the following controls:

- Label controls to identify the various elements on the UserForm
- A ComboBox control to select a resource
- A text box to enter the amount by which you want to increase or decrease the work for the selected resource
- OK and Cancel command buttons

When you have completed the UserForm, it should look like the one shown in Figure 24.12.

FIGURE 24.12

The Adjust Work dialog box based on the completed UserForm.

Label   Drop-down combo box

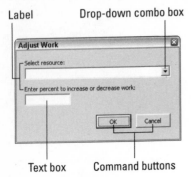

Text box   Command buttons

Label control

The UserForm won't be meaningful to the user unless he knows what the various controls do, so start by adding a Label control to the UserForm for the box where the user must select a resource. Click the Label button in the Visual Basic Editor Toolbox to select the Label control (see Figure 24.13). Then, on the UserForm, use your mouse to "draw" the control in the upper-left corner of the form by dragging from the upper-left corner to the lower-right corner of the location where you want the label control to appear (see Figure 24.14).

FIGURE 24.13

The Toolbox allows you to select the controls for the UserForm.

Text box

Label control   Drop-down combo box

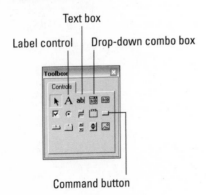

Command button

FIGURE 24.14

The Label control is displayed on the UserForm.

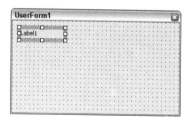

In the Properties window, set each of the properties for the Label control, as shown in the following table.

Property	Type the Following
(Name)	LblResource
Caption	Select Resource:
Height	12
Left	12
Top	12
Width	60

 The Label control has many other properties, but you can accept the default value for all the other properties.

ComboBox control

To select the resource whose work needs to be adjusted, you need a ComboBox control. Click the ComboBox button in the Toolbox and use your mouse to "draw" the control below the Label control (see Figure 24.15).

FIGURE 24.15

The ComboBox control is displayed on the UserForm.

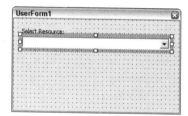

In the Properties window, set each of the properties for the ComboBox, as shown in the following table.

Property	Type the Following
(Name)	cboResource
Height	15.75
Left	12
Top	12
Style	1 – fmStyleDropDownList
Width	210

Add another Label control to the UserForm, just below the resource ComboBox control. Click the Label button in the Toolbox and use your mouse to "draw" the Label control below the resource ComboBox control (see Figure 24.16).

FIGURE 24.16

The second Label control is displayed on the UserForm.

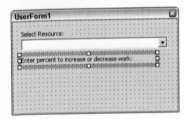

In the Properties window, set each of the properties for the Label control, as shown in the following table.

Property	Type the Following
(Name)	lblPercent
Caption	Enter percent to increase or decrease work:
Height	12
Left	12
Top	48
Width	192

TextBox control

Add a TextBox control to the UserForm just below the Label control that you just created. Click the TextBox button in the Toolbox and use your mouse to "draw" the TextBox control below the second Label control (see Figure 24.17).

The TextBox control is displayed on the UserForm.

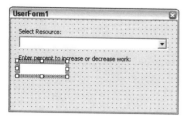

In the Properties window, set each of the properties for the TextBox control, as shown in the following table.

Property	Type the Following
(Name)	txtPercent
Height	15.75
Left	12
Top	60
Width	66

CommandButton control

Finally, add a CommandButton control — which represents the OK button — to the UserForm toward the bottom of the form. Click the CommandButton button in the Toolbox and use your mouse to "draw" the control below the previous TextBox control (see Figure 24.18).

FIGURE 24.18

The OK button is added as a CommandButton control on the UserForm.

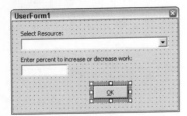

In the Properties window, set each of the properties for the CommandButton control as shown in the following table.

Property	Type the Following
(Name)	cmdOK
Accelerator	O
Caption	OK
Default	True
Height	19
Left	114
Top	90
Width	50

Now, add a CommandButton control next to the OK button that represents the Cancel button. Click the CommandButton button in the Toolbox and use your mouse to "draw" the CommandButton control next to the OK button (see Figure 24.19).

FIGURE 24.19

The Cancel button is added as a CommandButton control on the UserForm.

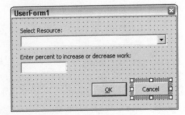

In the Properties window, set each of the properties for the CommandButton control as shown in the following table.

Property	Type the Following
(Name)	cmdCancel
Cancel	True
Caption	Cancel
Height	19
Left	174
Top	90
Width	50

Adding code to the UserForm

You now have the graphical user interface for the UserForm, but it isn't much more than a pretty face at this point. You need to add code to the UserForm so that it performs the functions that you need.

Adding code to display resource names

Initially, you need to add code to the UserForm so that when Project loads the form, the names of all the resources in your project appear as items in the Resource drop-down list. Follow these steps to add the appropriate code:

1. Click anywhere on the UserForm (other than directly on a control) and choose View ➪ Code. The Code window for the UserForm appears (see Figure 24.20).

2. From the Object drop-down box at the upper-left corner of the Code window, select UserForm (it will most likely already be selected).

3. From the Procedure drop-down box at the upper-right corner of the Code window, select Initialize.

4. In the Code window, type the following code between the lines Private Sub UserForm_Initialize and End Sub (you don't need to enter the lines Private Sub UserForm_Initialize and End Sub again):

```
Private Sub UserForm_Initialize()
Dim r As Resource
    For Each r In ActiveProject.Resources
        cboResource.AddItem r.Name
    Next r
End Sub
```

I review this code so that you understand how it works.

FIGURE 24.20

In the Code window for the UserForm, you can add code to make resource names appear to the ComboBox when Project loads the UserForm.

Procedure drop-down box

Object drop-down box   Code window

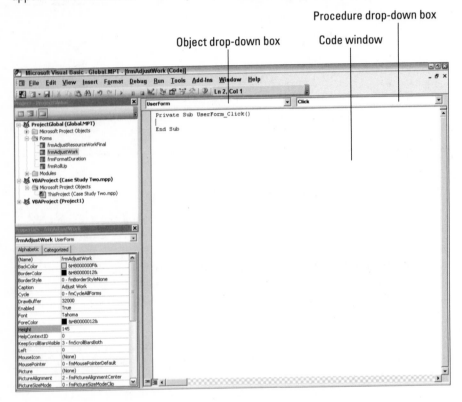

Because you want VBA to run this code before displaying the form, you place the code within the UserForm_Initialize procedure; VBA runs code in this procedure when loading the UserForm.

The line Dim r As Resource declares a variable named r, and you instructed VBA to create this variable as a resource object. Doing so allows you to manipulate a resource's properties and methods programmatically. An object's properties are the attributes that are associated with a type of object. A resource has many properties, including Name, Cost, and EMailAddress.

NOTE These properties are also fields that are associated with a resource in Project. In fact, *all* resource fields in Project are properties of a resource object in VBA.

A *method* is a procedure or action that VBA can perform on an object to achieve a particular result. For example, the resource object has the `Add` method, which allows you to add resources to a project, and the `AppendNotes` method, which appends notes to the resource's notes field.

The line `For Each r In ActiveProject.Resources` begins a section of code known as a *For . . . Next loop*. The line `Next r` closes the loop. The lines of code that appear within this loop run once for every resource in the project. The line `cboResource.AddItem r.Name` adds the `Name` property of the resource `r` as an item to the drop-down list. VBA reads the code in the loop for each resource in the project, adding each resource's name to the list.

You can now run the form and test some of its functionality. Choose Run ➪ Run Sub/UserForm (or press F5). The UserForm appears on the screen (see Figure 24.21).

FIGURE 24.21

The completed Adjust Work dialog box based on the UserForm.

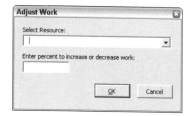

In the Adjust Work dialog box, click the Select Resource drop-down list and you see all the resources in your project. But when you try clicking the OK button or Cancel button, at this point nothing happens. In the following sections of this chapter, you will add code to the form that will be associated with clicking the OK button and Cancel button. For now, close the dialog box by clicking the X in the upper-right corner.

Adding code to the OK button to change work

You can add code to the OK button on the UserForm to accept the increased or decreased work for each task to which the selected resource is assigned. When the user clicks OK on the UserForm, the code that you're about to add will run.

Double-click the OK button on the UserForm in the Visual Basic window. The Code window appears (see Figure 24.22).

Using the Code window for the UserForm, you can add VBA code that will run when the user clicks the OK button.

Code window

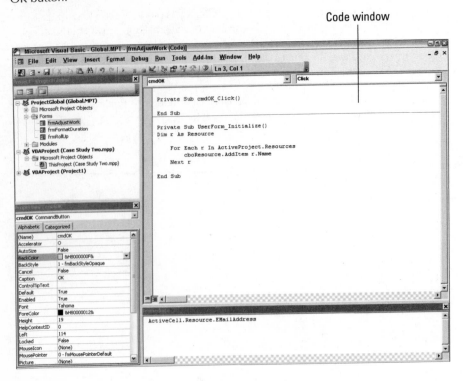

Add the following code between the lines `Private Sub cmdOK_Click` and `End Sub` (do not type in either of these lines; I included them so that you could see all the code that will ultimately appear in the Code window). Note the comments that precede each section describing the purpose of that section of code.

```
Private Sub cmdOK_Click ()
Dim t As Task
Dim a As Assignment
Dim Adjuster As Single

    'Make sure the user has typed a number
    If Not IsNumeric(txtPercent.Text) Then
        MsgBox "You must type a valid number in this field.",
vbInformation
        Exit Sub
    End If
```

```
        'Divide the number the user entered by 100, because the user
entered a percentage
        Adjuster = Val(txtPercent.Text) / 100

        'Loop through each task in the project
        For Each t In ActiveProject.Tasks
            'Skip over blank rows, if any
            If Not t Is Nothing Then
'Loop through each resource assignment in your project
            For Each a In t.Assignments
                'If the resource name is equal to the resource
the user selected,
                'then adjust the work by the Adjuster value
                If a.ResourceName = cboResource.Text Then
                    a.RemainingWork = a.RemainingWork +
(a.RemainingWork * Adjuster)
                End If
            Next a
        End If
    Next t

    'Display message confirming success
    MsgBox "The work has been adjusted successfully!",
vbInformation

    'Close the form
    Unload Me
End Sub
```

Let's review this code so that you understand how it works.

In this sub procedure, you declared three variables: t is a task object used as code loops through the tasks in the project, a is an assignment object used as the code loops through the assignments on a task, and Adjuster is a numeric variable with the data type of single that VBA uses to store the percentage that a user types in the UserForm to adjust the amount of work that's assigned to the task for the resource.

The section that begins with If Not IsNumeric(txtPercent.Text) verifies that the user has entered a valid number in the Enter Percent to Increase Or Decrease Work text box. This step is important because the sub procedure requires a valid number to perform the work adjustment. If the user enters a non-numeric character, VBA displays an error message.

The line Adjuster = Val(txtPercent.Text) / 100 uses the Val function in VBA to convert the value that the user enters to a rate by dividing the value by 100. For example, if the user types **20**, the Val function divides 20 by 100 to set the Adjuster variable to the rate of 0.2.

The line `For Each t In ActiveProject.Tasks` begins a section of code that loops through every task in the project to perform the set of actions listed within the loop. The line `Next t` closes the loop to identify the last action within the loop.

The line `If Not t Is Nothing Then` prevents errors if you run the code on a project that contains blank task rows. This line checks to make sure that the sub procedure is not on a blank row in the project's task list. If the sub procedure is on a blank row, this line makes the sub procedure skip that row as it loops through the tasks.

The line `For Each a In t.Assignments` begins a section of code that loops through each resource assignment of a task in your project to perform the actions listed within the loop. The line `Next a` closes the loop. Within this section of code, the line `If a.ResourceName = cboResource.Text Then` compares the name of the resource assignment to the name of the resource that the user selected from the drop-down list. If the two are equal, the code assigns the resource that the user selected to the current task in the loop. If the two are not equal, the code closes the loop.

The line `a.RemainingWork = a.RemainingWork + (a.RemainingWork * Adjuster)` sets the remaining work for the resource assignment equal to its current value *plus* the remaining work multiplied by the `Adjuster` variable. For example, if the resource assignment had 10 hours of work and the `Adjuster` variable was set to the rate of .5, the code would add an additional 5 hours to the 10 hours originally assigned for a total of 15 hours.

The `MsgBox` line displays a message to the user that the sub procedure has run successfully.

The line `Unload Me` closes the form (literally unloading it from memory), and `Me` is a reserved word that refers to the current form without having to specify its name.

Adding code to the Cancel button

You just added code that will run when the user clicks the OK button. You now need to add code to the Cancel button so that the UserForm closes when the user clicks this button without making any changes to the project. From the Code window, select the `cmdCancel` object from the Object drop-down list. Add the following code between the lines `Private Sub cmdCancel_Click` and `End Sub`:

```
Private Sub cmdCancel_Click ()
    'Close the UserForm
    Unload Me
End Sub
```

You have now added all the required code to the UserForm. Click the Save button on the toolbar at the top of the Visual Basic window to save the UserForm.

Adding a sub procedure to show the UserForm

You have now designed and coded the UserForm. You need only to add a simple sub procedure to make the UserForm appear.

> **ON the CD-ROM** The module that you create in these steps is available on the CD that accompanies this book. To add the module from the CD instead of creating it manually, choose File ▹ Import File, and browse for the file `modAdjustWork.bas`.

1. Choose Insert ▹ Module. VBA adds a new module to the project.

> **NOTE** A *module* is simply a container for one or more procedures.

2. In the Properties window, set the name for this module to `modAdjustWork`.

3. In the Code window, add the following sub procedure (see Figure 24.23):

```
Sub ShowAdjustWorkForm ()
    'Display the UserForm
    frmAdjustWork.Show
End Sub
```

FIGURE 24.23

The `ShowAdjustWorkForm` sub procedure displays the UserForm.

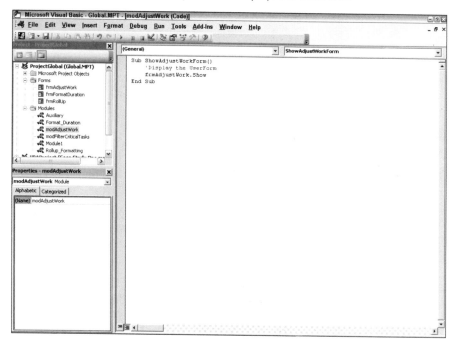

The purpose of this sub procedure is to display the UserForm called `frmAdjustWork`. This is the sub procedure that you will run whenever you want to run the code on the UserForm. To run this sub procedure, click any line within the sub procedure and press F5. The UserForm appears and is now functional.

TIP   To avoid having to choose Tools ⇨ Macro ⇨ Macros, you can assign your macro to a toolbar button or add it to a custom menu. See Chapter 23 for details on adding a macro to a toolbar or menu.

Example Three: Customizing the Project Guide

Microsoft first introduced the Project Guide in Project 2002 to make the software easier to use and more intuitive, especially for new users. The Project Guide interface appears on the left side of the main Project window (see Figure 24.24).

FIGURE 24.24

The Project Guide appears on the left side of the Project window.

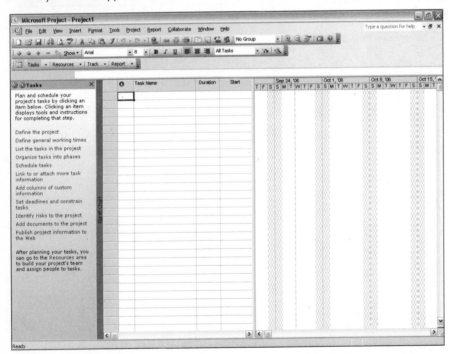

You can customize, extend, or build the Project Guide extended from scratch to meet your organization's requirements. Organizations can define and develop business processes and procedures and implement them by using a customized Project Guide. Because a Project Guide can be associated to a project plan or project template, you can develop different Project Guides for the various types of projects that your organization performs.

The Project Guide (see Figure 24.25) is comprised of three components: a toolbar, a side pane, and a main view area:

- **Toolbar:** The toolbar is the top level of the Project Guide's structure. The toolbar displays buttons for each of the guide's goal areas. *Goal areas* organize the project into logical groups of functions that correspond to the major activities associated with managing a project. The default Project Guide that comes with Project is made up of four goal areas: Tasks, Resources, Track, and Report.

FIGURE 24.25

The Project Guide features a toolbar, side pane, and main view area.

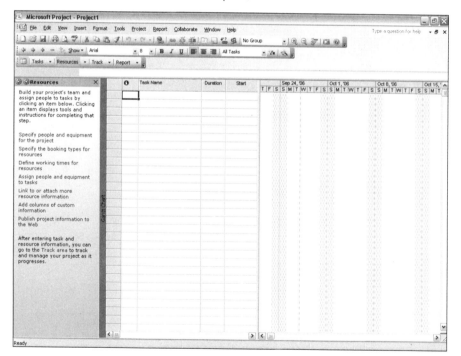

- **Side pane:** The side pane displays on the left side of Project's main screen. This pane displays a list of the tasks associated with a particular goal area when you click the button on the Project Guide toolbar for that goal area. For example, the Resources side pane lists, as links, each of the resource-related steps that you use to manage a project. When you click the <u>Specify people and equipment for the project resource</u> link, a screen appears in the side pane to lead you through all the required steps to add resources to a project.

- **Main view area:** The main view area refers to the main Project window that appears to the right of the side pane. The main view area usually displays a Project view, but it can also display a Web page from Project Web Access or even your organization's intranet. The main view area's content can change, depending on the task selected in the Project Guide's side pane.

Content of the Project Guide XML document

The structure and content for the Project Guide are defined within an XML file. You can use XML, or eXtensible Markup Language, to create dynamic content for your browser, and in this case, the Project Guide. The default XML document that Project uses for the Project Guide is a compiled document called Gbui.xml. You also can download an editable version from the Microsoft Web site as part of the Project Guide Software Developer's Kit (also known as the Project Guide SDK).

The SDK also contains the sample code for several Project Guide examples. You need only a basic ability to read and modify XML because the XML structure is fairly simple. To customize the Project Guide, you modify the XML document and replace the default Gbui.xml document with your own customized version. Then, you configure your project to use the new customized guide instead of the default Project Guide.

The Project Guide displays a series of HTML (HyperText Markup Language) pages in the side pane based on the XML document. HTML is the language that is widely used to display content for your browser. The level of complexity of the HTML pages that are used by the Project Guide depends on the complexity of the functionality being implemented.

Project Guide XML document elements

The Gbui.xml document is broken into many elements, each with a corresponding design and function within the Project Guide. Some elements invoke an action, such as navigating to an HTML page, whereas others define the Project Guide's organization and layout (see Figure 24.26). The elements of Gbui.xml are described as follows:

FIGURE 24.26

The Gbui.xml file is comprised of many elements.

- ViewChanges: This element defines how the Project Guide should respond as the user changes views in Project. Because the users can switch to a different Project view at any time, the content of the side pane must change in tandem with the Project view so that it is relevant to the view that the user has displayed. For example, if a user is working with the Gantt Chart view, the side pane may show steps that are related to creating task dependencies. If the user changes the view to the Resource Sheet view, the side pane content would need to be refreshed to be applicable to the new view.

- PageChanges: This element defines how the Project Guide should respond when the user displays Project Web Access pages within Project. For example, the PageChanges element responds whenever a user displays Project Web Access–based content, such as risks, issues, and documents, from within Project Professional.

- GoalArea: Each GoalArea element (see Figure 24.27) defines the Project Guide side panes that appear for the tasks or activities in that goal area and creates an entry in the Project Guide toolbar. The default Project Guide includes Tasks, Resources, Track, and Report as the GoalAreas. Each GoalArea element is made up of a GoalAreaID, GoalAreaName, GoalAreaDescription, URL, and RelevantViews. When a user selects a goal area in the Project Guide toolbar, a corresponding HTML page appears in the side pane that displays the steps that are associated to that GoalArea. A GoalArea element consists of the following items:

■ GoalAreaID: This is a unique identifier for the goal area.

■ GoalAreaName: This is the name of the goal area that is shown on the toolbar, such as Tasks.

■ GoalAreaDescription: This text is displayed at the beginning of a goal area side pane.

■ URL: This is the reference to the HTML page that is associated with the goal area. When the user clicks a goal area in the Project Guide command bar, the corresponding HTML page is displayed in the side pane. By default, this page displays the tasks within the goal area that are defined in the Gbui.xml document GoalAreaTasks.

■ RelevantViews: This element is used to define the views that are relevant to a particular goal area. If the user switches to a view that is not relevant, the ViewChanges element responds and switches the goal area or side pane. This ensures that the content in the side pane is always relevant to the view.

■ GoalAreaTask: This element corresponds to an individual Project Guide side pane task. Each GoalArea element can contain one or more GoalAreaTask elements, corresponding to all the tasks within that goal area.

The GoalAreaTask element (refer to Figure 24.27) consists of the following items:

■ TaskID: This is a unique identifier.

■ Title: This is displayed in the header area at the top of each Project Guide side pane.

■ TaskName: This displays in its associated goal area's side pane.

■ URL: This is the reference to the HTML page for GoalAreaTasks. Each GoalAreaTask has an HTML page that contains the content that appears in the side pane for that task.

■ TaskHelp: This is additional Help content for a GoalAreaTask. Project Guide side panes can offer help that can appear as a Help link at the bottom of the side pane. If you include TaskHelp, you must specify a HelpName that contains the URL of the custom help HTML page.

■ RelatedTask: This element references other GoalAreaTasks that may be related to the GoalAreaTask. RelatedTasks appear in the Next Steps and Related Activities menu.

■ RelatedActivity: This element references related activities that are not defined GoalAreaTasks in the Project Guide but that correspond to VBA methods that are available in Project. The purpose of this element is to provide access to any needed functionality from within Project, including custom VBA sub procedures that you have written. The RelatedActivity element consists of the following items:

■ ActivityName: This displays the activity in the Next Steps and Related Activities menu.

■ VBAMethod: This is the name of the Project Object Model method that should be executed for this activity.

FIGURE 24.27

The GoalArea element defines the tasks that appear in the Project Guide side panes.

GoalAreaTask

RelevantViews

GoalArea URL

GoalAreaDescription

GoalAreaName

GoalAreaID

TaskID

Title

TaskName

GoalAreaTask URL

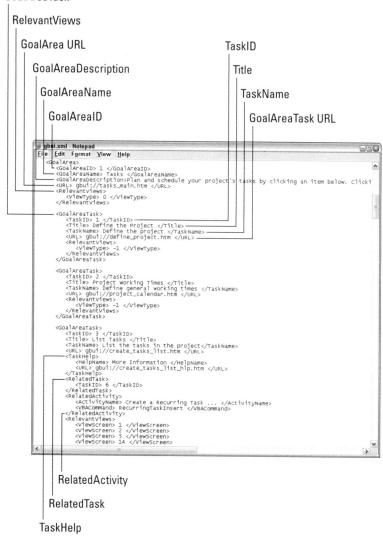

RelatedActivity

RelatedTask

TaskHelp

Defining the Project Guide for a project

Because a Project Guide is associated with a project, you must be able to define the Project Guide that a particular project plan should use; you use the Options dialog box to define the project's Project Guide. Choose Tools ➪ Options and click the Interface tab (see Figure 24.28). A user can change the Project Guide for a specific project or set the Project Guide for all projects by clicking the Set as Default button. In addition, the properties are also available in the Project Object Model, making these settings available to custom macros and VBA code.

Customizing the Project Guide to create a new project

When you start a project, you may want to collect certain project properties, such as the project title or project description. You also may want to base the new project on a particular template. You can customize the Project Guide to add a new task to the Tasks goal area called Create a New Project. The Create a New Project task would prompt the user for a project title, project category, and project description and display a set of option buttons from which the user could select a project template from the standard templates that come with Project.

FIGURE 24.28

The Options dialog box allows you to select the Project Guide that is to be used with your project.

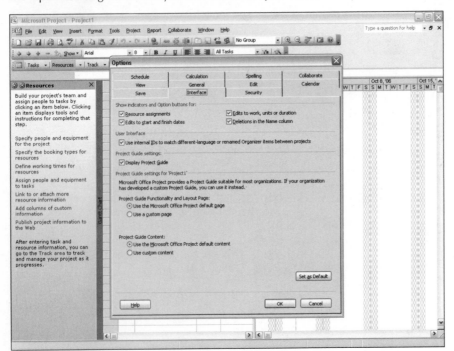

You can also design the project category interface to display a drop-down list of choices rather than require the user to enter this information. Upon completing this screen, Project copies the supplied information to the project properties, just as though you had entered this information directly in the Properties dialog box, and creates a new project plan using the selected template. To add this new task to the Project Guide, follow these steps:

1. Add a new task to the Tasks goal area by modifying the default XML document `Gbui.xml` and adding a new `GoalAreaTask` called Create a New Project.

2. Create a custom HTML page that displays in the side pane when the user clicks the new Project Guide task. This page will contain the necessary functionality to collect information, display a drop-down list of available categories, and populate the associated project plan properties. In this example, the HTML page scripts use JScript, a commonly used scripting language, and the VBScript language.

3. Configure the current project plan to use the custom Project Guide using the Interface tab in the Options dialog box.

NOTE After you create a custom Project Guide, you must make it available to the users in your organization by storing customized HTML pages, scripts, and XML documents locally on a user's computer, on a network share, or on an intranet or Internet server. After you select the location where you intend to store the HTML pages, scripts, and XML documents, make sure that all the custom URL references in the `Gbui.xml` document, HTML pages, and scripts point to the correct file share or URL in your environment.

Adding a new task to the Tasks goal area

The CD that accompanies this book contains sample code to add a new task, called Create a New Project, to the Project Guide. Using this code as a framework, you should ultimately be able to create your own code to add new tasks.

To add the new task to the Tasks goal area, follow these steps:

1. From the CD that accompanies this book, copy the folder `Examples\ProjectGuide\CreateNewProject` to the location where users can find your custom Project Guide.

NOTE The `Examples\ProjectGuide\CreateNewProject` folder includes files for a custom Project Guide with an additional task named Create a New Project in the Tasks goal area.

2. Download the `Gbui.xml` file as part of the Project Guide Software Developer's Kit and open it using Notepad or another text editor.

3. Add the following code in numerical order after the last `</GoalAreaTask>`.

```
<GoalAreaTask>
<TaskID> 100 </TaskID>
<Title> Create New Project </Title>
<TaskName> Create a new project </TaskName>
```

```
<URL> file://C:/Examples/Project
Guide/CreateNewProject/CreateNewProject.htm </URL>
<RelevantViews>
<ViewType> -1 </ViewType>
</RelevantViews>
</GoalAreaTask>
```

4. Change the line that begins with <URL> to reference the folder where you copied these files and save the file.

5. For each task that you want to add to your goal area, copy and paste the code from Step 2 in the Gbui.xml document, replacing the TaskID, Title, TaskName, and other elements that pertain to your new task.

The default XML document now has a new GoalAreaTask. Figure 24.29 shows the custom Project Guide content that appears in Project with the new GoalAreaTask, Create a New Project, included in the Tasks goal area.

FIGURE 24.29
_____

The custom Project Guide displays a new task called Create a New Project.

Creating a custom HTML page

After you have deployed your custom Project Guide and the user clicks the Create a New Project task, the Project Guide displays the HTML page CreateNewProject.htm, which is located in the Project Guide folder that you copied from the CD (see Figure 24.30). This file contains the code to create the graphical user interface and functionality for the Create a New Project task. You don't need to make changes to this file unless you want to add or modify the functionality on this page.

FIGURE 24.30

The Project Guide displays a custom screen called Create Project.

Project description

Project title

Create

In the Gbui.xml file, you can find a GoalAreaTask that references the HTML page Create NewProject.htm. Also, each GoalArea or GoalAreaTask page usually has its own *script file* associated with it. The script file contains functions and code that are specific to the new GoalAreaTask page. Notice how the code from the CreateNewProject.htm file, shown as follows, references the script file CreateNewProject.vbs. This .vbs file contains all the functionality for creating a new project.

> **TIP** It is a good programming convention to keep script and code separate from the content that displays on your screen. In other words, keep the underlying functionality in the .vbs or .js file, and place the user interface elements in the .htm file.

```
<script src="gbui://util.js" language="JScript"></script>
<link rel="stylesheet" href="gbui://ProjIE.css" type="text/css"
/>
</head>
<script src=" CreateNewProject.vbs" language="VBScript"></script>
```

> ## A Behind-the-Scenes Look: How Project Controls the Behavior of the Project Guide
>
> The previous code also references `util.js` and `ProjIE.css`. These items are part of the compiled Project 2007 application.
>
> - `Util.js` is a script file that contains some common functions that are used by the default Project Guide and includes functions for handling resizing and setting scroll bars. Including this reference from the default Project Guide allows your custom page to use functions that are already defined in the script file.
>
> - `ProjIE.css` is a *style sheet* that contains the descriptions that define the appearance of the default Project Guide's user interface elements. Including this reference allows the custom page example to inherit its appearance from the default Project Guide's style sheet.

The rest of the `CreateNewProject.htm` page contains the basic HTML elements and script that prompts the user for the information that is needed to populate the project properties.

The script file `CreateNewProject.vbs` demonstrates the capability of the custom Project Guide to perform actions on the current active project plan. The sub procedure `validateData()` sets a reference to the *Project Object Model* (the way that you programmatically interact with Project) using the code `window.external.application`. After this reference is established, you can use the same properties and methods that are used by custom macros and VBA code. In this example, you set a reference to the active project plan and populate the project properties with the information that is entered on the custom page. You also create a new project based on the template that the user has selected in the Project Guide.

```
sub validateData()
    dim currentApplication
    dim templateName
    dim errorMessage

'Suppress any excess script errors to avoid user confusion.
on error resume next

'Check for blank data
errorMessage = ""
  if trim(ProjectTitle.value)="" then
        errorMessage = "   Enter a Project Title." & chr(13) &
chr(10)
        ProjectTitle.value = ""
    end if
    if trim(ProjectNotes.value)="" then
        errorMessage = errorMessage & "   Enter a Project
Description." & chr(13) & chr(10)
```

```
            ProjectNotes.value=""
        end if

    'Set template name
      select case true
      case projectOffice.checked
            templateName = "C:\Program Files\Microsoft
Office\Templates\1033\PROJOFF.MPT"
          case newBusiness.checked
            templateName = "C:\Program Files\Microsoft
Office\Templates\1033\NEWBIZ.MPT"
        case infrastructure.checked
            templateName = "C:\Program Files\Microsoft
Office\Templates\1033\INFSTDEP.MPT"
          case softwareDevelopment.checked
            templateName = "C:\Program Files\Microsoft
Office\Templates\1033\SOFTDEV.MPT"
        case else
            errorMessage = errorMessage & "   Select a Project
Type." & chr(13) & chr(10)
        end select


      if errorMessage <> "" then
            errorMessage = "To continue you must:" & chr(13) &
chr(10) & chr(13) & chr(10) & errorMessage & chr(13) & chr(10)
            msgbox  errorMessage,,"Project Guide"
            exit sub
      end if
      set currentApplication = window.external.application
      currentApplication.FileOpen
templateName,,,,,,,,,"MSProject.MPT"
          currentApplication.Activeproject.Title = ProjectTitle.value
          currentApplication.Activeproject.ProjectSummaryTask.Notes =
ProjectNotes.value
          pNavigate 1,-1,"createPlan"
end sub
```

I review this code to give you a better understanding of how it works.

Each of the sections that begin with `case` evaluates the type of project template that is selected by the user in the Project Guide. The guide creates a new project based on the project template that is associated with the selected option.

The `FileOpen` method opens the template that the user selected in the Project Guide. When the user clicks the `Create` hyperlink, this triggers the `validateData ()` routine and completes the custom `GoalAreaTask`. Figure 24.31 displays the Project Properties window that contains the information that was entered in the custom Project Guide.

The Project Properties dialog box displays the information that was entered in the custom Project Guide.

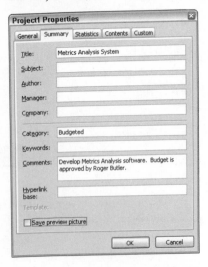

Deploying the customized Project Guide

After you have created a custom Project Guide, you need to configure Project to use the custom guide. Each user can choose Tools ➪ Options and click the Interface tab to point Project to the custom Project Guide. Another convenient way to ensure that a project references the correct Project Guide is to set the options within a project template, and any new project that is based on the template will use the correct Project Guide.

Summary

This chapter presented an introduction to VBA, particularly as you can use it in Project. You learned that VBA forms the foundation for macros and that you can easily produce VBA code by recording a macro. You followed through three examples of creating and modifying VBA code. In the first example, you created a filter to see critical tasks and their resource assignments. In the second example, you used code to adjust work. In the third example, you saw how to customize the Project Guide so that you can modify it to function the same way that your organization works.

In Chapter 25, you explore importing and exporting Project information.

Importing and Exporting Project Information

Sometimes you need to move information in and out of Project. Although you can do this by copying and pasting the information, you'll find that you make these moves primarily by using Project's import and export functions. You can import and export information using various file formats. For example, you can export a Project schedule as a graphic image to use in a graphics program or on a Web page, or to print on a plotter. Or, you may find it convenient to start a project in an Excel workbook, a WSS Project Tracking List, or Outlook's Task List.

> **NOTE** Project 2007 contains a wizard that enables you to generate an XML file.

Understanding General Importing and Exporting Concepts

Importing is the process of bringing information into a Project file from another program. *Exporting* is the process of sending information from Project to another program. When you import or export information, you use an import/export map. Project comes with a series of useful import/export maps that you can edit if necessary, or you can create a custom map. To view, copy, or edit any of the predefined import/export maps, or to create your own map, you use the Import/Export Wizard.

Think of an import/export map as a template that Project uses to correctly translate information from one program to another. An import/export map defines the information that you want to import or export and enables you to describe how to match the information in the Project file with the information in the other program's file. Whenever you import or export, you can use one of the predefined maps that comes with Project, or you can create a new map. Because the wizard walks you through the process, creating a new map is fairly easy to do.

Exporting Information

You can export information to Microsoft Office products, such as Excel workbooks, Access databases, or Word documents. You also can export some Project information to graphic images that you can use in a graphics program or as an image on a Web page. And you can export information to XML, text (.txt) files, or comma-separated value (.csv) files.

 Although the steps for each file type vary slightly, the process for importing or exporting is generally the same.

Saving reporting information in an OLAP Cube or an Access database

Project automatically creates OLAP cubes and an Access database when it produces visual reports, but you don't have direct access to the data when you create a visual report. In addition, when you close your project, Project automatically deletes these OLAP cubes and Access databases. If you want access to the cube or the database to prepare reports outside the context of visual reports, you can save the OLAP cube and the Access database.

To save an OLAP cube, start by choosing Reports ➪ Visual Reports. Then, click the Save Data button in the Visual Reports window to see the Save Reporting Data window, shown in Figure 25.1.

You can create any of the following cubes:

- Task Usage
- Resource Usage
- Assignment Usage
- Task Summary
- Resource Summary
- Assignment Summary

You also can customize the fields that will appear in the cube you select; click the Field Picker button in the Save Reporting Data window to display the Field Picker dialog box shown in Figure 25.2.

FIGURE 25.1

You can create a reporting OLAP cube when you create any visual report in Project.

FIGURE 25.2

Use this dialog box to identify the fields you want to include in the selected OLAP cube.

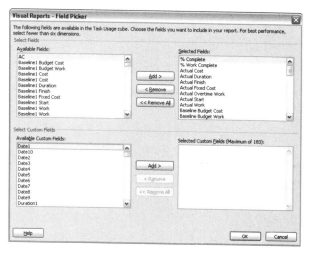

The fields that appear in the Field Picker dialog box depend on the type of cube you selected; task-related fields appear in the Task Usage and Task Summary cubes, but resource fields don't when you choose to create either of these cubes. To add a field, select it in the left column and click the Add button. To remove a field, select it in the right column and click the Remove button. To add and remove custom fields, use the same techniques in the bottom of the dialog box. Click OK when you finish to redisplay the Save Report Data window.

To save the cube, click the Save Cube button; Project displays the Save As dialog box (see Figure 25.3), supplies a default filename, and automatically sets the file type to .cub. If you want, change the filename; click Save to save the cube file.

FIGURE 25.3

Saving cube data.

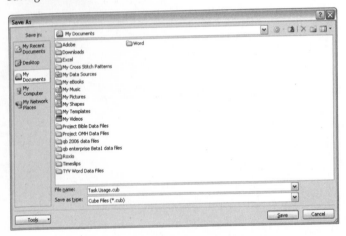

To save your Project file data in an Access database, click the Save Database button in the Save Reporting Data window. Project again displays the Save As dialog box, this time setting the file type to an Access database file (.mdb). You can change the default name suggested for the file; click Save to save the database.

Exporting to Office files

You can export information to Excel workbooks or include Project information in Word. You export information to Excel, but you don't use the export process to include Project information in Word.

Sending Project data to Excel

Using the Import/Export Wizard, you can easily send information to Excel. The wizard gives you the choice of creating a new map or using an existing map. Follow these steps to start the process of sending information to Excel:

1. Open the Project file that contains the information that you want to export.

2. Choose File ⇨ Save As to open the Save As dialog box.

3. Enter a name in the File Name list box for the file that you want to export.

4. Open the Save As Type list box and select Microsoft Excel Workbook or Microsoft Excel PivotTable.

NOTE When you create an Excel PivotTable file, Project creates two sheets in the workbook for each type of data that you export. One sheet contains the data that is used in the PivotTable and the other sheet contains the PivotTable. Project uses the last field in each map as the default field for the PivotTable, and all the other fields appear as rows in the PivotTable.

5. Click Save. Project starts the Export Wizard. Click Next.

6. Choose Selected Data and click Next.

NOTE You can choose Project Excel Template to export the entire Project file to Excel.

7. Choose New Map or Use Existing Map.

If you choose Use Existing Map, you see the Map Selection dialog box (see Figure 25.4).

FIGURE 25.4

Use this dialog box to select the map that you want to use to export your data.

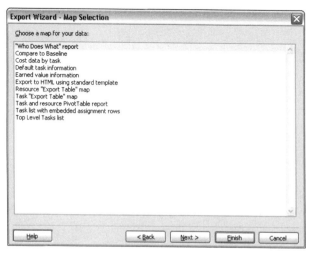

If you choose New Map, you don't see the Map Selection dialog box. Instead, when you click Next, you see the Map Options dialog box.

8. Select a map and click Next. The Export Wizard displays the Map Options dialog box.

9. Select the type of data to export (see Figure 25.5). The boxes that you select determine which wizard screens will subsequently appear when you click Next.

NOTE The map you selected in Step 8 contains a predefined collection of data. The boxes you check in Step 9 identify the type of data to export within the predefined collection.

FIGURE 25.5

Select the type of data to export in the Map Options dialog box.

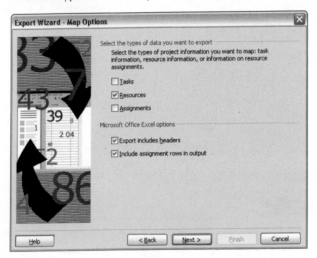

TIP If you want your Excel workbook to contain assignments that are listed under tasks or resources, similar to the Task Usage or Resource Usage views, select the Include Assignment Rows in Output check box.

10. When you click Next, you see one of the mapping dialog boxes. In this example, I selected Resources in the Map Options dialog box. The Resource Mapping dialog box appears (see Figure 25.6) and includes the following options:

- **Destination Worksheet Name:** This box contains the name that Excel will assign to the sheet in the workbook. You can change this name.

- **Export Filter:** Use this list box to select the tasks that you want to export. By default, Project assumes that you want to export all tasks, but you can export, for example, only completed tasks.

FIGURE 25.6

As you add fields in the Resource Mapping dialog box, a preview of the Excel worksheet that you're creating appears at the bottom of the Resource Mapping dialog box.

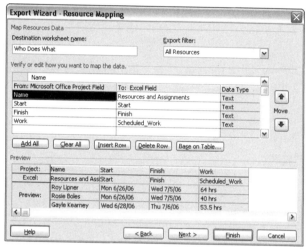

- **From: Microsoft Office Project Field:** Under this column, click any blank cell to add fields to export one at a time. After you click, you can use the list box arrow that appears to view a list of the fields that are available for exporting and to select a field.

- **To: Excel Field:** Select a field to export and click the column next to the field that you added. Project suggests a column heading for the field in the Excel worksheet; you can change this heading.

- **Data Type:** You can't change the data type for the field in the destination program, which appears in this column.

- **Add All:** To quickly add all the fields in the Project file, click the Add All button.

- **Clear All:** To remove all the fields that you added, click the Clear All button.

- **Insert Row:** If you decide to add a field between two existing fields, click the row that you want to appear below the new field. Then, click the Insert Row button, and Project inserts a blank row above the selected row.

- **Delete Row:** To delete a field, click anywhere in the row that contains the field and click the Delete Row button.

- **Base on Table:** To add all the fields in a particular Project table, such as the Entry table or the Cost table, click the Base on Table button. Project displays the Select Base Table for Field Mapping dialog box, from which you can select a table. When you click OK, Project adds all fields that are contained in that table to the list of fields that you want to export.

■ **Move:** You can use the Move buttons on the right side of the dialog box to reorder fields. Click the field that you want to move and then click either the Move Up arrow or the Move Down arrow.

NOTE If you selected the Tasks and the Assignments check boxes as well as the Resources check box in the Map Options dialog box (shown previously in Figure 25.5), when you click Next, the Export Wizard displays additional boxes that are almost identical to the Resource Mapping dialog box, but for each of these data types.

11. After you finish defining your map, you see the final box of the Export Wizard (see Figure 25.7). If you elect to save your map by clicking the Save Map button, Project displays the Save Map dialog box, as shown in Figure 25.8. Provide a name for the new map in the Map Name text box.

FIGURE 25.7

In the final dialog box of the Export Wizard, choose whether to save the map that you've defined.

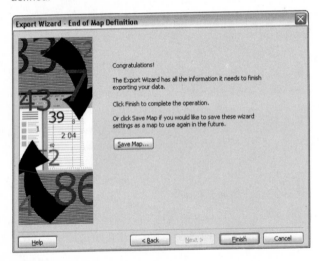

FIGURE 25.8

If you decide to save the map, provide a name for it in the Save Map dialog box, which displays a list of all existing maps.

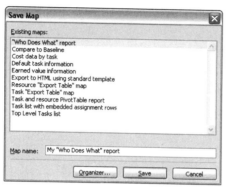

Sending Project data to Microsoft Word

Although you can't export Project data directly into Word, you can use the Windows Copy and Paste commands to incorporate Project text or table data into a Word file. For example, you can copy the columns in any table to a Word document. Start in Project and follow these steps to send Project data to Word:

1. Open the file that contains the information that you want to incorporate into a Word document.

2. Select the information. You can copy text information from the Notes tab of either the Task Information dialog box or the Resource Information dialog box. In addition, you can copy table columns (see Figure 25.9).

FIGURE 25.9

Select information to copy to Word.

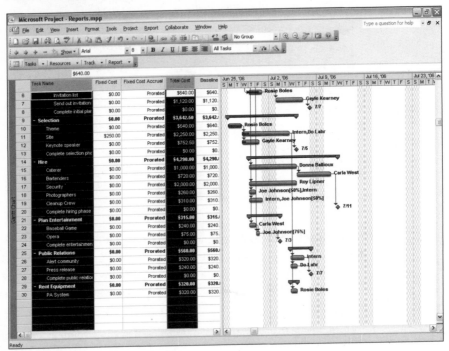

3. Click the Copy button on the Standard toolbar.

4. Open or switch to Word.

5. Position the insertion point where you want the Project information to begin.

6. Click Paste. The Project information appears in Word.

As shown in Figure 25.10, table information appears in Word as tab-separated columns. Using Word's Convert Text to Table feature (select the data and click the Insert tab and then the Table button; click Convert Text to Table), you can convert the information into a Word table.

FIGURE 25.10

Project table information as it appears when you copy it to Word.

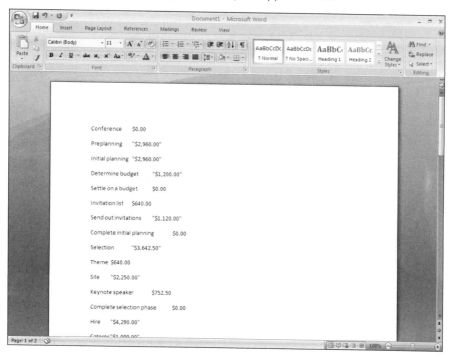

Exporting Project information to a graphic image

You can create a picture from your Project information and view the picture in any graphics program or save the picture in a Web-compatible file format. When you use the following technique, you copy Project information to the Windows clipboard. You can copy all or part of any view except the Task PERT, Task Form, and Resource Form views. Follow these steps to create a picture from Project information:

1. Select the view of which you want a picture.

2. Tell Project how much of your plan to copy. To copy only a portion of your plan, select the information that you want to copy. To copy all visible portions of your plan, don't select anything.

3. Click the Copy Picture button on the Standard toolbar. The Copy Picture dialog box appears (see Figure 25.11).

Use the Copy Picture dialog box to describe how you want to copy the picture.

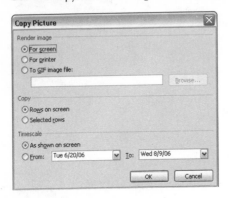

4. In the Render image section, select one of the following options to specify how you want Project to copy the picture:

   ■ **For Screen:** Select this option to copy the information for display on a computer screen.

   ■ **For Printer:** Select this option to copy the information for a printer to use.

   ■ **To GIF Image File:** Select this option to save the information as an image that you can use on a Web page and in other programs. If you select this option, also specify the path and filename in the box below this option.

5. (Optional) If you selected rows before you started this process because you want to copy only those rows, select the Selected Rows check box.

6. (Optional) To copy information for a range of dates other than those currently displayed, select the Date Option button (the last one in this dialog box) and then enter From and To dates.

7. Click OK.

To view an image that you copied as a screen or printer image, switch to the program in which you want to display the Project information and then paste the picture by using the program's Paste command. A copied image in Microsoft Paint appears in Figure 25.12.

FIGURE 25.12

A Project image that I pasted into Microsoft Paint.

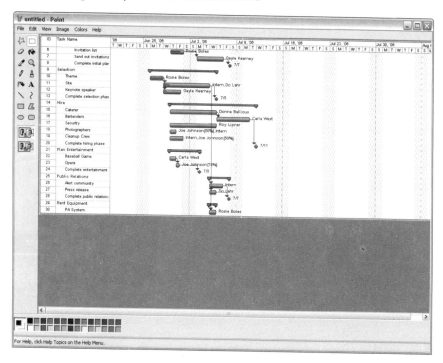

Exporting to text files

If you have a program that can read either a text (.txt) file or a comma-separated value (.csv) file, you can export information from Project to that program. You need to save the information that you want to export as either a text file or a .csv file in Project.

NOTE   This process uses the Export Wizard and closely resembles exporting information to Excel or Access.

Follow these steps to export information to a text file:

1. Open the Project file that contains the information that you want to export.
2. Choose File ➪ Save As to open the Save As dialog box.
3. Select Text or CSV, whichever format works best in the program to which you're exporting, in the Save As type box.
4. Type a name in the File name box for the file that you are exporting.

5. Click Save. The Export Wizard begins. Click Next.

6. Choose to create a new map and click Next. Project displays the Map Options dialog box (see Figure 25.13).

FIGURE 25.13

Select the options for the export map.

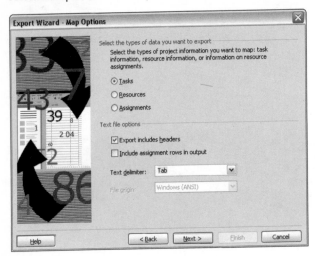

NOTE   If you choose to use an existing map, Project displays a list of available maps. Choose one and click Next to display the Map Options dialog box. If you choose to create a new map, you don't see the list of available maps — saving you a step.

7. Select the options for the export map and click Next. You see at least one of the mapping dialog boxes. The one(s) that you see depends on the information that you chose to export. Refer to the section "Sending Project data to Excel," earlier in this chapter, for details on completing this dialog box.

8. Click Next and complete the additional mapping dialog boxes as appropriate.

NOTE   You can click the Save Map button to save the map that you created.

Importing Information

You can bring information into Project from another Project file or from Microsoft Excel, Microsoft Access, or Microsoft Word. You also can import information that was created in any program that can save text (.txt) files or comma-separated value (.csv) files. When you import a Project file, you actually consolidate two Project files. When you import non-Project files, you use an import/export map to define the data that you want to import.

TIP You can import XML files into Project. In the Open dialog box, select the XML file. Project launches the Import Wizard, where you make one choice: You choose to append the data in the file to the active project, merge the data in the file with the data in the active project, or import the file as a new file.

Inserting another project

When you import one Project file into another, you don't use an import/export map. Instead, importing one Project file into another Project file is the same as consolidating Project files, which you read about in Chapter 15.

Importing Office files

You can import information from Excel workbooks, Access databases, or your Outlook Task List by using the Import Wizard and maps that define the way that the information should be viewed by Project. You can also include information from Word, but you don't use the import process.

Bringing Excel workbook information into Project

Want to start your project in Excel? You can use the Microsoft Project Task List Import Template and then easily transfer the information from Microsoft Excel workbooks to Microsoft Project files. The Microsoft Project Task List Import Template automatically installs to the Office template folder and is available when you start a new workbook in Excel.

 **NOTE** You cannot import an Excel 2007 file format (`.xlsx`) into Project, but you can save the Excel file to an Excel 97-2003 workbook (`.xls`) and then import the file into Project.

 NOTE You can't import an Excel PivotTable into Project.

If you already started your project in Excel without using the template, you can still use the Import Wizard to bring your Excel data into Project. Follow these steps to do so:

1. In Project, choose File ⇨ Open or click the Open button on the Standard toolbar.
2. Open the Files of Type list box and select Microsoft Excel Workbooks.
3. Use the Look In list box to navigate to the folder that contains the Excel workbook that you want to import.
4. Highlight the workbook and click Open. Project starts the Import Wizard.
5. Click Next. In the Map dialog box, choose New map.

NOTE If you choose the Use existing map option, Project displays the list of maps from which you can choose. After you select a map, Project imports your data.

6. Click Next. In the Import Mode dialog box, select the As a New Project option button.

NOTE If you select the Append the data to the active project option button, Project imports the data and places it after any existing tasks in the Project file. If you select the Merge the Data into the Active Project option button, you'll complete Steps 7 and 8, but in the Task Mapping dialog box, you'll click the Set Merge Key button to identify the field that's found in both the Excel file and the Project file.

7. Click Next. In the Map Options dialog box, select the types of data that you want to import (see Figure 25.14).

FIGURE 25.14

Select the types of data that you want to import.

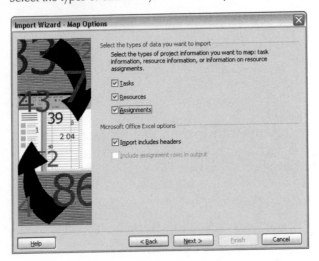

8. Click Next. In the Task Mapping dialog box, select a worksheet from the Source Worksheet Name list box, and Project attempts to resolve the column names in the worksheet with Project fields (see Figure 25.15). Look for fields that contain "(not mapped)" in the To: Microsoft Office Project field. Enter the Project field name or select that name from the list that appears when you click in the To: Microsoft Office Project field. You should also verify the mapping of all fields the first time you use a new map.

FIGURE 25.15

The Task Mapping dialog box shows the fields that Project expects to import from your workbook.

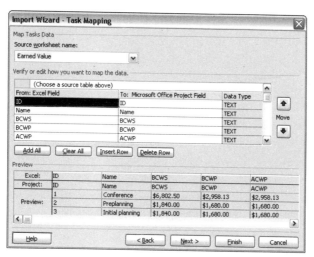

CROSS-REF For a complete list of the functions of each field in this dialog box, see the section "Sending Project data to Excel," earlier in this chapter.

9. Click Next. You see the final box of the Export Wizard, in which you can elect to save the map that you just defined.

NOTE If you selected the Resources and the Assignments check boxes as well as the Tasks check box in the Map Options dialog box (shown previously in Figure 25.14), then, when you click Next, the Export Wizard displays additional boxes for each of these data types that are almost identical to the Task Mapping dialog box.

10. To save your map, click the Save Map button, and Project displays the Save Map dialog box. Provide a name for the new map in the Map Name text box.

Bringing Access database information into Project

Importing Access 2003 or earlier databases into Project is similar to importing Excel workbooks, except that you can import all or part of an Access database into a Project file. Again, you use an import/export map to describe to Project the type of data that you're importing.

To import some or all of an Access database into Project, follow these steps:

1. Choose File ➡ Open or click the Open button on the Standard toolbar.

2. Open the Files of Type list box and select Microsoft Access Databases.

3. Use the Look In list box to navigate to the folder that contains the Access database that you want to import.

4. Highlight the database and click Open. Project starts the Import Wizard.

5. Click Next. In the Map dialog box, choose New Map.

> **NOTE** If you choose the Use Existing Map option, Project displays a list of available maps from which you can choose. After you select a map, Project imports the Access file.

6. Click Next. In the Import Mode dialog box, select the As a New Project option button.

> **NOTE** If you select the Append the Data to the Active Project option button, Project imports the data and places it after any existing tasks in the Project file. If you select the Merge the Data into the Active Project option button, you'll complete Steps 7 and 8, and in the Task Mapping dialog box, you'll click the Set Merge Key button to identify the field that's found in both the Access file and the Project file.

7. Click Next. In the Map Options dialog box, select the types of data that you want to import.

8. Click Next. If necessary, make changes to the Task Mapping dialog box,

> **NOTE** If you selected Merge the data into the active project in Step 6, you need to tell Project how to link the Access table with the project tasks. Highlight the field you will use to merge, typically the ID, and then click the Set Merge Key button.

9. Click Next. You see the final box of the Import Wizard, in which you can elect to save the map that you just defined.

> **NOTE** If you selected the Resources and the Assignments check boxes as well as the Tasks check box in the Map Options dialog box, then, when you click Next, the Export Wizard displays additional boxes for each of these data types that are almost identical to the Task Mapping dialog box.

10. If you elect to save your map by clicking the Save Map button, Project displays the Save Map dialog box. Provide a name for the new map in the Map Name text box.

Bringing Outlook task lists into Project

Perhaps you started a task list in Outlook's Task List and now you realize that your list of tasks is really a project, and you need the scheduling and cost features in Project. You don't need to start over; you can import the Outlook Task List into Project by following these steps:

1. In Project, choose Tools ➡ Import Outlook Tasks. Project displays the Import Outlook Tasks dialog box (see Figure 25.16).

FIGURE 25.16

In this dialog box, mark the tasks that you want to import into Project.

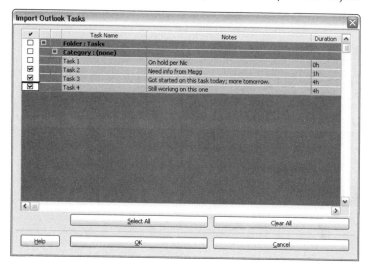

2. Check the tasks that you want to import and click OK. The tasks appear in Project. If the open project already contains tasks, Project appends the Outlook tasks to the task list.

Bringing Word document information into Project

In contrast to other types of files, you can't import Word files directly into Project. You can, however, include information in Word documents in a Project file by using one of the following techniques:

- You can paste information.
- You can link or embed information.

Pasting information from Word into Project

When you use the paste method, you can paste the information either into a table view or into a note in Project. Pasting eliminates the extra step of retyping information.

If you paste text into blank rows, Project treats the information as new tasks or resources. If you paste information into fields that already contain information, Project replaces the information in those fields with the pasted information. However, you can't paste information into Project fields that contain calculated values, such as some of the fields in a cost table.

NOTE You also can use the following technique to paste information from an Excel workbook into a Project table view, but first you must organize the information in your workbook to match the organization of a Project table. For example, suppose that you want to paste information into a resource sheet with the Entry table applied. Your workbook has 3 columns, but the resource sheet has 12 columns, and you want to paste the information into Columns 2, 5, and 8.

To paste this information, you need to create and apply a table in Project that displays only the fields that you intend to paste from your workbook. Make sure that the order and type of columns in the Project table match the order and type of information in the Excel table that you're pasting.

To paste information from Word into a Project table, follow these steps:

1. Open the Word document from which you want to copy information and then copy the information to the Windows clipboard (see Figure 25.17).

FIGURE 25.17

A Word document that you can paste into a Project table.

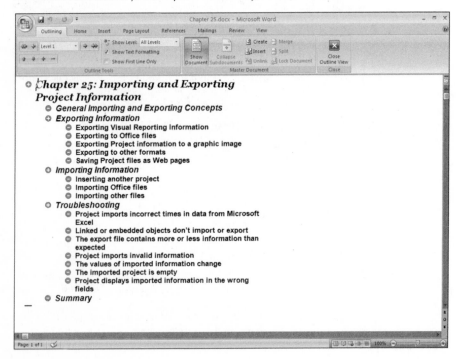

2. Switch to Microsoft Project.

3. Switch to the view into which you want to paste the information. If necessary, choose View ➪ More Views. From the More Views dialog box that appears, select the view that you need and then click Apply.

4. Select the table into which you want to paste information by choosing View ➪ Table ➪ More Tables. Choose the table that you want from the More Tables dialog box and then click Apply.

5. (Optional) If the table that you select has columns that you don't need or is missing columns that you do need, you can add or hide columns. You can also add rows if necessary.

6. Click the first field in which you want information to appear after you paste.

7. Click the Paste button on the Standard toolbar. The information that is stored on the Windows clipboard appears in the Project table, as shown in Figure 25.18.

FIGURE 25.18

The information from the Word document appears in Project.

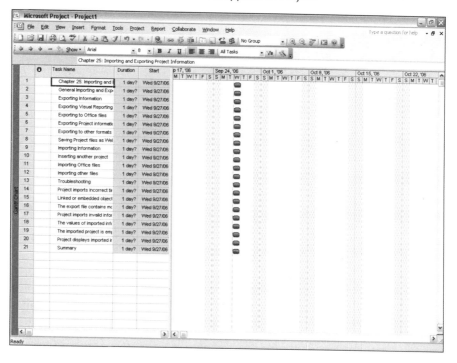

You can paste information from a Word document into a note in Project by using the same technique. Copy the information in Word to the Windows clipboard. Switch to Project and double-click either the task or the resource to which you want to add a note. In the Task Information or Resource Information dialog box that appears, click the Notes tab. Then, right-click the Notes area to display a shortcut menu and choose Paste (see Figure 25.19). The information from Word appears in the Notes area.

You can use a shortcut menu to paste information from the Windows clipboard into a task or resource note.

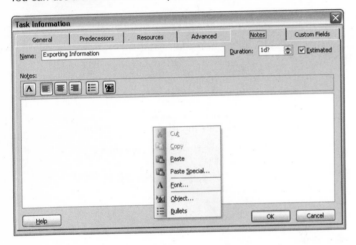

Linking or embedding a Word document in Project

When you link or embed a Word document in Project, you actually insert the document as an object into your Project schedule, as follows:

- When you link a Word document to a Project file, the Project file reflects any changes that you make to the Word document.
- When you embed a Word document in a Project file, the Project file does not reflect subsequent updates to the Word document.

Project views objects that you insert as graphics. Therefore, you can link or embed a Word document as a graphic element in any graphics area of a Project file. A *graphics area* is any area in Project that can display picture information, including task, resource, or assignment notes; headers, footers, and legends in views; headers and footers in reports; the chart portion of the Gantt Chart view; and the Objects box in a task or resource form.

To insert a Word document as a linked or embedded object, follow these steps:

1. Open a Microsoft Project file and display the graphics area into which you want to insert a document.

2. Open the Insert Object dialog box (see Figure 25.20).

TIP To open the Insert Object dialog box in a task, resource, or assignment note, right-click to display a shortcut menu and choose Object. To open the Insert Object dialog box in the Gantt Chart view, choose Insert ⇨ Object.

FIGURE 25.20

Use the Insert Object dialog box to link a Word document to a Project file or embed a Word document in a Project file.

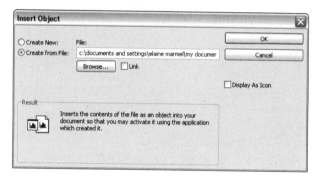

3. Select the Create from File option button.

4. Enter the path and filename of the document that you want to insert, or click Browse to locate and select the file.

5. Do one of the following:

    ▪ To link the object to the source document, select the Link check box.

    ▪ To embed the object, deselect the Link check box.

6. Click OK. Project displays a graphic image of your file (see Figure 25.21).

    You can use the handles around the image in the Task Information dialog box to move or resize the image.

FIGURE 25.21

A Word document inserted as a graphic image in a task note.

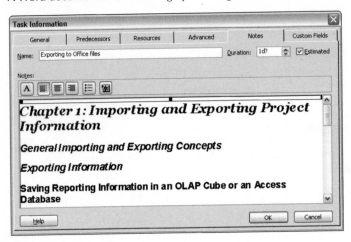

> **TIP** By default, Project displays the contents of the file that you insert rather than an icon that represents the file. To display the object as an icon, select the Display As Icon check box in the Insert Object dialog box.

> **TIP** You can delete the object by making sure that you see the handles that surround it and pressing Delete.

After you click OK, an icon appears in the Indicator column. When you slide the mouse over that icon, however, you don't see the contents of the note in the tip because it is a graphic image. Instead, you see a pair of single quotation marks, as shown in Figure 25.22.

Importing other files

If the information that you want to import comes from a program that can produce either Microsoft Project Exchange files or text files, you can import that information. Microsoft Project Exchange (.mpx) files are of the ASCII, record-based file format.

FIGURE 25.22

When you link or embed an object in the note of a task or resource, you can't reveal the contents of the note by pointing at it with the mouse pointer.

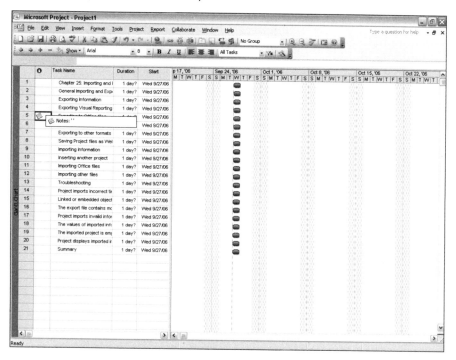

Importing Microsoft Project Exchange files

You can use the MPX file format to import information from older versions of Project into Project 2007. Some other project management software packages also support the MPX file format, so if you need to import information from another project management software package, you can save it as an MPX file and import it into Project. Importing an MPX file is similar to opening any project. Follow these steps to import an MPX file:

1. Choose File ➪ Open.

2. In the Open dialog box, open the Files of type list box and choose MPX.

3. Use the Look In list box to navigate to the appropriate file and click Open.

NOTE The currently recommended method of interchanging project data with other products is XML.

Importing text files

If you have a program that can create either a text file or a comma-separated value file, you can import information from that program into Project. You need to save the information that you want to import as either a text file or a CSV file in the native program. The Import Wizard walks you through the process. If the map that you need doesn't exist, you need to create it.

Follow these steps in Project to import the information:

1. Choose File ➪ Open or click the Open button on the Standard toolbar.

2. Open the Files of Type list box and choose Text (*.txt) or CSV (*.csv).

3. Use the Look In list box to navigate to the folder that contains the file that you want to import.

4. Highlight the file, and click Open. Project starts the Import Wizard.

5. Choose an existing map or create a new one. See the section "Bringing Excel workbook information into Project," earlier in this chapter, for details.

Troubleshooting

Importing and exporting can be tricky operations. Little things go wrong that cause these operations to fail. This section suggests ways to solve some of the problems that you may encounter while importing or exporting.

On a general note, use some common procedures when you export or import data. For example:

- Create a table on which to base your export/import map.

- Include unique identifier fields in export/import maps whenever possible to ensure traceability.

- Include descriptive fields to make the export/import easy to read.

- When updating existing project data, first import to a new project and use the Compare Project Versions utility to confirm correct mappings. Display the Compare Project Versions toolbar (right-click any toolbar and choose Compare Project Versions) and click the Compare Project Versions button. Project displays the dialog box that you see in Figure 25.23. Select the two projects and the task and resource tables to compare.

- Save the Map so that you can compare it easily.

None of the preceding techniques is trouble-free, but getting in the habit of creating repeatable and verifiable maps will help you avoid many problems.

FIGURE 25.23

Use this box to select two projects to compare.

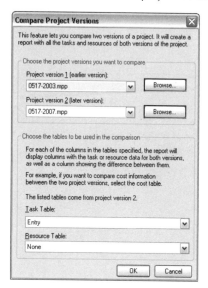

Project imports incorrect times in data from Microsoft Excel

In Excel, when you assign a date to a cell, Excel assigns a default time to the cell of 12:00 a.m. You may not see that time, but Excel has attached it to the cell. If the data that you import from Excel to Project contains dates without specific times, Project automatically uses Excel's default time of 12:00 a.m. If you don't want to use Excel's default time in Project, enter times in Excel before you import.

Linked or embedded objects don't import or export

You're not imagining things. Project does not import or export linked or embedded objects when exchanging data with Microsoft Excel or Microsoft Access. You need to relink or re-embed the objects after you complete the import or export operation.

The export file contains more or less information than expected

The information that you find in your exported file depends on the import/export map that you select, the table that you choose, and the filter that you apply. If you export more or less information than you expect, check the map, table, and filter.

Export/Import Maps are created and edited using the Export Wizard; you won't find an "Edit Map" menu command or button. To troubleshoot an existing map, choose File ⇨ Save As and specify a filename and file type to start the Export Wizard. On the Export Wizard – Map dialog box, select Use Existing Map and click Next. On the Export Wizard – Map Selection dialog box, select the map that was used to generate the export file that is in question and click Next. On the Export Wizard – Map Options dialog box, do not change any settings; simply click Next. Review the fields selected and the Export Filters on the Task, Resource, or Assignment Mapping dialog boxes.

Project imports invalid information

Project checks data that you import to ensure that the data types for each field are valid. If necessary, Project may modify the values of some fields to handle inconsistencies.

If Project warns that you are trying to import invalid data, check the import/export map that you've selected to make sure that you are importing the correct type of information into a Project field. Also, check the data in the import file and make sure that the field values are valid and within the acceptable range for the Project field into which you intend to import the data.

The values of imported information change

This situation is similar to the previous one, in which Project determines that the information that you're trying to import is invalid. Project checks (and changes, if necessary) the data that you import to ensure that the data types and the values for each field are valid. Project may also change data to make sure that it falls within ranges that are valid for Project fields and doesn't create inconsistencies between fields that depend on each other. Project also overrides values that you attempt to import into calculated fields by replacing the imported data with the calculated value.

The imported project is empty

As you know, importing depends on the import/export map that you select. If you choose the wrong map, no data may import. Also, make sure that you're looking at the correct view after importing. If you import task information, you may not see it if you're looking at a resource view.

Project displays imported information in the wrong fields

When imported information appears in the wrong Project field, you should check the import/export map. Make sure that you select the correct map and that the table you used contains the correct fields. Finally, check the mapping of the fields between the import file and your Project file.

Summary

In this chapter, you found out how to import and export information in Microsoft Project. In particular, you should now know how to do the following:

- Create and edit import/export maps
- Export information to Excel, Access, and Word
- Export information to graphics files, text files, HTML files, and other project management software files
- Import information from another project; from Excel, Access, or Word; or from text files
- Solve common problems that occur when you export or import information

Chapter 26

Project Case Studies

I n this chapter, I provide seven case studies featuring the use of Project 2000, Project 2002, and Project 2003 — sometimes in conjunction with an add-on product — to solve real-life problems. I deliberately include cases that run the gamut from small businesses to large corporations. For example, in one case you'll read about a nonprofit organization that used Project to solve a problem.

IN THIS CHAPTER

Real-life examples of using Project

Case 1

DEA Brown & Sharpe, part of Hexagon Metrology, the leading producer of coordinate measuring systems with world headquarters in Heathrow, UK, serves the measurement needs of industrial companies around the globe. DEA Brown & Sharpe offers the most complete source for metrology products anywhere in the world. Coordinate measuring machines, precision measuring instruments, software and post-warranty aftermarket services that keep measuring systems operating at peak performance levels are all available through a worldwide distribution channel and strategically located precision centers. Hexagon Metrology Group is a multinational group of companies that includes Brown & Sharpe GmbH, Brown & Sharpe Qianshao, CE Johansson, DEA, Mirai S.R.L, Quality Ltda, TESA, and Wilcox Inc.

The challenge faced by DEA Brown & Sharpe Limited was met by Technology Associates International, a global company with offices worldwide. Headquartered in the United Kingdom, Technology Associates is a Microsoft Project Premier Partner and a Microsoft Gold Certified Partner and specializes in Microsoft Project EPM solutions, services and deployment. The experience of Technology Associates in deploying Enterprise Project Management solutions across global companies is very extensive and was a key factor in providing confidence to senior management that DEA Brown & Sharpe would be able to successfully implement such a mission-critical solution. DEA Brown & Sharpe Limited was the first UK company to fully adopt the Microsoft Office Project 2003 EPM solution and was part of the Early Adopters program.

Problem statement

To gain and preserve a competitive advantage, DEA Brown & Sharpe must continually deliver and develop new products for its customers and maintain an outstanding level of customer service and support. When DEA Brown & Sharpe was faced with the expansion of its business, the challenge of dealing with customer support contracts and meeting the increasing demand for service personnel to be on-site, with the right skills and in the right location, within hours in some cases, was a big problem in itself. But the same personnel also are involved in installation and commissioning of new machines all over the world, and it is vital to get the right people at the right place at the right time. With more than 200 different products and a range that is increasing all the time, the problem was becoming ever more complex. In addition, the Senior Management at DEA Brown & Sharpe wanted to control product development projects more closely, especially from a financial perspective. DEA Brown & Sharp needed a solution that could handle a complex mix of projects, some long-term development and manufacturing projects and some projects that are very short term, service-support projects. The system also had to be flexible, customizable, and very adaptable.

Problem solution

During the initial discussions, it quickly became apparent that Microsoft Office Project 2003 would be the ideal solution, even though it was still in very early development. Through Technology Associates International, DEA Brown & Sharpe was invited to take part in the Rapid Adoption Program for Microsoft Office Project 2003 and the company enthusiastically accepted. Once enrolled on the program, Technology Associates worked closely with DEA Brown & Sharpe IT Manager Nick Ward and members of the senior management team to complete the system design and initial consultation process.

After considering the system design proposal, DEA Brown & Sharpe chose to implement Microsoft Office Project Professional 2003 and Microsoft Office Project Server 2003. Combined, these products make up the Microsoft Solution for Enterprise Project Management (EPM).

One key aspect of the solution is the new feature in Microsoft Office Project 2003 called multivalue fields. To meet the demands for engineers to respond to service calls for customers that may or may not have support contracts, it is vital that the company is able to quickly respond to demands for on-site support and prioritize those requests. The multivalue field provides an excellent way of setting up multiple skills for a service engineer — most service engineers can have skills in up to 40 different machines, out of a possible range of 200 or so. In addition, the level of skill required also had to be classified (Advanced or Competent) for each skill attributed to a resource.

Using multivalue fields, managers at DEA Brown & Sharpe can quickly identify the correct resources by matching a generic resource with the right machine skills to a list of named engineers with those skills. The Resource Breakdown Structure (RBS) also can be used to identify the location of service personnel by region, country, county, or city. This process enables resources to be identified efficiently and effectively by geographical location, minimizing travel time and maximizing the engineers' time on-site.

Service logs, job cards, and all relevant documentation can be uploaded and tracked using the document-tracking mechanism provided by Microsoft Office Project Server 2003 and Windows SharePoint Services (WSS), which can be integrated into the solution. When you use WSS, each project has its own SharePoint Web site so that project managers and team members are able to maintain all relevant documentation for a project (including CAD drawings, photographs, specifications, quality documentation, and control and change request documentation) in one easily accessible place. This collaborative workspace is easy for users to navigate to and utilize and is truly the focus of all documentation and information concerning each program or project.

When site engineers visit client premises to assess the site and location of a new machine, they produce site surveys. Site surveys are vital because some machines can weigh several tons and require special handling to ensure correct alignment of the large CMMs and avoid distortion of the precision-engineered table. Site engineers can arrive on-site with a digital camera, take video footage and still photographs of the site, and then upload the pictures to the SharePoint Web site for that project. The commissioning/installation team has ready access to this vital information almost instantly, and the whole process ensures an accurate transmittal of key information to the people who really need it, which is backed up by actual photographic or video evidence. Microsoft Office Project 2003 Server helps to keep project information secure because project managers can decide that only people directly involved with the project can have access to the related documents.

Accessing key corporate management data is a breeze because the management team can obtain a global view of development projects and the resources involved in those projects. And because the information is updated in real time, it is always accurate.

The solution uses customizable views such as the Project Center and Resource Center in Microsoft Office Project Web Access. These customizable views enable the management team to view high-level key performance indicators and then drill down to a more detailed level if the information presented seems to warrant further investigation. Before using the Microsoft EPM solution, the management team did not have such strong perception of ongoing projects, or have an effective control on costs or resource loading/capacity.

With a growing customer base, it is extremely important for DEA Brown & Sharpe to be able to determine whether a certain project is on schedule and evaluate the impact of slippage or reduced resource availability. DEA Brown & Sharpe also wants to be able identify the number of engineering resources being used by a project and whether the project is a cost-effective investment in terms of ROI.

Business benefits

Using the Microsoft EPM solution, DEA Brown & Sharpe can capture each element of a project more accurately, from the number of hours needed to design the new product to the development cost of the project. Managers are now better able to estimate how many resources a new project will require and whether the budget is budget to undertake a particular project at a certain point of the fiscal year.

Furthermore, Microsoft EPM allows users to capture best practices to create enterprise-wide project templates that ensure standardized reporting throughout the business. With consistent and accurate project reports, managers are able to make more informed business decisions, ultimately resulting in a better bottom line for the business in terms of profit, revenue, quality, control, and delivery as well as customer satisfaction.

The senior management team is able to review high-level project information and make strategic decisions about projects. Internally, project review meetings are now more focused and effective because of the information and tools at the disposal of managers. The meetings enable everyone to get a perspective on potential and current issues that might affect a particular project's progress and help everyone stay informed about the progress of all current development projects. The executive staff has a complete, high-level, enterprise-wide view of all ongoing development and service projects because of the portfolio management features in the Microsoft EPM solution that provide an overview of the status of all projects within an enterprise. In addition, if there are any issues with a project, Microsoft EPM enables executives to conduct "what if" analysis through the Portfolio Modeler and evaluate all the options available to get a project back on track.

The benefits of the solution have been tremendous. The solution was rolled out completely in a matter of just weeks. The vision for the business and the goals achieved by the company were to

- Develop a common, network-based method for planning and tracking projects on a company-wide basis

- Enhance management's view of the status of major development projects and resource use

- Provide a rapid decision-making model to enable the fast deployment of service personnel with correct skills

- Enhance the speed of execution, quality, effectiveness, and productivity of development projects and activities

- Provide effective tools to DEA Brown & Sharpe project managers that streamline their job of managing projects within their department, synchronizing with geographically dispersed personnel and generating useful management reports

- Improve speed of response to customers

Problem solvers

Technology Associates International (UK Office)
The Mansley Centre, Timothy's Bridge Road
Stratford Upon Avon, Warwickshire CV37 9NQ UK
Tel: +44 (0) 1789 292150 Fax: +44 (0) 1789 292191

Technology Associates International (U.S. Office)
Suite 3600, One Market, Spear Tower
San Francisco, CA 94105
Tel: (415) 449-3602; Fax: (415) 293-8001
Web Site: http://www.techassoc.com
E-mail: info@techassoc.com

Case 2

The challenge that this Fortune 100 company faced was met jointly by Ray Coker and Neal Boring
of The Southern Project Group.

Problem statement

One division within a major Fortune 100 company in the aerospace industry made the corporate
decision to use Microsoft Project to support widely adopted project management practices. After
a close look at Microsoft Project, the division found that the program didn't calculate certain
factors the way that the company needed. Specifically, the company wanted to report on progress
on a summary level, have progress bars drawn on the summary taskbars, and calculate the SPI
(Schedule Performance Index) metric to support the green light/yellow light/red light reporting
model that they use.

When calculating Percent Complete duration on a Summary Task, Microsoft Project weighs and aver-
ages durations of detail tasks below summary task without considering the effort (work) involved.
For example, Project weighs a three-day task that takes 5 hours of effort as heavily as a three-day task
that takes 50 hours when calculating Percent Complete on a Summary Task.

The company preferred to view Percent Progress rather than Percent Complete on Gantt Charts.
In the mathematical model that the company developed, Percent Progress considers both the dura-
tion of a task and the effort involved, and calculates SPI, the Budgeted Cost of Work Performed
(BCWP)/Budgeted Cost of Work Scheduled (BCWS). Project contains the information to calculate
SPI but doesn't calculate it.

Problem solution

The solution that Ray and Neil produced was a collection of menus and toolbars that managed the process for updating and reporting in Microsoft Project and the actual analysis or math in Excel. In other words, updated Project data was mapped to Excel, where formulas that calculate SPI, supplied by the company, are applied to the data. Finally, the data calculated in Excel is brought back into Project, updating the project for the company's reporting criteria.

An official for the company comments on the solution: "Microsoft Project, customized with our Schedule Tracking Tool, has provided our company with valuable tools that are used weekly to report progress against plan."

Problem solvers

Ray Coker
Project Direct
4523 Azeele Street West
Tampa, FL 33609
Phone: 813-282-8246
Email: ray@projectdirect.com

Southern Project Group
11206 Big Canoe
3292 Wood Poppy View
Big Canoe, GA 30143
Office: 706-579-2588
Mobile: 770-823-9130
Email: info@southernprojectgroup.com

Case 3

The challenge facing Longs Drug Stores was met by Sicun Management Group, Inc., using Microsoft Project and Project KickStart.

Problem statement

Longs Drug Stores' Human Resources Department had to implement a new Human Resources Information and Payroll System (HRIS) while going through an acquisition and conducting business as usual. For Longs, a delay in deploying the HRIS system was not an option for two primary reasons:

- The system was linked to a massive HR reengineering effort that would bring a new information system to the $3 billion company and its 16,000 employees.

- The existing HR/payroll system was almost 30 years old, had no additional capacity, and had year 2000 problems that couldn't be fixed, thus placing the majority of the burden for human resources on individual operating managers.

Problem solution

To ensure the success of this massive project, skeptical operating managers had to buy in to the transformation. Input from all participants involved in the project plan was paramount; with this concept in mind, a steering committee and a working staff group — both composed of representatives of operations and Human Resources — were established, and brainstorming sessions began.

Sally Cabbell of Sicun Management Group, Inc., used Project KickStart — a project planning tool that links to Microsoft Project — in order to capture ideas during brainstorming sessions. Project KickStart is ideal to use when a group is providing input; it allows for easy and rapid entry of Phases, Tasks, Resources, Notes, and some timing.

During the dynamic brainstorming sessions, Sally projected Project KickStart on a screen so that the task forces could see their ideas being captured. When the group was satisfied with its work each day, Sally printed the Project KickStart plan and each member of the group took away a beginning project plan. In this way, project-management discipline was introduced into a segment of the organization where project plans had never before been used.

Sally then dumped the Project KickStart data into Microsoft Project, where the more sophisticated project planning of resources, timing, dependencies, and baselines can be captured. Project KickStart fed beautifully into a Microsoft Project plan.

Microsoft Project was then used throughout the project, which lasted about 18 months. At the end of the project, the HR functional operations were completely transformed, including reassigned responsibilities and staffing the key jobs with new, internal operations people who were taught HR during the long transformation process.

The success of this project proved to the participants that managing change is a logical, methodical, carefully planned activity; and when done well, everyone benefits and no one loses — even when sweeping changes are implemented. Careful planning and rigorous management of the plan does not have to be disruptive but can actually improve productivity without the pain of an unproductive period due to the change.

Problem solvers

Sicun Management Group, Inc.
2255 Morello Ave., Suite 166
Pleasant Hill, CA 94523
Phone: 925-288-8755
Fax: 925-735-8071
E-mail: scabbell@sicun.com

Experience in Software
2000 Hearst Ave.
Berkeley, CA 94709-2176
Phone: (510) 644-0694
Web: www.projectkickstart.com

Case 4

The challenge that faced the Nebraska Arts Council was met by Barbee Davis of Davis Consulting.

Problem statement

Education budget cuts have, for the most part, been felt most strongly in the arts programs of most schools. Many schools have lost their music or art programs entirely or those programs have been cut back significantly. The Nebraska Arts Council received substantial grant money to be used to find a way to make arts basic to education through teacher education and school reform. The Nebraska Arts Council decided to use the money to reeducate classroom teachers at six schools to include the arts as part of the typical classroom curriculum—as opposed to relying on schools to provide separate arts programs. Initially, the Nebraska Arts Council ran into some challenges while trying to organize an effective approach to meet all the requirements of the various grant providers. So, Barbee Davis of Davis Consulting was hired as a project consultant to help the Nebraska Arts Council clarify and meet its goals.

Problem solution

Using the process in Microsoft Project for planning a project, Davis Consulting met with the Nebraska Arts Council and together they clarified the charge of the Nebraska Arts Council: to aid teachers in producing curriculum units that included visual arts selections, and to help produce a plan to sustain the production and use of curriculum units in the coming years when the funding was no longer available. In particular, they decided that they had to deal with four distinct issues:

- Ensure that the teachers finished the curriculum units as their final product to meet the grant requirements
- Motivate the teachers
- Get administrators to buy in and support the project
- Create a plan for sustaining the project

To meet the first goal, the Nebraska Arts Council chose a curriculum writing process and set up a "teach the teacher" program, in which several "mentor" teachers were trained. Then, the teachers attended a series of four classes/workshops where they learned a formal curriculum process and actually began to write their units under the supervision of their mentors.

To meet the second goal, the Nebraska Arts Council kicked the year off by offering up to ten people at each school a $400 trip to London to view the actual art pieces that the teachers were using in their curriculum units. The teachers paid $200 at the beginning of the year and signed a contract in which they agreed to produce the curriculum units. The terms of the contract stated that if the teachers met a series of performance goals during the year, they would pay the balance of the money due—(another $200) and the grant money would fund the rest of the trip.

To meet the third goal, the Nebraska Arts Council decided to allow each school involved in the program to send up to eight teachers and two administrators to London. The administrators had their own series of activities to complete to qualify for the trip.

To meet the fourth goal, the teachers put their units on a Web site for all Nebraska teachers and agreed to mentor other teachers to help develop additional curriculum units. They agreed to teach their curriculum units throughout the upcoming school year.

Davis Consulting and the Nebraska Arts Council created a plan in Microsoft Project and tracked and reported on the progress systematically. It was a great success: Every goal was met and the morale for the year was higher than it had ever been. Teachers who had been bored and some who had never really understood what the project was all about were awakened and involved.

Each teacher was set up as a subproject within the overall project and most of the dates had "Must Finish On" constraints; the final date was the trip to London. Each teacher's requirements were listed separately and not merged to an entire project because the successful completion of the project didn't depend on each person's completing his or her individual activities. If a teacher fell behind or dropped out of the program, other teachers signed up as alternates and stepped in.

In this case, Project wasn't used in the traditional way — that is, to set up task dependencies and determine a critical path to figure out when the project would end. Instead, Project was used to track tasks that needed to be completed by each teacher and by specified dates; if a teacher didn't complete the tasks, he or she was dropped from the program, but the project continued along.

This example is an important one because users of Microsoft Project often narrow their thinking to believe that it is only useful for construction, architecture, and manufacturing. In fact, it also is an extremely powerful software tool for organizing more esoteric projects and keeping them on track. Microsoft Project's feedback reports have credibility, whereas mere progress updates are soon forgotten. Microsoft Project helped to boost enthusiasm and buy-in for the project, which is critical to the success of any project. This case, which can also be used in any business environment, demonstrates a very effective use of Microsoft Project as a model for change management.

Problem solver

Barbee Davis
Davis Consulting
9524 Hascall
Omaha, NE 68124
Phone: (402) 397-4716
Cell: (402) 690-7066
Fax: (402) 397-1551
Email: barbeedavis@home.com

Case 5

The challenge faced by a large Asian conglomerate that needed a unique software application was met by John D. Callos of IdeaBridge, an international strategy and management consulting firm. Callos used Microsoft Project and Project KickStart, a Project add-on developed by Experience in Software.

Problem statement

An IdeaBridge client was in negotiations to sell its e-commerce company with a unique software application to a large Asian conglomerate that needed to use and integrate the IdeaBridge client's application in order to quickly establish a new market position. This project was a high-profile initiative, and it was vital that the solution/technology be integrated, checked, marketed, promoted, and launched within a three-month period.

The conglomerate's team called John Callos, Managing Director of IdeaBridge Consulting Group, to say that team members were coming over in a few days to try to close a deal with his client but they wanted to meet him to gauge his ability to assist the integration team. They wanted Callos to be involved because of his familiarity with the product and the target market. They gave him a few scant details and asked him to have a proposed project plan and integration timeline mapped out by the time their flight touched down in Los Angeles.

For this multimillion-dollar project, John had to be able to use Microsoft Project, which concerned him greatly; at the time, he was just a novice user of Microsoft Project.

John used the Internet to research project management approaches for a project of this magnitude and to look for some templates available for download to hit the ground running, but at first he wasn't able to find any that would have been viewed as an impressive platform from which to launch the project.

Problem solution

Ultimately, John found a program called Project KickStart that turned out to be perfect for what he needed. John instantly found the program capable of being used intuitively. He answered the series of questions that Project KickStart asked him, and the program then logically and simply walked him through all the project phases. The simplicity of Project KickStart was vital because John had no time to learn anything from scratch. John's job was made even easier because he could merge Project KickStart information instantly into Microsoft Project, which was a requirement of the project.

Within a few hours, John had a *very* detailed outline of the project plan. With this outline in hand, John augmented the plan with some bullet points he found on the Microsoft Project portion of the Microsoft Web site and other project management sites. By the time the prospective buyers had arrived, John was able to present them with an extremely detailed plan that took just a few hours to complete.

The prospective buyers were impressed with the detail of the plan and began negotiating for a role far beyond what they had initially envisioned, ultimately leading to John's full time, on-site management of the entire project team in Asia. During this time, John used Project KickStart's link to Microsoft Project to transfer his project plan to Microsoft Project and to e-mail the particulars to the team in Asia.

Using a full-time person to keep the project plan constantly updated, the project team integrated the various project plans of the technology development firm, the advertising and marketing firms, the business partners, the media people, and the opening day kick-off event planners. They developed an incredibly useful document that kept everyone on task and prevented things from falling through the cracks. The client was thrilled to be able to focus on other pressing matters, knowing that the project was 100 percent under control because John had a detailed project plan that included well over 500 distinct items. Anytime company employees have a similar project, they can refer to this plan and use it as a template to ensure that they have thought of everything that should be included in a project plan.

In this case, Project KickStart enabled John's firm to land a large international project with a well-known Asian conglomerate because Project KickStart helped John put together a project plan outline quickly — even before he learned Microsoft Project. And none of John's efforts were wasted thanks to Project KickStart's seamless integration with Microsoft Project.

Problem solvers

John D. Callos, Managing Director
IdeaBridge Consulting Group
5300 East El Prado Avenue, Suite B
Long Beach, CA 90815
Phone: (562) 986-1223
Web: www.IdeaBridge.com
Email: info@IdeaBridge.com

Experience in Software
2000 Hearst Ave.
Berkeley, CA 94709-2176
Phone: (510) 644-0694
Web: www.projectkickstart.com

Case 6

The challenge faced by this Fortune 100 company was met by Project Assistants, Inc., a Microsoft Project Certified Partner based in Wilmington, Delaware.

Problem statement

The IT division within a major Fortune 100 company was looking for a way to collect project management metrics data in a more consistent, accurate, and automated fashion. This data would be used to support trend analysis across all the projects within the organization. The company had initiated other programs previously to collect project management metrics, but these programs were always very time consuming and created considerable additional work for the project managers.

Project Assistants convinced the company to standardize on the use of Microsoft Project by demonstrating how the company would be able to collect the project management metric data directly from within Microsoft Project — without changing the current process used by the project managers. In this way, current work processes in Microsoft Project wouldn't be interrupted.

In particular, the company wanted to

- Collect metric data on schedule and work variances throughout the life of a project. This data would allow management to identify why some projects finish behind schedule or over budget and, in turn, improve the estimating accuracy over time.

- Collect methodology compliance data to determine whether a correlation existed between overall project quality and procedures that the organization had invested heavily in developing when project managers closely followed the standard methodology tools.

Problem solution

To solve these problems, Project Assistants developed a COM add-in to collect key metric data directly from within Microsoft Project. To address the company's first business requirement, the COM add-in collects metric data on schedule and work variances throughout the life of a project. The system calculates the finish variance and work variance at key stages of a project, and if the variance exceeds the allowed tolerance (for example, by 10 percent), the project manager must enter the reason that the variance is out of tolerance.

To address the company's second requirement, the COM add-in collects methodology compliance information, thus allowing project managers to map their project to one of the approved methodologies and in turn associate the required deliverables for the methodology to their corresponding tasks in the Microsoft Project plan. For example, the "Conceptual Data Model" deliverable would be mapped to the task "Create Conceptual Data Model" in the project plan. The metrics collection tool allows the project manager to report the status of these required deliverables to management, as well as provide a reason that the project manager may have chosen not to follow an approved methodology at certain points in the project.

The COM add-in also includes an automated status-reporting module that allows project managers to complete a questionnaire that focuses on key project management factors, such as scope, budget, and risk. Based on the answers to the questions, the project manager receives a "red light," "yellow light," or "green light" for his or her project. In this way, the company can measure the "health" of a project in a consistent and standard way throughout the organization.

Problem solvers

Project Assistants, Inc.
1409 Foulk Road, Suite 200
Wilmington, DE 19803
Phone: (302) 477-9711
Fax: (302) 477-9712
Web: www.projectassistants.com
E-mail: ibrown@projectassistants.com

Case 7

BCE Emergis caters to a client list that includes leading banks, insurance companies, and healthcare companies across North America, developing sophisticated, transaction-based Web applications to transform their customers' business processes and provide them with a competitive edge in the global economy. The challenge faced by BCE Emergis was met by Tenrox, Inc. — a Quebec-based developer of business-optimization software products — using Projeca and Microsoft Project.

Project statement

BCE Emergis has enjoyed tremendous success in quickly growing its business to 2,000 employees, but this growth has been accompanied by challenges. After several company acquisitions and offices in Montreal, Toronto and Greensboro, North Carolina, BCE Emergis quickly found itself with a mixture of multilingual reporting systems being used by its project managers. Because the company did not have a standardized bilingual management system in place to measure each project's time allocation and budget cost center, reporting results had to be manually combined and analyzed — a time-intensive and tedious effort.

Upper management found it very difficult to consolidate project information and track profitability. Management had no tools or metrics to reorganize groups according to workload and to improve productivity. Additionally, project managers were able to track only the amount of time spent on a project — as opposed to being able differentiate overtime hours.

BCE Emergis sought an affordable and easy-to-use turnkey solution that was designed to handle time management and expense management and would be compatible with all leading ERP, CRM, Project Management, Payroll, and accounting systems.

Project solution

Projeca — an out-of-the-box, pure HTML system developed by Montreal-based Microsoft Certified Partner, Tenrox — automates, optimizes, and helps standardize paper-intensive and time-consuming administrative tasks. Designed for integration with Microsoft Project (used by the majority of BCE Emergis project managers), Visual Basic, C++, SAP, and other popular systems, Projeca's deployment and implementation was painless and saved the company countless hours of training and replicating data. It also provides 250 reports that can be modified by using other software and allows users to create new reports with ease.

Problem solvers

Tenrox, Inc.
600 Boulevard Armand-Frappier
Laval, Quebec
Canada, H7V-4B4
Web: www.tenrox.com/
Phone: (450) 688-3444
Fax: (450) 688-7862

Summary

This chapter described some real-life situations in which Project helped provide a solution. The cases covered a variety of industries, including some in which you wouldn't expect Project to be used.

Part VII

Appendixes

Appendix A

What's on the CD-ROM

The CD-ROM that accompanies this book contains demos or demonstration/trial versions of several popular add-on products for use with Microsoft Project. In addition, this CD-ROM includes sample files for three of the most common types of projects that you can use as time-savers when you begin building similar schedules. You'll also find this book in Adobe Acrobat Reader (.PDF) format — along with Adobe Acrobat Reader — and a Web page of links to some Project partners

IN THIS APPENDIX

System requirements

Working with the CD

What software you'll find on the CD

Troubleshooting

System Requirements

Make sure that your computer meets the minimum system requirements shown in the following list. If your computer doesn't match up to most of these requirements, you may have problems using the software and files on the CD. For the latest and greatest information, please refer to the ReadMe file located at the root of the CD-ROM.

- A PC with a Pentium or faster processor; or a Mac OS X computer with a G3 or faster processor
- Microsoft Windows XP or later
- A CD-ROM drive

Using the CD

If you have AutoRun enabled on your computer, the CD should load automatically; you'll see an interface with links to view various components on the CD. If you don't have AutoRun enabled (or if you prefer to navigate on your own), you can view the contents of the CD manually. You'll find the contents of the CD organized into folders.

To install the items from the CD to your hard drive, follow these steps.

1. Insert the CD into your computer's CD-ROM drive. The license agreement appears.

> **NOTE** If the license agreement doesn't appear, click Start ➪ Run. In the dialog box that appears, type D:\start.exe. Replace D with the proper letter if your CD-ROM drive uses a different letter. Click OK.

2. Read through the license agreement and then click the Accept button if you want to use the CD.

3. The CD interface appears. The interface allows you to install the programs and run the demos with just a click of a button (or two).

Shareware programs are fully functional, free, trial versions of copyrighted programs. If you like particular programs, register with their authors for a nominal fee and receive licenses, enhanced versions, and technical support.

Freeware programs are free, copyrighted games, applications, and utilities. You can copy them to as many PCs as you like — for free — but they offer no technical support.

GNU software is governed by its own license, which is included inside the folder of the GNU software. There are no restrictions on distribution of GNU software. See the GNU license at the root of the CD for more details.

Trial, demo, or evaluation versions of software are usually limited either by time or functionality (such as not letting you save a project after you create it).

Software on the CD-ROM

This appendix describes the contents of the CD-ROM and, where necessary, gives instructions for installing programs on your computer. You can use the demo versions of these products to see how they fit your needs. Each listing includes contact information so that you can buy the software directly from the vendor.

> **NOTE** In some cases, these vendors did not have the fully updated version of their software for Project 2007 prepared in time for this book's publication. If you have access to Project 2003, you can test the early version and then order the Project 2007 version. If you no longer have access to Project 2003, you can contact the companies to get an updated demo or more product information.

PDF

You'll find a .PDF file of this book on the CD. You can use this file to electronically search for topics in the book. You'll also find a .PDF file of the forms in Appendix B of this book, which you can use to help you plan your project. You can read .PDF files with Adobe Reader, which you'll also find on the CD-ROM. If you open either file in Adobe Reader, you can easily search for topics or print the forms.

Empire TIME

Demo version, Windows

This suite of solutions includes Empire TIME for both Project Financial Management and Resource Skills Management. You can use Empire TIME, a multicurrency project time and expense accounting system, for internal chargebacks or external billing. Empire TIME is a high-performance, Windows-based client/server system that integrates with Microsoft Project, allowing managers to analyze time, staff assignments, costs, and revenue on their projects. Empire TIME is distinguished by its robust accounting capabilities for tracking and invoicing actual cost and revenue for time, expenses, services, and materials.

The Windows Support Group, Inc.
150 West 22nd St.
New York, NY 10011
Phone: (212) 675-2500
Web: www.wsg.com

Milestones Professional

Trial version

Milestones Professional is a front end for Microsoft Project. You can enter and manage project data in Milestones and then move (export) it into Project. You can also import Project data to Milestones. This approach enables you to better control the display of some Project data because you can make settings for the number of tasks per page, column and page layout, and OLE linking and embedding. You also can use Milestones Professional as a stand-alone scheduler for creating and updating simple Gantt or timeline schedules without using the resource management features of Project.

Kidasa Software
1114 Lost Creek Blvd., Ste. 300
Austin, TX 78746
Phone: (800) 765-0167
E-mail: sales@kidasa.com
Web site: www.kidasa.com

Milestones Project Companion 2006, from Kidasa Software

Trial version

Milestones Project Companion provides advanced Web publishing and reporting tools compatible with Microsoft Project 2007.

Kidasa Software
1114 Lost Creek Blvd., Ste. 300
Austin, TX 78746
Phone: (800) 765-0167
E-mail: sales@kidasa.com
Web site: www.kidasa.com

PERT Chart EXPERT

Demo version

PERT Chart Expert is a Windows-based application that enables you to create PERT charts from existing Project schedules, text files, or spreadsheets. As an add-on to Microsoft Project, PERT Chart EXPERT integrates with Project to generate presentation-quality PERT chart diagrams.

Critical Tools
8004 Bottlebrush Dr.
Austin, TX 78750
Phone: (512) 342-2232
Web: www.criticaltools.com

PertMaster Project Risk

Trial version

You can use this as stand-alone software or as an add-on for Microsoft Project to run schedule and cost risk analyses.

Pertmaster LTD
The Surrey Technology Centre
40 Occam Road
Guildford, Surrey
GU2 7YG
Tel: +44 (0)1483 685 190
Fax: +44 (0) 1483 573 704

Pertmaster
2100 West Loop South, Ste 1050
Houston, Texas 77027
Main Tel: +1 713 595 7656
Support: +1 713 595 7651
Fax: +1 713 595 7657
Web site: www.pertmaster.com

Project KickStart

Trial version

Project KickStart is the fast, easy way to plan and organize your projects. The software's seven-step icons quickly guide you through the process of building a strategic plan. You'll consider project goals, obstacles, resources, and other "big picture" issues. Use the Project KickStart "hot-link" icon to transfer your plan into Microsoft Project. Project data will appear in MS Project's Task column, ready for scheduling.

Experience in Software
2000 Hearst Ave.
Berkeley, CA 94709-2176
Phone: (510) 644-0694
Web: www.experienceware.com

WBS Chart Pro

Demo version

WBS Chart for Project is a planning tool that enables you to create projects by using a WBS (work breakdown structure) Chart. You can use this method to plan, manage, and display projects with a tree-style diagram. With WBS Chart for Project, you can sketch a project quickly and easily by dragging your mouse on the screen. You can then transfer the plans that you create in WBS Chart for Project directly to Microsoft Project or to any program that can read a Microsoft Project file format (*.mpp). You can also use WBS Chart for Project to automatically generate presentation-quality WBS charts from existing Microsoft Project files.

Critical Tools
8004 Bottlebrush Dr.
Austin, TX 78750
Phone: (512) 342-2232
Web: www.criticaltools.com

Project Sample Files

The CD-ROM also contains three sample files that give you a head start on typical projects. Copy these sample files to your hard drive, open them, save them with your own project name, and then add, delete, and change settings for the various tasks included here.

You need to create your own resources and assign them to tasks and add timing and dependency relationships between tasks. The three sample files are as follows:

- Publication sample file (`Publish.mpp`). This sample file is useful for any kind of publishing project, from a simple brochure to a product documentation manual. Phases for writing and editing content, design, layout, printing, and distribution give you the basis for your own publishing project.

- Meeting sample file (`Meeting.mpp`). Everybody plans meetings. Whether it's a regular weekly staff meeting or your company's annual meeting, this sample file provides the tasks that you need to arrange for location, transportation and lodging, invitations, catering, equipment, and speakers.

> **TIP**   Project 2007 comes with some predefined templates on which you can base projects. To use a template, choose File ⇨ New and click the On My Computer link. As do my sample files, the templates provide a starting place for projects that you enter into Project.

- Facility sample file (`Facility.mpp`). You can use this sample file to set up a new facility or to move to a new space. Tasks include planning space, coordinating movers, managing utilities, and setting up computer networks.

What's on the Web Site

The Project 2007 Bible Web page offers links to the sites of Microsoft Project partners who offer software that enhances Microsoft Project and assistance in using Microsoft Project. At several of the Web sites, you'll find Web-based demo products. All author-created material from this book that is included on the CD-ROM is also available at the book's companion Web site, which is located at www.wiley.com/go/project2007bible. So if you're out and about and find that you need access to the author files (and don't have the CD handy), go there and you can download the files. Also, if you purchased the eBook version of the book (and therefore did not receive the CD), feel free to download the author files so that you can more easily follow the examples.

Troubleshooting

If you have difficulty installing or using any of the materials on the companion CD, try the following solutions:

- **Turn off any anti-virus software that you may have running.** Installation programs sometimes mimic virus activity and can make your computer incorrectly believe that it is being infected by a virus. (Be sure to turn the anti-virus software back on later.)

- **Close all running programs.** The more programs you're running, the less memory is available to other programs. Installers also typically update files and programs; if you keep other programs running, installation may not work properly.

If you have trouble with the CD-ROM, please call the Wiley Product Technical Support phone number at (800) 762-2974. Outside the United States, call 1(317) 572-3994. You can also contact Wiley Product Technical Support at http://support.wiley.com. John Wiley & Sons will provide technical support only for installation and other general quality control items. For technical support on the applications themselves, consult the program's vendor or author.

Appendix B

Project Management Worksheet

This appendix provides worksheets that allow you to plan every phase of a project. Feel free to make copies of these pages and fill them in as you work through your project to be sure you've covered all the bases.

ON the CD-ROM You can find a copy of this appendix in the *Microsoft Project 2007 Bible* Forms folder on the CD-ROM of this book in .PDF (Adobe Acrobat) format to help you print and use these forms. You'll also find a copy of Adobe Acrobat Reader.

Phase I: Research

In this phase, you gather information about the scope and goals of your project; you determine parameters, such as dates, resources, and money available for your project; and finally, you specify deliverables.

1. Ask the following people or groups of people to define the goal of this project. Note any discrepancies in their goal statements and resolve them before you begin planning your project:

   - Your manager.

   - Your staff.

   - The manager of finance.

   - The person who manages the product or service that pertains to your project. For example, if you are setting up a new manufacturing unit, contact the production line supervisor. If you are organizing the move to a new facility, contact the office or facilities manager.

Write their responses here:

_____

_____

_____

_____

2. In the space provided, sketch the organizational chart of those who will implement your project. Indicate who reports to whom within your general organization and then specifically for this project (these two hierarchies may differ slightly). Who will expect to receive reports, communications, and deliverables?

3. To help you begin to build a project team, list the resources you may have available for your project in the following table, noting each resource's department, expertise, and availability.

Project Resources Table

Resource	Department	Expertise	Availability

4. Research timing for this project and answer the following questions:

    ■ How long have similar projects taken in your organization or your experience?

    _____

    ■ Are any of the dates related to your project unchangeable, such as a yearly inspection by an outside organization or the end of your fiscal year? List them here. Also make note of holidays and vacation times.

    _____

    _____

    _____

    _____

■ Rank the priority of the three major areas that typically affect a project: time, quality, and cost. In a crunch, the criterion that you rank highest here will take precedence.

___Time

___Quality

___Cost

Phase II: Planning

In this phase, you take some of the information that you gathered in Phase I and begin to see how those details will come together to form a project plan that can be the basis of your project schedule.

1. Write a goal statement. This one-sentence description states the desired result of all the efforts in your project. A sample goal statement may be as follows: "Our goal is to successfully launch a new software product into the marketplace."

_____

_____

_____

2. Write a scope statement. This statement should broadly outline the parameters of your project. A sample scope statement may be as follows: "We will finalize the software according to our internal quality standards and launch it in three major markets by the end of this fiscal year at a cost not exceeding $1.2 million."

_____

_____

_____

_____

_____

3. List the major phases of your project:

_____

_____

_____

_____

_____

4. List any milestones in your project. Milestones are tasks that mark a moment or accomplishment in your project.

   _____

   _____

   _____

   _____

   _____

   _____

   _____

   _____

   _____

5. Create a contact list for your project, including each resource's name, title, and department; each resource's manager, contact information, hourly rate or fee; and any other information that you consider useful. You can create this list in a word processing program, such as Microsoft Office Word, or begin to enter this resource information in Microsoft Office Project. Use the following entry as a model:

   Resource Name: John Smith
   Title/Department: Engineer/manufacturing department
   Manager: Sally Jones, manufacturing manager
   Phone: (444) 555-1111
   E-mail: jsmith@org.com
   Rate: $35 per hour
   Comments: Not available in December due to professional association commitments; assistant is Bob James, ext. 5567.

   _____

   _____

   _____

   _____

   _____

   _____

   _____

   _____

   _____

_____

_____

_____

_____

_____

_____

_____

_____

_____

_____

_____

_____

_____

6. Outline the standards that you will use for entering information into Microsoft Office Project, including the following:

■ How will you name resources (by name or title)?

_____

■ Who will track progress and how often?

_____

■ What are your organization's standard work hours and fiscal year? This information enables you to create an accurate calendar in Project.

_____

■ What regular reports will you generate and to whom will they go?

_____

_____

■ How will you track and account for overtime?

_____

_____

Phase III: Creating Your Project Schedule

In this phase, you enter information to begin building your project. Use this checklist to be sure that you are creating a comprehensive and accurate schedule.

Checklist for creating a Project schedule

_____ Enter general project information, such as the project name and start and finish dates.

_____ Make any calendar settings for your project based on your organization's workday, week, or year.

_____ Enter the names of major phases of your project.

_____ Enter the first level of individual tasks in each phase, including task name and timing. If this level task will have subtasks, don't bother to enter timing because the task timing will be derived from subtasks.

_____ Enter any subtasks and include timing information.

_____ Enter any regularly recurring tasks, such as monthly project meetings.

_____ Add resource information to individual tasks, including costs and availability.

_____ Establish dependencies between tasks.

_____ Study and resolve resource conflicts by using the resource leveling and contouring tools in Project.

_____ Determine whether Project is giving you an acceptable finish date. If it isn't, consider using the following actions:

  ■ Add resources to reduce duration. (However, this action is likely to add costs.)

  ■ Request additional time to complete the project.

  ■ Use resource downtime more efficiently.

  ■ Adjust dependencies.

  ■ Start the project earlier.

_____ If possible, add some slack time to tasks to allow for delays.

_____ Set up any workgroup resources with whom you will be using Project's TeamAssign, TeamStatus, and TeamUpdate features.

_____ When the project schedule is acceptable, set the baseline and save the file.

Phase IV: Tracking Your Project

Tracking your project involves entering actual time expended on tasks. Use this checklist to help in tracking projects. Don't forget to set a baseline before beginning to track activity on your project.

Tracking procedures checklist

_____ Enter actual start and finish dates for tasks that have been completed.

_____ Enter resource effort expended on tasks.

_____ Enter actual fees or charges incurred on tasks.

_____ Set remaining durations and percent complete for individual tasks.

_____ Use various tracking views in Project, information about earned value and resource usage, and filters, such as critical paths, to analyze the status of your project. Pay careful attention to how much time and money remains by comparing your original estimates and actual activity on the project.

_____ Make any adjustments necessary to keep your project on track, such as adding or reassigning resources, extending your final deadline, or reassessing the remaining budget available for the rest of the project based on cost overruns.

_____ Send out TeamStatus and TeamUpdate messages to keep your team informed of project progress.

Phase V: Preparing for the Next Project

After you've completed a project, don't forget to analyze the project's activities so that you can improve your estimation and tracking ability for your next project. Use this worksheet to analyze your completed project.

1. List your baseline start and finish dates and actual start and finish dates for your entire project:

  - Baseline start:_____

  - Baseline finish:_____

  - Actual start:_____

  - Actual finish:_____

2. Write a statement about the major factor that affected your timing and a conclusion about whether you could have anticipated or avoided that factor. Be honest about your own failings. It's the best way to become better at what you do.

  _____

  _____

  _____

3. Enter your baseline total costs and actual total costs for the project:

  - Baseline costs:_____

  - Actual costs:_____

4. Write a statement about the major factor or factors influencing your final costs, including what you can do to avoid cost overruns on a future project (or, if you're lucky, what you can do to have similar cost savings on future projects). What did you do or not do to keep costs in line?

   _____

   _____

   _____

5. Analyze how resources performed on your project. Are there people or vendors you would *not* recommend for use on future projects? Are there people or vendors you feel did exceptionally well? Make a record of them so that you and others in your company can plan resources for future projects appropriately.

   ■ Vendor issues on current project:

   _____

   _____

   _____

   ■ Recommended resources for future projects:

   _____

   _____

   _____

6. List three things you can do more efficiently as a project manager on your next project to improve performance and efficiency:

   _____

   _____

   _____

7. List three things your manager or organization could provide you to make your next project more successful:

   _____

   _____

   _____

8. List three ways you can improve your tracking procedures on future projects:

   _____

   _____

   _____

9. Write statements of what worked and what didn't work in your management of resources in these areas:

- Communication:

  _____

  _____

  _____

- Accuracy of time estimates for resources to complete tasks:

  _____

  _____

  _____

- Resource management:

  _____

  _____

  _____

Appendix C

Available Fields and Functions for Custom Field Formulas

This appendix contains three tables that help you identify the fields and functions that you can use when creating formulas to include in custom fields. Table C-1 contains a list of all the Task fields that you can include in a formula. The fields are listed according to the submenu on which they appear when you click the Fields button in the Formula dialog box. Table C-2 contains the same information for Resource fields. In each of these tables, the first column contains a field category. The second column contains either fields within the category or a subcategory. If the second column contains a subcategory, then the fields appear in the third column. Table C-3 lists the functions that you can include in a formula, as well as a description of the function's purpose.

TABLE C-1

Task Fields Available for Custom Field Formulas

Category	Subcategory or Field	Field
Cost	Actual Cost	
	Actual Overtime Cost	
	ACWP	
	Baseline Cost	Baseline Cost, Baseline1 Cost – Baseline10 Cost, Baseline Budget Cost, Baseline 1 Budget Cost – Baseline10 Budget Cost
	BCWP	
	BCWS	
	Budget Cost	
	Cost	
	Cost Variance	
	CPI	
	Custom Cost	Cost1 – Cost10
	CV	
	CV%	
	EAC	
	Enterprise Custom Cost	Enterprise Cost1 – Enterprise Cost10
	Enterprise Project Custom Cost	Enterprise Project Cost1 - Enterprise Project Cost10
	Fixed Cost	
	Overtime Cost	
	Remaining Cost	
	Remaining Overtime Cost	
	SPI	
	SV	
	SV%	
	TCPI	
	VAC	
Date	Actual Finish	
	Actual Start	

Category	Subcategory or Field	Field
	Baseline Finish	Baseline Finish, Baseline1 Finish – Baseline10 Finish
	Baseline Start	Baseline Start, Baseline1 Start – Baseline10 Start
	Constraint Date	
	Created	
	Custom Date	Date1 – Date10
	Custom Finish	Finish1 – Finish10
	Custom Start	Start1 – Start10
	Deadline	
	Early Finish	
	Early Start	
	Enterprise Custom Date	Enterprise Date1 - Enterprise Date30
	Enterprise Project Custom Date	Enterprise Project Date1 - Enterprise Project Date30
	Finish	
	Finish Variance	
	Late Finish	
	Late Start	
	Preleveled Finish	
	Preleveled Start	
	Resume	
	Start	
	Start Variance	
	Stop	
Duration	Actual Duration	
	Baseline Duration	Baseline Duration, Baseline1 Duration – Baseline10 Duration
	Custom Duration	Duration1 – Duration10
	Duration	
	Duration Variance	
	Enterprise Custom Duration	Enterprise Duration1 - Enterprise Duration10
	Enterprise Project Customer Duration	Enterprise Project Duration1 - Enterprise Project Duration10

continued

Category	Subcategory or Field	Field
	Finish Slack	
	Free Slack	
	Leveling Delay	
	Remaining Duration	
	Start Slack	
	Total Slack	
Flag	Confirmed	
	Critical	
	Custom Flag	Flag1 – Flag20
	Effort Driven	
	Enterprise Custom Flag	Enterprise Flag1 - Enterprise Flag20
	Enterprise Project Custom Flag	Enterprise Project Flag1 - Enterprise Project Flag20
	Estimated	
	External Task	
	Group By Summary	
	Hide Bar	
	Ignore Resource Calendar	
	Level Assignments	
	Leveling Can Split	
	Linked Fields	
	Marked	
	Milestone	
	Overallocated	
	Recurring	
	Response Pending	
	Rollup	
	Subproject Read Only	
	Summary	
	TeamStatus Pending	
	Update Needed	

TABLE C-1 (continued)

Category	Subcategory or Field	Field
ID/Code	Custom Outline Code	Outline Code1 – Outline Code10
	Enterprise Custom Outline Code	Enterprise Task Outline Code1 - Enterprise Task Outline Code30
	Enterprise Project Custom Outline Code	Enterprise Project Outline Code1 - Enterprise Project Outline Code30
	ID	
	Outline Number	
	Predecessors	
	Successors	
	Unique ID	
	Unique ID Predecessors	
	Unique ID Successors	
	WBS	
	WBS Predecessors	
	WBS Successors	
Number	% Complete	
	Constraint Type	
	Custom Number	Number1 – Number20
	Enterprise Custom Number	Enterprise Number1 - Enterprise Number40
	Enterprise Project Custom Number	Enterprise Project Number1 - Enterprise Project Number40
	Objects	
	Outline Level	
	Physical % Complete	
	Priority	
	Resource Type	
	Status	
	Type	
Project	Date	Creation Date
		Current Date
		Default Finish Time
		Default Start Time

continued

853

TABLE C-1	(continued)	
Category	**Subcategory or Field**	**Field**
		Last Update
		Project Finish
		Project Start
		Status Date
	Number	Minutes Per Day
		Minutes Per Week
		Resource Count
		Task Count
	Text	Author
		Project Calendar
		Subject
		Title
Text	Contact	
	Custom Text	Text1 – Text30
	Enterprise Custom Text	Enterprise Text1 - Enterprise Text40
	Enterprise Project Custom Text	Enterprise Project Text1 - Enterprise Project Text40
	Hyperlink	
	Hyperlink Address	
	Hyperlink Href	
	Hyperlink SubAddress	
	Name	
	Notes	
	Project	
	Resource Group	
	Resource Initials	
	Resource Names	
	Resource Phonetics	
	Subproject File	
	Task Calendar	

Category	Subcategory or Field	Field
Work	% Work Complete	
	Actual Overtime Work	
	Actual Overtime Work Protected	
	Actual Work	
	Actual Work Protected	
	Baseline Work	Baseline Work, Baseline1 Work – Baseline10 Work, Baseline Budget Work, Baseline1 Budget Work – Baseline10 Budget Work
	Budget Work	
	Overtime Work	
	Regular Work	
	Remaining Overtime Work	
	Remaining Work	
	Work	
	Work Variance	

TABLE C-2

Resource Fields Available for Custom Field Formulas

Category	Subcategory or Field	Field
Cost	Actual Cost	
	Actual Overtime Cost	
	ACWP	
	Baseline Cost	Baseline Cost, Baseline1 Cost – Baseline10 Cost, Baseline Budget Cost, Baseline1 Budget Cost - Baseline10 Budget Cost
	BCWP	
	BCWS	
	Budget Cost	
	Cost	
	Cost Per Use	

continued

TABLE C-2	*(continued)*	
Category	**Subcategory or Field**	**Field**
	Cost Rate Table	
	Cost Variance	
	Custom Cost	Cost1 – Cost10
	CV	
	Enterprise Custom Cost	Enterprise Cost1 - Enterprise Cost10
	Overtime Cost	
	Overtime Rate	
	Remaining Cost	
	Remaining Overtime Cost	
	Standard Rate	
	SV	
	VAC	
Date	Available From	
	Available To	
	Baseline Finish	Baseline Finish, Baseline1 Finish – Baseline10 Finish
	Baseline Start	Baseline Start, Baseline1 Start – Baseline10 Start
	Custom Date	Date1 – Date10
	Custom Duration	Duration1 – Duration10
	Custom Finish	Finish1 – Finish10
	Custom Start	Start1 – Start10
	Enterprise Custom Date	Enterprise Date1 - Enterprise Date30
	Enterprise Custom Duration	Enterprise Duration1 - Enterprise Duration10
	Finish	
	Start	
Flag	Can Level	
	Confirmed	
	Custom Flag	Flag1 – Flag20
	Enterprise Custom Flag	Enterprise Flag1 - Enterprise Flag20
	Linked Fields	
	Overallocated	

Category	Subcategory or Field	Field
	Response Pending	
	TeamStatus Pending	
	Update Needed	
ID/Code	Custom Outline Code	Outline Code1 – Outline Code10
	Enterprise Custom Outline Code	Enterprise Resource Outline Code1 - Enterprise Resource Outline Code29, RBS
	ID	
	Unique ID	
Number	Accrue At	
	Custom Number	Number1 – Number20
	Enterprise Custom Number	Enterprise Number1 - Enterprise Number40
	Max Units	
	Objects	
	Peak	
	Type	
	Workgroup	
Project	Date	Creation Date
		Current Date
		Default Finish Time
		Default Start Time
		Last Update
		Project Finish
		Project Start
		Status Date
	Number	Minutes Per Day
		Minutes Per Week
		Resource Count
		Task Count
	Text	Author
		Project Calendar
		Subject
		Title

continued

TABLE C-2	(continued)	
Category	**Subcategory or Field**	**Field**
Text	Base Calendar	
	Code	
	Custom Text	Text1 – Text30
	E-mail Address	
	Enterprise Custom Text	Enterprise Text1 - Enterprise Text40
	Group	
	Group By Summary	
	Hyperlink	
	Hyperlink Address	
	Hyperlink Href	
	Hyperlink SubAddress	
	Initials	
	Material Label	
	Name	
	Notes	
	Phonetics	
	Project	
	Windows User Account	
Work	% Work Complete	
	Actual Overtime Work	
	Actual Work	
	Baseline Work	Baseline Work, Baseline1 Work – Baseline10 Work, Baseline Budget Work, Baseline1 Budget Work – Baseline10 Budget Work
	Budget Work	
	Overtime Work	
	Regular Work	
	Remaining Overtime Work	
	Remaining Work	
	Work	
	Work Variance	

TABLE C-3

Functions Available for Custom Field Formulas

Function Category	Function	Description
Conversion	Asc(string)	Returns an Integer representing the character code corresponding to the first letter in a string.
	CBool(expression)	Coerces an expression to a Boolean.
	CByte(expression)	Coerces an expression to a Byte (0–255).
	CCur(expression)	Coerces an expression to a Currency value.
	CDate(expression)	Coerces an expression to a Date.
	CDbl(expression)	Coerces an expression to a Double.
	CDec(expression)	Coerces an expression to a Decimal.
	Chr(charcode)	Returns a string containing the character associated with the specified character code.
	CInt(expression)	Coerces an expression to an Integer.
	CLng(expression)	Coerces an expression to a Long.
	CSng(expression)	Coerces an expression to a Single.
	CStr(expression)	Coerces an expression to a String.
	CVar(expression)	Coerces an expression to a Variant.
	DateSerial(year,month day)	Returns a Variant (Date) for a specified year, month, and day.
	DateValue(date)	Returns a Variant (Date).
	Day(date)	Returns a Variant (Integer) specifying a whole number between 1 and 31, inclusive, representing the day of the month.
	Hex(number)	Returns a String representing the hexadecimal value of a number.
	Hour(time)	Returns a Variant (Integer) specifying a whole number between 0 and 23, inclusive, representing the hour of the day.
	Minute(time)	Returns a Variant (Integer) specifying a whole number between 0 and 59, inclusive, representing the minute of the hour.
	Month(date)	Returns a Variant (Integer) specifying a whole number between 1 and 12, inclusive, representing the month of the year.

continued

TABLE C-3	*(continued)*	
Function Category	**Function**	**Description**
	Oct(number)	Returns a Variant (String) representing the octal value of a number.
	ProjDateConv(expression, dateformat)	Converts a numeric value to a date in an optionally specified format.
	ProjDurConv(expression, durationunits)	Converts a numeric value to a duration value in the specified units.
	Second(time)	Returns a Variant (Integer) specifying a whole number between 0 and 59, inclusive, representing the second of the minute.
	Str(number)	Returns a Variant (String) representation of a number.
	StrConv(string, conversion, LCID)	Returns a Variant (String) converted as specified.
	TimeSerial(hour, minute, second)	Returns a Variant (Date) containing the time for a specific hour, minute, and second.
	TimeValue(time)	Returns a Variant (Date) containing the time.
	Val(string)	Returns the numbers contained in a string as a numeric value of appropriate type.
	Weekday(date, firstdayofweek)	Returns a Variant (integer) containing a whole number representing the day of the week.
	Year(date)	Returns a Variant (Integer) containing a whole number representing the year.
Date/Time	Cdate(expression)	Coerces an expression to a Date.
	Date()	Returns a Variant (Date) containing the current system date.
	DateAdd(interval, number, date)	Returns a Variant (Date) containing a date to which a specified time interval has been added.
	DateDiff(interval, date1, date2, firstdayofweek, firstweekofyear)	Returns a Variant (Long) specifying the number of time intervals between two specified dates.
	DatePart(interval, date, firstdayofweek, firstweekofyear)	Returns a Variant (Integer) containing the specified part of a given date.
	DateSerial(year, month, day)	Returns a Variant (Date) for a specified year, month, and day.
	DateValue(date)	Returns a Variant (Date).
	Day(date)	Returns a Variant (Integer) specifying a whole number between 1 and 31, inclusive, representing the day of the month.

Function Category	Function	Description
	Hour(time)	Returns a Variant (Integer) specifying a whole number between 0 and 23, inclusive, representing the hour of the day.
	IsDate(expression)	Returns a Boolean value indicating whether an expression can be converted to a date.
	Minute(time)	Returns a Variant (Integer) specifying a whole number between 0 and 59, inclusive, representing the minute of the hour.
	Month(date)	Returns a Variant (Integer) specifying a whole number between 1 and 12, inclusive, representing the month of the year.
	Now()	Returns a Variant (Date) specifying the current date and time according your computer system's date and time.
	ProjDateAdd(date, duration, calendar)	Adds a duration to a date to return a new date.
	ProjDateDiff(date1, date2, calendar)	Returns the duration between two dates in minutes.
	ProjDateSub(date, duration, calendar)	Returns the date that precedes another date by a specified duration.
	ProjDurValue(duration)	Returns the number of minutes in a duration.
	Second(time)	Returns a Variant (Integer) specifying a whole number between 0 and 59, inclusive, representing the second of the minute.
	Time()	Returns a Variant (Date) indicating the current system time.
	Timer()	Returns a Single representing the number of seconds elapsed since midnight.
	TimeSerial(hour, minute, second)	Returns a Variant (Date) containing the time for a specific hour, minute, and second.
	TimeValue(time)	Returns a Variant (Date) containing the time.
	Weekday(date, firstdayofweek)	Returns a Variant (Integer) containing a whole number representing the day of the week.
	Year(date)	Returns a Variant (Integer) containing a whole number representing the year.
General	Choose(index, expression1, expression2,...)	Selects and returns a value from a list of arguments.

continued

861

TABLE C-3	*(continued)*	
Function Category	**Function**	**Description**
	Ilf(expression, truepart, falsepart)	Returns one of two parts, depending on the evaluation of an expression.
	IsNumeric(expression)	Returns a Boolean value indicating whether an expression can be evaluated as a number.
	IsNull(expression)	Returns a Boolean value that indicates whether an expression contains no valid data.
	Switch(expression1, value1, expression2, value2,...)	Evaluates a list of expressions and returns a Variant value or an expression associated with the first expression in the list that is True.
Math	Abs(number)	Returns a value of the same type that is passed to it specifying the absolute value of a number.
	Atn(number)	Returns a Double specifying the arctangent of a number.
	Cos(number)	Returns a Double specifying the cosine of an angle.
	Exp(number)	Returns a Double specifying e (the base of natural logarithms) raised to a power.
	Fix(number)	Returns the integer portion of a number. If the number is negative, Fix returns the first negative integer greater than or equal to number.
	Int(number)	Returns the integer portion of a number. If the number is negative, Int returns the first negative integer less than or equal to the number.
	Log(number)	Returns a Double specifying the natural logarithm of a number.
	Rnd(number)	Returns a Single containing a random number.
	Sgn(number)	Returns a Variant (Integer) indicating the sign of a number.
	Sin(number)	Returns a Double specifying the sine of an angle.
	Sqr(number)	Returns a Double specifying the square root of a number.
	Tan(number)	Returns a Double specifying the tangent of an angle.
Microsoft Office Project	ProjDateAdd(date, duration, calendar)	Adds a duration to a date to return a new date.
	ProjDateConv(expression, Dateformat)	Converts a numeric value to a date in an optionally specified format.

Function Category	Function	Description
	ProjDateDiff(date1, date2, calendar)	Returns the duration between two dates in minutes.
	ProjDateSub(date, duration, calendar)	Returns the date that precedes another date by a specified duration.
	ProjDurConv(expression, durationunits)	Converts a numeric value to a duration value in the specified units.
	ProjDurValue(duration)	Returns the number of minutes in a duration.
Text	Asc(string)	Returns an Integer representing the character code corresponding to the first letter in a string.
	Chr(charcode)	Returns a String containing the character associated with the specified character code.
	Format(expression, format firstdayofweek, firstweekofyear)	Returns a Variant (String) containing an expression formatted according to instructions contained in a format expression.
	InStr(start, string1, string2, compare)	Returns a Variant (Long) specifying the position of the first occurrence of one string within another.
	LCase(string)	Returns a String that has been converted to lowercase.
	Left(string, length)	Returns a Variant (String) containing a specified number of characters from the left side of a string.
	Len(string)	Returns a Long containing the number of characters in a string or the number of bytes required to store a variable.
	LTrim(string)	Returns a Variant (String) containing a copy of a specified string without leading spaces.
	Mid(string, start, length)	Returns a Variant (String) containing a specified number of characters from a string.
	Right(string, length)	Returns a Variant (String) containing a specified number of characters from the right side of a string.
	RTrim(string)	Returns a Variant (String) containing a copy of a specified string without trailing spaces.
	Space(number)	Returns a Variant (String) consisting of the specified number of spaces.
	StrComp(string1, string2, compare)	Returns a Variant (Integer) indicating the result of a string comparison.
	StrConv(string, conversion, LCID)	Returns a Variant (String) converted as specified.

continued

TABLE C-3	(continued)	
Function Category	**Function**	**Description**
	String(number, character)	Returns a Variant (String) containing a repeating character string of the length specified.
	Trim(string)	Returns a Variant (String) containing a copy of a specified string without leading and trailing spaces.
	UCase(string)	Returns a Variant (String) containing the specified string, converted to uppercase.

Appendix D

Project Management Resources

Project management is a detailed methodology and intricate system of requirements that has evolved over many years for various industries and disciplines. Project management as a topic encompasses concepts of leadership and team building, charting and analysis of data, cost and schedule control, and more.

Many useful resources for project management information, tools, and support can help you work with Microsoft Project. This appendix contains five resource categories: Associations, Publications, Education, Online, and Software Products. It provides phone numbers and, when available, address and fax information. As you can see from this list, project management is an extremely international discipline. Remember to dial country codes before any phone number outside the United States.

IN THIS APPENDIX

Associations

Publications

Online

Software products

Associations

The following associations provide support and information for both general and industry-specific project management issues.

- **Association for the Advancement of Cost Engineering:** Counts among its membership those interested in cost engineering and cost estimating.

  209 Prairie Ave., #100
  Morgantown, WV 26505
  Phone: (800) 858-COST
  http://www.aacei.org/

- **Association of Proposal Management Professionals:** Can assist you in developing proposals for your projects, whether you bid for government or industry contracts. APMP has local chapters, as well as a newsletter and task force on Electronic Procurement.

  Barry Fields
  Fax/Voice Mail: (406) 788-9840
  E-mail: apmpmemserv@msn.com
  http://www.apmp.org/

- **Association for Project Management:** Based in England and has chapters in both the United Kingdom and Hong Kong. This association has a certification program for project management professionals.

  150 West Wycombe Rd.
  High Wycombe
  Buckinghamshire
  HP12 3AE
  Phone: 0845 458 1944
  Fax: +44 (0) 1494 528937
  E-mail: services@apm.org.uk
  http://www.apm.org.uk/

- **American Society for Quality:** Focuses on quality issues in project management. This organization offers certification in a variety of specializations related to quality.

  P.O. Box 3005
  Milwaukee, WI 53201-3005
  U.S. Phone: (800) 248-1946 (United States and Canada only)
  International Phone: 414-272-8575
  http://www.asq.org/

- **Construction Management Association of America:** As their mission statement, this organization "promotes professionalism and excellence in the management of the construction process."

  7918 Jones Branch Drive, Suite 540
  McLean, VA 22102
  Phone: (703) 356-2622
  Fax: (703) 356-6388
  http://cmaanet.org/

- **Educational Society for Resource Management:** (Formerly American Production & Inventory Control Society and still referred to as APICS) Specializes in support and information for those wanting to improve or maximize their resource management skills.

  5301 Shawnee Rd.
  Alexandria, VA 22312-2317
  Phone: (800) 444-2742
  http://www.apics.org/

PMI Special Interest Groups

PMI offers a variety of special interest groups, or SIGs, that focus on different aspects of project management. SIG members are required to pay a small fee to support the group, and all members must also belong to PMI.

These SIGs are either currently available or under consideration:

- Aerospace & Defense
- Automation Systems
- Automotive
- Consulting
- Design-Procurement-Construction
- Diversity
- eBusiness
- Education & Training
- Financial Services
- Government
- Healthcare Project Management
- Human Resources
- Information Systems
- Information Technology & Telecommunications
- International Development

- Manufacturing
- Marketing & Sales
- Metrics
- New Product Development
- Oil, Gas & Petrochemical
- Pharmaceutical
- Program Management Office
- Quality in Project Management
- Retail
- Risk Management
- Service & Outsourcing
- Students of PM
- Troubled Projects
- Utility
- Women in Project Management

- **International Project Management Association (IPMA):** A multinational nonprofit confederation of project management associations based primarily in European countries. It offers international conferences on project management.

  International Project Management Association
  PO Box 1167, 3860 BD Nijkerk, The Netherlands
  Tel: +31 33 247 3430
  Fax: +31 33 246 0470
  info@ipma.ch
  http://www.ipma.ch/

- **Project Management Institute:** The premier United States project management association. It has chapters across the country, educational programs, a long list of publications, and online discussion forums. In addition, PMI has a monthly magazine called *PM Network* and a quarterly called *Project Management Journal*. Its publication, *A Guide to the Project Management Body of Knowledge* (PMBOK Guide), is a bible in the project management world.

  Project Management Institute Headquarters
  Four Campus Boulevard
  Newtown Square, PA 19073-3299
  Phone: (610) 356-4600
  Fax: +610-356-4647
  Web: www.pmi.org
  E-mail: customercare@pmi.org

Publications

A great many books, newsletters, and journals are devoted to project management and its many facets. Some of the publications in this list are from small presses or associations. You can use the ISBN number — a publishing industry code — to order many of the books from your local bookstore.

Books

The following books provide guidance on general project management principles and industry-specific project management advice. You can search for these books, read descriptions of them, and find locations to by them by using the ISBN database found at http://isbndb.com/.

- *The AMA Handbook of Project Management*
  Author: Paul C. Dinsmore
  Publisher: Amacom Books, A Division of AMA
  ISBN: 0-8144-0106-6

- *Cost Estimator's Reference Manual*
  Authors: Rodney D. Stewart, James D. Johannes, Richard M. Wyskida, eds. Publisher: John Wiley-Interscience.
  ISBN: 0-471-305103

- *Effective Project Management Through Applied Cost and Schedule Control*
  Authors: James A. Bent and Kenneth K. Humphreys
  Publisher: CRC
  ISBN: 0-8247-9715-9

- *5-Phase Project Management*
  Authors: Joseph W. Weiss and Robert K. Wysocki
  Publisher: Project Management Institute
  ISBN: 0-201-56316-9

- *Fundamentals of Project Management*
  Author: James P. Lewis
  Publisher: Amacom Books, A Division of AMA
  ISBN: 0-8144-7835-2

- *Managing High-Technology Programs and Projects*
  Author: Russell D. Archibald
  Publisher: John Wiley & Sons, Inc.
  ISBN: 0-471-51327-X

- *Project Management: Strategic Design and Implementation*
  Author: David I. Cleland
  Publisher: McGraw-Hill Professional Book Group
  ISBN: 0-07-012020-X

- *Project Management for the 21st Century*
  Authors: Bennet P. Lientz and Kathryn P. Rea
  Publisher: Academic Press
  ISBN: 0-12-449966-X

- *Project Management Memory Jogger: A Pocket Guide for Project Teams*
  Author: Paula Martin
  Publisher: Project Management Institute
  ISBN: 1-57681-001-1

Journals and magazines

Many of the associations listed in the first section of this appendix publish magazines or journals. Some of those are listed here, along with a phone number to contact for additional information. Note that many of these publications are available only to members of the organization.

- *APICS Magazine*
  Association for Operations Management
  http://www.apics.org/Magazine/default.asp

- *International Journal of Project Management*
  Elsevier Science
  http://www.elsevier.com/inca/publications/store/3/0/4/3/5/index.htt

- *Journal of Quality Technology*
  Quality Management Journal
  Software Quality Professional
  Quality Engineering
  Technometrics
  AQP's Journal for Quality and Participation
  American Society of Quality Control
  `http://www.asq.org/pub/index.html#journals`

- *Project Management Journal*
  Project Management Institute
  `http://www.pmi.org/info/PIR_PMJournal.asp`

Online

You could spend days online and never run through all the project management and project management–associated Web sites. However, the following list offers a few good places to begin surfing. Please note that Web sites and addresses change frequently; those listed here were current as this book went to press.

ON the CD-ROM   You'll find links to all these sites on the *Microsoft Project 2007 Bible* Web page included on this book's companion CD-ROM.

- **American Production and Inventory Control Society:** `www.apics.org`
- **Architecture, Engineering, Construction Business Center:** `www.aecinfo.com`
- **Center for Coaching and Mentoring:** `http://coachingandmentoring.com/`
- **Earned Value Management:** Sponsored by the Office of the Under Secretary of Defense (Acquisition & Technology) Systems Acquisition/Performance Management. `www.acq.osd.mil/pm`
- **FedWorld:** `www.fedworld.gov/`
- **Heuristic Management Systems:** `http://www.hmssoftware.ca`
- **The Project Management Forum:** `www.pmforum.org/`
- **Project Management Institute:** `www.pmi.org`

Software Products

In addition to the excellent software products in demo or trial version form on the companion CD-ROM, the following section lists some other project management tools worthy of investigation:

ON the CD-ROM   You'll find the links to all these sites on the *Microsoft Project 2007 Bible* Web page included on this book's companion CD-ROM.

■ **Innate Multi-Project:** Innate Multi-Project extends Microsoft Project to a complete program management system, giving a view across projects, offering resource capacity planning, and supporting your business processes whether top-down or bottom-up.

Innate, Inc. Saracens House
25 St. Margarets Green
Ipswich, Suffolk IP4 2BN
England
E-mail: mikew@innate.co.uk
www.innate.co.uk
Phone: +44 1473 251550

ON the CD-ROM You'll find demos for Innate products on the CD-ROM that accompanies this book. Also on the CD-ROM, on the *Project 2007 Bible* Web page, you'll find a link to Innate's Web site that you can use to locate and order Multi-Project from Innate.

■ **Project Administration and Control System (PACS):** The project management portion of a larger financial software suite called Renaissance C/S Financial Applications. If you want to integrate your project costs into your general ledger, check this one out.

Herkemij & Partners
Cypresbaan 6
2908 LT Capelle a/d Ijssel
The Netherlands
Phone: 31 10 4580899
Fax: 31 10 4508233
http://www.herkemij.nl

■ **Graneda:** A professional graphics add-on package with which you can create exciting project charts. The application includes extensive printer and plotter drivers for printing your charts.

■ **Project Visuals:** Project Visuals is a simple and powerful project management graphics add-on application that gives you additional Gantt options, including logic Gantt charts, multiple bars/symbols on the same line (optimized), multiple levels of grouping, all sorts of formats, filters, and views. Using this package, you can create time-phased PERT diagrams, zoned/banded or clustered, with numerous types of node box formats, colors, and filters. You also can use Project Visuals with you Microsoft Project data to produce WBS/OBS diagrams.

Knowledge Relay, Inc.
5212 Katella Ave., Ste. 104
Los Alamitos, CA 90720
Phone: (562) 795-0147
Fax: (562) 795-0152
http://www.netronic-us.com/

- **Artemis:** Offers a bi-directional interface between Microsoft Project and the Artemis Views enterprise project and resource management solution.

  Artemis Management Systems
  Newport Beach, United States
  Telephone: 800.477.6648
  Fax: 949.660.7020
  www.aisc.com

- **Enterprise Advantage Toolset:** Proprietary software that interfaces with Project Server. In June, 2006, Mantix was acquired by W S Atkins plc.

  Mantix Limited
  3 America Square
  London
  EC3N 2LR
  Telephone: 020 7480 0620
  Fax: 020 7709 7666
  E-mail: programmes@mantix.com
  http://www.mantix.com

- **Risk +:** Integrates seamlessly with Microsoft Project to quantify the cost and schedule uncertainty associated with project plans. Anyone familiar with Microsoft Project can easily conduct a sophisticated risk analysis to answer questions such as, "What are the chances of completing this effort by 2/28/00?" or "How confident are we that costs will remain below $9 million?" or "How likely is this task to end up on the critical path?" Single point estimates for task duration and cost tend to be optimistic and provide no insight into the uncertainty associated with a task. With Microsoft Project alone, you are forced to make statements such as, "Task X will complete in 10 days." Adding Risk + allows you to make and assess the far more realistic statement, "Task X will take between 8 and 12 days to complete, and will most likely take about 10 days." With Risk +, you are able to identify the high-risk areas of your project, determine the likelihood of risk materializing, assess the impact of possible risk, and more importantly, have the information and opportunity to mitigate risk long before it impacts your project.

  C/S Solutions, Inc. (C/SSI)
  111 N. Sepulveda, Suite 333
  Manhattan Beach, CA 90266
  Tel (850) 269-3260
  Fax (850) 269-3270
  www.cs-solutions.com/

- **Hans Tørsleff IPW TimeReg 2006:** A time registration system that updates Microsoft Project with Actual Work entered by the individual resource, sparing the project manager the manual update of the project plan and giving more time to the real management of the project.

- **Hans Tørsleff Project Manager:** Allows you to decentralize the planning of the project and resource management but maintain the bird's-eye perspective provided by a centralized project management tool. It includes reporting and a Virtual Project generator.

Hans Tørsleff Management Systems A/S
Gl. Kongevej 161
1850 Frederiksberg C
Denmark
Phone: +45 70 20 08 16
Fax: +45 70 22 08 07
E-mail: mail@htms.dk
http://www.htms.dk/

- **Project Partner:** Functions as an add-on application with Microsoft Project to present the scheduling data in several very useful graphic formats. The three main options include a timescaled network diagram, an earned-value spending curve, and a resource or cash flow by period summary. Project Partner is designed to increase a project team's ability to easily communicate complex project status information.

Bluewater Project Management Services, LLC
500 S. 336th Ave., Ste. 204
Federal Way, WA 98003
Phone: (253) 874-8884
Fax: (253) 838-1798
http://www.bluewaterpm.com/solutions/solutions.asp

EPK Suite 4.1: Based on Project Server, this software offers an integrated approach to planning for your projects. You can inventory resources, prioritize projects, control processes and more with EPK Suite.

EPK Group LLC
6671 W. Indiantown Rd.
Suite 56, PMB 153
Jupiter, FL 33458
(561) 310-7279
(561) 658-0979 Fax
Web: http://epkgroup.com/

- **QuantumPM** offers a selection of professional project and portfolio management tools as well as custom solutions, including Budget Forecast Tool, EPK, EVM4, QuantumPM Schedule Auditor (QSA), QSA Portfolio, and Time-Phased Analysis Program

QuantumPM Corporate Headquarters
Denver, Colorado
9085 E. Mineral Circle, Suite 235
Centennial, CO 80112
Voice: (303) 699-2334
Fax: (303) 699-3329
www.quantumpm.com
info@quantumpm.com

- **Smart EPM**: Offers an end-to-end EPM solution built using the Microsoft Office System stack. SMART EPM offers specific functionality and benefits for demand management, portfolio management, project management, operational management, collaboration, and business intelligence.

  LMRS olutions Inc.
  5860 Owens Ave, 130
  Carlsbad, CA 92008
  Phone: (760) 603-9990
  Fax: (858) 225-0685
  http://www.lmrsolutions.com/
  info@lmrsolutions.com

- **Fast Tracks**: Four out-of-the-box solution configurations called Fast Tracks are available from ProSight. While the Fast Track solutions are ready to use as-is, customers typically make modest customizations so that the Fast Track products fully support the customer's organizational objectives and fully comply with their processes.

  ProSight
  Corporate Headquarters
  9600 SW Barnes Road, Suite 300
  Portland, OR 97225-6665
  877.531.9121 (503.889.4800)
  http://www.prosight.com
  prosightinfo@prosight.com

Glossary

ACWP (actual cost of work performed) Cost of actual work performed to date on the project, plus any fixed costs.

ALAP (as late as possible) A constraint placed on a task's timing to make it occur as late as possible in the project schedule, based on its dependency relationships.

ASAP (as soon as possible) A constraint placed on a task's timing to make it occur as early in the project as possible, based on its dependency relationships.

BAC (budget at completion) The total of planned costs to complete a task (also referred to as *baseline costs*).

BCWP (budgeted cost of work performed) Also called *earned value;* this term refers to the value of work completed. A task with $1,000 of associated costs, when 75 percent complete, has a baseline value of $750.

BCWS (budgeted cost of work scheduled) The planned completion percentage multiplied by the planned cost. This calculated value reflects the amount of the task that is completed and the planned cost of the task.

CV (earned value cost variance) This variance indicates the difference between the planned costs (baseline costs) and the costs after taking into account actual costs to date and estimated costs going forward (scheduled costs). The difference between these two values produces either a positive (overbudget) or negative (underbudget) cost variance.

EAC (estimate at completion) The total scheduled cost for a resource on a task. This calculation provides the costs incurred to date plus costs estimated for remaining work on the task.

WBS (work breakdown structure) Automatically assigned numbers for each task in a project outline designed to specify an order to complete the project. Government project reports often include WBS codes.

actual A cost or percentage of work completed and tracked as having already occurred or been incurred.

actual cost of work performed See *ACWP.*

as late as possible See *ALAP.*

as soon as possible See *ASAP.*

base calendar The default calendar on which all new tasks are based, unless a resource-specific calendar is applied.

baseline The snapshot of a project plan against which actual work is tracked.

baseline cost The total of all planned costs on tasks in a project before any actual costs have been incurred.

budget at completion See *BAC.*

budgeted cost of work performed See *BCWP.*

budgeted cost of work scheduled See *BCWS.*

calendar The various settings for hours in a workday, days in a work week, holidays, and nonworking days on which a project schedule is based.

circular dependency A dependency among tasks creating an endless loop that can't be resolved.

collapse To close a project outline to hide subtasks from view.

combination view A Project view with the task details showing at the bottom of the screen.

constraint A rule that forces a task to fit certain parameters. For example, a task can be constrained to start as late as possible in a project.

cost A cost can be applied to a task in a project. The cost of the task may be fixed, or you can apply a cost to a task by assigning resources, which can be equipment, materials, or people with associated hourly rates or fees.

critical path The series of tasks that must occur on time in order for the overall project to meet its deadline.

critical task A task on the critical path.

crosstab A report format that compares two intersecting sets of data; for example, you can generate a crosstab report showing costs of critical tasks that are running late.

cumulative cost The planned total cost for a resource to date on a particular task. This calculation provides the costs already incurred on the task, plus the costs planned for the remaining, as yet uncompleted, portion of the task.

cumulative work The planned total work of a resource on a particular task. This calculation provides the work already performed on the task plus the work planned for the remaining, as yet uncompleted, portion of the task.

current date line The vertical line in a Gantt Chart indicating today's date and time.

demote To move a task to a lower level in the project outline hierarchy.

dependency A timing relationship between two tasks in a project. A dependency can cause a task to happen after another task, to happen before another task, or to begin at some point during the life of the other task.

detail task See *subtask*.

duration The amount of time it takes to complete a task.

duration variance A field displaying the variation between the planned (baseline) duration of a task and the current estimated task duration, based on activity to date and remaining activity to be performed.

earned value Also called *budgeted cost of work performed*. Earned value refers to the value of work completed. For example, a task with $1,000 of associated costs, when 75 percent complete, will have a baseline value of $750.

earned value cost variance See *CV*.

effort driven An effort-driven task has an assigned amount of effort to complete it. When you add resources to these tasks, the effort is distributed among those resources.

elapsed duration An estimate of how long it will take to complete a task, based on a 24-hour day and 7-day week.

estimate at completion (EAC) The total scheduled cost for a resource on a task. This calculation provides the costs incurred to date, plus costs estimated for remaining work on the task.

expand Opening a project outline to reveal sub-tasks as well as summary tasks.

expected duration This calculation estimates the actual duration of a task based on performance to date.

external task When tasks are linked between projects, Project displays tasks from the external project in the current project. The external task represents the linked tasks without having to leave the current project.

finish date The date on which a project will be completed.

finish-to-finish relationship A dependency relationship in which the finish of one task depends on the finish of another task.

finish-to-start relationship A dependency relationship in which the start of one task depends on the finish of another task.

fixed cost A cost that does not increase or decrease based on the time a resource spends on a task. A consultant's fee or permit fee are examples of fixed costs.

fixed date A task that must occur on a certain date. Fixed-date tasks do not move earlier or later in the schedule because of dependency relationships.

fixed duration The length of time required for a task remains constant, no matter how many resources are assigned to it. Travel time is a good example of a fixed-duration task.

float See *slack*.

Gantt Chart A standard project management tracking device that displays task information alongside a chart that shows task timing in a bar chart format.

gap See *lag*.

ID number The number assigned to a task based on its sequence in the schedule.

lag The result of dependency relationships among tasks. Lag is a certain amount of downtime between the end of one task and the start of another.

leveling See *resource leveling*.

linking Establishing a connection between two tasks in separate schedules so that changes to tasks in the first schedule are reflected in the second. Linking is also a term applied to establishing dependencies among tasks in a project.

milestone A task of zero duration that marks a moment of time in a schedule.

network diagram A standard project management tracking form that indicates workflow among the tasks in a project.

node Boxes containing information about individual project tasks in the Network Diagram view.

nonworking time Time when a resource on a project is not available to work. On the project calendar, time specified as time resources won't be working.

outline The structure of summary and subordinate tasks in a project.

overallocation When a resource is assigned to spend more time than its work calendar permits on a single task or combination of tasks occurring at the same point in time.

overtime Any work scheduled above and beyond a resource's standard work hours; overtime work can have a different rate assigned to it than a resource's regular rate.

percent complete The amount of work on a task that has already been accomplished, expressed as a percentage.

predecessor In a dependency relationship, the task that is designated to occur before, or precede, another.

priorities Project uses the priorities that you assign to tasks when it performs resource leveling to resolve project conflicts; a higher-priority task is less likely than a lower-priority task to incur delay during the leveling process. You also can assign priorities to projects.

progress lines Gantt Chart bars that overlap the baseline taskbar and indicate tracked actual progress on the task.

project A series of steps to reach a specific goal. A project seeks to meet the triple constraints of time, quality, and cost.

project management The discipline that studies various methods, procedures, and concepts used to control the progress and outcome of projects.

promote To move a task to a higher level in a project's outline hierarchy.

recurring task A task that is repeated during the life of a project. Typical recurring tasks are regular meetings of project teams or regular reviews of project output.

resource A cost associated with a task. A resource can be a person, piece of equipment, materials, or a fee.

resource contouring Changing the time when a resource begins work on a task. You can use contouring to vary the amount of work that a resource does on a task over the life of that task.

resource driven A task whose timing is determined by the number of resources assigned to it.

resource leveling A process used by Project to modify resource assignments to resolve resource conflicts.

resource pool A centrally located, shared collection of resources. Many organizations share the resources in their resource pool among all their projects.

roll up The calculation by which all subtask values are "rolled up" or summarized in a summary task.

slack Also called *float*. The time you have available to delay a task before that task becomes critical. You have used up slack on a task when any delay on that task will cause a delay in the overall project deadline.

split tasks When progress on a task is interrupted or delayed because the task has been placed on hold, you can split the task into two tasks. When you split tasks, the downtime between the two is not allocated to the total time taken to complete the task.

start date The date on which a project begins.

start-to-finish relationship A dependency relationship in which one task can't start until another task finishes.

start-to-start relationship A dependency relationship in which the start of one task depends on the start of another task.

subproject An inserted copy of a second project that becomes a phase of the project in which it is inserted.

subtask Also called a *subordinate task*. A task providing detail for a specific step in the project. This detail is rolled up into a higher-level summary task.

successor In a dependency relationship, a successor task is scheduled to begin after another task in the project.

summary task A task in a project outline that has subordinate tasks beneath it. A summary task rolls up the details of its subtasks and has no timing of its own.

task An individual step to be performed to reach a project's goal; a project is composed of tasks.

template A format in which a Project file can be saved; the template saves elements such as calendar settings, formatting, and tasks. New project files can be based on a template.

timescale The area of a Gantt Chart view that indicates the units of time being displayed.

tracking The act of recording actual progress in terms of both work completed and costs accrued on tasks in a project.

variable rate A shift in a resource's cost that can be set to occur at specific times during a project. For example, if a resource is expected to receive a raise or if equipment lease rates are expected to increase, you can assign variable rates for those resources.

work breakdown structure See *WBS*.

workload The amount of work that any resource is performing at any given point in time, taking into account all tasks to which the resource is assigned.

workspace A set of files and project settings that can be saved and reopened together so that you can pick up work on a project or projects at the point at which you stopped.

Index

Q

T

what-if analysis *(continued)*
    Optimistic Gantt view, 184–185
    PERT Weights view, 186–187
    Pessimistic Gantt view, 186
    tables, viewing, 162
    views, 182–183
Who Does What report, 415, 416
Who Does What When report, 415, 417
wide-area network (WAN), 510
Windows Authentication, Forms Authentication versus, 545
Windows security accounts
    Application Pool security account, 531
    creating, 532–534
    described, 530–531
    instance administrator account, 532
    shared service provider administrator account, 532
    site collection owner account, 531
    Windows SharePoint Services Service account, 531
Windows SharePoint Services
    account, 531
    documents, sharing, 678–681
    managing, 548–550
    Project Server installation and configuration, 534–539
Windows taskbar icons, 708–710
wizards
    Define the Project Wizard, 24–25
    Gantt Chart Wizard, 257–260
    Import Project Wizard, 616
    Resource Substitution Wizard, 629–633
Word (Microsoft)
    exporting information to, 793–795
    Gantt Chart, inserting in document, 284–286, 289–290
    importing information, 803–808
    linking or embedding information, 806–808
    pasting information from, 803–806
work
    action items, creating, 44
    allocating during project, 134–135
    availability
        box, 145
        time, calculating, 146
    Cost table for, 380
    costs versus
        for resources, 458–459
        for tasks, 457–458
    default filters, listed, 243–244
    delays, Leveling Gantt view, 170–171
    displaying and hiding, 75–78
    Earned Value table for, 457–458
    goal area, adding new task to, 779–780

group, setting in Gantt Chart view, 176–177
information, sharing with other software, 13
linking across projects, 491–493
in network diagram (nodes), 10–11
new project, entering, 61–64
OK button to accept increased or decreased, 767–770
outline
    adjusting to, 70–73
    copying, 73–75
Overbudget reports, 409
priority, setting, 337–338
Project Center
    adding, 665–667
    reassigning, 667–668
recurring, 96
removing from display, 227
resources, assigning to, 141–142
splitting to resolve scheduling conflicts, 309–311
Tasks in Progress report, 413
Tasks Starting Soon, progress report, 410, 412
Tasks Status Report, 443–444
Tasks with a Task Calendar Assigned filter, 243
Tasks with Attachments filter, 243
Tasks with Deadlines filter, 243
Tasks with Estimated Durations filter, 243
Tasks with Fixed Dates filter, 243
Tasks/Assignments with Overtime filter, 243
time on, entering, 663–664
timing with Gantt Charts, 9
views, sorting, 229–231
work assignments
    Calendar, importing, 675–676
    details, viewing and changing, 663–664
    progress report
        available reports, 415
        Overallocated Resources, 418–419
        To Do List, 418
        Who Does What report, 415, 416
        Who Does What When report, 415, 417
    Project Center
        adding tasks, 665–667
        described, 661–662
        reassigning tasks, 667–668
        task updates, submitting, 664–665
        time on tasks, entering, 663–664
    resource, modifying, 475
    Resource Usage view, 194–195
work breakdown structures (WBS)
    described, 8
    illustrated, 10

920

Office heaven.

Get the first and last word on Microsoft® Office 2007 with our comprehensive Bibles and expert authors. These are the books you need to succeed!

978-0-470-04691-3

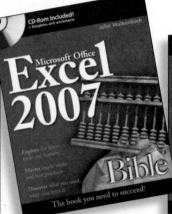

978-0-470-04403-2

978-0-470-04689-0

978-0-470-04368-4

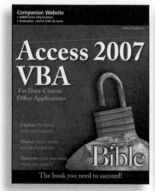

978-0-470-04702-6

978-0-470-04645-6

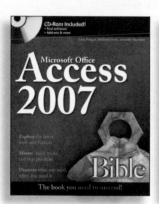

978-0-470-04673-9

978-0-470-00861-4

WILEY
Now you know

Available wherever books are sold

Wiley Publishing, Inc.
End-User License Agreement

READ THIS. You should carefully read these terms and conditions before opening the software packet(s) included with this book "Book". This is a license agreement "Agreement" between you and Wiley Publishing, Inc. "WPI". By opening the accompanying software packet(s), you acknowledge that you have read and accept the following terms and conditions. If you do not agree and do not want to be bound by such terms and conditions, promptly return the Book and the unopened software packet(s) to the place you obtained them for a full refund.

1. **License Grant.** WPI grants to you (either an individual or entity) a nonexclusive license to use one copy of the enclosed software program(s) (collectively, the "Software") solely for your own personal or business purposes on a single computer (whether a standard computer or a workstation component of a multi-user network). The Software is in use on a computer when it is loaded into temporary memory (RAM) or installed into permanent memory (hard disk, CD-ROM, or other storage device). WPI reserves all rights not expressly granted herein.

2. **Ownership.** WPI is the owner of all right, title, and interest, including copyright, in and to the compilation of the Software recorded on the physical packet included with this Book "Software Media". Copyright to the individual programs recorded on the Software Media is owned by the author or other authorized copyright owner of each program. Ownership of the Software and all proprietary rights relating thereto remain with WPI and its licensers.

3. **Restrictions on Use and Transfer.**

    (a) You may only (i) make one copy of the Software for backup or archival purposes, or (ii) transfer the Software to a single hard disk, provided that you keep the original for backup or archival purposes. You may not (i) rent or lease the Software, (ii) copy or reproduce the Software through a LAN or other network system or through any computer subscriber system or bulletin-board system, or (iii) modify, adapt, or create derivative works based on the Software.

    (b) You may not reverse engineer, decompile, or disassemble the Software. You may transfer the Software and user documentation on a permanent basis, provided that the transferee agrees to accept the terms and conditions of this Agreement and you retain no copies. If the Software is an update or has been updated, any transfer must include the most recent update and all prior versions.

4. **Restrictions on Use of Individual Programs.** You must follow the individual requirements and restrictions detailed for each individual program in the "About the CD" appendix of this Book or on the Software Media. These limitations are also contained in the individual license agreements recorded on the Software Media. These limitations may include a requirement that after using the program for a specified period of time, the user must pay a registration fee or discontinue use. By opening the Software packet(s), you agree to abide by the licenses and restrictions for these individual programs that are detailed in the "What's on the CD-ROM" appendix and/or on the Software Media. None of the material on this Software Media or listed in this Book may ever be redistributed, in original or modified form, for commercial purposes.